THE MEDIA: AN INTRODUCTION

Third Edition

Cobley

Longman
is an imprint of

PEARSON

Harlow, England • London • New York • Boston • San Francisco • Toronto
Sydney • Tokyo • Singapore • Hong Kong • Seoul • Taipei • New Delhi
Cape To... ... • Paris • Milan

Pearson Education Limited

Edinburgh Gate
Harlow
Essex CM20 2JE
England

and Associated Companies throughout the world

Visit us on the World Wide Web at:

www.pearsoned.co.uk

First published 1998
Second edition published 2002
Third edition published 2010

ISBN 978-1-4058-4036-1

British Library Cataloguing-in-Publication Data
A catalogue record for this book is available from the British Library

Library of Congress Cataloguing-in-Publication Data
The media : an introduction / edited by Daniele Albertazzi and Paul Cobley. - 3rd ed.
    p. cm.
  The 2nd ed. was edited by Adam Briggs & Paul Cobley.
  Includes index.
  ISBN 978-1-4058-4036-1 (pbk.)
 1. Mass media. I. Albertazzi, Daniele, 1968- II. Cobley, Paul, 1963-
  P90.M364 2010
  302.23-dc22

                                                    2009031551

10 9 8 7 6 5 4 3 2 1
13 12 11 10 09

Typeset in 9.5/12.5 pt Stone Serif by 73.
Printed and bound in Great Britain by Ashford Colour Press Ltd, Gosport, Hants

The publisher's policy is to use paper manufactured from sustainable forests.

Contents

List of figures, photos and tables   vii
Contributors   x
Acknowledgements   xix
Publisher's acknowledgements   xx

Introduction   1
Daniele Albertazzi and Paul Cobley

Part 1 UNDERSTANDING THE MEDIA   13

Introduction   13
Daniele Albertazzi and Paul Cobley

1 Approaches to the Media   15
Joanne Sayner

2 Media Form   35
John Corner

3 Models of Media Institutions   46
Stylianos Papathanassopoulos

4 The Media in Europe   60
Hans J. Kleinsteuber

Part 2 WHAT ARE THE MEDIA?   75

Introduction   75
Daniele Albertazzi and Paul Cobley

5 Comics   77
Roger Sabin

6 Photography   88
Stephen Bull

iii

7   Book Publishing   106
      Beverley Tarquini

8   Public Relations   120
      David Miller

9   Newspapers   140
      Raymond Kuhn

10   Magazines   153
      Anna Gough-Yates

11   Radio   165
      Guy Starkey

12   Television   176
      Dorothy Hobson

13   Cinema   190
      Anne Jäckel

14   Popular Music   206
      Roy Shuker

15   The Internet and the Web   220
      Lorenzo Cantoni and Stefano Tardini

16   News Agencies   233
      Oliver Boyd-Barrett and Terhi Rantanen

17   News Media   246
      Jackie Harrison

18   Advertising   258
      Iain MacRury

Part 3   THE MEDIA ENVIRONMENT: POLICY, ECONOMICS AND INSTITUTIONS   277

Introduction   277
Daniele Albertazzi and Paul Cobley

19   Economics   281
      John Sedgwick and Guglielmo Volpe

20 Policy   293
Marco Gambaro

21 Public Service Broadcasting in Europe   306
Jérôme Bourdon

22 Censorship and Freedom of Speech   318
Julian Petley

Part 4   AUDIENCES, INFLUENCES AND EFFECTS   333

Introduction   333
Daniele Albertazzi and Paul Cobley

23 Administrative Research of Audiences   335
Michael Svennevig

24 Effects   354
Guy Cumberbatch

25 Impacts and Influences   369
Jenny Kitzinger

26 Active Audiences   381
Joke Hermes

Part 5   MEDIA REPRESENTATIONS   393

Introduction   393
Daniele Albertazzi and Paul Cobley

27 Sexualities   397
Charlotte Ross

28 Gender   410
Rosalind Gill

29 Social Class   427
Karima Laachir

30 Race and Ethnicity   444
Sarita Malik

Contents

31 Media and Religion 457

Leen d'Haenens and Jan Bosman

32 Youth 471

Bill Osgerby

33 The Body, Health and Illness 485

Andy Miah and Emma Rich

34 Nationality 505

Barbara O'Connor

35 Sport 519

Neil Blain and Raymond Boyle

36 Sex Acts 534

Brian McNair

Index 546

List of figures, photos and tables

Figures

15.1	Centralised, decentralised and distributed networks	222
15.2	The website communication model (WCM)	225
17.1	Definitions and layers	248
18.1	Expenditure on advertising media: percentage of total advertising expenditure for print, TV, radio, outdoor and cinema and internet. Global comparisons 1997–2006/UK compares 2001–06	259
18.2	Internet advertising expenditure UK 1997–2006 (£m)	265
19.1	Movies as a system of provision	283
19.2	Audience sizes of the most popular 150 programmes broadcast during week ending 6 January 2008, ordered by rank	290
23.1	TV viewing shares (February 2002–August 2008)	342
23.2	Radio listening diary page	344
23.3	UK cinema admissions 1992–2008	347
31.1	Articles on Islam and Muslims in the Dutch press in 2005 (N = 1,130)	464
31.2	Attitude towards Muslims and non-Muslims in the reporting as a reaction to the events of 11 September 2001 and 2 November 2004	466
31.3	Framing of Islam as a reaction to the events of 11 September 2001 and 2 November 2004	467

Photos

Chapter 6

Diagram of *camera obscura*. Athanasius Kircher: Large Portable Camera Obscura, 1646	89
Kodak advertisement, 1888	92
Alexander Chadwick: Evacuating through tube tunnel	97
Gregory Crewdson, *Untitled* (*Ophelia*), 2001 (from the series Twilight)	98
Corinne Day, *Kate Moss, Kate's Flat*, 1993	100
Front cover of *Heat* magazine, 31 July–8 August 2004	101

Chapter 27

This is arguably the most visible form of female sexuality
   in mainstream Italian media today   404
Front cover of *Il Cassero*, May-June 2006   406

Chapter 28

Front cover of the *Sun*, 20 December 2007   415
Clinton's 'tears' were endlessly discussed in the media   416
Attacking the beauty myth . . . to sell beauty products   420
Are men's bodies now equally objectified as women's?   423

Chapter 29

Front cover of *Le Nouvel Observateur*, 10-16 November 2005   434
Front cover of *Le Point*, 10 November 2005   435
Front cover of *Le Point*, 17 November 2005   436
Front cover of *Le Nouvel Observateur*, 30 March-5 April 2006   438

Chapter 33

Front cover of *Time* magazine, 31 July 1978   489
Genetic test for athletic performance (2004)   490
Ron's Angels website   491

Chapter 34

Guinness advertisement: Born of Our Land   506

Tables

4.1	The global players in the media market (2006)	72
7.1	Market share (%) of publishing groups for consumer sales 2007	110
7.2	Market share (%) of publishing groups for consumer sales 2003	110
7.3	Change in source of GB consumer purchases 2001-05	112
7.4	Translations from original languages	114
7.5	Comparison of bestseller lists (%)	114
9.1	Number of newspapers sold per 1000 inhabitants aged 15 or more	143
11.1	UK weekly reach and share listening data for three digital radio platforms	167
13.1	Film production investments 1996 and 2002-06 (million US dollars)	194
13.2	Film production figures 1996 and 2003-06 (of which co-productions)	198

18.1 Overall increase in advertising expenditure 260

18.2 Ingredients in the emergence of the modern advertising industry 266

18.3 Strengths and weaknesses of main media for advertisers 270

19.1 Market shares (%) in the UK TV industry 288

19.2 Programme ratings for week ending 6 January 2008 289

23.1 Viewing figures: five UK terrestrial channels and Sky 1
(week ending 25 January 2009) 339

23.2 Top 20 most-visited websites in the UK 350

23.3 Top 10 company websites visited and patterns of use by
UK home internet users 351

Contributors

Daniele Albertazzi is Senior Lecturer in European Media at the University of Birmingham and writes about the communication strategies, styles of propaganda and mass media use of political parties in contemporary Europe, as well as Italian and Swiss politics. He has recently co-edited two volumes: *Twenty-First Century Populism: The Spectre of Western European Democracy* with Duncan McDonnell (Palgrave Macmillan, 2008) and *Resisting the Tide: Cultures of Opposition under Berlusconi (2001–2006)* with Clodagh Brook, Charlotte Ross and Nina Rothenberg (Continuum, 2009). He is currently writing a monograph on *Populists in Power: Actions and Reactions* with Duncan McDonnell.

Neil Blain is Professor of Media and Culture and head of the Department of Film, Media and Journalism at the University of Stirling. He has written extensively on questions of the media and collective identity in Europe, and co-edited *Sport, Media, Culture: Global and Local Dimensions* (Frank Cass, 2003). He co-authored *Media, Monarchy and Power* (Intellect, 2003) and co-edited *The Media in Scotland* (Edinburgh University Press, 2008). He is joint editor of *The International Journal of Media and Cultural Politics*.

Jan Bosman is Associate Professor at the Department of Communication of the Radboud University of Nijmegen, the Netherlands. He teaches on the effects of media, with a special interest in the effects of advertising and on marketing theory and consumer behaviour. His research interests include the validity of self image, brand image theory, and the (low involvement) psychological mechanisms underlying product placement and sponsoring effects.

Jérôme Bourdon is head of the Department of Communications at Tel Aviv University and associate researcher with the Center for the Sociology of Innovation (CSI-CNRS) in Paris. He works on the theory and global history of television, on the relations between collective memory and the media. He also produces historical documentaries. His most recent book is *Le récit impossible. Les médias et le conflit israélo-palestinien* (De Boeck Université, Paris, 2009). His recent articles in English include 'Unhappy Engineers of the European Soul: The Politics of Pan-European Broadcasting', *Gazette*, 69(3), 2007 and 'Soft Despotism: Reality Television and the New Subject of Politics', *Framework: The Journal of Cinema and media*, 49(1), 2008.

Oliver Boyd-Barrett acquired his doctorate from the Open University (UK) and is currently Professor of Journalism at Bowling Green State University (USA). He has published extensively on issues of international news flow, news agencies and educational media. His books include *Communications Media, Globalization and Empire* (as editor and contributor) (John Libbey, 2007), *The Globalization of News* (as co-editor and contributor) (Sage, 1999), *Contraflow in Global News* (co-author) (John Libbey, 1992) and *International News Agencies* (Constable, UK, 1980 and Sage, US, 1980). His current area of specialty is media coverage of war. He has held a variety of academic and administrative positions in the UK and USA.

Raymond Boyle is a Professor of Communications at the Centre for Cultural Policy Research at the University of Glasgow. He has published widely in the area of media sports, and his recent books include *Power Play: Sport, the Media and Popular Culture*, second edition, with Richard Haynes (Edinburgh University Press, 2009), *Sports Journalism: Context and Issues* (Sage, 2006) and *Football in the New Media Age*, with Richard Haynes (Routledge, 2004). He is currently leading an AHRC funded project looking at representations of entrepreneurship on television and also sits on the Editorial Board of the journal *Media, Culture and Society*.

Stephen Bull is a writer, artist and lecturer. He is course leader for BA (Hons) Photography at the University of Portsmouth. Stephen is the author of *Photography* in the *Routledge Introductions to Media and Communications* series (Routledge, 2009) and since 1995 has contributed articles and reviews to magazines including *Source: The Photographic Review*, *Photoworks* and *Creative Camera*. He has exhibited at Tate Britain and The Photographers' Gallery, London and published books of photographs including *Meeting Hazel Stokes* (Neroc'VGM, 2006). Stephen has led courses at Tate Modern in 'Photography as Art', 'Photography and the City' and 'Photography and Celebrity'.

Lorenzo Cantoni graduated in philosophy and holds a PhD in Education and Linguistics. He is full professor at the Università della Svizzera Italiana (USI, University of Lugano, Switzerland), Faculty of Communication Sciences, where he teaches eLearning and eGovernment. He is vice-director of the Institute of Institutional and Educational Communication, director of the laboratories webatelier.net: production and promotion over the Internet, NewMinE Lab: New Media in Education Lab; is executive director of TEC-Lab: Technology Enhanced Communication Lab and scientific director of eLab: eLearning Lab. His research interests are where communication, education and new media overlap, ranging from computer mediated communication to usability, from eLearning to eTourism and eGovernment. He is the co-author with Stefano Tardini of *Internet* (Routledge, 2005).

Paul Cobley is Reader in Communications at London Metropolitan University. His publications include *The American Thriller: Generic Innovation and Social Change in the 1970s* (Palgrave, 2000), *Narrative* (Routledge, 2001) and, as editor, *The Communication Theory Reader* (Routledge, 1996), *Communication Theories* (4 vols., Routledge, 2006), *The Routledge Companion to Semiotics* (Routledge, 2009) and *Realism for the 21st Century: A John Deely Reader* (University of Scranton Press, 2009). He is series editor of *Routledge Introductions to Media and Communications* as well as *Semiotics, Communication and Cognition* (Mouton de Gruyter). He is also the co-editor of two journals, *Social Semiotics* and *Subject Matters*, and is associate editor of *Cybernetics and Human Knowing*.

John Corner is currently Visiting Professor in Communication Studies at the University of Leeds. He has written extensively on media history, institutions and forms in books and journals and is an editor of the journal *Media, Culture and Society*. Recent work includes an historical study of current-affairs journalism, *Public Issue Television*, co-authored with Peter Goddard and Kay Richardson (Manchester University Press, 2007). Current research interests include political culture and documentary film and television and he is preparing a book on the interconnections of power, representational form and subjectivity.

Dr Guy Cumberbatch is a chartered psychologist and Director of the Communications Research Group in Birmingham. He has specialised in media psychology for over three decades, particularly the effects of media violence and the representation of minority groups. Guy is proud that half of his work has been commissioned by regulators (such as Ofcom, the Council of Europe, BBFC) and half by broadcasters and production companies (such as the BBC and Warner). Before establishing CRG at Aston Science Park, Guy was Senior Lecturer in Applied Psychology at Aston University.

Marco Gambaro is Associate Professor of Media Economics and Communication Economics in the Department of Economics and Business at Università degli Studi di Milano. Previously he taught at IULM University in Milan and Università di Trento. His research focuses on industrial economics, the regulation in telecommunication, the television industry, the Italian and international film industry, competition in communication markets, the economics of information and advertising, and demand for cultural goods. He has published several books on these topics, as well as working as a consultant for private and public institutions.

Rosalind Gill is Professor of Social and Cultural Analysis in the Faculty of Arts and Humanities, King's College London. She is author of *Gender and the Media* (Polity, 2006) and co-editor of *Secrecy and Silence in the Research Process: Feminist Reflections* (Routledge, 2009) and *New Femininities* (Palgrave, 2010). She is currently conducting research in two fields: work in the cultural industries and children's engagements with 'sexualised' culture. She is also writing a book about mediated intimacy.

Anna Gough-Yates is Associate Head (Research) in the Department of Applied Social Sciences at London Metropolitan University. Her research interests focus on the 'economic' processes and practices of the media industries, and their relationships to cultural meanings and effects. In particular, her work has explored the interactions between media, feminist politics and understandings of femininity. Amongst her main publications are the co-edited collection *Action TV: Tough Guys, Smooth Operators, and Foxy Chicks* (Routledge, 2001), and the monograph *Understanding Women's Magazines: Publishing, Markets and Readerships* (Routledge, 2003). She is also currently a consultant for the BBC Trust and Audience Councils.

Leen d'Haenens is Associate Professor at the Centre for Media Culture and Communication Technology, Catholic University of Leuven, Belgium, and at the Department of Communication, Radboud University Nijmegen, the Netherlands. She teaches on media policy, on media and minorities, and analysis of media texts. Her research interests include ethnic minority youth as digital citizens, media responsibility and accountability mechanisms. She recently co-edited *Western Broadcast Models: Structure, Conduct and Performance* (Mouton de Gruyter, 2007).

Jackie Harrison is Professor of Public Communication, Head of Department of Journalism Studies and Chair of the Centre for Freedom of the Media at the University of Sheffield. She is currently researching the civil power of news. She is the author of *News* (Routledge, 2006) and *European Broadcasting Law and Policy* (Cambridge University Press, 2007) and is co-editor of *Mediating Europe: Mass Media in Contemporary European Culture* (Berghahn, 2009).

Joke Hermes is a professor of practice-based research in Media, Culture and Citizenship at INHolland University in the Netherlands. Qualitative research, media audiences and popular culture are ongoing themes in her work. Her interest in well-theorised, empirically grounded work in media and cultural studies is also central to the *European Journal of Cultural Studies* of which she is one of the three founding editors. Her key international book publications are *Rereading Popular Culture* (2005) and *Reading Women's Magazines* (1995).

Dorothy Hobson is Senior Lecturer in Media, Communications and Cultural Studies at the University of Wolverhampton where she is course leader – MA Contemporary Media. Her main teaching and research interests are popular television genres particularly soap opera, drama series, news, and audiences and broadcasters. Her publications include *Soap Opera* (Polity, 2003) and *Channel 4: The Early Years and the Jeremy Isaacs Legacy* (I. B. Tauris, 2007). Her recent contributions are to *Young People, Television and Reality TV*, edited by C. von Feilitzen (Nordicom Gotenburg University, 2004), *Porcupines in Winter* edited by A. Buonofina and G. Mulgan (The Young Foundation, 2006), *Television and Criticism*, edited by S. Davin and R. Jackson (Intellect, 2008). She is a Fellow of the Royal Television Society.

Anne Jäckel is a former Senior Lecturer (now retired) and Visiting Research Fellow at the University of the West of England. Her main interests are European film policy and cinematograpic co-productions with European partners both within and outside Europe. She is the author of *The European Film Industries* (BFI, 2003) and of numerous book chapters and journal articles published in *Cineaste, Media, Culture & Society, European Journal of Communication, National Identities, Historical Journal of Film, Radio and Television* and *Modern & Contemporary France*.

Jenny Kitzinger is Professor of Media and Communication Research at Cardiff University. She specialises in researching the media coverage, and audience reception, of health and scientific issues. Her most recent book is *Human Cloning in the Media: From Science Fiction to Science Practice* (Routledge, 2008) (co-authored).

Previous books include *Framing Abuse: Media Influence and Public Understanding of Sexual Violence Against Children* (Pluto Press, 2004), *Developing Focus Group Research* (Sage, 1999), *The Mass Media and Power in Modern Britain* (Oxford University Press, 1997) and *The Circuit of Mass Communication in the AIDS Crisis* (Sage, 1999).

Hans J. Kleinsteuber is Professor (Emeritus) in Political Science and Communication at the University of Hamburg, where he teaches in the Erasmus Mundus Master programme: Journalism and Media within Globalisation. He has been director of the Research Centre for Media and Politics for 20 years. His teaching and research interests include comparison of media systems in Europe and North America, media politics, economics and technology. He has written books on Europe as a communication space and media policy in Europe. His latest books are *A Handbook of Journalism and Media* (2005), as well as *Introduction to Travel Journalism* (2008) and *Radio* (2009). He is a longstanding member of the Euromedia Research Group.

Raymond Kuhn is Professor of Politics at Queen Mary, University of London, where he is course convenor for the second year course on Politics and the Mass Media. He has written widely on French media policy and political communication, including a single authored study *The Media in France* (Routledge, 1995). He is also the author of *Politics and the Media in Britain* (Palgrave, 2007).

Karima Laachir is a lecturer in Literary and Cultural Studies at SOAS and convenor of the MA Cultural Studies in Africa, Asia and the Middle East. She has worked and published extensively on the North African Diasporas in France and issues of exclusion and marginalisation as well as how diasporic cultural productions have changed the cultural and political scene in France. Currently, she is working on comparative postcolonial literature (Arabophone, Francophone and Anglophone), Arabic popular culture with a focus on media and cinema, and Arab Diasporas in Europe. Her forthcoming monograph will be on *Contemporary Arab Women Writers: Gender, Sexuality and the Politics of Freedom*.

Iain MacRury is Principal Lecturer in Cultural Studies and Creative Industries at the University of East London. He is the author of *Advertising* (Routledge, 2009) and co-editor of *The Advertising Handbook* (Routledge, 2009). He is also co-editor of *Olympic Cities: 2012 and the Remaking of London* (Ashgate, 2009). He is co-author of *The Dynamics of Advertising* (Harwood Press, 2000) and co-editor of *Buy This Book: Studies in Advertising and Consumption* (Routledge, 1997). He has contributed a number of papers and chapters on advertising and other related topics to edited books and journals.

Sarita Malik lectures, researches and writes on representation and identity within the context of media, cinema and the creative industries. Her publications include *Representing Black Britain: Black and Asian Images on Television* (Sage, 2002) and numerous academic and journalistic articles on racial and cultural identities – both in relation to screen representation and social change. She is on the MeCCSA Committee and Chair of the MeCCSA Race Network.

Brian McNair is Professor of Journalism and Communication at the University of Strathclyde. He is the author of many books and articles on media themes, including *Mediated Sex* (Arnold, 1996), *Striptease Culture* (Routledge, 2002) and *Cultural Chaos* (Routledge, 2006). He has contributed essays on pornography to Feona Attwood's *Mainstreaming Sex* (I. B. Tauris, 2009) and Darren Kerr's *Hard To Swallow* (Wallflower Press, 2010). In addition to work on sexuality and the media, he writes about journalism and political communication. His most recent book is *Journalists in Film* (Edinburgh University Press, 2010).

Andy Miah is Chair in Ethics and Emerging Technologies in the Faculty of Business and Creative Industries at the University of the West of Scotland, Fellow of the Institute for Ethics and Emerging Technologies, USA and Fellow at FACT, the Foundation for Art and Creative Technology, UK. He is author of *Genetically Modified Athletes* (Routledge, 2004) and co-author with Emma Rich of *The Medicalization of Cyberspace* (Routledge, 2008) and editor of *Human Futures: Art in an Age of Uncertainty* (Liverpool University Press and FACT, 2008).

David Miller is Professor of Sociology in the Department of Geography and Sociology at the University of Strathclyde in Glasgow, Scotland. He is also the co-founder of Spinwatch.org, a website publishing public interest reporting on spin, deception and lobbying and the editor of an associated wiki database spinprofiles.org. David also chairs the 'Teaching About Terrorism' Special Interest Group of the Higher Education Academy's Centre for Sociology, Anthropology and Politics. Recent publications include: *A Century of Spin: How Public Relations Became the Cutting Edge of Corporate Power*, co-authored with William Dinan (Pluto Press, 2008) and *Thinker, Faker, Spinner, Spy: Corporate PR and the Assault on Democracy*, edited with William Dinan, (Pluto, 2007).

Barbara O'Connor is Senior Lecturer in the School of Communications at Dublin City University. She has an academic background in sociology and social anthropology and her main teaching and research interests include international/intercultural communication, media audiences/consumption, and popular cultural forms and practices such as tourism and recreational dance. She has published widely in each of these areas and her most recent publication is a co-edited collection, *Mapping Irish Media: Critical Explorations* (University College Dublin Press, 2007). She is currently Director of the University Designated Research Centre for Society, Information, and Media (SIM).

Bill Osgerby is Professor of Media, Culture and Communications at London Metropolitan University. His research focuses on 20th century British and American cultural history, and his books include *Youth in Britain Since 1945* (Blackwell, 1998), *Playboys in Paradise: Youth, Masculinity and Leisure-Style in Modern America* (Berg/New York University Press, 2001), *Youth Media* (Routledge, 2004), and a co-edited anthology, *Action TV: Tough-Guys, Smooth Operators and Foxy Chicks* (Routledge, 2001).

Stylianos Papathanassopoulos is Professor in Media Organisation and Policy at the Faculty of Communication and Media Studies at the National and

Kapodistrian University of Athens. He has written extensively on media developments in Europe and especially on television issues. His research interests are on European communications and new media policies as well as political communication. Among his recent books: *Television in the 21st Century* (Kastaniotis, 2005), *Media and Politics* (Kastaniotis, 2004), *European Television in the Digital Age: Issues, Dynamics and Realties* (Polity Press, 2002), *European Communications: The Policies of European Union in the Communication Domain*. (Kastaniotis, 2002).

Julian Petley is Professor of Screen Media and Journalism in the School of Arts at Brunel University. His most recent publications are *Censoring the Word* (Seagull Books/Index on Censorship, 2007), *Censoring the Moving Image* (Seagull Books/Index on Censorship, 2008), which was co-written with Philip French, and *Censorship: A Beginner's Guide* (Oneworld, 2009). He is a member of the boards of *Index on Censorship* and the *British Journalism Review*, principal editor of the *Journal of British Cinema and Television*, and chair of the Campaign for Press and Broadcasting Freedom.

Terhi Rantanen is Professor in Global Media and Communications and Director of the MSc programme in Global Media and Communications at the London School of Economics and Political Science. She has published extensively on a range of topics related to global media and especially news. Her publications include *The Globalization of News* with O. Boyd-Barrett (Sage, 1998), *The Global and the National: Media and Communications in Post-Communist Russia* (Rowman & Littlefield, 2002), *The Media and Globalization* (Sage, 2004) and *When News Was New* (Wiley-Blackwell, 2009).

Emma Rich is a senior lecturer in Body and Physical Culture, School of Sport and Exercise Sciences, Loughborough University. Her research focuses on public pedagogy and health, examining how people learn about the body and health through different social contexts. She is co-author of *The Medicalization of Cyberspace* (Routledge, 2008) and *Education, Disordered Eating, and Obesity Discourse: Fat Fabrications* (Routledge, 2008). She is also co-editor of the forthcoming text, *The Obesity Debate* (Palgrave, publishing 2010).

Charlotte Ross is a lecturer in Italian Studies at the University of Birmingham, where she also convenes the MPhil in Gender Studies. Her main research interests are in gender, sexuality and the body, in both literature and society. She is co-editor with Daniele Albertazzi, Clodagh Brook and Nina Rothenberg of *Resisting the Tide: Cultures of Opposition under Berlusconi (2001–06)* (Continuum, 2009) and with Loredana Polezzi of *In corpore: Bodies in Post-Unification Italy* (FDUP, 2007).

Roger Sabin is the author of several books about comics, including *Adult Comics: An Introduction* (Routledge, 1994) and *Comics, Comix and Graphic Novels* (Phaidon, 1996), and reviews graphic novels for the national press. He currently lectures at Central Saint Martins College of Art and Design, University of the Arts London, where he is Reader in Popular Culture.

Joanne Sayner lectures in cultural theory and German studies at the University of Birmingham. She also convenes a course on media, culture and communication. Her main research interests are in gender, memory and cultural representations of the past. She has published several feminist literary historiographies and a monograph entitled *Women without a Past? German Autobiographical Writings and Fascism* (Rodopi, 2007).

John Sedgwick is Professor of Film Economics, as well as Director of the Centre for International Business and Sustainability, at London Metropolitan University. He researches into the economic history of film and has published in the journals *Economic History Review*, *Journal of Economic History*, *Explorations in Economic History* and *Journal of Cultural Economics*, as well as written numerous book chapters. He has published a monograph entitled *Popular Filmgoing in 1930s Britain* (University of Exeter Press, 2000) and edited an anthology of papers *The Economic History of Film* (Routledge, 2005). He was a Leverhulme Research fellow in 2000, a Menzies Research Fellow in 2006 and a RMIT/AFTRS Visiting Research Fellow in 2007. He is currently working on a book on the Australian market for movies in the 1930s, as well as researching the idea of film consumers as risk takers.

Roy Shuker is Associate Professor in Media Studies at Victoria University of Wellington, New Zealand. His main teaching and research interests are in popular music studies, cultural consumption, and media policy. His publications include *Popular Music: The Key Concepts* second edition (Routledge, 2005) and *Understanding Popular Music Culture*, third edition (Routledge, 2008).

Guy Starkey is Professor of Radio and Journalism at the University of Sunderland, where he is also the Head of the Department of Media. A former radio producer and presenter, he worked at radio stations in the United Kingdom, Europe and the Middle East. He is the author of *Radio in Context* (Palgrave Macmillan, 2004) and *Balance and Bias in Journalism: Representation, Regulation and Democracy* (Palgrave Macmillan, 2007), as well as co-author with Andrew Crisell of *Radio Journalism* (Sage, 2009). His research interests include journalistic representation, political economy, distribution technology and the pedagogy of radio.

Michael Svennevig is Senior Research Fellow in the Institute of Communications Studies at the University of Leeds. He has worked at senior level in audience research for the BBC – helping in developing the 'EastEnders' concept – and at the former Independent Broadcasting Authority, where he undertook a range of studies including an examination of the role of the media in religious activity and belief, followed by several years as a freelance media researcher. At Leeds, he has researched the evolution of the internet in the UK, and undertaken content analysis for the BBC Trust. He also lectures on the audience and audience research methods.

Stefano Tardini is researcher at the Università della Svizzera Italiana (USI, University of Lugano, Switzerland), Faculty of Communication Sciences, where he is also the managing director of eLab: eLearning Lab. His research interests include ICT mediated communication, eLearning, (online) communities and social networks, cultural semiotics and argumentation theory. He is developing his research in three interrelated directions: an approach to ICT mediated communication from a socio-historical perspective; an analysis of the impact of the introduction of eLearning activities and tools into given communities; an elaboration of a semiotic approach to online communities and social networks. He has co-authored, together with Lorenzo Cantoni, the book *Internet*, in the series *Routledge Introductions to Media and Communications* (2006).

Beverley Tarquini is a Senior Lecturer and Programme Leader for the MA in Publishing in Publishing Media at the Oxford International Centre for Publishing Studies, Oxford Brookes University. Her teaching interests are in editorial, rights management and new product development, at both undergraduate and postgraduate level. Her research focuses on aspects of educational and academic publishing as well as the assessment and expectations of students within Higher Education. She works as a freelance editor for several publishers.

Guglielmo Volpe is a Senior Lecturer in economics education with the Department of Economics at Queen Mary, University of London. He holds a PhD in Economics from Dundee University and has taught economics modules at both undergraduate and postgraduate level. His research interests lie in the areas of economic growth and of economic education. In 2003 he won the student-nominated award for best economics lecturer from the Economics Network of the Higher Education Academy. In 2004 he was awarded a National Teaching Fellowship from the HEA and in 2008 he won the Queen Mary, Economics Department best teacher award.

Acknowledgements

We are indebted to all those who helped us since we embarked on the mission of producing the third edition of this volume. Firstly, we would like to thank our contributors who, during the run-up to RAE2008, were nevertheless sufficiently committed to the subject area to spend time writing for the good of our future students. Secondly, we thank our colleagues in communication, media, cultural and European studies at London Metropolitan University and the University of Birmingham with whom we have discussed media, cultural and research issues over the years. Paul Cobley would like to thank Jon Baldwin, James Bennett, Sara Cannizzaro, Mike Chopra-Gant, Nick Haeffner, Paul Kerr, Gholam Khiabany, Anna Gough-Yates, Peter Lewis, Bill Osgerby, George Paszkiewicz, Luke Tredinnick and Wendy Wheeler. Daniele Albertazzi would like to thank Ron Speirs, Karima Laachir, Berny Sèbe, Joanne Sayner, Charlotte Ross, Clodagh Brook, Mike Caesar, Gerry Slowey, Clelia Boscolo, Paolo De Ventura, Ita MacCarthy, Monica Borg and Anna Maria Bucci. Thanks should go to the referees and questionnaire respondents who have given feedback since the first edition appeared, as well as those who have given informal feedback. Andrew Taylor at Pearson initiated the third edition and deserves special thanks for staying with it and demonstrating utmost patience.

The publishers would like to thank all those who kindly reviewed previous editions of the book and thereby contributed to the thinking for this edition. We would also like to thank the contributors and editors for their work on the third edition.

Paul Cobley would also like to thank a number of people for allowing this book to come to fruition. Firstly, my erstwhile co-editor, Adam Briggs, who helped evolve the concept and my tenacious co-editor, Daniele Albertazzi, who helped evolve it further. Liz Hogan offered hospitality, tolerance and patience at a crucial stage. More patient, still, though, have been Alison Ronald, Stan Ronald Cobley and Elsie Ronald Cobley – they put up with a lot.

Daniele Albertazzi would like to thank Paul Cobley for inviting him on board and for being such good fun to work with and Liz Hogan for being there throughout and reading his drafts.

Daniele Albertazzi
Paul Cobley

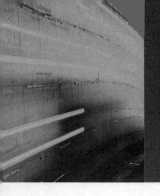

Publisher's acknowledgements

We are grateful to the following for permission to reproduce copyright material:

Figures

Figure 15.1: Adapted from *On Distributed Communications: I. Introduction to Distributed Communications Networks* (Baran, P., 1964). Copyright © 1964 by Rand Corporation, reproduced with permission of Rand Corporation in the format Textbook via Copyright Clearance Center; Figure 15.2: Adapted from *Comunicazione, Qualità, Usabilità,* Apogeo: Milano, Italy (Cantoni, L., Di Blas, N. and Bolchini, D., 2003), Reproduced with permission from Apogeo Srl; Figure 18.1: After *World Advertising Trends 2007,* WARC Ltd (www.warc.com); Figure 23.1: Adapted from Broadcasters Audience Research Board Ltd (BARB), TV Viewing Shares (February 2002–August 2008), www.barb.co.uk/report/index, Copyright © 2009 BARB Limited; Figure 23.2: Facsimile page of a Radio Joint Audience Research Ltd (RAJAR) radio listening diary, www.rajar.co.uk/docs/about/RAJAR_diary_example_page.pdf. Reproduced with permission from RAJAR Ltd; Figure 23.3: From CAA / Gallup / Nielsen EDI. Copyright © 2008 Cinema Advertising Association (CAA).

Tables

Table 7.1: Adapted from Nielsen BookScan, www.nielsenbookscan.co.uk. Data sourced from the TCM (Total Consumer Market) as measured by Nielsen BookScan representing over 90% of consumer purchases in the UK for the period 31 December 2006-29 December 2007; Table 7.3: Adapted from BML Books and the Consumer, www.bookmarketing.co.uk. Copyright © BML/TNS. Accessed from The Booksellers Association www.booksellers.org.uk, 10 August 2008; Table 7.4: Adapted from UNESCO Index Translationum, www.unesco.org/culture/xtrans (accessed 31 July 2008). Used by permission of UNESCO; Table 9.1: After *La Presse Quotidienne Nationale: Fin de Partie ou Renouveau,* Éditions Vuibert (Eveno, P. 2008), p. 18. Reproduced by Permission; Table 11.1: Adapted from 'Listening Via Platform – All Radio', *RAJAR Quarterly Summary of Radio Listening,* Quarter 4 (Radio Joint Audience Research Limited, 2007) (www.rajar.co.uk/docs/2007_12/2007_Q4_Listening_via_platform.pdf). Reproduced with permission from RAJAR Ltd; Table 19.1: From Broadcasters Audience Research Board Ltd (BARB) Annual % Shares of Viewing (Individuals) 1981–2008 (www.barb.co.uk/facts/annualShareOfViewing); Table 19.2: From Broadcasters Audience Research Board Ltd (BARB) Weekly Top 30 Programmes (www.barb.co.uk/index1.cfm) (accessed 28 February 2008); Table 23.1 from Broadcasters Audience Research Board Ltd (BARB) Weekly Top 10 Programmes (www.barb.co.uk/report/weeklyTopProgrammes); Table 23.3: Adapted from The Nielsen Company, http://uk.nielsen.com. Copyright © The Nielsen Company.

Text

Page 40: Extract from 'We Got Down to the Outside and It Was Like an Apocalypse', *Guardian,* 12 September 2001, p. 6 (Ellison, M., Vulliamy, E. and Martinson, J. 2001), Copyright © Guardian News & Media Ltd 2001; 321: Extract from 'Berlusconi, the Media and the New Right in Italy', *Harvard International Journal of Press/Politics,* 1(1), pp. 87–105 (Statham, P. 1996). Copyright © 1996 by Sage Publications, reprinted by permission of Sage Publications; 328: Extract from 'All Hail Berlusconi', *Observer,* 18 January 2004 (Carlin, J.). Reproduced with permission from John Carlin.

Photos

Page 89: © Bettmann / Corbis; 92: Courtesy of Kodak Ltd (UK); 97: Alexander Chadwick / AP / Press Association Images; 98: Courtesy of White Cube, London and Gregory Crewdson; 100: Corinne Day / Maconochie Photography; 101: Courtesy of Bauer Consumer Media; 404: Livio Valerio / LaPresse / Press Association Images; 406: Courtesy of Cassero, Bologna; 415: Copyright © News Group Newspapers Ltd; 416: Elise Amendola / AP / Press Association Images; 420: The Advertising Archives; 423: The Advertising Archives; 434: Courtesy of Le Nouvel Observateur; 435: Courtesy of Le Point; 436: Courtesy of Le Point; 438: Courtesy of Le Nouvel Observateur; 489: Copyright © 1978 Time, Inc.; 506: © Fred Gambino 2008 / Diageo Ireland.

In some instances we have been unable to trace the owners of copyright material, and we would appreciate any information that would enable us to do so.

Introduction

Daniele Albertazzi and Paul Cobley

Anyone who seeks to underestimate the centrality of media in contemporary European life does so at their peril. Today, arguably more than at any time in the past, media are the key players in contributing to what defines reality for the citizens of Europe and beyond. The media comprises major industries within the general European economy, systems of representations, a forum for debate and the expression of desires, a source of potential influence and objects for analysis and understanding of society. This book provides an introduction to the way that the media occupies such a position of prominence in contemporary human existence.

To introduce this book it is necessary to do two things. Firstly, to focus attention on understanding what this thing 'the media' is whilst also fostering a recognition of the difficulties of producing a comprehensive definition during:

- a period of digitisation and the rapid development it allows;
- a period of profound social and economic change in Europe and globally.

Secondly, it is necessary to attempt to help the reader use this book as an effective study tool. This introduction gives information on how this volume is structured, what it contains and how it can be most fruitfully read. If this volume is successful, and if it is used astutely, it should offer the means to gain a foundational knowledge of the numerous ways in which today's media in Europe operate. This will enable the student to proceed to more dedicated and specific study.

Contemporary European media and media study

Like the media, the *study* of media is constantly expanding and developing. Where media scholars of the past might have been concerned to study media in its national setting, current study of the media is coming to the recognition that the path to greater understanding leads beyond national boundaries. This book (and the previous editions of it) is concerned to enhance an understanding of the

1

media in Europe. Since it appeared in its first edition, the relevant knowledge resources and the environment have changed so as to assist this ambition. Thus, the focus on Europe in this volume is developed further and the essays which make up the volume allow a comparative perspective. Media study is expanding. If some UK media scholars have been parochial in the past, many are less parochial now. During the past decade there has been an increase in the numbers of foreign language scholars in UK universities working on media. In addition, British media studies has started to recognise more fully the burgeoning sphere, as well as the quality, of media study in other European countries (especially the big three of France, Germany and Italy, but also Denmark and the Netherlands).

Yet these are not the only reasons why a strong focus on Europe is needed now to understand contemporary media. This volume features contributors from across Europe (and around the world), recruited for the purposes of analysing the media (including the UK media) with a keen eye on the important matter of its specific social context: the European Union (EU). In a number of (sometimes problematic) ways, the EU embodies European traditions of governance and culture which have created the environment for a 'media system' or 'media culture' which gives European media, in all their diversity, some unity. The EU is a very important context within which to understand the media because, to some extent and in some countries, it provides a counterbalance to the influence of America – the EU both regulates, and sometimes actively seeks to develop, the media in Europe.

Of course, as this book clearly shows, media systems are still very much nationally based and remain diverse across the continent. As Hans Kleinsteuber puts it succinctly in Chapter 4, 'The media systems of Europe clearly reflect the fragmented history of the European continent; in terms of media structures Europe appears to be a laboratory of media experiences and diversities' (see p. 60). This statement refers to a number of broad observations that can be made about the diversity and differences between media in different European countries:

- There are several different models of 'public service broadcasting' (PSB). That is, there are nationally-bound ways by which European citizens can, as part of their experience of mass media, gain access to publicly (state) funded media that is regulated by governments and offers programming of different levels of diversity. The British model of PSB, it is worth noting, has provided some inspiration for other European countries.

- The newspaper and magazine industries exercise varying degrees of influence on political and social life in different countries.

- Satellite and cable technologies have been taken up at different speed in different parts of the continent during the past 25 years, which means that traditional, terrestrial television still exercises considerable influence on national cultures (and on the political process).

- The few European-wide TV channels (as opposed to national channels) that currently exist continue to enjoy very small audiences.

- The *size* of a nation state has a huge impact on how its media system develops – compare, for instance, the cases of Luxembourg (very small) and France (very large).

- Different European countries have implemented policies to support and regulate the media, usually deriving from very different national contexts, traditions and prevailing political circumstances.

In the face of the diversity of European media systems, English-speaking media study has often focused on the media in the UK alone. When a comparative perspective has been introduced to the study of UK media, it has frequently involved comparison with the USA (which, putatively, shares a language with the UK).

Yet, despite the disparities and discrepancies across the continent, it is reiterated here that the media in Europe are also marked by several common features, affinities and histories and are, to some extent, developing in similar ways. Consider the following:

- Chapter 21 (below) on PSB in Europe *does* reveal the existence of very different models of PSB and posits a 'North–South divide'. Nevertheless, broadcasting in Europe almost always revolves around (or leaves a considerable space to) PSB. Across the continent public service broadcasters face similar problems: they have experienced erosion of their viewing shares and revenue, while the logic of imposing a licence fee to guarantee their existence has been challenged. As a consequence, a number of European public service broadcasters (starting with the BBC) have pursued commercial opportunities of their own and seem increasingly locked in a battle with commercial broadcasters to retain influence and market shares.

- The state has always intervened (more or less forcefully) to regulate and, in some cases, defend and foster the media (for instance, in almost every European country the national movie industry is subsidised to an extent – see Chapter 13, below – with newspapers often also getting public support and finance).

- Technological advances (principally, in recent years, digitisation) have affected all media systems.

- So, too, has increasing competition to terrestrial and analogue media from differently delivered media (this competition, resulting from, of course, the arrival of satellite, cable and, again, digital technologies).

- European states (and the EU) agree that media are crucial to foster democracy and participation. There has been a flurry of regulation by both the EU and European nation-states which affects media industries in different ways according to the perceived importance of those industries. These have included content restrictions, both in advertising and in editorial content, yet within a widespread framework of freedom of expression guaranteed since 1953 by the European Convention on Human Rights.

- Cross-media concentration and convergence have also left a mark Europe-wide. As this book shows, the influence of media barons in the political process has been noticeable in several countries. As Julian Petley, writing on censorship, notes 'in pursuit of policies friendly to their business interests, media owners have shown themselves all too ready to employ their own media for their own purposes, backing those governments which support their economic interests and excoriating those which do not. All of these factors give rise to forms of censorship and restriction which are best described as structural and systemic, but which are no less damaging to media freedom for being less immediately obvious than cuts, bans and other more "old-fashioned" forms of overt proscription' (Chapter 22, p. 318).

All of the above amount to a persuasive argument in favour of the study of European media or, at the very least, studies of national media which recognise both their limitations and the wider context.

One of the factors differentiating European nations is history. National histories are important to the analyses that make up the contributions to this volume since national media are inseparable from them. Nevertheless, the focus of essays in this volume is squarely on the contemporary moment. Frequently, the study of media has surveyed the history of one medium, or media in general, by charting technological changes and their impacts. Although the current volume does not have the space or time to pursue such an approach, it does concern itself with recent developments in media technology that have demanded attention, particularly digitisation.

Digitisation and its effects

The 'effects' of digitisation of media are much debated. Media study has not reached a consensus on the matter, much as it has not reached agreement on whether media in general have 'effects' on audiences (see Chapters 24, 25 and 26, below). However, there is little doubt that digitisation has allowed some significant developments to take place in respect of media and its consumers. Broadly, digitisation has:

- effected the re-distribution towards erstwhile consumers of at least a modicum of power previously monopolised by media corporations; that is, modest resources are now required in order for individuals or small groups – as opposed to large corporations – to send messages that might be received by large numbers of people (through podcasting, desktop publishing, uploading one's own music to websites, blogs, continually revised multiple author channels such as wikis, webcams, citizen journalism, multiple text messaging); furthermore, some of these practices are specifically geared to, or indirectly have the effect of, presenting an alternative to the perspective offered by media corporations (not to mention those technologies which allow theft of copyrighted messages such as illegal DVD or CD burning or peer-to-peer file-sharing which can produce copies of artefacts produced by media corporations without any of the quality depreciation which often characterised theft in the older media).

- affected entire media industries and the way they operate; that is, media corporations have sought to exploit the potential offered by digitisation, through such innovations as IPTV (television content offered through the internet), podcasting and downloadable television programmes from the major television companies, pay-per-view, music and video download sites, e-books, interactive digital television services, HD-television, and so forth.

In light of these two broad changes (and the many associated sub-changes) in the media landscape, all contributions to this volume have been compelled to take digitisation into account. Digitisation has wrought major changes in media production and use, and has been swift in doing so; indeed, it is instructive in this respect to consider the media landscape at the time of the preparation of the last edition of this volume. There were some pages devoted to downloads ('music: on the internet' in the index), but only one reference to a technology that is now commonplace in European households, the DVD. Although it is less than a decade ago, the world of the previous edition of this book had not seen podcasting, youtube.com, Facebook, MySpace, Flickr, Twitter, World of Warcraft, the BBC iPlayer, Second Life, Radio 7, the iPhone, affordable 6 megapixel domestic digital cameras, Nintendo DS, USB memory sticks, flat screen televisions and had only witnessed a fledgling iTunes site with digital rights management firmly intact. (Moreover, offering a sense of the speed of media development and leaving the issue of digitisation aside just for the duration of this sentence, the geopolitical world of the last edition of this book had not seen 9/11, an event whose effects were to be pretty much integral to the transformation of media in the past decade, especially in the sphere of representations.)

Digitisation demands consideration because its opportunities for wresting at least some potential from the grasp of the established and wealthy media industries constitutes a serious threat, in the opinion of many media producers, to their sovereignty. As Roy Shuker points out in Chapter 14, below, the mainstream music industry has been increasingly alarmed at this prospect since the end of the last century and has since taken concerted action against the file-sharing site, Napster. Beyond the threat to established media producers, however, is the new set of possibilities for media production in general. A good example of this is the phenomenon known as web 2.0 which is usually characterised with references to increasing use of audio-visual material and interactivity in contrast to old print-dominated websites. Yet, the media theorist David Gauntlett offers a much more illuminating evaluation of web 2.0 by describing its facilitating participatory qualities. Whereas web 1.0 in the decade after 1994–95 promoted 'uploading to', 'publishing' or creating a website in a manner which was like the cultivation of separate gardens for others to view – a large corporation had such a website, a group of friends or colleagues had one, an individual had one – with each garden divided by a fence, web 2.0 was more like an allotment: 'different people coming together and working on the same thing' (Gauntlett 2008). Wikipedia is an obvious example of this. For Gauntlett, though, the important matter to note is that such participatory digital intervention constitutes a potential sea change in the entire process of media production and consumption.

That digitisation holds such massive potential has not gone unnoticed by the established media industries in Europe. In the UK, for example, the inexorable movement to digital switchover of television in 2010 has also been accompanied by exploitation by the established media owners of a series of possibilities digitisation offers, from Sky+ to HD services to downloadable programmes, as well as a proliferation of the number of television channels now available. The participatory element of digitisation noted by Gauntlett has also been exploited by established media – user generated content (UGC) is now a frequent component of news and magazine programmes, for example, even if it arrives in the lowly form of a text message sent by mobile phone. Taking another, less obvious, example from this volume, Beverley Tarquini argues that: 'The improvements in price, quality and format in other recent electronic devices such as the Amazon "Kindle Reader" and Sony's portable Reader have enabled inroads into publishing and may threaten the continued existence of the printed book' (see Chapter 7, p. 106). These devices have been taken up and developed regardless by companies that have previously made profit from the printed word but see yet more profit in the potential of digitisation.

Perhaps unsurprisingly, digitisation has also affected specific media-related tasks. Newsrooms and news broadcasts, for example, have changed dramatically in the past five years (see Chapter 17 below). In particular, there have arisen 'convergent' newsrooms, where the content produced is then immediately adapted in a multimedia environment for a variety of partially different formats (e.g. to be uploaded on websites, sent out as text messages, etc.) – in short, not solely delivered by television. Conversely, UGC, as noted above, has carried on the process in the opposite direction.

As with much technological innovation, there is the potential for some human operatives in the media message chain to suffer from digitisation. In major media organisations digitisation has seen redundancies in media organisations and this is one aspect of the debate on EU regulation of digitisation and the extent of the possibilities offered by digital production and distribution technologies. Indeed, it should be said that this book appears at a pivotal moment for the development of media in Europe. Despite technological possibilities unfolding in the second decade of the 21st century, media industries are still attempting to recover from the crisis caused by the decline of advertising revenue at the beginning of the century, which was itself compounded by the ultimate failure of the so-called 'dot.com' boom. In addition, Europe is beginning to suffer more fully the effects of the global economic crisis. The implications and potential of digitisation remain; however, the cost of realising them quickly might be too much.

But what *are* the media?

In addition to foregrounding the importance of current media technology and the European context of media, this volume is also designed to address the even more fundamental questions about what actually constitutes the media. Sharp readers will notice that this introduction has alternated between references to 'the media' in the plural (a collection of industries) and in the singular (a monolith). It is often forgotten that the term 'media' is the plural of 'medium' and that 'the media' (implying singular) is actually a diverse collection of industries and practices, each with their own methods of communication, specific business interests, constraints and audiences. At the same time, though, it is worth acknowledging that 'the media' (singular) is an important facet of the popular imagination, responsible for messages that may not be 100 per cent trustworthy and dictated by a set of economic and political interests which, especially with trans-national cross-media ownership (Rupert Murdoch's News International empire is an obvious example), traverse more than just the one medium.

As a collection of commonalities the media *can* therefore be conceived as:

- a collection of industries;
- a collection of practices;
- a collection of representations;
- a collection of the products of economic and statutory regulations;
- a collection of audiences' understandings;
- a means of delivering audiences to advertisers (or is it a public service?);

and, latterly, in the throes of digitisation:

- a collection of individuals or small groups sending messages to other individuals, small groups or much larger groups.

Yet, even with these definitions it is important to note that the media is/are in perpetual flux. Consumers of media know very well that the media's content changes from day to day. Additionally, media outlets are continually being bought, sold and created. Regulations change; so do technologies and audiences.

One way of achieving a broad overview of the media is by reference to the communications process. What all media entail is a process that involves senders, messages and receivers as well as a specific social context in which they operate. Thus:

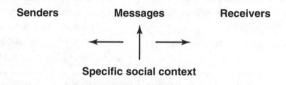

understood as consisting of (at least) the following:

Senders	
Pre-digitisation	*Post-digitisation*
'Senders' of media messages could usefully be understood as institutions.	'Senders' of media messages can be institutions (as left), but not necessarily; nevertheless, they must possess relevant technology to reach 'receivers'.
Resource-rich senders – institutions – use established and new media (including the internet) with the pronounced likelihood that they will reach large numbers.	Resource-poor senders tend to use technologies such as the internet where it is possible they reach large numbers.
Institutions	Resource-poor senders
• are economic entities which have to maintain a sufficient cash flow to continue/expand their activities; • work within legal and governmental frameworks of regulation; • are peopled by professionals implementing specialised practices; • facilitate the transmission of certain messages embodying certain worldviews (and not others).	• are not necessarily economic entities and do not necessarily desire to continue/expand their activities; • work within legal and governmental frameworks of regulation, but also sometimes operate outside these; • sometimes require and possess only a small amount of technological competence; • facilitate the transmission of certain messages embodying certain worldviews (and not others).

(*continued*)

Messages

- Differ from medium to medium.
- Are not simple reflections of the world.
- Are thoroughly constructed entities.
- Emanate from 'senders' operating within the parameters noted above.
- Are often aimed at target audiences.
- Are often rich and open to interpretation.
- Are subject to political, cultural and legal constraints (but, in post-digitisation, sometimes find it possible to evade them).

Receivers

Pre-digitisation	*Post-digitisation*
The 'receivers' of media messages	The 'receivers' of media messages
<ul><li>are commodities sold to advertising agencies;</li><li>have demographic characteristics;</li><li>are not passive consumers or 'cultural dupes';</li><li>make meaning of messages according to pre-existing values, attitudes and experiences;</li><li>sometimes apprehend depictions of themselves in messages and assess the nature of these depictions, sometimes fail to apprehend depictions of themselves and sometimes notice their absence from messages;</li><li>are often only able to effect feedback in indirect or protracted ways.</li></ul>	<ul><li>are not only commodities sold to advertising agencies when they can be generally identified by the media corporation;</li><li>have demographic characteristics (but these are sometimes hidden);</li><li>are not passive consumers or 'cultural dupes';</li><li>make meaning of messages according to pre-existing values, attitudes and experiences;</li><li>sometimes apprehend depictions of themselves in messages and assess the nature of these depictions, sometimes fail to apprehend depiction of themselves and sometimes notice their absence from messages;</li><li>are often able to effect feedback directly.</li></ul>

Specific social context: contemporary Europe

Europe has

- its own models of media operation and regulation;
- diverse national traditions, languages and audiences;
- diverse traditions of representation;
- an ambiguous relationship to American media.

Thinking of the media in terms of these components of the communication process should help in establishing a preliminary understanding of what the media is/are. If these components are understood now, it will also assist in the most efficient use of this book.

How to use this book

This book is divided into five parts: one part helping to come to terms with how to approach the media; one part on what the media are; one part on the contemporary environment in which media operate; one part on how audiences experience the impact of media and how we can go about the study of this; one part on the analysis of the representations which make up the 'content' of media. In more detail, Part 1, 'Understanding the Media' contains essays about analysing media, different forms of media and an overview of different media systems in Europe. Contributions in this part offer an analytic introduction and overview which will serve in understanding the following sections and chapters. Part 2, 'What are the Media?', as the part title suggests, describes the media as a series of *separate* and *distinct* industries and practices rather than as a monolithic entity. It contains essays on the specific media themselves, the practices that characterise them and the industry that surrounds them. In sum, it offers accounts of what the media in Europe are. Part 3, 'The Media Environment: Policy, Economics and Institutions' contains explorations of issues which are, strictly speaking, 'external' to the media but which directly impinge on them. These are the factors that determine and embody the media economically, politically and institutionally. The essays – on economics, policy, PSB and censorship – emphasise the ways in which these matters affect the content and subsequent consumption of media. Part 4 'Audiences, Influences and Effects' presents debates about audience measurement and media audiences as consumers, media audiences as the subjects of psychological effects, audiences as subjects in media cultures and representations, and audiences as participants in the process of producing/consuming media texts. The final part, 'Media Representations' examines some of the things that actually appear (and *do not* appear) in the media. The essays in this part deal with the manner in which different media represent different facets of the 'real' world. Representations are a key issue in the study of media and a matter of considerable debate. Thus, the essays cover the important areas of concern regarding representation in Europe: sexuality; gender; social class; race and ethnicity; religion; youth; the body, health and illness; nationality; sport; and sex acts.

Despite the wide range of topics and the attempt to be representative in the volume as a whole and within each chapter, it is better *not* to simply use this book to gain a little information on one specific media topic which harbours personal appeal. More will be learned from reading about other topics covered in this volume, over and above those in which there might be a personal or specific interest. Such a reading strategy will enable the reader to:

● compare, contrast and thereby recognise the distinctiveness of a given topic, and
● identify consistencies across topics.

As well as providing introductions, each chapter allows the pursuit of further study by offering subjects for discussion (in the form of a few questions) and by suggesting further reading. In all cases references to published works in the main body of the chapter are to be found. This can serve two purposes: for the author of the article the reference supplies details of the evidence being used; for the reader, it supplies a source for further study in whatever facet is under discussion. The index provides comprehensive cross-referencing of topics.

The media, studying the media and media studies

There can be no doubt that the study of media is rapidly expanding. One reason is that, in the second decade of the 21st century, the media are increasingly a central part of people's lives, people's cultures and global economies. Another reason, not unconnected to this, is that the study of media remains vibrant.

'Media studies' emerged in the 1970s in Europe, evolving from sociology, 'mass culture' theory and the study of 'mass communications', all of which had already gained a firm grip in US universities. While often attempting to be 'pluralist' and open, in general media studies tended to incorporate the agendas which were already embedded in its ancestors. Throughout the 1980s and 1990s media studies in Europe consolidated itself as a discipline even though, like other disciplines such as sociology before it, media studies had to weather a storm in which many people outside universities (as well as a few within) tried to suggest that it was not 'a proper subject'. For some, the media was too trivial to be taken as an object of study; for others, media study was assumed to be exclusively hostile in its analyses of media products; for yet others, media studies did not provide enough of a practical education in the skills necessary for working in the media industries. All of these suspicions proceeded from false premises.

Firstly, what is trivial – celebrity culture, for example – is by no means always insignificant. Trivialities can perfuse everyday life to the extent that they play a large part in creating perceptions of the world at large. Secondly, an effective and credible vocational emphasis in the study of media cannot exist without a 'critical' component. 'Critical' here does not necessarily entail an endless catalogue of media sins against humanity; instead, it points to the acquisition of a thorough-going insight into the media, their uses, their significance in contemporary life and their modes of operating. Media studies graduates, whether they enter the media industries or not, will:

- benefit from a knowledge and understanding of media institutions as economic and professional entities;
- they will also gain much from a prior knowledge of the diversity of media audiences and what brings audience members together as possible constituencies;
- they will also be well-placed if they are equipped with an understanding of the social realities of audiences and how this impacts on media consumption (who likes popular science books? what makes who purchase items online, change channel, go to the cinema, switch off, click through, cancel a subscription, start a blog, switch newspaper, illegally download rather than use a legitimate music website, etc? what kind of things do people want to hear, see, surf through, download, read, subscribe to, upload, share, etc.?);
- they will also benefit from an understanding of how media products, as commodities, are delivered to audiences (or not) and how they are filtered (through economics, policy, national media models and even through censorship procedures).

What makes the study of contemporary media special is that the ubiquity of media, and the human engagement that it allows, means that whoever consumes media is, already, in a sense, an expert. Indeed, there have recently been suggestions from media scholars that digitisation has moved so fast that media studies has scant hope of catching up with it and that its users currently know more about media than its analysts (see Merrin 2008). However, in some ways, this has always been the case: analysis and understanding cannot move at the same speed as the phenomena that are its objects. Thus, this book seeks to go beyond the knowledge that accrues as a consequence of our daily media consumption. It goes, instead, into a realm much different from our *experience* of consuming radio, film, books, TV, newspapers, magazines, etc. The consuming of various media products is a different activity to the *understanding* of what those products consist of and how they have come about. The *production* of media products is not like its consumption, either – it is much slower. Since the media are so diverse, since their products are so numerous, since they are distributed across different media systems, the *study* of media needs to be likewise variegated. This book attempts to provide the first steps, for media students, towards this goal.

Questions

1 Using knowledge gained from this book and elsewhere try to construct a list of possible
   (a) media 'senders'
   (b) media 'messages'
   (c) media 'receivers'
   (d) media 'contexts'.
   Do not worry if your lists become very long.

2 List all the things that the creator of any media representation may need to know before embarking upon the creative process. Leave your list for a while and then re-read it, adding components where necessary. Will the list need to be substantially changed for different kinds of representation (e.g. news as opposed to 'fiction')?

3 Make some notes on contemporary digital media (downloading, virtual worlds, photo-sharing). Then try to imagine the world before the internet, mobile telephony and digital cameras. Although we are less than two decades away from that world, how difficult is the task?

References

Gauntlett, D. (2008) 'Participation Culture – Part 1' Inaugural lecture, University of Westminster, 12 November, www.youtube.com/watch?v=-I1ccF2UXVw (accessed 25 February 2009).

Merrin, W. (2008) 'Media Studies 2.0 – my thoughts . . .' Media Studies 2.0 blog, 4 January. http://mediastudies2point0.blogspot.com/search?q=media+studies+2.0 (accessed 25 February 2009).

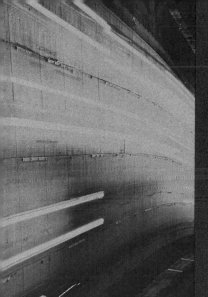

Part 1

UNDERSTANDING THE MEDIA

Introduction

Daniele Albertazzi and Paul Cobley

We have said already that this book is not meant to be read from cover to cover. Instead, you should consult parts of it for your own purposes and be dictated by your own needs (although, on the other hand, keep in mind that a little curiosity always pays off in the end). If there is only one part of this book that you have decided to read in its entirety, however, then by all means make it this one. Part 1 works as a long introduction to the whole volume and we see it as invaluable in enabling you to make the best use of what follows.

The first thing you will learn from Part 1 is that both the production and the study of media takes place within, and is informed by, specific perspectives. It is not difficult to understand how this happens to be so in the case of the production of mediated messages, as media proprietors and media institutions will inevitably be characterised by specific interests and views that they may want (or, when times get tough, even *need*) to promote, and doing so through the 'all powerful' media is a temptation that many seem unable to resist. What may be easier to miss, however, is the extent to which research *into* the media (whether funded by advertisers, private companies and the media industries themselves, or whether carried out by scholars, or both) inevitably reflects approaches, intellectual interests and beliefs that will inescapably generate different forms of understanding. While these interests may all be legitimate, in dealing with them, and in thinking about the possible consequences for the production of knowledge that they entail, you *must* enquire about what agendas they might in the end serve. This part thus starts with a chapter on 'Approaches to the Media' which will help you refine your theoretical tools by making you aware not only of which theoretical approaches have informed the study of media since 'media studies' started taking shape as a discipline, but also, importantly, of the political reasons why such approaches have been deployed (or else have been contested and maybe even rejected). Do not be fooled by the bad press some of the 'isms' presented in Chapter 1 usually get: not only are they are important (for the reasons mentioned above) but they also have very 'practical' applications. When properly understood, therefore,

Marxist cultural criticism, for instance, will force you to interrogate the extent to which the mediated text inevitably reveals something about (and, in turn, is shaped by) the (often forgotten) material and social conditions of its production, while feminism will help you uncover the extent to which 'society constructs and maintains unequal relations between the sexes, what are called patriarchal (male centered) relationships of power' (Chapter 1, p. 13) also, although not exclusively, through the communication process.

Following this discussion about how the media have been studied and were conceptualised in different contexts and for different purposes, the following chapter focuses on the 'forms' of representation with which audiences engage. Whatever the mediated 'content' you decide (or are 'volunteered' by your lecturer) to approach, such content 'is only rendered through the form' (Chapter 2, p. 35), i.e. a specific combination of signs, in which it is expressed. The chapter thus illustrates what is involved in formal analysis and explains why you should, as students, care to find out about it. The short answer to this question is that the relationship between 'form' and 'content' is far from being a simple one and yet remains inescapable, whatever the media we might be using.

Part 1 then proceeds to consider different 'Models of Media Institutions', since, after all, these are the very entities that make the production of mediated content possible in the first place. Taking television as a case study, Chapter 3 will reveal several differences in the way this medium has developed in Europe. Focusing on the extent to which institutions reflect and, in turn, affect 'political systems, political philosophies, cultural traits and economic conditions' (p. 46), the chapter discusses the effects recent processes of 'liberalisation' of the airwaves have had on the quality of programmes, the economics of television, media regulation and the development of public service broadcasting. The existence of a 'dual television system' (i.e. based on a model of private television vs. public service broadcasting) is shown to be typical of European broadcasting and crucial to fostering pluralism – a major preoccupation of European nations, and the EU as a whole. In revealing how this dualism is being challenged across Europe by the deployment of new technologies, this analysis opens the way to debating the final topic covered by this first part, i.e. the extent to which it is possible to compare national media systems at all and even talk about a 'Europeanisation' of national media in recent years (Chapter 4). As we have signalled in the introduction, and as Chapter 3 itself shows, although the media in Europe remain very national, and even parochial, there are many features of media systems across the continent (an obvious example being the determination with which sectors such as television are subject to regulation, or the extent to which public service broadcasting is still seen as vital) which now look truly 'European'. Moreover, the EU has indeed provided a framework that is lending European media some unity, while also helping to develop and defend those media. While the issue of the unity of European media still needs discussion, this book works from the observation that Europe provides the specific social context within which national media systems (including the UK one) need to be considered and conceptualised. Chapter 4 will provide you with the grounding to understand why this is the case.

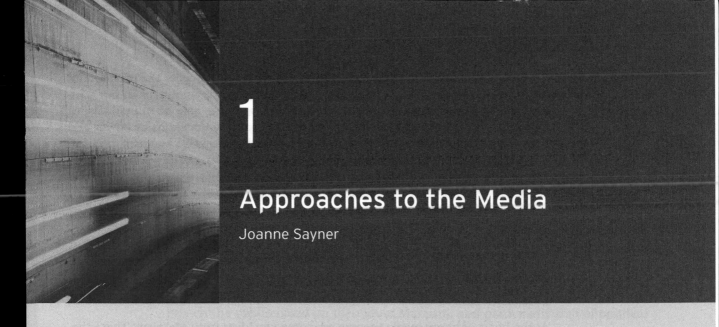

1

Approaches to the Media

Joanne Sayner

Chapter overview

This chapter considers a variety of theoretical approaches to the media. It suggests why they have been useful and what their limitations might be. It emphasises that contemporary media theorists often combine approaches and that their choice depends not only on their case studies but also on their political point of view. The chapter considers the continued influence of Marxism on approaches to media and looks at theories based on political economy and the work of the Frankfurt School. Approaches which focus on reception and the consumption of media, for example ethnography and uses and gratifications theory, are looked at alongside those which posit a more universal understanding of how individuals and language work, for example psychoanalysis and semiotics. The chapter ends by looking at the continued relevance of feminist approaches and also suggests areas which have yet to be developed fully by theorists of the media.

Introducing the terrain

There is no single approach to the media. Media critics have become adept at using all the tools at their disposal to interrogate their diverse and complex case studies. What is required of a media critic today is a willingness to question the usefulness of different theories, to test out their appropriateness for a constantly changing media landscape. This requires an ability to combine different approaches.

No media theories exist in a vacuum and the links, parallels and similarities between them inevitably make the picture more complex. Very often approaches to media are responses to what has gone before. They tackle what are perceived to be past limitations and criticisms. The aim of this chapter is to explain some of the key ideas of some of the key approaches. It will point to why these approaches are, or have been, productive. The following narrative emphasises similarities and links – it could have been told in many different ways and many other theories could have been included.

system and was maintained in complex ways involving both consent and resistance. Using ideas from Marx and Friedrich Engels, these cultural theorists looked at the way in which the ideas of the ruling classes become universalised and normalised, that is, they become universally accepted as being the only 'sensible' or 'common sense' option.

Vital to an understanding of these approaches are ideas by Marxists Antonio Gramsci and Louis Althusser. Both theorists understood society to be divided into two sets of institutions: on the one hand are those which use force in order to make us behave in certain ways (think of the police, the courts, the military, what they referred to as 'political society'); on the other are institutions which instead persuade us to consent to dominant ways of thinking arising from a particular type of social, economic order (think for example of schools, parents, churches, what they referred to as 'civil society'). Althusser described the former as 'Repressive State Apparatus' (RSAs) and the latter as 'Ideological State Apparatus' (ISAs) (2004: 43). Now obviously many of these institutions have both repressive and ideological functions, but important for theorists of media is that our systems of television, radio, film and print media would all belong to the ISAs.

Following Althusser, our media perpetuate the ideology of a society by a process of 'interpellation' (2004: 46), that is, calling to us (or, to use Althusser's term, 'hailing' us). As individuals we then respond to representations in a way which reinforces dominant ideology. For example, in the contemporary capitalist economy of Britain, women are interpellated by a large cosmetics firm to conform to expectations of femininity and buy lots of make-up 'because we're worth it'. By, literally, buying into the idea the advert promotes we become both a particular type of individual (or subject) and a supporter of a particular social order. This process of interpellation, according to Althusser, happens numerous times to each and every one of us every day on an unconscious level. Althusser's theories have proved particularly useful for media approaches to advertisements (Williamson 1978; Winship 1980).

Following Gramsci, the media, as constitutive elements of civil society, also induce us to consent to a particular economic system and to the leadership of the ruling classes within this system. This process, which he termed 'hegemony', has been pivotal for media theorists looking at how certain ideas become dominant and are maintained. To take a contemporary British example, an investigation of New Labour using such analysis would look at the role the media played in constructing, supporting and disseminating ideas about social equality, state intervention and the rights of the individual. It would highlight the ways in which such ideas have progressively been subjugated to the rationale of the capitalist system.

As these two brief examples suggest, integral to any contemporary approaches using these theories is the ability of the consumer or media producer to resist dominant ideology. To what extent can a woman ignore, challenge or subvert the hail of the cosmetics industry? Althusser's opinion on the matter was rather bleak and he implies that it is almost impossible to contest dominant ideology. For Gramsci, in contrast, the potential for resistance, or the possibility of forming a 'counter-hegemony', was an integral part of his analysis. As Raymond Williams has explained, for Gramsci a 'lived hegemony is always a process' (Williams 1977: 112) which constantly has to be defended. This is why Gramsci's ideas found particular resonance for theorists looking to explain the existence of different, competing cultures in society. The possibility for change is one of the reasons that it continues to be relevant for contemporary media approaches (McRobbie 1994).

As part of the battles between the different approaches above, some media critics responded to what they saw as ideas about passive consumption of media and decided to focus their approaches more directly on the reception of media texts.

'Going native?': ethnographic approaches to media

An ethnographic approach involves the exploration of lived cultures. It has its origins in the work of anthropologists who used to travel to investigate other cultures. Ethnography is therefore 'the analysis of how culture is used and understood by actual individuals and groups' (During 2005: 22). Methods employed can be quantitative (for example, those focused on measuring, like surveys and questionnaires) and/or qualitative (for example, those with more interpretative elements like interviews and participant observation). There are many accessible texts which can help the potential ethnographer to recognise the prerequisites and potential pitfalls of such research (Deacon *et al.* 1999; Marsen 2006). In the past, cultural studies has found such approaches to be particularly successful in examining ideas of resistance both in subcultures (Cohen 1972; Hebdige 1979) and working class cultures (Hoggart 1958; Willis 1977).

In media terms, ethnographic researchers set out to investigate the multiple ways in which texts are received by their audiences. Such work has often been referred to as 'new audience research', although as Boyd-Barrett points out, it is not new in its insistence on the fact that 'different readers read texts differently' (Boyd-Barrett and Newbold 1995: 499). Such methods are based on empirical approaches, that is, gaining evidentiary data and statistics from which understandings about people's behaviour can be drawn. Advocates of these approaches importantly point to the culturally constructed nature of any such interpretation.

However, the use of the term ethnography to describe what media critics are doing is contentious because studies relying on ethnographic approaches often examine texts and audiences out of context. For example, one of the most famous surveys of audience reactions, David Morley's *The Nationwide Audience* (1980), confronted groups of people with the news programme in a setting quite unlike that in which they usually watched it. Subsequent studies, for example Dorothy Hobson's examination of the soap opera *Crossroads* (1982), analysed behaviour in the home but still focused only on one aspect of consumption, rather than placing it within the context of 'social histories' as ethnographers would try to do (Turner 2003: 124). For this reason, contemporary approaches tend either to be more explicit about the limitations of their purpose, while still seeing value in these methods, or they broaden their remit (Turner 2003: 108–42).

Histories of such audience research show developments in relation to theoretical approaches, the types of media under investigation, and in terms of theme (Abercrombie and Longhurst 1998; Alasuutari 1999; Tulloch 2000; Schroder *et al.* 2003). Firstly, there has been a theoretical shift towards models which insist on a complexity of audience responses to media (Turner 2003: 72–7). These approaches have moved from the 'territory of audience reception to a broader analysis of cultural consumption' (Turner 2003: 138; Gauntlett and Hill 1999). Secondly, in terms of media technologies, past studies have particularly focused on television and its use in the home (Ang 1985). More recent studies consider domestic settings and wider media use but in relation to changing media forms (Bull 2000; Brown and Green *et al.* 2005; Hamill and Lasen 2005). Finally, thematically, contemporary approaches often focus on responses to sex (particularly pornography) and violence, questions of celebrity, and fandom.

What characterises several of the above studies is their incorporation of two often distinct lines of inquiry: questions of interpretation of media texts and questions of use (Hall cited in Turner 2003: 119). The extent to which media critics are interested in use often depends upon how much credence they give to what is called a uses and gratifications approach.

'I can't get no satisfaction': uses and gratifications approaches to media

One approach to media which focuses directly on consumption is uses and gratifications theory. This is a theory which asks the question 'how does the audience use the media to satisfy their needs?' Asking this question firstly involves defining what people's needs might be and how the media can help to fulfil them. The terms use and method are also important, as shown below. Information gleaned through this approach is clearly of interest for media producers who want to encourage us to consume certain things. Media critics who draw on these theories are not only able to suggest how media producers respond to our needs but even create new needs so that we consume certain products in order to fulfil them. As James Lull states: 'Need is a concept that can even be manipulated for profit' (2002: 103).

Different theorists have discussed uses and gratifications in different terms but many begin with a definition of 'need'. This can be seen as a basic requirement for human survival (for instance food, drink or shelter); however, arguably there are also 'higher level needs' which 'become salient when biological and safety needs are met' (Lull 2002: 103). Such needs are, to a large extent, culturally constructed. What we need in a Western, developed country is most certainly understood differently to that which is needed in a developing country, and not just because of the economic imbalance, but also because of centuries of different traditions and cultural expectations.

Needs can be fulfilled, or gratified, by certain methods, that is, the ways and means in which we go about achieving something. As part of any method we might use media. For example, an important human need is the feeling of belonging. There are many ways in which we could fulfil this need through interaction – popping round to the neighbours, having a dinner party or going to bingo. However, it is also possible that we sign up to Facebook or Bebo and spend several hours each day in virtual contact with others. Media use therefore becomes part of the method of gratifying a need.

James Watson suggests that consumers need the media for various reasons. He defines these in terms of diversion, personal relationships, personal identity and surveillance (2003: 62). He argues that the media satisfies these needs in turn by providing methods of escapism, identification with characters, enabling us to see parallels with our own lives, and by giving us the opportunity to have opinions about things. However, not all consumers have all of these needs and not all types of media satisfy needs in the same ways. Lull broadens the category of use examining how we consume the media within our daily routine, what he calls 'structural use', and how it corresponds to our personal relations (1980). For example, do we watch the television 'for company' and to what extent can this tell us about the domestic sphere in a globalised society?

Arthur Asa Berger, avoiding clear distinction between needs, uses and gratifications, suggests yet more reasons that we might consume media: from experiencing pleasure, beauty or other emotions in a safe environment, to satiating our curiosity by gaining information, that is, for educational reasons. Within his 24 point list of reasons people use the mass media, he points to religious or political reasons for consumption and suggests that media can fulfil a need to have our values affirmed or questioned. The media, he argues, provide us with authority figures and role models that might otherwise be lacking in our lives (2005: 125–32). He claims that it is possible to investigate media texts by looking at which elements gratify which needs (2005: 133).

As I suggested above, media critics looking at uses and gratifications have highlighted the ways in which media producers attempt to create the idea of a need in order to sell products. This creation of need was examined by the Frankfurt School theorist Herbert Marcuse in his text *One Dimensional Man* (1964), where he criticised the ways in which capitalist systems create 'false needs' in order to make profit, that is, they make us believe that we cannot survive without something.

Uses and gratifications theory therefore focuses on the reader of media texts. Its critics argue that it does so to the exclusion of the texts themselves – the texts are in many ways irrelevant to the discussion as different people consume different texts in different ways. In contrast, two approaches which focus instead on meanings within texts and the ways they are interpreted are those of psychoanalysis and semiotics.

'All about my mother': psychoanalytical approaches to media

In contrast to the approaches mentioned above, what characterises psychoanalysis is its ahistoricism. That is, it supposedly provides critics with a set of tools which are applicable regardless of social context or economic environment. This does not, however, mean that these theories are not a product of a specific historical time period or that their uses by media critics have not developed in response to changing social conditions. Rather, it suggests a set of theories which are applicable to understanding all human behaviour.

Psychoanalytical approaches to media are based on the premise that 'we are not [. . .] aware of everything that is going on in our minds' (Berger 2005: 76). These approaches use Sigmund Freud's theories as their starting point, theories which investigate the relationships between that which we are aware of, the conscious, and that which is in our minds but which we are unaware of, the unconscious. Such approaches try to understand why we make certain decisions about what media we produce and consume and how we produce and consume it. This information is obviously of great use for producers and advertisers who want us to consume in particular ways, but also for media critics who want to make such decisions apparent.

Critics have used key concepts from psychoanalysis to explore media in different ways; for example, Freud's hypothesis that the mind is divided into the 'id', the 'ego' and the 'superego' (1927). The id is responsible for our drives, the superego represents our moral framework, or conscience, and the ego is the part of our mind which negotiates between the other two in response to the environment we find ourselves in. According to Freud our mind prevents us becoming conscious of certain things because of the negative feelings we would experience if it did not. In Freud's terms, we 'repress' certain ideas, thoughts and feelings, for example, the desire to steal, because of the consequences that would result from acting upon it.

Berger argues, albeit rather reductively, that it is possible both to interpret media texts by looking for 'id' figures (the villains) and 'superego' figures (the superheroes), and to identify 'id' and 'superego' genres (for example, television or radio programmes, books, or films dealing with questions of sexuality, or law and justice respectively (2005: 87)). Berger also points to the ways in which psychoanalytical approaches look for (hidden) meanings in texts. He draws attention to the psychoanalytical belief that our unconscious desires are hidden in symbols; these symbols therefore in fact represent something which our superego would disapprove of (2005: 88). Very often these symbols occur in dreams and Berger draws parallels between the interpretation of dreams and the ways in which media critics interpret a particular media form by asking 'What is going on? What disguises are there? What gratifications do we get? What do the various symbolic heroes and heroines tell us about ourselves and our societies?' (2005: 89, 91–4).

Media critics have found Freud's work on sexuality to be particularly productive, although it is often the source of controversy. The perceived usefulness depends on the interpretation of his writings. Freud's work can offer a framework for understanding gendered identities and sexuality. Freud describes how an infant develops into a boy or girl. This involves the repression of an inherent bisexuality and the progression into 'normal' heterosexuality. During this process, called the Oedipal stage, an infant begins to separate itself from its mother and to recognise differences between male and female bodies. Jacques Lacan, a theorist who further developed Freud's theories, called this stage the 'mirror' stage (the child can recognise him/herself as a distinct person in the mirror) and he argued that this is the point when the child begins to enter into language with all the cultural codes that this entails (2004). These ideas about the processes of separation from the parents, the transference of feeling onto others through looking and identifying with others around us have proven pivotal for media applications of these theories.

A classic example of the use of psychoanalytical theory is a text by Laura Mulvey called 'Visual Pleasure and Narrative Cinema' (1975). Relying on concepts of the unconscious, repression, scopophilia (pleasure in looking) and narcissism (a preoccupation with oneself), Mulvey argued that 'mainstream Hollywood cinema in the post-war years primarily sets out to satisfy the unconscious desires of men' (Burston and Richardson 1995: 5). Referring to what she calls 'the male gaze' she argues that women are subject to objectification by male viewers and that women spectators must also adopt this position if they are to take pleasure in the films. Since its publication in 1975 Mulvey's article has been criticised by feminists for its emphasis on heterosexuality and its inherent essentialism (reducing all women to the same 'essence'), issues Mulvey herself addressed in her later essays (1989). However, the controversy generated by the article has proved of fundamental importance for subsequent feminist and queer approaches to the media (Burston and Richardson 1995).

'I saw the sign': semiotic approaches to media

All media practice is comprised of types of 'language'. Not just spoken and written language as we usually understand it, but a complex system of codes which depend on their contexts. Semiotic approaches investigate how these languages work. More specifically, semiotics is the 'general science of sign systems and their role in the construction and reconstruction of meaning' (Watson and Hill 1993: 169). While semiotics in media studies often involves finding out what a particular text means, semiotics more broadly investigates how it is possible for texts to mean at all (Marsen 2006: 54). Like psychoanalysis, semiotics looks for regular patterns.

Following Ferdinand de Saussure's *Course in General Linguistics* (1916), semioticians believe that language is comprised of signs. We can interpret these signs as they occur in our written and spoken language, but can also apply Saussure's theories more generally to interpret other signs, such as visual images, present in the media. According to Saussure signs are made up of a 'signifier' and a 'signified'. The signifier has come to be understood as the spoken sound, the writing on the page or the image. Hearing or seeing the signifier causes us to have a mental image or idea about what it refers to and it is this what Saussure calls 'the signified'. For example, if you read or hear the word 'television' you will be imagining what a television looks like. Unless you have a pictorial signifier (a photo or drawing) in front of you, it is quite likely that your mental image of a television will be different to mine but we would both understand what we meant. If, on the other hand, you saw or heard the word 'Fernsehen', unless you spoke German, you would not be able to relate this signifier to a signified (this word also means 'television'). However, the fact that English uses the word 'television' and German 'Fernsehen' is what semioticians call the arbitrary nature of the relation between the signified and the signifier; there's no particular reason why it should be one word and not the other, except for nearly a century of culturally specific tradition and usage. A visual signifier, in contrast, might be either a photograph or a symbol. A photograph might specify exactly the signified, whereas a symbol would be more likely to involve some interpretation of what it means and knowledge of context. Nevertheless, symbols are not purely arbitrary as they bear some resemblance to the signified. In all cases though, a reader has to be able to interpret the sign to be able to assign meaning to it.

Approaches based on semiotics look at the interaction or relationship between different signs in the creation of meaning. These relationships are important because Saussure emphasised that signs work on the basis of opposition and difference; we understand 'black' in relation to 'white', 'peace' in relation to 'war', 'old' in relation to 'young'. When applied more broadly, the concept that all signs signify in relation to all others means that media semioticians are on the look-out for intertextuality. This 'describes the borrowing by a text of content or stylistic features that were present in a previously produced text' (Marsen 2006: 61). There are many filmic examples which quote from previous cultural texts in different ways.

Using theories about the sign, Louis Hjelmslev distinguished between 'denotative' and 'connotative' meaning. Denotative, or primary meaning, is the literal description of something. The connotative meaning is the cultural meaning, the secondary associations that are attached to it. Roland Barthes used these concepts to investigate the links between signs and specific social contexts. His work was to prove invaluable for media critics, not least for approaches to visual images in everyday phenomena, including music, dance, food and fashion. His short, entertaining investigations in *Mythologies* were first published in 1957. He reminds us that material culture always signifies. For example, on a denotative level, an Aston Martin is an expensive, British-made, classic car. On a connotative level, it is a car driven by James Bond and spectacularly crashed in *Casino Royale* (2006). Its use in the film, at least the producers of the car hope, imbues it with connotations of glamour, adventure and sex. Using this example, a media critic could explore such connotations as part of investigations of contemporary portrayals of masculinity and heterosexuality.

Using theories of semiotics a media critic can therefore examine any aspect of a given cultural text or practice for what is being signified. For example, a television advertisement can be explored, scene by scene, by looking at the spoken words, the images, the camera angles, the music, the backdrop, and the actors' clothes, hair styles and body 'language' (Goldman and Papson 1996). Advertisers rely on us being able to understand what the signs signify, both denotatively and connotatively, in order to sell their products (Nadin and Zakia 1994).

Important to media analyses based on semiotics is whether the critic chooses to adopt a synchronic or a diachronic approach. A synchronic approach involves taking a snapshot of meanings at a particular point in time (think of synchronised swimmers who must, at any given moment, be doing exactly the same thing), whereas a diachronic approach takes an historical look at how meanings have changed or progressed over time. For example, a synchronic investigation of the connotations of the use of the phrase the 'War on Terror' might look at 30 articles published in American newspapers on 21 September 2001. A diachronic approach might also take 30 articles which use the same phrase but they would be selected over the course of the past eight years in order to examine any changes in what is being connoted.

It is also possible to use diachronic and synchronic approaches within media texts in syntagmatic and paradigmatic ways. A syntagm 'is defined as a system of interrelated, consecutive units' (Marsen 2006: 62). A sentence is a syntagm, as is a pop song, film or news report. So, a syntagmatic analysis of the latest Hollywood blockbuster would look at the way these units are organised throughout the film; such analysis is usually diachronic. A paradigm, in contrast, is 'a class of elements that are semantically homogenous' (ibid. 63). For example, in the sentence: 'Peace talks were interrupted by demonstrators', the word 'demonstrators' could have been replaced by 'protestors', 'terrorists', or 'conscientious objectors' – all of these words have the same function grammatically but have very different meanings. As Jostein Gripsrud writes: 'Paradigms may be thought of as "storage shelves" where one finds and takes out the words one needs to fill certain places in the sytagms' (2006: 24). Just as we can fill a place in a sentence with different alternatives which make sense, we could also do the same in other syntagms familiar to media critics, for example a news report; within a sequence, or syntagmatic structure, which describes flooding in Gloucester we might replace an image of a news reporter in a flooded street with a bird's-eye view of the area from a helicopter. These alternatives are the paradigms. Paradigmatic analysis is synchronic and it involves highlighting oppositions, or choices within a text. These oppositions can then be investigated for ideological significance. For example, when deciding on a new character to be introduced into a long-running radio series, the producers have the choice of a male or female character, someone old or young, someone from the country or city, etc. Investigations of such paradigmatic decisions can be used to highlight themes in media texts. A theme is 'a sign that has a non-physical signified: that is, a signified that does not refer to a concrete object in the world' (Marsen 2006: 60). For example, the choice of an elderly female character might be part of a theme of emancipation, loneliness or love.

Saussure's ideas have been important for media critics and are referred to as being semiotic approaches. However, it is in fact more accurate to refer to Saussure's work as semiology (although semiotics and semiology are now often used interchangeably). The term semiotics came from another theorist, Charles Sanders Peirce. While a Peircean approach to media is still in its infancy, it can potentially be of importance for addressing a key criticism of a Saussurean approach: that it focuses on the message alone and not on the reception of it. Integral to Peirce's definition of the sign is the 'interpretant', in other words the sense made of the sign by the recipient (Marsen 2006: 57). Peirce further maintained that signs can be categorised in three ways according to the relation of objects: 'iconic', 'indexical' and 'symbolic'. Iconic signs, for example maps or photographs, closely resemble what they are describing. Indexical signs work by causality, for example sound, such as that of traffic on a movie soundtrack might be caused by items being caught by the recording. Symbols, in contrast, bear no resemblance to what they supposedly signify but we understand them because of convention; for example a red rose signifies love in a British context, a white carnation signifies death in a German context. As Gripsrud has argued, Peirce's definitions are relevant for media theorists when considering the issue of digital photography and the extent to which it can be seen as both iconic and indexical (2006: 30–1, 35–9).

As can be seen from the above discussion, this approach to media is particularly useful for 'its ability to deal with sound, image and their interrelation' (Turner 2003: 16). The value of semiotics for media critics lies in the attention it draws to the processes of signification. These have been influential in combination with different media theories, from those focusing on ideology to those engaged in audience research.

The final approach is one which it is almost impossible to separate from the discussion above. Although it has very distinct characteristics, it always draws on, and contributes to, the approaches already mentioned. This is an approach based on theories of feminism.

'Girl power?': feminist approaches to media

'Feminism', as Chris Weedon insists, 'is a politics. It is a politics directed at changing existing power relations between women and men in society. These power relations structure all areas of life, the family, education and welfare, the worlds of work and politics, culture and leisure. They determine who does what and for whom, what we are and what we might become' (1995: 1). Feminists therefore begin with the assumption that society constructs and maintains unequal relations between the sexes, what are called patriarchal (male centred) relationships of power. Investigations of the complexity of such power are at the heart of the feminist project. Feminists examine the status attached to women in society and the value attributed to women's experiences.

The impact of feminism was particularly felt in the 1970s and it has progressively become a more dominant set of methods for approaching the media. However, as Rosalind Gill points out, while 'feminist ideas have become a kind of common sense [. . .] feminism has never been more bitterly repudiated' (2008: 1). Often it is said that we are now in a 'postfeminist' age, one in which the feminist gains of the past are being actively undermined (McRobbie 2006: 59). While some theorists believe that it is popular media culture which is 'perniciously effective' in the undoing of feminist agendas (McRobbie 2006: 59; Brunsdon 2005) others remind us that 'feminism now happens *in* the media' (Gill 2008: 40, my emphasis).

Inevitably, feminist criticism is linked to the societies it examines, so as the role of women in society and feminist agendas have shifted so have feminist media theories (van Zoonen 1991; Brunsdon 1993; van Zoonen 1994). Carter and Steiner summarise this move of the 'contours of feminist media theory from the "images of women in the media" approaches prevalent in the 1970s through to contemporary discussion of masculinity, globalization and cyber culture' (2004: ix). As this suggests, contemporary feminist analyses have responded to the proliferation of complex and competing constructions of gendered identity and to investigations of both the roles of women and men.

Several key historical ideas of feminism are still relevant today, although not every media theorist subscribes to them in the same ways. Firstly, an important claim of feminism is that 'the personal is the political'. That is, there is no area of our lives untouched by gendered politics, and this especially applies to areas traditionally defined as 'private', such as the home. Feminist approaches can highlight how the media often helps to thematise such boundaries and bring important issues to a wider public. For example: episodes of talk shows like *Oprah* and *Tricia* play a role in confronting subjects which in the past have belonged 'behind closed doors'; the British soap opera *EastEnders* has several times confronted 'personal' issues such as rape and domestic violence, the representation of which has led to large increases in calls to the national helpline numbers listed at the end of the programmes; and ethnographic investigations in the domestic sphere have often shown how media consumption is affected by gender hierarchy (Morley 1980; Gray 1992).

Secondly, feminists have traditionally distinguished between the terms female and feminine; where female refers, generally, to a biological category, and feminine refers to 'a set of culturally defined characteristics', that is, the characteristics of what a woman 'should' be (Moi 1989: 117). While recent theorists, including Judith Butler, have challenged the idea of 'sex' being biologically determined, arguing instead that it is similarly socially constructed and regulated by the medical profession (1990), there remains a focus (McRobbie 2006) on the cultural construction of what it means to be a woman. Critics consider the ways in which femaleness and femininity are created in the media, that is, they examine the restricted stereotypes of women presented. Feminists believe that given the preponderance of images in the media it is unlikely that these ideas about femininity 'would have no impact on our own sense of identity' (Gauntlett 2002: 1). The extent to which they affect us, and the extent to which this can be measured, is of course open to debate but the prevalence of visual images in the media have provided, and still provide, fertile ground for such analyses (Goffmann 1979; McRobbie 1999; Blackman 2006; Gill 2008). Vital to contemporary analysis is an understanding that representations of femininity have become increasingly complex. More recently, approaches focusing on visual images of femininity have been joined by critical discussion of masculinity (Benwell 2003).

Thirdly, a focus of feminist investigations is the issue of female pleasure and its relationship to ideology. Linked to examinations of consumption and approaches based on uses and gratifications, early investigations looked particularly at genres enjoyed by women (Modleski 1982; Ang 1985; Radway 1987). Media theorists must negotiate the difficulties of analysing media which women enjoy but which perpetuate sexist ideologies (Gill 2008: 13–16, 195–8). For example, the current, controversial use of irony within various media forms, especially advertising, which perpetuates sexist media messages while attempting to forestall feminist criticism (McRobbie 2006; Gill 2008).

Feminist approaches combine these issues with the other approaches discussed in this chapter. For example, feminist semioticians have pointed to binaries that construct our language and contain inherent hierarchies which subordinate the female. Other critics have paid close attention to the ways in which language signifies in our media and have applied semiotic theory not only to written and spoken language but to visual images and cultural products (for example, McRobbie 1977). Many feminists believe that there are links between capitalism and

29

patriarchy. They have drawn on theories of ideology to critique hegemonic ideas of femininity and masculinity (McRobbie 1977; Winship 1978). Materialist feminist approaches and approaches drawing on theories of political economy have also proven illuminating. Eileen Meehan has looked, for example, at the ways in which sexist assumptions made by television conglomerations about the compositions of their target audiences affect the production and support of certain types of programmes and channels (2002).

Notwithstanding the continued use of ideas of hegemony and ideology, feminists have increasingly turned to Michel Foucault's ideas of discourse as their theoretical models (Gill 2008: 60–4). Foucault's understanding of how subjectivity is formed and his insistence on complex networks of power and knowledge which characterise our societies has led in part to a shift away from understandings of consolidated blocks of power like patriarchy (McRobbie 2006: 60). This has led to a productive diversification of feminist approaches, but arguably at the expense of a unified political force. Vitally, though, this shift focuses attention on the fact that integral to any understanding of gendered identities is also the issue of ethnicity or 'race'. That is because 'what one learns when one learns one's gender identity is the gender identity appropriate to one's ethnic, class, national and racial identity' (Spelman 1988: 88). Media critics interested in these areas need to be constantly aware of their own positionality in relation to hierarchies of gender, ethnicity and class. Gendered approaches to the media have been challenged by feminist critics of colour who have demanded a rethinking of analytical models (Gill 2008: 27). Much work remains to be done using postcolonial approaches to media. While some of the key elements to such analysis are similar to that of feminism, including the thematisation of binary relations and the necessity of antiessentialism, media critics can profit from theories of 'Othering' and identity. Approaches informed by postcolonialism are more commonly being linked to investigations of political economy, not least because of their focus on globalisation and changing ideas of community (Gill 2008: 67–9).

'The end is just the beginning'

As the choice of approach to the media will be determined by the case study in question, it is not possible to suggest one approach as the most useful for examining the contemporary media landscape. However, with the increasing globalisation of the media, studies which investigate new technologies and their relationships to issues of identity are particularly relevant. All of the approaches discussed above are potentially useful in this respect; however there seems to be increasingly a trend towards combining approaches in order to benefit from the insights accorded by all.

Questions

1 Why are issues of media concentration and of privatisation of public service broadcasting important for political economists?

2 What can Marxist approaches to media learn from contemporary feminism?

3 What, in your view, is the most productive approach for studying audience consumption of contemporary soap operas and why?

Further reading

Ang, I. (1991) *Desperately Seeking the Audience*, London: Routledge. An ethnography study of television audiences which draws on both American and European contexts.

Barthes, R. (1970) *Writing Degree Zero and Elements of Semiology* (trans. A. Lavers and C. Smith), Boston: Beacon. Two books bound together in which Barthes looks at how language creates meaning. He focuses especially on the links between writing, society and politics. The second book is an influential 'primer' giving Barthes take on Saussure's observations on the sign.

Chomsky, N. and **Herman E.** (1988) *Manufacturing Consent: The Political Economy of the Mass Media*, New York: Pantheon. A classic, controversial text which uses ideas of hegemony in its criticism of the US press system.

Kellner, D. (1997) 'Critical Theory and Cultural Studies: The Missed Articulation', in J. McGuigan (ed) *Cultural Methodologies*, London: Sage, pp. 12–41. A useful analysis of the parallels and similarities of the approaches of the Frankfurt School and British Cultural Studies.

McRobbie, A. (2009) *The Aftermath of Feminism: Gender, Culture and Social Change*, London: Sage. In this text McRobbie questions whether we have entered a post-feminist age and takes contemporary media and celebrity case studies as the basis for arguing that a 'new form of sexual contract' has emerged.

Williams, R. (1977) 'Ideology', in *Marxism and Literature*, Oxford: Open University Press, pp. 54–71. An accessible and insightful examination of the competing definitions of ideology still used as the basis for many discussions by media critics today.

References

Abercrombie, N. and Longhurst, B. (1998) *Audiences*, London: Sage.

Adorno, T. W. and Horkheimer M. (1997) *Dialectic of Enlightenment*, London: Verso.

Adorno, T. W. (1975) 'Culture Industry Reconsidered' (trans. A. Rabinbach), *New German Critique* (6): 12-19 [first published in German in 1967].

Alasuutari, P. (ed) (1999) *Rethinking the Media Audience: The New Agenda*, London: Sage.

Althusser, L. (2004) 'Ideology and the Ideological State Apparatuses', in A. Easthope and K. McGowan (eds) *A Critical and Cultural Theory Reader*, Maidenhead: Open University Press, pp. 42-50.

Ang, I. (1985) *Watching Dallas: Soap Opera and the Melodramatic Imagination*, London: Methuen.

Barthes, R. (1972) *Mythologies*, New York: Hill & Wang [first published 1957].

Benwell, B. (ed) (2003) *Masculinity and Men's Lifestyle Magazines*, Oxford: Blackwell.

Benjamin, W. (1999) 'The Work of Art in the Age of Mechanical Reproduction', in A. Arendt (ed) *Illuminations*, London: Pimlico, pp. 211-44.

Berger, A. A. (2005) *Media Analysis Techniques*, 3rd edition, London: Sage.

Blackman, L. (2006) '"Inventing the Psychological": Lifestyle Magazines and the Fiction of the Autonomous Self', in J. Curran and D. Morley (eds) *Media and Cultural Theory*, London: Routledge, pp. 209–20.

Boyd-Barrett, O. and Newbold, C. (eds) (1995), *Approaches to Media: A Reader*, London: Arnold.

Brown, B. and Green N., *et al*. (eds) (2005) *Wireless World: Social and Interactional Aspects of the Mobile Age*, London: Springer.

Brunsdon, C. (1993) 'Identity in Feminist Television Criticism', *Media, Culture and Society* 15 (2): 309–20.

Brunsdon, C. (2005) 'Feminism, Post-feminism: Martha, Martha and Nigella', *Cinema Journal* 44 (2): 110–16.

Bull, M. (2000) *Sounding out the City: Personal Stereos and the Management of Everyday Life*, Oxford: Berg.

Burston, P. and Richardson, C. (eds) (1995) *A Queer Romance: Lesbians, Gay Men and Popular Culture*, London: Routledge.

Butler, J. (1990) *Gender Trouble: Feminism and the Subversion of Identity*, London: Routledge.

Carter, C. and Steiner, L. (2004) *Critical Readings: Media and Gender*, Maidenhead: Open University Press.

Chakravartty, P. and Zhao, Y. (2007) 'Introduction: Toward a Transcultural Political Economy of Global Communication', in P. Chakravartty and Y. Zhao (eds) *Global Communications: Toward a Transcultural Political Economy*, Lanham: Rowan and Littlefield, pp. 1–19.

Cohen, P. (1972) 'Subcultural Conflict and Working-Class Community', *Working Papers in Cultural Studies*, 2.

De Saussure, F. (1960) *Course in General Linguistics*, Bally, C. and Sechehaye, A. (eds) in collaboration with Riedlinger, A., London: Owen [first published 1916].

Deacon, D. *et al*. (1999) *Researching Communications: A Practical Guide to Methods in Media and Cultural Analysis*, London: Arnold.

Durham, M. G. and Kellner, D. (2006) *Media and Cultural Studies; Keyworks*, 2nd edition, New York: Wiley-Blackwell.

During, S. (2005) *Cultural Studies: A Critical Introduction*, Abingdon: Routledge.

Freud, S. (1927) *The Ego and the Id*, (trans. J. Riviere), London: Hogarth.

Gauntlett, D. and Hill, A. (1999) *TV Living: Television Culture and Everyday Life*, London: Routledge.

Gauntlett, D. (2002) *Media, Gender and Identity: An Introduction*, London: Routledge.

Gill, R. (2008) *Gender and the Media*, Cambridge: Polity.

Goffmann, E. (1979) *Gender Advertisements*, London: Macmillan.

Goldman, R. and Papson, S. (1996) *Sign Wars: The Cluttered Landscape of Advertising*, New York: Guilford.

Gray, A. (1992) *Video Playtime: The Gendering of a Leisure Technology*, London: Pandora.

Gripsrud, J. (2006) 'Semiotics: Signs, Codes and Cultures', in M. Gillespie and J. Toynbee (eds) *Analysing Media Texts*, Maidenhead: Open University Press, pp. 9–42.

Hamill, L. and Lasen, A. (2005) *Mobile World: Past, Present and Future*, London: Springer.

Hebdige, D. (1979) *Subculture: The Meaning of Style*, London: Methuen.

Hoggart, R. (1958) *The Uses of Literacy*, London: Penguin.

James, D. E. (1996) 'Is There a Class in the Text?', in D. E. James and R. Berg (eds) *The Hidden Foundation: Cinema and the Question of Class*, Minneapolis; London: University of Minnesota Press, pp. 5–23.

Lacan, J. (2004) 'The Mirror Stage', in A. Easthope and K. McGowan (eds) *A Critical and Cultural Theory Reader*, Maidenhead: Open University Press, pp. 81–6 [first published 1949].

Lull, J. (1980) 'The Social Uses of Television', *Human Communication Research* 6: 197–209.

Lull, J. (2002) *Media, Communication, Culture: A Global Approach*, 2nd edition, Oxford: Blackwell.

Mansell, R. (2004) 'Political Economy, Power and New Media', *New Media & Society* 6 (1): 96–105.

Marcuse, H. (1964) *One Dimensional Man: Studies in the Ideology of Advanced Industrial Society*, London: Routledge and Kegan Paul.

Marsen, C. (2006) *Communication Studies*, Basingstoke: Palgrave.

McChesney, R. W. (2008) *The Political Economy of Media: Enduring Issues, Emerging Dilemmas*, New York: Monthly Review Foundation.

McRobbie, A. (1977) 'Jackie: An Ideology of Adolescent Femininity', CCCS Occasional Paper, Birmingham: University of Birmingham.

McRobbie, A. (1994) *Postmodernism and Popular Culture*, London: Routledge.

McRobbie, A. (1999) *In the Culture Society*, London: Routledge.

McRobbie, A. (2006) 'Postfeminism and Popular Culture: Bridget Jones and the New Gender Regime', in J. Curran and D. Morley (eds) *Media and Cultural Theory*, London: Routledge, pp. 59–70.

Meehan, E. R. (2002) 'Gender the Commodity Audience: Critical Media Research, Feminism and Political Economy', in E. R. Meehan and E. Riorden (eds) *Sex and Money: Feminism and Political Economy in the Media*, Minneapolis: University of Minnesota Press, pp. 209–22.

Modleski, T. (1982) *Loving with a Vengeance: Mass Produced Fantasies for Women*, New York: Routledge.

Moi, T. (1989) 'Feminist, Female, Feminine', in C. Belsey and J. Moore (eds) *The Feminist Reader*, Basingstoke: MacMillan, pp. 117–32.

Morley, D. (1980) *The Nationwide Audience*, London: British Film Institute.

Mosco, V. (1998) *The Political Economy of Communication*, London: Sage.

Mulvey, L. (1975) 'Visual Pleasure and Narrative Cinema', *Screen* 16 (3): 6–18.

Mulvey, L. (1989) *Visual and Other Pleasures*, Basingstoke: Macmillan.

Nadin, M. and Zakia, R. (1994) *Creating Effective Advertising Using Semiotics*, New York: Consultant University Press.

Negus, K. (2006) 'Rethinking Creative Production Away from the Cultural Industries', in J. Curran and D. Morley (eds) *Media and Cultural Theory*, London: Routledge, pp. 197–208.

Radway, J. (1987) *Reading the Romance: Women, Patriarchy and Popular Literature*, London: Verso.

Schroder, K., Drotner, K., Kline, S. and Murray, C. (2003) *Researching Audiences*, London: Arnold.

Spelman, E. V. (1988) *Inessential Woman: Problems of Exclusion in Feminist Thought*, Boston: Beacon Press.

Tulloch, J. (2000) *Watching Television Audiences*, London: Arnold.

Turner, G. (2003) *British Cultural Studies: An Introduction*, 3rd edition, London: Routledge.

Van Couvering, E. (2004) 'New Media? The Political Economy of Internet Search Engines' http://personal.lse.ac.uk/vancouve/IAMCR-CTP_SearchEnginePoliticalEconomy_EVC_2004-07-14.pdf (accessed 20 August 2008).

Watson, J. (2003) *Media Communication: An Introduction to Theory and Process*, Basingstoke: Palgrave Macmillan.

Watson, J. and Hill, A. (1993) *A Dictionary of Communication and Media Studies*, London: Arnold.

Weedon, C. (1995) *Feminist Practice and Poststructuralist Theory*, Oxford: Blackwell.

Williams, R. (1977) *Marxism and Literature*, Oxford: Open University Press.

Williamson, J. (1978) *Decoding Advertisements: Ideology and Meaning in Advertisements*, London: Marion Boyars.

Willis, P. (1977) *Learning to Labour: How Working Class Kids Get Working Class Jobs*, Farnborough: Saxon House.

Winship, J. (1978) 'A Woman's World, Woman: an Ideology of Femininity', Women Studies Group (ed) *Women Take Issue*, London: Hutchinson, pp. 133-54.

Winship, J. (1980) *Advertising in Women's Magazines: 1956-74*, Birmingham: Centre for Contemporary Cultural Studies.

Zoonen, L. van (1991) 'Feminist Perspectives on the Media', in J. Curran and M. Gurevitch (eds) *Mass Media & Society*, London: Edward Arnold, pp. 33-54.

Zoonen, L. van (1994) *Feminist Media Analysis*, London: Sage.

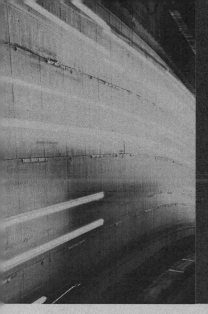

2

Media Form

John Corner

Chapter overview

What is involved in formal analysis? How does it relate to other aspects of media inquiry? How important is attention to form for our broader understanding of media processes? Addressing these issues, this chapter relates form to matters of content, interpretation and impact. By way of an example it looks at different depictions of the attack on the New York World Trade Center on September 11, 2001.

Introduction

In this chapter I want to look at why the study of form, of the way in which media texts work as crafted pieces of communicative performance, is of great importance in any programme of media study. This will require some attention to be paid to definitions of form and also to ideas about its analysis and to the way in which it is linked to other phases of communication through the media. Getting clear some ideas about media form will, I hope, provide a useful preliminary to engaging with those issues of process, structure and variety of representation that are discussed and illustrated elsewhere in this book.

The kind of attention given to questions of form varies considerably across the international range of studies concerned with media. In some cases form is a regular point of reference and exploration, in others it is only touched on, if at all, as a secondary matter. This variation indicates a broader pattern of divergence within the whole field of media studies, one between Humanities and Social Science modes of inquiry, with form a much more established term in the first of these areas. However, I am convinced that only by making questions about form a routine part of studying the media, from whatever perspective, will significant progress be made on most of the important matters we need to know more about. As other chapters in this book amply illustrate, media forms are subject to constant development in response to factors such as technology, the organisation of

35

production, the structure of markets and the social and cultural contexts in which audience expectations develop. Therefore working with form also means working close to the dynamics of media as agencies of cultural change.

Form and content

I talked above of the 'crafting' of communication. By 'form' I mean the particular organisation of signs, sometimes simple, sometimes complex, sometimes seemingly spontaneous, sometimes highly considered and strategic, that constitute any specific piece (text or act) of media communication – for instance, an advertising poster, an episode of a situation comedy on television, the opening remarks of a radio host, an article in a newspaper or a website home page with its text and images. Inevitably, such sign use is *conventional,* drawing selectively on what may well be a large range of communicative conventions (established 'rules of practice') for doing what it is trying to do and for being what it is trying to be. These conventions will inform word choice and order (as for instance in a popular newspaper front-page lead), they will be behind the ways in which images are lit and photographed and the ways in which items depicted in it are composed within a given frame and perspective and (in film, television and video) connected together as coherent moving sequences. Even if the communication is designed to read, sound or look highly 'original', conventions of form will be an important constitutive element (perhaps informing decisions about what is omitted, what is added or what is done with a significant difference).

The basic 'content' of any communication could, in most cases, be articulated by the use of any one of a number of different formal choices. For instance, there exists a wide range of visual techniques and styles by which to shoot, for the opening of a television programme, the main waterfront buildings of Liverpool. On the other side of the equation, the formal means used in depicting waterfront Liverpool will have a relative independence from their employment in this particular instance. They are likely to have a much wider application as a way of using television cameras effectively. Following the two different lines of possibility opened up here is a key feature of formal analysis – noting how *this* instance might have been communicated differently and noting how *different* instances have been communicated similarly.

One objection to what I have said so far might come from someone firmly committed to the view that it is impossible to separate 'form' from 'content', with the implication that even to use these terms at all is to slip into self-deception. This seems to me to be an over-reaction to those analysts who have gone on about 'form' without much regard for 'content' and those who have studied 'content' without paying much if any attention to 'form'. We can agree that any study should connect with *both*, but it is absolutely necessary to analytic progress to see the two as separate. Only this way can we understand their closeness of interconnection. Some writers on the media make the mistake of asserting the fusion of things that, illogically, they also wish to claim are related (only separate things can be related).

The form–content relationship is a complicated one. We can talk about specific formal strategies, devices and techniques in a way that is illuminating across a variety of different kinds of content but we should not forget the shaping influence that particular content will exert over the particular use of form. To put it the other way round, content is an analytically separable element too, but in any given media artefact it has a high level of form dependency (*it is rendered through the form* just as we can say that the form *expresses and projects the content*). In certain contexts, an emphasis solely on content may be relatively easy for the purposes of conducting an argument (for example, about the number of appearances in British television drama of Black police officers in comparison with Black criminals). Elsewhere, argument about content without close attention to form may be deeply misleading (as for instance, in analysis of television war reporting, where just *how* something is shown may be more important than simply noting *what* is shown). It is worth recognising how the division between 'fictional' and 'factual' forms operates here. Fictional forms, for instance film and television drama, have a history of both being enjoyed and discussed in relationship to their form, since they present themselves to viewers as *artifice*, as creative invention. Matters to do with their narrative structure and pacing, their use of the camera in exploring the imagined world on offer, their construction of character and their acting performances, etc. will inform most talk about them, ranging from that of professional critics to everyday conversation. It would perhaps be useful if some of the ways in which we talk about fiction, giving open attention to its formal devices, were used more often, albeit with adaptation, in talking about factual output.

To summarise, my view is that while content and form indicate elements of communication which cannot usefully be considered in isolation from each other – in many instances the interconnections and dependencies are too close for that – they are analytically separable in a way that allows us to engage with the nature of their relationship in any particular case.

Form and interpretation

Other chapters in this book refer in more detail to the ways in which study of the variables of interpretation has figured in recent media enquiry. A realisation of the extent to which the meanings of the media are dependent upon *acts of interpretation* rather than being a property inherent to media artefacts themselves and simply projected outwards from them, has been an important point of development in media research. It has given rise to a number of challenging lines of study into the social conditions of interpretability as they vary among different readerships and audiences. It has also broken forever any direct linkage between media items and influence, since it has introduced variables of meaning into the research perspective and correctly regarded mediation as a form of *symbolic transaction* in which the terms are both complex and dependent upon many factors. Research on influence has always been aware of the importance of variables but it has generally related these to a 'message' whose basic meaning was highly stable even if the use made of it or its function in prompting behaviour were not.

An emphasis on the way in which interpretative activity is pivotal in giving meaning to what we see and hear on the media in no way reduces the need for media research to pay attention to questions of form. Far from it. We will develop our understanding of meaning-making from media items only if we deepen and refine our knowledge of media forms in all their fascinating ways of facilitating and directing the ways in which we make meanings. This will also help us understand media production better, its criteria of quality and its ideas of what 'works' and what does not.

The scope of reader/viewers to vary in their interpretations of the same item is largely a function of social and biographical factors informing the interpretative framework they use in making sense of the item. It should be obvious that someone who has only been in Britain for a year, having come from Poland to find work, may well interpret a television news item on European immigration very differently from a UK citizen who has lived most of their life in a small English village with no overseas newcomers. However, although media texts do not 'close off' the meanings that different people will produce from an item, they nevertheless exert a shaping influence over our primary levels of understanding. They do this simply by their use of known words in a given language or even of familiar kinds of image or story pattern. If the news item I mentioned above finished with a shot of a newly arrived immigrant sleeping rough in the streets because of a failure to find a job and rent lodgings, it would be hard for anyone not to interpret this as projecting a broader *problem* – too many immigrants arriving for too little available work – whatever information was carried elsewhere in the story or whatever the variations in the way this meaning related to the viewer's own perceptions and values. If the reporter went as far as to run a voice-over comment across the scene, 'But this will not stop many more entering Britain to see if they can find a better life here,' it would be very difficult to imagine much interpretative variation among viewers as to *what was meant*, although there would definitely be differences in social and political response to it, including the possibility of complaints to the broadcasting authorities about unacceptably negative judgements on immigration being made by the reporter. Meanings are attributed by us to media items in a way that shows variations. But these items also have a high degree of efficiency in directing and organising common pathways through the cultural and communicative frameworks (the systems of meaning) we have internalised as members of a culture and speakers of a language. Is it therefore surprising that, when it comes to discussing last night's news, film or comedy show with friends, we have a lot of meanings to *share* as well as to dispute? Indeed, without some sharing there could be no dispute.

Elements of formal analysis

Analysis of communicative form has been undertaken in a wide range of disciplines; literary criticism, linguistics and art history have lengthy traditions of enquiry while film studies, cultural studies and media studies have more recent bodies of work. One of the key factors differentiating the analytic approaches is their level of systematic formulation – the degree to which they self-consciously follow procedures. Many literary critics analysing a poem, for instance, will do so with extremely close attention to its character as word arrangement, but with little by way of explicit procedure. Linguists, on the other hand, often analyse language with careful regard to their own analytic scheme and its categories, which are made clear in the analysis. Such a difference is partly a product of the different *aims* of enquiry – in the one case an artistic appreciation, in the other a description of language structures – but many types of communicative analysis combine a number of aims, so distinctions of this kind can prove troublesome. Semiotics, the science of signs, has, to many, seemed to offer the most general and rigorous system for analysing communication. Its emphasis on structural interrelations provides a framework of procedures for use across a whole range of different forms, including visual texts. In the study of media, the work of Roland Barthes (especially Barthes 1972) has been highly influential. However, the very precision of this kind of semiotics has been a problem insofar as it assumes too rigid and stable a communicative system, blocking out variation, and frequently ignores that process of interpretation, described above, by which meaning is also finally the product of specific, socially situated acts of reading and viewing. Despite some excellent and suggestive work, the tradition of media semiotics best known in English speaking academia (as opposed to semiotics generally) has not consolidated itself as a confident and fully coherent approach to formal analysis and it is now unlikely to do so as its systemic rigidities become further out of alignment with an interdisciplinary emphasis on variation, context and usage and on ideas that connect better with this emphasis.

Another general problem for formal analysis has been posed by visual texts. Clearly, the study of visual depiction, whether in drawing, photography, film, television or whatever, requires different tools from the study of written and spoken language (on this, see Messaris 1994). With language, the signifying units of words and the rules of combination (syntax) provide a core of relatively stable meanings. A dictionary and a grammar primer are indications of this. The units and combinatory rules of photography are far harder to grasp as a formal system. For a start, in a photograph we have no obvious signifying unit to compare with the word. Second, we face the problem that while a sentence is clearly a communicative device capable of generating all sorts of propositional and evaluative information, a photograph of a car in a street may just seem to be showing a car in the street. In other words, it may appear to have no communicative project at all apart from presenting us with a 'likeness'. Barthes' (1977) insightful discussion of the photograph as appearing to be 'a message without a code' takes up this very point. We may recognise that there is much more communicative work going on than this, and that indeed the 'message' is 'coded', but specifying the code system and its particular local application has often, not surprisingly, proved to be a formidable and controversial task.

All I will say here on this difficult question is that any serious project of formal analysis must have reasonably consistent, and preferably explicit, criteria for *identifying* distinctive components of communication. It must have a way of providing a *description* of communicative organisation that attends to how these components work in different combinations (the 'rules' for using them, however flexible these may be). There is much work that takes this approach but indicative examples might include Clive Scott (1999) on the relations between text and photographs, Karen Lury (2005) on television genres (see also the suggestions for further reading at the end of this chapter), the many editions of David Bordwell and Kristin Thompson (2006) on filmic organisation and Martin Montgomery (2008) on news discourse. The project should then be able to offer *explanations* that can address the link between particular examples of communicative practice (form in relation to content and *vice versa*) and the meanings actually registered by readers and audiences, even though these are likely to show variations according to context.

Having drawn attention to some of the principal analytic issues, I want to look at how what I have discussed so far relates to a particular instance.

'9/11'

The fact that these two numbers, spoken or written together, for many people in the world now immediately evoke a major event, one which will perhaps shape geopolitics for decades, suggests the symbolic intensity at work in all representations of what happened on the date they so concisely indicate.

The following extract is taken from a UK newspaper, the *Guardian*, on the day following the attack on the World Trade Center in 2001. Most of the paper was given over to various kinds of reporting on the event, its context and consequences. The extract is from a much longer account co-authored by three journalists. It attempts to document the *experience* of the event by drawing on eye-witness accounts, sometimes in direct quotation, sometimes not.

Geoff de Lesseps was on the telephone at 8.45 am, talking to his wife from his office on the 80th floor of the northern tower of the World Trade Center in lower Manhattan. 'I was meant to be going on a business trip tomorrow and she had this strange feeling about airplanes, I swear to God', said the 37-year old chief executive officer.

Then the first of the kamikaze planes hit the building a few floors above, cutting a cartoon-like outline into the 1,362 ft building, once the tallest in the world. The most spectacular terrorist attack on the United States had begun.

Twenty minutes later another plane hit the second tower of the complex. Soon people were hanging on for their lives – and falling – 1,000 ft above the ground under blue skies and a pale half-moon.

Forty-five minutes later people were still clinging on to windows, clearly visible from the street below, still against the ruptured symbol of US power and influence, debris fluttering like ticker-tape and stricken birds, catching the sunlight as it twisted to the ground. Finally, the unluckiest of the thousands who work each day in the towers lost their grip or jumped from the smoke and flames.

'I'm moving from this city', one man shouted as he ran. A homeless woman, shuffling along West Broadway, muttered: 'They're doing this for what? To save the world from what?' Now both towers were ablaze, columns of smoke billowing into the blue.

Schoolchildren stood in the streets; some of those working close by ran from the scene. Most just stared, in the middle of the broad boulevards, stung.

But as the crowds stood paralysed, one of the towers did the unthinkable; it suddenly disappeared into a cloud of its own making, and, in slow motion, collapsed to the ground with a deadly, horrible thud – punctured by screams on the streets: 'Holy Shit – it's gone!'

Source: From Ellison, M., Vulliamy, E. and Martinson, J. (2001) 'We Got Down to the Outside and It Was Like an Apocalypse', *Guardian*, 12 September: 6.
Copyright © Guardian News and Media Limited 2001. Reproduced with permission.

These are only the opening few paragraphs but the power of their formal organisation, the way they organise our perception and response to the situation they describe, is clear. There is strong chronology, given by the sequence 8.45, 'then', 'twenty minutes later', 'forty five minutes later', 'finally' and 'But as the crowds . . .' The irruption of the hugely abnormal event is grounded in a first paragraph about normality and routine, the telephone call recounted concisely but with a detail that works to consolidate its reality as a datum point in an object world, as well as a social world, about to be radically transformed.

The piece is doing its descriptive work in a context where most readers will already be terribly familiar with the event as a visual phenomenon, through the replays of varied television material the previous day and photographs of the kind that feature on the paper's own front page. Nevertheless, the awesome character of what happened is still a necessary reference point for any experiential account and for any relaying of emotional responses too. So central and overwhelming is this visibility that the piece works almost as an elaborative commentary on the picture that will be in almost every reader's mind. The 'cartoon-like' outline of the damage to the building, the 'blue skies', the 'pale half-moon' intensify our sense of a basic image we already hold. The description extends itself to a restrained metaphoric level, with the 'ruptured symbol' and the analogy with 'ticker-tape' and 'stricken birds'. The sheer horrifying *aesthetics of the spectacular* is so powerful here that noticing the way in which debris was caught in rays of sunlight does not figure as inappropriate. Into this sequence of visualised occurrences, localised voices of response, frightened or questioning, are placed – a human context for the objective disaster unfolding. The dominant feeling of simply watching, a feeling which connects witnesses on the ground with readers of the piece, is brought across powerfully in the last lines of the extract, as one of the towers slowly does the 'unthinkable'. It is the *particularity* of disaster, conveyed partly by using language to convey the local, unfolding moments of its perception, that gives this writing its strength.

How does this compare with a photograph of the event, one of the many, often very similar, photographs taken of the burning towers at stages during the attack? We can take the photograph by Spencer Platt for Getty Images that appeared on the front page of the *Guardian* on 12 September 2001 with the headline 'A Declaration of War', as well as on the front pages of many other newspapers in Britain and throughout the world (for a good reproduction of the Platt image itself without any titles see www.washingtonpost.com/wp-srv/photo/attack/newyork/2.htm). Within Britain alone, it was used by *the Independent* (headline: 'Doomsday America'), the Scottish newspaper *the Herald* (headline: 'The War of the Worlds'), *the Daily Telegraph* (headline: 'War on America') and *the Sun* (headline: 'The Day That Changed the World'). The image captures the disaster at a moment when both towers are still standing, though both have been hit, and it shows the South Tower just seconds after the impact of the second aircraft. Formally, the image gains strength from the way in which the two towers dominate the photograph in their full height, portrayed almost directly head on, without the angles that other published images introduce. The towers are near enough to give a sense of closeness without losing a sense of their full presence as giants of the cityscape, with a height position for the camera that allows the 'head on' gaze. The huge plume of smoke from the North Tower drifts across the top of the picture, 'capping' the South Tower. An explosive fireball around the entry point of the second aircraft bursts from the South Tower, pushing out both towards us and across the front of the North Tower. The second impact has also produced a huge burst of smoke and fire from the left of the South Tower. Underneath the main fireball, running the length of the image, there is a broad layer of debris, thinning out as it scatters down to the bottom of the frame. This is an astonishing image of urban modernity in devastation and it is not surprising that many people had recourse to the idea of 'disaster movie' in attempting to describe not only the appalling scale of the event but also their sense of it as a visual experience. The effect produced by the formal organisation of such movies, their aesthetics of 'tricks' and special effects and their extensive use of models and props, was here reproduced in reality. The photograph bears witness to this frightening sense of a kind of event already familiar from the iconography of fiction becoming a fact. Its own formal composition 'carries' the reality in a way that gives the (literally) monumental catastrophe that it portrays an overpowering degree of visual presence as the twin silver columns of the towers are linked together both by the black smoke at the top and the orange flame in the middle. We should remember, too, that almost everyone who saw this image would by then have known that the towers subsequently collapsed and therefore it 'carries', as part of its pictorial rendering, a sense of an impending further stage of the disaster not yet made visible.

We can make a striking comparison here with the formal handling of the 9/11 events in Michael Moore's feature documentary *Fahrenheit 9/11* (Dog Eat Dog, 2004). After a lengthy pre-credit sequence concerning the US elections of 2000, and the 'scandal' surrounding the final count, Moore opens the film proper with a minute of black screen, a 'non-space' in which we hear the sounds of aircraft, explosions, screams, the urgent voices of emergency services and sirens. As this minute elapses, the visuals return to show us faces in grief looking upwards, people holding each other for comfort or sitting on the ground in distress. People moving under a shower of falling debris are shown in slow motion, the fall of the debris itself finally taking up the whole of the screen. Then the camera tracks alongside a notice-board displaying photographs of missing persons. Over this, Moore opens his commentary:

> On September eleventh, 2001, nearly 3,000 people, including a colleague of mine, Bill Weems, were killed in the largest foreign attack ever on American soil . . .

Moore gets signifying power into his depiction by absolutely denying the viewer the central 'spectacle' of the burning towers which was a necessary feature of the contemporary news accounts, including photojournalism. By using a blank (black) screen and sounds, he invites the viewer to *imagine* the horror of the event, 'subjectivising' it in a way that scenes of the external devastation would not do. He can rely on his audience already having a mediated visual memory of the externalities, he wants to get us closer to the scale of the psychic impact and significance. It is interesting how this strategy continues even when vision returns. We are 'cued' towards the spectacle of the towers by the uplifted, anguished faces of the crowd but what they are seeing is kept back from us. Once again, we draw on the knowledge we already have to continue the lines of uplifted gaze to their awful focus of attention.

Each of these three ways of portraying the attack – the newspaper account, the celebrated photograph and Moore's film – show formal choices being made as to *how* to deploy word, image and sound to represent the event. Each could have been done in a variety of very different ways, even allowing for a central commitment to be 'true' to external physical facts. In assessing how they work, we have to attend to their formal organisation as media artefacts as well as recognising their *documentary* power, as accounts of reality.

Images and accounts of 9/11, both factual and fictional, continue to circulate internationally, including on *YouTube*, providing narrativised and visualised 'versions' of what happened. They have become 'iconic' for a whole range of purposes, including that of prosecuting 'the war on terror'. We could spread our analysis out to include a wider range of photographs (see for instance, the range of newspaper front pages from all over the world collected at www. september11news.com). We could also look at television programmes, movies, journalism, novels, paintings and even cartoons. Moore's treatment, for instance, could be interestingly compared with that of Paul Greengrass in the film *United 93* (Working Title Films 2006), where the main event is portrayed, visually and in radio and phone reports, through a primary focus on the unfolding drama in another hijacked plane and in New York air traffic control. We could look at the variations of portrayal and use across national boundaries, within Europe and then beyond. We would find that close formal analysis got us closer to how the event was 'made to mean' within different vocabularies of media practice and within the different interpretative frames, including frames of national identity, available to readers and viewers.

The future of form in media study

My fundamental argument is that the symbolic exchange managed by communicative form is a pivotal moment in media processes, the moment around which both production capacities and intentions and consumer expectations and interpretations gather. This is true for all media. Studies of the internet are showing a greater recognition of the web as a symbolic, not merely informational, medium and we can look forward to more attention being paid to the formal organisation of websites and the kinds of experience – linguistic, iconic, spatial and temporal – that they offer (see, for instance, the introductory accounts in Gauntlett and Horsley 2004). If media systems exert power as well as give pleasure, then it is primarily through the organisation of that which appears on page and screen (and, by implication, through the absence of that which does not) that such power is exercised. In investigating this process, questions about form (about *how communication is done*) are central and they are therefore essential to any full consideration of media practices and their consequences.

The analysis of form poses challenges for the analyst but this is no good reason for not giving full attention to meeting them. Doing so will advance our knowledge of the various professional 'languages' and communicative resources of media and at the same time give us a richer, deeper and more self-conscious engagement with the changing symbolic environments within which we all live.

Exercises

1 Record television news of the same lead story from two channels and by examination of visual and verbal organisation (e.g. sequencing of segments, visualisation, phrasings, captions) consider the impact of formal differences upon the interpretative options made available to viewers (including to yourself).

2 Take front pages from three different national newspapers that lead with the same story. How do their headlines and use of photographs differ and what are the implications of the differences for the meaning of the story and the positions of reaction and judgement that we are cued towards?

3 Take a magazine advert that you think works well and one that you think does not and briefly list the reasons for your judgements. Ask a friend to assess the same examples without knowing your opinion and then compare the results in the way they highlight formal features that carry implications for a reader's sense of the product's values and attractiveness.

Note

At points in this account, I have drawn for illustration on analyses that I have published elsewhere in greater detail, notably in Corner (2007).

Further reading

Books with good introductory material on matters of form include:

Deacon, D., Pickering, M., Golding, P. and Murdock, G. (2007) *Researching Communications*, 2nd edition, London: Arnold. A helpful account of some of the principal approaches to studying communication, addressing questions both of concept and method.

Hariman, R. and Lucaites, J. L. (2007) *No Caption Needed: Iconic Photographs, Public Culture and Liberal Democracy*, Chicago: University of Chicago Press. A suggestive study of the public and political power of photography. The book looks at a selection of photographs which have gained 'iconic' status within American public life and explores their construction, contexts, reworkings and variable interpretation. See also the website at www.nocaptionneeded.com.

Keeble, R. (2006) *The Newspapers Handbook*, 4th edition, London: Routledge. A useful attempt to provide students with a sense of the complexity of newspaper layout and language use.

Lury, K. (2005) *Interpreting Television*, London: Arnold. A clear and stimulating look at television form across a number of genres, offering many examples and raising important questions about how television programmes work to provide both knowledge and pleasure.

References

Barthes, R. (1972) *Mythologies* (trans. A. Lavers), London: Jonathan Cape.

Barthes, R. (1977) 'The Rhetoric of the Image' in his *Image-Music-Text*, London: Fontana.

Bordwell, D. and Thompson, K. (2006) *Film Art: An Introduction*, 8th edition, New York: McGraw-Hill.

Corner, J. (2007) 'Documentary expression and the physicality of the referent: observations on writing, painting and photography', *Studies in Documentary Film. 1.1*, pp. 5–19.

Ellison, M., Vulliamy E. and Martinson, J. (2001) 'We Got Down to the Outside and It Was Like an Apocalypse', *Guardian*, 12 September: 6.

Gauntlett, D. and Horsley, R. (eds) (2004) *Web Studies*, 2nd edition, London: Hodder Arnold.

Lury, K. (2005) *Interpreting Television*, London: Hodder Arnold.

Messaris, P. (1994) *Visual Literacy: Image, Mind and Reality*, Boulder, CO: Westview.

Montgomery, M. (2008) *The Discourse of Broadcast News: A Linguistic Approach*, London: Routledge.

Scott, C. (1999) *The Spoken Image: Photography and Language*, London: Reaktion Books.

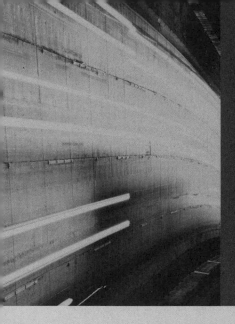

3

Models of Media Institutions

Stylianos Papathanassopoulos

Chapter overview

Although media systems in Europe have developed at about the same time, each national system still differs in many respects when compared to others. The same applies to broadcasting institutions, since they reflect the differences among political systems, political philosophies, cultural traits and economic conditions, resulting in different broadcasting models. Since the 1980s, most European broadcasting systems have faced a similar set of issues, such as technological advances, increasing competition and consolidation of their ownership status. These new developments have created a new market and altered the dynamics of the existing media structure.

Introduction

The study of media institutions aims to explore their structure and performance, as well as the conditions that have shaped and transformed them. In effect, each national broadcasting system represents a particular arrangement, which, in turn, reflects the politico-economic environment that operates within it. Governments regulate media systems in ways that reflect attitudes towards economic organisation, the rights of individuals, political traditions, and so on. Moreover, governments may treat different media in significantly different ways (Seymour-Ure 1987). In countries that have experienced repressive regimes in their modern history, such as Spain, Greece and Portugal, the media, especially broadcasting, have usually been, directly and/or indirectly, under the tight control of the state and regarded as a mouthpiece of the government of the day. Consequently, changes in forms of government bring about enormous changes in media institutions. Concurrently, the economic development of each country affects the performance of its media system to the extent that 'media development is a function of economic development' (Sanchez-Taberno 1993: 35).

Another factor is that of media consumption. Across Europe there are some significant differences among countries when it comes to the penetration and consumption of the printed and electronic media. This, too, impacts on the range and development of different media. Nevertheless, political and economic conditions and culture are the circumstances that mainly influence the development and the structure of most media systems and institutions. According to Hallin and Mancini (2004) the development of media systems are dependent on four variables:

1 the development of media markets;
2 the degree and nature of the links between the media and political parties;
3 the development of journalistic professionalism and journalistic autonomy; and
4 the role of the state in the function of the media.

The aim of this chapter is to explore changes within European broadcasting and to trace the dynamics and realities of the new developments. To do that, the chapter divides the developments in two periods according to the mode of television transmission. At first, it describes and assesses the restructuring of the European television landscape during the era of analogue transmission; it then reviews the development of digital television in Europe, while exploring the old and the emerging models of broadcasting in both eras.

The age of analogue television

Since the mid-1980s, Western European broadcasting has entered a period of tremendous and continuous change, following developments in television technology and implementing public policies favouring the liberalisation, privatisation and commercialisation of television systems. Until then, broadcasting organisations (in countries like Spain, Portugal, Greece) were either 'state-owned' or state-controlled; in others, like Britain, broadcasting organisations were either publicly funded or funded (wholly or partially) through a licence fee paid by all television set owners; finally, in some others, like Germany, France, Italy, they were funded by a combination of public and private (i.e. commercial advertising) funds. In all European countries, however, broadcasting was defined as a public service run by public entities which in turn were subject to public regulations. Traditionally, this was justified on political, economic, social and cultural grounds. The *de jure* monopoly status of public broadcasters was regarded as necessary in order to cope with the scarcity of radio frequencies, the fear that broadcasting could lead to the dissemination of subversive ideas, and to preserve free access to opinions rather than a free marketplace for advertisers. These political and economic rationales were challenged as a result of the profound changes of the 1980s (McQuail and Siune 1986; Negrine and Papathanassopoulos 1990). Generally speaking, three different European 'models' of public broadcasting can be identified during this period of time.

The 'old' models of broadcasting

In the *integration* model, public service broadcasters were funded mainly through a licence fee and enjoyed a *de jure* monopoly. This model had its roots in the idea that broadcasting could be treated as a natural monopoly and the belief that only this sort of structure could uphold the 'public interest'. Such a model did not rely on either journalistic or advertising competition for the provision of diversity but was based, in theory, on the notion of 'internal pluralism'. That is, the councils or committees which were directly or indirectly responsible for programming would be made up of representatives of various political, social and cultural groups in society ('internal pluralism') and this would ensure that a wide variety of perspectives were represented by the broadcasting authorities. Despite the political influence that was exerted on these broadcasting organisations, there was a basic consensus on this form of regulation and with regard to this structure of broadcasting. Most countries in Europe chose this model, i.e., a funding structure that mixed commercial advertising revenue and licence fee within each broadcasting institution.

The *duopoly* model, favoured by Britain from the 1950s onwards, was a hybrid model. In this case one finds the co-existence of public and private broadcasters who do compete for audiences but not for the same sources of revenue: thus, the BBC relies solely on the licence fee, whilst commercial companies rely solely on commercial funding. However, the nature of the duopoly required some mechanism to ensure that a full range and variety of genres and opinions were transmitted and that the competition between broadcasting services did not standardise the output. This has been achieved by the setting up of regulatory agencies such as Ofcom for the commercial broadcasting sector, with the BBC overseeing the public, non-commercial sector. Significantly, both private and public authorities pursue broadly similar public service broadcasting obligations.

The third, and in reality marginal, model was the *private sector monopoly*. The exclusive example was that of the Grand Duchy of Luxembourg. Hemmed in by its larger neighbours of Germany, France and Belgium and too small to become a significant media player, Luxembourg adopted a policy of creating internally a base for international broadcasting since the 1950s. Thus, it created 'an appropriately lax regulatory environment so that its national private commercial operator (CLT/RTL) could cream off advertising from its neighbours' (Dyson and Humphreys 1988: 7). It was a policy which inevitably brought it into conflict with other European countries such as Britain who wanted to preserve its cultural dominance and programming policies. Some countries, notably France, which were also likely to lose out financially, as funds flowed to Luxembourg, overcame the problem by acquiring stakes in CLT.

As noted, the 1980s was a period that was associated with changes in broadcasting policy as well as a series of technological developments, which had directly or indirectly, an impact on policy choices towards television. Since media systems differ, each country dealt with the issues and pressures for media change in a variety of ways. What united them was the sense that these issues and pressures were common to them all. These included:

- uncertainty over the direction of future technological change in respect of the 'new media';
- the spiralling costs of programme production and administration at a time of pressure on licence fees in relation to a growing political and economic pressure for the re-conceptualisation of broadcasting as a marketplace rather than as a cultural entity;
- the emerging demand for the liberalisation of previous monopolies particularly in the field of telecommunications (Negrine and Papathanassopoulos 1990).

The pace of deregulation

The most obvious manifestation of that change was the transformation of the mon-opolistic public service broadcasting corporations from the sole broadcasters to only one amongst many in a more competitive broadcasting market. In fact, since the 1980s, new commercial broadcasters came into existence. For example, in 2006 the total number of channels in Europe exceeded 5000 compared to less than 90 in 1989. Moreover, more than three-quarters of today's channels are private.

Some took advantage of the new technologies by broadcasting through satellite or cable; others took advantage of a more liberal approach to broadcasting which allowed for the development of terrestrial television systems. But all, one way or another, took advantage of the more liberal set of rules which were now governing their audiovisual landscape: rules, for example, which allowed commercial broadcasters to carry nothing but entertainment or to broadcast large quantities of imported material. In this way, what had initially been a fairly closed, state controlled system, characterised by a small number of public broadcasters, now became a large competitive environment, with a knock-on effect on the nature of the public broadcasters, on funding systems, on broadcasting cultures, and so on (Brants and De Bens 2000; Papathanassopoulos 2002).

The pace of broadcasting liberalisation in Europe followed various phases. According to Tunstall and Machin (1999: 190), there were several deregulatory waves of television systems in Europe. They were:

- The initial wave of injudicious deregulation which included Italy, Luxembourg, France and Germany; all four countries had committed themselves to massive deregulation by 1986.
- The second wave (around 1988–95), which included the UK and some heavily cabled nations such as the Netherlands and Belgium. Following the UK in the 1990s it was the turn of the smaller nations in Scandinavia and the Mediterranean, including Sweden, Greece, Portugal and Spain.
- The final wave involved a number of newly independent and newly ex-communist nations in Eastern and East-Central Europe, following the fall of the Soviet Union at the beginning of the 1990s.

The effects of broadcasting deregulation

The restructuring of the Western European television systems has also changed the relationship between the private and the public broadcasting sector. Where once only a few channels existed, now there are many, and there are many more yet to come. The effects of broadcasting liberalisation are now being felt across Europe with new commercial players and forces coming into play, although the processes of liberalisation and its impact has varied from country to country. There are, however, some common effects. These are summarised below (Papathanassopoulos 2002):

- The economics of European television have changed dramatically. The new audiovisual landscape has led to an increase in *competition* and an increase in demand for programmes, while the existing broadcasters (private and public) have been forced to meet the challenge of the newcomers in order to retain their audiences. This has resulted in a sharp increase in the total cost of content rights, especially for films and sports (mainly related to the aggressive competition policy of pay-TV channels). At the same time, private channels and interests have put pressure on regulatory agencies to relax the framework surrounding television advertising, sponsorship and bartering.

- Despite the increase in European audiovisual production, at the beginning of the 21st century, the USA remains the world leader in TV-programming exports. In the European Union, the annual trade deficit with the USA in this sector has been more than €8 billion (CEC 2003). US productions account for 60 to 90 per cent of the audiovisual markets of member states (receipts from cinema ticket sales, video cassette sales and rentals, and sales of television fiction programmes), whilst the corresponding European share of the US market is of the order of 1 or 2 per cent (CEC 2003). In fact, the European system of quotas has not been able to stem the 'Dallasification' of television content, and US fiction succeeds in breaking through all cultural barriers in Europe (De Bens and de Smaele 2001).

- A direct result of the liberalisation and subsequent commercialisation of the broadcasting system is an obsession with TV ratings and pressure from advertisers for larger audiences.

- There has been a widespread concern regarding the quality and range of programmes. Broadly speaking, a television culture led by market forces tends towards the maximisation of profit and the minimisation of financial risk, resulting in imitation, blandness and the recycling of genres, themes and approaches regarded as most profitable (McQuail 1998: 119–20; Ouellette and Lewis 2000: 96). In the search for larger audiences, broadcasters, especially the commercial ones, have not refrained from using whatever means they can to increase the popularity of their offerings (de Bens 1998: 27).

- A similar side effect of the liberalisation and intense competition of commercial television channels has been the proliferation of TV news programmes. Since the late 1980s, news programming has undergone a revolution. Competition at the international, regional and local level has mushroomed, and news output has expanded considerably. Compared to that of the past, the news of the 21st century has much more 'value added': not only do channels inform viewers of the facts; they are also preoccupied in how to sell information to them. In other words, TV channels pay more attention to news *presentation* rather than to the *content* of news, while traditional news values have been undermined by 'infotainment' values (Franklin 1997).

- Public broadcasters have faced erosion of both their viewing share and their revenue; that erosion has been more severe for some than for others. A number of European public broadcasters have responded to the challenge from commercial broadcasters by pursuing commercial opportunities of their own such as co-productions, international sales or joint ventures, within the limits of national and EU regulations. However, their future will rest in their way of funding. This, in close association with the digital threats, will be the most important issue for European public broadcasters.

- The liberalisation of television has led to the creation of larger and fewer dominant groups and as a result the sector is becoming more concentrated and populated by multimedia conglomerates. The trend towards a complex form of cooperation between media and telecommunications groups in Europe has raised fears of excessive concentration of ownership (Murdock and Golding 1999). Mergers, acquisitions and common shareholding, led in most instances by telecommunications groups, have created a web of common interests across the European media, though even here the pattern is not uniform. Although the EU has failed to harmonise ownership regulations for the European media, its interest in this area indicates a concern about the economic forces behind the media and the risk these pose for diversity and pluralism.

- The liberalisation, privatisation and commercialisation of television have had implications not only nationally but also locally and internationally. Although regional and local television is not new in Europe, liberalisation has brought a multiplication of regional and local private channels in most countries (see Moragas Spa and López 2000).

- The liberalisation of European broadcasting in the 1980s has led to new formalised procedures – for example, *the foundation of new regulatory bodies* and procedures to license new (mainly commercial) broadcasters and to oversee their behaviour. This has often led to different rules (sometimes stricter, sometimes less strict) being enacted. The emergence of regulatory bodies, almost non-existent in Europe before the 1980s, is a result of 'regulatory capitalism' and is grounded in the delegation of regulatory competencies to authorities that are partly independent from direct political control (Gilardi 2005). In the broadcasting field, there is great diversity among these regulatory authorities. Broadcasting regulation usually encompasses the power to license broadcasters, to monitor whether broadcasters are fulfilling their legal obligations, and to impose sanctions if they fail to carry them out. To these traditional functions can be added those of organising and coordinating the broadcasting landscape. Since 1998 regulatory authorities have started cooperating in order to coordinate their approaches and avoid divergent policies. The function, structure and jurisdiction of such authorities vary. In most countries there are separate regulatory bodies for supervising broadcasting and telecommunications industries.

● As television has become the dominant medium, viewing time rose when audiences were first offered an alternative to the state fare. In 2006 the average daily television viewing time in Europe was 222 minutes, much lower compared to North America (271 minutes). One significant change in the European television household has been the transition from collective family viewing of two or three generalist channels to a new reality where individual family members watch television alone or surf the internet (Papathanassopoulos 2002; Idate 2007). Moreover, with a much broader range of channels on offer, European viewers have become less loyal to channels as a result of the almost absolute penetration and heavy use of remote controls. Additionally, more and more European TV households now own two or three TV sets (EAO 2006). Although TV viewing time and programme preferences differ throughout Europe, European viewers seem to give preference to sports (especially soccer), news, films (in most cases US films), sitcoms and, recently, reality TV programmes (such as *Big Brother*) (Mediametrié 2007).

Towards the digital era

Since the late 1990s, European television has been experiencing a new deregulatory wave led again by technological developments. With the advent of digital television one notes a second wave towards further liberalisation of the already deregulated television environment, regardless of the side effects of the first deregulatory wave of the 1980s. As Chalaby and Segel note: 'Digitisation is transforming not only the way we watch television, and the way we use television, but also the way television is made' (1999: 352).

By and large, the arrival of digital television, either terrestrial, cable or satellite, was seen to profoundly transform the media system and its institutions. However, the full implications of the digitalisation of television are still the subject of much speculation, hype and uncertainty. As the history of European television has shown, the successful development of any new technology and form of television has to do with the content and the perceived value added that they offer to the viewers.

The development of digital television had not been easy. Although in the mid-1990s, large European media companies announced their plans for digital satellite pay-TV channels, the reality was different. In fact, 2002 could be seen as an important year concerning the hype for digital television in Europe, since it witnessed the successive bankruptcy of various digital operators – such as the UK's ITV Digital, Spain's Quiero TV and Greece's Alpha Digital; the merger of Spain's two satellite packages – Canal Satélite Digital and Vía Digital; the merger-takeover of Italy's leading operator Telepiù by its rival Stream; the re-launch of the new Polish digital satellite platform, Nowa Cyfra, which was born of the merger of Cyfra Plus and Wizja TV; the continued financial decline of cable operators, including NTL and UPC; the bankruptcy of Leo Kirch's media empire, which was mainly based on the heavy losses of its ill-fated digital pay-TV venture Premiere; and, finally, the official merging in 2007 of the French pay-TV platforms Canalsatellite and Télévision par Satellite (TPS).

In the first decade of the 21st century, Digital Terrestrial Television (DTT) has been considered as one of the main motors of digital growth in Europe. In effect, the so-called 'digital switchover' (i.e. the transition from analogue to digital broadcasting) has been a top priority in the EU agenda which aims for its accomplishment before 2012 (Iosifidis 2006). But the 'road to digital' is uneven. At the end of 2006, average DTT penetration in Europe was just under 12 per cent. DTT penetration was highest in the UK (31.7 per cent) and Finland (31.3 per cent). Spain (21.6 per cent), Italy (20.3 per cent) and Sweden (21.7 per cent) were not far behind. France, which came late to DTT but is rapidly making up for lost ground, was at 14 per cent. Penetration in Germany (4.9 per cent) and the Netherlands (3.8 per cent) was well behind, but in both countries most households receive television via cable. The Netherlands was the first country to switch off analogue terrestrial transmissions in December 2006 (*Screen Digest* 2007).

However, economic considerations often seem to be ignored when making projections regarding the transition to digital. The huge capital costs associated with launching digital services bring higher prices for programmes and make them 'think twice' before entering the new digital ventures. Some suggest that digital TV is riskier than the sudden rush to launch free TV in the 1980s. In fact, the Western television industry is not as it used to be in the 1970s and the 1980s, when many private TV channels sprang up. The prices paid were not huge, but distributors had an interest in building up competition to the monopoly state broadcaster. The new digital services had tangibly different content to offer in order to stimulate and retain consumer interest, and this required large investments in premium programming, especially films and sports.

On the other hand, the European Union recommended in December 2005 that its member states cease all analogue television transmissions by 2012 and strongly advised that those members that have not launched DTT services should do so. This means that Europe will more speedily proceed to digital terrestrial than to digital satellite television. In effect, compared to the US, European DTT penetration is ahead, since free digital terrestrial reached 1 per cent of households at the end of 2005 in the US. Cable and satellite penetration are much higher and the US is not relying on DTT to meet its analogue switch-off deadline of 2009. On the other hand, Australia and Japan are ahead of both the US and Europe in terms of DTT penetration, but have set conservative switch-off dates: Japan's target is 2011, while Australia has delayed switch-off to 2010 in cities and 2012 in rural areas.

Additionally, one also has to take into account that the partners in the consumption of audiovisual and multimedia products are changing. In the US, trends indicate that time spent watching television is declining, with more time being spent surfing the internet or using other multimedia services. Broadcasters are trying to meet this challenge by broadening the scope of their services and expanding their activities onto the internet and multimedia areas. According to a recent survey by Burst Media (2007) consumers' online habits are changing TV viewing patterns. In effect, more than 75 per cent of the respondents who watch television while online visit websites directly related to the programme they are watching, and 6 per cent of respondents combine online and offline 'all the time'. Moreover, about 42 per cent of respondents watch less television today than one year ago. The decrease in TV viewership is most pronounced among respondents of 18–24 years. Among this group, half watch less television today than one year ago. Additionally, nearly one-half of women of 25–34 years and 35–44 years watch less television today than they did one year ago. As far as Europe is concerned, although average viewing time is stable, it is too soon to establish a direct link between changes in the consumption of the two media. However, according to an Ofcom study, television in Britain is of declining interest to young people aged 16–24 years. On average, they watch less than the average viewer. Instead, the internet plays a central role in their daily lives. More than 70 per cent of 16–24 year olds interviewed in 2006 used a social networking website (Ofcom 2006: 39–40). In terms of viewing choices, one of the dominant trends in European television in 2005–06 was the increasing audience shift to new digital channels.

The evolving model

Television has fuelled most of the advertising spend growth in the 1980s and 1990s and may continue to do so over the next few years. This is due to a combination of several factors: the continued growth of private channels; the expansion of digital television leading to an increased multichannel universe; increased local production, which will stimulate viewership and television advertising; improved economic conditions; and cutbacks in advertising on public channels that will lead to more television advertising on private channels in several countries.

In fact, the television advertising supply for private broadcasters has increased considerably in most countries across Europe since the late 1980s. This has been due to the decrease in the public broadcasters' share and the creation of 'inspill' advertising windows. But, with more competition in television, especially from digital TV, leading to the erosion of the market share, advertising revenue has to be shared out amongst even more broadcasters. In fact, conditions differ considerably compared to the 1980s. The first reason is that commercial free television has grown faster than the advertising sector average. In other words, more channels, generalist and niche-advertiser-supported channels, have to compete for the same source of revenue. This fragmentation of the advertising market and of audiences poses a significant threat to both established and new broadcasters. In effect, advertisers nowadays are much more selective. They may be reluctant to pay the high price of ad-slots that command large audiences when a good proportion of those viewers may not be interested in buying their products. As Bughin and Griekspoor (1997: 91–2) argue, the days when free commercial broadcasters found it easy to make money because they dominated their national markets have gone. Although the launching of a channel nowadays might be easier than it was 15 years ago, the chances of success are slimmer.

The direct impact of audience fragmentation – the downward pressure exerted upon the cost of advertising slots – is not, however, the only cause for concern. There is a broader concern among both broadcasters and the advertising agencies that clients regard advertising as an ineffective way of interacting with consumers. It has been noted that one reason for this is that while competition does exert a downward pressure, the fragmentation of audiences may mean that advertisers have to buy more advertising in order to reach the number of homes they had been used to in the past (Brown 1997). Furthermore, intense competition for programmes has increased the costs of programme acquisitions while, at the same time, it has increased the power of advertisers to negotiate for better prices and a greater range of audiences. Additionally, economic recession and the after-effects of terror attacks and the war in Iraq has led to a decline in advertising revenues, especially for Europe's major commercial broadcasters. It is not, therefore, surprising to find European private broadcasters, on the one hand, challenging public broadcasters for carrying advertising and, on the other, putting pressure on regulatory agencies to relax the framework surrounding television advertising, sponsorship and bartering.

These developments have led media analysts to argue that in the future advertising will play a much smaller role in television funding. In this respect, it is argued that the funding model for television is set to change, as thematic channels will allow advertising to be better aimed at target groups (Davis 1999). Various studies foresee that the strongest growth in television revenues will come through direct consumer expenditure, with rapid expansion of pay-TV and on-line multimedia services. In effect, a range of advertising and marketing techniques are already possible with digital technology, including the placing of direct orders by consumers during programmes, virtual advertising and product placement, and the insertion of internet hyperlinks in TV programmes.

It is also foreseen that the introduction of digital television will not only offer an expansion of free-to-air opportunities but it will also expand the market for subscribed TV services and will extend the sector into a new world of pay-per-view (PPV) and additional interactive services. Media analysts point out that with viewers able to interact with digital TV advertising and e-commerce applications and request more information on an advertisement by using a control device, advertisers can look forward to added value. By and large, it is forecasted that in the digital era, TV subscription will play a major role in the funding of broadcasting and the balance between advertising income and subscription for television services, mainly premium services and transactions, is shifting in favour of subscription.

However, this will be an incremental procedure. Although pay-TV is the growth sector in broadcasting, it is already very competitive and will become even more so as digitalisation brings down the cost of entry into this market. Even if the extra number of channels available leads to viewers watching more television, which is unlikely, there are only a finite number of hours and channels any single viewer can realistically watch. Moreover, the size of the potential market is particularly important in television because of the very high fixed costs incurred before a single viewer or subscriber is signed up (Brown 1997: 45). This also means that small markets are less viable for pay-TV than larger ones, and Europe mainly consists of small markets. Economies of scale make it difficult for broadcasters in small markets to make money unless they can persuade subscribers to spend much larger sums for their television service than they would normally have to pay in larger markets.

Advertising will remain television's largest source of funding in the near future. One could say that the television industry cannot survive without advertising, so it has to find ways to accommodate advertisers even in the form of interactive TV advertising and similar applications. Similarly, advertisers cannot ignore mass audience channels because these channels 'will continue to be more cost-effective in reaching the entire population compared to purchasing time on several niche channels to aggregate the equivalent of a mass audience' (Honing 2004: 11).

But in one way or another, in the 'third age of commercialisation associated with the digital revolution' (Iosifidis, Steemers and Wheeler 2005: 46), pay-TV's influence is increasing steadily, even if advertising and public funding still account for the lion's share of television revenue in Europe. Most studies foresee that in the next decade, pay television will continue to grow, digital channels will gradually learn to attract new advertisers offering them the ability to reach only their targeted customers at prices well below those charged by the major general interest channels (Idate 2003), and there will be wider consumer acceptance of pay-per-view for significant events.

In this context, the future of public broadcasting may become more complicated since it has to face the digital challenge, too. The proliferation of channels, due to the advent of digital television, will further fragment audiences and decrease the public broadcasters' advertising revenue – if it stays unchallenged. Furthermore, in the new digital environment, public broadcasters may witness a further decrease in their audiences, which will certainly pose questions about the legitimacy of their main source of income, the licence fee. Additionally, the introduction of digital television means higher costs in the short and medium term as public broadcasters try to upgrade their infrastructure and purchase new equipment, to buy or produce more competitive and thus more expensive programming, including the launch of new channels, while at the same time their revenues are essentially stagnant. The difference for public broadcasters in comparison to private media groups is that their income (especially the licence fee) is not only static but, according to the EU, it cannot be easily used for digital ventures. However, public broadcasters are responding to challenges.

By and large, public broadcasters in Europe, although they rely on a certain number of significant assets, such as their social mission, quality programming, etc., face the most difficult challenge in their long history. This, however, is not only the side effect of the arrival of digital television; it is also the outcome of public policies, either on a national or EU level, which only rhetorically support the real future of public broadcasters. This is because most public policies give preference to the private sector. Public broadcasters have demonstrated that if left alone, they can react with success, but as soon as they become more competitive, new challenges are posed to their revenue; in the meanwhile, they are not being given the opportunity to prepare themselves for the digital era, as telecommunications operators did in the last decade.

Summary

Television has been used as a paradigm case of the models of media institutions in Europe. While in the past European television used to be dominated by public broadcasters operating under strict national regulation, since the 1980s television in Europe has resulted in a dual system consisting of a strong private sector, exclusively funded by advertising in its various forms (such as conventional commercials, sponsoring and bartering), and a public sector, mainly funded by the licence fee and to a lesser extent by advertising. By and large, this 'dual television system', largely recognised as a distinctive feature of the broadcasting landscape in Europe (McQuail 2007) and an integral part of the European model of society, seems to have been challenged. This is due to new developments of market forces as well as the development and application of new technologies, such as digital television. With new technologies, TV channels are now able to charge their viewers/customers on an individual basis, while the fragmentation of the TV market poses new problems to the funding of the generalist private channels.

Questions

1 Describe the main models of the European broadcasting system before deregulation and compare it with that of your country.

2 Describe the consequences of broadcasting deregulation in Europe and explore whether they apply in the case of a national broadcasting system you choose to analyse.

3 Do you believe that in the future advertising will remain the main source of income for television stations?

Further reading

Humphreys, P. (1996) *Mass Media and Media Policy in Western Europe*, Manchester: Manchester University Press. This provides a coherent overview and analysis of the changes of media systems in Europe prior to the advent of digital television.

Kelly, M., Mazzoleni, G. and McQuail D. (eds) (2004) *The Media in Europe*, London: Sage. A country-by-country analysis by the Euromedia group concerning the changes in the broadcasting systems of many European countries.

McQuail, D. and Siune, K. (eds) (1998) *Media Policy; Convergence, Concentration and Commerce*, London: Sage. One of many overviews of change across Europe produced by a group of European media scholars. Later volumes update information.

Sinclair, J. and Turner, G. (eds) (2004) *Contemporary World Television*, London: BFI. This book contains a full discussion of the developments of broadcasting systems across Europe and other parts of the world.

References

Brants, K. and De Bens, E. (2000) 'The Status of TV Broadcasting in Europe', in J. Wieten, G. Murdock and P. Dahlgren (eds) *Television Across Europe: A Comparative Introduction,* London: Sage, pp. 7-22.

Brown, C. (1997) *The New Economics of Audiovisual Production: Film and TV Financing, Production and Distribution in the Digital Age,* London: FT Media and Telecoms.

Bughin, J. and Griekspoor, W. (1997) 'A New Era for European TV', *McKinsey Quarterly,* 3: 90-102.

Burst Media (2007) 'Multi-Tasking Media Consumers Are Merging the Internet with Other Media', 5 November, www.burstmedia.com (accessed 1 March 2008).

CEC (2003) 'The Future of European Regulatory Audiovisual Policy, Communication from the Commission to the Council, the European Parliament, the European Economic and Social Committee and the Committee of the Regions', Brussels, 15.12.2003, COM (2003) 784 final.

Chalaby, J. K. and Segell, G. (1999) 'The Broadcasting Media in the Age of Risk: The Advent of Digital Television', *New Media and Society,* 1 (3): 351-68.

De Bens, E. (1998) 'Television Programming: More Diversity, More Convergence?', in K. Brants, J. Hermes and L. van Zoonen (eds) *The Media in Question: Popular Cultures and Public Interest,* London: Sage, pp. 27-37.

De Bens, E. and de Smaele, K. (2001) 'The Inflow of American Television Fiction on European Broadcasting Channels Revisited', *European Journal of Communication,* 16 (1): 51-76.

Dyson, K. and Humphreys, P. (eds) (1988) *Broadcasting and New Media Politics in Western Europe,* London: Routledge.

EAO (European Audiovisual Observatory) (2006) *Trends in European Television,* European Audiovisual Observatory: Paris.

Franklin, B. (1997) *Newszak and News Media,* London: Arnold.

Gilardi, F. (2005) 'The Institutional Foundation of Regulatory Capitalism: The Diffusion of Independent Regulatory Agencies in Western Europe', *Annals of the American Academy of Political and Social Science,* 598 (1): 84-101.

Hallin, D. C. and Mancini, P. (2004) *Comparing Media Systems; Three Models of Media and Politics,* Cambridge: Cambridge University Press.

Honing, D. (2004) 'What Kind of Future for Television?', *Intermedia,* 32 (4): 10-15.

Idate (2003) (Institut de l'Audiovisuel et des Télécommunications en Europe) 'Thematic channels facing network digitisation', (256), 10 April.

Idate (2007) *Personal TV.* Report/Focus, Strasbourg: Idate.

Iosifidis, P. (2006) 'Digital Switchover in Europe', *International Communication Gazette,* 68 (3): 249-68.

Iosifidis, P., Steemers, J. and Wheeler, M. (2005) *European Television Industries.* London: BFI.

McQuail, D. (1998) 'Commercialization and beyond' in D. McQuail and K. Siune (eds) *Media Policy; Convergence, Concentration and Commerce,* London: Sage, pp. 107-27.

McQuail, D. (2007) 'Introduction: Reflections on Media Policy in Europe', in A. W. Meier and J. Trappel (eds) *Power, Performance and Politics; Media Policy in Europe,* Baden-Baden: Nomos.

McQuail, D. and Siune, K. (1986) *New Media Politics: Comparative Perspectives in Western Europe,* London: Sage Publications.

Mediametrié (2007) *2006: One Television Year in the World,* Eurodata TV Paris: Mediametrié.

Moragas Spa, de M. and López, B. (2000) 'Decentralization Processes and the "Proximate Television" in Europe' in G. Wang, J. Servaes and A. Goonasekera (eds) *The New Communications Landscape: Demystifying Media Globalisation,* London: Routledge, pp. 33-51.

Negrine, R. and Papathanassopoulos, S. (1990) *The Internationalisation of Television*, London: Pinter.

Ofcom (Office of Communications) (2006) *The Communications Market 2006*, London: Ofcom, (www.ofcom.org.uk/research/cm/cm06/cmr06_print/).

Ouellette, L. and Lewis, J. (2000) 'Moving Beyond the "Vast Wasteland": Cultural Policy and Television in the United States', *Television and the New Media*, 1 (1): 95–115.

Papathanassopoulos, S. (2002) *European Television in the Digital Age*, Cambridge: Polity Press.

Sanchez-Tabernero, A. (1993) *Media Concentration in Europe*, European Institute for the Media Monograph 16, Dusseldorf: European Institute for Media.

Seymour-Ure, C. (1987) 'Media Policy in Britain: Now You See It, Now You Don't', *European Journal of Communication*, 2: 269–87.

Screen Digest (2007) 'DTT Take-up Accelerates in Europe', May: 136.

Tunstall, J. and Machin, D. (1999) *The Anglo-American Media Connection*, Oxford: Oxford University Press.

4

The Media in Europe

Hans J. Kleinsteuber

Chapter overview

This chapter reflects critically upon the different media systems of Europe. It defines the notion of 'media system' and considers whether and how systems can be compared across the continent, focusing in particular on the media in Britain, Germany and France. Attention will also be devoted to former communist countries and the media systems of small states. Finally, the chapter will assess the extent to which one can talk of 'Europeanisation' with reference to national media in recent years.

Introduction

Europe is moving together. But the media landscapes of its member states are still amazingly national. Since 1989 – with the publication of the directive 'Television without Frontiers' – the European Union (EU) has attempted to introduce some sort of Europe-wide media policy that could provide a common European audiovisual space. However, not much has changed since then, and to understand the continent one still needs to think in terms of different media systems. This issue is made even more urgent by the fact that there are hardly any pan-European media to accompany the political process of integration and harmonisation (like, for instance, the TV-channels Euronews and Eurosport). For example, if we consider the coverage of the activities of the European Commission, it becomes apparent how the reporting is done by the national media of 27 member states, which inevitably view Europe through the lenses of their national cultures. As a consequence, Europe lacks a common public sphere.

This chapter presents the central facts about the national media systems of the European Union, as well as mentioning some of the systems beyond its borders. The following questions will be asked:

- What is a media system?
- How can media systems be compared to one another?

- What are the characteristics of the major European media systems: Britain, Germany, France?
- What about the systems in the former communist countries of Europe and the specific characteristics of media systems in small states?
- Is there a process of Europeanisation occurring?

What is a media system?

Generally speaking, a system is a collection of individual elements that together constitute a whole, where each element interacts with the others, as well as the outer world. On this basis, different publishing entities – news agencies, the print press, broadcasting, websites – together constitute a national media system that relates to others. In addition, every media system is also distinct from the political, economic and cultural systems of the nation it belongs to. A media system is always characterised by strong inner relations, with elements seemingly at the system's periphery assuming great importance, e.g. agencies provide news for different media, such as the press or electronic media, which compete with each other for audiences for the same news as well as simultaneously cross-promoting their own activities.

Media systems often operate within the borders of a nation-state; the majority of companies and organisations are based in the state where the market they target also resides. But the media can choose to operate at many different levels: while some media might be limited to local distribution others, as a result of processes of Europeanisation and globalisation, have increasingly become global players and their headquarters can be located beyond the borders of the nation from which they originated. In most European states the media are still predominantly national and, as such, may look quite similar to one another. However, in reality there are important differences. Some nations have a strong local press (especially in Northern Europe); in others the press is mainly national (in Southern Europe); in some the press is widely read (e.g. Britain); in others its consumption is mainly limited to the intellectual elite and the middle class (e.g. Italy). This article attempts to describe a few common patterns, as well as differences, among European media systems.

How to compare media systems

If one is interested in more than one media system, the common way to describe them is by comparing them to one another. A comparison is – to put it in very general terms – a method for looking at similarities and differences among units of analysis, in this case the units that make up national media (Kleinsteuber 2004). Rather than simply comparing the systems of two nation-states, it is usually much more interesting to include several, because only then it is possible to understand some of the common features (the similarities) and the tremendous variations that are also a peculiarity of Europe (the differences).

Classifications of European media systems

The central focus of this chapter is the array of media systems in Europe: how they emerged, what is special about them and what we can learn by looking at them. It makes sense to cluster these systems into groups (or 'theories' or 'models', as authors have put it) in order to highlight similarities and differences. The result is the following classification.

The comparative study of media systems started with a contribution by American scholars more than 50 years ago. They grouped the 'press' (we would say the media) as they found it in the 1950s into four 'theories' (that we would call models today):

- the 'authoritarian theory': control over the media by repressive regimes;
- the 'libertarian theory': free enterprise and freedom from government interference;
- the 'social responsibility theory': government supports freedom and actively promotes it;
- the 'Soviet Communism theory': control over media by the Communist party.

(Based on Siebert *et al.* 1956)

These four 'theories' described Europe's situation up to half a century ago. The authoritarian model refers to Europe's past, when early newspapers were licensed and censured by political authorities, a policy that gradually disappeared in some countries quite early on (e.g. the Netherlands, the UK), and was destroyed by revolutionary change (France in 1789) or gradually ended much later (Germany and Italy in the 19th century).

Siebert *et al.* saw a mixture of the 'libertarian' and the 'social responsibility' model realised in the media systems of Western Europe. But during that era, the continent was divided between Western media models and 'Soviet Communist' systems in the East. With the disappearance of the Soviet Union and its empire around 1990, this theory lost some of its relevance, although it still helps in understanding how the media have recently developed in Central and Eastern Europe (see below).

To describe the present situation in Western Europe, reference is made to the groundbreaking work of Hallin and Mancini. In their study of comparative media systems in Western democracies they have developed three different 'models' that can be found in the West, the North and the South of the continent.

- the 'liberal model': dominance of market mechanisms and strong commercial media (Britain, Ireland);
- the 'democratic corporatist model': media tied to social and political groups; relatively active but legally limited role of state (Scandinavia, Germany);
- The 'polarised pluralist model': integration of media into party politics, strong role of the state (France, Italy).

(Based on Hallin and Mancini 2004)

This classification focuses on the Western part of the continent. If we want to also include the media systems of Central and Eastern Europe, it makes sense to introduce a fourth model, i.e. the 'Post-Communist model'.

Leading media systems in Europe: Britain, France and Germany

Although there have been attempts to provide comprehensive descriptions of all media systems in Europe, even in the handbooks that are available some systems are left out (Terzis 2007; Kelly *et al.* 2004). With reference to the classification of Hallin and Mancini (described above), the leading media systems of the three models in the West (Britain), North (Germany) and the South of Europe (France) are discussed below.

These countries have some features in common. For instance, they are characterised by a long tradition of newspaper production: the oldest newspaper in Germany was published in 1607, while the London *Times* is more than 200 years old. To give an idea of how interrelated Europe's media history was, consider the origins of news agencies. France was the first country where news were distributed by a specialised agency, the Agence Havas founded in 1835 by Charles-Louis Havas (1783–1858), known today as Agence France Press (AFP). Two of Havas' employees brought this idea to other European countries: these were the Germans Paul Julius Reuter and Bernhard Wolff. Reuter (1816–99) established his agency first in Aachen (1850), and then moved to London: Reuters is still a leading agency, even though Thomson Reuters recently transferred its headquarters to New York. Wolff (1811–79), founded his Wolffs Telegraphisches Bureau in Berlin in 1850. Much later, this company was ruined by the Nazi regime; its successor today is Germany's Deutsche Presse Agentur (dpa).

All three agencies are today among the news leaders of the world, maintain global networks of correspondents and provide services in different languages, also competing with each other (see, also, Boyd-Barrett and Rantanen, in this volume). This gives a good example of how, even in the early days, although developing on a national level, media systems could still show similarities between one-another.

Below are some common features of the three countries mentioned above that are also typical of the rest of Europe:

● a well-developed press system which includes national, as well as local, titles;

● a highly diversified market for magazines of all kinds serving the national market. Increasingly, well-known magazines (*Vogue*, *Cosmopolitan*) are available in nationally adapted editions (i.e. they are being 'cloned'); as such, some of them are increasingly becoming a European phenomenon;

● a well developed dual system in broadcasting, meaning that public service broadcasters, financed by a universal fee (and sometimes also by advertising) compete with commercial broadcasters financed mainly by paid commercials;

- the existence of Pay TV, most successful in countries that show little diversity in the traditional media. When cable and satellite penetration is high and there are many television channels, pay TV seems less attractive.

- the presence of digital radio and TV, although these are not successful everywhere to the same degree; Britain is the world leader, in some Eastern countries the service is not available;

- leading off-line media companies mostly controlling the world of online publications;

- a high ratio of media concentration, with patterns of media control being quite different in different systems.

Despite these similarities, there are also striking differences between the three leading European countries.

The UK: motherland of public service

General characteristics:

- a long and uninterrupted tradition of press freedom;
- the mother country of public service broadcasting (PSB);
- high penetration of digital media;
- strong Anglo-American connection in terms of production and ownership of media.

Following Hallin and Mancini (2004), Britain (together with Ireland) provides the best example of the 'libertarian' model, within which media activities are left largely to the market. Britain is characterised by a long tradition of little regulation of media and it is also the hub for American media conglomerates acting out of London and providing television services to various European countries (e.g. CNN or MTV Europe).

As for the press, the UK has a long tradition of free newspaper publishing, with the London *Times* having been published without interruption since 1788. Today, the dominant press titles are based in the capital, even though a lively regional and local press does exist. Most copies are sold by the tabloids (for instance, the *Sun*) and the British press is famous for being disrespectful of public figures. The British have a strong tradition of newspaper reading, even though circulation is declining. There is a high degree of newspaper concentration; the largest two companies own 55 per cent of the national press, the top four 85 per cent. The situation is not different for the local press and magazine publishing (Bromley 2007).

As for broadcasting, in contrast to the determination of media activities by the market, British public service broadcasting still provides the model for the rest of the world. The British Broadcasting Corporation (BBC), first established as a company in 1922, became a corporation in 1927 when it was first granted a Royal Charter, thus becoming a public institution of great prestige. Its founder, the Scotsman Sir John Reith (1889–1971), made sure that it provided news and education, as well as entertainment. Essential to the BBC's philosophy is that it is financed by a licence fee and does not transmit adverts in its national programmes.

A Royal Charter – the last one having been renewed in 2007 – and an accompanying Agreement guarantee the editorial independence of the BBC, but also require the corporation to make its purposes and aims public. At present, there is an ongoing debate in Britain concerning the notion and principles of public service and how these can be maintained in a digital world. The supervising authority, the Office for Communication (Ofcom), has developed a model of public service that is based on the following assumptions:

- PSB should deliver high levels of content;
- meet the changing demands of the audience;
- reach a broad audience with content that is free at the point of use;
- provide diverse content;
- serve all communities; and, finally,
- be sufficiently flexible to respond to future developments. (www.ofcom.org.uk)

Already in 1954 – very early by European standards – a commercial broadcaster, Independent Television (ITV), was introduced. It was totally financed by advertising, however it still had to meet public service obligations. Today, a number of general and specialised BBC channels, as well as several commercial channels, are freely available. Because the number of universally accessible programmes was rather limited until recently and cable not well developed, pay TV, where individual broadcasts or programmes are accessed by a one-off payment, seemed attractive to British viewers and the satellite broadcaster BSkyB became a prominent player. It is controlled by the Australian–American mogul Rupert Murdoch, who is also an important global press tycoon. All in all, today about 500 channels are available in the UK, most of them digital, many of them free (through Freeview and Freesat) which makes the UK the country in Europe with the highest penetration of digital broadcasting (reaching over 70 per cent of households).

Germany: media federalism

General characteristics:

- a history of both controlled and free media;
- a federalised political system, mirrored by a decentralised media system;
- high cable penetration and strong free media;
- a degree of media control by family clans.

Germany is the most populous country of the EU (with 82 million inhabitants) and it is located at the heart of a German-speaking area which includes Austria and parts of Switzerland (i.e. about 100 million people). This makes the country the most attractive market in the EU. Institutionalised press freedom was first and firmly established relatively late, only through a press law of 1874. This legislation did not survive the Nazi regime and after the Nazi defeat following World War Two a totally new media system was established in the four occupation zones of the country. A media system thus emerged in the Soviet occupation zone that followed the Soviet communist pattern of media and later disappeared during the unification process of 1989–90, mostly following the patterns of transformation explained below (Kleinsteuber and Thomass 2007).

The most important feature of the country is its highly decentralised tradition, as reflected in the early re-establishment of the Länder-states, which already existed before the Federal Republic of Germany was founded in 1949. Later, the Federal Constitutional Court interpreted the constitution (Basic Law or *Grundgesetz*) in such a way so as to give the Länder-states the final say in all questions of broadcasting. The press system is also based on Länder-laws (that are similarly phrased, on the basis of the *Grundgesetz*).

Germany's tradition of decentralisation is clearly reflected in the press system. About 90 per cent of all subscription dailies are published locally and focus mainly on local affairs. Only the rest, about 10 per cent of newspapers, are considered national quality papers. A special case is the tabloid *Bild* (selling more than 3 million copies per day), as the national edition is accompanied by regional sections. Springer, by far the largest newspaper company in Germany and in Europe, controls more than 20 per cent of the newspaper market (including *Bild*) and is strong in other media markets as well. In the magazine industry, four companies control about 60 per cent of the total market (Springer being, again, among them). Major media companies are usually family-owned.

The tradition of decentralisation is also reflected by public service broadcasting, built up by the various Länder-states after 1945 and still existing in this form. There are nine regional broadcasters, such as WDR in North-RhineWestphalia (with its main centre in Cologne). These joined together to offer the First ARD-TV channel in1954 (ARD being the network of regional broadcasters). In addition, regional broadcasters built up regional culture programmes and other specialised channels. The second channel, ZDF, is also unique, as it originates from an agreement made between all 16 Länder-states. It is run by an independent company in Mainz. These public broadcasters are financed by a licence fee and strictly limited advertising. Control of the organisation rests with the 'Broadcasting Councils', which include representatives of 'socially relevant groups', i.e. politicians, business associations' spokespersons, representatives of trade unions and churches, as well as representatives of the sporting and cultural worlds. Even though the number of politicians is limited, their influence is significant, as many of the groups represented in these bodies have links to one of the two major parties (Christian Democrats and Social Democrats). As a result, the Councils end up representing the two major political currents ('black' and 'red'), something which is intended to guarantee some degree of balance in the organisation's output. This situation has led Hallin and Mancini to classify the system as 'democratic corporatist' – where corporatism refers to a social arrangement in which power is shared by interest and civic organisations that are integrated into the policy-making process.

The trend towards deregulation that characterised Western European economies in the 1980s made it possible for commercial radio and commercial television to be born in Germany, too. Licences are now handed out by regulatory bodies that, once again, have been established by the Länder-states and, again, are controlled by 'socially relevant groups'. Two 'broadcasting families' control about 90 per cent of the commercial market share today. One 'family' of RTL channels is owned by the Bertelsmann company, the largest media conglomerate in Europe (and outside the USA), with headquarters in the provincial town of Gütersloh – this being another symbol of media decentralisation. The other 'family' is ProSiebenSat.1, built up by the media tycoon Leo Kirch, who after seriously mismanaging his businesses went bankrupt. His assets were later taken over by Anglo-American investment funds. All in all, the four central actors in the television business (ARD, ZDF, RTL, ProSiebenSat.1) provide for a multi-channel environment and more than 90 per cent of the population receive at least 30 German-language channels via cable or satellite. Because of this multi-channel environment of choice, pay TV (with its individually priced programmes) had a somewhat more difficult start than in the other countries analysed here. International investors control the central pay-provider Premiere and, from 2007, Rupert Murdoch started to take over the company renaming it Sky.

France: quotas and subsidies

General characteristics:

- a centralised political and media system with Paris at its centre;
- strong influence of the government (the President) upon media;
- policy of subsidies and quotas;
- media dominated by French non-media companies.

The French Revolution (1789–95) transformed France into a modern nation-state and also introduced the idea of individual freedom in the country. Freedom of expression was secured in a law of 1881. A proud history, an admired culture and the desire to protect the French language in a world where English has become the lingua franca, have led to France's reliance on the principle known as 'l'exception culturelle'. This includes the state's duty to actively defend values associated with 'French exceptionalism', an idea that may be found in many elements of the national media policy of the country (Lamizet and Tétu 2007).

For hundreds of years the centre of France has been Paris, the intellectual metropolis of the country. It is also the centre of media production, management and distribution. Newspapers with a high circulation are based in the capital, covering the whole political spectrum from right to left. Traditional papers are in a crisis, as they have to compete with aggressive free sheets in a country in which reading papers is not as common as in most of the countries of Northern Europe. However, the French are intensive magazine readers.

Broadcasting is seen as a playground for political interests. The president, Nicolas Sarkozy, a powerful figure directly elected by the population in 2007, exerts continuous influence over the media. President Sarkozy is keen to get broadcasting time and his initiatives often get positive coverage on television. Public service broadcasting has a relatively strong standing and is considered a bulwark against foreign influence. However the funding provided to PSB in France is comparatively lower than in the other countries mentioned above and much of the revenue has come from advertising, a situation that is being changed by Sarkozy in 2009.

During the 1980s a dual system of broadcasting was established in France, as in other European countries. In a unique development, the first channel, TV 1, was sold to a big French company that had a leading position in the construction sector. The remaining two public service channels are France 2 and France 3, with the latter putting strong emphasis on regional reporting. A small number of commercial channels have been licensed to cover the whole country, and a pay-TV channel, Canal+, started transmissions, too. Cable penetration has been low and whoever wants more choice has to switch to packaged digital pay TV, mainly provided by Canal+, which is quite successful. Digital TV reaches no more than one third of the population.

One feature of the typically French understanding of culture is that broadcasting is subject to a variety of specific regulations. Indeed, France is also known as the country of quotas: licences stipulate how much French content has to be shown on television, how much French music has to be played on the radio and how many French films Canal+ is obliged to offer. Media regulation makes sure that the major media outlets are in the hands of French companies. In fact, media concentration is high and non-media conglomerates, especially those that heavily rely on state orders or are heavyweights in the defence sector, control much of the national media. President Sarkozy, who often favours his friends in the upper ranks of large companies, has been treated well by the media so far.

Another feature of France is the high rate of subsidies for the press (total about €1 billion per year); the film industry, one of the largest in Europe, is also well financed. French citizens go more often to movie shows than most other Europeans, and the cinemas show a comparatively high proportion of national productions. The government and political parties exercise some degree of control over the system; in the terminology of Hallin and Mancini (2004), the outcome of this is what they call 'polarised pluralism'. The term pluralism in this context refers to a political style that proposes to share power among different groups in society which themselves promote diversely yet, at the same time, promote the idea of consensus among groups. 'Polarised pluralism' therefore amounts to a pluralist ethos which is nevertheless controlled, ultimately, by government.

Media systems in Central and Eastern Europe and the Post-Communist model

General characteristics:

- common past as states belonging to the Soviet sphere of influence;
- short democratic tradition, with changes still taking place;
- adoption of Western standards;
- constant problems caused by governmental influence;
- high percentage of media owned by foreign companies.

Up to 1989, Europe was divided into two large blocs which were separated by an 'Iron Curtain'; as a consequence, two totally different clusters of media systems were present here. In Western Europe, the media were putatively free and responsible, characterised by a mixture of the 'libertarian' and of the 'social responsibility' models as described by Siebert *et al.* (1956). In Eastern Europe, the former Soviet Union had established a system of satellite states in which the monopolistic Communist party demanded total control over the media. Siebert *et al.* (1956), therefore, spoke of a 'Soviet Communism model', too. According to the founder of the Soviet Union, Vladimir Ilyich Lenin (1870–1924), the media had to play the role of propagandists and agitators for the party. In fact, the press and broadcasting received strict guidance by the party, censorship was common and Communist states attempted to stop 'undesirable' information from accessing the country. Not all Eastern states totally closed their doors to Western influence, and some underground media were active in several of these countries.

With the breakdown of the Soviet system at the end of the 1980s, the states of Central and Eastern Europe had the chance to embrace democracy, in a process that was known as 'transformation'. During those years of transformation, the journalists and the media often played a crucial role in criticising the old power structures and opening up the country to new ideas. For a number of years, since 1990 onwards, journalists worked in a kind of power vacuum, during which they could pretty much report whatever they wanted. However, soon the post-Communist authorities sold many of the news media to investors and a new age of competition swept through. In addition, new publications entered the market. Western media companies soon moved in, bought up or founded new publications (often adaptations of their own successful products). An example of this is the best-selling Polish newspaper *Fact*, published by the German Springer Company and inspired by its tabloid *Bild*.

The former state broadcasters were usually transformed into public service organisations, but often the tradition of strong governmental influence somehow survived in post-Communist times. Everywhere in Eastern Europe, commercial competition also plays a relevant role. The Central European states that acquired membership status of the EU (like Poland or the Czech Republic) and the Baltic states (like Lithuania) have introduced media legislation and enjoy relatively free media systems today. Some minor differences may be found in South Eastern European states (such as Bulgaria and Romania) (Jakubowicz 2008).

The situation is different in the former Soviet Union. Here, in the late 1980s Mikhail Gorbachev pursued a new policy of 'openness' known as 'glasnost', calling for an opening up of the Soviet system, a development in which the media were meant to play an essential role. Subsequently, the old Soviet empire broke down and Russia passed a new constitution. Here, foreign influence remained minimal and the state – especially since the Presidency of Vladimir Putin (2000–08) – gained control of many of the influential media, first and foremost the omnipresent television. The media that are not directly controlled by the government are mostly under the control of so-called 'oligarchs', a small number of powerful people owning large shares of Russia's wealth. These two categories of media make sure that Putin and his ruling circle enjoy positive coverage while providing little discussion of the initiatives of the opposition. The system is not free, but also not as closed it was in communist times, for example, access to international information is not a problem and the internet has become the leading medium carrying dissent and criticism.

The situation is certainly worse in newly independent states that had been part of the former Soviet Union. In countries like Belarus or countries in Central Asia, there is virtually no press freedom and journalists are constantly in danger of being prosecuted or even murdered. The exception to this rule is Ukraine where, after the 'orange revolution' of 2004–05, free elections have been held and the media system is mostly free.

The media systems of small states

General characteristics:

- access to the same services as in large countries;
- high cross-border influence;
- presence of protective measures, e.g. strong public service or subsidies;
- presence of small national companies and high foreign ownership.

So far, the discussion has focused mainly on large European states. However European countries come in very different sizes, from large ones (like Russia and Germany, with respectively 142 and 82 million inhabitants) to very small ones (such as Luxembourg, with 470,000 inhabitants). Whereas large countries such as Russia in the East and Germany, Britain or France in the West are able to control most media activities within their borders, the situation is different in small countries: here the media of neighbouring countries are often freely available and might seem quite attractive to people since they often offer more choice and more TV channels than national ones. This is a problem especially for small countries that are part of a larger language space dominated by one of the major European powers. In Ireland, for example, 20 per cent of the newspaper market is taken by titles imported from the UK. In Austria, a German media company controls the two most popular newspapers and most TV programmes come straight from Germany. Countries that live behind high language walls and where the languages spoken are not widespread outside their borders (e.g. Finland or Hungary) may find it easier to 'protect' their identities from outside influence. While countries like Greece seem to be at ease with their peripheral position, a country such as Portugal suffers the influence of Brazil – a major media power that exports many of its telenovelas, for instance, to Portugal.

In some of the smaller European countries the resulting situation is seen as a potential threat to their national identities, so protective policies are relied on – without affecting the freedom of the media. Typically, public service broadcasters in small countries tend to be heavily supported. This is generally seen as some kind of 'safety measure' in defence of national uniqueness. The European country that comparatively spends most to support public service is Switzerland, where the broadcasting organisation SRG SSR idée suisse consists of four separate organisations that offer programming in the four official languages of the country. As already suggested by the name, the SRG, calling itself the 'Swiss idea', the largest media unit of the country, mirrors the diversity of Switzerland and is seen as a central unifying force.

Another element of national protection is financial support to keep the local media alive against the background of increasing international competition. Besides France (see above), subsidies to print media are mainly granted by smaller European countries like Sweden and Austria in order to safeguard local cultures and some degree of diversity.

The situation in Europe becomes even more complicated if we also consider the 'mini-states'. Interestingly, at times the tiny Grand-Duché de Luxembourg played a crucial role in the commercialisation of the European broadcasting industry. While in the larger countries a public service monopoly was still maintained, the commercial Radio Télévision Luxembourg (RTL) Company beamed radio and later TV programmes into large parts of the continent. Only when the resistance to commercial broadcasting was broken, production moved into the respective countries, in order to operate closer to the market. Luxembourg lost its importance as a media hub and today only the headquarters of the RTL Group (owned by Bertelsmann) remains in Luxembourg and the L in RTL still reminds us of its origins.

Conclusion

The media systems of Europe clearly reflect the fragmented history of the European continent; in terms of media structures Europe appears to be a laboratory of media experiences and diversities. There are two organisations, Freedom House (FH) and Reporters Without Frontiers (RwF), which rank countries according to the degree of media and journalistic freedom to be found within its borders. Freedom House rates nearly all EU countries as 'free'; only Bulgaria and Romania are seen as 'partly free'. RwF's ranking features only European countries in the top 14 places; between one and 50 (out of 169 countries that are ranked) only two members of the EU are not listed (i.e. Bulgaria and Poland). But even among members of the European Union there are differences, with Italy being defined as only 'partly free' once in recent years, mainly due to the actions and conflict of interests of its PM, the media tycoon Silvio Berlusconi. Freedom House also emphasises that some Eastern European countries (like Belarus) are among the worst abusers worldwide (www.freedomhouse.org; www.rsf.org).

There are similarities among the largest and most influential countries in Europe, but also some important differences. Clearly, Britain stands for the introduction of the idea of public service. The German tradition of decentralised governance is reflected in a system of federalised public service. In France, there is wide consensus about the need to safeguard France's civilisation (its language and culture) through relatively strong state intervention. In democratic Central and Eastern European countries, much of what may be found in the West was adopted, including an independent press and a dual broadcasting system. Today, some of the Central European countries rank higher than their Western counterparts as far as press freedom is concerned, according to the organisations cited above.

Table 4.1 The global players in the media market (2006)

Organisation	€billions
1. Time Warner, Inc., New York, USA	35,221
2. The Walt Disney Company, Burbank, California, USA	27,306
3. Viacom, Inc./CBS Corporation, New York, USA	20,709
4. News Corp. Ltd., Sydney, Australia	20,171
5. Comcast Corporation, Philadelphia, USA	19,884
6. Bertelsmann AG, Gütersloh, Germany	19,279
7. NBC Universal, Inc., New York, USA	12,893
8. Sony Corporation, Tokyo, Japan	12,389
9. Vivendi, Paris, France	9,389
10. Cox Enterprises, Inc., Atlanta, Georgia, USA	8,283

Source: Institut für Medien- und Kommunikationspolitik, www.medienpolitik.eu/cms/index.php?idcatside=189&mod7_1= (accessed 12 October 2007)

As for media concentration, this is a problem affecting the whole continent. Five of the Big Six, the largest media companies active on a global scale, are located in the US (see Table 4.1). The sixth one is the German Bertelsmann, the largest book publisher in the world.

All global companies are – in one way or another – active in Europe, with American media companies usually operating out of London. Increasingly, Global Players are also entering national markets: Murdoch's News Corporation, for instance, now offers pay-TV in Britain, Italy and – lately – in Germany, too. Bertelsmann's RTL group is active in at least 10 European TV markets. A group coalescing around Pro7Sat.1, controlled by Anglo-American investments funds, now rivals it and has increasing interests in Europe as well. Foreign ownership of national media is especially widespread in Eastern Europe, where large chunks of media are often controlled by Western European and/or American companies.

Europe's national media might not be able to retain their importance in the future. Hallin and Mancini argue that the notably different Western European models all move in one direction; these scholars see a process of 'homogenisation' taking place, a convergence in the direction of the 'liberal model' as well as increasing commercialism (Hallin and Mancini 2004: 251–95). This means that the 'libertarian theory' of Siebert *et al.*, which mainly reflected the situation of the USA 50 years ago, arguably provides us with a snapshot of the future, too. Continuously growing media companies are spreading their activities across the continent, as part of a general process of globalisation. The influence of national regulation will wither away, while transnational companies from outside Europe, as well as those based in Europe, look at the continent as an increasingly attractive market for expansion.

At the same time, the idea of public service – as we have seen, a uniquely European idea – is now more under pressure than ever before. This seems to pose a real danger to PSB; however, on the other hand, we also find plenty of ideas in Europe about how to protect local and very diverse identities. The question that remains unanswered is what does it all mean for the necessary establishment of a European public sphere.

Questions

1 What constitutes a media system and how may systems be compared to one another?

2 Why is the landscape of European media systems so diverse?

3 Name at least two similarities and two differences between the media systems of Britain, Germany and France.

4 Look up the ranking of your country on the Freedom House and Reporters Without Frontiers websites. How does it compare to the rest of Europe?

Websites

www.freedomhouse.org – The website of the New York based non-governmental organisation Freedom House that ranks the world media systems according to their degree of freedom every year. It represents mainly the views of publishers.

www.rsf.org – The non-governmental organisation Reporters Without Borders, operating in Paris, ranks the media systems of the world, giving special consideration to the perspective of journalists.

www.ejc.nl – The European Journalism Centre in Maastricht offers an interactive website focused on the European media landscape with descriptions of all media systems on the continent from Armenia to the United Kingdom.

References

Bromley, M. (2007) 'The United Kingdom Media Landscape' in G. Terzis (ed) *European Media Governance*, Bristol: Intellect, pp. 43–54.

Hallin, D. C. and Mancini, P. (2004) *Comparing Media Systems: Three Models of Media and Politics*, Cambridge: Cambridge University Press.

Jakubowicz, K. (2008) 'The Eastern European/Post-Communist Media Model Countries. Introduction' in G. Terzis (ed), *European Media Governance*, Bristol: Intellect, pp. 303–13.

Kelly M., Mazzoleni, G. and McQuail, D. (eds) (2004) *The Media in Europe. The Euromedia Handbook*, London: Sage.

Kleinsteuber, H. J. (2004) 'Comparing Mass Communication Systems' in F. Esser and B. Pfetsch (eds) *Comparing Political Communication: Theories, Cases and Challenges*, Cambridge: Cambridge University Press, pp. 64–86.

Kleinsteuber, H. J. and Thomass, B. (2007) 'The German Media Landscape' in G. Terzis (ed), *European Media Governance*, Bristol: Intellect, pp. 111–23.

Lamizet, B. and Tétu, J.-F. (2007) 'The French Media Landscape' in G. Terzis (ed) *European Media Governance*, Bristol: Intellect, pp. 225–37.

Siebert, F. S, Peterson, T. and Schramm W. (1956) *Four Theories of the Press,* Urbana, IL: University of Illinois Press.

Terzis, H. G. (ed) (2007) *European Media Governance: National and Regional Dimensions,* Bristol: Intellect.

Part 2

WHAT ARE THE MEDIA?

Introduction

Daniele Albertazzi and Paul Cobley

A volume such as this one inevitably needs to ask the question of what the media actually *are* (taking into account that our introduction has defined the media as a diverse collection of industries and practices, each with their own methods of communication, specific business interests, constraints and audiences). To put it bluntly, how did different industries develop, and what were the pressures (economic, legislative, etc.) that affected such development in this or that direction? Also, how are different industries organised and how do they work? Who owns/controls them and who manages to dominate specific markets? Moreover, and given how quickly media landscapes have converged, to what extent can we still even draw a clear line *between* media industries and highlight ways of dealing with the public that can still be said to be specific to some media and not others?

This part of the book covers a variety of industries, some of which embody a medium in its entirety (e.g. TV or cinema), while others span a variety of different media (e.g. pop music, advertising, public relations and others). Contributors to this part have focused on the specific features of different industries, outlining their characteristic agendas (where they could be identified) and, in keeping with the intentions of the volume, have done so within a comparative perspective. While all chapters concentrate on the state of the current industry, attention has also been given to recent developments, as well as what developments can be foreseen for the immediate future. The latter exercise inevitably involves a certain amount of speculation; however, we can be fairly sure that convergence *will* keep impacting on the way each of the media industries discussed in this part operates in the foreseeable future. (An obvious example discussed in this volume is news agencies and news organisations and the variety of ways in which they can now re-package and re-use information thanks to the opportunities afforded to them by new technologies.) In other words, the only thing we can be certain about when considering what the media might be *today* is possibly the fact that they still are very much 'in flux'.

You should take care to use this section to give you a basic understanding of what any medium – for example, the internet – is before you proceed to talk about it.

5

Comics

Roger Sabin

Chapter overview

This chapter seeks to explore the role of comic books in Europe. The focus is on European 'album' culture and its history. By examining the ways in which the economics of comics production have influenced their reception, we can begin to understand why they have attained such a high level of cultural respectability (in France, they are known as 'the ninth art'). A secondary theme of the chapter is to ask why in the UK comics have never been accepted as an artform in the same way.

Introduction

This chapter is about comic books. Why, you may ask, should such a subject be relevant to a book about media studies? The answer is simple, but commonly not expected: that comics constitute 'a medium' just like film, television, novels and any other narrative medium you care to mention, and are therefore equally worthy of consideration within the parameters of media studies. They have their own properties, and generate their own 'kick': they are not 'movies on paper', and nor are they some half-way house between 'literature' and 'art'. Rather, they involve a co-mingling of words and pictures that can rival any other medium for depth of expression. (On the mechanics of how comics work, see McCloud 1994; Groensteen, 2007. For an alternative definition, arguing against the idea of a 'medium', see www.emaki.net.) In other words, comics matter.

In Europe, comics matter more than in most parts of the world, and in keeping with the focus of the rest of this book, our attention will be turned to this aspect. There are, of course, notable comics traditions elsewhere (most of the histories available focus on the USA); but in Europe, the form has become culturally respectable in a way that is unmatched anywhere in the world, with the possible exception of Japan. This is a bold claim to make in some ways because there are as many comics traditions in Europe as there are countries – 27 member states of the

EU as of 2008. Mapping a 'cultural geography' of comics is therefore a complicated task, especially bearing in mind that some countries have distinct traditions within their own borders, for example Belgium, with its Flemish and Francophone heritage. (For more on this, see de la Iglesia (2007).) Yet, it is still fair to talk of a unified European comics market, and this is because comics here share properties that are distinct from any other region in the world: these include not just cultural status, but also kinds of format, and, above all, underlying economics.

One European country, however, has never fitted into this template: namely, the UK. In comics, as in politics and so much else, the UK remains separate. A secondary theme of this chapter, therefore, is what makes UK comics so different, and why the country has never become part of the 'European Comics Community'.

Albums for all tastes

The most immediate way to obtain a sense of the place of comics in European life is to make a few basic observations. First and foremost, European comics culture is essentially an 'album' culture. This is to say that comics are produced as hardback books, usually of about 48 pages in length, containing a single self-contained story, with high-quality production values and full colour throughout. The artwork is often superb, and they have an aesthetic value that until recently was virtually unknown in the UK and the USA. This is duly reflected in the price (between roughly €12 and €28), and the fact that they are sold not from newsagents, but from bookshops. These comics are not intended to be read and thrown away after one sitting, but to be kept on bookshelves and returned to.

There are some exceptions to this rule. There exist, for example, monthly comics magazines that consist of anthologies of serialised stories. However, they are, again, usually of a much higher quality than their UK and American counterparts, and the publishers' aim is typically to 'pre-publish' stories so that they can then be collected into album form at a later date. This system has a long history in Europe, and originally had the advantage of 'testing the waters' in the sense that if a story did not prove popular in the magazine, it would not make it into hardback. Today, however, stories are almost always guaranteed to be released as albums, and the magazines play a less significant role. Moreover, the trend since the mid-1980s has been for first publication to be in album form, thus circumventing the magazines altogether.

In terms of content, we can also observe that the subject matter covered by the comics includes 'something for everybody'. A quick scan of the shelves in a typical Parisian bookshop, for example, reveals an extensive range, from 'funny animal' stories for young children to, for example, hard porn for adults. In between, the storytelling styles can encompass the dumbest-of-dumb pulp fiction to hyper-literate meditations on philosophy and art. The point is better made by considering a random handful of hit albums dating from the 1980s to 2008:

- *The Town That Didn't Exist* (in translation through Titan Books). Written by acclaimed French novelist Pierre Christin (also a Professor of Journalism at Bordeaux University), with artwork by Enki Bilal (born in former Yugoslavia), the story revolves around the impossibility of building a utopia. In an (unspecified) age of industrial decline, a mysterious wheelchair-bound woman inherits a fortune and proceeds to spend it on constructing a city where no one need work ever again. A downbeat, often very weird, allegory for the contradictions of Marxist theory.

- *The Towers of Bois Maury: Babette* (in translation through Titan). Written and illustrated by Belgian 'Hermann' (Hermann Huppen), this historical drama, set in the early medieval period, concerns the rape of a peasant girl by a noble, and the murderous events this sets in train. Plenty of action – swordfights, jousting and hideous torture – all rendered in exquisite photo-referenced linework, and held together by a meticulously researched script.

- *Blueberry: Chihuahua Pearl* (in translation through Epic Comics). Written by French novelist Jean-Michel Charlier and illustrated by fellow countryman Jean Giraud, one of the most acclaimed artists in the industry, this gritty Western has the feel of a Sergio Leone movie. Long coats, cigar-chewing, and stubble are *de rigueur* for both goodies and baddies, as US cavalryman Lieutenant Blueberry investigates misdeeds across the Tex–Mex border.

- *The Incal: Volume 1* (in translation through Titan). Written by Chilean filmmaker Alexandro Jodorowsky and illustrated by 'Moebius' (a pen-name for Jean Giraud, as above), this first part of a science fiction 'cosmic epic' features the adventures of a private detective on a faraway planet. New Age and Tarot card references add colour to this Philip K. Dick-influenced story, packed with violence, grotesque monsters and vast spaceships. Narratively drivesome, but a feast for the eyes.

- *Pixy* (in translation through Fantagraphics). Written and drawn by Dane Max Andersson, the frankly indescribable story involves a procession of bizarre characters and inventions, including buildings that eat people and gun-toting foetuses. There is a satirical theme underpinning the strangeness, but this is basically an ultra-violent surrealist nightmare.

- *Remembrance of Things Past* (in translation through NBM). Marcel Proust's 'impossible to adapt' novel, adapted by Stephane Heuet in a series of albums (up to Part 3 as of 2008), and published as part of a 'Comics Lit' imprint. The artwork offers a wealth of period detail, and makes Proust more accessible without becoming a cartoon Cliff's Notes.

You might notice that this selection of titles is essentially aimed at a teenage and adult audience. This is a fair reflection of the bulk of European comics publishing in recent years, at least in terms of numbers (for reasons we shall explore in a moment). However, it is important to add that the really big hitters in regard to sales rely on more traditional formulas, and are orientated towards a juvenile and family readership. In particular, two characters dominate: Tintin and Astérix. Both have been around for decades (Tintin since the 1920s, Astérix since the 1950s), and such is their fame, both in the UK and the USA, that we need not detail their history here (on Tintin, see Thompson 1991; Peeters 1992; on Astérix, see Kessler 1995). Suffice to say that between them, the be-quiffed boy-reporter and the diminutive ancient Gaul have sold more comics than any other characters put together (sales of Tintin albums alone are estimated to be in the hundreds of millions). Today, although the creator of Tintin (Georges 'Hergé' Remi) and the writer of Astérix (René Goscinny) are dead, the back-catalogues for both characters continue to sell extraordinarily well, and they are also stars of stage, screen, television, computer game, and – in the case of Astérix – a theme park.

Other big sellers after Tintin and Astérix also tend to be marketed towards a juvenile/family audience, and are worth mentioning in passing. For example, translations of Disney comics do very well throughout Europe (famously, Eurodisney is in bitter competition for punters with the Astérix park), while other successful European-originated titles include The Smurfs (from the Netherlands), about cute blue elves; Lucky Luke (from France), about a gormless cowboy; and Blake and Mortimer (from Belgium), about a pair of time-travelling English detectives. Most of these comics have also developed huge adult followings on top of their intended young readership.

Continuing our survey, we can tell one more thing simply by looking at the titles available in the shops: that some countries are more important than others in terms of who publishes what. It soon becomes clear, for example, that France is the centre of the Eurocomics world. More titles are published here than anywhere else, and there is a long tradition of cartoonists from all over Europe being published by French houses (it is fair to say that the easiest route for a Portuguese cartoonist to be published in Portugal is to be first published in France, where the French publisher will then sell the book rights to a Portuguese house). Companies like Dargaud (who publish Astérix), Flammarion (who publish Tintin), and Glénat are prolific and powerful, but smaller outfits like L'Association (which, like other European small presses, e.g. Avant Verlag, Optimal, Sins Entido, prefers to publish books that are more experimental, and in black and white) can have major hits. Perhaps the best known success from the French 'indie' sector was the two volumes of *Persepolis* – originally published by L'Association, available in English through Pantheon (published in 2003 and 2004) – which concerned Marjane Satrapi's autobiographical account of growing up in pre-revolutionary Iran: to date, they have sold over 500,000 copies worldwide.

It is difficult to say which country comes next in the ranking order. The Benelux countries certainly have strong industries (it is a point of pride among Belgians that statistically more comics are sold per head here than in any other part of Europe). The north of Europe, including Scandinavia and Germany, is served by the giant corporation Carlsen, based in Germany, which often publishes translations of titles originated elsewhere in Europe. Meanwhile, Italy and Spain are certainly big comics consumers, and have thriving indigenous titles.

Moving away from the specific comics in the shops, we can also observe that in Europe, due to such a wide-ranging industry, there has developed a culture surrounding the form that is unique. For example, people commonly learn to read using comics, and continue to buy them throughout their lives. There is no 'cut-off' point as there has been traditionally in the UK and the USA. Thus, many comics characters become household names, and their exploits permeate everyday parlance. Perhaps the most visible expression of this love of comics is the comics festivals, which take place every year in most European nations. These tend to be large-scale events, not just for committed fans, but for all members of the family. The biggest, in Angoulême in south-western France, takes over the whole of the town for a period of several days, with exhibitions, talks, film shows, stalls, and, of course, artists' signing sessions (if you're lucky you get a sketch too). Angoulême markets itself very much as 'pour la famille', and regularly attracts over 125,000 visitors: in other words, roughly 20 times as many as the comparable (fan-orientated) event in the UK, and slightly more than in America. Other no less lively festivals are held in Lucca (Italy), Brussels (Belgium), Grenoble (France) and Frankfurt (Germany).

Respectability: a 'ninth art'?

That's probably as far as we can go in analysing the European scene just by looking in this way. To dig a little deeper, we need to explore two areas that are not immediately obvious: the comics' history and their underlying economics. Both themes are very closely linked, of course, and both are essential elements of any media studies investigation. Let us begin with the extraordinary level of intellectual respect that comics command in Europe, something that has influenced their history quite considerably. It is true to say that they are written about and deconstructed in the same way as any other artform. To give the most prominent example of a scholar with an interest: whenever the Italian Umberto Eco (author of *The Name of the Rose*) holds forth about contemporary culture, in books, TV and radio documentaries and newpaper columns, he invariably includes comics. (Eco's best-known book (in translation) to deal with comics is *The Role of the Reader* (1981), which includes a classic essay on Superman.) He's not the only one: academics all over Europe have made comics an integral part of degree courses. There are serious critical magazines about the subject, and specialist archives and study centres (such as those in Angoulême and Brussels).

This embracing of comics by Europe's 'intellectual class' (as it is still often referred to there) itself has a history. The trend dates back to the 1960s (although before this it is possible to find erudite discussions of titles like *Tintin*), and in particular to the French 'rediscovery' of early American comic strips. Comics study groups started to emerge, which focused primarily on strips like 'Little Nemo', 'Krazy Kat', 'Flash Gordon' and 'Dick Tracy'. A similar process had started in the late 1950s, when French intellectuals started to take American movies seriously – at the time, a very unusual concept. Now comics were being given the same treatment, and it was not long before critical and theoretical magazines were founded, and exhibitions organised. Undoubtedly an important moment in the growth of the movement was an exhibition of (largely American) comics at no less prestigious a venue than the Louvre in 1967 (the catalogue for the exhibition was published as a book: Couperie *et al.* 1968).

The co-option of comics into serious cultural debate continued into the 1970s. European intellectuals increasingly concentrated on European rather than American comics, and the new decade saw the form being referred to in France as 'the ninth art' (film and television had been added to the list a few years earlier). More than this, and partly as a result, the whole notion of what constituted 'culture' *per se* was being reconfigured. Old notions dating from the Victorian era that culture essentially meant 'high culture' – for instance, fine art, classical music, opera, and literature drawn from a 'respected' canon of authors (Shakespeare, Goethe, etc.) – were being challenged as (mainly) French intellectuals progressively elevated elements of 'low culture' (movies, television, jazz and rock music, and, of course, comics) to the status of bona fide artforms. It was an exciting period in intellectual history, and perhaps had its ultimate flowering in the works of French philosopher Roland Barthes, who argued that culture should include everything, and that the distinctions between 'high' and 'low' were outdated (see in particular Barthes 1977). Barthes, too, discussed comics.

Cultural crossovers

A corollary of this shifting of cultural priorities was that there developed close links between European comics and other artforms – especially with movies. It is possible to argue that the same kind of thing happened in Britain and America: but in these countries, comics, because of their low cultural status, were primarily seen as 'raw materials' to be stolen from at will by movie-makers. In Europe, a far more respectful tradition took shape whereby comics creators and film-makers collaborated and shared ideas. The career of the great Italian movie director Federico Fellini is very instructive in this respect. He was a founder member of an important comics study group in the early 1960s (The 'Centre d'Etudes des Literatures d'Expression Graphique', or CELEG for short), and frequently paid homage to comics in his films. Later in his career, he would collaborate with comics artists to produce comics albums, notably *Trip to Tulum* (1989), drawn by Milo Manara, which was based on a once-discarded film script. Other European film-makers closely associated with, and influenced by, comics include the Frenchmen Alain Resnais and Jean-Luc Godard. Equally, comics creators often work in the movies: Enki Bilal, for instance, directs his own films, including science-fiction yarns like *Bunker Palace Hotel* (1990) and *Immortal* (2005). Most recently, *Persepolis* has become an animated feature, co-written and co-directed by Marjane Satrapi, and was joint winner of the Grand Prize at Cannes in 2007.

A similar process was evident with regard to novelistic fiction. Writers of comics would also pen novels, while novelists would try their hand at comics. For example, in our list of hit comics albums above, two of the writers happen also to be internationally recognised novelists: Pierre Christin and Jean-Michel Charlier. There are many more such examples, notably Jerome Charyn, a Europhile American author, whose collaborations with French artist Francois Boucq (*The Magician's Wife, Billy Budd: KGB*) have produced some of the best thriller comics.

Because of this relative parity among the artforms, comics creators command a level of respect in Europe that is comparable to film directors or novelists – again, a concept that would be alien to the comics scene in the UK or USA. Sometimes, it is even true that star creators assume the status of 'auteurs' (a French word denoting a creative artist who has a controlling influence over their work). Such is the case with the above-mentioned Jean ('Moebius') Giraud, and to a lesser extent with Enki Bilal and Milo Manara. In the case of these creators, comics can be marketed on the basis of their names, just in the same way as novels are sold as 'the new Dave Eggers' or films as 'the new Tarantino'.

Economic factors

These factors have greatly influenced, and have been influenced by, the economics of comics production in Europe. Because of the cultural respect that comics command, creators have never been exploited in the same way that they have in the UK and USA. Rather, comics have traditionally been a natural place for upcoming creative talents to ply their trade – as natural as working in movies, novels, advertising, illustration and so on. The crucial issue has always been rates of pay: for, whereas in the USA and the UK creators have until quite recently been paid a flat fee calculated by the page, in Europe, creators receive royalties as well: in other words, they earn a split of any profits their work may make.

The development of the album system was a major step forward in this respect. It was the Tintin albums that established the form, in the 1930s. What was unusual about them was that they were published by a Catholic publisher, Casterman (who were bought by Flammarion in 2000), whose code of practice evidently entailed a 'moral obligation' to pay creators a decent royalty. Thus, not only did Tintin's creators receive a royalty when strips appeared first in magazine form, but also a second royalty when they were collected together as albums. This system has endured through the decades since, throughout the European comics industry, and has ensured not only a reasonable living for creators but also a higher standard of work. For it stands to reason that if creators are paid well, then they take more pride in what they are doing: this in turn means that it is easier to take comics seriously as an artform.

Most creators also retain copyright over their creations, which means that they rather than the publishers determine what happens to them. For example, if a creator decides to stop producing stories starring a particular character, then there is no way a publisher can step in and hire another creator to continue the strip without the originator's permission (which would additionally require financial remuneration). This is why Tintin stories ended with the death of Hergé, in contrast to Superman stories, which have continued long past the death of his creators (Siegel and Shuster). More than this, control of copyright means that it is the creator who benefits from any film or TV adaptations – always very important in the world of comics, as we have seen.

Other historical factors have also combined to bolster the economics of the comics industry. For example, there has been a more successful history of unionisation and collective bargaining among comics creators in parts of Europe than in the USA and the UK. This has meant that when disputes arise, they are settled in a manner which at least takes the views of creators into account (very rare in the latter countries). Also, the intervention of governments in some European countries has meant certain advantages for the industry. For instance, after World War Two, the French government introduced a law which limited the importation of comics from abroad: the French industry was thus protected against foreign competition, and allowed to develop at its own pace. More recently, governments in some countries have actually subsidised the comics industry. The most famous example of this was the construction of a sizeable museum and study centre in France (Centre nationale de la bande dessinée et l'image, or CNBDI), part-funded by the government to the tune of millions of francs. Once again, the fact that comics have cultural kudos was a major factor in the government's decision: the centre was opened by the then Minister for Culture, Jack Lang.

The position of the UK

So we can see that economics and cultural acceptance have combined in Europe to create a unique comics culture. But the question remains, what about the UK? Of course, the UK is a part of Europe in many respects; but in terms of comics, there is different sensibility at work. Certainly, the UK industry has produced its own classic titles in the past – *The Beano, Eagle, 2000AD* and *Viz* to name just a few (see Gravett and Stanbury 2006). But it can be argued that these have been successful despite the production system rather than because of it. For in the UK, comics have traditionally been culturally despised as either lowest-common-denominator trash, or as literature for children, or both. Underlying this prejudice, as we have seen, there has existed an iniquitous economic situation that has meant that comics have usually been the last place anybody would want to work.

Thus, the comics tradition in the UK has been dominated by titles aimed at an 8-to-12 age-range, produced on cheap, poor-quality, paper, and designed to be binned after one read. As for the contents, despite some notable exceptions, the norm has been mediocre storylines, produced to string the reader along for week after week, and unexceptional artwork. In other words, the work-for-hire, fee-per-page, system that has prevailed in the UK has ensured that comics remain largely the preserve of hacks, and thus have never acquired any kind of cultural respectability. Many of the beneficial aspects of comics production that we have discussed with regard to European comics, and which are largely taken for granted there – the collecting of stories into albums, the way in which royalties are split among creators, how they retain copyright, and so on – have (historically) barely made an impact on the UK scene. Arguably this is one reason why the UK industry has shrunk from its heyday in the 1960s to its present level, consisting of merely a handful of publishers of weekly and monthly product (notably Rebellion, publishers of *2000AD*; IFG Ltd, publishers of *Viz*; and DC Thomson, publishers of *The Beano*), plus a few book publishers who put out a limited range of 'graphic novels' – more about which in a moment.

Yet recently, things have been changing. With the growth since the late 1970s of a network of specialist shops orientated towards hard-core comics fans (usually, it should be said, fans of American superhero titles), there has developed a more European approach to the economics of comics production. Today, many publishers offer creators royalty splits, plus control over copyright – concessions that were very rare only two decades ago. Part of this evolution has been due to the particular economics of the specialist shop system (see Sabin 1992: Chapter 5), but partly it has been due to the influence of the European industry itself. For example, people involved in the UK scene have become more aware of working conditions in Europe since the mid-1970s, when fan shops began to import European albums aimed at an adult and teenage audience. This was followed by a spate of translations of top albums by small UK and US publishers, and the emergence of a UK fan following for Eurocomics (albeit a very limited one). This gradual rise in awareness prompted some publishers to question previous employment practices, and some creators to press for change.

The rise of the 'graphic novel' in the UK and USA in the 1980s and 90s was part of this process. Graphic novels are basically lengthy comics in book form – in other words, an indigenous version of the European album. Although other factors were involved in their origination, the European paradigm was certainly influential: UK and US creators had long sought the opportunity to experiment with longer stories and more sophisticated artwork in tune with their European counterparts. So, too, the European idea of selling comics from bookshops was exploited more fully: graphic novel shelves were erected, and efforts were made to ensure that they were reviewed in the literary pages of the newspapers. In this way, a readership was solicited which might not otherwise have come across comics – the kind of readership that publishers in Europe had been serving for decades.

Thus, the question of whether the UK can ever join the European Comics Community is not entirely closed. Graphic novels and European albums can be pretty much the same in terms of format, quality and price, and this does mean that the comics are more easily sellable across the markets. Yet, when it comes to content, it is still true that the UK has a lot of catching up to do before publishers can offer the same range of subject matter as exists in Europe. Things are improving, and there have been a few UK hits across the Channel (the recent books by Posy Simmonds being an example) just as there have been a few Euro-hits in the UK. But any realistic appraisal of the situation would have to conclude that in 2009, UK readers still prefer UK and American comics, while European readers prefer European comics. In the end, each continues to find the other 'a bit too foreign'.

Continuing marginalisation

So, what is the future for Eurocomics? The industry is changing all the time, as we have seen, and the internet is making an impact, as it is everywhere else. 'E-comics' are becoming more popular across the continent, but although there are possibilities for cheap and easily accessible translations into English, this path has not yet been exploited bar a few low-key experiments. Elsewhere, publishers' sites and fan sites devoted to individual creators are often appearing in multi-lingual versions, and this is opening things up. But in general, the main impact of digital technology so far has been in the realm of print-to-order publishing for very small publishers, and as an advertising tool (especially the web) for the very large ones.

Movie adaptations of Eurocomics will continue to have some sway, and one very important example is scheduled for a 2011 release. *The Adventures of*

Tintin: Secret of the Unicorn is the long-awaited, and hugely budgeted, Dreamworks collaboration between Steven Spielberg and Peter (*Lord of the Rings*) Jackson. It is being produced using a 'motion capture' process, and will star Jamie Bell. However, it is already the focus of some controversy due to the source material being accused of racism (the UK's Campaign for Racial Equality said of *Tintin in the Congo* that 'the "savage natives" look like monkeys and talk like imbeciles'), and due to the reputation of Hergé himself coming under renewed fire for his alleged collaboration with the Nazis during the war. Time will tell whether the juggernaut of the movie's PR can overcome such criticisms. In any case, the effect on the comics industry is likely to be circumscribed: an inevitable spike in Tintin album sales, but not necessarily for other kinds of eurocomic.

Questions

1 How far is there a unified 'European Union' when it comes to comics?

2 Why is the UK comics industry distinct from the rest of Europe?

3 What are the key Eurocomics albums, and why?

Further reading

Eurocomics are still much under-researched. However, the 1990s and 2000s have seen a number of high quality studies in English, mostly about Francophone BD. These include Bart Beaty's *Unpopular Culture: Transforming the European Comic Book in the 1990s* (Toronto: University of Toronto Press, 2007); McQuillan, E., Forsdick, C. and Grove, L. (eds) *The Francophone Bande Desinée* (Amsterdam: Rodopi, 2005), Laurence Grove's *Text/Image Mosaics in French Culture* (Aldershot: Ashgate, 2006), Matthew Screech's *Masters of the Ninth Art: Bandes Desinées and Franco-Belgian Identity* (Chicago: University of Chicago Press, 2005), and Ann Miller's *Reading Bande Dessinée* (Bristol: Intellect, 2007).

The most detailed and up-to-date information is available in fanzines, and readers are encouraged to track down the regular column 'Eurocomics for Beginners' by Bart Beaty in the American zine *The Comics Journal* (Seattle: Fantagraphics).

The more academic *International Journal of Comic Art* (Drexel Hill: John A. Lent) has frequent, useful articles. The internet is also a good source, though sites tend to come and go without much warning: one reliable example is: *European Comics on the Web* (http://ifarm.nl/strips/) which has links to a variety of specialist sites.

For an overview of comics available in English, see Randy Scott's *European Comics in English Translation* (Jefferson: McFarland and Co, 2002). Some of the glossier surveys of comics in general contain sections on European material, for example Paul Gravett's *Graphic Novels: Stories to Change Your Life* (London: Aurum, 2005) and Roger Sabin's *Comics, Comix and Graphic Novels* (London: Phaidon, 1996).

References

Barthes, R. (1977) *Mythologies*, Harmondsworth: Penguin.

Eco, U. (1981) *The Role of the Reader*, London: Hutchinson.

Gravett, P. and Stanbury, P. (2006) *Great British Comics*, London: Aurum Press.

Groensteen, T. (2007) *The System of Comics*, Jackson, MS: University of Mississippi Press.

Iglesia, de la, M. (2007) 'Geographical Classification in Comics', *International Journal of Comic Art*, 9 (2): Fall/Winter 2007 (Drexel Hill: John A. Lent).

Kessler, P. (1995) *Astérix Complete Guide*, London: Hodder.

McCloud, S. (1994) *Understanding Comics*, London: HarperCollins.

Peeters, B. (1992) *Tintin and the World of Hergé*, Boston, MA: Little, Brown.

Sabin, R. (1992) *Adult Comics: An Introduction*, London: Routledge.

Thompson, H. (1991) *Hergé and His Creation*, London: Hodder & Stoughton.

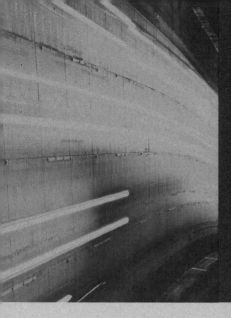

6

Photography

Stephen Bull

Chapter overview

This chapter examines what the identity of photography is perceived to be and the ways by which photographs communicate. These ideas influence how photographs are employed and the chapter introduces the key debates about some of the main ways in which the medium of photography is put to use. It discusses popular photography, photography for sale, art photography and the relation of photography to celebrity.

Introduction

Photography is everywhere. It would be extremely difficult to get through a day without seeing a photograph. Indeed it is more usual to see hundreds or thousands of them, in print and on screen. Advertising photographs, snapshots, images for identification, photojournalism, art photography, fashion, pictures of celebrities looking bad: these are the kinds of photographs that surround us all the time in the West.

Yet despite its ubiquity, photography remains a mysterious and fascinating medium, hard to pin down. This chapter begins with two sections examining what the identity of photography is perceived to be and the ways by which photographs communicate. These ideas influence how photographs are employed, and in the following shorter sections the chapter introduces the key debates about some of the main ways in which the medium of photography is put to use.

Identity and meanings

The identity of photography

Although the existence of photography was officially announced in Europe in 1839, most historians make a point of noting that its origins lie centuries earlier

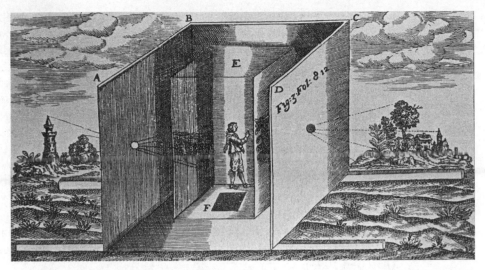

Diagram of *camera obscura*. Athanasius Kircher: Large Portable Camera Obscura, 1646
Source: © Bettmann / Corbis

and in many other places (see Marien 2006; Rosenblum 2008). At least since the 1600s, and probably hundreds of years before, the *camera obscura* (Latin for 'dark chamber') was used to help make accurate images of the world. The *camera obscura* is a large sealed room or box with a small hole in one side. If what is outside the *camera obscura* is brightly lit then an image of it is projected through the hole into the room or box and can be traced. However this relies on the human hand to record what is projected, which takes skill and time.

As the photography historian Geoffrey Batchen has meticulously detailed, between 1790 and 1839 a number of what he refers to as 'proto-photographers' were trying to find ways to permanently fix the image projected within the *camera obscura* so that it could be recorded instantly and without the need for a skilful hand (Batchen 1997). Batchen argues that this reflects an era when nature was seen to be coming increasingly under the control of human culture (for example, by harnessing the power of natural light). To Batchen, when proto-photographers such as Nicéphore Niépce in France and William Henry Fox Talbot in Britain succeeded in fixing the image, they also fixed within the identity of photography itself this combination of ideas about nature and culture. This is summed up by the very word 'photography': photo- from the Greek *phos* meaning light (occurring in nature), and -graphy from *graphè* meaning writing or drawing (practices cultivated by humans).

This integration of opposing ideas within the identity of photography is evident in a divide between critical approaches to the medium in the 20th century. Modernists such as John Szarkowski, the curator of photography at the Museum of Modern Art, New York from 1962 to 1991, argued that photography has an inherent and unchanging nature that anyone using a camera plays a part in discovering. Focusing on aesthetics, the look of the photograph, in a 1960s book and exhibition Szarkowski famously refined the nature of photography down to a combination of five aspects: the thing itself, the detail, time, the frame, and the vantage point (Szarkowski 2007).

In the 1920s Walter Benjamin observed that the mass reproducibility of photographs via the negative/positive process Talbot pioneered, coupled with 20th century mechanical technology, meant pictures could simultaneously appear in a potentially infinite number of times and in a potentially limitless amount of places (which Benjamin examined from a Marxist perspective as a way of distributing information to a vast audience) (Benjamin 1999). Taking their cue from Benjamin – and influenced by a 'postmodern' approach – in the 1970s and 1980s writers such as Victor Burgin, Rosalind Krauss and John Tagg refuted Szarkowski's ideas about aesthetics and instead emphasised the cultural contexts of photographs (Burgin 1982; Bolton 1989; Tagg 1988).

More recently Batchen has argued that at their respective extremes Modernism isolates photographs from the cultural context outside the frame of the image, while postmodernism regards photographs only as vessels for ideas and ignores the content of what is inside the frame; he suggests that in any analysis of photography both the context and content of photography must be taken into account (Batchen 1997).

The meanings of photographs

Since the 1960s the most influential approach to analysing the meanings of photographs has been a version of semiotics incorporated into English-speaking academic debate from 'semiology'. The French writer Roland Barthes developed semiology in essays such as 'Rhetoric of the Image' where he analyses the denotation and connotation of a photographic advert (Barthes 1977). The denotation of the photograph is what the viewer immediately recognises in the image's content. However the viewer also immediately 'reads' meaning into what they see: this is the connotation of the image. Connotation comes from the cultural context of the photograph and the cultural background of the viewer. The connotations of the image (photographs are what Barthes calls 'polysemic' – they have a number of possible meanings) are not just limited by the content of the image (its denotation) but are also refined by the use of text. It is rare to see a photograph that has no text to accompany it. For Barthes, text functions in two main ways: anchorage, where the text describes what is in the picture, precisely defining the meaning of the photograph the way an anchor moors a boat in place; and relay, where the text and image articulate different messages, working together to create meanings that are often still open to a greater degree of interpretation.

The fact that the advert Barthes analyses uses a photograph to communicate is vital: it makes the visual argument more convincing, despite its obvious staging (this is what Barthes means by the 'rhetoric' of the image). As Andre Bazin wrote in the 1940s, photographs are regarded as being closer to reality, more 'natural', than a drawing or painting because the photograph is seen to have a direct connection with what it represents (Bazin 1980). (When photography was first announced, the painter Paul Delaroche reportedly exclaimed 'From today painting is dead!' (Batchen 1997: 260n).) The linguist and founder of semiology, Ferdinand de Saussure, argued that the basic element of communication is the linguistic 'sign', while the philosopher Charles Sanders Peirce founded modern semiotics through categorising signs of all kinds according to the way they are perceived. He gave photography as an example of an 'indexical' sign: one that is regarded as a direct trace of its cause (in roughly the same way that a footprint is seen as a direct trace of a foot) (Sturken and Cartwright 2001: 10–44). Applying the concept of indexicality to photographs has been subject to a great deal of debate, much of it mistaken and ill-informed regarding Peirce's work (see Elkins 2007). Nevertheless the idea that when we look at a photograph our gaze often seems to join with the look of the camera's lens, positioning our point of view 'within' the image as if we were actually there, represents a significant element of photography's power; it is also an issue often applied to the analysis of gender or race in photography (Burgin 2003; McGrath 2003).

In Barthes' final book, *Camera Lucida*, he names two aspects of photographs: what he calls the 'studium', broadly the general meaning of a photograph that most viewers will understand, and the 'punctum' a personal meaning that will be unique to specific viewers (Barthes 2000). Time is integral to the idea of the punctum: the examples Barthes gives, such as a photograph of his recently deceased mother, all relate to the way that photographs record people, places, objects and moments that will pass. While Barthes' approach is often melancholic, Bazin sees photographs more positively as a way of snatching moments 'from the flow of time' and preserving the instant (even though time actually continues) (Bazin 1980). As well as semiotics, psychoanalysis has also been used to analyse photographs, often in a similar way to which Freud examined fantasies and dreams (Burgin 1986; Freud 1991). Christian Metz, fusing semiology and psychoanalysis, has argued that the Freudian concept of the fetish, an object that stands in for something else, is applicable to photography: indeed a photograph almost always replaces something (a person, place, object, moment) that is otherwise absent (Metz 2003).

During the late 1980s and early 1990s the increasing use of digital cameras and the computer manipulation of photographs led to debates about whether the perceived indexicality of photographs was going to disappear (Mitchell 1992; Ritchin 1999; Wombell 1991). Often these discussions centred on the idea that digital technology had fundamentally changed the nature of photographs; 'From Today Photography is Dead' exclaimed one article in the early part of the decade, paraphrasing Delaroche's words (Mitchell 1993). By the end of the 1990s a second wave of analysts argued instead that photographs had always been manipulated and that the same basic idea of photography continued: digital photography was not a revolution but an evolution in a technologically ever-changing medium (e.g. Batchen 1997; Manovich 2003). It could also be contended that a digital image, projected or viewed on a screen, represents a purer version of photography (as 'writing with light') than an image on a piece of paper (see Sassoon 2004). Michel Frizot argues that whether light is recorded by film or digital sensors, a photograph is still a direct trace of the world (Frizot 2007). In the 21st century the mass digital reproduction of photographs, their online transmission, and the fact that they are encountered via screens as much as they are in print has taken Benjamin's ideas much further than he is likely to have imagined (see Sassoon 2004). The fixed photograph is now mobile. And yet in its travels from screen to screen and its potential for alteration or instant deletion, it is also more transient and ephemeral than ever before. The digital photograph is everywhere and nowhere.

Selling photography

Photography for sale

1839 is the date photography went on sale. As soon as photography was made public it became a commodity. By the 1850s portrait studios were all over Europe and America. Portrait photographers developed the *carte-de-visite*, multiple images on a single glass plate negative, which made the costs of production cheaper and allowed people who could not afford the initially expensive and complicated apparatus required for making photographs to have accurate renditions of themselves produced (Ramamurthy 2009). It is with the proliferation of *carte-de-visite* portraits that the family photo album emerges (see below). In 1888 George Eastman invented flexible roll film, which meant that 100 images could be exposed on a single strip. The film was sold ready-loaded in easy to use 'box' cameras. Once the film was finished the whole camera was sent to Eastman's company and developed. The prints were then returned along with the camera reloaded with a new roll of film (see Marien 2006). Eastman's photographic company Kodak (its name a universally usable word with no specific meaning) began the process of making photography accessible to the masses with its slogan 'You Press The Button, We Do The Rest'.

Much analysis of photography often forgets the camera equipment with which the image was made. In 1980, before digital photography became available to the general public, Don Slater examined how the mass marketing of camera technologies helped to define the kinds of photographs people make, as well as promoting distinctions between snapshooters, hobbyists, semi-professionals and professionals, each of whom is sold different types of equipment via, for example, different photography magazines (Slater 1997). In the 1990s Slater analysed debates about the selling of software for computer manipulation and hardware for storage, arguing that the flow of information was becoming central in a digital age (Slater 1995). Despite the increased viewing of photographs on screens, companies such as PhotoBox, the website where customers upload digital files from their camera or camera phone and then receive their prints (or their images on birthday cards, mugs, etc.) in the post, has combined digital technology with the desire for hard copies.

Kodak advertisement, 1888
Source: Courtesy of Kodak Ltd (UK)

Photographs themselves are commodities too. From the pictures made by professional wedding photographers to sports photography, images of celebrities caught by paparazzi to the art photographs that now regularly sell for millions of dollars (Badger 2007: 201–32), from the photojournalism and portraiture owned by image banks such as Getty or Corbis, to the same companies' stock photography that accounts for around 70 per cent of the images used to sell products to us (Frosh 2003), photographs are for sale.

Photography for selling

The advertising slogan for *Kodak* is an excellent example of connecting the consumer (*You* Press The Button) with the company (*We* Do The Rest). The relationship that photographs have with the viewer (the point of view of the camera's lens blending apparently seamlessly with their own look) makes photography an ideal tool for selling. In her study of advertising images Judith Williamson argues that viewers are invited to identify with the scenes depicted in the adverts that are an unavoidable part of contemporary life (Williamson 2002). Williamson draws on Jacques Lacan's psychoanalytic concept of the 'mirror phase'. Lacan claims that a child learns to recognise what it sees as its 'self' through identifying with images – and that an identification with certain images continues throughout adult life. Advertisers use the rhetoric of the photograph to persuade audiences to identify with what is shown and so believe that the product and lifestyle being offered is for them. At the same time the photograph also offers the viewer identification with a shared set of beliefs – in Marxist terms an 'ideology' (Burgin 1982; Ramamurthy 2009) – such as the belief that consuming products will improve our lives, or more recently that to buy a product will make us 'ecologically sound' (Myers 1999). In response to this proliferation of photographic images, jarring 'subvertisements' have been published by organisations including Adbusters. Meanwhile photography-based stencil graffiti by artists such as Banksy has appeared in city streets across the world, using the rhetoric of the photographic image to parody and suggest alternatives to the dominant ideology (Banksy 2006).

Popular photography

Say cheese! The nature and culture of snapshots

Alongside advertising, the most common form of photography is the domestic snapshot. Although it was not until the 1950s that photography truly became available to all, the accessibility and marketing of the medium meant that in the 1980s, a century after the formation of Kodak, 80 million films (producing on average 24 or 36 negatives each) were being bought each year in the UK alone (Slater 1997). Yet the lack of critical study about the kinds of everyday snapshots that most people in the world make and appear in means that the subject remains surprisingly overlooked. In a rare and detailed study in the 1960s, sociologist Pierre Bourdieu argued that the central subject of photography is the family and that photographs play a vital role in cultivating unity among families (Bourdieu 1990). From childhood we quickly learn how to perform for photographs – and soon afterwards when to take them and how to organise people for our own snaps. Adopting a similar approach to Szarkowski, Graham King and Dave Kenyon have (in separate studies) attempted to define the nature of the snapshot (King 1986; Kenyon 1992). Graham focuses on aesthetics, listing such qualities as tilted horizons, unconventional cropping and the distant subject as characteristic of the snap; while in an analysis of the contents of family albums Kenyon identifies the most common themes of domestic photography: family, Christmas (for which we could substitute equivalent festivals), holidays, weddings and the natural environment.

As Kenyon's study demonstrates, despite all the billions of snapshots that are made across the world every year, the types of subject matter photographed are generally limited to celebratory moments. Writers such as Annette Kuhn and the photographer and author Jo Spence have analysed snapshots to reveal the complex personal and political meanings that are hidden within or kept outside the frame of the domestic photograph (Kuhn 2002; Spence 1995). Spence also developed the technique of phototherapy where photography is used to recreate and explore issues such as childhood memories.

Beyond the snapshot, but still outside of professional photography (i.e. images made to be sold), camera clubs have traditionally been the place for amateur hobbyists to display and discuss their work (Bourdieu 1990). Part of this process often involves the judging of photographs, where comments are made on images and marks often assigned (Bull 1999). With the use of digital photography, websites such as Flickr now perform a comparable function, with hobbyists' photographs eliciting remarks from viewers around the world.

Mobile photographs: camera phones and social networking

Go to any pop concert, football match or comedy gig and you will be surrounded by members of the audience taking pictures on their mobile phones (indeed you may well be taking them yourself). By 2003 sales of camera phones had reached over 150 million worldwide (2005) and it is now unusual for a mobile phone not to include a camera. More than ever before, we are all photographers: although Damian Sutton (2005) has suggested that the same kinds of snapshot photographs still predominate.

Sutton argues that the mobility of the camera phone continues the portability of the Kodak box camera (Sutton 2005). But as he also notes, and as I have already argued here, the digital photograph itself is portable, too. While picture messaging from mobiles was initially less popular than companies such as Nokia may have predicted, the mobility of the snapshot online is now a key element of photography in the 21st century. Some of the main environments in which such images appear are moblogs (mobile phone photograph blogs) and social networking sites such as Facebook. Founded in 2004, Facebook allows members to put information about themselves online alongside a profile picture to represent them. Within the Facebook page members can also create photo albums where images are uploaded, organised and 'tagged' with popup text to identify who or what has been photographed. If given permission other users can view the albums and comment on the pictures. The once private photo album, tucked away in a cupboard or under a bed, has become publicly available.

The photograph as document

Evidence

The commonly perceived indexicality of photography has, since the 19th century, resulted in it being employed to provide evidence. Tagg has demonstrated how medical, educational and legal institutions have made use of photography to record the people who pass through them (Tagg 1988). To Tagg this operates as social control, placing the subjects under a form of surveillance. He connects this to Michel Foucault's discussion of Jeremy Bentham's idea of the Panopticon, a design for an ideal prison where each inmate is potentially being watched by unseen guards at any time, which Foucault uses as a metaphor to describe power in contemporary society. Tagg notes how the use of photography by the police has progressed in parallel to developments in photographic technology. The UK police now have a Crimestoppers website where images of most wanted criminals are made available to the public. The combination of visual and textual information on these webpages is similar to that of the records kept by medical and educational institutions or even the pages of sites based on leisure such as *Facebook*. While the online applications Google Earth and Google Maps provide an apparently democratic power to survey the world in great detail via a patchwork of satellite photographs, some governments have requested that certain areas of their countries remain pixelated from view.

Elizabeth Edwards has studied how the use of photography to gain knowledge and power over its subjects was particularly pronounced in 19th and early 20th century colonial imagery as Western countries continued to 'discover', map, and attempt to possess the rest of the world (Edwards 2001). The idea of self identity deriving from Lacan's concept of the mirror phase, briefly examined above, is here contrasted with the combination of anxiety (including fear and disgust), and desire (of a sexual kind and not always acknowledged) connoted by photographs of those perceived to be unfamiliar, different and 'Other'. In the 1980s the way photographs can be instruments of anxieties and desires simultaneously was demonstrated in an analysis by Kobena Mercer, who identified the legacy of colonial imagery in white photographer Robert Mapplethorpe's overtly sexualised images of the Black male nude, indicating photography's power to represent ambivalent feelings about the 'Other' (Mercer 1999).

Documentary

Although there are many precursors to the documentary photograph in such work as Roger Fenton's 1850s images of Crimean War landscapes showing the aftermath of battles, 'documentary' as a word and concept began to be defined in

1926 when the British film-maker John Grierson described a film by fellow director Robert Flaherty as having 'documentary value' (Solomon-Godeau 1991a). Like Grierson, Flaherty made films about real lives that established the dominant mode for documentary: the revealing of subjects to an audience unlikely to share the same experiences, and often about which that audience might be concerned. A now classic example of 'concerned' documentary photography occurred during the American economic depression and droughts of the 1930s when a team of photographers were assigned by the Farm Security Administration to document the starving farmers migrating to find work. The resulting images were mass re-produced in widely read US photo-magazines such as *Life* and helped create awareness of the farmers' plight, although they could also be interpreted as examples of what Martha Rosler has referred to as 'victim' photography (see Rosler 2003). This kind of photojournalism was meant to be as objective as the reports that it accompanied (in principle at least).

After the World War Two, documentary photography became more independent of magazine editors. The photo agency Magnum was set up in 1948 to give its members control over the publication of their images. In the decades that followed, photographers such as Magnum member Henri Cartier-Bresson (who promoted the idea of the 'decisive moment' where the photographer captures an activity at precisely the right fraction of a second in an ideally composed shot) and Robert Frank (who photographed America in the mid 1950s) visualised their own subjective opinions about what they depicted. By the 1980s British documentary photographer Martin Parr was able to fully acknowledge that his witty and colourful photographs of everyday culture, made using a snapshot aesthetic, were consciously 'prejudiced' (Brittain 2000; Williams 2002), while late 20th century images by photographers such as Nan Goldin and Richard Billingham were diaries in a loosely documentary form.

David Campany has argued that the speed by which documentary photography conveyed events to the public had been fully superseded by television and the web well before the turn of the millennium (Campany 2003a). The combination of photojournalistic and televised coverage of the Vietnam War could be seen as marking this transition. Rather than capturing decisive moments, documentary – in the form of what Campany calls 'late photography' – has instead re-turned to recording the aftermath of events in images that Campany suggests might be just a bit too beautiful (such as Joel Meyerowitz's pictures of Ground Zero in the days following 9/11) (2003a). Other photographers including Jeff Wall and Gregory Crewdson make elaborately staged images for an art context that are 'documentary' in appearance but actually involve the recreation or total fabrication of events (see below for an examination of art photography).

In complete contrast to late photography and staged scenes, digital photography has led to the rise of 'citizen journalism' where members of the public document events on their mobiles (for example, Alexander Chadwick's photographs of the London bombings in 2005), often distributing and selling the images themselves via the web (see Chapter 17). In an even more startling shift, instead of photojournalism the central war photographs in the early 21st century Iraq conflict were those taken by US soldiers using digital cameras documenting their own humiliating abuse of Iraqi prisoners.

Alexander Chadwick: evacuating through tube tunnel
Source: Alexander Chadwick / AP / Press Association Images

Photography as art

What makes a photograph art?

'Pictorialist' photographers in the 19th and early 20th century attempted to establish the medium as an art by using techniques such as soft focus and retouching to mimic the look of painting, coupled with the traditional subject matter of paintings such as landscapes, nudes, religious scenes and elaborately staged fantasies. During the early 1900s, influenced by the contemporary style and subjects of Modern artists including Pablo Picasso, some photographers turned instead to 'straight' photography and up-to-date subjects. Images such as Alfred Stieglitz's pioneering *The Steerage* (1907) and Paul Strand's *Wire Wheel, New York* (1917) utilise the technical qualities of photography: they are sharply focused, employ no retouching to imitate paint, and crop what is in front of the camera, sometimes creating pictures that are almost abstract. By the 1930s a group of American photographers including Ansel Adams, Imogen Cunningham and Edward Weston formed the technically centred Group f64 (named after the aperture which gives the greatest amount of detail). The work they made, along with their counterparts in Europe and Russia such as the Surrealist Man Ray, New Objectivity photographer Laszlo Moholy-Nagy and the Constructivist Alexander Rodchenko, helped to establish a visual language of technique, angle and cropping specific to Modernist photography, often with the emphasis on formal qualities (from which Szarkowski was to extrapolate many of his ideas about the intrinsic nature of photographs).

Contemporary art photography

Modernism in visual culture reached a peak in the mid-20th century without photography having fully established its credentials as an art form. However, conceptual and performance artists in the 1960s and early 1970s often recorded their largely ephemeral actions using photography (Campany 2003b). Some of these artists, such as Keith Arnatt and Gilbert and George began to focus on photography itself as their medium. Postmodernism in the late 1970s and 80s continued contemporary art's attempts to connect art with popular culture: accordingly artists including Barbara Kruger, Richard Prince and Cindy Sherman made use of the popular medium of photography in their work. Often these practitioners applied techniques of appropriation, either by using photographs that already existed and reinterpreting them through cropping and the application of text or, as in the case of Sherman's series of *Untitled Film Stills*, by mimicking the look of other images (Solomon-Godeau 1991b).

In the 1990s artists that used photography, such as Andreas Gursky, became central to contemporary art. Gursky is one of a number of well-known contemporary photographers who were taught by Bernd and Hilla Becher at the Düsseldorf Art Academy. The Bechers' straight-on typologies of water towers and other industrial architecture (referred to in the title of their first book as *Anonymous Sculptures*) were inspired by August Sander's attempt to document a cross section of German life in the 1920s and 1930s via a series of portraits of German social 'types'. In turn the Bechers inspired the school of what Charlotte Cotton refers to as 'deadpan'

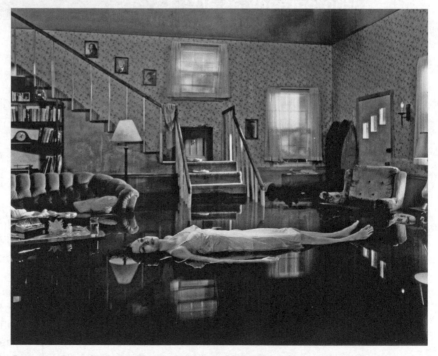

Gregory Crewdson, *Untitled (Ophelia)*, 2001 (from the series Twilight)
Source: Courtesy of White Cube, London and Gregory Crewdson

art photography: a practice that has extended far beyond their own students (Cotton 2004).

More recently artists such as Wall, Crewdson, Thomas Demand and Tom Hunter have used photography to stage 'performative' images, where scenes and events are elaborately set up just for the picture and well in advance of the photograph being made. Some of this work also recreates the look of documentary photography and/or elements from the kind of pre-Modernist painting that influenced the Pictorialists (see above) (Bull 2004). It is via the work of artists since the 1960s, along with major exhibitions of photography in art galleries in the first decade of the 21st century, that photography has not become art but instead, as Campany puts it, 'art has become increasingly photographic' (Campany 2003a: 14).

Photography as entertainment

Photography in fashion

Like fashion itself, fashion photography has cyclical trends. Ideas and images become popular and then disappear, only to be revived a few years later. The main context for fashion photography is the magazine (Barthes 1990; Jobling 1999). As late as the 1950s photographs in fashion magazines were mostly highly staged, studio-based and static, recalling the style of the drawn illustrations that preceded them. Both the models and photographers were part of an elite. In the 1960s London-based photographers from working class backgrounds including David Bailey and Terence Donovan took fashion photography onto the streets, often blending their shoots with a documentary aesthetic (Harrison 1991). Such images helped contribute to notions of social mobility and an increased access to fashion, heightened by the collaboration between photographers and models from similar backgrounds such as Jean Shrimpton and Twiggy. Sometimes referred to as 'waifs' these models are often shown leaping and jumping in dynamic images that Hilary Radner has argued represent an idea of female independence, although she notes that fashion photography is ultimately about selling clothes: the freedom apparently represented is a freedom to consume within a capitalist ideology (Radner 2000).

The 1970s and 1980s saw the return of more staged imagery in the sometimes explicit images of Guy Bourdin and Helmut Newton. At the time these pictures were criticised from a feminist perspective because of their stereotyping of women and sometimes violent fragmentation of the female body (see Brooks 1997), although recent histories of fashion photography have reappraised them (Harrison 1991; Williams 1998). In complete contrast the 1990s saw apparently casual snapshots of thin models not leaping or jumping, but leaning on walls and slumping on sofas, such as the pictures by Corinne Day of Kate Moss that appeared in *Vogue* and started the debate about whether these kinds of images promoted eating disorders and drug abuse (Arnold 2001). Over the decade the developing digital manipulation of images of the body in fashion magazines ran parallel with an increased

Corinne Day, *Kate Moss, Kate's Flat,* **1993**
Source: Corinne Day / Maconochie Photography

modification of the physical body itself (de Perthuis 2005). Fashion photography in the 21st century – now sharing many stylistic qualities with art photography and exhibited in major galleries – once again involved highly theatrical images, often with celebrities as the models (Bright 2007; Kismaric and Respini 2004).

Photography and celebrity

The 21st century is arguably a celebrity-obsessed era and photography plays a major part in both creating celebrities and revealing them to be human. In the 19th century photography put faces to the names of those already famous for their achievements such as the British poet Sir Alfred Lord Tennyson (Hargreaves 2001). The mass reproduction of photography in newspapers and magazines, along with other forms of reproduction such as film, television and recorded sound enabled performers including Elvis Presley and Marilyn Monroe to achieve global fame in what might be called The Golden Age of Celebrity during the middle years of the 20th century. The publicity images of these stars showed them as perfect, almost godlike and inhuman in their perfection (Muir 2005).

The emergence of paparazzi in the 1950s and 1960s, beginning in Rome and named after a photographer in Federico Fellini's film *La Dolce Vita* (1960), led to very different images of celebrities caught off-guard being reproduced in magazines and newspapers (Squiers 1999). Karin E. Becker has defined the characteristics of the paparazzi photograph as being badly composed, out of focus, often including intrusive foreground objects, and capturing strange poses and facial expressions. Becker argues that these qualities suggest the image is not staged and therefore exposes what the celebrity is really like (Becker 2003). Tabloid newspapers, celebrity gossip websites and British magazines such as *Now*, *Heat* and *Closer* (which had a combined weekly circulation in 2005 of 1.5 million) use photography and text to show celebrities as only human in images that often focus on

Front cover of *Heat* magazine, 31 July–8 August 2004
Source: Courtesy of Bauer Consumer Media

bodily 'flaws': a process Chris Rojek has referred to as the 'mortification' of celebrity (Rojek 2001).

Simultaneously, in a culture where celebrity is often seen as an achievement in its own right, a form of global fame can now be gained simply by appearing in images. A snapshot photograph of 16-year-old Xiao Pang became an 'internet meme' when it travelled the web and was manipulated in a variety of ways during 2006, including a series where Pang's face was 'Photoshopped' into film posters. Pang has since hired a manager and is aiming for a career in the entertainment industry. Photography began by mass reproducing images of those already famous for their achievements. The mass digital reproduction of photographs is now a route to achieving celebrity itself.

Whether they are selling commodities, idealising families, identifying individuals, documenting wars, hanging on gallery walls, making clothes fashionable, stitching up or establishing celebrities, photographs combine the facts of what they record with the fictions created by how they are used. Returning to the ideas that Batchen argues were embedded in the very identity of photography at its conception, we might conclude that photographs are nature mediated by culture.

Questions

1 Analyse the denotation and connotation of two photographs. What are their potential meanings? How does any accompanying text affect your interpretation of them? Can the two photographs be connected?

2 Under what circumstances might a photograph represent the truth about what it depicts?

3 Has digital technology changed photography? If so, how? If not, why?

Further reading

Batchen, G. (1997) *Burning With Desire: The Conception of Photography,* Massachusetts, MIT. A meticulously detailed, groundbreaking approach to defining the medium.

Bull, S. (2009) *Photography*, London: Routledge. An accessible introduction to photography for the 21st century.

Cotton, C. (2004) *The Photograph as Contemporary Art*, London: Thames & Hudson. Recent art photography concisely overviewed and well illustrated.

Marien, M. W. (2006) *Photography: A Critical History*, London: Lawrence King. The most up-to-date history of the medium.

Wells, L. (ed.) (2003) *The Photography Reader*, London: Routledge. A vital handbook of critical ideas.

Journals

Aperture

Photographies

Photography and Culture

Photoworks

Portfolio

Source

Websites

www.lensculture.com

www.zonezero.com

References

Arnold, R. (2001) *Fashion, Anxiety and Desire: Image and Morality in the 20th Century*, London: IB Tauris.

Badger, G. (2007) *The Genius of Photography: How Photography Has Changed Our Lives*, London: Quadrille.

Banksy (2006) *Wall and Piece*, London: Century.

Barthes, R. (1977) 'Rhetoric of the Image' in *Image/Music/Text*, London: Fontana.

Barthes, R. (1990) *The Fashion System*, California: University of California.

Barthes, R. (2000) *Camera Lucida*, London: Vintage.

Batchen, G. (1997) *Burning with Desire: The Conception of Photography*, Cambridge, MA: MIT.

Bazin, A. (1980) 'The Ontology of the Photographic Image' in A. Trachtenberg (ed) *Classic Essays on Photography*, New Haven, CT: Leete's Island Books.

Becker, K. E. (2003) 'Photojournalism and the Tabloid Press' in L. Wells (ed) *The Photography Reader*, London: Routledge.

Benjamin, W. (1999) 'The Work of Art in the Age of Mechanical Reproduction' in J. Evans and S. Hall (eds) *Visual Culture: The Reader*, London: Sage.

Bolton, R. (1989) *The Contest of Meaning: Critical Histories of Photography*, Massachusetts: MIT.

Bourdieu, P. (1990) *Photography: A Middle-Brow Art*, Oxford: Polity.

Bright, S. (2007) *Face of Fashion*, London: National Portrait Gallery.

Brittain, D. (2000) 'I'm Buggered Without My Prejudices' (interview with Martin Parr) in *Creative Camera: 30 Years of Writing*, Manchester: Manchester University Press.

Brooks, R. (1997) 'Fashion: Double-Page Spread' in J. Evans (ed) *The Camerawork Essays: Context and Meaning in Photography*, London: Rivers Oram.

Bull, S. (1999) 'The Après-Garde' in *Creative Camera*, No. 357, April/May: 10-13.

Bull, S. (2004) 'Documentary Photography in the Art Gallery', *Engage*, 14 (Winter): 14-20.

Burgin, V. (ed) (1982) *Thinking Photography*, London: Macmillan.

Burgin, V. (ed) (1986) 'Seeing Sense' in V. Burgin, *The End of Art Theory*, London: Macmillan.

Burgin, V. (2003) 'Looking at Photographs' in L. Wells (ed) *The Photography Reader*, London: Routledge.

Campany, D. (2003a) *Art and Photography*, London: Phaidon.

Campany, D. (2003b) 'Safety in Numbers: Some Remarks on Problems of "Late Photography"' in D. Green (ed) *Where Is the Photograph?*, Brighton: Photoforum and Maidstone: Photoworks.

Cotton, C. (2004) *The Photograph as Contemporary Art*, London: Thames & Hudson.

de Perthius, K. (2005) 'The Synthetic Ideal: The Fashion Model and Photographic Manipulation', *Fashion Theory*, 9 (4): 407-24.

Edwards, E. (2001) *Raw Histories: Photographs, Anthropology and Museums*, Oxford: Berg.

Elkins, J. (ed) (2007) *Photography Theory*, London: Routledge.

Freud, S. (1991) *The Essentials of Psychoanalysis: The Definitive Collection of Sigmund Freud's Writing*, London: Penguin.

Frizot, M. (2007) 'Who's Afraid of Photons?' in J. Elkins (ed) *Photography Theory*, London: Routledge.

Frosh, P. (2003) *The Image Factory*, Oxford: Berg.

Hargreaves, R. (2001) 'Putting Faces to the Names' in P. Hamilton and R. Hargreaves, *The Beautiful and the Damned: The Creation of Identity in 19th Century Photography*, Aldershot: Lund Humphries.

Harrison, M. (1991) *Appearances*, London: Jonathan Cape.

Jobling, P. (1999) *Fashion Spreads: Word and Image in Fashion Photography Since 1980*, Oxford: Berg.

Kenyon, D. (1992) *Inside Amateur Photography*, London: BT Batsford.

King, G. (1986) *Say Cheese! The Snapshot as Art and Social History*, London: Collins.

Kismaric, S. and Respini, E. (2004) *Fashioning Fiction in Photography Since 1990*, New York: Museum of Modern Art.

Kuhn, A. (2002) *Family Secrets*, London: Verso.

Manovich, L. (2003) 'The Paradoxes of Digital Photography' in L. Wells (ed) *The Photography Reader*, London: Routledge.

Marien, M. W. (2006) *Photography: A Critical History*, London: Lawrence King.

McGrath, R. (2003) 'Re-Reading Edward Weston' in L. Wells (ed) *The Photography Reader*, London: Routledge.

Mercer, K. (1999) 'Reading Racial Fetishism' in J. Evans and S. Hall (eds) *Visual Culture: The Reader*, London: Sage.

Metz, C. (2003) 'The Photograph as Fetish' in L. Wells (ed) *The Photography Reader*, London: Routledge.

Mitchell, W. J. T. (1992) *The Reconfigured Eye: Visual Truth in the Post-Photographic Era*, Massachusetts: MIT.

Mitchell, W. J. T. (1993) 'From Today Photography Is Dead!', *Creative Camera* No. 321, April/May 1993: 54-7.

Muir, R. (2005) *The World's Most Photographed*, London: National Portrait Gallery.

Myers, K. (1999) 'Selling Green' in C. Squiers (ed) *Over Exposed: Essays on Contemporary Photography*, New York: New Press.

Radner, H. (2000) 'On the Move: Fashion Photography and the Single Girl in the 1960s' in S. Bruzzi and P. C. Gibson (eds) *Fashion Cultures: Theories, Explorations and Analysis*, London: Routledge.

Ramamurthy, A. (2009) 'Spectacles and Illusions: Photography and Commodity Culture' in L. Wells (ed) *Photography: A Critical Introduction*, London: Routledge.

Ritchin, F. (1999) *In Our Image: The Coming Revolution in Photography*, New York: Aperture.

Rojek, C. (2001) *Celebrity*, London: Reaktion.

Rosenblum, B. (2008) *A World History of Photography*, New York: Abbeville.

Rosler, M. (2003) 'In, Around, and Afterthoughts on Documentary Photography' in L. Wells (ed), *The Photography Reader*, London: Routledge.

Sassoon, J. (2004) 'Photographic Materiality in the Age of Digital Reproduction' in E. Edwards and J. Hart (eds) *Photographs Objects Histories: On the Materiality of Images*, London: Routledge.

Slater, D. (1995) 'Domestic Photography and Digital Culture' in M. Lister (ed) *The Photographic Image in Digital Culture*, London: Routledge.

Slater, D. (1997) 'Marketing the Medium: An Anti-Marketing Report' in J. Evans (ed) *The Camerawork Essays: Context and Meaning in Photography*, London: Rivers Oram.

Solomon-Godeau, A. (1991a) 'Who Is Speaking Thus? Some Questions About Documentary Photography' in *Photography at the Dock: Essays on Photographic History, Institutions, and Practices*, Minnesota: Minnesota University Press.

Solomon-Godeau, A. (1991b) 'Living With Contradictions: Critical Practices in the Age of Supply-Side Aesthetics' in A. Solomon-Godeau, op. cit.

Spence, J. (1995) *Cultural Sniping: The Art of Transgression*, London: Routledge.

Squiers, C. (ed) (1999) *Over Exposed*, New York: New Press.

Sturken, M. and Cartwright, L. (2001) *Practices of Looking: An Introduction to Visual Culture*, Oxford: Oxford University Press.

Sutton, D. (2005) 'Nokia Moments' in *Source* No. 43, Summer: 44–7.

Szarkowski, J. (2007) *The Photographer's Eye*, New York: Museum of Modern Art.

Tagg, J. (1988) *The Burden of Representation: Essays on Photographies and Histories*, London: Macmillan.

Williams, V. (1998) *Look At Me: Fashion and Photography in Britain 1960 to the Present*, London: British Council.

Williams, V. (2002) *Martin Parr*, London: Phaidon.

Williamson, J. (2002) *Decoding Advertisements: Ideology and Meaning in Advertising*, London: Marion Boyars.

Wombell, P. (1991) *Photo-Video: Photography in the Age of the Computer*, London: Rivers Oram.

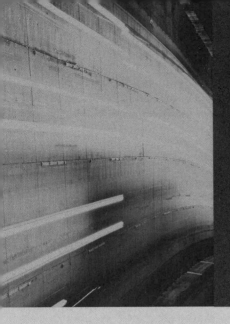

7

Book Publishing

Beverley Tarquini

Chapter overview

This chapter looks at the nature of book publishing, gives a brief account of its history, looks at categories of books and publishers, international rights and digital issues and concludes with an assessment of the future of the book in the 21st century. Examples from countries throughout Europe will be given where relevant and where statistics are available.

Background

There is no future for the printed book . . . this and many other such headlines have frequented the media throughout Europe for much of the last five years but how accurate are they? This chapter looks at the future of book publishing whilst taking into account the immense changes currently taking place within the industry. The processes of producing publications, from production (including the composition and physical transformation of material), editorial (the formation of content into accessible form) to sales, marketing and distribution channels have all undergone radical transformations and publishers need to constantly evaluate how relevant these processes are in the 21st century and to what extent they need to be adapted in this digital age.

Statistics show a mature industry with stable book sales per capita across many European countries but in a competitive market facing challenges from other media, particularly the web, book publishers need to find new ways to attract readers, increase their turnover and protect the diversity of their products.

A brief history

The history of book production dates back to ancient times with the proliferation of manuscripts which were handwritten and circulated locally, leading to the production of the codex, in which folded sheets were bound together. As a commercial activity it had been recorded in both Ancient Greece and Rome with manuscript trading popular amongst the literate. In China and the Far East it was evident in the *Jlandu*, in which wooden strips or bamboo were inscribed with ink, around 600 BC.

Significant developments occurred in the late 15th century when the German goldsmith, Johann Gutenberg, invented typographical printing and produced the first printed book, an edition of the Bible in Latin around 1454. Other printings followed, most notably of religious or scholarly texts and there followed a gradual process of technological modernisation and a period of mass production. This developed dramatically in the 18th and 19th centuries and combined with a growth of literacy and prosperity, ensured a rise in popularity for the printed word. A gradual widening of the supply chain developed between book producers and their audience with improved transportation methods, ensuring accessibility to readers outside of major cities.

Matters of censorship became the subject of much political debate, as did the question of ownership of written work. A succession of international treaties were produced, notably the 1886 Berne Convention for the Protection of Literary and Artistic Property and the 1996 World Intellectual Property Organization (WIPO), aimed at protecting an author's intellectual property. They became increasingly important as copyright infringements within the international book community were vigorously challenged, in a bid to protect authors' integrity and earnings as well as publishers' financial turnover and profits.

Flourishing in the 20th century, despite the pressures of 'new media' such as television, book publishing was aided by initiatives such as the paperback revolution, initiated by the publishers Allen Lane in the 1930s, which paved the way for the mass market appeal of books produced at affordable prices to the consumer. The streamlining and outsourcing of production processes also made many more titles economically viable, combined with creative and sophisticated marketing campaigns which raised the profile of the industry. Publishing became an important global business and in the 1970s European publishers expanded their global market share through a succession of mergers and acquisitions with US publishers. For example, the family-owned media group Bertelsmann AG acquired US publisher Bantam Books in 1980 and Doubleday in 1986, becoming the world's largest publisher in 1998 when it then purchased the US publisher Random House. In 2007 it was ranked third, in terms of revenue, behind the Pearson and Thomson conglomerates. The new millennium has seen further evidence of the acquisitions of US publishers by European companies, with many of the former relinquishing the book side of their businesses and concentrating on other media interests such as the internet and television.

In the UK, although it is the smallest segment of the domestic publishing media with an estimated 22 per cent of the total market compared to 44 per cent taken by newspapers and 34 per cent by magazines (Richardson 2007), book publishing is the fastest growing international business. The heavy dependence on advertising by the other media has meant that book publishing can concentrate solely on the quality of its products; however, it is a highly competitive industry where many titles fail to sell each year and it is estimated that around one third of adults do not buy a book at all. Throughout Europe the largest markets for book publishing are in Germany, UK, France and Italy, with the UK producing the greatest number of titles per year per million of population. In 2006 UK publishers sold a diverse range of 787 million books (both in the UK and in export markets) with a value of £2.81 billion and a total of 115,522 titles published, compared with 94,500 in 1996 (Richardson 2007).

National book policies exist in some countries with clear statements of intent. For example, the mission statement of the Börsenverein, the official Publishers and Bookseller's Association of Germany, clearly relates economic policy for the book industry to the importance of a cultural agenda (www.boersenverein/de).

Categories of books

The United Nations Educational, Scientific and Cultural Organisation (UNESCO) defines a book as a 'a non-periodical printed publication of at least 49 pages, exclusive of the cover pages, published in the country and made available to the public' (UNESCO 1964: 144). With its clear emphasis on the book as a physical object, this definition naturally takes no account of the digital developments of the past few decades, most notably with the rise of the e-book and the rapid technological changes taking place within the publishing industry. A more relevant definition might be 'the sharing and making public of a range of information in either printed or digital form'.

Publishing relies on categorisation and books are registered and allocated within an International Standard Book Number or ISBN. Thus each product is unique but categories vary across EU member states and many differ in terms of sales, distribution and markets, as do statistical methods for measuring the business.

Categories of publications are often listed as:

1 Consumer or Trade – written for a general audience and separated into fiction and non-fiction, their profile and success is often driven by discount requirements of retailers. A sub-section of this category could be children's publishing, though many companies have completely separate divisions. A large market and traditionally more vulnerable to market pressures, it is more likely to benefit from subsidies.

2 Educational or schools – textbooks for nursery to college education and affected by government policies on education, often sold through non-retail channels such as specialist schools suppliers and protected by issues of educational curriculum and language.

3 Academic – monographs and textbooks for university level and above. International sales are often subject specific.

4 Business and Professional – a range of practical and technical works and general management books.

5 Reference – sometimes amalgamated into the two categories above, yet retaining distinctive qualities in both composition and sales methods. The category includes encyclopaedias and dictionaries.

6 Electronic – a relatively new category, encompassing all digital products.

Few industries can boast such a wide range of products, from the million copy best-selling novel to the smaller (yet still profitable) more specialised book with worldwide sales of only 400 copies. The market is dominated by a small number of best-selling titles holding a large share of the market, particularly in the area of fiction and non-fiction. In this highly competitive arena publishers need to maximise sales of existing titles, not only with initiatives for sales and marketing promotions but by flexibility and adaptability with content. 'Classic' texts of out of copyright works remain popular but this area is dominated by large conglomerates with recognised brands such as Penguin and Oxford University Press: the challenge for other publishers is to provide some added value to the product. For example, Weidenfeld and Nicolson publishers launched a list of edited classics in 2007, Compact Editions, with 'sympathetically' edited novels of reduced word length, aimed at encouraging readers to engage with titles. The essential elements which made the book a classic are, the publisher claims, retained. Other initiatives include the production of manga versions of classic stories by London publisher Metro Media to appeal to a younger audience and to tap into the fashionable interest in graphic style novels.

Branding has increasingly played a part in establishing the success of particular authors, particularly celebrities, who – often aided substantially by ghost writers – capitalise on the fame they have achieved in other media such as newspapers and television to launch a range of publications, from autobiographies, to self help books and novels. The publications issued under the name of model and television personality Katie Price, otherwise known as Jordan, have increased her profile internationally and much publicity was generated by the news that her novel *Crystal* outsold the whole of the combined Booker Prize shortlist in its first year of publication.

Publishers

There is a growing polarisation between large publishing houses which are often part of international conglomerates and small/medium sized firms. In a fragmented industry most companies are likely to publish an average of 35 titles per year. Large firms may be divided into divisions, sharing brands and focusing on different markets. In the UK the mid-1980s showed a change in the composition of some medium sized companies with many mergers and acquisitions and now a small number of large international groups control over 50 per cent of the home market. Led by the British, Dutch, French and German, there has also been a large rise in the ownership of US based publishers. See Table 7.1.

A similar situation exists in Germany with around 74 per cent of the market dominated by four companies. Germany has a smaller number of companies than France, Italy or the UK despite being a larger market in terms of sales value and the second largest in the world outside of the US. See Table 7.2.

There is increasing polarisation between the large conglomerates and smaller (often subject niche based and with low overheads) publishing companies. Medium sized publishers do not have the advantages of the economies of scale,

Table 7.1 Market share (%) of publishing groups for consumer sales 2007

Publishing group	UK market share (%)
Hachette (Hodder Headline/Little, Brown/Orion)	14.3
Bertelsmann (Random House/Transworld)	13.8
Pearson (Penguin and Dorling Kindersley)	11.2
News Corporation (HarperCollins)	7.9
Holtzbrinck (Pan Macmillan)	3.1
Bloomsbury	2.5
Oxford University Press	2.0
Others	45.2

Source: Adapted from Nielsen BookScan, www.nielsenbookscan.co.uk. Reproduced with permission. Data sourced from the TCM (total consumer market) as measured by Nielsen BookScan representing 90% of consumer purchases in the UK for the period 31 December 2006–29 December 2007.

Table 7.2 Market share (%) of publishing groups for consumer sales 2003

Publishing group	German market share (%)
Bertelsmann	32.6
Holtzbrinck	17.3
Bonnier/Piper	13.1
Verlagsgruppe Luebbe	10.9
Other	26.1

Source: Publishing Market Watch 2004

particularly in production, sales and marketing, shared by larger companies, nor can they take advantage of the lower overheads enjoyed by smaller competitors.

Subsidies and prices

Books are regarded as both economic and cultural products by European governments and publishers have traditionally differentiated their products from other commercial activities and have benefited from subsidies such as grants for particular publications and reduced rates of value added tax (VAT), ranging from 0 per cent (as in the UK) to 25 per cent. The Association of European booksellers argues that any increase in VAT will be reflected in the price of books, thus discouraging purchases, and that EU states have the right to apply their own policies. In France, the National Centre for Books supports diversity in the market by providing £25 million in loans and subsidies for particular projects and smaller countries such as Austria had, in the early 1990s, a subsidy programme providing £2.2 million per year.

The debate about fixed prices or resale price maintenance (RPM) is ongoing within the industry. In the UK the Net Book Agreement allowed publishers to set the retail price of the book (termed the 'net price') and meant that retailers were not allowed to sell books below that price and use the discounts which were available to other sorts of products. Abandoned by the UK in 1995 amidst growing pressure from other retail sectors, it nevertheless continues in various forms throughout European countries, such as Germany, where the only discounted books are referred to as 'damaged'. Opponents of RPM argue for the benefits of a free market economy and the fact that lower prices of books attract larger sales and make products available in a wide variety of selling outlets. They argue that retail outlets such as supermarkets often sell products to those who would not buy from traditional outlets and therefore the overall market is expanded. Supporters claim that RPM provides support for small publishers of quality books and small bookstores which would otherwise find it hard to compete with large outlets, which tend to stock mainly bestsellers at vastly reduced prices. Price management plays an important part in the success of building bestsellers but is undercutting the price of these titles healthy for the book trade in general?

For example, in the UK, the final title in the *Harry Potter* series was sold in several major supermarket chains at (it was suggested) cost price, leaving smaller outlets unable to compete and thus losing a large part of their turnover. The question for the industry is: does this policy encourage or limit diversity? In countries with non-fixed prices such as the UK and Finland the number of titles purchased per million of the population is higher than the fixed price markets of Germany or France. However, if book publishing is essential to a country's cultural as well as economic well being then the survival of smaller, independent companies both in the production of books as well as distribution is arguably vital to increase diversity and innovation. Some countries embrace both arguments, for example Belgium, which, for many years, imposed self-regulation where discounts were restricted for six months following publication, after which pricing is unrestricted. The debate continues and each European country has its own cultural or historical reasons for fixed or free pricing.

Sales outlets

Books are increasingly sold outside of traditional bookshop outlets, particularly in supermarkets. This reliance on third parties to sell products means that sales value can rise while publishers' turnover falls, owing to the discounts demanded by distributors. This can particularly affect smaller companies who cannot match the discounts agreed by large conglomerates and thus lose out on floor space and marketing opportunities. The reliance in non fixed price countries of discounting has encouraged a plethora of marketing opportunities. For example, in the UK many chain bookshops operate a '3 for 2' policy where publishers pay a fee to have their titles displayed prominently and discounts are passed on to the consumer who is given an additional title if two others are bought.

Utilising other types of media to promote books has always been undertaken by publishers. Serialisation of trade publications in newspapers and magazines has traditionally aided both marketing strategies by increasing a book and its author's exposure and leading to increased sales, sometimes dramatically. A book by the British politician David Blunkett was successfully serialised in both a tabloid and broadsheet newspaper simultaneously; by concentrating on different aspects (private life versus public) the publisher maximised media exposure, appealing to readers at different ends of the reading spectrum. The television book club on the Channel 4 UK daily chat show *Richard and Judy*, following the format of the Oprah Winfrey book club in the US, ensured that all books chosen for weekly discussion shot straight to the top of the best selling charts. For example, the first winner of the book club award, Joseph O'Connor's *The Star of the Sea*, had sold 14,000 copies in paperback when first recommended in 2004. It has now sold over 600,000 copies worldwide. Many other titles have become international best sellers and titles recommended by the club are now responsible for over 25 per cent of the sales of the top 100 books in the UK. The internet has also helped to promote book sales through a variety of methods such as setting up author blogs to raise the profile of trade authors, by providing ancillary material linked to textbooks at schools and universities and reaching new readers by internet based marketing campaigns. Benefits to consumers include sales of second hand books which provide a threat to the sale of new titles, particularly expensive hardcover reference works and student textbooks, although the latter frequently change editions within five years, thus making previous copies obsolete.

The change within patterns of book purchasing within the UK book trade and the rapid rise in popularity of supermarkets and the internet is summarised in Table 7.3.

The increase in sales on the internet is more and more prevalent in European countries without fixed prices. In a study of Swedish book publishing, Ann Steiner (2006) discusses the success of book sales on the internet and questions their effect on diversity within the industry. Sweden is similar in many respects to the UK with no fixed prices and a high literacy rate. In 1997 the first Swedish internet bookstore opened and soon Sweden had one of the highest percentage of internet users in Europe with an estimated 15 per cent of the book market compared to 17 per cent in the UK and 4–5 per cent in Germany, whose internet sales remained regulated by fixed prices. Internet sales in Sweden appeared to be gained at the expense of book clubs, subscriptions and supermarkets (making up approximately half of the book buying market) rather than 'regular' bookshops. Internet sales had received an initial boost as until 2001 Sweden had a 24 per cent VAT on books,

Table 7.3 Change in source of GB consumer purchases 2001-05

Outlet	Change (%)
Chain bookshops	+18
Bargain bookshops	−14
Independent bookshops	−16
Supermarkets	+90
Other retail	−12
Direct mail	−25
Internet	+183

Source: Adapted from BML, *Books and the Consumer* (accessed through the Booksellers Association, www.booksellers.org.uk, 10 August 2008). Copyright © BML/TNS. Reproduced with permission.

but this could be avoided to some extent by buying books online; the government then lowered the rate to 6 per cent and sales grew by 20 per cent in the first year and this higher rate was maintained in the following year, too. One of the main perceived threats from internet sales was the dominance of English language publications at the expense of smaller languages, but most internet bestsellers are Swedish publications, rather than translations from foreign languages (50 per cent versus 30 per cent in 2005). Thus cultural diversity appears to be intact, although the prominence of English language titles has been strengthened at the expense of German, French and other languages.

A further argument in favour of internet book sales is highlighted by Steiner with reference to Chris Anderson's 'Long Tail' theory (2006) which argues that a wider range of titles can be offered online than in a large bookshop, due to the latter's constraints of space. For example, the internet provider Adlibris claimed that in 2004 the 1000 best selling titles accounted for only 25 per cent annual sales and 40 per cent sales were for titles which are not available in traditional bookstores. Thus the life span of backlist titles can be prolonged and the claim that all of the low sellers combined provide a much larger market than that provided by bestsellers further adds to the claims of greater choice and diversity, refuting the claims that consumers are only interested in bestsellers. Many purchasers of books embrace the physicality of the purchasing experience in a traditional bookshop but Steiner highlights the 'communal' reading 'experience' (Steiner 2006: 136) often provided online where suppliers record previous purchases and then direct consumers to other books which may be of interest, arguing that 'sensual practices like touching and smelling are excluded' but replaced by a feeling of belonging to a 'communal experience' (ibid.). An enterprising publisher recently sent all purchasers of an electronic textbook a 'scratch and sniff' piece of paper which replicated the smell and feel of a book, when its research discovered that students missed the physical sensation of handling a printed object.

The general consensus within the publishing world appears to embrace the concept of booksellers and internet providers working in tandem to satisfy the needs of the consumer, with the former providing website opportunities and online marketing opportunities as well as providing the face to face expertise which has been an essential element in other retail sectors faced with internet competition.

Rights and territories

Two of the key questions facing publishers are: what rights have been granted for the ownership and use of the intellectual property or content of a book and where and in what form can the work be distributed and sold? The trade in translations, rights and licences can be used to measure international cultural diversity and the former in particular provides an interesting barometer of the importance of particular countries within the international publishing community. In terms of translations, English, French and German are the top three source languages, accounting for 75 per cent of all translations worldwide.

UNESCO provides Table 7.4 illustrating the cumulative translations from original languages registered since 1979.

Table 7.4 Translations from original languages

Original language	Number of translations
English	984,569
French	183,473
German	167,485
Russian	93,227
Italian	54,766
Spanish	42,793
Swedish	30,316
Latin	16,476
Dutch	15,835
Danish	15,797

Source: Adapted from UNESCO (2007) *UNESCO Index Trans-lationum*, www.unesco.org/culture/xtrans (accessed 31 July 2008). Reproduced with permission from UNESCO.

Translation of Chinese publications are growing steadily, currently numbering over 7000 and it will be interesting to observe its year on year progress over the next decade as China becomes increasingly dominant economically and its language is now studied in many schools. English accounts for more than half of all books translated from original languages but the UK imports far fewer titles than its European neighbours. Germany is the strongest buying market for translations with around 75 per cent translated books from English and 10 per cent from French but exports only 6 per cent translation rights into the English language.

The Swedish book trade magazine *Svensk Bokhandel* compared 10 European bestseller lists and the US list from May 2004 to April 2005 (See Table 7.5). In most

Table 7.5 Comparison of bestseller lists (%)

Country	Domestic authors	US authors	UK authors	Other authors
US	91	91	9	0
Finland	80	10	10	0
Sweden	61	15	12	12
UK	61	39	61	0
France	60	29	2	9
Spain	60	16	3	21
Norway	44	17	17	22
Netherlands	41	30	5	24
Denmark	40	25	6	29
Germany	24	29	8	39
Austria	19	22	5	54

Source: From Svensk Bokhandel, www.svb.se.

European countries, authors from their own country are the most read (an average of 60 per cent), but in the US it is as high as 91 per cent. No translations appeared in the US and the UK lists. The dominant author during this period was the US writer Dan Brown.

Digital developments

In 2007 there were estimated to be over 320 million households with broadband access worldwide and technological advances continue to revolutionise the nature of book publishing. Procedures in the composition and production of books are increasingly streamlined and outsourced to countries such as India to provide maximum efficiency at the lowest possible price. Recent developments such as 'print on demand' (POD) mean that single copies of books can be printed economically thus ensuring that more specialised works continue to be available in print form and rendering the term 'out of print' practically obsolete.

The arrival and growth of electronic books – e-books – is regarded as both an opportunity and a threat to book publishing. There were some initial problems, with Barnes and Noble's e-book store and electronic publishing imprint which launched in 2001 closing within two years and Sony's Libris failing to take off in Japan in 2004. However, growing success can be found in Amazon's Digital Audio book provider which has an international presence with four sites around the world in the US, UK, Germany and France, and is the leading provider of spoken information on the internet. Consumers can download audio to their computers and then transfer the audio to devices such as MP3 players or transfer or 'burn' the content to audio CDs. The software is also bundled with new iPods and the distributors claim that sales of traditional audio books on tapes or CDs are not affected as the product is appealing to a different market. The standard of light and formatting on computer screens is improving dramatically to enable titles to be more easily accessed on screens although it remains to be seen whether these devices will capture the public's imagination to the extent that iPods have for the music industry. Out of copyright classics can be downloaded free of charge in projects such as Project Gutenberg whose repository currently holds over 330,000 free e-books.

Academic publishers have for a number of years produced e-books, originally for institutional libraries but later as customised textbooks for specific markets. Digital sales have to date grown faster in particular areas such as reference titles – encyclopaedias and dictionaries and also in travel with satellite navigation systems replacing maps for many consumers. The global VLE (Virtual Learning Environment) market for educational books was established and is used for access to content by many in educational and academic institutions. The European Commission is to make many European books available online in its i2010 programme and have set aside €36 million for research into digitisation. The Chinese government has announced that all of their 165 million students will be supplied with e-readers to avoid the cost of buying physical copies of textbooks.

Consumer publishers were spurred into action in 2004 when Google announced it would scan and index books from libraries as part of its Book Search Tool.

This controversial move prompted the mass digitisation of backlist books and the creation of libraries of digital files with publishers working both independently and alongside Google and others to make information available on the internet. With downloads to electronic devices such as iPods and mobile telephones now in preparation with the latter already prevalent in Japan, future developments remain unclear but some consumer publishers feel that digitisation of consumer titles will see a rapid rise over the next decade.

However, the problem of regulating and protecting intellectual property continues to challenge the book industry. The difficulty of defining the format of intellectual property is illustrated by the wording of many current publishers' contracts which ask authors to assign electronic rights 'in forms either known or assumed in the future'. In other words the format of some projects remains unknown. Many works contracted pre-2000 took no account of issues of electronic rights and had to be renegotiated and publishers are now wary of being too specific in the wording of their agreements.

The problems of supplying information in an electronic form have been also vigorously debated within the 'Open Access movement'. The definition of this term can be summarised in synthesising the documents arising from the Budapest Open Access initiative (BOA) in 2001, the Bethesda Statement on Open Access Publishing (2003) and the Berlin Declaration on Open Access to Knowledge in the Sciences and Humanities (2003). Essentially it refers to information of a scholarly nature which is freely accessible online and has clear implications for publishers of academic and scholarly work, but also relates to the move by internet search engines such as Google to digitise and make available books from other categories both in and out of copyright on the web.

The improvements in price, quality and format in other recent electronic devices such as the Amazon 'Kindle Reader' and Sony's 'eReaders' also question the likely long-term dominance of the printed word. The latter holds up to 350 books in its internal memory and hundreds more in its external memory and is available in a lightweight, pocket-sized format, where pages are turned by touch rather than buttons. In response to this competition Random House and Hachette who control 30 per cent of the British book market began, in 2008, to offer downloadable versions of a range of titles from best selling cookery writer Delia Smith to novelists such as Ian McEwan.

There are fears that the problems caused to the music business by illegal downloading are beginning to affect the book trade. Unlicensed free digital copies of individual chapters or even entire books, not only best-selling fiction but also cookery books and poetry, can be accessed without regulation on the internet. 'In July 2007 scanned pages from *Harry Potter and the Deathly Hallows* appeared on the internet four days before its release and a Chinese translation appeared free online weeks before the official Chinese language version reached bookshops' (Hoyle 2008). Whilst increasing readership of books online, unless this practice is regulated by revenue producing procedures the growth of such activities will have repercussions for the whole publishing industry – for authors' royalties, publishers' turnover and ultimately the range of titles offered to the consumer. Other problems include pricing policies which remain inconsistent.

The future of the book

In 1995, the writer Nicholson Baker referred to the book as a highly efficient 'random access device' and wrote: 'We've come up with a beautifully browsable invention that needs no electricity and exists in a readable form no matter what happens' (cited in McCrum 2006). The environmental lobby canvassing against the mass culling of trees for the manufacturing of paper argue that alternatives must now be offered to the printed word and the digital revolution has provided powerful alternative means of accessing information in electronic form. However, is print versus digital the only challenge facing book publishing in the 21st century?

In a recent UK survey by Book*Facts* (2008) twice as many children as adults (17 per cent versus 8 per cent) gave as a reason for not reading books the alternative use of electronic media. Questions as to what extent the printed book can compete as a leisure or learning item will continue to be asked and in attracting new readers publishers will need to utilise all available means at their disposal.

In trade publishing the combination of promotable authors and media savvy agents along with increasingly high profile marketing campaigns, has seen a rise in the utilisation of different media outlets, most notably newspapers, magazines, television and radio, to promote book campaigns. The role of the small publisher remains precarious when faced with competition from conglomerate brands and large discount demands from sales outlets, yet with niche products and inventive marketing campaigns there remain opportunities to establish new companies and achieve success.

The flexible provision of content in other categories through digital means, such as customised academic and reference publications in which selected chunks of content can be purchased, means that customers have increasing choice in their purchases. The role of the internet providers with their value added role of directing consumers to a wider range of titles has arguably increased accessibility and choice for book buyers, but the emergence of e-books and its dominance of the book publishing market has yet to be proved and publishers are cautious as to estimates of success, mindful of the declining market for CDRoms which were much heralded in the 1980s, but declined as their technology was replaced by the internet. The territorial and regulatory aspects of downloading book titles from the web need to be constantly monitored if publishing is to avoid the widespread illegality found in the music industry.

There are challenging times ahead within the digital age for book publishers who are no longer simply custodians of authors and specific works but managers of a range of content, competing within a multi-media industry. Digitilisation may not replace paper based publishing but will certainly displace a segment of its market. However, although considerations of format, be it printed or electronic, and methods of distribution of their products may be up for debate, the key questions for publishers remain: how do they maintain and attract new readers, establish successful profit margins and ensure diversity within their products?

Questions

1 Should book publishing be subject to the demands of a free market economy or can the use of subsidies in this particular branch of media be justified?

2 The protection and regulation of intellectual property is the most important issue facing the book industry. Discuss.

3 What are the major challenges facing publishers in the 21st century and is there a future for the book in printed form?

Further reading

Baverstock, A. (2008) *How to Market Books: The Essential Guide to Maximizing Profit and Exploiting All Channels to Market*, 4th edition, London: Kogan Page. A complete overview of how books are marketed, including an examination of the impact of internet sales on the book business.

Clark, G. and Phillips, A. (2008) *Inside Book Publishing*, 4th edition, Abingdon: Routledge. A guide to all aspects of the book publishing industry, which includes case studies and contributions from leading industry experts.

Cope, B. and Phillips, A. (eds) (2006) *The Future of the Book in the Digital Age*, Oxford: Chandos Publishing. A stimulating collection of essays about the role of the printed book in a digital world.

Owen, L. (2006) *Selling Rights*, 5th edition, London: Routledge. Containing details of the historical and legal protection of intellectual property, this accessible guide looks at all aspects of selling rights and co-publications from English-language territorial rights, book club and paperback sales through to serial rights, translation rights, dramatisation and documentary rights, electronic publishing and multimedia.

Richardson, P. (2007) *UK Publishing Profile*, London: The Publishers Association. A complete overview of the state of the UK publishing industry, examining a range of categories and markets, backed up by up to date statistics and analysis.

Squires, C. (2007) *Marketing Literature: The Making of Contemporary Writing in Britain*, Basingstoke: Palgrave Macmillan. An original study of the publishing of contemporary writing in Britain, which analyses the changing social, economic and cultural environment of the publishing industry in the 1990s and 2000s and investigates its impact on genre, format, packaging, authorship and reading.

References

Anderson, C. (2006) *The Long Tail: How Endless Choice Is Creating Unlimited Demand*, London: Random House.

Book*Facts* Online (2008) 'Expanding the Book Market', www.bookmarketing.co.uk/index.cfm (accessed 7 July 2008).

Booksellers Association (2008a) UK Publishing Groups – Consumer Sales 2005–2008, *BA Reports Library*, January, www.booksellers.org.uk/industry/display_report.asp?id=3825 (accessed 10 August 2008).

Booksellers Association (2008b) UK Book Sales – Retail 1999–2008, *BA Reports Library*, April, www.booksellers.org.uk/industry/display_report.asp?id=3789 (accessed 10 August 2008),

Booksellers Association (2008c) Comparison of Bestseller Lists, *BA Reports Library*, August, www.booksellers.org.uk/industry/display_report.asp?id=3888 (accessed 4 August 2008).

Hoyle, B. (2008) 'Internet Book Piracy Will Drive Authors to Stop Writing', *The Times*, 31 March. http://entertainment.timesonline.co.uk/tol/arts_and_entertainment/books/article3648813.ece (accessed 1 August 2008).

McCrum, R. (2006) *E-read all about it*, 15 January 2006, *the Observer*, www.books.guardian.co.uk/ebooks/story/0,11305,1686540,00.html (accessed 15 January 2006)

Richardson, P. (2007) *UK Publishing Profile*, London: The Publishers Association, www.publisher.org.uk (accessed 1 July 2007).

Steiner, A. (2006) 'Diversity, or Is It All the Same? Book Consumption on the Internet in Sweden' in B. Cope and A. Phillips (eds) *The Future of the Book in the Digital Age*, Oxford: Chandos Publishing.

Svensk Bokhandel Magazine in Booksellers Association Reports (2008) http://www.booksellers.org.uk/industry/reports.asp (accessed 4 August 2008).

UNESCO (1964) *Records of the General Conference 13th session Paris,* http://portal.unesco.org/en/ev.php-URL_ID=13068&URL_DO=DO_PRINTPAGE&URL_SECTION=201.html (accessed 30 June 2006).

UNESCO (2007) *Index Translationum*, http://databases.unesco.org/xtrans/xtra-form.shtml (accessed 31 July 2007).

8

Public Relations

David Miller

Chapter overview

This chapter examines the rise of public relations as a philosophy and an industry and debates how to understand its increased importance in the era of neoliberalism. It notes the key importance of the state and business in disseminating and suppressing information as well as the countervailing tactics which are used by pressure groups and other activists. The chapter examines the relative success of various tactics and groups in managing the news and how this relates to the exercise of political and economic power. It points to contemporary developments in ownership and control of the media and promotional industries and argues that these tend to narrow the space for free debate. As corporate power both increases and is·increasingly subject to challenge, the question of curbing 'promotional culture' is raised.

Introduction

Contemporary society has become more promotional. Public relations (PR) and promotional strategies are now central concerns of government, business, trades unions, popular movements and even the smallest single-issue protest group. The rise of 'promotional culture' (Wernick 1991) parallels, and is intimately intertwined with, the expansion of the role of the media in societal decision making and development. As Robert Jackall has remarked: 'Few areas of our social lives are untouched by the visual images, narratives, jingles, rhetorics, slogans, and interpretations continuously produced by these experts with symbols' (Jackall 1994: 7). In Britain, the US and many other countries, the sheer amount of media space demanding to be filled has markedly expanded since the end of the 1970s. But the rise of public relations (and related activities such as lobbying) is also related to the rise in prominence of corporate power, often described as 'neoliberalism', meaning 'the doctrine that market exchange is an ethic in itself, capable of acting as a guide for all human action' (Harvey 2005). So how should we understand the relationship between public relations, the media and power in society?

News and media strategies

In liberal pluralist theory the media provide a public space in which information is shared and the public informed. By this it is meant that the free media function as a watchdog on the actions of government. Free competition for media space and political power ensures that a variety of voices are heard in the media (Gans 1980; Blumler and Gurevitch 1995; Sigal 1986). In contrast, much Marxist theory sees the media as agencies of class control in which official messages are reproduced by journalists, the masses are indoctrinated and the stability of capitalism assured (see Curran 1991; Curran and Seaton 1995, Chapter 16).

It has been widely noted, however, that the identification of these two positions as self-contained opposites can rather overstate the difference between them (Curran *et al.* 1982). While some differences between the approaches remain, until recently both have been highly 'media-centric' (Schlesinger 1990: 64) in their analyses and explanations of public relations strategies. They have tended to assess the public relations activities of sources by either examining media content or interviewing journalists and have therefore failed to examine 'source–media relations from the perspectives of the sources themselves' (Schlesinger 1990: 61; Ericson *et al.* 1989: 24).

The use of media-centric methods of research has affected the kinds of analysis of source power available. In one variant of Marxist theorising about the media, often referred to as 'structuralist', it is argued that the opinions of the powerful receive a 'structured preference' in the media and become 'primary definers' of media coverage (Hall *et al.* 1978). This approach has tended to overemphasise the power of official sources and to underestimate the extent to which pressure groups and others can manage the news (Miller 1993). Crucially it also assumes that managing the news is tantamount to exercising power in society.

By contrast, pluralist approaches tend to underemphasise the crucial importance of official sources of information and overplay the fluidity of competition. An approach which moves beyond 'media-centrism' and directly examines the promotional strategies of government, business and interest or pressure groups has been advocated and a wide range of number of studies now exist (e.g. Anderson 1991, 1997; Cook 1989; Davies 2000a, b, 2002, 2003, 2007; Deacon 1996, 2003; Deacon and Golding 1994; Dinan and Miller 2007; Ericson *et al.* 1989; Manning 1998; Miller 1994; Miller *et al.* 1998; Miller and Dinan 2008a; Schlesinger *et al.* 2001; Tilson 1993). But media-centrism is not only a methodological question. Taken seriously the study of communicative strategies by powerful and lowly organisations also suggests that power is exercised not just through the mass media but outside and sometimes despite the media. For example most lobbying activities are secretive and involve the planning of communicative strategies for influence. They attempt to pursue direct influence rather than using the media to convince their targets.

The following sections of this chapter review some of the important issues in understanding promotional strategies and their relationships with the media and power in society. First we briefly examine the rise of public relations and promotional culture.

The rise of 'promotional culture'

The rise of public relations as a specific profession occurred around the turn of the 20th century in the USA, in Britain and in Germany. The development of propaganda and public relations suggests that public opinion became more important in this period. 'Within the life of the generation now in control of affairs', wrote the most important US theorist of the trend, Walter Lippmann, 'persuasion has become a self conscious art and a regular organ of popular government' (Lippmann 1921: 158). Lippmann approved of what he termed the 'manufacture of consent' by public relations. But why did public opinion suddenly become so important that it needed to be managed?

The extension of the franchise between 1880 and 1920, giving most adults the vote for the first time, as well as other democratic reforms, were key factors in increasing the influence which could be exerted by the populace on decision making. In other words, the rise of public relations as a specialism was a *response* to the modest democratic reforms of this period (Miller and Dinan 2008a). Edward Bernays was amongst the first to make a profession out of what he called the 'conscious and intelligent manipulation' of the beliefs and behaviour of the public. Those who 'manipulate this unseen mechanism' of society were, he wrote, an 'invisible government which is the true ruling power of our country' (Bernays 1928: 9). This kind of manipulation also emerged in the UK at the same time. Political scientist Graham Wallas pioneered the idea that society was now too complex for the masses to properly comprehend. Meanwhile business activists such as Dudley Docker formed organisations called Business Leagues and later 'National Propaganda' dedicated to resisting democracy with propaganda. 'If our league succeeds' wrote Docker in 1911, 'politics would be done for. That is my object' (cited in Miller and Dinan, 2008a: 40).

Public relations offices have tended to be established at moments of crisis for the powerful, whether at war, under attack from colonial possessions or organised labour. For example, the Foreign Office and the armed forces first appointed press officers during World War One and in 1919 Prime Minister Lloyd George's aide set up a covert propaganda agency to incite hostility against trades unionism, part-funded by employers (see Middlemass 1979; Miller and Dinan 2008a). Business PR became more important after the end of World War Two. An organisation called Aims of Industry was founded by business leaders in 1942–43 and it soon saw action assisting the medical profession in resisting the introduction of the National Health Service and campaigning against the nationalisation of the sugar and iron and steel industries (Kisch 1964). In the US it has been argued that the conservatism of the 1950s was 'politically constructed' in part by the 'intellectual reconquest' of the US by big business (Fones-Wolf 1994: 285). Since 1945 we have witnessed the growth of information posts in British government (Tulloch 1993), both in civil ministries (Crofts 1989) and in colonial counter-insurgency (Carruthers 1995), leading latterly to the rise of the 'public relations state' (Deacon and Golding 1994: 4) and in the political parties the emergence of the 'spin doctor' (Jones 1995, 1997, 1999). Corporate PR has also expanded and adapted to new challenges, such as the threat to business interests of the environmental movement. According to some accounts the PR activities of, for example, McDonald's (Vidal 1997), British Airways (Gregory 1996), and consultancies like Burson Marsteller (Hager and Burton 1999) have often strayed over the line of good faith and even legality (Beder 1997, 2006a, 2006b; Rampton and Stauber 2001; Stauber and Rampton 1995).

The Conservatives' release of the free market from 1979 had an explosive impact on PR. Between 1979 and 1998 the PR consultancy industry in the UK increased elevenfold in real terms (Miller and Dinan 2000). PR consultancies expanded on the back of the mass privatisations of publicly owned assets and the increased international mobility of capital fostered by neoliberal regimes in the UK, the USA, Japan and elsewhere.

In the political world, too, PR and marketing techniques have become much more important. The obsession with controlling image and perception evident in the Labour Party under Blair and Brown led to the jettisoning of Labour's distinctive policy platform (Heffernan and Marqusee 1992), to be replaced by spin and presentation. The accounts of this period which have thus far appeared make it clear that a small group of modernisers around Blair (especially pollster Philip Gould and spin doctors Peter Mandelson and Alastair Campbell) conspired to reshape the party in a new market-friendly guise (Gould 1998; Macintyre 2000; Routledge 1999). It has been widely agreed that centralised and politicised information control by Blair's press secretary Alastair Campbell, surpassed that experienced under the Thatcher administration (Jones 1999; Oborne 1999) and the prognosis for the Brown administration appeared to be no better (*Financial Times* 2008; Price 2008).

With the growth of PR have come myriad specialisms such as media relations, public affairs, issues management and lobbying (Moloney 1996). Lobbying is a secretive and largely covert industry in which lobby firms or corporations communicate directly with MPs, civil servants, ministers and other power brokers to pursue their interests. Much of this occurs without much recourse to the use of the mass media. It is these kind of communicative activities that have the possibility of exerting direct power, that are often missing from 'media centric' accounts of power relations. Lobbying has become more important as government has become more market friendly and as marketisation of government has opened up more space for direct corporate power. The activities of lobbyists themselves became a major public issue following the exposure by the media of the cash-for-questions controversy when some MPs were revealed to be secretly working for undeclared lobbying interests (Greer 1997; Leigh and Vulliamy 1997). Soon after the election of the New Labour government in 1997 the tight networks of power around New Labour were exposed when Labour-friendly lobbyists offered direct ministerial access to an undercover journalist posing as a businessman. In a similar sting in 1999 lobbyists targeting the new Scottish Parliament were also exposed as offering access to ministers for cash (Schlesinger *et al.* 2001). The covert and media-shy activities of lobbyists have unquestionably become more important in policy making (Hollingsworth 1991; Silverstein 1998), but calls to regulate British lobbyists have so far gone unheeded. The European Parliament voted in favour of lobbying registration in early 2008, but the European Commission has made only half hearted moves to introduce a voluntary register in June 2008 (Kanter 2008). UK developments in 2007–08 focused on the inquiry into lobbying conducted by the Public Administration Select Committee (Miller and Dinan 2008b; PASC 2007; Hall 2008).

It was only in the 1970s that organisations such as trades unions started to appoint PR officials and prioritise media relations (Jones 1986). As the media have become increasingly important or as other avenues for influence or change are closed off, so pressure groups and other campaigners have been forced to try to attract the attention of the media in order to pursue their aims. Since the 1970s there has been a change in the character of protest. Mass marches and demonstrations have become less popular and are increasingly seen as ineffective (Engel 1996; Porter 1995). Instead radical or countercultural movements increasingly understand the value of smaller and more focused actions which are more likely to have televisual appeal (Grant 1995; Vidal and Bellos 1996). This can be seen particularly in the campaigns against Genetically Modified (GM) food, where campaigners have damaged crops wearing protective clothing and with TV cameras in tow.

The focus of much lobbying and public relations activity has also shifted from the centres of power in the nation-state to transnational bodies. In Europe, Brussels has become a much more important target for both pressure groups (Greenwood 1997; Mazey and Richardson 1993) and the PR industry (Dinan and Miller 2006). The global level has also become markedly more important. Corporations are increasingly able to move capital globally to seek higher and quicker profits. Consequently institutions of global governance such as the World Bank, International Monetary Fund and World Trade Organization have become more important in regulating the 'free trade'. But in the wake of the globalisation of capital has come the globalisation of protest. The protests in Seattle against the WTO and in Prague against the IMF in 2000 signalled the public emergence of a heterogeneous assemblage of different interests from the developed and developing world united by their opposition to the free market and the dominance of predominantly US multinationals. Anti-capitalist protests have occurred across the world as the global reach of corporations has made clear the interconnectedness of local protests. One key aspect of the protests is a specific opposition to the marketing, PR and advertising strategies of multinationals. This is expressed by pressure groups such as the Canadian adbusters group (http://adbusters.org) and chronicled in Naomi Klein's anti-branding polemic *No Logo* (Klein 2000). This has been expressed in campaign websites such as PRwatch.org and Spinwatch.org and latterly in European and UK campaigns for lobbying transparency such as The Alliance for Lobbying Transparency and Ethics Regulation EU (ALTER-EU – www.alter-eu.org) and the Alliance for Lobbying Transparency in the UK (www.lobbyingtransparency.org).

Promotional resources

The contemporary experience is that government, business and pressure groups actively compete for media space and definitional advantage. However, in the competition for access there are very marked resource inequalities between organisations. One obvious way in which this is the case is in financial and personnel budgets. Government promotion is carried out by the Government Information and Communication Service, which employs more than 1200 information officers, plus support staff and has a budget running into hundreds of millions of pounds. The top 150 PR consultancies earned £765 million in fee income in 2007 up from £440 million in 1995 (*PR Week* 2008; Miller and Dinan 2000: 11). It is only government, corporations and the bigger interest groups who can afford long-term support from PR consultancies. In other words, the central institutions of the state and big business enjoy structured advantages in the competition. By resources, however, we also mean the extent to which an organisation is institutionally secure. For example, the central institutions of the state are plainly among the most institutionalised, whereas government-created statutory bodies are less institutionally secure. Outside the ambit of the state are major pressure groups such as Greenpeace or professional associations such as the British Medical Association. These are long-term bodies, which may not always be fully secure. The least institutionalised organisations are those with little formal organisation, arising out of specific campaigns or circumstances, whether as a result of attempts to block new motorways or bypasses or to stop the closure of a local school. A third type of resource is cultural. Respectability, authoritativeness and legitimacy are all key elements here. These are largely decided by and dependent on the perceptions of others and can decisively influence the credibility of an organisation. Cultural capital resides even in the smallest feature of personal presentation such as the accent of the speaker and how they dress. On the basis of the unequal distribution of resources we can identify some groups as 'resource-poor' (Goldenberg 1975) or 'resource-rich'. However, the resources available to the institutions of the state also exist in the context of broader structures of power and authority. Both the state and business have markedly more power to police disclosure and enclosure than others.

Policing enclosure and disclosure

The state is a key site for the policing of information. It controls a huge bureaucratic machinery for the production of research, official statistics and public information. The backbone of the machinery of media management in Britain is the system of mass unattributable briefings, known as the lobby system by which journalists receive the latest 'off-the-record' comment and political spin on the stories of the day. These appear in news reporting with the source of the information disguised in phrases such as 'the government believes' or 'sources close to the Prime Minister suggest'. The advantage for the government is that since the information is not attributed it is, as one minister put it, 'no skin off anyone's nose if it turns out to be wrong' (Cockerell *et al.* 1984: 33; see also Cockerell 1988; Franklin 1994; Harris 1990; Ingham 1991). The production of government information can itself be influenced by party political or class interests and there have been a number of controversies in Britain about the accuracy of official statistics (Levitas and Guy 1996). Furthermore, the accuracy of government information in general has been increasingly questioned. From the massaging of the figures for unemployment in the 1980s and 1990s, to disinformation in relation to the invasion of Iraq in 2003, state personnel regularly involve themselves in misinformation.

Successive cabinet secretaries have provoked opprobrium for their slippery definitions of the concept of truth. Sir Robert Armstrong famously acknowledged in an Australian court in 1988 that he had been 'economical with the truth' in the British government's attempt to suppress the book *Spycatcher*. In the Scott inquiry into the Arms to Iraq affair, his successor Sir Robin Butler maintained that Parliament had not been misled even though it had only been given partial information. 'Half the picture can be true' he stated (see Norton-Taylor 1995: 91).

Iraq: the use of propaganda and PR activities

The case of Iraq is instructive in examining the use of propaganda and PR activities. Seen from the point of view of 'media centric' approaches, the issue of propaganda is one of media reporting of claims and the extent to which journalists are misled or go along with the lies. But there is much more to see than this partial interest would suggest. Propaganda strategies are planned for particular reasons and they should be judged in relation to their intentions and not just in relation to how well they do or do not manage the media. There are three main points to make here.

The propaganda campaign to suggest that the incumbent Iraqi regime of Saddam Hussein posed a threat to the West was a compound deception, fusing carefully selected elements to present an entirely untrue account in which it was suggested that the Iraqi regime was a threat. This involved stories about mobile chemical labs, weapons of mass destruction available for use in 45 minutes and fictitious links with al-Qaeda (Miller 2004a). This was not based on faulty intelligence but on a determined and deliberate propaganda campaign, the aim of which was not to convince the British or US public as a whole, but to create enough of a coalition for those in favour of war to put their policy into action (Miller 2004a).

Seen from the media centric view, the campaign was effective in managing a good deal of the mainstream media, but was not a success in the blogosphere or amongst the public. While such conclusions are justified they neglect to look at the intentions behind and the ultimate outcomes of the propaganda – to invade Iraq and take control of its resources. That element of the propaganda campaign was stunningly successful in the face of unparalleled opposition from much of the population of the world.

A second point to make is that this campaign could only be put in place by very substantial investments of time and resources. Both the Bush and Blair governments invested heavily in new propaganda organisations, with Bush creating the Office of Global Communications to coordinate activities worldwide and across time zones (Miller 2004b).

A third point is that we need to understand the philosophy of the propaganda. Powerful agents like states – though the point applies to corporations too – see propaganda and public relations simply as weapons in a battle. This is normally discussed as the 'battle of ideas', but if this suggests that the ideas element is not fully integrated with strategies involving coercion and violence, then it is not quite right. The philosophy of propaganda in the age of the 'war on terror' is part of a philosophy of 'total spectrum dominance'. The US and UK military and civilian planners see what they call 'information dominance' simply as a constituent part of dominance over land, air, sea and space. This means that all information – whether it is the command and control systems of a military opponents or the pages of the mainstream press – have the potential to be 'weaponised'. If such information does not have the capability of adding to 'dominance', the philosophy dictates that the aim is to 'deny, degrade or destroy' information perceived as 'unfriendly'(Miller 2004c). Some have argued that propaganda is not a suitable term to describe all of these strategies (Corner 2007). There is some merit to that argument in that the traditional term is perhaps not capacious enough to encompass all the uses to which governments put it. But the consequence of not using it – of abandoning it without anything to put in its place – at precisely the period in history where there has been unparalleled investment in and success for propaganda, seems less than persuasive.

Promotional strategies: lobbying versus media relations

Resources determine the strategies which organisations are able to employ. But resource-rich organisations do not always devote the main part of their efforts to managing the media. It may be that low-profile and discreet lobbying in Whitehall, Brussels or at the WTO is seen as a more effective way of pursuing interests. Indeed it has been suggested that the groups most able to implement this type of 'insider' strategy (Grant 1995) are by definition resource-rich since they have superior contacts and are perceived as more respectable, credible and authoritative or representative. Furthermore, given that British society is characterised by marked inequalities of wealth, power and status, the defenders of the current order are only likely to need to engage in media management in so far as change is threatened or desired. This is one explanation of the observation that business tends not to be as visible as its critics in the media (Tumber 1993).

Both of these factors influence the strategies of resource-poor groups. An absence of contacts with government and the aim of political or cultural change can condemn resource-poor groups to strategies and tactics which resource-rich organisations would rarely even consider. Moreover, resource-poor groups may not wish to become entangled in consultative procedures with government for ideological or strategic reasons (Grant 1995).

More prosperous groups tend to concentrate on more orthodox media relations. Nevertheless, resource-poor groups are sometimes able to gain coverage in the media and can on occasion influence public debate. This is particularly the case with issue-based campaigning groups which appear to gain a higher profile than those which simply attempt to raise resources or their own profile (Deacon 1996).

For example, Peter Tatchell of the lesbian and gay activist group Outrage has commented:

> We produce very good quality press releases that back up what we say with hard facts and statistics. It makes it much easier for people to take us seriously.
>
> (Cited in Miller and Williams 1993: 132)

The imaginative and highly controversial tactics of Outrage allowed them to capture the media spotlight for lesbian and gay issues at an unprecedented level in the 1990s. It is this kind of skill and innovation in campaigning strategy which can help the resource-poor group even in marginalised parts of the developing world. A similar tale can be told about some of the tactics of climate change campaigners in 2007–08 such as in Plane Stupid or at the Kingsnorth Climate Camp in their attempts to draw attention to the pressing issue of environmental crisis (PR Week Reporters 2008; Plane Stupid, nd).

But however sophisticated their public relations skills, small alternative groups are unlikely to be able to gain sustained positive media coverage in the face of strong competition from resource-rich organisations.

Problems of coherence and division

Conversely, resource-rich organisations are not always able to plan and execute coherent and unified promotional strategies. All organisations, whatever their resources, are likely to contain a variety of competing agendas, political perspectives and professional rivalries. In government departments, for example, there is a history of rivalry between promotional professionals and administrative civil servants (Miller 1993). Furthermore, the involvement of a variety of official bodies in a particular issue can lead to, or be symptomatic of, serious disputes over strategy and tactics. The rivalry between different government agencies in Northern Ireland such as the police, the army, the various intelligence bodies and the Northern Ireland Office are well known and in 1974 the divisions were so serious that a strike by Protestant workers succeeded in bringing down a power-sharing assembly in the face of the government's inability to speak with one voice (Miller 1993).

Too much publicity can be dangerous for radical organisations. Success in gaining media coverage may lead to internal dissent as spokespersons become media-friendly. The suspicion within the organisation that the newly visible spokesperson might become infatuated with their own celebrity and have 'sold out' is never far from the surface (see Anderson 1993; Gitlin 1980; Miller *et al.* 1998). Furthermore, divisions over strategy and tactics are common, especially in radical or countercultural movements or groups. Divisions within environmental and animal rights groups have increasingly appeared as some become more mainstream. The divisions between organisations campaigning for rights for people with disabilities are absolutely typical. Here the old style of incremental campaigning now competes with the more radical direct action approach of organisations such as the Disabled People's Direct Action Network (DAN), which eschews the gradualist approach and agitates for civil rights rather than 'charity' and sympathy.

One campaign slogan, fusing radical politics with newsworthy punchiness, reads 'piss on pity'. For the old-style campaigners such tactics are more likely to alienate policy makers. According to one: 'if you go up to an MP with that on I don't think he or she's likely to warm to you – if they're not already interested' (Parker 1995: 6). For the radicals such an approach smacks of tried and failed reformism. Such differences of emphasis on strategy, tactics and goals are of course partly genuine political differences, but can also indicate strategies of 'product differentiation' and a means of generating extra pressure on decision makers.

Of course, there are occasions on which it is seen as better to cooperate on particular issues. Resource-poor groups can enter tactical or long-term alliances with their resource-rich competitors or even with their apparent enemies. But more commonly pressure groups will join other statutory and non-statutory bodies to create a common strategy, perhaps at the European or global levels (Dinan and Miller 2006).

Media factors

The media operate within a complex set of pressures of ownership, editorial control and economic interest. Journalists do have some measure of autonomy in their daily work routines. But this varies greatly between radio, television and the press, between different channels or newspapers and even between different formats, be they news, current affairs or discussion programmes in the broadcast media or news, features, columns and editorials in the press. These variations are in part a result of variations in news values, but they also reflect the promotional networks which form around varying journalistic beats. At the pinnacle of the news values of broadcasting, the broadsheet press and some elements of the tabloid press is hard news. This typically revolves around the news beats of central government which are covered by political correspondents or lobby journalists. Down a notch in terms of news value are more peripheral government departments such as Defence, Education, Agriculture or Health, which typically have their own corps of specialist journalists. As a result of this form of organisation the bulk of political news originates with the central bureaucracies of Whitehall and the political party's news management apparatus. However, the specialist correspondents are also engaged in attempting to cover the major policy debates or new developments in their field. Furthermore, they may have a special page devoted to their output in broadsheet newspapers such as the health, science or education pages. Such factors do mean that specialists can be more interested in the intricacies of policy debates or in the activities of resource-poor groups than their non-specialist colleagues on the news desk. As a result resource-poor groups who target specialist journalists can often build up a valuable relationship with them and will tend to gain more access to the inside specialist pages than to other sections of the paper. The relationship also has advantages for the specialist journalist in that pressure groups can be used as a research resource. On the other hand, specialists do tend to gravitate towards official sources in their area and may be less likely to view pressure group stunts as newsworthy than their news desk.

Deacon and Golding (1994) suggest that journalists tend to see news sources as either *advocates* of a point of view or constituency who can be used to give a 'balancing' comment, or as *arbiters*, as 'expert witnesses' who can judge the significance or import of events. Both rich and poor groups can move between these designations though achieving arbiter status is harder than advocate status. Groups at the poorer end of the resource spectrum may only be designated arbiters by specialists. When an issue leaves the specialist pages to move higher up the news agenda to the front pages, most likely when official pronouncements or action are involved, an organisation may have to contend with reverting to advocate status. Such differences are also inflected by varying news values across the media. For example, 'cuddly charities', the ones which deal with animals, children or health, are more heavily featured in tabloid and television coverage (Deacon 1996). But the media are increasingly subordinate to commercial imperatives. In the press investigative journalism has declined, to be replaced by lifestyle and consumer writing. On television 'reality TV' has squeezed out programmes which periodically make powerful interests uncomfortable or provide the public with useful information (Barnett and Seymour 1999; Cohen 2000; Stone 1999). Furthermore, in TV news the obsession with 'liveness' is substituted for explaining the world (Snow 2000).

The impact and success of promotional strategies

The success and impact of promotional strategies are hard to measure, first, because they have myriad aims which are not always clearly conceptualised. Second, they work at different levels. That is, some groups target local opinion, while others simply want to raise funds.

The self-denying status of propaganda, the behind-the-scenes nature of lobbying and the endemic secrecy surrounding the policy process in Britain are further reasons why evaluations of success or impact are difficult. Finally, we should beware of judging success in terms simply of the amount or quality of media coverage, since media coverage does not necessarily or straightforwardly translate into influence (cf. Cracknell 1993).

Governments, business and interest groups try to manage the media because of a widespread recognition that media reporting can impose limits on organisational action and provide opportunities for influencing public opinion, and the distribution of power and resources in society (Walsh-Childers 1994: 827; Linsky 1986). However, one of the key limitations of much media and cultural studies is the reluctance to examine the outcomes of successful (or unsuccessful) media management (Philo and Miller 2001: 70–1). The influence of media reporting on public opinion and, most importantly, government and corporate decision making demand to be directly investigated.

Media strategies have helped to sell government policies such as the privatisation of British public utilities in the 1980s (Miller and Dinan 2000; Philo 1995). Conversely, even flagship policies of strong governments such as the Poll Tax can fail despite concerted marketing campaigns (Deacon and Golding 1994). In the longer term the strategies of social movements and associated struggles can lead to marked changes in the status and power of social constituencies such as women, Black people and lesbians and gay men. The emergence of issues like racism, violence against women, child sexual abuse, homophobia and even the environment were preceded by long and, on many occasions, apparently unsuccessful campaigns to raise awareness and change society (cf. Tiffen 1989: 197–8).

Changing trends?

Those parts of the media industry which are run by private corporations – that is most of the industry – are increasingly integrated into the global corporate power structure. The increase in the size and power of corporations means that directors of media firms are also directors of other firms too. The biggest media companies are now owned by corporations with many other interests. So, 'Rather than scrutinize the merchants of militarism, large news organizations have been inclined to embrace them. In some cases, as with General Electric and NBC, the arms contractor and the network owner are one and the same. The Pentagon's key vendors can rest assured that big TV and radio outlets will function much more as allies than adversaries' (Solomon 2000).

The convergence between the media and PR business is visible especially in companies like United Business Media, which owns CMP a provider of events, print and online publications. UBM is also a major shareholder of ITN (20 per cent) and the Press Association (17.01 per cent) (UBM 2007). But UBM also owns PR Newswire, a publicity service for corporations and the PR industry which distributes content to news outlets such as ITN and the Press Association. PR Newswire is also the parent of another subsidiary, eWatch, a controversial internet monitoring agency which advertised a service to spy on activist groups and corporate critics. After it was exposed by *Business Week* in 2000 the page promoting this was removed from the eWatch website and eWatch even claimed that it had never existed (Lubbers 2002: 117).

The interests of the media corporations as corporations also means that they are politically active. The media industry is very active in lobbying around issues like healthy eating and obesity as the regulation of advertising would directly impact on their bottom line. Pearson, the media firm which owns the *Financial Times* and *The Economist* funds neoliberal think tanks like Demos and the Social Market Foundation. *The Times* newspaper has funded the Science Media Group the organisation set up to manage coverage of science in – amongst other places – *The Times*. Journalists from Reuters and other news outlets have attended the Bilderberg group, the secretive elite policy planning group and most notably were active participants in the LOTIS (Liberalisation of Trade in Services) committee set up to lobby for the opening up of markets in services. Leaked minutes show that three separate Reuters staff attended the meetings and debated how best to counter protestors against GATS (the programme of opening up world markets in services). The minutes record that Henry Manisty of Reuters 'wondered how business views could best be communicated to the media. In that respect, his company would be most willing to give them publicity' (Wesselius 2001).

The integration of the PR and media industries is in its early stages. But it is a tendency which undermines the possibility of independent media. This tendency is reinforced by the rise of 'infomediaries' and 'fake news'. Amongst the developments are the trend towards the direct corporate control of information media. This has been something that PR operatives in the UK have been conscious of and trying to influence for some time. An early example of this was the joint venture between ITN and Burson Marsteller, one of the biggest and least ethical PR firms in the world. Corporate Television News was based inside ITN headquarters with full access to ITN archives and made films for Shell and other corporate clients (Brooks 1995; Monbiot 1998; Whitehead 1998).

PR firms have also been busy developing their own channels. One venture, pioneered by Brunswick, one of the most secretive PR companies in the UK – which is also close to both Gordon Brown and David Cameron, provides what it calls 'London's premier business presentation centre' within their own expensive offices in Lincoln's Inn Fields in London. The Lincoln Centre is a subsidiary of Brunswick and provides webcasting service to companies such as Atkins, Spirent, Diageo and Compass Group (Lincoln Centre, nd).

The PR industry is quite open about the reasons for this trend in their trade press. *PR Week* reports that they are 'enthusiastic' about it: 'it avoids the embarrassing howlers that a press conference can create', says Keren Haynes, a founding director of Shout! Communications. Citing the 1990s example of corporate 'fat cat' Cedric Brown of British Gas being 'torn into by journalists' when trapped in a lift, Haynes notes that had Brown 'been at the other end of a webcast, such a situation would never have happened' (Gray 2006: 26). This kind of total message control is handled by PR agencies as well as a new breed of fake news providers. BAA, for example commissions the controversial firm World Television to produce its webcasting programme. World Television is the company behind a British government fake news service called British Satellite News (Miller 2006).

An initiative by one of New Labour's favourite PR people, Julia Hobsbawm, attempts to blur the lines between spin and journalism even further. It is titled Editorial Intelligence (ei) and involves a range of journalists, PR people and lobbyists such as the disgraced former lobbyist Derek Draper. Reports suggest that Editorial Intelligence was offering journalists £1000 a year to sit on its advisory board, and £250 a time to appear on discussion panels, while, according to the *Sunday Times*, 40 organisations 'such as the Royal Mail and Vodafone have paid £4000 each to join the club in the hope of getting their agendas across to Britain's "most influential commentators"' (Fixter 2006).

Editorial Intelligence is simply one example among an impressive variety of initiatives. Before Editorial Intelligence, Hobsbawm floated the idea of a 'truth commission' an Orwellian-sounding project in which a number of key journalistic and market ideologues were involved including John Lloyd, who has written a book about how it is the media (rather than government or the market) which is destroying politics (Lloyd 2004). Lloyd and Hobsbawm were also involved in the discussion leading to the formation of the new journalism think tank at the LSE/LCC. Called 'Polis', a key inspiration was the academic Roger Silverstone whose work on the media and morality chimed well with Hobsbawm and Lloyd's distaste for independent journalism. In his last – posthumously published – book Silverstone refers to the 'trashing of trust' in which the media are held to have a central role (Silverstone 2006: 163). Silverstone also proposed the importance of media literacy as a means to ensure 'media justice'. He puts this clearly at one point: 'The slogan? Let's say "Education, not regulation!"' (2006: 185) – a slogan which is music to the ears of corporate lobbyists everywhere. He also notes that 'it would be good' to reduce 'conflict, repression, discord' (2006: 187). The opposing view is that journalism and PR have differing interests and attempting to bring them closer can only damage the potential independence of journalism.

Lloyd founded the Reuters Institute at Oxford with a £1.75 million grant from the media monolith, the Reuters Foundation. The trend to fund think tanks and the setting up of focused journalism centres operates in parallel with the rise of fake news. But a similar development is the rise of 'journo-lobbyists'. The aim is the same – to dominate the information environment. This development is furthest advanced in the US, and is unsurprisingly the province of the extensive network of think tanks, lobbying firms and front groups associated with neoliberal and neoconservative tendencies. One pioneering example is Tech Central Station which appears at first glance to be a kind of think tank cum internet magazine. Look a little deeper and it is apparent that TCS has 'taken aggressive positions on one side or another of intra-industry debates, rather like a corporate lobbyist' (Confessore 2003: 2). 'But', writes Nicholas Confessore,

> TCS doesn't just act like a lobbying shop. It's actually published by one – the DCI Group, a prominent Washington 'public affairs' firm specializing in P.R., lobbying, and so-called 'Astroturf' organizing, generally on behalf of corporations, GOP politicians, and the occasional Third-World despot. The two organizations share most of the same owners, some staff, and even the same suite of offices in downtown Washington, a block off K Street. As it happens, many of DCI's clients are also 'sponsors' of the site it houses. TCS not only runs the sponsors' banner ads; its contributors aggressively defend those firms' policy positions, on TCS and elsewhere.
>
> (Confessore 2003: 2)

James Glassman, who runs Tech Central Station has 'given birth to something quite new in Washington: journo-lobbying'. Confessore notes:

> It's an innovation driven primarily by the influence industry. Lobbying firms that once specialized in gaining person-to-person access to key decision-makers have branched out. The new game is to dominate the entire intellectual environment in which officials make policy decisions, which means funding everything from think tanks to issue ads to phony grassroots pressure groups. But the institution that most affects the intellectual atmosphere in Washington, the media, has also proven the hardest for K Street to influence – until now.
>
> (Confessore 2003: 2)

The wider project of the PR industry of which the direct takeover of the channels of communication is part, is to abolish the possibility of independent journalism, whilst maintaining the appearance of independent media.

Conclusion

This brings us back to debates about the effects of 'promotional culture' on the democratic process. On the one hand, it can be argued that there has been an increasing sophistication in news management on the part of the powerful, especially in government and business. On the other, that some countervailing pressure has been exerted and that particular social constituencies have to some extent advanced their position in our culture. This seems to speak of an increasing sophistication of promotional strategies on the part of the powerless, too. Yet, before we embrace the comforting pluralist notion of relatively open competition for power and resources we should examine the relative prominence of official sources in the media and the results of promotional strategies on the distribution of rewards and resources in society – meaning specifically levels of poverty and inequality and the distribution of power. While winners and losers vary and the type and extent of inequality in contemporary society does change, it is clear that Western countries remain radically inegalitarian societies. Indeed in some cases (such as Britain), whatever the victories of the resource-poor in the media, inequalities of wealth and power have actually become dramatically wider since the beginning of the 1980s (Philo and Miller 2001). In other words wealth can be systematically moved from poor to rich even as the media are awash with stories about corruption in big business or government.

Contemporary corporate and governmental public relations activities are terminally lacking in good faith, they debase the political language and stride forward hand in hand with an increasingly commercialised media – ever ready to take handouts from PR operatives. The campaign against corporate promotion is gathering pace. From Seattle and protests against war to critiques of New Labour 'spin', there is resistance to the misinformation and distortion which are central to the PR business. There are possibilities for pressure groups and the powerless to intervene in this process. It is also possible to plan and execute promotional strategies on behalf of the powerless which do not compromise either radical politics or a respect for truth. The key question for the future is whether the systematic distortions of promotional culture can be curbed in the interests of democratic deliberation and decision making.

Questions

1 How do multinational corporations manipulate the media to safeguard their interests?

2 Are pressure groups condemned to rely on publicity stunts to promote their aims and, if so, why?

3 Does spin work? Is it successful in (a) managing the media; (b) influencing public opinion; (c) legitimising government policies?

4 Using an example selected from contemporary news coverage, analyse the promotional strategy of one or more of the following: a government department, a corporate organisation, a pressure group and attempt to assess the relative success or failure of the strategy.

Further reading

Beder, S. (2006) *Suiting Themselves: How Corporations Drive the Global Agenda*, London: Earthscan. The best account of corporate management of global governance.

Carey, A. (1995) *Taking the Risk Out of Democracy*, edited by Andrew Lohrey, Sydney: University of New South Wales Press; (1997) Urbana, IL: University of Illinois Press. A critical examination of the beginnings of PR in the USA, UK and Australia.

Dinan, W. and Miller, D. (eds) (2007) *Thinker, Faker, Spinner, Spy: Corporate PR and the Assault on Democracy*, London: Pluto. Case studies of the role of public relations and think tanks in power politics.

Miller, D. and Dinan, W. (2008) *A Century of Spin: How PR Became the Cutting Edge of Corporate Power*, London: Pluto. An historical overview of how business power arose and how democracy declined.

Stauber, J. and Rampton, S. (1995) *Toxic Sludge Is Good for You: Lies, Damn Lies and the Public Relations Industry*, Monroe, ME: Common Courage. A popular account of what is wrong with the PR industry.

Websites

www.prwatch.org – Center for Media and Democracy. Publishers of *PR Watch* which provides public interest reporting on the PR industry.

www.sourcewatch.org – CMD also hosts Sourcewatch a 'wiki' database on PR and spin.

www.spinwatch.org – Spinwatch, a public interest reporting site on spin and propaganda, based in the UK.

www.spinprofiles.org – Spinwatch also hosts a wiki on lobbying, spin and propaganda.

References

Anderson, A. (1991) 'Source Strategies and the Communication of Environmental Affairs', *Media, Culture and Society*, 13 (4): 459–76.

Anderson, A. (1993) 'Source-media Relations: The Production of the Environmental Agenda' in A. Hansen (ed) *The Mass Media and Environmental Issues*, Leicester: Leicester University Press.

Anderson, A. (1997) *Media, Culture and Environment*, London: UCL Press.

Barnett, S. and Seymour, E. (1999) *A Shrinking Iceberg Travelling South . . ., Changing Trends in British Television: A Case Study of Drama and Current Affairs*, London: Campaign for Quality Television.

Beder, S. (1997) *Global Spin: The Corporate Assault on Environmentalism*, Totnes, Devon: Green Books.

Beder, S. (2006a) *Free-Market Missionaries: The Corporate Manipulation of Community Values*, London: Earthscan.

Beder, S. (2006b) *Suiting Themselves: How Corporations Drive the Global Agenda*, London: Earthscan.

Bernays, E. (1928) *Propaganda*, New York: Horace Liverwright.

Blumler, J. and Gurevitch, M. (1995) *The Crisis of Public Communication*, London: Routledge.

Brooks, R. (1995) 'ITN "Has Fingers in Both Pies" on Video News', *Observer*, 10 September: 4.

Carruthers, S. (1995) *Winning Hearts and Minds: British Governments, the Media and Colonial Counter-Insurgency 1944-1960*, Leicester: Leicester University Press.

Cockerell, M., Hennessy, P. and Walker, D. (1984) *Sources Close to the Prime Minister*, London: Macmillan.

Cockerell, M. (1988) *Live from Number 10*, London: Faber.

Cohen, N. (2000) *Cruel Britannia: Reports on the Sinister and the Preposterous*, London: Verso.

Confessore, N. (2003) 'Meet the Press: How James Glassman Reinvented Journalism – as Lobbying', *Washington Monthly*, December, www.washingtonmonthly.com/features/2003/0312.confessore.html.

Cook, T. (1989) *Making Laws and Making News,* Washington, DC: Brookings Institution.

Corner, J. (2007) 'Mediated Politics, Promotional Culture and the Idea of Propaganda', *Media, Culture and Society,* 29 (4): 669-77.

Cracknell, J. (1993) 'Issue Arenas, Pressure Groups and Environmental Agenda' in A. Hansen (ed) *The Mass Media and Environmental Issues*, Leicester: Leicester University Press.

Crofts, W. (1989) *Coercion or Persuasion: Propaganda in Britain after 1945*, London: Routledge.

Curran, J. (1991) 'Rethinking the Media as a Public Sphere' in P. Dahlgren and C. Sparks (eds) *Communication and Citizenship*, London: Routledge.

Curran, J. and Seaton, J. (1995) *Power without Responsibility*, 4th edition, London: Routledge.

Curran, J., Gurevitch, M. and Woollacott, J. (1982) 'The Study of the Media: Theoretical Approaches', in M. Gurevitch, T. Bennett, J. Curran and J. Woollacott (eds) *Culture, Society and the Media*, London: Methuen.

Davis, A. (2000a) 'Public-relations Campaigning and News Productions: The Case of the "New Unionism" in Britain', in J. Curran (ed) *Media Organisations and Society*, London: Arnold.

Davis, A. (2000b) 'Public Relations, News Production and Changing Patterns of Source Access in the British National Media', *Media, Culture and Society*, 22: 39-59.

Davis, A. (2002) *Public Relations Democracy: Public Relations, Politics and the Mass Media in Britain*, Manchester: Manchester University Press.

Davis, A. (2003) 'Whiter Mass Media and Power? Evidence for a Critical Elite Theory Alternative', *Media, Culture & Society*, 25 (5): 669-90.

Davis, A. (2007) *The Mediation of Power: A Critical Introduction*, London: Routledge.

Deacon, D. (1996) 'The Voluntary Sector in a Changing Communication Environment: A Case Study of Non-official News Sources', *European Journal of Communication* 11 (2): 173-99.

Deacon, D. (2003) 'Holism, Communion and Conversion: Integrating Media Consumption and Production Research', *Media, Culture & Society*, 25 (2), 209-31.

Deacon, D. and Golding, P. (1994) *Taxation and Representation*, London: John Libbey.

Dinan, W. and Miller, D. (2006) 'Transparency in EU Decision Making, Holding Corporations to Account: Why the ETI needs mandatory Lobbying Disclosure' in T. Spencer and C. McGrath (eds) *Challenge and Response: Essays on Public Affairs and Transparency*, Brussels: Landmarks Publishing.

Dinan, W. and Miller, D. (eds) (2007) *Thinker, Faker, Spinner, Spy: Corporate PR and the Assault on Democracy*, London: Pluto.

Engel, M. (1996) 'Protest Locale That Can't Square the Circle', *Guardian*, 25 March: 2.

Ericson, R., *et al.* (1989) *Negotiating Control: A Study of News Sources*, Buckingham: Open University Press.

Financial Times (2008) 'Rise of "PR Week Crowd" Dismays Prime Minister's Loyal Footsoldiers', *Financial Times*, 28 June, www.ft.com/cms/s/0/7798449e-44ad-11dd-b151-0000779fd2ac.html.

Fixter, A. (2006) 'Editorial Intelligence Splits Trade as It Pays for Journos', *Press Gazette*, 7 April, www.pressgazette.co.uk/story.asp?sectioncode=1&storycode=33727.

Fones-Wolf, E. (1994) *Selling Free Enterprise, The Business Assault on Labor and Liberalism, 1945–60*, Urbana, IL: University of Illinois Press.

Franklin, B. (1994) *Packaging Politics*, London: Edward Arnold.

Gans, H. (1980) *Deciding What's News*, London: Constable.

Gitlin, T. (1980) *The Whole World is Watching*, Berkeley, CA: University of California Press.

Goldenberg, E. (1975) *Making the Papers: The Access of Resource-Poor Groups to the Metropolitan Press*, Lexington, MA: D. C. Heath.

Gould, P. (1998) *The Unfinished Revolution, How the Modernisers Saved the Labour Party*, London: Abacus.

Grant, L. (1995) 'Just Say No', *Guardian*, 3 June: 12–22.

Grant, W. (1995) *Pressure Groups, Politics and Democracy in Britain*, 2nd edition, Hemel Hempstead: Harvester Wheatsheaf.

Gray, R. (2006) 'Webcasts deliver the Results', *PR Week*, 17 March: 26.

Greenwood, J. (1997) *Representing Interests in the European Union*, Basingstoke: Macmillan.

Greer, I. (1997) *One Man's World: The Untold Story of the Cash-for-Questions Affair*, London: Andre Deutsch.

Gregory, M. (1996) *Dirty Tricks: British Airways' Secret War Against Virgin Atlantic*, revised edition, London: Warner Books.

Hager, N. and Burton, B. (1999) *Secrets and Lies, The Anatomy of an Anti-environmental PR Campaign*, Nelson, NZ: Craig Potton Publishing.

Hall, I. (2008) 'MPs Split Over Need for Action as PASC Inquiry Sessions End', *Public Affairs News*, www.publicaffairsnews.com/issues/articleview.asp?article_id=570.

Hall, S., Critcher, C., Jefferson, T., Clarke, J. and Roberts, B. (1978) *Policing the Crisis: Mugging, the State and Law and Order*, London: Macmillan.

Harris, R. (1990) *Good and Faithful Servant*, London: Faber.

Harvey, D. (2005) *A Brief History of Neoliberalism*, Oxford: OUP.

Heffernan, R. and Marqusee, M. (1992) *Defeat from the Jaws of Victory, Inside Kinnock's Labour Party*, London: Verso.

Hollingsworth, M. (1991) *MPs for Hire: The Secret World of Political Lobbying*, London: Bloomsbury.

Ingham, B. (1991) *Kill the Messenger*, London: HarperCollins.

Jackall, R. (ed.) (1994) *Propaganda*, London: Macmillan.

Jones, N. (1986) *Strikes and the Media*, Oxford: Blackwell.

Jones, N. (1995) *Soundbites and Spin Doctors*, London: Cassell.

Jones, N. (1997) *Campaign 1997, How the General Election Was Won and Lost*, London: Indigo.

Jones, N. (1999) *Sultans of Spin, the Media and the New Labour Government*, London: Victor Gollancz.

Kanter, J. (2008) 'EU Opens Voluntary Registry for Lobbyists, but No Great Rush to Sign Up', *International Herald Tribune*, 23 June, www.iht.com/articles/2008/06/23/business/lobby.php.

Kisch, R. (1964) *The Private Life of Public Relations*, London: MacGibbon and Kee.

Klein, N. (2000) *No Logo*, London: Flamingo.

Leigh, D. (1980) *The Frontiers of Secrecy*, London: Junction Books.

Leigh, D. and Vulliamy, E. (1997) *Sleaze: The Corruption of Parliament*, London: Fourth Estate.

Levitas, R. and Guy, W. (eds) (1996) *Interpreting Official Statistics*, London: Routledge.

Lincoln Centre (nd) retrieved on 11 June 2007 from www.thelincolncentre.co.uk/home.html.

Linsky, M. (1986) *Impact: How the Press Affects Federal Policymaking*, New York: W. W. Norton.

Lippmann, W. (1921) *Public Opinion*, New York: Free Press.

Lloyd, J. (2004) *What the Media Are Doing to Our Politics*, London: Constable.

Lubbers, E. (ed) (2002) *Battling Big Business*, Totnes, Devon: Green Books.

Macintyre, D. (2000) *Mandelson and the Making of New Labour*, London: HarperCollins.

Manning, P. (1998) *Spinning for Labour: Trade Unions and the New Media Environment*, Aldershot: Ashgate.

Mazey, S. and Richardson, J. (1993) 'Pressure Groups and the EC', *Politics Review*, 3(1): 20–4.

Middlemass, K. (1979) *Politics in Industrial Society: The Experience of the British System Since 1911*, London: Andre Deutsch.

Miller, D. (1993) 'Official Sources and Primary Definition: The Case of Northern Ireland', *Media, Culture and Society*, 15(3): July, 385–406.

Miller, D. (1994) *Don't Mention the War: Northern Ireland, Propaganda and the Media*, London: Pluto.

Miller, D. (ed) (2004a) *Tell Me Lies: Media and Propaganda in the Attack on Iraq*, London: Pluto Press.

Miller, D. (2004b) 'The Propaganda Machine' in D. Miller (ed) *Tell Me Lies: Media and Propaganda in the Attack on Iraq*, London: Pluto Press.

Miller, D. (2004c) 'Information Dominance: The Philosophy of Total Propaganda Control', in Y. Kamalipour and N. Snow (eds) *War, Media and Propaganda: A Global Perspective*, Lanham, Maryland: Rowman and Littlefield, pp. 7–16.

Miller, D. (2006) 'The Propaganda We Pass Off as News Around the World. A British Government-funded Fake TV News Service Allows Mild Criticism of the US – All the Better to Support It', *Guardian*, 15 February, www.guardian.co.uk/politics/2006/feb/15/media.television.

Miller, D. and Dinan, W. (2000) 'The Rise of the PR Industry in Britain 1979–98', *European Journal of Communication*, 15(1): 5–35.

Miller, D. and Dinan, W. (2008a) *A Century of Spin: How PR Became the Cutting Edge of Corporate Power*, London: Pluto.

Miller, D. and Dinan, W. (2008b) 'Corridors of Power: Lobbying in the UK' in 'Les Coulisses du Pouvoir' Sous la Direction de Susan Trouvé-Finding, Special Issue of *L'Observatoire de la Société Britannique* No. 6, 2008.

Miller, D. and Williams, K. (1993) 'Negotiating HIV/AIDS Information: Agendas, Media Strategies and the News', in J. Eldridge (ed) *Getting the Message*, London: Routledge.

Miller, D., Kitzinger, J., Williams, K. and Beharrell, P. (1998) *The Circuit of Mass Communication, Media Strategies, Representation and Audience Reception in the AIDS Crisis*, London: Sage.

Moloney, K. (1996) *Lobbyists for Hire*, Aldershot: Dartmouth.

Monbiot, G. (1998) 'Dressed for the Job', *Journalist*, July/August: 20–1.

Norton-Taylor, R. (1995) *Truth Is a Difficult Concept: Inside the Scott Inquiry*, London: Guardian Books.

Oborne, P. (1999) *Alastair Campbell, New Labour and the Rise of the Media Class*, London: Aurum.

PASC (Public Administration Select Committee) (2007) 'PASC Launches Lobbying Inquiry' *Press Notice* 38, Session 2006–07, 21 June 2007, www.parliament.uk/parliamentary_committees/public_administration_select_committee/pasc0607pn38.cfm.

Parker, I. (1995) 'Spitting on Charity', *Independent on Sunday Review*, 9 April: 4–6.

Philo, G. (1995) 'Television, Politics and the Rise of the New Right', in G. Philo (ed) *The Glasgow Media Group Reader*, Vol. II, London: Routledge.

Philo, G. and Miller, D. (2001) *Market Killing, What the Free Market Does and What Social Scientists Can Do About It*, London: Longman.

Plane Stupid (nd) Plane Stupid website, www.planestupid.com/.

Porter, H. (1995) 'Crowd Control', *Guardian,* 12 October: 2–3.

PR Week (2008) Top 150 PR Consultancies 2008, 25 April.

PR Week Reporters (2008) 'Activists Target Edelman in Climate Change Protest', *PR Week*, 17 July 1, www.prweek.com/uk/home/article/832313/FRONT-PAGE-Activists-target-Edelman-climate-change-protest/.

Price, L. (2008) 'Team Brown – Where Are You? As the Government Lurches from One Crisis to Another, the String-pullers and Spin Doctors Are Noticeable by Their Absence', *Guardian*, 16 June, www.guardian.co.uk/media/2008/jun/16/media.gordonbrown.

Rampton, S. and Stauber, J. (2001) *Trust Us, We're Experts: How Industry Manipulates Science and Gambles with Your Future*, New York: Jeremy P. Tarcher.

Routledge, P. (1999) *Mandy: The Unauthorised Biography of Peter Mandelson*, London: Pocket Books.

Schlesinger, P. (1990) 'Rethinking the Sociology of Journalism: Source Strategies and the Limits of Media-centrism' in M. Ferguson (ed) *Public Communication: The New Imperatives*, London: Sage.

Schlesinger, P., Miller, D. and Dinan, W. (2001) *Open Scotland? Journalists, Spin Doctors and Lobbyists*, Edinburgh: Polygon.

Sigal, L. (1986) 'Who? Sources Make the News', in R. K. Manoff and M. Schudson (eds) *Reading the News*, New York: Pantheon.

Silverstein, K. (1998) *Washington on $10 Million a Day: How Lobbyists Plunder the Nation*, Monroe, ME: Common Courage Press.

Silverstone, R. (2006) *Media and Morality: On the Rise of the Mediapolis*, Cambridge: Polity.

Solomon, N. (2000) 'Broadcasters Celebrate Big Gains from Violence and Greed', *FAIR, Media Beat*, 14 September (retrieved on 11 June 2007 from www.progress.org/archive/sol51.htm).

Snow, J. (2000) 'Journalism, the Techno Revolution, and the Art of Disinformation', *The Hetherington Lecture*, 1 November, Stirling Media Research Institute, Stirling University. www-fms.stir.ac.uk/Hetherington/2000/index.html.

Stauber, J. and Rampton, S. (1995) *Toxic Sludge Is Good for You: Lies, Damn Lies and the Public Relations Industry*, Monroe, ME: Common Courage.

Stone, J. (1999) *Losing Perspective: Global Affairs on British Terrestrial Television 1989-1999*, London: Third World and Environment Broadcasting Project, www.ibt.org.uk/4tv%20Research/Losing%20Perpective/losing.html.

Tiffen, R. (1989) *News and Power*, Sydney: Allen and Unwin.

Tilson, D. (1993) 'The Shaping of "Eco-nuclear" Publicity: The Use of Visitors Centres in Public Relations', *Media, Culture and Society*, 15(3): 419-36.

Tulloch, J. (1993) 'Policing the Public Sphere: The British Machinery of News Management', *Media, Culture and Society*, 15 (3): 363-84.

Tumber, H. (1993) ' "Selling Scandal": Business and the Media', *Media, Culture and Society*, 15(3): 345-62.

UBM (United Business Media) (2007). Regulatory Announcements REG – United Business Media: Final Results Part 1. 2 March, www.unm.com/ubm/ir/rns/rnsitem?id=117281830nPrr2FF3Ea&t=popup (accessed 11 June 2007).

Vidal, J. (1997) *McLibel: Burger Culture on Trial*, Basingstoke: Macmillan.

Vidal, J. and Bellos, A. (1996) 'Protest Lobbies Unite to Guard Rights', *Guardian*, 27 August: 5.

Walsh-Childers, K. (1994) ' "A Death in the Family" – A Case Study of Newspaper Influence on Health Policy Development', *Journalism Quarterly*, 71 (4): 820-9.

Wernick, A. (1991) *Promotional Culture*, London: Sage.

Wesselius, E. (2001) 'Liberalisation Of Trade in Services: Corporate Power at Work'. www.gatswatch.org/LOTIS/LOTIS.html (accessed 11 June 2007).

Whitehead, B. (1998) 'Why Did ITN Kill My Story?', *Journalist*, October/November: 14-15.

9

Newspapers

Raymond Kuhn

Chapter overview

This chapter provides an analytic framework for an examination of national newspaper industries in Europe based on eight key features: market dominance of national or regional titles; market segmentation; circulation and readership; finance; ownership patterns and rules; content regulation; partisanship; and newspaper power. Using examples from the British, French, Italian and German newspaper markets, the chapter highlights the overlapping challenges facing traditional paid-for hard copy newspapers, notably from free papers and the internet. The future success of newspapers, particularly in attracting younger readers, will depend on content adaptation and a user-friendly online presence.

Introduction

Of the main news media functioning in Europe today, newspapers have by far the longest history. Sales of newspapers to a mass public generally started in the second half of the 19th century, underpinned on the demand side by the spread of literacy and the extension of the electoral franchise and on the supply side by innovations in production technology, such as the rotary press, and improvements in distribution through new means of transportation, notably railways. Newspapers catering for elite readerships go back even further in time, with the publication of many European daily papers originating in the 18th century (Sassoon 2006: 194–9). Yet despite, or perhaps because of, their longevity as a mass medium, newspapers across Europe now face a series of interlocking and overlapping challenges to their ongoing prosperity. Indeed, in the eyes of some industry analysts, their long-term survival – at least in their traditional form – is seriously at risk.

Newspapers produced in hard copy and financed through a combination of advertising and direct payment by the consumer are more then ever before engaged in a battle for audiences and income in highly competitive media markets. The huge expansion of radio and television provision over the past 20 years (including rolling news services), the increase in household take-up of broadband internet and the growing availability of free newspapers – all pose a challenge to the economic sustainability and social relevance of the traditional paid-for press. The two main objective symptoms of the difficulties facing national newspaper industries in Europe are circulations and share of advertising revenue relative to other media sectors. In addition to these quantitative indices, one can also find qualitative evidence of public disaffection with newspaper content and widespread concern among newspaper journalists about their professional role in the digitised information age.

The main objectives of this chapter are to analyse and evaluate selected key aspects of contemporary newspaper industries in Europe, using France, the UK, Italy and Germany as examples. These four national markets are not presented here as a reflection in every detail of developments across Europe as a whole. However, it is clear that national newspaper industries in Europe are encountering a largely common set of problems that are reasonably well illustrated with reference to the experience of these, its four largest countries.

National newspaper industries: a framework for analysis

Every national newspaper industry in Europe can be analysed in terms of certain key features. Although the following is by no means an exhaustive list, it does include the most important variables:

- market dominance of national or regional titles
- market segmentation
- circulation and readership
- finance
- ownership patterns and rules
- content regulation
- partisanship
- newspaper power.

The first variable – whether a particular newspaper market is dominated by national or regional titles – is important because it is likely to have significant implications for the nature of newspaper content and in particular whether this is 'nationally inclusive' or 'regionally differentiated'. In respect of this variable, for instance, the French and UK newspaper industries show strong elements of contrast. In France regional dailies, centred on a provincial conurbation, dominate the market. Of the 10 million total print run of daily newspapers in France, around 7 million are regional titles and fewer than 3 million are national titles produced in Paris. The biggest selling daily is *Ouest-France* (Rennes) with a circulation of over 700,000. Other high circulation regional dailies include *La Voix du Nord* (Lille), *Sud-Ouest* (Bordeaux), *Le Progrès* (Lyons) and *Le Dauphiné libéré* (Grenoble). The great importance attached to local identity in France has no doubt contributed to the powerful position of these regional papers in their particular geographic areas. Whatever the explanation for their success, one result of their market dominance is that three out of four French adults *never* read a national newspaper (Tableaux Statistiques de la Presse 2002: 97). In contrast, in England and Wales (Scotland and Northern Ireland have their own market specificities) the most important newspapers in terms of audience reach are the national titles produced in London, some of which – notably the *Sun, Daily Mail* and *Daily Mirror* – have nationwide circulations of over one million. These national papers provide the primary print-based source of political information on national and international issues and events to their readers, who tend to use local and regional papers as a supplement to – rather than a substitute for – reading a national title (Kuhn 2007). As a result, the UK has 'by far the largest national newspaper press in Europe' (Deacon 2004: 10).

The German press system is somewhere in between the French and British. The major players in circulation terms are 'national' titles in that they are available nationwide. However, most are produced not in the capital, Berlin, but in major regional cities such as Frankfurt and Munich and, reflecting Germany's federal political system, they contain a significant amount of regional (*länder*) as well as national and international news (Humphreys 1994). The newspaper industry in Italy is also decentralised in terms of production, with national papers produced in Turin (*La Stampa*) and Milan (*Corriere della Sera*) as well as in Rome (*La Repubblica*).

The second variable – market segmentation – refers to how the supply of newspapers is socio-economically differentiated in terms of target audiences. Here too the French, UK, German and Italian newspaper industries can be usefully compared. The UK has a stratified national market with 'quality' newspapers such as the *Guardian* and the *Independent* at the top, popular tabloids ('red tops') including, the *Sun* and the *Daily Mirror* at the bottom and mid-market papers ('black tops') such as the *Daily Mail* in between, even if there is some evidence of the blurring of the boundaries between these different strata in recent years in terms of both content and format. In contrast, because of the dominance of regional dailies, France lacks a national popular tabloid: there is no French equivalent of the *Sun*. Italy too lacks a flourishing tabloid sector. In sharp contrast, Germany has the biggest selling tabloid title in Europe, *Bild*, with a circulation of just under 4 million in 2005. All four countries have at least one daily newspaper catering for business elites (*Financial Times, Les Echos, Il Sole 24 Ore* and *Financial Times Deutschland*). France and Italy also have big selling sports dailies (*L'Equipe, La Gazzetta dello Sport* and *Lo Stadio*), while the huge coverage of sport in generalist newspapers has prevented the emergence of a similar niche daily in the UK.

Whatever the geographic or socio-economic configuration of their particular national markets, the most obvious cause for concern for national newspaper industries across Europe relates to the third variable – circulation and readership. Table 9.1 provides some cross-national statistical data regarding newspaper circulations. Two points are particularly worthy of note. First, mainly because of their large tabloid readerships, the UK and Germany hugely outperform France and Italy. Second, despite increased levels of formal educational qualifications in all four countries, newspaper sales in relation to population declined between 1960 and 2005 – dramatically so in the UK and France, marginally in Germany and Italy.

Table 9.1 Number of newspapers sold per 1000 inhabitants aged 15 or more

	1960	1990	2005
UK	514	393	348
Germany	307	343	305
France	252	155	159
Italy	122	118	114

Source. Eveno, P. (2008) *La Presse Quotidienne Nationale: Fin de Partie ou Renouveau*, Paris: Éditions Vuibert, p. 18. Reproduced with permission.

For many people reading a newspaper remains a daily ritual. Observance of this ritual is, however, less widely maintained than previously. Of all the sociological variables – educational qualifications, gender, ethnic origin, employment status – potentially linked to the decline in newspaper reading, age is the single most important. Young people are particularly resistant to paying for a newspaper and there is a fear among newspaper owners and journalists that the current generation of young people may never properly acquire the habit of regular newspaper reading even as they grow older. If so, we are witnessing a generational change in media consumption patterns to which newspapers will be obliged to respond if they are quite simply not to go out of business. Interestingly, the magazine sector across Europe has in general held up well, showing that there is no inevitability about the decline of all print-based media in the digital era. If magazines can continue to prosper in an environment where audiovisual media are clearly in the ascendancy why, one may ask, is the same not true of newspapers?

This leads us to consider the fourth variable: newspaper finance. Most newspapers are financed from a mix of commercial advertising and consumer payment. One obvious factor in suppressing demand for newspapers is their cover price. Newspapers remain expensive to produce and distribute in their traditional hard copy form. The introduction of new printing technology in the last quarter of the 20th century did not lower production costs as much as had been hoped and did nothing to reduce distribution costs. In France the price of daily newspapers is particularly high, with some titles costing over £1 per copy. In the UK the sensitivity of readers to price was well illustrated in the 1990s when the Murdoch press group launched a price war against its competitors and many readers transferred their allegiances to a cheaper Murdoch-owned newspaper.

Reducing the price of newspapers as a way to boost sales is not, however, within the capacity of most press companies in Europe, since they simply lack the scale of media interests to sustain significant price cuts over time. In any case, while high cover prices may deter potential readers, they may still be necessary for the newspaper's economic balance-sheet since a large element of production and distribution costs are fixed irrespective of the length of print runs. In short, lowering the unit price of newspapers to gain more readers may not make financial sense, while raising the price increases consumer disaffection and depresses sales even further.

Most newspapers in Europe rely on advertising for some of their income, although the extent of this dependence varies from title to title. In respect of advertising funding the health of the newspaper sector within the wider national media market depends on the interaction of two factors: the total amount of resources devoted to advertising across all media sectors (television, radio, the press, cinema, internet, etc.) and the percentage share of the media advertising budget that newspapers manage to secure. The worst case scenario for newspapers is a 'double whammy': a reduction in the total amount of expenditure spent on media advertising combined with a reduced percentage share for newspapers – in other words, a smaller slice of a shrinking cake.

The French and Italian newspaper sectors receive comparatively small amounts of finance from advertising in comparison to their UK and German counterparts. In part this is due to less advertising in their respective national economies – the share of advertising in national GDPs in 2005 was 0.61 per cent in France, 0.62 per cent in Italy, 0.75 per cent in Germany and 0.98 per cent in the UK (Eveno 2008: 205). It was also because a smaller slice of advertising in the media goes specifically to their newspaper sectors – in 2005, for instance, the share of media advertising secured by newspapers was 13 per cent in France and 18 per cent in Italy, compared with 30 per cent in Germany and 33 per cent in the UK. In part this is related once again to the lack of mass market tabloids in France and Italy. It is also a result of the attractive advertising rates offered by private sector broadcasters in both these countries.

The fifth variable concerns patterns of newspaper ownership. The extent of concentration in both national and regional newspaper markets varies from one European country to another. With regard to the market for national newspapers, Germany is highly concentrated with three press groups having over 87 per cent share between them in 2004. Germany was followed by the UK with over 70 per cent market share in the hands of the three leading press groups; France with 70 per cent; and Italy, by far the least concentrated, with just under 45 per cent (Ward 2004: 8). These statistics need to be linked to specific features of these countries' press systems. In the German national newspaper market, for instance, due to the overwhelming circulation dominance of the *Bild*, its owners, the Springer group, had over 72 per cent share on their own. In UK national newspapers Rupert Murdoch's News International is by itself a major player with over 32 per cent market share through its ownership of the *Sun, The Times, News of the World* and *Sunday Times*. In France ownership of *national* newspapers is reasonably diverse, with no significant concentration of national titles in the hands of any single press group. The main ownership concentration issue in France is at the *regional* level: not so much because a single press group owns lots of regional titles nationwide (although this is beginning to take place), but rather because in any particular region a single newspaper frequently enjoys a de facto monopoly position and is usually well able to protect its fiefdom against potential competitors. In Italy the daily newspaper sector is dominated by two major groups: RCS Media-Group, which publishes the biggest selling national paper *Il Corriere della Sera* and the third best-selling title *Gazzetta dello Sport*, and Gruppo Editoriale L'Espresso which owns the country's second most popular newspaper *La Repubblica* and a host of local titles, mostly in the north of the country.

Concentration of media ownership is not just an issue confined to the newspaper sector. Faced with a difficult market for their product, some newspaper companies have sought to extend their ownership interests into other, potentially more lucrative media sectors such as magazines, radio, television and the internet. Such a strategy aims to spread risk by offsetting the potential of economic downturn in one area of activity against the likelihood of growth in another. The resultant concentration of ownership may allow for economies of scale and scope as synergies are created across previously distinct media sectors (Doyle 2002). Such concentration may also allow countries to develop 'national media champions', able to compete more effectively in transnational and global markets. At the same time, critics point to potential problems for editorial pluralism and diversity of content when such cross-media diversification leads to a country's previously distinct media markets being dominated by a very small number of companies.

In the UK the most obvious example of this cross-media diversification is Rupert Murdoch's News Corporation, which began to diversify in the 1980s with the launch of its Sky satellite television service. Since the 1990s the supply of direct-to-home satellite television to the British market has been dominated by BSkyB, in which Britain's most powerful newspaper group has clearly been the controlling force. Murdoch's media interests also span the globe. His UK newspaper interests are thus only a small part of a multi-media, global empire.

There is no equivalent of Murdoch's News Corporation in France, in terms of either domestic cross-media diversification or transnational implantation. No French newspaper group is a major player in global media markets, while the financial weakness of national newspaper companies has in general prevented them from being successful major players in other domestic media sectors, especially national television. While with the development of local television as part of the digital switchover, several regional newspaper groups in France have moved to take a stake in the supply of local television programming, the lack of significant cross-media diversification by newspaper groups at the national level in France remains striking. In Italy the two main press groups have diversified into radio, but not into television where the private sector is dominated by Mediaset, controlled by Silvio Berlusconi. In Germany the main newspaper groups do not have majority controlling interests in the broadcasting sector at either national or regional level.

The details of regulatory regimes on media ownership, whether specifically in the newspaper sector or across media sectors, vary from country to country. There is no single overarching piece of European Union legislation on this issue, aside from general competition rules (Harcourt 2005). The tendency across national markets in recent years has been towards a liberalisation of media ownership rules so as not to impede the emergence of powerful multi-media conglomerates. Governments and legislators across Europe have tended to prioritise economic objectives over concerns about pluralism and diversity. At the same time, for political reasons policy makers are frequently keen to retain key media interests in the hands of their own national companies. The main ownership actors in the newspaper sector in France, Germany and Italy are national companies, in contrast to the UK where Murdoch (not a UK citizen) has become a major player since the 1970s.

This leads us to consider the sixth variable – content regulation. In comparison to the broadcasting sector newspapers across Europe have long been subject to light touch regulation of their content. In both France and the UK newspapers won their 'freedom to publish' in the second half of the nineteenth century when the state brought a formal end to a variety of practices, including censorship, legal restraints on content and restrictive financial measures, all of which had curtailed press freedom in the past. In France the key reform was the press law of 1881, while in the UK the abolition of the so-called 'taxes on knowledge' in the 1850s and 1860s marked a rupture with the previous system of state-imposed controls. Press freedom in Germany and Italy was effectively abolished by the pre-war Nazi and Fascist regimes and had to be reinstituted as part of a wider reconstruction of liberal democracy in both countries after World War Two (Williams 2005: 38).

In all European countries there are still state-imposed limitations on what newspapers may cover in their columns and how they may report stories. Newspaper editors and journalists have to be careful that, for example, they do not infringe libel laws or legislation proscribing incitement to racial hatred. No newspaper is wholly free to publish what it likes. Unlike the UK, France also imposes legal restrictions on the media to protect the private lives of its citizens, including politicians and celebrities, from unwarranted intrusion. As a result, French newspapers have abstained from covering the sexual improprieties of their political elites. For example, the existence of President Mitterrand's illegitimate daughter, Mazarine, was kept a secret from the French public for many years, as journalists and state officials colluded in keeping the story out of the public domain.

The seventh variable concerns newspaper partisanship. In contrast to radio and television, where balance and due impartiality tend to be the guiding regulatory principles with regard to political content, newspapers across Europe are free to support whichever political parties and candidates they wish. Close organisational ties between newspapers and political parties have in the main long since disappeared as papers became more commercial and less party political entities in the second half of the 20th century. Mainstream newspapers owned by – or enjoying close organisational ties with – political parties are largely a thing of the past. Even *L'Humanité* now has a less close link with the French Communist party than for much of its existence when it effectively acted as the mouthpiece of the party.

This lack of formal organisational links between newspapers and political parties is not, however, synonymous with depoliticisation. In election campaigns many newspapers adopt an overtly political stance by endorsing the campaign of a party or leadership candidate. Through their editorial columns they also often retain a more or less pronounced partisan identification with a particular party, or at least tend to be associated in the minds of their readers with certain political values. *Le Figaro* and the *Daily Telegraph* are conservative newspapers, while *Le Monde*, the *Guardian* and *La Repubblica* are papers of the centre-left.

A newspaper's partisanship may be influenced by a variety of factors: the views of its owner, the paper's history and brand image, the party preferences of its readership and the political conjuncture of the moment. Such a cocktail of factors means that the partisanship of any particular newspaper is not necessarily set in stone. It is increasingly likely that newspapers too closely associated editorially with a particular political party will find it hard to prosper. This form of editorial partisanship is now on the wane. In part, this is a reflection of less intense ideological differentiation at the level of party competition in Europe. It is also driven by commercial considerations, since unconditional loyalty on the part of a newspaper towards a party will tend to alienate a section of the paper's potential readership. It is likely that in the future newspaper partisanship will be more conditional, volatile and issue-oriented than previously.

The final variable relates to the power of newspapers. The days are long gone when newspapers enjoyed a virtual monopoly as suppliers of information in the mediated public sphere. They now face stiff competition from other media for access to sources, content, advertising revenue and audiences. In addition, surveys of public opinion show that audiences consider newspapers on the whole to be less accurate and trustworthy in their news coverage than the broadcasting media. On the face of it, therefore, the power of newspapers to influence audiences appears weak.

Yet it would be a mistake simply to write newspapers off as irrelevant commentators on events. They continue to perform key functions, notably agenda-setting and watchdog, even if it is frequently difficult precisely to evaluate the extent of their influence, particularly in the thorny realm of their impact on voting behaviour. In the UK, for example, national newspapers undoubtedly exercise an important agenda-setting function for the broadcasting media, politicians and the public with regard to the salience of issues. Recent examples might include asylum seekers and the EU constitution. In France, despite their comparatively low nationwide circulations, the Paris-produced dailies are in many respects the dominant agenda-setters, especially with reference to the concerns of elites. In particular, the quality national dailies such as *Le Monde* and *Le Figaro* exercise a strong influence among key economic and political decision makers, as well as acting as a major forum for the discussion of new ideas in social and cultural matters. Similar claims might be made for the quality dailies in Germany (*Die Welt, Frankfurter Allgemeine Zeitung* and *Die Zeit*) and Italy (*Il Corriere della Sera* and *La Repubblica*).

Local and regional titles may also influence the content and tone of national political debate. Not surprisingly, French politicians are always keen to harness the support of a regional daily in their campaigns, with Jacques Chirac even declaring his candidacy for the 1995 presidential election via a regional newspaper, *La Voix du Nord*. In the UK local and regional newspapers played an important role on the issue of the 'poll tax' during the last years of the Thatcher premiership, when local newspapers acted as a channel for the expression of popular and elite dissent (Deacon and Golding 1994).

Newspapers are often in the vanguard in the performance of the media's role as watchdog on behalf of the public, whether as citizens or consumers. Sometimes newspapers take the initiative through investigative journalism in exposing political scandal or corruption. More frequently, they act as an echo chamber for other political actors, such as pressure groups and the judiciary, by giving publicity to particular campaigns. In Italy, for example, in the early 1990s newspapers cooperated with judicial officials in publicising the financial corruption associated with the ruling Christian Democrat party and Socialist party in the so-called *Tangentopoli* ('Bribesville') investigations (Hibbert 2008: 98).

Some newspapers regard their watchdog function as an integral part of their civic responsibilities. However, it is also the case that the critical coverage of a particular personality may frequently be a self-serving exercise in prurient muck-raking designed to boost circulation figures. In a democracy there may be a fine line between legitimately serving the public interest and unacceptable intrusion into the private lives of public figures. The balance to be struck between public interest and the protection of privacy continues to remain an issue of political and legal debate across Europe as the 'freedom of expression' of newspapers comes up against the 'right to privacy' of those in public life.

Newspapers in the information age

Paid-for newspapers in their traditional hard copy form face two principal challenges in the contemporary information age.

The first comes from free newspapers. These have become hugely popular with readers across Europe in recent years, mainly as a result of the spread of the *Metro* chain which originated in Sweden in 1995. A Norwegian group, Schibsted, later launched its own rival free paper, *20 Minutes*, across a smaller group of European countries. Distributed in urban centres, notably at underground and railway stations, these free newspapers are particularly popular with women and the young. In France, for example, in 2007 *20 Minutes* was the most popular daily newspaper (2.53 million readers per day), while its competitor *Métro* was not far behind (2.32 million readers per day) (*Le Monde*, 12 March 2008: 14). Italy also shows a particularly high readership of free newspapers with an estimated daily circulation of around 2 million (compared with about 6 million for paid-for newspapers) (Ward 2004: 97).

The attitude of traditional newspaper companies to the arrival of free newspapers has been mixed. While originally opposed to this new and unexpected challenge, some established press groups have become involved in their ownership, for instance the Ouest France group in France and the RCS MediaGroup in Italy. Free newspapers have not yet had a major negative impact on total paid-for sales in national markets, although undoubtedly some paid-for titles have been harder hit than others. Indeed, from one perspective free newspapers can be seen as a valuable addition in the battle facing the newspaper industry as a whole against other media sectors. They are popular with consumers and are one of the few growth areas in hard copy newspapers. Supporters argue that they provide a useful way of attracting new readers, especially among the young, who it is hoped will then migrate over to paid-for newspapers as the habit of reading a daily paper takes hold. In contrast, opponents have argued that free newspapers are the cuckoo in the nest of the newspaper industry, as they undermine the economics of traditional production and distribution. Their content has been criticised for its superficiality, while the reliance on advertising places a premium on what some condemn as 'journalism lite' largely based on a cut-and-paste of press releases.

The second challenge comes from the internet and is more complex than that posed by free newspapers. By making information instantly available to users the internet is often the first port of call for audiences seeking up-to-date news about moving events in real time. This is an area in which hard copy newspapers cannot hope to compete – indeed it could be said that this is simply an extension of the problem of being 'first with the news' that newspapers have had to face since the arrival and spread of radio (1920s–1930s) and television (1950s–1960s). In addition, for a growing number of people the internet is a more attractive and user-friendly source of information than hard copy newspapers. This is particularly the case with certain sections of society, notably the young.

The internet also provides information in a non-linear fashion, which allows users to augment and deepen their information search at will. News sites provided by internet portals such as Google and Yahoo! provide new – and from newspapers' perspective unwanted – competition. To many the internet's combination of visual and audio text, its interactive function through chat rooms and its capacity to allow users to be producers and not just consumers of information make hard copy newspapers look tired and out of date. The expansion of internet reach into domestic households has also led to advertising revenue – both brand and classified – moving away from the 'old media', including newspapers, as advertisers chase changing patterns of media usage among their target audiences in, for example, the purchase of goods and services.

The initial response by many newspaper executives to the advent of the internet was simply to publish an on-line replica of the hard copy newspaper (or in the most extreme cases to do nothing by pretending that the internet did not exist!). This strategy quickly revealed its limitations as it became clear that a huge swathe of linear text was not the way to attract users to a newspaper's website. Several newspaper companies have invested significant resources in creating multi-faceted websites which serve to propagate the newspaper brand, while at the organisational level newsrooms are increasingly integrated in the production of both hard copy and on-line versions. One of the most successful on-line media ventures in France is the website Le Monde.fr, which provides archival resources, discussion sites for users and links to other relevant websites. In the UK the *Guardian* has developed a network of special interest sites under the umbrella title of Guardian Unlimited, covering news, film, sport, work, education, shopping, books and money among other topics.

A major issue facing newspaper management in the online sector is whether to charge the user for services or to provide them for free. There is evidence that young people in particular have become accustomed to not paying for access to certain services (for example, the downloading of music) and that this is creating a new relationship between provider and user in the online world. While some newspapers charge users for access to at least some of their services (for example, access to their archives), it is likely that newspapers will increasingly try to secure advertising funding for their online services so as to reduce, or better still eliminate, the direct costs of website access to the consumer. The financing of web-based content will be a major issue for newspaper organisations over the coming years.

For journalism the internet brings some notable advantages. It allows ordinary citizens to contribute to the production process through submission of photos and video footage as well as text. It permits access to a wider variety of sources than in the past and should, therefore, help create a more level playing field between traditional official sources and more marginal socio-political actors in terms of news coverage. It allows journalists to publish information and opinion across a range of websites and in different formats. The internet can thus be seen to democratise information production and distribution.

However, the internet may also de-professionalise the activity of journalism. Blogs at their worst become sites of unsubstantiated rumour and gossip where the rules of ethical journalism do not apply. One major advantage that some (though certainly not all) newspapers have in the eyes of the public is their credibility – they are trusted as suppliers of accurate information. It is not surprising, therefore, that some newspaper websites such as those of *Le Monde* and the *Guardian* feature among the most popular in terms of usage, and not just among their respective national audiences.

Conclusion

Are newspapers in crisis? Times are certainly difficult for many newspaper titles. The financial model of traditional newspaper publishing has been hit by a combination of technological, economic and social factors – most notably, the internet, shrinking advertising budgets, competition from free newspapers and disaffection among the younger generation to the product in its hard copy, paid-for form. Undoubtedly some individual titles will go out of business in the next few years, unable to adjust to new market conditions. Of course, there is nothing new in the closure of individual newspaper titles. What is new is that such titles are now unlikely to be replaced in the market as tended to be the case in the past.

Yet although not masters of their fate, neither can newspapers just assume the posture of helpless victim. To survive, and better still prosper, in the digitised information age will require a focus by newspaper management on two key strategic elements. The first is content. Although news reportage will continue to be a staple part of their contribution to information dissemination, hard copy newspapers have long since lost the capacity to be the first source of news. Yet the success of many niche-oriented magazines suggests that the print medium still has a role to play in providing entertainment, features and commentary. Upmarket newspapers will continue to emphasise the depth of analysis and quality of their columnist journalism, while incorporating different supplements – economy, finance, literature, the arts – to boost sales on specific days of the week. Certain genres of coverage – such as sport, culture and lifestyle – now occupy greater space than in the past, as do stories and features aimed at women readers. Even in traditional genres, such as domestic politics, there is a tendency towards the inclusion of a more 'human interest' approach to political coverage that emphasises the concerns of 'ordinary voters' and the personal attributes of politicians. Coverage of popular culture, including television 'soaps' and reality programmes such as *Loft Story* (France) and *Big Brother* (UK) have become an integral part of newspaper coverage (and not just in the tabloid press), as newspapers attempt to attract young readers.

The second strategic element concerns the successful transition of the newspaper to the world of online media. The internet needs to be seen not as a replacement for newspapers, but rather as providing these with an additional platform for the provision of a broader range of services to existing and new audiences. Several newspapers in Europe enjoy a strong brand image which is already serving them well in the online world. Newspaper organisations that fully embrace the potential of the internet can reasonably hope to enjoy commercial success, provided that the economics of newspaper publishing on the internet can be satisfactorily resolved. At the same time, newspapers in their traditional hard copy form are not doomed to disappear. What now constitutes a 'newspaper' may be more difficult to define than it used to be, but newspapers in both online and paper forms will remain an integral part of the supply chain in European media markets for the foreseeable future.

Questions

1 What is the future for newspapers?

2 What more could newspapers do to attract young adult readers?

3 What are the arguments for and against concentration of ownership in the newspaper industry?

Further reading

Hallin, D. and Mancini, P. (2004) *Comparing Media Systems*, Cambridge: Cambridge University Press. An advanced comparative study of the media in English-speaking and European democracies from a political science perspective.

Kelly, M., Mazzoleni, G. and McQuail, D. (eds) (2003) *The Media in Europe*, London: Sage. A country by country profile of media systems in 23 European states.

Williams, K. (2005) *European Media Studies*, London: Hodder Arnold. Organised thematically with a chapter devoted to the press in Europe.

References

Deacon, D. (2004) 'Politicians, Privacy and Media Intrusion in Britain', *Parliamentary Affairs*, 57 (1): 9-23.

Deacon, D. and Golding, P. (1994) *Taxation and Representation: The Media, Political Communication and the Poll Tax*, London: John Libbey.

Doyle, G. (2002) *Media Ownership*, London: Sage.

Eveno, P. (2008) *La Presse Quotidienne Nationale: Fin de Partie ou Renouveau*, Paris: Vuibert.

Harcourt, A. (2005) *The European Union and the Regulation of Media Markets*, Manchester: Manchester University Press.

Hibbert, M. (2008) *The Media in Italy*, Maidenhead: Open University Press.

Humphreys, P. (1994) *Media and Media Policy in Germany*, Oxford: Berg.

Kuhn, R. (2007) *Politics and the Media in Britain*, Basingstoke: Palgrave Macmillan.

Sassoon, D. (2006) *The Culture of the Europeans*, London: Harper Press.

Tableaux Statistiques de la Presse: Edition 2002 (2002), Paris: La documentation française.

Ward, D. (2004) *A Mapping Study of Media Concentration and Ownership in Ten European Countries*, Hilversum: Commissariaat voor de Media.

Williams, K. (2005) *European Media Studies*, London: Hodder Arnold.

10

Magazines

Anna Gough Yates

Chapter overview

This chapter is concerned with the contemporary magazine industry in Europe. It notes the current crisis of the magazine industry, its broad determinants and the fate of the magazine as a medium. It identifies the key magazine industry sectors – not only the consumer sector but, in addition, the all-important trade press. Among the key issues it discusses for magazines since the turn of the 21st century is the growth of 'celebrity culture' as a driver for magazines' focus.

Magazines in Europe

In a recent edition of the *Guardian* newspaper, the journalist and magazine consultant David Hepworth described a chance encounter with a well-known veteran of the magazine industry. Hepworth asked him whether he would be purchasing any of the magazine titles currently up for sale by the international media group EMAP. '"I wouldn't buy a magazine these days," came the reply. "Not even in a newsagent"' (Hepworth 2007: 6). According to Hepworth, this type of gallows humour is common in the magazine industry today. Whilst the major magazine companies and corporations in America and Europe continue to produce a wide range of titles, the industry is widely understood to be at a 'turning point', with all sectors witnessing stagnation or decline in sales and profits (Robinson 2007: 10).

There are a number of events that have contributed to the weakening of the industry. First, magazine publishers have to deal with a shifting media landscape, and there is increasing competition for a finite proportion of consumer time from other media including television, the internet and computer games. Second, with the growth of commercial media, advertisers across Europe are moving some of their spending from magazines to other vehicles, such as interactive television and the internet, which many believe are more effective at targeting specific groups of consumers. Lastly, since the worldwide economic slump that began in

2001, there has been a decline in the amount of money that companies are willing to spend on advertising overall. In other words, the cake has become smaller, and so has the slice of it that magazine publishers are receiving (TSE/Rightscom 2005: 76–7).

Despite these threats to magazine publishing, the picture is not all gloom and doom. Whilst profits may not be as high as they have been in the past, 70 per cent of people in Europe are thought to read magazines on a regular basis, and in some countries the figure may be as high as 95 per cent (TSE/Rightscom 2005: 89). Furthermore, the magazine industry has historically been a very creative and adaptable one, and whilst it has made profits in the past from magazines for general readerships, it now produces wide ranges of magazines for audience segments that it hopes will appeal to advertisers. Thus magazines exist for almost every consumer sector imaginable, not only a variety of magazines for target groups of men, women and children, but also an amazing selection for groups that include model makers, Francophiles, dog owners, computer game players, food lovers, amateur genealogists, and mountain and hill walkers! The industry is also very competitive, and there are often several magazines produced by different publishers that target similar groups of consumers – motorcyclists, for example, have a wide choice of titles including *Bike, Classic Bike, Fast Bikes, Motorcycle News, Performance Bikes, RiDE,* and *Two Wheels Only*. In the UK, there are over 3000 titles aimed at consumer groups, and over 5000 aimed at businesses. Across Europe there are around 28,000 magazines for consumers, and over 17,000 titles aimed at the professions and businesses, and the industry is estimated to have an annual turnover of €37 billion (TSE/Rightscom 2005: 20).

The quantity of launches and closures also indicates that the European magazine industry remains dynamic. When publishers have identified new market groups, they have launched and re-launched titles for them with content, design and promotions intended to appeal. The development and employment of new technologies has also helped them to do this with increased speed, and many publishers are now innovating with online services as well. There are other forms of innovation too – including the development of new magazine formats, new promotional tools for advertisers, and diversification of brands into other media, such as radio. And when markets are saturated at home, publishers increasingly look to expand their brands to other languages and countries, not only in Western Europe, but also to Eastern Europe and Asia (TSE/Rightscom 2005: 108). While the degree of future profits for magazine publishers in Europe may remain uncertain, the extent of activity in the industry indicates that it is anything but complacent.

The magazine business

The publishing industries in Europe today have tended to grow out of early 20th century businesses that were owned by a small coterie who went on to develop large publishing empires that now dominate business and consumer magazine publishing. Some of these empires have traded on the stock exchange, and must therefore be receptive to the wishes of, and remain accountable to, their shareholders, who hope to make considerable amounts of money from their investments. Others have chosen to remain privately owned by individuals, families, or groups of private investors. Because privately owned magazine empires are not required to publicise their earnings, they enjoy a greater degree of autonomy, and privacy if they desire, than those that are publicly owned (Johnson and Prijatel 1998: 177–9).

The first phenomenally successful magazine publisher in Britain was George Newnes, who launched the magazine *Tit-bits* in 1882, which literally re-printed 'tit-bits' from other publications of the period. Through a combination of attractive content, and the use of ingenious advertising schemes to promote the magazine (such as offering readers £100 free insurance against railway accidents, and clues for a treasure hunt for tubes of sovereigns), *Tit-bits* achieved enormous circulation figures of 700,000. Newnes followed these with the popular monthly *Strand Magazine* (1891–1950), the 'true-adventures' title *Wide World Magazine* (1898–1965), and the society news magazine, the *Daily Courier* (1896) (Herd 1952: 233–4). Alfred Harmsworth followed suit, with a combination of popular magazines and newspapers for the middle and working classes including the magazine *Answers to Correspondents on Every Subject Under the Sun* (1888–1956), latterly just *Answers*; a penny weekly aimed at young women, *Forget-Me-Not* (1893–1918), and the *Daily Mail* (1896-present). Arthur Pearson, too, set up newspapers and magazines for this audience, including *Pearson's Weekly* (1890–1939) and the *Daily Express* (1896-present). By 1963 Newnes, Harmsworth and Pearson had merged with Odhams' Press and the Mirror Group to become the publicly owned International Publishing Corporation (IPC) – the largest UK magazine corporation of the 20th century. By the early 21st century, IPC had been bought up by Time Inc., the publishing division of AOL Time Warner in a multi-million pound deal. It currently controls over 22 per cent of the UK magazine market (Quinn 2008).

Other publishers have attempted to rival IPC by building up, and acquiring portfolios of magazines. Indeed, it is increasingly unusual for a single trade or consumer magazine to be produced by a single publisher. Formed in 1947, the regional newspaper group, East Midlands Allied Press (EMAP), for example, soon diversified into magazines and by 2007 it had 18 per cent of the newsstand magazine market in the UK, and was the second biggest publisher in France (Quinn 2008). Foreign publishers too have attempted to enter the British magazine market, hoping to build upon their capital and history of publishing expertise. In the 1980s, for example, Germany's biggest publishers, Bauer, Gruner and Jahr (owned by Bertelsmann), made successful forays into the women's domestic monthly and weeklies markets, prompting worried competitors to speak of a 'German Invasion' (Braithwaite 2002: 28). Although Gruner and Jahr withdrew from the UK market in 2000, selling its titles to the National Magazine Company, Bauer recently bought the consumer magazine arm of EMAP (which was broken up and sold off due to financial difficulties) and now controls 25 per cent of the UK market, making it the largest privately owned magazine publisher in Europe (Quinn 2008). The National Magazine Company itself was taken over by the American tycoon, William Randolph Hearst, in 1911, and is still part of the privately owned Hearst Corporation, which is the world's largest publisher of magazines. The National Magazine Company controls around 3 per cent of the consumer magazine market in Britain (Arnold 2007). The trend, therefore, seems to be for vast international corporations to sell, and to buy, large portfolios of magazine titles.

Most UK publishers are now owned by foreign groups, with only the BBC, Future and Dennis Publishing having British ownership. Publishers therefore increasingly license or produce foreign editions of their successful titles to sell abroad. The American media corporation, Hearst, for example, has been publishing a UK edition of *Cosmopolitan* since as early as 1886, and now licenses local editions of it in over 30 countries. German publisher Bauer also licenses editions of its titles abroad, with magazines familiar on the UK market such as *Closer*, *Top Santé* and *FHM* being found across Europe and in the US.

Production and distribution

From the late 19th century until the late 1970s, a formal division of labour existed in magazine publishing. On the one hand, there were the publishing houses themselves. On the other, there were a host of independent production firms on which the publishers relied – typesetters, printers, repro-houses and so on (Driver and Gillespie 1992: 149–50). By 1945, many publishers, including IPC, had decided that independent production firms were too costly, and consolidated their structures through the development of large, in-house printing divisions. By the late 1970s, however, the magazine industry was finding that a new economic environment was making these systems of production increasingly moribund. Economic recession, coupled with growing competition from other media (especially television) was having a significant negative impact on magazine circulation. There was also growing competition for advertising, which meant that advertising revenue was ebbing from the industry, forcing many magazines to introduce higher cover prices that made them less attractive to potential buyers. Fearing that the market for magazines might all but disappear, publishers desperately sought to cut costs, and one of the ways they did this was by streamlining and rationalising through the implementation of new technologies. The pre-press and some parts of the pre-press sector were badly affected by these changes, and there were many job losses during the 1980s and 1990s (Driver and Gillespie 1992: 156–7).

Typesetters in the pre-press sector had traditionally been responsible for inputting copy. Word processors and computer based publishing systems changed all of this, making it possible for journalists to input their text directly. The gradual erosion of the traditional systems of magazine production continued throughout the 1980s as new technologies, such as desktop publishing systems, became available. This ultimately transformed the traditional networks of production within magazine publishing. From their computer terminals, magazine journalists can now pass copy to sub-editors and departments, where computer programs can be used to lay out the pages, with gaps left for the later insertion of pictures. Pages and picture transparencies can then by sent electronically to the repro house where they are downloaded. After pictures and text are merged through the use of high resolution digital scanners, an image setter can then produce film separations from which a proof copy of the magazine can be made for the publisher's approval before the film is finally sent to the printers (Driver and Gillespie 1992: 152–7). In an effort to reduce printing costs, magazine publishers also sold off their colour printing companies in the 1980s. Cheap print operations began to emerge in suburban locations, and publishers now have print and paper buying departments which can help them to secure discounts on bulk orders for paper and to bargain for cheaper print deals (Driver and Gillespie 1993a: 58).

Cost-cutting measures since the 1980s have also been focused on the immediate working practices of journalists. Many companies established more de-centralised forms of business organisation during this period, setting up semi-autonomous satellite companies, and contracting out ancillary services that had previously been undertaken in-house (Driver and Gillespie 1993b: 188). Undermining the journalists' unions, the numbers of journalists employed on permanent contracts has also diminished, while many work as freelancers. Journalists are also now expected to be multi-skilled, not only taking on the role of copy-inputting from the typesetter, but also operating as technicians, researchers and so on.

Publishers have also sought to boost the speed and efficiency of their distribution, since the majority of profits can only be made when titles are stocked on retailers' shelves. Traditionally distribution had been the responsibility of the publisher, who delivered copies of magazines to wholesalers such as Smiths, Menzies and Dawson, who in turn supplied them to retailers. Retailers received the magazines under a 'firm sale' agreement, which made them liable for any copies left unsold. A gradual shift to 'sale or return' agreements has, however, allowed retailers to buy magazines on credit from the wholesaler and to return any unsold copies. In turn, this has made retailers more ambitious in their ordering of titles.

Diversification in the field of distribution has also become a logical step for the larger magazine companies wanting to maximize their sales in the most cost-effective way. Because of this, the role of the 'distributor' emerged during the 1980s, responsible for communicating the publisher's perceptions of their target readers to retailers targeting similar groups of consumers. Whilst independent distributors exist, IPC's Marketforce, for instance, has become one of the largest distribution concerns, distributing not only all of IPC's own titles, but also titles for a range of smaller publishers. Britain's leading distributor, COMAG (a joint venture between the National Magazine Company and Conde Nast) also distributes third party titles, as does Frontline, which is jointly owned by Bauer, BBC Worldwide, and Haymarket Media. The financial benefits for publishers involved in magazine distribution have been considerable. Substantial revenues can be gained by distributing the magazines of smaller companies, and they in turn are keen to use the muscle of large publishers to achieve sales (Bland 1989: 19).

The most visible outlets for purchasing magazines are newsstands, newsagents, and supermarkets. With the quantity of magazines on the market, however, many retailers restrict the range of magazines that they will stock, opting for the most profitable titles that will appeal to their customer base. This fierce competition means that many magazines, particularly those produced by new or smaller publishers, never make it to the retailers, and they can therefore find it difficult to survive. Because of the competition for retailer space, most magazines are largely, or exclusively, purchased on subscription, and are therefore posted to their readers. This applies particularly to business magazines and professional journals, but also includes popular titles such as *Reader's Digest, Saga Magazine*, and *National Geographic Magazine*, which are almost exclusively distributed on subscription (see PPA 2008; Johnson and Prijatel 1998: 150–1). Other magazines are distributed free, given out in public places, posted directly to people's homes and to targeted work addresses or (in the case of local magazines) placed strategically in retailers.

Magazine industry sectors

An investigation of the terms 'consumer', 'organisation', and 'business-to-business' can provide us with a broad picture of today's magazine field when seen through the eyes of the magazine professional (see Johnson and Prijatel 1998: 14–19). Indeed, the terms 'consumer', 'organisation' and 'business-to-business' refer not only to the content of magazines, but to the commercial constituencies they hope to attract. Consumer magazines, therefore, are sold to consumers via the newsstand or by subscription, marketed to consumers through advertising and PR, and usually contain advertising. Consumer magazines make a substantial proportion of their revenue (estimated to be around 30 per cent) through consumer advertising. It is perhaps not surprising, therefore, that a number of critics and commentators have argued that the content of consumer magazines is as much determined by the needs of advertisers as by the perceived desires of the magazine's readers (see, for example, Curran 1986; Curran and Seaton 1988). Many of the magazines with the highest circulations are consumer magazines. In Europe it tends to be the general interest consumer magazines that top the circulation stakes. These include titles such as *Kampioen*, a family magazine from the Netherlands, with staggering circulation figures of around 3.8 million per week; *Télé Z*, a French television listings magazine with circulation figures in excess of 1.7 million per week, and the German general news magazine, *Stern*, with weekly circulation figures of over 1 million. In the UK, it is the television magazines that achieve the highest figures, with *What's On TV* and *TV Choice* regularly selling above 1.4 million copies each (FIPP/Zenith Optimedia 2007).

Organisation magazines are titles that are published by organisations for members of their society or association, as public relations for the organisation, or for customers of an organisation. They are usually designed to appeal to a tightly defined readership, with specific interests, information needs, or purchasing habits. Whilst you may not have heard of many organisation publications, for their target constituencies these magazines are very familiar. Indeed, some organisation magazines in Europe, such as the UK's *Skymag*, a magazine for subscribers to Sky television services, are distributed to many more households than the highest selling consumer magazines. Other organisation magazines that are familiar to us are those provided free to travellers on airlines or trains, such as Virgin Trains' onboard magazine, *Hotline*, or the magazine for travellers on the SBB rail service in Switzerland, *Via*. Another type of organisation magazine tends to be familiar only to employees or regular clients of large companies or institutions. The John Lewis

Partnership, which is the UK's largest department store group, for example, produces an in-house national magazine for employees called the *Gazette*, and local magazines for employees called *Chronicle*.

Business-to-business magazines are sometimes known as the trade press. These magazines target readerships from particular occupations or professions, and are often sold simultaneously by subscription and on the newsstand. *Revolution, Marketing*, and *PR Week* for example, are magazines for those working in the UK advertising, marketing, and public relations industries, and provide information on new campaigns, media vehicles, and market research to those in the business. *Computing* (UK), *PC Expert* (France), and *Computerworld* (Poland) are also nationally distributed business-to-business magazines that are targeted at those in the IT industries. They provide information on new developments and launches in personal computing, software, hardware, and accessories, for example. Indeed, whilst many of us may not have heard of these business-to-business titles, some have very sizeable circulations of over half a million copies every week (FIPP/Zenith Optimedia 2007).

Within these sectors, magazines are targeted towards a diverse range of readerships that are understood by publishers to have an equally diverse range of information requirements. This has an impact on all of the magazine content, including the cover, articles, photographs, and the advertising that the magazine attempts to attract. Thus a magazine for the over 50s like *Saga* would not run with an article on nightclubbing in Ibiza, and nor would it aim to attract advertising from Club 18–30! The market 'niches' that magazines target, therefore, are increasingly tightly defined, and their market research departments often define the 'ideal' reader or readers, distinguished by gender, age, income, location and occupation, and by less tangible factors such as values, attitudes and beliefs. This type of market research and targeting is commonly known as 'lifestyle'. With business-to-business magazines, for example, the target readership is in a specific occupation or profession, and readers will want information to help them be successful. But over and above this information, they will want a magazine that seems to 'speak' to them, both in content and visually. *Campaign* magazine, for example, is a title for those working in the advertising and commercial media industry that aims to cover industry developments as they happen. However, it is also a magazine that is well known for its distinctive design, which is an important tool for attracting readers from this field.

In the marketing of consumer magazines, publishers also focus on the characteristics of the individuals they hope to reach. The woman targeted by *Good Housekeeping* (UK), for example, is upper or upper-middle class, and over 45 years of age. Her 'lifestyle', however, is described by the publishers as involving 'a partner, a home and family. Quality is her byword. She is a modern and discerning consumer who is prepared to invest time and effort in making the best choices' (Natmag 2008). The 'lifestyle' market targeted by the Russian magazine *Domachniy Ochag* (a licensed version of *Good Housekeeping*) on the other hand, is defined rather differently because it is targeting an audience in a different culture. Aimed at women between the ages of 25–44, with 'high purchasing power', the main motto of the magazine is 'practicality'. A typical magazine reader 'is a modern woman who loves her home and family, and who devotes much of her time to them.'

The publishers also state that the magazine is read by different generations of women in the family, and is equally popular with all of them (Independent Media 2008).

Whilst the diversity of magazine titles available may be welcomed by many readers, who enjoy magazine content that they perceive to be targeted at them, we must not forget that magazine publishing is primarily a commercial endeavour. The quantity of magazines on sale is evidence of this, and publishers continually launch (or re-launch) magazines for particular market 'niches' in an attempt to reach both readers and advertisers. In the UK, there has been a 40 per cent increase in the number of magazines on the market over the past decade. It is the circulation figures of the magazine that are important to publishers, as they are concrete evidence of the numbers of people buying the magazine title and can be used to attract advertising and promotions. In most European countries, therefore, circulation figures are audited independently. In the UK, for example, circulation figures are verified by the independent, industry funded, Audit Bureau of Circulation (ABC), and similar bodies exist in many European countries. Another means of monitoring the success of a magazine is the National Readership Survey (NRS), which analyses the lifestyles, status, and incomes of different groups of magazine readers. Publishers and advertisers can use the NRS to verify just how successful individual magazines actually are in reaching the target 'lifestyle' group.

Market research is, of course, not an exact science, and many magazine titles fail to spark with readers. In such cases, publishers often attempt to 're-launch' a title towards a slightly altered 'lifestyle' group of readers. Publishers prefer to do this as opposed to closing a title, because magazine launches are extremely costly, and if a few people are reading your magazine it is better to attempt to grow the readership, as opposed to starting from scratch again. Sometimes, however, publishers find it necessary to close a title. In the UK, for example, the once highly successful women's glossy magazine, *New Woman*, was closed in 2008 after 20 years on the newsstands. Other titles have not even reached such a ripe old age. The news and celebrity women's weekly, *First*, closed in 2008 after only two years on the market, whilst the weekly music title, *Popworld Pulp*, swiftly bowed out of the market after just two issues (Hepworth 2007: 6).

Strategies for success? Celebrity culture in magazines

The growing percentage of media space that is given over to 'human interest' content, and the fact that it attracts more readerships than news and current affairs has long been noted in relation to the popular press (Curran, Douglas and Whannel 1980). The distinctions between information and entertainment have also been understood to undergo erosion, with much contemporary news media drawing upon codes and conventions traditionally employed by entertainment. Magazines such as *Time* and *Newsweek*, for example, increasingly use photographs from the paparazzi, as well as images from tabloid newspapers to illustrate their articles. Entertainment media also draw upon news content. In the realm of magazines, for example, we have the UK's political satire magazine, *Private Eye*, and the US's *The Funny Times* being just two of the many that are irreverent towards politicians and the news.

One important area where contemporary magazines have burgeoned is in the sphere of 'celebrity'. In relation to television, John Langer (1981) has argued that it is the growth and maturation of the television landscape that has led to the emergence of a personality-centred culture, where there is what he terms a 'will to ordinariness'. Whilst Hollywood developed a 'star system' (see Ellis 1991), Langer argues that television developed a more intimate, domestic 'face' focused upon the 'personality'. The personalisation and growing self-referentiality of the media has, in turn, contributed to the development of what has been termed the 'celebrity culture', or a culture where the phenomenon of celebrity permeates and redefines the public and the private realms (Geraghty 2000). In an American context, James Autry has observed the increase of what he terms 'celebrity journalism' within all forms of media, including fashion, news and sport. Magazines since the late-20th century, he argues, have been particularly driven by 'celebrity' as it has proved to be a sure-fire way of improving sales in recessionary conditions (Autry 1998: 341–2). Certainly in recent years the re-orientation of magazines towards a 'celebrity' focus, and the success of launches of new 'celebrity' titles have been notable. In the US, for example, celebrity magazines such as *US Weekly* and *Star* have had notable success with readers in recent years. In the UK, celebrity weeklies such as *Heat* and *Reveal* have been increasingly popular with women with busy lifestyles, who have been understood to enjoy relaxing with a weekly glossy as a 'my time' treat which could offer some escapism through the celebrity content (Mintel 2006). Spain too has seen major growth in the popularity of magazine titles in this area, and has witnessed a growth of readership for existing titles such as *¡Hola!* , as well as interest in more down-market titles such as *Diva* and *Gala* (Bueno *et al.* 2007). For a brief period in the early years of the 21st century, 'celebrity' therefore appeared to hold the key to arresting the decline in magazine sales.

Despite celebrity magazines appearing to be a growth area, publishers cannot escape the fact that, on the whole, overall sales figures of magazines are falling year on year, and the magazine industry's share of advertising revenues is in a downwards spiral. There are, of course, growing numbers of actual titles on the market. This does not, however, mean that there is a growing audience of readers. Competition between magazine publishers is therefore increasingly intense. Yet it should hardly have come as a surprise to magazine publishers that readers are not buying more magazines. And it is not simply that our modern lives are too busy to allow us time to read them. Indeed the challenge for magazine publishing is that our media usage is changing and fragmenting.

Firstly, the magazine industry has experienced an increase in direct competition for its traditional audiences from some newspaper titles. Not only have we seen an erosion of the distinction between information and entertainment in the news, but also many newspapers have launched their own glossy magazine supplements. The *Sunday Times*, for example, has a glossy magazine supplement that features celebrity coverage, fashion, and home-interest features. The benefits for the newspapers are twofold, in that they not only maintain their readership, but also attract the financial benefits from high spending, luxury good advertisers

(Mintel 2006). Second, and particularly in relation to the women's magazine market, there is increasing competition from book publishers, who have revived their fortunes by featuring titles targeted at women, or 'chick lit' titles such as *Bridget Jones's Diary*. Indeed, market research by Mintel in 2006 suggested that 52 per cent of consumers reading weekly celebrity titles also regularly read such books (Mintel 2006). Last, but definitely not least, there have been significant technological advances that mean that magazine readers can now access the staple diet of magazines in a wider range of media, including radio and television, but most worryingly for magazine publishers, the internet (Mintel 2006).

Recent research by Ofcom has indicated that between 10 and 20 per cent of adults in the UK believe that they read magazines less often since they began using the internet, which has increased in line with the growth of high speed internet use in the home (Robinson 2007: 10). Moreover, in August 2007, Ofcom reported that there had also been a 'feminisation' of the internet, with women in the 25–49 age bracket spending more time on the internet than men, the most popular sites being Bebo for social networking, and the auction site eBay (Allen 2007). Where consumers go, advertisers of course, follow.

Some in the magazine industry have remained resolutely positive about the commercial possibilities the internet offers them. They point, for example, to the power they already have in their existing brand names, and to the success of the men's music site, NME.com, and to profitable ventures that include vogue.co.uk. Websites are also cheaper to produce, and the content is easier to distribute when compared to the magazine market (Robinson 2007: 10). Some publishers are even tentatively stepping into the realm of the internet only magazine, with the National Magazine Company (Natmag), for example, re-launching a celebrity gossip based web magazine, handbag.com, with facilities for readers to build their own groups in a way similar to social networking site MySpace. IPC's chief executive, Sylvia Auton, has also argued that the print magazine still has a good future for at least the next 10 years, as most households still don't have broadband internet access, and of those that don't, many are resistant to it (Auton cited in Robinson 2007: 10).

Others, however, believe that the difficulties for the magazine industry are structural, and that the internet is therefore a major problem for the industry. Websites largely give their content away, and a site such as vogue.co.uk is only profitable because its content comes largely for free – from the magazine itself. The amount that advertisers expect to spend on buying space on the internet is also low when compared to that spent on magazine space, and many predict they will stay low because internet sites do not have scarcity value. If advertisers find the cost of advertising in an online magazine too high, they have a myriad of other appropriate sites they can go to in order to reach their target markets (Robinson 2007: 10).

At the time of writing, it does seem possible that our growing attachment to the internet will result in the decline of print magazines. Some magazine publishers are clearly attaching high hopes to being able to carve out new market niches for online readers. Others argue that, at their best, magazine websites will be successful only if they are complementary to a top-selling print edition. Magazine websites may be interactive and immediate. But print magazines are easily portable, and can be read when we are travelling to work on public transport, for example. Moreover, magazine publishers have long known that the feel of the smooth paper, combined with sophisticated design and relevant editorial, are the main attraction of magazines for their readerships. Call me 'old fashioned', but the combination of sensory experience, portability, and high quality design in the glossy print magazine are going to be impossible for publishers to replicate online. In a market that is crowded with media channels, the majority of magazines may well be reduced to niche publications. Yet, while the print magazine may witness a decline in circulation, it will not, I would wager, die out entirely.

Questions

1 Compare two magazines about television, the consumer magazine *Radio Times* and the business-to-business magazine *Broadcast*. How does each treat television programmes, what does this tell you about television and what does it tell you about the different audiences for those magazines?

2 Take one contemporary European magazine and scrutinise it from start to finish. What do the following items in the magazine tell you about its mission: the articles, any editorial material (e.g. a leader), any advertisements, any classified ads?

3 Compare a UK edition of any magazine also published in any other European country. What are the differences and similarities in each edition of the magazine?

Further reading

Audit Bureau of Circulations, www.accessabc.com/ (accessed 3 March 2009). Indispensable resource for understanding current magazines and their circulations.

Gough-Yates, A. (2002) *Understanding Women's Magazines*, London: Routledge. Discussion of contemporary magazines targeted at women with particular attention to issues to do with the development of consumer culture.

Machin, D. and van Leeuwen, T. (2004) 'Global Media: Generic Homogeneity and Discursive Diversity', *Continuum: Journal of Media and Cultural Studies* 18 (1): 99–120. Revealing study of how global magazines work, part of a larger project on *Cosmopolitan*.

References

Allen, K. (2007) 'It's Arrived: The Feminisation of the Net', *Guardian*, 23 August.

Arnold, B. (2007) 'Hearst', Ketupa.net, Braddon, Australia, www.ketupa.net/hearst.htm (accessed 27 August 2008).

Braithwaite, B. (2002) 'Magazines: The Bulging Bookstores' in A. Briggs and P. Cobley (eds) *The Media: An Introduction*, Harlow: Pearson Education.

Bueno, M., Cardenas, M. L. and Esquivias, L. (2007) 'The Rise of the Gossip Press in Spain', *Journalism Studies* 8 (4): 621-33, www.informaworld.com/smpp/title~content=t713393939~db=all~tab=issueslist~branches=8-v8.

Curran, J. (1986) 'The Impact of Advertising on the British Mass Media' in R. Collins (ed) *Media, Culture and Society: A Critical Reader*, London: Sage.

Curran, J. and Seaton, J. (1988) *Power without Responsibility*, 3rd edition, London: Fontana.

Curran, J., Douglas, A. and Whannel, G. (1980) 'The Political Economy of the Human Interest Story' in *Newspapers and Democracy*, London: MIT Press.

Driver, S. and Gillespie, A. (1992) 'The Diffusion of Digital Technologies in Magazine Print Publishing: Organisational Changes and Strategic Choices', *Journal of Information Technology*, 7 (1): 149–59.

Driver, S. and Gillespie, A. (1993a) 'Structural Change in the Cultural Industries: British Magazine Publishing in the 1980s', *Media, Culture and Society*, 15 (2): 183–201.

Ellis, J. (1991) 'Stars as a Cinematic Phenomenon' in J. Butler (ed) *Star Texts: Image and Performance in Film and Television*, Detroit, IL: Wayne State University Press.

FIPP/ZenithOptimedia (2007) *World Magazine Trends 2006/2007*, London: FIPP/ZenithOptimedia.

Geraghty, C. (2000) 'Re-examining Stardom: Questions of Texts, Bodies and Performance', in C. Gledhill and L. Williams (eds) *Reinventing Film Studies*, London: Arnold, pp. 183–201.

Hepworth, D. (2007) 'Have the Glossies Lost Their Shine?', the *Guardian*, 17 December, p. 6.

Herd, H. (1952) *The March of Journalism: The Story of the British Press from 1622 to the Present Day*, London: George Allen and Unwin.

Independent Media (2008) *'Domachniy Ochag'*, Moscow: Independent Media., www.goodhouse.ru (accessed 25 August 2008).

Johnson, S. and Prijatel, P. (1998) *The Magazine From Cover to Cover: Inside a Dynamic Industry*, Chicago, IL: NTC Publishing Group.

Langer, J. (1981) 'Television's Personality System', in T. O'Sullivan and Y. Jewkes (eds) *The Media Studies Reader*, London: Arnold, pp. 165–7.

Mintel (2006) *Women's Magazines*, London: Mintel.

Natmag (2008) *Natmag Direct Media Guide 2008: The Best Magazine Brands in Great Britain*, London: Natmag.

PPA (2008) 'Subscription Trends', London: PPA, www.ppa.co.uk/cgi-bin/wms.pl/68 (accessed 31 December 2008).

Quinn, A. (2008) 'Magazine Publishers', UK: Magforum, www.magforum.com/magazinepublishers.htm (accessed 27 August 2008).

Robinson, J. (2007) 'Net Closes in as Glossy Magazines Lose Their Lustre', *Observer: Business and Media*, 12 August: 10–11.

TSE/Rightscom (2005) *Publishing Market Watch: Final Report*, Brussels: European Commission.

11

Radio

Guy Starkey*

Chapter overview

Radio continues to expand at national, regional and local levels, exploiting the new platforms of cable, satellite, digital transmission and the internet. The last decade has seen a renaissance in the medium, with a greater choice of programming available today than ever before. Now over a hundred years old, radio is rising - albeit hesitantly - to the challenge of a mediatised society and through both themed and mixed-programming, its listeners are uniquely enriched.

Radio's first centenary: sound in health?

On the face of it, radio – in the UK at least – is thriving as never before. The publicly funded BBC, which tradition places at the heart of the broadcasting system, has four national FM networks, one national AM network, and 40 regional and local stations – many of them commanding respectable audiences. The latter are normally calculated in terms of 'weekly reach', the number of people who listen to a particular station for at least five minutes in an average week. At the end of 2007 Radio 1's weekly reach was 10.7 million listeners, Radio 2's 12.8 million, Radio 3's 2 million, Radio 4's 9.3 million, and Radio 5 Live's 6.1 million – while the combined weekly reach of the regional and local stations was 9.8 million, just ahead of Radio 4 (RAJAR 2008). More modest audiences are achieved by the BBC's digital-only stations, 1Xtra (453,000), 6Music (493,000), 5 Live Sports Extra (630,000), and BBC7 (853,000) which launched in 2002. Even the BBC World Service, which grew out of the Empire Service of old (Starkey 2007: 117–18), has found a new domestic audience of 1.2 million, largely due to the development of Digital Audio Broadcasting (DAB).

*This chapter is based in part on an original contribution to the second edition, by Professor Andrew Crisell.

But thanks to the Broadcasting Act of 1990 the most remarkable expansion of radio has been in the 'independent' or commercial sector ('independent' was a sly term devised for commercial television at its inception in the 1950s: the aim was to disguise its money-making intentions and at the same time to imply that its rival was feebly dependent on government largesse!). Whereas in 1984 the public could tune to a mere 48 independent radio stations on FM and AM, by 2008 there were 247 on FM and 61 on AM, outnumbering the BBC's by more than six to one. The expansion of independent radio during the 1990s was significant not just in numerical terms but for the levels of its provision: for the first time listeners could tune in to legal, home-based, *national* commercial stations, as opposed to the continental stations of the 1930s and 1950s and the offshore pirates of the sixties and seventies (Crisell 1994: 22; 30–1). Classic FM launched in 1992, Virgin 1215 in 1993, and Talk Radio UK (now broadcasting as talkSPORT) in 1995. Also for the first time, *regional* commercial stations could be heard on FM, as well as vastly more stations at *local* level. In 1996 commercial radio's total audience at last caught up with that of the BBC, and investors in the now burgeoning private sector were not unreasonably looking forward to taking the lion's share of the market. (The other key indicator of a radio station's performance in audience ratings terms is its share of all listening, a figure derived from the total number of hours listened in a week to all the stations in a particular survey area.)

A paradox of the new competition designed by its free-marketeer architects to reduce the BBC's dominance of the radio industry is that commercial radio has signally failed since 1999 to retain, let alone build on, that brief majority share. The reasons for this are manifold and include a cynical failure to invest in distinctive, quality programming on local commercial FM and AM services (Starkey 2003). However, commercial radio is fighting back and far from conceding to the BBC its now well-established lead of around 12 per cent in share terms, many in the sector see networking of programmes with high profile presenters as a way to ratings success. Yet, also paradoxically, it is a slow migration by listeners to digital radio (rather than networking with all the false economies and loss of localness that may entail) that has proven to be their saving grace. Since November 1999 the commercial sector has boasted its own national digital multiplex service, Digital One, and in a rare outbreak of solidarity, both sectors, public and private, have attempted to stimulate the growth of DAB through the Digital Radio Development Bureau (DRDB). By February 2008 the Radio Authority and its successor Ofcom had between them awarded licences to 46 local and regional commercial digital multiplexes bringing 85 per cent of the UK within reach of a far superior choice of listening than had ever been possible through the analogue broadcast bands, AM and FM, where a scarcity of frequency argument had always been used to stifle creativity and innovation.

Despite some spectacular failures, including national music stations Core (for teens), Life (for 18–35s) and Prime Time (for over-50s) and the literary-focused speech station One Word, among the surviving offerings from the commercial sector were Planet Rock (563,000 listeners) and the Jazz (364,000), both of which provided noteworthy extensions to the musical repertoire on offer, but which were nonetheless threatened with closure at the time of writing. Many other stations lack national coverage but are available in several regions, where they add considerable additional choice. Examples in 2008 include Traffic Radio, provided by the Highways Agency, an ambient music service, Chill, and two offerings from United Christian Broadcasters (UCB), but the most obvious differences between stations relate to musical genre, and despite its sporadic launches and closures a far wider range is on offer on DAB than on FM. Some local DAB multiplexes relay local or regional FM services from outside the region, hence Geordies in North-East England may listen in to 'London's biggest conversation', LBC, or hear indie and new music on XFM. Most larger FM stations are simulcast on DAB, and the greater clarity the technology offers AM stations means many of them are winning new, discerning audiences willing to try again golden oldie stations such as those in the Magic network in northern metropolitan areas and those in the larger Gold network. They began life as the original simulcasts of the very first Independent Local Radio franchisees (Baron 1975). The mainstream digital services, Smash Hits Radio and The Hits attract audiences of 966,000 and 1.4 million respectively, and while they don't represent any significant broadening of musical choice, they do demonstrate the growing potential of digital-only stations.

In all, the commercial sector alone has injected almost £150 million into programming for the DAB platform in the UK (*Radio Magazine* 2008). This is of course additional to the sums spent on investment and cross-subsidy by the BBC. Meanwhile, as the delicate balance between receiver price and consumer demand (Hendy 2000: 50–2) had begun to tip in the direction of mass production around 2003, and with the price of a receiver dropping to £30 from an initial £300, by 2008 cumulative sales of DAB radios had reached 6.5 million. Despite earlier predictions of radio's demise, DAB radio sets became one of the more compelling consumer purchases of Christmas 2007, and one national retailer, John Lewis, reported that they were outselling fashionable, branded MP3 players at a rate of six per minute, compared with five iPods per minute (Mackenzie 2008). DAB is though, in radio terms, not the only show in town. Despite governmental reluctance to set an analogue switch-off date for radio (perhaps 2015, just as television which was given a protracted period of four years to 2012 for a phased transfer to all-digital), today radio listening increasingly takes place by other means. Table 11.1 demonstrates the popularity by 2007 of new ways of listening to radio services, and the importance of the other main digital transmission platforms, Sky and Freeview. Even though listening through a television set rather obviates one of radio's biggest selling points – its portability – the 78 radio stations currently available through Sky's Electronic Programme Guide (EPG) are clearly finding audiences.

Table 11.1 UK weekly reach and share listening data for three digital radio platforms

	All digital	DAB	Digital via TV	Internet
Weekly reach (% of UK population)	30	16.8	10.3	5.7
Weekly share (% of UK radio listening)	16.6	10	3.1	1.9

Source: Adapted from Radio Joint Audience Research Limited (2008) Listening via platform – all radio, *RAJAR Quarterly Summary of Radio Listening*, Quarter 4. Reproduced with permission.

Many of these are simulcasts of FM, AM or DAB services but many more are only available through Sky and the internet. Again, most are distinguished only by their variation on a musical format, but a minority offer speech services, among them WRN with its digest of international services from around the world. Freeview, on the other hand, also includes radio stations in its offer, but the greater limitations on bandwidth on this digital *terrestrial* platform mean they are restricted in number to 32.

The expansion of the independent sector from 1992 brought with it a long-awaited boom in radio advertising (Horsman 1996: 17). Until the 1990s radio's meagre share of the total UK advertising market led it to be regularly derided as the '2 per cent medium'. Then, advertising revenue rose from £141 million in 1992 to £481 million in 2000 (source: Radio Advertising Bureau). Although advertisers naturally tend to exaggerate, one promotional slogan for the medium at the time seemed no more than the strict truth: 'Commercial radio. Its time has come.' Between 1993 and 1996 the annual increase of revenue was 23 per cent, and radio became an attractive prospect for companies which already had substantial holdings in other media and were keen to expand into new sectors. It was made even more attractive by the Broadcasting Act of 1996, which relaxed many of the remaining rules on cross-media ownership. Unfortunately, more recently this growth has stalled, and gloomy predictions of catastrophic falls in advertising revenue, while so far proving largely over-pessimistic, have dampened down expectations of the sector and been a considerable disincentive to further investment. When the internet overtook radio in terms of its share of the advertising market, apocalyptic warnings of the imminent demise of the commercial sector failed to acknowledge that newspaper advertising had also been surpassed in 2006 (Allen, 2007), with television soon to fall victim, too.

Yet paradoxically the full story of radio's recent growth has still not been told. For some years the Radio Authority and, since 2003, its successor Ofcom have licensed a large number of restricted service licences (RSLs), which allow particular institutions, locations or events to make low-powered broadcasts, usually for a limited period. The main beneficiaries of the RSLs have been hospitals and educational establishments, but commercial operators have also run 'trial' services to demonstrate demand in areas unserved – or, they claimed, *under*served – by commercial radio. In a typical year, several dozen such temporary stations have taken to the airwaves, mainly on FM, although modest budgets and short lifespans severely limit their ability to build audiences. Many areas with large Asian communities have benefited from Radio Ramadan RSLs. The most recent development has reinforced the 'community radio' sector. Since 1983 campaigners have formally lobbied for a permanent, legal 'third force' in UK radio (Lewis and Booth 1989), and following the Communications Act 2003 the Community Media Assocation has largely been granted its wish. An initial 2002 pilot project of 15 so-called Access Radio stations led to a rolling programme of licensing not-for-profit radio stations meeting very specific criteria around social gain for specified communities and the training of volunteers in the skills of radio production. Staffed almost entirely by keen amateurs, these stations certainly bring variety to the radio spectrum, although others may well struggle to earn the kind of reputation quickly established by London's Resonance FM for its 'experimental' programming. Where funding relies too heavily on donations the sector may struggle financially, too.

But despite its slow start one of the most important of the recent developments is internet radio, whose nature and potential can be summarised thus. Even the smallest, most localised station can achieve almost worldwide reach – and relatively cheaply. The territorial boundaries that until recently restricted a station to a particular editorial area are gone, as are regulatory controls on scope of operation and content (Barnard 2000: 253). It is now a commonplace irony that stations which have been issued temporary RSL licences to broadcast by Ofcom, or denied community radio licences because they have failed to meet some criterion or other in their applications can quite legally use the internet to reach listeners on the far side of the globe. RSLs may use the web to continue broadcasting long after their licences have expired and their FM transmitters have been switched off. Though often widely scattered, the audiences for internet stations are not necessarily large but they gain the potential for interactivity: they can download music and other material, join online chat groups, and order merchandise. Mainstream broadcasters can also benefit from such a relationship, often enhancing their programming with material derived from their diasporic audiences (Crisell and Starkey 2006). Many internet-only radio stations are effectively bedroom broadcasters: amateur enthusiasts using automation software to play out sequences of music and station identifications from their hard drives, while some more sophisticated websites, such as Live 365, provide online facilities for their subscribers to schedule such stations and brand them in their own names. Even though internet listening may be only very slowly catching on, taking a share of less than 2 per cent of all listening in 2007 (see Table 11.1), the experience may be particularly intense in the case of diasporic listening, where for example a Polish migrant worker living in the UK may enjoy accessing the broadcasts of Polskie Radio online, or a fan of Liverpool football club may relish tuning in to Radio Merseyside's partisan match commentaries while living in New York (Crisell and Starkey 2006).

Yet it must be a matter of some uncertainty whether, in coexisting with computer images, internet radio *is* radio in the strict sense. Do the images merely complement the radio output or – as may be more likely since sight is our dominant faculty – does the radio output become an adjunct to the images, the mere soundtrack of a broader 'multi-media' experience? Of course, unless we are unsighted or listening with our eyes shut, even traditional radio is a constant accompaniment to the things we are looking at, such as dishes in the sink or traffic on the road ahead. But the crucial point is that its output has *no need of* these images: it is quite unrelated to what we can see – in its own terms, self-sufficient. This is why, notwithstanding those scholars who discount its significance (Shingler and Weiringa 1998: 1; Crook 1999: 62), blindness is the crucial, indeed determining, feature of the radio medium (Starkey 2004a: 25–6). Listeners to internet radio may, of course, ignore any associated images on their screens or listen to it while accessing other, unrelated material from their computers. But even if we are still happy to regard it as the genuine article there are two key aspects of the internet radio experience which mean it differs considerably from mainstream listening. First, it is for the time being much less portable and flexible than radio which is heard through conventional receivers (although mobile phones linked to the internet and dedicated wi-fi internet radio sets are already extending its portability, while listening through television sets is also spatially limiting). Second, in the UK at least, the vast majority of listening – over 98 per cent – is still through *regulated* analogue and digital broadcasting platforms using broadcast frequencies. Unlike the relatively unregulated internet, these frequencies are controlled by either Ofcom or the BBC Trust – the latter under powers delegated to it through the BBC's renewable Royal Charter (Crisell 1994: 21; Starkey 2007: 22–3).

Public service and commercial competition: an enduring duopoly?

For those very reasons we shall focus on the familiar BBC/commercial duopoly in the radio sector, one first established in 1973 – which as we have already noted has been marked since the early 1990s by an absolute increase in the number of stations, and since then by competition between the sectors at all three geographical levels. The 'third force' of community radio and RSLs together will hardly even dent their domination of the market; moreover, much internet listening is to simulcast streams of BBC and Ofcom-regulated stations. But to what extent has the numerical increase in the number of stations really brought with it a commensurate increase in choice? Certainly commercial radio has enriched its output in one or two genres, notably pop and rock music, as well as classical 'favourites' and 'dance' music, but not in many others that are typical of the medium, such as documentary, features, drama, comedy and light entertainment, where the BBC's near-monopoly has, until the time of writing, been left largely unchallenged. The BBC has enhanced its own offer, through the additional sporting commentaries on Five Live Sports Extra, better broadcast quality of Five Live itself on the various digital platforms and the popularly-acclaimed service of repackaged archive comedy and drama that makes up the bulk of BBC7's output, but the Corporation remains woefully negligent of its duty to children, begrudgingly allocating them a meagre four hours a day on that same BBC7 (Starkey 2004b). If a true challenger to the BBC's long-standing monopoly of high-production value speech radio were to emerge, it could only be the 2007 winner of the contest to operate the second national commercial multiplex, 4Digital. A subsidiary of the publicly-owned, commercially-funded television broadcaster Channel Four, and as such relatively distinct from both the BBC and the commercial companies, 4Digital's offer of 10 new national DAB services included a commitment to breaking the mould of speech radio. Inevitably, though, the market would decide the fate of 4Digital, and whether it truly was a challenge to the old duopoly – just as only months before, the market brought about the demise of Channel Four's first foray into DAB, when it purchased and then quickly disposed of a 50 per cent stake in One Word. This pioneering speech station with its mixed diet of book readings, author interviews and film and book reviews struggled to draw audiences even one fifth the size of BBC7's, and as advertisers proved similarly elusive it folded in 2008 having made seven-figure losses.

The apostles of consumer sovereignty, such as Professor Sir Alan Peacock, would be unfazed by this. In 1985 Professor Peacock was appointed by the government to chair a committee to consider new ways of financing the BBC (Peacock, 1986). Though the committee recommended the short-term retention of the Corporation's television licence fee it proposed the adoption of subscription funding as more TV and radio channels became available, thus introducing a closer connection between supply and demand. The essence of Peacock's view was that types of programming should stand or fall entirely on the strength of consumer demand for them, and indeed we are witnessing this phenomenon as DAB struggles to establish itself as the premier radio platform, rather than the Betamax of radio (as an efficient but obsolete technology), which some say it will become. However, it could be claimed that demand and choice are a more complex and elusive matter than free market economists might assume – a claim which Peacock half acknowledged when he conceded that consumers are sometimes willing to pay as taxpayers and voters for what they are not prepared to buy as consumers (McDonnell, 1991: 99). What we choose and what we esteem are not always the same thing: choice is often made on the basis of ignorance and timidity, of pleasure rather than benefit. We might greatly enjoy or gain from what we would not freely have chosen to listen to, and few would agree with the proposition that the best programme is defined by what is preferred by the greatest number.

However, we might have welcomed 4Digital to the airwaves although remaining conscious of the uncertainties in predicting a robust future for DAB. If we look back over the history of broadcasting (Crisell 1997) we can see how a purely quantitative approach to audience choice has led not only to a lack of it with respect to certain *types* of programme but to an overall reduction in the *number* of those programmes. As we noted earlier, only BBC radio has continuously broadcast features, plays and comedy, but whereas these could once be found on each of the three networks it operated, they are now largely confined to one: Radio 4. In fact the trend towards formats has been all but unstoppable. When Independent Local Radio (ILR) began, its regulator, the Independent Broadcasting Authority (IBA), was expected by the government to impose public service requirements on the stations in the form of some programming variety. Such variety was, however, completely at odds with commercial radio's need to target consumers, and in order to stay afloat most of the stations soon moved to (mainly pop and Top 40) formats, with the reluctant consent of the IBA. BBC Radio 5 tried to buck the trend in 1990 by launching as a mixed programme channel, but it failed to win a coherent audience and was obliged to re-launch four years later in the news and sport format of Radio 5 Live (Starkey 2004b).

Whither radio – or will radio wither – in the digital age?

Predicting the futures of rapidly-evolving media, especially in the relatively durable context of a book, is notoriously unwise. Institutional developments, especially around the issue of ownership in the private sector, can occur unexpectedly and within timescales so short that they render the medium of print very vulnerable to being overtaken by further events. For example, in the time that has elapsed between completing the first draft of this chapter and the final amendments before it goes to print, the largest group of commercial radio stations in the UK, GCap Media plc, has been bought by a smaller rival, Global Radio, for £375 million. Global (a private company as opposed to a plc that is publicly-listed on the London Stock Exchange), had come into being with the purchase of Chrysalis Radio just a year earlier. Meanwhile the Jazz has closed, while Planet Rock has been bought for a 'nominal sum' by a consortium of ageing rock stars led by a millionaire 'rock fan and radio enthusiast', all keen for the station to survive and willing to invest money until it breaks even (Plunkett 2008). The German magazine publisher Bauer has bought the second largest radio group from EMAP (McNally 2007), Virgin Radio has changed ownership in a deal depriving the station of the Virgin brand (necessitating a re-launch as Absolute Radio) and 4Digital has abandoned plans for the launch of its own multiplex. Then, a surprise recession finished off a dozen or so small unprofitable FM stations. Yet, despite the often frantic pace of institutional change, we can observe trends, identify the phenomena behind them and base broad predictions upon some reasonable conclusions. This, of course, is complicated by external factors, such as the development of other media: who, for example, could have predicted with any certainty before their time the popularity of email, texting, search engines, wikis and social networking sites?

Certainly, the BBC's future was secured in the medium term by the renewal of its Charter in January 2007, so despite occasional demands from the commercial sector for parts of its radio operation to be privatised, in UK radio the duopoly looks certain to continue. Yet, a paradox of the duopoly is that until the promises of 4Digital, competition had failed to *stretch* the medium. Despite the faltering progress of DAB, among the huge majority of stations that are now formatted, most are devoted to mainstream pop. Some stations do offer specialist or ethnic music (Classic FM, BBC Asian Network, Sunrise Radio, BBC Radio Cymru, Choice FM), and a relatively tiny number offer continuous speech formats, such as LBC, talkSPORT, City Talk in Liverpool and Talk 107 in Edinburgh (now closed down). Although in the provision of pop music there is a greater diversity than before (yet not, perhaps, quite the diversity that is implied by the proliferation of musical genres: indie, reggae, ragga, house, hard core, trance, garage, hip-hop, jazz-funk, punk, nu-metal, rap-metal, and so on), formats produce radio stations which are individually uniform and predictable in what they provide. This is, of course, their whole point: it is always open to individuals to introduce their own elements of relief or variety by tuning to another channel – but what is largely lost to the continuous listener is the exposure to new radio experiences *by chance*.

Paradoxically, the purchase of Planet Rock, effectively by some of its listeners, may be an isolated phenomenon or one of some significance. Homogeneous output – 'classic' rock music – of appeal to a (male, 40–60 plus) demographic largely underserved by commercial radio, together with intelligent and informed speech content related solely to the musical format, made this digital-only station so compulsive a listen to its audience that during the three months of uncertainty over its future, spontaneous online campaigns were mounted to support it. Such intense support by a newly-formed community of listeners to save the station contrasts markedly with the more usual indifference towards less distinctive music radio stations. Whether listener power extends more often beyond reaching for the on/off button, changing station or using radio's new-found interactivity via the web to customise the medium remains to be seen.

To a greater extent, though, 'national' has largely overshadowed 'local'. Syndication of off-peak and even in some cases peak programmes, 'co-location' of stations for different editorial areas within a single studio building that is outside most of those areas, and increased use of automation are also reducing localness. Some commercial radio owners think their salvation in the ratings war with the BBC lies in attracting nationally-known presenters from television to present syndicated programmes across their networks of local and regional stations, but others perceive localness of content to be their trump card. A single FM network, Radio 4, swims against the current of modern radio in a highly distinctive and significant way (Hendy 2007). In the variety and nature of its output it presupposes a *listener*, not someone for whom radio is merely an accompaniment in the background. Certain of its programme genres paradoxically demonstrate radio's strengths by pushing against its limitations. Drama, which is normally a spectacle, something to be watched, thrives here by stretching the listener's imagination (Crook 1999). Comedy, another genre which normally depends on the visual, must on radio literally live by its wits, survives on its more cerebral ability to create laughter through words alone. What Radio 4 still does is to reclaim for its audiences something of the archaic value and pleasure of listening to intelligent speech.

Mixed programming requires the listener's passive, old-fashioned submission to a selection of material which is made by others who presumably 'know better', the acceptance of a hierarchy of expertise and values which neatly complements the patrician approach of the early BBC. But its ultimate consequence is intellectual enlargement, the exposure to a much wider range of knowledge and experience, and thus the basis for autonomy of another kind. Mixed programming exalts the individual because it assumes that in the potentially infinite nature of their interests, listeners transcend the simple categories of market research: they are human beings even more than they are 'types of consumer'.

Radio may still be the Cinderella medium, because its budgets may be dwarfed by those of other media. Despite the proliferation of networks and stations there are ever more competing media threatening to diminish its audiences. Notwithstanding the uncertainty of its digital future, radio's final paradox provides its greatest strength: much may be achieved on radio at little expense – in the way that radio drama may transport its listeners to distant galaxies without the ubiquitous and expensive computer-generated imaging (CGI) of television and film. One hundred years old, radio still affords much food for thought: its enduring popularity, its relatively recent, tentative steps into the digital domain and its inherent characteristics mean it is still a vibrant, modern and relevant medium. Aptly, one of the latest arrivals on DAB is branded Amazing Radio. Straddling the institutional pillars of public service and commercial competition, having repeatedly adapted to changing contexts and still growing, radio clearly remains full of potential.

Questions

1 Most television commercials make great use of the varied visual resources of the medium. Select a radio commercial which in your opinion effectively compensates for, or even exploits, sound broadcasting's lack of vision, explaining how you think it does so.

2 Listen over a period of time to the output of Classic FM and then attempt some detailed analysis of it. In its presentation and promotion of classical music how far does the station resemble, and how far does it differ from, a conventional pop music station? What can you infer about the identity of its target audience?

3 Listen to a studio discussion programme on the radio and then watch a similar programme on the television. What difference did the visual dimension make? In enabling you to distinguish the speakers more clearly do you feel that it enhanced or detracted from your concentration on, and understanding of, the issues that were being discussed?

Further reading

Chignell, H. (2009) *Key Concepts in Radio Studies*, London: Sage. A welcome addition to the Sage series of 'Key Concepts', this detailed text provides an encyclopaedic approach to the practice and theory of radio.

Briggs, A. (1995) *The History of Broadcasting in the United Kingdom, Volume 5: Competition 1955-1974*, Oxford: Oxford University Press. This final volume of what, despite the title, is almost exclusively a history of the BBC, gives a useful account of the launch of Radio 1 and of the reorganisation of BBC network radio in 1970.

Crisell, A. (ed) (2004) *More Than a Music Box: Radio Cultures and Communities in a Multi-Media World*, Oxford: Berghahn. The distinguished broadcasting historian and theorist, Professor Andrew Crisell, leads and edits a collection of erudite chapters addressing a range of radio issues, from institutions and programming practice to technological development.

Donovan, P. (1992) *The Radio Companion*, London: Grafton. An alphabetical guide to radio from its inception to the beginning of the 1990s. Contains entries on many of the historical matters referred to in this chapter.

Fleming, C. (2002) *The Radio Handbook*, London: Routledge. The second edition of a popular volume first written by P. Wilby and A. Conboy and published in 1994. A celebration of radio in its many forms, with extensive contextualisation from the late 1990s and some interesting case studies.

Reith, J. (1924) *Broadcast Over Britain*, London: Hodder and Stoughton. The BBC's first director-general's first attempt to articulate his philosophy of 'public service' broadcasting.

Scannell, P. (ed) (1991) *Broadcast Talk*, London: Sage Publications. A collection of essays which analyse the character and purposes of talk in radio and television and suggest its overall importance.

The Radio Journal: Studies in Broadcast and Audio Media, Bristol: Intellect Books. The regular journal of the Radio Studies Network (**radiostudiesnetwork.org.uk**), which was founded in the UK but demonstrated openness to radio academics worldwide.

References

Allen, K. (2007) 'Online Advertising Share Overtakes Newspapers', *Guardian*, 28 March.

Baron, M. (1975) *Independent Radio*, Lavenham: Dalton.

Barnard, S. (2000) *Studying Radio*, London: Edward Arnold.

Brook, S. (2008) 'Global Radio Buys GCap for £375m', *Guardian,* 31 March.

Crisell, A. (1994) *Understanding Radio*, 2nd edition, London: Routledge.

Crisell, A. (1997) *An Introductory History of British Broadcasting*, London: Routledge.

Crisell, A. and Starkey, G. (2006) 'News on Local Radio', in R. Franklin (ed) *Local Journalism and Local Media*, London: Routledge.

Crook, T. (1999) *Radio Drama: Theory and Practice*, London: Routledge.

Hendy, D. (2000) *Radio in the Global Age*, Cambridge: Polity.

Hendy, D. (2007) *Life on Air: A History of Radio 4*, Oxford: Oxford University Press.

Horsman, M. (1996) 'On Radio Advertising's Boom', *Independent,* 16 April: (2) 17.

Lewis, P. M. and Booth, J. (1989) *The Invisible Medium: Public, Commercial and Community Radio*, London: Macmillan.

Mackenzie, Y. (2008) 'Digital radio penetration up 1m', *Broadcast,* 23 January, London: EMAP.

McDonnell, J. (1991) *Public Service Broadcasting: A Reader*, London: Routledge.

McNally, P. (2007) 'Bauer buys Emap consumer magazines and radio', pressgazette.co.uk, 7 December, London: Wilmington Business Information.

Peacock, A., *et al.* (1986) *Report of the Committee on Financing the BBC*, Cmnd 9824.

Plunkett, J. (2008) 'Planet Rock: GCap Station Sold to entrepreneur Malcolm Bluemel', *Guardian*, 4 June.

Radio Advertising Bureau website www.rab.co.uk.

Radio Joint Audience Research Limited (2008) Listening via platform – all radio, *RAJAR Quarterly Summary of Radio Listening*, Quarter 4 (www.rajar.co.uk).

Radio Magazine (2008) 'DAB: Running Out of Runway', *Radio Magazine*, 825, 30 January, Rothwell: Goldcrest Broadcasting.

Shingler, M. and Wieringa, C. (1998) *On Air: Methods and Meanings of Radio*, London: Edward Arnold.

Starkey, G. (2003) 'Are Radio Audiences Choosing to Reject Greater Choice?', in S. Ralph, C. Lees and H. Manchester (eds) *Diversity or Anarchy?* Luton: University of Luton Press.

Starkey, G. (2004a) *Radio in Context*, London: Palgrave.

Starkey, G. (2004b) 'BBC Radio 5 Live: Extending Choice Through "Radio Bloke?"', in A. Crisell (ed) *More Than a Music Box: Radio Cultures and Communities in a Multi-Media World*, Oxford: Berghahn.

Starkey, G. (2007) *Balance and Bias in Journalism: Representation, Regulation and Democracy*, London: Palgrave.

12

Television

Dorothy Hobson

Chapter overview

This chapter will look at the medium of television and attempt to explain key aspects which are integral to an understanding of the subject as it is currently developing, examining various elements which are distinct but inextricably linked. In this chapter I aim to explain the relationship between television as an industry, through its programmes and with its audience, and its importance as a focus for academic study.

What is television?

Television is an all embracing word which covers both the industry which produces the programmes and the programmes themselves. By 2012 when the UK digital switchover is complete, there will be a major change in the sets on which British viewers receive programmes. All television receivers in Britain will need to be replaced or be fitted with a set-top box or viewers will need to subscribe to a satellite or cable provider or else they will receive no signal at all. Lifestyle choices will also determine which sets viewers purchase for their homes. The existing analogue signals will be no more: British viewers will be watching television on computers, tiny mobile phones, public screens, and on whatever amazing television sets new technology might offer us in the next phase of its unrelenting development.

Studying television involves a multitude of different elements which all feed into the subject: making the connections between the different parts will result in a better understanding of the whole. Understanding television is an important part of an understanding of society and of the representations and ideologies which reflect and shape beliefs and cultures. Over 50 million people watch and appreciate television in the UK without studying it from an academic perspective and in this chapter I will aim to explain the relationship between television as an industry, through its programmes and with its audience, and its importance as a focus for academic study.

While this chapter will concentrate on the current state of television, it is perhaps useful to take a rapid journey through the development of television in the UK until it reached the position it occupies in the present. Below I have discussed elements which I think are relevant and important at this time in studying television; in the end, of course, the choices of specific factors which relate to the development of television are partly subjective. The suggestions for further reading that are included with all contributions to this volume will, in this case, cover additional perspectives, discussions and theories which can be related to the overall topic for future work.

A 20th century development

Nowadays it might be hard to imagine a world without any form of media except for newspapers, journals, cinema and the telegram; yet in the early 20th century this was all that was available. Telecommunications had been vital during World War One and when the war was over, at the beginning of the 1920s, the wireless manufacturers were left with the equipment that they had developed and for which there was a danger that there would be no use. The beginning of the pattern of the development of technology 'in search of products to distribute' came from that time. The development of broadcasting was relatively slow in the UK and each new channel was preceded by a government committee to decide whether introducing it was in the public interest. A brief account of the development of the UK channels is as follows:

- 1936: BBC Television begins broadcasting from Alexandra Palace to the London area.
- 1955: ITV starts broadcasting in the London area. BBC TV reaches the East and Northern Ireland: 95 per cent of the UK can now receive television.
- 1964: BBC2 launches.
- 1982: Channel 4 begins broadcasting.
- 1983: BBC Breakfast Time starts; 15 days later a new ITV company, TV-am, begins to broadcast a breakfast programme.
- 1990: April – Launch of British Satellite Broadcasting; 1 November The Broadcasting Act; 2 November Sky TV and BSB merge to form British Sky Broadcasting (BSkyB).
- 1997: March – Channel 5 goes on the air.

(*Royal Television Society Handbook* 2002–3)

This is a very broad outline of the developments and the length of time which it took for British television to have five channels and two breakfast-time services. In the past 10 years, however, the number of channels and the provision of programmes have exploded until there are now hundreds of channels all competing for viewers.

As well as the explosion of channels there has also been an explosion of means of watching programmes and although in the past it could be argued that these were just alternative means of distributing material, the big change is that now there is a change in provision of content and programmes which may be watched on many different outlets. It is important to differentiate between the programmes which are provided by professional programme-makers and the content made and sent out by individuals who have access to the new social networks such as MySpace and YouTube which are transmitted usually via the internet. The internet marks a significant change because these new offerings are part of what television has to compete with for the time and attention of its viewers.

The rest of this chapter will concentrate on changes which have happened in the past 20 years in the UK as a result of yet another Broadcasting Act, which had profound effects on broadcasting.

The 1990 Broadcasting Act

As the Conservative government of Mrs Thatcher continued its pursuit of deregulation across many public institutions in the 1980s, broadcasting did not escape her attention. The 1990 Broadcasting Act (HMSO 1990) changed the ecology of broadcasting in Britain. The main purpose of the Act was to bring in deregulation of broadcasting and to allow for the expansion of satellite and cable broadcasting. This it achieved. It also changed the way that television and radio was regulated as the new regulatory body, the ITC (Independent Television Commission) took over from the IBA (Independent Broadcasting Authority). The most significant change in its duties was that it regulated *after* the event, so although companies could be fined and censured for breaking the codes of practice, they did not have to submit programmes to any form of scrutiny or control before transmission. It can be argued that this effectively began the downward spiral in terms of the protection of viewers from the over-enthusiasm or commercially driven exuberance which might tempt broadcasters to gain higher audience figures for a programme. That is, broadcasters would see censure or fining after the event to be worth the risk.

Deregulation also affected the development of programmes and genres, the methods of production, in the process changing the whole nature of television in Britain. The 1980s might be seen as the halcyon days of television with the coming of Channel 4 and the expansion of innovative programmes across all four terrestrial channels. However, this was a short-lived period and the changes which were to occur as a result of the 1990 Broadcasting Act had results which were not universally envisaged. The Act heralded a huge expansion of channels and changes in the broadcasting landscape, both in the number of channels and their blatant commercialism. While being designated as the legislation which brought in deregulation and offered extended choice to viewers, in fact, the Act's effect was crucial in stifling the expansion of the creative development of existing channels. For the overall effect on creativity was that the expansion of choice split the audience and ensured that the race towards commercially driven ratings-seeking programmes became the dominant trend of television.

The move towards the popular became the rationale of the commercially driven terrestrial channels. In order to compete with the unfettered popular programming available across the range of satellite channels, it was necessary for terrestrial channels especially to adapt their programming strategies to try to keep their audiences. Whatever they might have aspired to achieve, the commercial imperatives played a major part in their future plans. For instance, most sport which had been free to air was lost to the subscription channel, Sky, and there was also a diminution of certain genres. As an example, whereas there has been a wide range of documentaries throughout the history of broadcasting, this genre changed its character and 'Popular Factual' or 'Contemporary Factual' became the genres of choice, meaning that the programme makers stopped making old-style diverse documentaries. Some developments were productive, however, with the emergence of new hybrid genres.

In 2003 the new multi-purpose regulator Ofcom was brought in as a result of the Communications Act. Ofcom controls television, radio, telephone and telecommunications in the UK; the new basis for regulation centres on the concept of viewers as consumers and citizens. The latters' rights had to be protected as citizens, but so did the commercial rights of the providers. The regulation from Ofcom was designed to take place 'after the event', but their control of broadcasting was greater than that of the ITC, with the main sanctions being financial fines once complaints had been investigated (see below). Ofcom's website provides a wealth of information which is invaluable in understanding these elements of television. They do not just regulate – they also conduct research on many aspects of television which have an influence on policy and debate (www.ofcom.co.uk).

Television now – programmes: content is king

While channels and platforms (televisions, internet, mobile devices, etc.) proliferate for the public it is content which determines what viewers think of the services. Arguably the most important aspect of television, both to audiences and broadcasters, is the set of programmes available to view. Audiences have always watched programmes rather than channels and now, with the multiplicity of means of distribution and viewing, this is even more evident. The expansion of satellite channels referred to above resulted in changes in programme production and development of new forms. However, some of the long established genres remain at the top of the viewing figures across the main popular channels. These are the creative gems which broadcasters need to maintain their positions, in order to be commercially viable and fulfil the public service requirements that are demanded by the Royal Charter (in the case of the BBC). It is worth making a note of those genres now.

Drama, a perennial genre on UK television

Soap operas remain the top rated programmes on UK television with *EastEnders* (1985, BBC), *Coronation Street* (1960, ITV), and *Emmerdale* (1989, Yorkshire Television for ITV; formerly *Emmerdale Farm* (1972–89) attracting viewers on a regular basis for BBC1 and ITV. Channel 5 recently paid an astonishing £300 million to show the Australian soap opera *Neighbours* (1985, Fremantle Media for BBC and Five)*;* much more than the BBC were prepared to pay to continue to air the series. Soap operas are essential for broadcasters to retain audiences both for public service and commercial value (Hobson 2003). Popular series like *Casualty* (1986, BBC), *Holby City* (1999, BBC), *Dr. Who* (2005, BBC), *Robin Hood* (2006, BBC), *and Heartbeat* (1992, Yorkshire Television for ITV) are part of the strong drama genre which both remained stable and, at the same time, innovative and from which developed new hybrid programmes like *Doctors* (2000, BBC), combining the elements of medical, police and serial drama into a new daytime form. Classic serials including the nightly *Little Dorrit* (2008, BBC) and *Cranford* (2007, BBC) were examples of high quality public service broadcasting from the BBC. The innovative new drama *Life on Mars* (2006, BBC) showing the police force exhibiting politically incorrect behaviour in the year 1973, was a great success both in terms of audience figures, critical acclaim and industry recognised awards. Across the board drama remains one of the major achievements of British television and an attraction for audiences.

Lifestyle

Lifestyle programming developed from the 1980s with a range spanning 'makeover programmes' for houses and gardens, to programmes which were about personal appearance and personal lives. However the genre developed fully in the late 1980s and progressed to its current height through the 1990s. Series which pointed out the faults of participants and told them how to improve, and sometimes paid for that improvement, became the staple diet across channels. Viewers were told *How to Look Good Naked* (2006, Maverick Television for Channel 4), how to look *10 Years Younger* (2004, Maverick Television for Channel 4), or that *You Are What You Eat* (2004–07, Celador for Channel 4); these were accompanied by programmes which are much more extreme and didactic in terms of how to improve various aspects of people's lives. Other programmes patronised hapless and harassed parents by telling them how to look after their children, and even in the sensitive area of child rearing there were examples of programmes which were worse than patronising; their didactic attitudes could be seen as verging on the dangerous (see Chapter 33). It could also be asked of any programme which showed children behaving in a way that was deemed out of control, who was protecting the children from being shown on television and being seen by millions of people? (See Lury 2009.)

At a much more acceptable level, *Jamie's School Dinners* (2005, Fresh One for Channel 4) achieved a level of public service by teaching the nation what dangerous junk food their children had been eating in schools as the eponymous TV chef, Jamie Oliver, set out to change eating habits and inspire the provision of food which was healthier for children. As he informed government of the harm that unhealthy food was causing to children, Jamie Oliver provided an example of responsible and creative programming. Lifestyle in some cases became the new public service but in other cases it appeared voyeuristic and cruel. Clearly, there are an array of views on the positive and negative aspects of lifestyle television (Palmer 2008).

Reality TV

The fastest growing genre in television over the past few years has been that of Reality TV. Hybridism is rampant in the genre. What began as a genre derived from 'fly-on-the-wall' documentaries and which followed police or other emergency services as they pursued their everyday jobs, developed into programmes made from emergency services' own footage. The hybrids of the form take the best elements from different genres and develop new programmes which combine entertainment, education and information. One form involves round-the-clock observation of the interaction of individuals (sometimes 'celebrities') in a confined environment where they are compelled to carry out daily tasks (see discussion of *Big Brother*, below). One of the most popular variants of Reality TV has been the entertainment reality shows like *I'd Do Anything* (2008, BBC), *The X Factor* (2004, Talkback Thames and SYCOTV for ITV), *Britain's Got Talent* (2007, ITV), which give opportunities to talented people who might not otherwise be able to be seen by producers and directors. Some people put themselves forward who have no obvious talent and that of course, adds to the entertainment value of the programme; but the *aim* of this variant of the Reality TV show, supposedly, is *not* to humiliate the participants. In the end, winners emerge who might end up making a career in their chosen occupations; even those who do not win are often given other opportunities in their chosen field. While it is easy to be critical of these programmes it is again necessary to differentiate between those which are cruel and voyeuristic and those which have some point to them other than the humiliation of contestants and participants.

There is nothing wrong with popular programming, of course; indeed it is the lifeblood of television; but the quality within genres and programmes always needs to be considered when criticising television. Being able to discern the quality from ill-judged or poor quality programmes which are designed to merely fill slots in the TV schedules is an important critical faculty. Without dismissing popular genres, the benefits of studying television as an academic discipline should enable you to differentiate and discriminate between the good and the indifferent. That is, where creativity has been facilitated by the medium and where it has been curtailed, impeded or is absent.

Talent – writers and performers

Talent is also very important to the industry, as the cases of a writer like Russell T. Davies, who created the current incarnation of *Dr. Who* or the writer Andrew Davis who has adapted many classic serials to successful television scripts, clearly demonstrate. Broadcasters have to pay for the talented people they use to gain audiences but sometimes just as important is the fact that they prevent other channels from having them. Presenters are both poached by, and move between, channels. The chat show host Paul O'Grady chose to move from ITV in 2005 with his previous show *The Paul O'Grady Show* (2004–05, Granada for ITV) renamed *The New Paul O'Grady Show* (2005, Olga Television for Channel 4) which has successfully brought in good audiences and won awards in its new incarnation on Channel 4 since it began transmissions in 2006. Successful and popular presenters, actors and production companies are the fuel which drives the industry in its attempt to reach and please audiences. Sometimes presenters or performers are paid large sums of money to move to a rival channel and are then locked in by so-called golden handcuffs, with little to do but without the freedom to appear on other channels. Producers want to use their talent, but if they cannot find the right vehicle for them, they would rather that the talent did nothing instead of appearing on another channel attracting viewers. Whatever their fee it is the performers who attract audiences and the writers and producers who can create and devise successful formats across the range of genres who are the most valuable asset for broadcasters. They, together with the most successful programmes, are what achieve the successes which television needs to compete with other media and other providers.

The growth of 'the ordinary' and the death of serious programming

More by accident than design there was a development in programming which had repercussions across the whole of television. This was the growth of the 'ordinary' and the inclusion of so-called 'ordinary' people in all aspects of television. The trend came from perfectly laudable beginnings. Since the 1980s there had been a call from outside pressure groups to include so-called 'ordinary people' in television programmes. The call was for women, the working classes, gays and lesbians, ethnic minorities who had previously been denied access to the screen, to be allowed a voice. Indeed this was one of the reasons for the creation of Channel 4 (Lambert 1982; Hobson 2003). Some of those who were previously denied access, are now represented and appear on television; but the so-called ordinary people have not become major participants in television programmes.

In order to be a participant in any programme, it is usually necessary to be *extra-ordinary* and to have some 'over the top' personality traits. It is open to discussion whether television has really become more democratic in its choice of participants. In fact, ordinary people have not become part of the grammar of television. However, notions of ordinariness have spread to so-called celebrities or professional presenters who now are in programmes trying to show how they can do other things, besides those they are known for, or not (as the case may be). Their dancing and skating prowess is displayed in *Strictly Come Dancing* (2004, BBC) and *Dancing on Ice* (2007, ITV) and these are programmes which draw huge audiences on a regular basis. Critics may deplore the genres but the hybridity of the ordinary and celebrity and minor achievements from struggling performers, is a success with audiences. Of course, only the programmes which would give ordinary people the opportunity to show and develop their talents can really be seen as progressive in terms of the democratisation of television which was envisaged with the expansion of channels (Evans and Hesmondhalgh 2005; Holmes and Jermyn 2003; Hill 2005, 2007).

Composition of the industry

Television has changed in the UK, both in the way it is viewed and the number of channels which now exist. BBC, ITV, Channel 4 and 5 all have extra digital channels and an ever increasing number of satellite channels. The provision of programmes has also changed, with the growth of independent production being a major development since the birth of Channel 4. However, all is not as might have been expected when Channel 4 began and independent production became a major part of British television.

While the idea was that many new television companies would emerge to service the channel, in fact the independent sector has gone through various stages and has not resulted in the massive growth which was hoped for. Many of the companies which were the most successful have formed themselves into the so-called 'super-indies' or acquisitors such as IMG Media, EndemolUK, Shine and the RDF Media Group. They have taken over a number of smaller companies, as have some of the broadcasters. New companies are formed and develop each year. Some are successful but according to the television industry journal *Broadcast* (Anon. 2003: 23), 'It's the consolidators that are growing. For the first time, their combined turnovers are more than the combined incomes of the non-acquired indies.' It is a complicated story and although new indies emerge and are successful every year, they lead a very precarious life, as they are always seeking new commissions to keep the businesses going. However, the growth of independent production has changed the nature of commissioning by broadcasters. Independent producers now compete and have their own allocated percentages of commissions by broadcasters.

Recent events: 2007 a remarkable year

In the past two years there have been some serious issues relating to issues of governance and accountability across a range of terrestrial broadcasters in the UK. At the beginning of 2007 no one could have envisaged the traumas which were to beset British television. Although they affected all of the channels and they were on the surface not connected, there was a theme which underlaid many of the problems and which was perhaps indicative of a moment of coalescence of changes which had taken place over the years since the 1990 Broadcasting Act. The seemingly disparate incidents combined to make a difficult year across British broadcasting. Some incidents were directly related to programmes, others were connected to voting by the public in different competitions. These incidents have been covered at length because they have, at one level, dominated the thinking about television although, at another, they are just part of the ongoing incidents which have been part of the immediate recent history of television.

Channel 4 and *Celebrity Big Brother* – racism and bullying

If one programme can be seen to epitomise the arguments about the popular, the extra-ordinary and the commercialisation of television, it is the Channel 4 programme *Big Brother*. Launched in 2000 it became the flagship programme of the channel. The format of the show is that 12 strangers are locked in a house for what began as a period of nine weeks – this has extended with every series in an attempt to maximise the audience. They are observed by hidden cameras and are asked to perform tasks and undergo ritual humiliation at the hands of Big Brother, that is, the Big Brother producers. Each week someone is voted out until the winner emerges at the end of the series. While the series began with contestants who simply did not know what was likely to happen to them, over the years producers have selected contestants who are perceived to have extra-ordinary, flamboyant and sometimes deliberately outrageous personalities. Such a precedent of 'extra-ordinariness' was already set by the majority of the contestants chosen for the TV dating programme that started in the 1980s, *Blind Date* (1985). Yet *Big Brother* contestants demonstrate an even more flamboyant collusion in their own sense of display and humiliation for the opportunity to appear on television.

From the outset, *Big Brother* gained a huge audience in Channel 4 terms and heralded the beginning of a number of similar Reality TV shows across television. As well as the ordinary *Big Brother*, the channel launched a celebrity edition, where minor or nearly forgotten celebrities revealed their vulnerability and 'ordinariness'. In January 2007 Channel 4 launched its latest *Celebrity Big Brother* and nine celebrities entered the Big Brother House. The programme began slowly as the contestants started to get to know each other. Ratings were not high. On the third night Jade Goody, a previous contestant on the main *Big Brother* show in 2003, entered the house as a surprise guest with her boyfriend Jack and her mother Jackiey, someone with no claim to celebrity except that she was the mother of Jade.

Jade's own status is an example of the cult of celebrity which has dominated the television industry during the last decade. Although she did not win the series when she first appeared she was one of the first people to achieve a high profile and she did develop herself into a celebrity who opened a beauty salon and produced a perfume. Well aided by the tabloid press and television programmes she became a successful business woman but retained her pre-*Big Brother* persona which belied her obvious drive and talent for self promotion. During her own appearance in *Big Brother* in 2003 the production company revealed their interest in humiliation and showed Jade stripping naked in a card game. Cruelty has been endemic in the series and it was not surprising that it jumped up and shocked viewers in the fated 2007 series.

A précis of the events is as follows (see Hobson 2007: 202–5 for a fuller version). Jade, her mother (until she was quickly evicted by the public vote) and two other housemates, Jo O'Mara and Danielle Lloyd, engaged in acts of bullying using racist terms to attack and humiliate another inmate, the Bollywood actress, Shilpa Shetty. Besides calling her names, such as 'the Indian' and 'Mrs Poppadom', giggling and discussing imagined eating habits which were without question fuelled by ignorant racist feelings, they also, crucially, ignored her. The channel overlooked this behaviour, as did the production company Endemol, and it was not until the public voiced their disgust to Ofcom that action was taken. The press caught the mood and the story became part of the media circus which surrounds Reality TV when it crosses its self-imposed boundaries. Some 46,000 people complained to Ofcom and ratings climbed to 5.7 million viewers by 20 January (*The Today Programme*, BBC Radio 4, 20 January 2007). This incident snowballed with 300 articles published in the UK, 1200 English language websites covering it, 3900 around the world, and the then Chancellor of the Exchequer Gordon Brown having to answer questions about the event as he visited India and met with mass demonstrations and national offence at the treatment of Shetty and the perceived national insult which was perpetrated against her.

The programme continued and the contestants were spoken to by the channel; when they were voted out they faced the wrath of the British press and public and their own public humiliation. The channel and Ofcom meanwhile put into place their own enquiries and discussed whether or not they should have intervened and whether there had been racism. These were embarrassing and futile discussions because the behaviour was clearly unacceptable and that it was allowed to continue was negligent. It brought into focus the gap between the broadcasters and programme-makers and their viewers. Whilst the viewers knew what was wrong with the programme, the regulator and the broadcaster needed to discuss and consider the matter before recognising the obvious.

Phone-ins and problems of trust

Channel 4 was still investigating the *Celebrity Big Brother* affairs when they encountered a new problem. Their tea-time magazine programme *Richard and Judy* had an item entitled *You Say We Pay* in which viewers rang a dedicated line with high call charges to be selected to compete in a competition that day. The problem arose when it was discovered that even after contestants had been selected for a particular day, the 'would-be' contestants would still be allowed to phone in and their money would still go on being taken. Again Ofcom was alerted and another investigation was put in place.

Soon, other channels began to find out that they too had problems with their 'phone-in' programmes. GMTV and ITV, for instance, had also invited viewers to phone a premium phone number to take part in competitions, leaving the lines open after the chosen viewer had been selected. Ofcom fined GMTV an unprecedented £2 million and criticised them for 'gross negligence'. GMTV was making 35–40 per cent of its annual profits from the operation of its competitions and they were accused of paying comparatively little attention to their compliance responsibilities (Anon. 2003). The chief executive of GMTV, Paul Corley, resigned before the fine was imposed and the channel took full responsibility for the breaches.

ITV, too, was found to have not overseen its voting process appropriately in some of its most popular programmes, including the flagship entertainment shows fronted by Ant and Dec. It was fined £6 million for serious breaches of the Broadcasting Code.

Questions of trust

2008 began for the BBC with the inauguration of a new system of management and control. Out went the Board of Governors, substituted by the newly formed BBC Trust with responsibility for the governance of the BBC, which immediately encountered a new set of problems. The most serious of these was the so-called 'Queensgate Affair', concerning a programme about a year in the life of Her Majesty the Queen made by an independent production company. A trailer of the programme created for a press launch, which had been edited to show the Queen apparently leaving her photographic session looking angry, was the item that raised concerns. If the programme had been made in-house at the BBC, then it is most unlikely that it would have been edited in the way it was, as the editor would have questioned why the producer was letting the edited programme give a misleading impression. In short, it can be assumed that a hierarchy of control would have been in place. The trailer was deliberately edited to appear as if the Queen was rather annoyed with the behaviour of the photographer, rather than, as was actually the case, she was walking in at a busy pace to get on with the session. The editing could be seen as a breach of film-making integrity. However, it also looked as though it was designed to give the programme a greater publicity edge, despite its mendacity.

The consequences were serious and an investigation conducted by Will Wyatt, a previous managing director of the BBC, resulted in a confidential report into the affair identifying clearly what had happened. It called for BBC staff to work 'collaboratively with independents to bring the best possible programmes to the screen and to promote them effectively and honestly' (Wyatt 2007: 21). The incident resulted in the resignation of Stephen Lambert, the executive in charge at RDF, someone who had spent most of his working life as a respected and award winning BBC documentary producer. Peter Fincham, controller of BBC1 also resigned but within a few months was appointed to the top job of director of television at ITV.

Events and what they tell us about the medium of television

The serious financial and ethical issues which were brought to light during 2007 might have come as a surprise to those outside the television industry, but it is possible to see them as a result of cumulative changes which had taken place over the preceding years both in the methods of television production and in the fight for television viewers. The need for television to attract viewers to different programmes and channels led to the inclusion of simplistic competitions within programmes where viewers phoned in to register to take part. Little skill was required but large revenues were accrued for the broadcasters. This was hardly at the forefront of creativity and it is ironic that it was because of these pathetic competitions that companies lost their credibility with viewers and incurred the wrath of the press and the regulators. Some of these competitions were even outside the immediate control of the television companies because they were operated by outside contractors. However, there were people within the broadcasting organisations who were theoretically responsible for ensuring that the competitions were run with integrity; these were the ones who were ultimately deemed responsible.

Loosening and losing control

One of the effects of the major expansion of provision of content to embrace a large percentage of programmes from independent production companies and outside companies running the phone-in competitions was loss of control by the broadcasters. This was inevitable. The philosophical basis on which Channel 4 was founded was that the channel would act as a broadcaster/publisher whose programmes were the editorial responsibility of the companies who made them. Jeremy Isaacs, first director of Channel 4, knew that this changed the nature of broadcasting but did not see it as a problem. In 1987 when talking to me about the fact that the chief executive of a broadcaster no longer had to be responsible for everyone and everything that was shown on their channel (Hobson 2007:180), he claimed that when one publishes other people's work, one cannot be fully responsible for it. Enabling many voices to speak means that the broadcaster cannot be fully in control of every programme. While Isaacs was referring to the editorial content of programmes, it has become obvious that one of the problems which has beset television over the last year or two has been the loss of control of both editorial and peripheral issues. The loosening and losing of control over independent production is inevitable once programmes move outside the command and, more importantly, the culture of the broadcasting institutions. It is one of the major areas where broadcasters have had to tighten their regulations. And yet the whole point of independent production would seem to be to have programmes which are not controlled by the broadcasters. It is a dilemma for television and this dilemma must inform our understanding of how the medium operates in the UK today. It is also a dilemma of control and governance which now has to be confronted and has to be satisfied by regulators and broadcasters.

The future is digital – content and distribution

These lapses in the relationship of broadcasters with viewers were regrettable and serious. However, the real issues of television are the provision of programmes and the work which broadcasters have to do to attract, retain and increase their audiences. One of the major issues which has affected the provision of television over the past few years has been the means of delivery, and as technology has revolutionised the industry, so programmes have all become subject to different modes of delivery. While the satellite channels from Sky and other providers are available by subscription, the terrestrial channels have also expanded their digital channels and, in fact, they provide expanded digital and high definition services via FreeSat.

Terrestrial channels have suffered badly from the expansion of satellite provision but the explosion of channels enabled by the 1990 Broadcasting Act means it is important to fully understand the way that audiences view television in Great Britain. While we have noted that there are no longer viewing figures for individual programmes in the 17 and 18 million region like in the past (think of soap operas in the 1980s), there is an enduring myth that satellite television has stolen the whole audience. The cumulative effect of the satellite channels has made great dents into the figures for terrestrial channels, but individual viewing figures for satellite channels are very small. In fact, the terrestrial channels are still the most viewed of all, their own digital channels being the most successful in the digital world.

As the means of distribution of television programmes proliferates, the future of the medium is a matter of great concern to broadcasters. They have embraced all the available technological means to deliver programmes to their audiences and to meet the needs and expectations of their viewers. They have had important ethical issues to deal with and need to keep their heads and maintain what is unique about their programming. The five terrestrial broadcasters are the bedrock of British television, underpinned by the BBC and its licence fee. In order to maintain the strength of the industry these are seen as the foundations of the television system which need to be protected and preserved.

Questions

1 What has the audience lost in the expansion of channels and means of distribution? What has it gained? Could things have been done differently? Have commercial interests resulted in viewers losing some programmes or genres?

2 Do you think that questions of trust are as important to viewers as the regulator Ofcom and the broadcasters think is the case? If so, consider why do you think this. If not, what do you think are the most important issues for audiences?

3 As broadcasters work to maintain their audiences they are aware that their audiences will also watch content on sources other than the television set. How do you think viewing will be take place in the next 10 years? Try to think of the different ways that different members of the audience will choose to watch. Will the mobile phone ever supersede the 50-inch flat screen as the main method of viewing television programmes in the future?

Further reading

Newcomb, H. (ed.) (2006) *Television: The Critical View*, 6th edition, New York: Oxford University Press. Regularly updated collection containing some classic essays and sections on production contexts, television texts and reception contexts.

Olsson, J. and Spigel, L. (eds) (2005) *Television after TV: Essays on a Medium in Transition*, Chapel Hill: Duke University Press. Collection of essays by some of the leading analysts of contemporary television.

Williams, R. (1974) *Television: Technology and Cultural Form*, Glasgow: Fontana. Still one of the best books on the medium of television despite its brevity and age. Many of the features of television it discusses have either come to pass or promise to come to pass.

Useful trade journals

Broadcast, EMAP Communications, London – weekly.

Television – Journal of the Royal Television Society, London – monthly.

Websites

www.bbc.co.uk

www.itv.com

www.channel4.co.uk

www.fivetv

www.ofcom.org.uk

www.barb.com

References

Anon. (2003) *The Annual Survey of the UK's Independent TV Producers, Broadcast*, 14 March 2008.

Evans, J. and Hesmondhalgh, D. (2005) *Understanding Media: Inside Celebrity*, Open University: Berkshire.

HMSO (1990) *Broadcasting Act*, London: HMSO.

Hill, A. (2005) *Reality TV: Audiences and Popular Factual Television*, Abingdon: Routledge.

Hill, A. (2007) *Restyling Factual TV: Audiences and News, Documentary and Reality Genres*, Abingdon: Routledge.

Hobson D. (2003) *Soap Opera*, Cambridge: Polity.

Hobson, D. (2007) *Channel 4: The Early Years and the Jeremy Isaacs Legacy*, London: I. B. Tauris.

Holmes, S. and Jermyn, D. (eds) (2004) *Understanding Reality Television*, Abingdon: Routledge.

Lambert, S. (1982) *Channel 4: Television with a Difference?*, London: BFI.

Lury, K. (2009) '"For Crying Out Loud": The Repression of the Child's Subjectivity in *The House of Tiny Tearaways*', *Semiotica*, 173 (1–4): 491–507.

Palmer, G. (ed) (2008) *Exposing Lifestyle Television*, Hampshire: Ashgate.

Royal Television Society (2002) *Royal Television Society Handbook 2002-3*, London: Royal Television Society.

Wyatt, W. (2007) *Investigation into 'A Year with the Queen'*, BBC Internal Document, London: BBC.

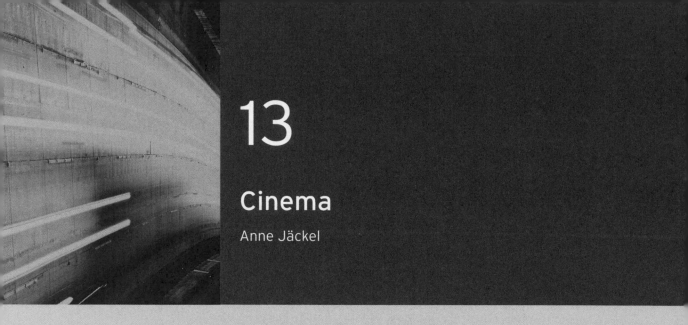

13

Cinema

Anne Jäckel

Chapter overview

The chapter examines the role played by Europe-wide and national funding institutions in film production, distribution and exhibition in Europe. State aid remains at the core of film production in the European Union. Benefiting from a strong regulatory framework and a comprehensive support system, France has consistently been the only European country that could claim both a prolific film industry and a strong film culture. Along with the French cinema industry, the chapter looks at some of the strategies adopted by other European film industries/players in order to compete in the global and rapidly changing audiovisual environment.

Introduction

European cinema has been defined and promoted in terms of 'art cinema' and of 'auteur cinema'. It is in Europe that cinema was first elevated to an art form and that a strong tradition of film culture has developed and flourished through specific art movements whether international (avant-garde, surrealism) or national (Soviet cinema, German expressionism, the British documentary movement, Italian neo-realism, the French and Czech new waves). Gaining critical recognition from film journals, theoreticians and intellectuals in the 1960s, the tradition of 'auteur cinema' – often sanctioned by national/regional funding agencies – has served the national cinemas of Europe well. Even though in its country of origin, 'auteur cinema' is likely to be more opposed to its national commercial cinema than it is to Hollywood films, on the international scene, reputed film directors such as Ingmar Bergman, Federico Fellini, François Truffaut or more recently Lars von Trier and Pedro Almadovar have brought status and prestige to – and become icons of – their national cinema. As European co-productions almost became the norm, by the mid-1990s Ginette Vincendeau (1995: xiv) could write 'film directors like [the late] Kieslowski and Wim Wenders have almost ceased to be Polish or German, and become "European"'.

It has been argued that what had united the European film industries in the 1980s and early 1990s was not a common identity but a 'shared situation and set of problems which certain forms of European collaboration [might] help alleviate' (Hill 1994: 67). Such collaboration has been fostered by the European and pan-European programmes MEDIA and Eurimages.

Public support for cinema in Europe

European and pan-European Funds

In the late 1980s, two major funding initiatives were set up at the European level to help the film industry: MEDIA (Measures to Encourage the Development of the Audio-visual Industry) under the aegis of the European Community, and the Council of Europe's Fund, Eurimages. While MEDIA was set up to provide aid and encourage initiatives designed to fulfil the needs of the entire audio-visual sector, Eurimages is a pan-European fund supporting (fiction and documentary) film co-productions and their distribution. From a pilot scheme of 10 projects in 1988 (ranging from script-writing to the creation of the European Film Academy), MEDIA grew into fully fledged Community programmes under the names of MEDIA 92, MEDIA II (1996–2000) and MEDIA Plus (2000–06). MEDIA's aim is to create 'cross-borders synergies' by establishing networks of cooperation among professionals. The numerous initiatives developed over the years (e.g. for research and development, finance, training, production, distribution and the encouragement of minority languages) have been regularly trimmed down and/or replaced by new ones designed to meet the new challenges facing the audio-visual industries.

Eurimages was developed within the Council of Europe's cultural programme with the remit to support 'works which uphold the values that are part and parcel of the European identity'. Initially, the Fund supported only low- and medium-budget films co-produced between partners from three member states. In 1998, it was open to bi-partite films.

Regularly assessed and scrutinised, MEDIA and Eurimages endorsed a more commercial approach to the film industry in the late 1990s. For example, MEDIA now supports production companies to develop a slate of films rather than a single project and stresses the importance of a business plan. Multilateral arrangements have been encouraged by both MEDIA and Eurimages and the growth of co-productions involving European partners (from 144 in 1990 to 369 in 2007 in an enlarged Europe) has largely been responsible for the upward path taken by European productions since the early 1990s. Two thirds of MEDIA-supported projects originate from 'countries with low audio-visual capacity' (MEDIA Desk France 2007) where the likelihood of an indigenous film making a profit at home is small. It is not only for Greek, Portuguese, Belgian or Scandinavian film-makers that co-production has become a way of life. Almost half of Romanian films made since 2000 are co-produced with other European partners.

It has been estimated that each euro from the MEDIA budget attracts six euros of private investment in the audio-visual industry (MEDIA Desk France, 2007). Between 2001 and 2006, MEDIA Plus and MEDIA Training supported more than 8000 projects representing an investment of €500 million (ibid.). Since its establishment, Eurimages has supported 1165 co-productions for a total amount of just under €343 million. In 2006, a report on the Czech Republic Cinematography quoted the country's contribution to Eurimages at €186,000 and the total benefit for the Czech Republic at €308,000. The author of the report contended that 'the importance of Eurimages transcend[ed] mere financial assistance; the fund helps our filmmakers overcome the limits of the domestic market, establish necessary contacts, acquire know-how and get their films into foreign distribution networks' (Ministry of Culture of the Czech Republic 2006: 11).

Whether one looks at the thousands of projects and hundreds of networks they have helped set up, the number of producers and distributors they have encouraged or the range of ventures supported (fiction, animation and documentary films, festivals, dubbing and subtitling, etc.), the results are extremely valuable. The increasing number of applications to the funds as well as the number of states willing to become members represent another measurement of their success. Eurimages membership has grown from the original 12 founding member states to 33 in 2007, 14 of which are from the former eastern bloc. (The UK briefly joined in 1993 and withdrew in 1995.)

Europa Cinemas

Almost half the films produced in Europe today are shown outside their country of origin with the support of the European Union programme (MEDIA Desk UK, 2007). Funded under the MEDIA programme, Eurimages and France's Ministry of Foreign Affairs, Europa Cinemas, has become the prime international network of cinemas (677 cinemas housing 1682 screens in 386 cities in 44 countries, in 2007).

North-South relations have also developed with the creation of Euromed Audiovisuel and Africa Cinemas. (Europa Cinemas operates Euromed, a Mediterranean network supporting exhibitors, distributors and festival directors in 12 Mediterranean countries, as well as Africa Cinemas – in collaboration with various French agencies – to facilitate the circulation of African films in Africa.)

Many of the films supported by MEDIA and/or Eurimages have been invited to and received awards at the major international film festivals (Cannes, Berlin, Karlovy Vary, Venice, San Sebastian). Award-winners include Luc and Jean-Pierre Dardenne's *La Promesse* (1996), Danis Tanovic's *No Man's Land* (2002), Hany Abu-Assad's *Paradise Now* (2005) and Cristian Nemescu's *California Dreamin'* (2006). However, outside the festival and the art-house circuits, theatrical release continues to be a major problem for European film.

Distribution: a new priority

The network of cinemas created by Europa Cinemas is impressive but, with the exception of British and other European English-language films (e.g. *The Queen, Goya's*

Ghosts) and a small number of non-English language large-budget co-productions (*Astérix et Obélix: Mission Cléopâtre*), non-national European films continue to find it difficult to cross their national borders on the large screen. US-financed heavily promoted blockbusters (*The Pirates of the Caribbean* films, the *Harry Potter* films, *The Da Vinci Code*, etc.) continue to dominate European as well as global box office. Occasionally, local films – particularly comedies – manage to enter the top 10 films in their country of origin (e.g. in 2006, *Les Bronzés 3* in France, *Das Parfum* in Germany and *Il Mio Migior Nemico* in Italy) but the European market remains fragmented. A strong and effective distribution system does not exist and Europeans have not enthused over the European Film Academy Awards (Felix).

Taking this into consideration, MEDIA 2007, the successor of MEDIA Plus, has given the major share of its budget to distribution (55 per cent). In an enlarged European Union, MEDIA 2007 has been allocated a budget of €755 million over seven years. (Annual grants will increase from €75 million in the first year to €107 million in 2013.) One of the first recipients of the new distribution budget was *Das Leben der Anderen* (*The Lives of Others*). Voted Best Film at the European Film Academy Awards and Best Film in a Foreign Language at Hollywood's Academy Awards in 2007, Florian Henckel's film received over €500,000 from the MEDIA programme to assist its distribution in cinemas and on DVD outside Germany. By placing distribution at the core of the new programme, MEDIA 2007 aims 'to enhance the performance of non-national European audio-visual works in participating countries and to increase the visibility of diverse cultures in the global arena' (MEDIA Desk UK, 2007). The rest of MEDIA 2007 budget goes to development (20 per cent) – with no obligation for producers to reinvest MEDIA support in a subsequent development project – promotion (including support to festivals) (9 per cent), training (7 per cent) and new technologies (4 per cent). Since 2007, Eurimages is also operating a new digitisation support scheme aimed at the production of 2K (minimum) digital masters intended for digital cinema projection, VoD, satellite distribution and high resolution internet distribution.

Covering 31 countries, the new MEDIA budget is equivalent to the whole budget France allocated to the support of its cinema in 2007. Operating on shoestring budgets and given the scale of their operations, neither Eurimages nor MEDIA 2007 are likely to achieve all of their goals. This partly explains why national governments continue to set up their own initiatives to help their domestic film industries.

State aid

Estimating at 600 the number of film support schemes operating across the EU, a European Audiovisual Observatory report stated:

> In the four years 2002–2005, they [EU Member States] provided over €6.5 billion of state aid for film production, which helped to produce over 3,600 films. France provides the highest overall amounts of State aid for films, followed by the UK, Germany, Italy and Spain. Public support in these five countries is accounting for 83 per cent of the total. (Broche 2007: 1)

France: a case study

France has the most prolific film industry in Europe. Figures from the Centre National de la Cinématographie (CNC) indicate that the country produced 240 films in 2005 and 203 in 2006. Co-productions with foreign partners represent between half and a third of films produced in France (see Table 13.1).

Considered as a viable alternative to Hollywood for a long time, the French support system has not only served French cinema well over the years but it has also encouraged – through co-production agreements and various funds set up to help lesser privileged artists and cinematographies in various parts of the world – the

Table 13.1 Film production investments 1996 and 2002-06 (million US dollars)

	1996	*2002*	*2003*	*2004*	*2005*	*2006*
Austria	18.73	33.8	27.0	57.9	67.5	87.6
Belgium	35.70	18.8	33.8	74.9	127.9	73.5
Denmark	39.65	28.9	76.0	79.7	133.7	58.1
Finland	9.58	11.3	14.3	25.6	27.1	19.7
France	642.52	813.0	1,304.6	1,303.5	1,601.3	1,444.7
Germany	309.59	447.2	577.1	702.7	845.3	1,035.2
Greece	5.94	9.8	13.4	15.0	11.4	15.8
Ireland	83.97	39.9	56.8	75.6	42.4	57.3
Italy	243.96	261.9	341.4	353.7	266.9	323.2
Luxembourg	3.45	1.1	6.7	3.7	4.4	6.7
Netherlands	29.41	49.8	91.4	85.1	79.7	100.1
Portugal	4.20	20.8	26.4	29.9	25.9	33.9
Spain	157.88	304.3	286.5	392.0	459.4	603.0
Sweden	40.25	30.4	47.8	78.4	104.4	100.3
UK	842.78	851.6	1,895.6	1,486.6	1,057.6	1,552.9
EU (15)	2,467.61	2,922.8	4,798.6	4,764.4	4,854.7	5,512.1
Bulgaria	–	2.5	5.6	5.5	3.6	6.9
Croatia	–	–	–	–	–	–
Czech Rep.	–	9.1	14.2	14.0	21.1	34.0
Estonia	–	1.0	1.1	2.8	5.2	6.0
Hungary	–	14.2	10.8	10.3	14.3	18.3
Latvia	–	0.5	0.7	0.8	1.2	1.7
Lithuania	–	0.6	0.8	0.8	1.7	0.9
Poland	–	8.3	13.7	16.2	31.8	54.8
Romania	–	3.6	8.0	11.3	13.6	15.4
Slovakia	–	2.8	4.8	2.2	6.1	3.9
Slovenia	–	5.0	4.1	6.1	10.3	8.4
EU (25)	–	2,932.5	4,812.1	4,783.5	4,881.6	5,538.5
US	–	14,661.0	14,607.0	14,716.0	13,945.0	14,742.0

Source: Figures compiled from *Screen Digest*, July 2007; European Audio-visual Observatory (OBS), 2006; *CNC Info* May 2007.

development of a certain 'world cinema' (e.g. the now defunct 'Fonds ECO' has aided co-productions with the countries in the former Eastern bloc until 1997 and the Fonds Sud helps African countries as well as film-makers from South and Latin America and South East Asia). French cinema owes its specificity to a strong regulatory framework (dating back to 1946) and a comprehensive support system with automatic and selective aid mechanisms for the production, distribution and exhibition sectors. While automatic aids tend to reward success (by favouring commercially successful producers), selective aids provide support to an essentially cultural strategy (by helping first-time film-makers as well as *auteurs* of challenging films and/or films with artistic merit). Over the years, France has been remarkably consistent and innovative in adapting its regulations (by raising a tax on television channels, blank videotapes and video-on-demand) and devising new incentives (creation of tax shelters, increasing participation of the regions and support to 'art et essai' theatres and film festivals) to help cinema through its various crises (Creton and Jäckel 2004).

However, today, the French model is described as a system 'running out of steam' even by its supporters. Production trends have been significantly affected by the restructuring of Canal+ – a crucial financing partner for French cinema since its inception in 1984 – the development of new satellite channels and other modes of delivery for films. The French have actively sought ways to regulate content and to fight piracy. Given the international nature of the new media platforms, French legislation faces an uphill battle. Moreover, France's generous support system to cinema, along with other national governments' initiatives, is now coming under the scrutiny of outsiders (the European Commission and the WTO).

Film policy and cultural specificity

Film has long been at the heart of cultural policies and the debate continues to take place at the highest level. Taking into account that globalised trade has an innate drive towards homogenisation, with the more powerful dominating the weak, UNESCO raised the issue of cultural diversity in a convention that came into force in 2007. The principle was supported by almost all nations in the world but pointedly opposed by the USA. Like the exclusion of audio-visual works from the General Agreement on Tariffs and Trade – in which France played a leading role – in 1993, the policy is driven by the fear that 'Hollywood' represents a threat to local industries and culture, particularly language.

Regulations

Both at national and European levels the origin of a film is the key to access public funds. According to EU regulations, 'the benefit of aid schemes cannot be restricted on the basis of nationality' (Broche 2007: 2). Yet the responsibility to ensure that 'the content of the aided production is cultural according to verifiable criteria' rests with each Member State. Each country has set up its own criteria (usually based on a sophisticated points system) to establish the nationality and/or the cultural specificity of a film.

Recently the European Commission has insisted on 'cultural tests' to underpin government subsidies. In late 2006, the new UK and German film support schemes were approved by the European Commission. (The cultural tests designed by the German authorities focus not only on domestic content but also on European cultural content.) To be approved, the UK Cultural Test had to be revised 'to ensure that the aid would be directed towards a culturally British product' (Broche 2007: 4). In the revised test, the two sections cultural content and cultural contribution (comprising cultural diversity, heritage and creativity) account for 65 per cent of the overall points available. The four criteria of the cultural content section include: 'extent to which the film is set in the UK, what proportion of the main characters are British citizens or residents, whether or not the subject matter or underlying material of the film is British and the extent to which the original dialogue is English' (ibid.: 5). France's eligibility criteria which also include points for 'European cultural content' to access its production support fund are still to be examined.

Co-financing and co-productions: a challenge to regulations

Scrutiny of national regulations and other forms of public support for films by the European Commission has occasionally provoked anger. In 2000, for example, the chairman of the European Producers Club Jean Cazès successfully challenged Brussels' 50 per cent restriction on public support to *Dancer in the Dark* (a co-production involving more than 10 public funding agencies), arguing that Lars von Trier's successful film would have never been possible if public aid mechanisms had been capped at 50 per cent (quoted in Frodon 2000).

Co-financing and co-production arrangements make the origin of film problematic. There have been intense debates over the 'Frenchness' of Luc Besson's English-language films *Leon* and *Joan of Arc*, the 'Britishness' of *Casino Royale* or the 'Irishness' of Ken Loach's film *The Wind that Shakes the Barley*. In 2004, a French court ruled against the CNC decision to accord its agreement – a condition to access French funds – to Jean-Pierre Jeunet's film *Un long dimanche de fiançailles* (*A Very Long Engagement*) on the grounds that it was mainly produced by a subsidiary of Warner Bros. In 2006, Austria's submission in the Best Foreign Language category *Caché* (*Hidden*) was rejected because Michael Haneke's film was not in the principal language of the country. The previous year, the multi-nationality of Christian Caron's *Joyeux Noël* (*Merry Christmas*), a co-production involving the participation of France, Germany, Belgium, Romania, Eurimages and MEDIA, had also prevented the film from entering the competition for an Oscar.

In 1996, the European Producers Club had suggested the adoption of a proposal allowing producers based in countries operating automatic support schemes to access each other's schemes as long as the films made could be defined as European (Jäckel, 2003: 55). Conversely, the EC's tests applied 10 years later are to ensure state aid is limited to locally spent investment. When a number of agencies are prepared to open out their funds to the wider regional economy, the introduction of a 'territorialisation' principle is at odds both with the call for the harmonisation of incentives across Europe and with the principle of 'cultural diversity'. It also fails to recognise that, in the age of globalisation, film is more than ever a transnational phenomenon.

Globalisation and competition

Film historian Michel Marie asserts that 'the future history of cinema will inevitably be transnational' (Marie 2006: xiv). Over the past 20 years, film studies have shifted from the investigation of cinema as a national (Higson 1989; Hayward 1993) and European (Sorlin 1991; Wayne 2002; Elsaesser 2005) to a transnational (Naficy 2001; Ezra and Rowden 2006) phenomenon. Transnational by definition, a large number of co-productions made since the creation of the European and pan-European Funds appear to fulfil the Council of Europe's mandate 'to strengthen human rights, racial tolerance and multicultural acceptance' (Council of Europe 1991: 9). One of the first co-productions to receive Eurimages funding was *Reise der Hoffnung* (*Journey of Hope*) (1991). The film of the Swiss director Xavier Koller depicts the tragic efforts of illegal immigrants (a Turkish family) to reach 'Paradise somewhere in Europe'. *Lamerica* (Amelio 1994), *Tirana Year Zero* (Koçi 2001), *Code Unknown* (Haneke 2001), *Dirty, Pretty Things* (Frears 2002), *Beur, Blanc, Rouge* (Zemmouri 2006), *Auf der anderen Seite* (Fatih Akin 2007) offer other examples of transnational films, films with a strong identity addressing cultural diversity and the socio-economic problems facing Europe today (e.g. the integration and/or acceptance of individuals or group of individuals within a wider community). In supporting those films, Europe's public funds have helped European cinema to remain at the forefront of the contemporary cultural forms through which the parameters of emergent questions of cultural identity and representation – in terms of ethnicity, socio-economic position, race, gender and youth – are articulated. Moreover, by helping film-makers from nations of contested status or with disputed borders and displaced peoples – whether from Palestine, Lebanon or the former Yugoslavia – public funds such as Eurimages, ARTE or the French Fonds Sud have made a significant contribution to the development of a truly 'transnational cinema' (Jäckel 2007). Yet, those transnational films do not automatically cross borders or necessarily make a profit. Another type of transnational film is needed for a film industry to survive, one that only the larger European players in the industry can provide.

The corporate business of film

Today, even France's regulatory and financing systems are not enough to maintain a relatively healthy French cinema. The 1990s saw the emergence of new major independent players (StudioCanal, EuropaCorp and Wild Bunch) who, in order to meet the challenges of globalisation and conquer new markets, have developed initiatives combining high-budget international production with ambitious distribution and marketing strategies. France is not unique: other countries (Germany, Spain, Italy) also have a small but significant number of companies with an international portfolio that includes film production and distribution. Backed by international financing, their films are often made in English with

Table 13.2 Film production figures 1996 and 2003–06 (of which co-productions)

	1996	2003	2004	2005	2006
Austria	15 (2)	17 (3)	24 (15)	24 (13)	32 (10)
Belgium	12 (6)	12 (11)	23 (20)	28 (26)	19 (16)
Denmark	21 (8)	24 (12)	26 (–)	41 (20)	20 (9)
Finland	11 (2)	10 (1)	15 (5)	13 (5)	14 (2)
France	134 (60)	212 (107)	203 (73)	240 (114)	203 (75)
Germany	64 (22)	80 (26)	87 (27)	103 (43)	122 (44)
Greece	17 (10)	22 (3)	22 (3)	16 (3)	21 (2)
Ireland	18 (12)	10 (4)	12 (0)	12 (4)	12 (0)
Italy	99 (22)	117 (19)	134 (38)	98 (30)	116 (26)
Luxembourg	5 (5)	3 (3)	2 (2)	2 (2)	3 (1)
Netherlands	18 (6)	29 (4)	24 (–)	24 (5)	29 (14)
Portugal	8 (6)	17 (13)	15 (9)	16 (7)	19 (16)
Spain	91 (25)	110 (42)	133 (50)	142 (53)	150 (41)
Sweden	18 (15)	27 (13)	40 (14)	54 (15)	51 (8)
UK	111 (52)	175 (102)	132 (108)	131 (92)	134 (84)
EU (15)	638	865 (363)	892 (364)	944 (432)	945 (348)
Bulgaria	7	12 (2)	7 (1)	4 (0)	7 (3)
Croatia	6	1 (0)	5 (0)	5 (1)	8 (–)
Czech Rep.	20 (3)	16 (3)	16 (1)	20 (7)	20 (5)
Estonia	0	3 (2)	4 (1)	4 (2)	8 (4)
Hungary	20	21 (1)	21 (4)	26 (9)	28 (3)
Latvia	1	2 (0)	3 (2)	2 (2)	4 (2)
Lithuania	1	1 (0)	1 (1)	2 (2)	1 (1)
Poland	17	20 (2)	17	29 (6)	37 (1)
Romania	9	17 (10)	21 (12)	20 (11)	20 (8)
Slovakia	2	5 (3)	2 (1)	5 (4)	3 (2)
Slovenia	3	6 (1)	7 (1)	10 (1)	7 (3)
EU (25)		942 (378)	965 (377)	1,045 (466)	1,055 (369)

Source: Figures compiled from *Screen Digest*, July 2007; European Audio-visual Observatory (OBS), 2006; *CNC Info* May 2007.

international stars and personnel, shot in foreign locations and heavily promoted. Technical innovation represents another strategy developed by a small but
significant number of European post-production and editing companies which
have become experts at designing software and using state-of-the-art digital tools
for special effects. With the growth of digital technologies, the number of animation films produced in Europe has also increased. So has merchandising. (For
example, Luc Besson not only produced and directed *Arthur and the Invisibles* but
also wrote a series of bestselling *Arthur* comic books. There were also video games
and toys.) The strength of the documentary sector (*Etre et Avoir, March of the
Penguins, Children of the Decree, Zidane: A 21st Century Portrait*) has also grown.

The production of films with a strong export potential – whether large-budget
films with special effects or ambitious comedies – has played a substantial part in

the inflation of film budgets. In France, the box office receipts of a small number of those films explain the relatively high market share (45 per cent in 2006) of domestic films. Elsewhere in Europe, the share of domestic films remains below 30 per cent (from a high 29.5 per cent in the Czech Republic to 0.4 per cent in Slovakia in 2006). Yet, at home, 'French films' shot in English along with films with special effects 'are often reduced to an unavoidable process of Americanisation or globalisation, met by critical indifference or perceived as a threat to cultural diversity (and/or French cultural specificity)' (Vanderschelden 2007: 38).

Despite the numerous protests against Hollywood domination and fears of loss of creative control in films co-financed with American partners, Europe has welcomed American investment and Europeans have invested both in American films and in the American film industry. Hollywood's interest in European directors, stars and (cheaper) locations is nothing new but, with overseas territories now accounting for the highest proportion of the studios' total earnings (60 per cent in 2006), most of the major American companies have established production bases and deals in Europe. As the large markets of India and China become more attractive, they are also moving eastwards.

In Europe, investments in film production have substantially grown over the past 10 years (see Table 13.2).

For the more ambitious European producers, the international – particularly the American – market plays an increasingly important part in their film revenues. Citing both *Pan's Labyrinth* and *The Queen*, industry analyst Leonard Klady (2007: 24) contends that today 'the most acclaimed international films [. . .] generate more money in North America than in any other country outside their producing nation'. He also argues that 'it's often the case that European and Asian films are sold internationally because of the attention they receive in the US' (ibid.).

Competition

In a global environment, the film industry has not only become big business but also a highly mobile business. The trend to attract foreign productions is growing. Policy makers are now urged to introduce tax incentives and other enticements as well as to start building their own studio facilities where they do not exist – and to increase tax credits and improve facilities where they do – in order to attract film and television production.

Even the UK – the most successful country in Europe at combining a strategy of attracting overseas productions and integrating its production methods into the local economy – introduced 'purposeful tax reliefs to stimulate indigenous film production and to generate inward investment by the major US studios' (Woodward 2006: 1). With a maximum limit to the grant available per film (€4 million, or up to €10 million in exceptional cases), Germany is less attractive for large budget films than the UK. Similar restrictions are also applied in France and Spain.

In the 1990s, many industry professionals in the West feared that studio work would be lured to the expansive and inexpensive facilities of Central and Eastern Europe. A significant number of films and television series have been shot in

Poland, the Czech Republic (the Barrandov studios near Prague), Hungary (the Mafilm Studio in Budapest), Slovakia (with the Koliba studios in the capital Bratislava) along with Romania (particularly for films requiring a large cast of extras). However, competition has intensified and those countries are now feeling the brunt.

Being competitive is essential to survive in the film business and competition is now on a global scale. Today film studios all over Europe are not only competing among themselves but also with the rest of the world, notably cheaper facilities and labour costs in Asia (India, China) and South America. At a 2007 Venice Film Festival Seminar, Elisabetta Brunella asserted 'there [were] several signs that the centre of gravity in world cinema [was] moving east' (MEDIA Salles 2007). Yet digital technologies may pose an even greater challenge than competition to European cinema.

Challenges and opportunities for cinema in Europe in the digital age

It is widely accepted that fast-changing technology is forcing all sectors of the film industry to face radical changes.

Production

While it is true that digital production tools are bringing the cost of moving image production down and facilitate wider access to the means of production, to date, they have had little effect on film style, genre or structure. The 'desktop aesthetic' that was supposed to change the face of cinema (e.g. Mike Figgis' split-screen feature *Time Code* (2000)) seems to have evaporated and, until now, few film-makers have explored the interactive possibilities inherent in the medium. However, in the face of increasing user-generated content, the emergence of new models for film production is likely as film-makers start to explore moving-image forms of varied lengths (including shorts suitable for mobile phones).

Distribution and exhibition

Despite the claim made at European level that 'the new technologies should be at the service of cinema' (Jens Rykaer, President of MEDIA Salles, quoted in Brunella 2007: 1), there is already sufficient evidence that digital cinemas can and will diversify the content of programming to include live concerts, operas, sports events, educational events and conferences. Today, cinema operators are not only struggling to meet the cost of digital equipment but they are also concerned with the effect of piracy and changes in window releases.

Digital piracy (including both sales of illegal copies on DVD and online piracy, in particular file sharing through peer-to-peer networks) is on a global scale and on the rise. Its costs to the industry are high. National and international organisations (including the US Motion Picture Association) are working together to introduce anti-piracy measures and limit authorised access and copying. However law enforcement is proving difficult and copyright offences continue to be reported all around the world despite the imposition of stricter penalties (*Screen Digest* 2007: 132).

The arrival of VoD is challenging the principle of windows release and threatening the position occupied by the film theatre as well as its right of exclusivity. Until now, there has been an informal agreement on an industry standard on media release timetable. Deemed necessary in order to maximise revenues during the various windows for exhibiting a film, such a timetable implies a territory-specific exploitation of the rights, window by window. France, a strong advocate of the *droit d'auteur* (author rights), has long had stricter rules than its European counterparts. Yet in 2007 when Twentieth Century Fox decided to reduce the DVD release window for *Night at the Museum*, German, Italian and UK exhibitors took a stand against what they perceived as an erosion of their position and withdrew the film from their screens. This has not stopped Disney offering its new productions on the iTunes site during their week of release in cinemas. Other powerful distributors are bound to follow.

At European level, there is no European-wide common practice and no detailed regulation. The Draft Directive AVMS Article 3f(1) states:

> Member States shall ensure that on-demand services provided by media service providers under their jurisdiction promote, where practicable and by appropriate means, production of and access to European works. Such promotion could relate, inter alia,
> - to the financial contribution made by such services to the production and rights acquisition of European works or
> - to the share and/or prominence of European works in the catalogue of programmes proposed by the service. (Quoted in NPA Conseil 2007)

The ambiguous wording of the Draft Directive on on-demand services and the promotion of European films – like that of the Television Without Frontiers Directive – leaves ample room for interpretation.

The majority of European films require long runs in cinemas to enable them to benefit from word of mouth. At a time when national television channels are buying fewer films, VoD may well, as a delegate at the 2006 Europa Cinemas Conference argued, reinforce the presence of European productions. To date, in European countries where online movie services have been readily adopted (the Nordic countries, France and Germany), cinema admissions have remained stable. It may not be coincidental that those countries also have both business (e.g. *à la carte* subscription) models and regulations in place for downloading films.

Elsewhere, the findings of the UK Film Council in 2006 do not augur well for the next few years. Reviewing the situation and looking to the future, the authors of the report write:

> . . . the initial effect of the latest digital revolution has been to compress rather than to expand film audiences. [. . .] Audiences are racing into the new digital entertainment arena while the film industry struggles to overcome barriers such as slow download speeds, unresolved rights and security issues, and undeveloped platforms. In a few years, these will be overcome, but in the meantime a proportion of consumer time and money has migrated away

from film into the expanding world of opportunity offered by the Internet and its associated devices.
(UK Film Council 2006/7: 1)

However, all may not be bleak. The lack of visibility of non-national European films is nothing new. The internet is proving a powerful tool to facilitate the mobilisation of minority interests. For 'specialised products' such as non-national European (particularly foreign-language) films, it could also be an important promotion tool and a powerful means of reaching audiences. The increasing number of and interest in film festivals is another reason to remain optimistic. Festivals have become an important alternative to the commercially oriented film distribution but public support – whether at regional, national or European level – remains crucial to the continuation of both the art-theatre and the festival circuits.

The increasing number and popularity of festivals screening European films both in and outside Europe testify to the long standing status of European film. The awards bestowed upon films from Central and Eastern Europe (e.g. Christian Mungiu's Cannes Palme d'Or winner *4 Months, 3 Weeks and 2 Days*) at the beginning of the 21st century also show that the cinemas of those countries have contributed much to sustaining and reinforcing the reputation of European cinema as a cinema that displays a verve and originality that challenges stereotypes. While a significant number of American films now escape Hollywood formulae, European cinema is still largely promoted as an 'auteur cinema'. Authenticity and an overt directorial presence – along with a medium or low budget – continue to distinguish most European films from films made elsewhere. However, as the recent films of the (Turkish-German) Fatih Akin (*The Edge of Heaven*), (French) Laurent Cantet (*Human Resources*), (German) Christian Petzold (*Yella*), (Hungarian) György Sláma (*Taxidermia*), (Romanian) Chriti Puiu (*The Death of Mr. Lazarescu*) or (Serbian) Srdan Golubovic (*The Trap*) show, focusing on the relationship between space, history and identity, European film-makers today express their personal, social and political concerns and confront their fragmented – regional, national, European and global – identities in an ever-increasing variety of challenging ways.

Conclusion

The belief that competition and digital technology will deliver diversity is widespread. 'Our aim is to see that the growing number of distribution platforms help provide audiences with more chances [. . .] to enjoy a broader range of films', stated the Chief Executive Officer of the UKFC in 2007 (Woodward 2007: 1). Similar claims were made at the end of the 20th century to develop multiplex cinemas. The more powerful players in the film industry argued then that a larger number of screens would provide greater diversity, more choice. Digital distribution offers a wider choice and has the potential to promote cultural diversity. However, online distribution and the internet may give film-makers a greater chance to have their work seen but the sheer volume of material online makes it difficult to notice and identify talent. Moreover, that digital technology has empowered the consumer has led to the fear that the larger players may use it to make audience-driven – and/or formula-led – products, compromising artistic vision.

New modes of film financing and production are calling into question not only the opposition between 'Hollywood' and Europe – or indeed the rest of the world – but also the definition of what constitutes a national, European or Hollywood film. Furthermore, the rapid development of digital technologies is not only calling into question 'the future of cinema and television as independent and exclusively designated sites of visual consumption' (Bergfelder 2006: 246) but also blurring distinctions between media-transmitted images. As competition intensifies and a new set of parameters emerge, new measures are being taken to ensure the survival of cinema, extend the reach of European films and safeguard cultural diversity in Europe. The emphasis of national, European and pan-European policies is now clearly making the shift from production to distribution. The European market and Europe's variegated film industries remain fragmented despite public – and private – efforts at European level. Cinema in Europe is diverse. In the digital age, fragmentation and diversity are not a handicap. The potential exists to expand niche markets for 'specialised films', to use the UKFC terminology, (e.g. 'films characterised by an innovative cinematic style and by an engagement with challenging subject matter'). Those films, often produced with the help of public funding, constitute a major part of European output. However, technology itself cannot safeguard cultural diversity. The different countries/regions of Europe all have different approaches (including their own set of regulations) as to how best to help cinema face its current crisis. The limited resources made available by the European funds are unlikely to fulfil the ambitious goals set in the MEDIA and Eurimages programmes. In the world of multi-media platforms, film may no longer occupy a privileged place but the cinema experience remains unique. In a fast-changing world, regulatory frameworks need to be flexible. However difficult it may be to enforce legislation, there is an urgent necessity not only 'to *keep* asserting the need for regulations' (Knight 2006: 362) but also to reassert the role of public funding institutions to support cinema in Europe.

Questions

1 To what extent can films be defined in terms of their origins (financial, technical and artistic input)?

2 What issues are raised by the criteria for assessing the national identity of film and accessing national and European film funds?

3 Can national and/or European support to the film industry be sustained when the very concept of what constitutes a film is changing?

4 Can cinemas survive in the digital age?

Further reading

Aitken, I. (2001) *European Film Theory and Cinema: A Critical Introduction*, Edinburgh: Edinburgh University Press. Explores the major theories and movements within European cinema.

British Film Institute (2006) *BFI Film and Television Handbook 2006*, London: BFI. Yearly publication which records statistics and views on the previous year's output.

Cahiers du Cinéma (2006) special issue, January, n.608. Collection of essays and interviews with film professionals on European cinema (in French).

Ezra, E. (ed) (2004) *European Cinema*, Oxford: Oxford University Press. Combining artistic analysis with attention to industrial context, provides overviews of key movements and traditions in European film history.

Henning, V. and Alpar, A. (2005) 'Public Aid Mechanisms in Feature Film Production: The EU MEDIA PLUS Programme', *Media, Culture & Society*, 27 (2): 229–50. Critical analysis of state aids for film production in EU countries.

Iordanova, D. (2003) *Cinema of the Other: The Industry and Artistry of East Central European Film*, London: Wallflower Press. Explores the main historical stages of development across the region and examines how the cinema of Eastern Europe is still excluded and largely under-explored.

Petrie, D. (ed) (1992) *Screening Europe: Image and Identity in Contemporary European Cinema* London: British Institute. Focuses on the questions of how European films are shaped and are being shaped by the changes that take place in Europe.

Statistical Yearbook: Cinema, Television, Video and New Media in Europe (2006). Strasbourg: European Audio-visual Observatory (OBS). Yearly publication of statistical data on cinema, television, video and the new media in the various countries of Europe.

Vitali, V. and Willemen, P. (eds) (2006) *Theorising National Cinema*, London: BFI. Addresses the complex relationship between national cinema and national identity. Also considers the future of national cinema in an age of transnational culture flows.

Willis, H. (2005) *New Digital Cinema, Reinventing the Moving Image*, London: Wallflower Press. Offers a survey of the diverse currents coursing through the circuits of digital cinema and also explores the issue of national identity and cinema in various parts of the world.

Websites

www.bfi.org.uk/ (British Film Institute)

www.cnc.fr/ (France's French film centre)

www.ukfilmcouncil.org.uk

www.europa-cinemas.org

mediasalles.it (explores current cinema exhibition issues)

www.coe.int/t/e/cultural_co-operation/eurimages

www.obs.coe.int/ (European audio-visual observatory)

References

Bergfelder, T. (2006) *International Adventures, German Popular Cinema and European Co-Productions in the 1960s*, New York and Oxford: Berghahn.

Broche, J. (2007) 'State Aid for Films – A Policy in Motion?', *Competition Policy Newsletter*, 1.

Brunella, E. (2007) 'New Digital Experiences at DGT 2007', *European Cinema Journal*, n2, ix.

Council of Europe (1991) *The Council of Europe and the Cultural Heritage*, Information Documents, Strasbourg: COE.

Creton, L. and Jäckel, A. (2004) 'The Business of Film: A Certain Idea of the Film Industry' in M. Temple and M. Witt (eds) *The French Cinema Book*, London: British Film Institute, pp. 209-20.

Elsaesser, T. (2005) *European Cinema Face to Face with Hollywood*, Amsterdam: Amsterdam University Press.

Eurimages News (2000) available at www.coe.int/t/e/cultural_co-operation/eurimages.

Ezra, E. and Rowden, T. (eds) (2006) *Transnational Cinema: The Film Reader*, London and New York: Routledge.

Frodon, J. M. (2000) 'Jean Cazès et l' Aide aux Films', *Le Monde*, 25 October: 36.

Hayward, S. (1993) *French National Cinema*, London and New York: Routledge.

Higson, A. (1989) 'The Concept of National Cinema', *Screen* 30 (4): 36-46.

Hill, J., McLoone, M. and Hainsworth, P. (eds) (1994) *Border Crossing: Film in Ireland, Britain and Europe*, London: British Film Institute.

Jäckel, A. (2003) *European Film Industries*, London: British Film Institute.

Jäckel, A. (2007) 'The Inter/Nationalism of French Film Policy', *Modern & Contemporary France*, 15 (1): 21-36.

Klady, L. (2007) 'Land of Opportunity?', *Screen International*, n1616, October issue.

Knight, J. (2006) 'Local Film Culture, Global Exchange: Conference Review', *Convergence*, 12 (3).

Marie, M. (2006) 'Preface' in P. Powrie (ed) *The Cinema in France*, London and New York: Wallflower Press.

MEDIA Desk France (2007) available at www.mediadeskfrance.fr.

MEDIA Desk UK (2007) April, available at www.mediadesk.uk.

MEDIA Salles (2007) Seminar on Venice Film Festival, MEDIA Salles News, available at www.mediasalles.it/dgt_online_informer_254/news25.htm.

Ministry of Culture of the Czech Republic (2006) *Report on the State of Czech Cinematography (2005)*, Ministry of Culture of the Czech Republic, Department of Media and Audiovisual Services, available at www.oea_publ/eurocine/CZ_2006.html.

Naficy, H. (2001) *An Accented Cinema: Exilic and Diasporic Filmmaking*, Princeton, NJ and Oxford: Princeton University Press.

NPA Conseil (2007) *Video on Demand in Europe*, Study for the European Audiovisual Observatory and the Direction du Développement des médias (DDM-France), Strasbourg: OEA.

Screen Digest (2007) 'Global Video Piracy Still Strong', May.

Sorlin, P. (1991) *European Cinemas, European Societies 1939-1990*, London: Routledge.

UK Film Council (2006/7) *RSU Statistical Year Book*, London: UK Film Council.

Vanderschelden, I. (2007) 'Strategies for a "Transnational"/French Popular Cinema', *Modern & Contemporary France*, 15: 1.

Vincendeau, G. (ed) (1995) *Encyclopedia of European Cinema*, London: British Film Institute.

Wayne, M. (2002) *The Politics of Contemporary European Cinema: Histories, Borders, Diasporas*, London: Intellect.

Woodward, J. (2006) *Film in the Digital Age, UK Film Council Consultation on Policy and Funding Priorities*, London: UKFC.

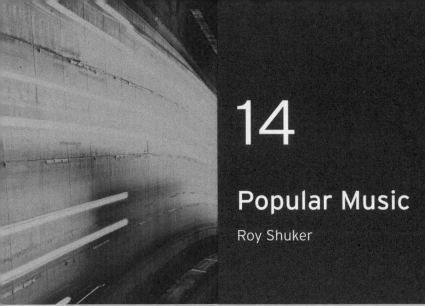

14

Popular Music

Roy Shuker

Chapter overview

This chapter presents an overview of the music industry in the UK, with some reference to the comparable European situation. The industry is seen as a network of revenue streams, with associated gatekeepers and cultural intermediaries. These include the record companies – historically the dominant sector – music retail, film and television, MTV, the music press and live music. The relative importance of these has shifted with the impact of the internet on every aspect of music production, distribution and consumption. However, despite claims for the consequent demise of the traditional music industry business model, the major labels are now repositioning themselves in order to maintain their dominant position.

Introduction

During 2007, a series of moves by big-selling music acts to bypass traditional record companies' market dominance, led to claims that these indicated the 'death knell of the old music industry' (*The Times* 2007). Paul McCartney quit EMI for the new record arm of coffee retail chain Starbucks. In July, Prince's new album *Planet Earth* was given away with the *Mail on Sunday*. Prince was heavily criticised by his record company, HMV, and by music retailers, but defended his move as simply 'direct marketing'. In October, Radiohead, now out of contract with the EMI Group, allowed fans to name their own price – an 'honesty box' system – when downloading their latest album *In Rainbow*s from the band's website. Late in the year, Madonna left Warner Music Group after 25 years with the company, to sign a US$120 million deal with concert promotion firm Live Nation. The star headed Forbes list of the 'Cash Queens of Music' for the period June 2006 to June 2007, with earnings of US$72 million. Reflecting the now standard range of activities among top performers, this income was generated less from album sales, but rather from her *Confessions* world tour, her fashion line with H&M, and a lucrative deal with NBC network to broadcast her concert at London's Wembley Stadium.

During the same period, sales of online music increased, but not sufficiently to make up for the continued decline in CD sales. The British Phonographic Industry, which represents the UK recorded-music business, noted that total music download sales for the year topped 77 million, a 50 per cent increase over 2006, while CD sales had dropped during the same period. In January 2008, British-based EMI announced it was slashing its staff numbers, and reshaping its artist roster.

To many observers, these were indications of a traditional music industry in crisis. Yet, at the same time, music was more prevalent than ever before in daily life, with exposure through live concerts, radio, ring tones, music television, video games, television advertising, YouTube, MySpace, internet downloading and the ubiquitous iPod. Clearly we are consuming more music than ever, but are less likely to pay for it.

The claims of an industry crisis reflected a tendency to equate the 'music industry' with the sound recording companies, who develop and market artists and their 'records' in various formats, including digital. This sector has historically been at the heart of the music industry (Barfe 2004) and certainly remains a very significant part of it. In a broader sense, however, the music industry embraces a range of other institutions and associated markets, and can be best regarded as a series of revenue streams. The most important of these are music publishing; music retail; the music press; music hardware, including musical instruments, sound recording and reproduction technology; tours and concerts and associated merchandising (posters, t-shirts, etc.); and royalties and rights and their collection/licensing agencies.

As the International Federation of the Phonographic Industries (IFPI) observes:

> The recorded music industry is the engine helping to drive a much broader music sector, which is worth more than US$100 billion globally. This is over three times the value of the recorded music market, and shows music to have an economic importance that extends far beyond the scope of record sales.
>
> (IFPI 2006b)

Gatekeepers and cultural intermediaries

The music industry includes a number of industry gatekeepers or cultural intermediaries: institutions, companies, and personnel who 'stand between' consumers and the musical texts, once it has been produced as a commodity. I use the phrase 'stand between' as shorthand for what are complex processes of marketing and consumption. The sound recording companies include staff making the initial decision about who to record and promote, and filtering material at each step of the process involving the recording and marketing of a song (Negus 1999; Hesmondhalgh 2002). There are a number of other gatekeepers, primarily various music media, with an historical progression of these. Based in the established sector of sheet music sales, retail shops were where sound recordings could first be listened to and purchased. Later, film and radio provided cultural spaces where music could be experienced, informing and shaping consumption. The music press, established in the 1920s, played a similar role, especially in the emergence of 'rock culture' in the 1960s. The introduction of television in the 1950s, followed by MTV in the 1980s, provided new sites of mediation. Most recently, the internet has dramatically altered the relationship between the sound recording industry and the manufacture, distribution and consumption of music.

The record companies

The increased concentration of the culture industries is a feature of late capitalism, and the music industry has been part of this process of consolidation. Reflecting the economies of scale and global integration required to compete on the world media market, a small group of internationally based large corporations have spread their interests across a variety of media, including sound recording, resulting in multi-media conglomerates (Schiller 1999; Herman and McChesney 1997). This is illustrated by German media giant Bertelsmann AG, which owns book publishing (Random House); magazines and newspapers (Grune+Jahr); printing and media services (Arvato Printing); direct marketing groups (book and CD clubs); online interests (CDnow); and, the heart of the company, Bertelsmann Music Group (BMG). In 2006, BMG publishing, the world's third largest music publishing company (with 2005 revenue of €371 million) was sold to Universal Music. Yet, indicating the huge scope of Bertelsmann's interests, that figure only accounted for about 2 per cent of the company's total revenue.

The majors

The international record industry is dominated by a small group of large international record companies. Commonly referred to as the majors, all are part of large international media conglomerates. Their market dominance has been to a degree undermined by shifts in the organisation and operating logics of the wider industry, with the impact of the internet (of which more later), but they remain in a powerful position within the broader music industry. In the late 1990s, there were six of these (Hull 2004). By 2007 further consolidation and mergers had left four: Warner Music Group is part of AOL-Time Warner; Universal Music Group is owned by Vivendi Universal of France; Sony-BMG is jointly owned by the Japanese Sony Corporation and Bertelsmann AG, who merged in 2004; EMI Ltd is a UK firm. (For an outline of the organisation and activities of each of the majors, see Bishop (2005); for the contemporary situation, see the websites listed at the end of this chapter.)

Estimates of the degree of market control and market share exercised by the majors are difficult to determine, but various authorities place their share of the global production, manufacture and distribution at between 80 and 90 per cent in most national markets (Hull 2004). There is considerable debate over the economic and cultural implications of such market dominance, especially the strength of local music industries in relation to marked trends toward the globalisation of the culture industries (Azenha 2006; Bishop 2005). At issue is the consequent question of control of the media and whose interests it operates in, and the relationship between diversity and innovation in the market. Free market economists argue that innovation will occur more frequently under conditions of oligopoly (increased concentration, fewer producers), since larger firms are better able to finance innovation and pass the costs and benefits along to consumers. Conversely, other analysts argue that conditions of oligopoly mean a lack of incentive for firms to depart much from the tried and tested, resulting in a high level of product homogeneity (Ross (2005) provides an accessible summary of the debate and its major contributors). The crucial question in this debate is how does such concentration affect the range of opportunities available to musicians and others involved in the production of popular music, and the nature and range of products available to the consumers of popular music?

The independents

While the 'majors' dominate the recorded music market, the 'independents', or 'indies' play an important role, too. These are generally small record labels that are independent of the majors (at least in terms of the artist acquisition, recording, and promotion), though frequently still reliant on a major for distribution and more extensive marketing. These labels are frequently considered to be more flexible and innovative in their roster of artists, and have been associated with the emergence and popularisation of new genres: UK examples include Island and reggae (in the 1970s); Stiff and punk (1980s); and Creation and Britpop (1990s). In other European countries, Sweden's Burning Heart Records has a reputation for garage bands, while Italy's Sonic Belligeranza has specialised in breakcore and conceptual noise music.

The term 'indie' denotes not just a type of economic entity, but a musical attitude, with both linked to a set of dominant musical values, with authenticity at their core (Fonarow 2006). Independents have a rich and often lauded role in the history of popular music (Kennedy and McNutt 1999), and continue to be an important part of the music industry, often acting as developers of talent for the majors. While there are a huge number of independent labels, and they produce two-thirds of the titles released, their market share remains small, usually around 15 to 20 per cent (Hull 2004).

The operation of the independents and the precise nature of their relationship with the majors is open to debate. It is clearly a dynamic process, and the examples of Creation and the career of Oasis (Harris 2003), and Rough Trade (Hesmondhalgh 2002) in the UK during the 1990s illustrated a definite blurring of the boundaries between the independents and the major companies.

Music retail

Music retail includes the sale of sheet music, musical instruments, music-related merchandise, concert tickets, music DVDs, music magazines and books. Primarily, however, the term 'music retail' refers to the sale of sound recordings to the public, initially through shops selling sheet music and musical instruments. In the UK in the early 1900s, chains of department stores began supplying hit songs, along with sheet music. Later, smaller, independent and sole proprietor shops emerged. By the 1950s, record retailers included independent shops, often specialising in particular genres; chain stores; and mail order record clubs. The subsequent relative importance and market share of each of these has reflected the broader consolidation of the music industry, along with shifts in recording formats and distribution technologies. The advent of electronic bar coding in the 1990s enabled retail, distribution, and production 'to be arranged as an interconnected logistic package', allowing 'music retailers to delineate, construct and monitor the "consumer" of recorded music more intricately than ever before' (du Gay and Negus 1994: 396). A similar process now occurs with the tracking of browsers and purchasers' preferences in online shopping.

As with the culture industries generally, increased concentration of ownership has been a feature of the music retail industry. An increasing proportion of recordings are sold through general retailers, and mega stores such as Tower and HMV. This concentration influences the range of music available to consumers, and the continued economic viability of smaller retail outlets. Brennan (2006) documents how the increased concentration of music retail in the UK constrains the availability of releases from indie and specialist genre labels. The general retailers frequently use music as a loss-leader: reducing their music CD and DVD prices to attract shoppers whom they hope will also purchase other store products with higher profit margins. This situates music as only one component of the general selling of lifestyle consumer goods. What this means for consumers, however, is a relatively restricted range of music on offer, with a heavy emphasis on the discounted chart-oriented recordings, which are available only on CD. Smaller local music chains have been forced to retrench by consolidating shops and 'downsizing' staff, or have kept operating through niche marketing and their increased use of the internet, as is the case with Think Indie, a British consortium of independent record retailers (www.thinkindie.com).

Traditional music retail has continued to be hard hit by the decline in sales of (non-digital) recorded music. In June 2007, HMV announced that its profits had halved over the past year, while discount CD chain Fopp went out of business. Music shops now display a much greater range of music related products, including DVDs, memorabilia, and music press publications, and frequently act as sales points for concert tickets.

Radio and the charts

Historically the enemy of the record industry during the disputes of the 1930s and 1940s around payment for record airplay, radio subsequently became its most vital promoter. As Barnard's study of British music radio shows (Barnard 1989), until the advent of MTV in the 1980s, radio was indisputably the most important broadcast medium for determining the form and content of popular music, and has continued to play a central part in determining and reflecting chart success. Radio can also play an important role in sustaining 'local' music. In the Netherlands, for example, in the mid-1990s, Radio Noordzee Nationaal played 90 per cent Dutch national music and gained a market share of some 10 per cent of the local radio market. Web radio and new broadcasting technologies have fostered an explosion of radio stations, even although many have a very localised signal. In the commercial sector, digital technologies have produced new production aesthetics and reshaped the radio industry, with a drop in terrestrial radio's audience (Hull 2004).

The concern to retain a loyal audience assumes fairly focused radio listening. Paradoxically, while the radio is frequently 'on', it is rarely 'listened' to, instead largely functioning as aural wallpaper, a background to other activities. Yet high rotation radio airplay remains important in exposing artists and building a following for their work, while radio exposure is also necessary to underpin activities like touring, helping to promote concerts, and the accompanying sales of recordings, whatever their format. The very ubiquity of radio is a factor here. It can be listened to in a variety of situations, and with widely varying levels of engagement, from personal stereos to background accompaniment to activities such as study, domestic chores, and reading.

The charts provide a crucial link between music retail and radio. The first UK chart appeared in 1928 (the *Melody Maker* 'Honours List'), and such charts quickly became the basis for radio 'Hit Parade' programmes, most notably the 'Top 40' shows. In the UK, the charts are produced by market research organisations sponsored by various branches of the media. The associated data collection is now substantially computerised and based on comprehensive sample data (Hull 2004: 201–2). Airplay information is compiled from selected radio stations, sales information from wholesalers and retailers, assisted by bar coding. This represents a form of circular logic, in that the charts are based on a combination of radio play and sales, but airplay influences sales, and retail promotion and sales impacts on radio exposure. Historically there has been frequent controversy over attempts to influence the charts, and debate still occurs over perceived attempts to manipulate them. The decline of the single format in the 1980s influenced the way the charts were constructed in the UK: in 1989 the industry reduced the number of sales required to qualify for a platinum award (from one million to 600,000) to assist the promotional system, and ensure charts continued to fuel excitement and sales.

The physical nature of the single, and its relation to promotion and the charts, underwent a radical change during 2005–06 as the music market moved online. In the UK, by early 2006, digital singles made up some 80 per cent of the singles market as a whole, up from 23 per cent in 2004. The availability of downloads transformed the way in which consumers obtained music, giving them greater direct input into the charts, and at much less cost.

The music press

The music press plays a major part in the process of selling music as an economic commodity, while at the same time investing it with cultural significance. Music magazines include a variety of publications: industry reference tools, musicians' magazines, record collector magazines, fanzines, 'teen glossies', 'the inkies', style bibles and the new tabloids. Although these publications have many features in common, each serves a particular place in a segmented market, in which journalism becomes collapsed into, and often indistinguishable from, music industry publicity (Shuker 2008: Chapter 9). Despite this symbiosis, popular music critics continue to function as significant gatekeepers and as arbiters of taste (Gorman 2001).

The majority of popular music magazines focus on performers and their music, and the relationship of consumers and fans to these. These fall into a number of fairly clearly identifiable categories, based on their differing musical aesthetics or emphases, their socio-cultural functions, and their target audiences. In the UK, 'teen glossies' emphasise vicarious identification with performers whose music and image is aimed at the youth market (e.g. *Smash Hits*); the 'inkies' (*New Musical Express*) have historically emphasised a tradition of critical rock journalism, with their reviewers acting as the gatekeepers for that tradition (Hoskyns 2003); and the 'style bibles' (*The Face*), which emphasise popular music as part of visual pop culture, especially fashion. Several relatively new magazines offer a combination of the inkies' focus on an extensive and critical coverage of the music scene and related popular culture, packaged in a glossier product with obvious debts to the style bibles (*MOJO, Q, UNCUT*). The European music press is differentiated in a similar fashion. It includes, for example, *Les Rockuptables* (France), oriented towards indie bands; *Puls Furore* (Norway), mainly covering rock, but also techno, roots, and jazz music; and *Popcorn*, a Bulgarian magazine aimed at younger readers, covering teen pop artists and styles. Currently, there is a clear split between inclusive magazines, attempting to cover a broad range of musical styles, and those magazines that are genre or style specific, e.g. *The Wire, Kerrang!, Mixmag*. The majority frequently reference audio weblinks; they also have substantial websites, with additional material to their print versions.

Fanzines are a significant part of the popular music press. Despite their essentially non-commercial and often ephemeral nature, they represent a cultural space for the creation of a community of interest, producing and maintaining particular musical styles and scenes (on punk rock, see Savage 1991; on progressive rock, Atton 2001). The internet has provided a new medium for the international dissemination of fanzines; through their 'printing' of contemporary concert reviews and tour information, such 'e-zines' have an immediacy that provides a form of virtual socialisation for fans.

Film and television

Film has an important historical relationship to popular music. Early silent films often had a live musical accompaniment (usually piano); and with the 'talkies' musicals became a major film genre in the 1930s, and continued to be important into the 1960s. Composers and musicians, primarily stars, provided a source of material for these films, as did Broadway musicals. The various genres of popular music, its fans and performers have acted as a rich vein of colourful, tragic and salutary stories for film-makers. Over the past 40 or so years, considerable synergy has been created between the music and film industries; film soundtracks and video games represent another avenue of revenue for recordings, including the back catalogue, and help promote contemporary releases.

Broadcast television has also been an important mode of distribution, promotion and formation for the music industry, through the popular music programmes in channel schedules: light entertainment series based around musical performers, music documentaries, and the presentation of musical acts as part of television variety and chat/interview shows (*Popular Music* 2002).

The introduction of public broadcast television in the UK in the 1950s coincided with the emergence of rock 'n' roll. Television helped popularise the new music, and established several performers, most notably Cliff Richard (and Elvis Presley in the US), as youth icons. Indeed, for some fans, along with film television was their only access to 'live' performance. Television was quick to seize the commercial opportunities offered by the emergent youth culture market of the 1950s, with advertising featuring products aimed at the teenage consumer. The main popular music shows on British television were *Juke Box Jury* and *Top of the Pops*, both starting in the late 1950s, and *The Old Grey Whistle Test* (launched by the BBC in 1971, and aimed at more album-oriented older youth). In 1963 *Ready Steady Go!* (RSG) began showcasing new talent, who usually performed live. In addition to the music, such shows have acted as influential presenters of new dances, image and clothing styles. Several of these shows are now marketed as sell-through videos or DVDs, documenting historically significant performers and styles (e.g. *The Best of the Old Grey Whistle Test*, BBC DVD, 2001), and showcasing contemporary acts (*Later . . . with Jools Holland*).

Popular music on television is increasingly competing against other genres for scheduling space and advertising revenue, while the demographic significance of the youth audience has declined since the 1990s. Many shows have now ended, including the iconic *Top of the Pops* in 2006. To a degree, their place has been taken by music related reality television shows. A hybrid genre, reality television draws on and reworks generic codes and conventions from a variety of sources, using new technology (e.g. camcorders) to convey a sense of immediacy and authenticity to viewers. Popular music has provided a significant vehicle for reality television. Popular series such as *S Club 7 in Miami* in the late 1990s reinforced the public profiles and commercial success of their performers, and foreshadowed the later *Pop Idol, Popstars* and *Rock Star* series. These musical talent quests, based on audience votes but with a key role played by judging panels (especially in the initial selection of participants), have become an international phenomenon. They have created new pop and rock stars, although the career of some has been short-lived (Shuker 2008: 153–4).

MTV

The US based cable channel, 'MTV: Music Television', founded in 1981, has made its logo synonymous with the music video form. It is currently owned by Viacom International, the third largest communications conglomerate in the world

(Bishop 2005: 452). MTV is credited with boosting a flagging music industry in the 1980s. It captured a considerable share of the advertising directed at the youth and young adult/yuppie market, and solved the perennial problem of cable television – how to generate enough revenue for new programming – by having the record companies largely pay for the 'programmes' by financing the video clips (Banks 1996). The channel now claims to reach some 300 million households worldwide.

MTV's success spawned a host of imitators in the US, and a number of national franchises and imitations around the globe. These raised the issue of the place of local music in a context dominated by international repertoire, especially from the North American music market. MTV Europe, launched in 1988, reserves a proportion of its airtime for European performers. While music videos remain the staple of its programming, the channel also screens concerts, interviews, and music oriented news and gossip items, acting as a visual radio channel (www.mtv.com).

Live music

As CD sales continue to fall, and online music sales remain relatively small, artists are focusing more on the growing markets of endorsements, merchandising, and live music. As fans are spending less on an artists recorded music, they are paying unprecedented sums to hear them in concert. In the 1980s, a concert for a major act was equivalent to the cost of a CD album. In summer 2007, 'you could have bought Madonna's entire catalogue for less than half what it cost to see her perform at the Wembley arena' (Sandall 2007: 7). Mama Group, which manages the Kaiser Chiefs and Franz Ferdinand, among many groups, saw more than two million people pass through the doors of its 18 UK venues in 2007 (Telegraph Group 2008).

Smaller, newer acts are increasingly looking to live music to build a fan base and generate sales. Rave metal band Enter Shikari released their debut album *Take to the Skies* on its own label Ambush Reality, yet it entered the British charts at number four. The band had played nearly 700 gigs since forming in 2003, and this combined with word of mouth and the now obligatory presence on MySpace, created a receptive market for the album (Sandall 2007).

Music festivals remain a feature of the live music scene. Major, long-established European festivals include Roskilde in Denmark, Paleo in Switzerland, and Sziget in Hungary. Sziget, a week-long festival held in Budapest, had 385,000 visitors in 2005. There was an explosion of music festivals scheduled in the UK during 2007, with 450 such large-scale events, ranging from Glastonbury to a one-day Underage Festival in Hackney London.

The music industry goes online

As this discussion of key dimensions of the music industry indicates, the internet has added a major new dimension to the marketing, accessing and consumption of popular music. In this final section, I want to look more closely at the industry's move online, and the accompanying debates, especially in relation to copyright.

The web includes sites for purchasing online retail music, for downloading music as digital files, for record companies and performers, online music magazines, online concerts and interviews, web radio and, finally, bulletin boards. These represent new ways of inter-linking the audience/consumers of popular music, the performers and the music industry; however, these developments also raise issues of copyright and control. Since 1999–2000, the mainstream music industry showed increasing alarm at the impact on their market share of Napster *et al.* and practices such as the downloading of MP3s and P2P (person to person) file sharing (Garofalo 2003). The copyright violation and consequent loss of revenue led several artists (notably the band Metallica) and record labels to sue Napster for breach of copyright. The issues involved were complex and the litigation process was a lengthy and very public one. Napster was forced to close down, but was re-launched as a legitimate service in late 2003 (Napster 2.0). Newer technologies and providers moved things to another level, allowing direct user-to-user (peer-to-peer) connections involving multiple file types, expanding the scope of file sharing activity and making it extremely difficult to track users or the files they choose to share.

The impact of downloading on 'legitimate' recording sales has been keenly debated. From the industry point of view, and some observers, downloading was clearly hurting the industry (Hull 2004). Others were not so convinced, and several academic studies found that those who copy music do not stop buying records or purchasing legal downloads (see Jones and Lenhart 2004; Kusek and Leonard 2005; Millard 2005). Market control was central to the debate around Napster and its successors: were artists and the recording companies being disempowered, and consumers (end-users) being empowered by the increasing availability of online music (McLeod 2005)?

The battle over P2P file sharing continued, with the music industry targeting new, post-Napster services, and individual consumers whom they perceived as infringing copyright. An alternative industry strategy also emerged, when in 2000, record companies began establishing copyright deals with internet music producers. In 2003 the entry of Apple into the music marketplace, with its iTunes service, met with considerable success, encouraging the development of further such services, most notably eMusic, which only sells music from independent labels. In 2004 music continued to shift online, with legal downloading taking an increasing market share (Hull 2004: 258–9), made even more attractive by the development of the iPod and its competitors, portable music systems capable of storing huge numbers of songs in digital format. In 2006, a major IFPI Report on Digital Music, a comprehensive review of the development of the digital music market internationally, presented some impressive statistical evidence. It showed that the online shift had actually gained momentum, with two million songs now available online, and mobile music now accounting for approximately 40 per cent of record company digital revenues. The report concluded that 'digital music now accounts for about 6 per cent of record companies' revenues, up from practically zero two years ago' (IFPI 2006a). IFPI Chairman and CEO John Kennedy said:

Two years ago, few could have predicted the extraordinary developments we are seeing in the digital music business today. Record companies are licensing their music prolifically and diversely. A new wave of digital commerce, from mobile to broadband, is rolling out across the world. It is generating billions of dollars in revenues, and it is being driven, to a large extent, by music - by the people who create music, who produce it and who invest in it.

(IFPI 2006a)

He went on to observe, however, that this growth faced challenges from piracy and called for 'more cooperation from service providers and music distributors, to help protect intellectual property and contain piracy' (IFPI 2006a). This view was challenged by those uncomfortable with the shift to longer periods of copyright and the greater industry regulation and prosecution of those breaking it. There is a basic tension between protecting the rights and income of the original artists and the restriction of musical output. In a recent collection of papers, the editors noted 'a recurring skepticism' about the benefits of copyright, with many of the contributors concluding that 'the current copyright regime was of limited benefit to the musical practitioners they describe' (Frith and Marshall 2004: 15). Although the contributors at times adopted contradictory views, there was convergence on two significant points: that the role of the creators of music should be given more prominence, as a bulwark against commercial pressure; and that the term of copyright has become too long.

While articles and exchanges continue to proliferate around the impact of new technologies and the internet upon the nature and operation of copyright in an era of new technologies, the playing field is looking to be increasingly weighted in favour of the industry. Copyright was originally conceived as a mechanism to balance private and public interests by eliminating perpetual monopolies over creative works. Today, as Bishop documents, the media conglomerates 'use their power and [intellectual] property to influence national and international laws in order to lock down culture and control creativity' (Bishop 2005: abstract; also Frith and Marshall 2004).

This is part of a series of moves whereby 'Major labels are currently repositioning themselves in ways that maintain or enhance their gate-keeping powers' (Azenha 2006). Traditional business retrenchment is part of this: in early 2008, EMI announced plans to centralise staff and cut up to a third of its workforce, and cull its roster of 14,000 artists, given that roughly 85 per cent of the music that the company releases never makes a profit. Chairman Guy Hand's controversial plans also hinge on making existing artists more profitable by concentrating on single digital tracks rather then full albums.

New strategies include taking a fresh look at subscription services (such as Rhapsody and Yahoo! Music Unlimited), which provide a steady revenue stream. These are presently hampered by technological limitations, especially underdeveloped high-speed cell-phone networks, and difficulties with licensing provisions and costs. Current initiatives suggest that these can be met, with the promise of streaming unlimited music for a monthly fee, rather than selling it track by track (*Rolling Stone* 2007). Companies are also maximising the range of products they produce, to take advantage of the new digital environment: 'Just five years ago, you'd release a handful of products from every album, meaning three singles, a couple of 12-inch remixes. Maybe up to about 10. Now, for the last Justin Timberlake album [Future Sex/Love Games 2006] we released 181 products. And 140 of them were digital: ringtones, wallpaper, soundtracks for games' (Ged Doherty, head of Sony BMG, cited by Sawyer 2008).

The recording industry is now going through a new phase, characterised by the impact of digital music and the decentralising of the means of recording, reproduction and distribution. At the same time, there is increasing consolidation and integration of the music industry as a whole, as part of a global cultural industry.

Questions

1 Investigate a music industry website (see the list below). What economic and cultural changes does it suggest for the future of popular music production, distribution and consumption?

2 Any new medium or technological form changes the way in which we experience music, with implications for how we relate to and consume music.
   (a) Interview a friend who owns an iPod (or write an account of your own practices), asking them why, when and where they use it, in comparison with other ways they listen to music.
   (b) Interview a friend who downloads music (or write an account of your own practices) asking them why they prefer this method of acquiring music, the genres and artists downloaded, and their attitude towards the debates around downloading. (Protect their anonymity if necessary.)
   Background reading: Jones (2005); Jennings (2007).

3 Undertake a content analysis of a music magazine (either online or published), having decided what aspects of its coverage you want to investigate. Include reference to its target audience, advertising, scope, and the language and critical stance present in its reviews.

Further reading

Hull, G. P. (2004) *The Recording Industry*, 2nd edition, New York and London: Routledge. While the statistical data has obviously dated, this remains the most accessible and comprehensive overview of the music industry.

Jennings, D. (2007) *Net Blogs and Rock'n'Roll: How Digital Discovery Works and What It Means for Consumers, Creators and Culture*, London and Boston: Nicholas Brealey Publishing. A provocative discussion of the impact of digital music; frequently hostile to the 'mainstream' record companies.

Shuker, R. (2005) *Popular Music: The Key Concepts*, 2nd edition, London and New York: Routledge. An A to Z 'beginner's guide', with particular attention to genres.

Websites

Industry

www.bpi.co.uk – The British Phonographic Industry

www.riaa.com – Recording Industry Association of America

www.ifpi.org.uk – International Federation of the Phonographic Industries (IFPI)

www.emo.org – European Music Office

Labels

www.timewarner.com – AOL Time Warner

www.bertelsmann.com – Bertelsmann AG

www.emigroup.com – EMI Group

www.islandrecords.com – Island Records

www.sonymusic.com – Sony Music

www.wmg.com – Warner Music Group

www.belligeranza.c8.com – Sonic Belligeranza

Periodicals; music press

www.uncut.net – UNCUT

www.nme.com – NME

www.q4music.com – Q

www.thewire.co.uk – The Wire

www.mixmag.net – Mixmag

www.kerrang.com/ – Kerrang!

www.froots.mag.com – fRoots

References

Azenha, G. (2006) 'The Internet and the Decentralisation of the Popular Music Industry: Critical reflections on Technology, Concentration and diversification', *Radical Musicology*, (1) www. radical-musicology.org.uk/2006/Azenha.htm (accessed 17 June 2008).

Banks, J. (1996) *Monopoly Television: MTV's Quest to Control the Music*, Boulder, CO: Westview Press.

Barfe, L. (2004) *Where Have All the Good Times Gone? The Rise and Fall of the Record Industry*, London: Atlantic Books.

Barnard, S. (1989) *On the Radio: Music Radio in Britain*, Milton Keynes: Open University Press.

Bishop, J. (2005) 'Building International Empires of Sound: Concentrations of Power and Property in the "Global" Music Market', *Popular Music and Society*, 28 (4): 443-72.

Brennan, M. (2006) 'This Rough Guide to Critics: Musicians Discuss the Role of the Music Press', *Popular Music*, 25 (2): 221-34.

Fonarow, W. (2006) *Empire of Dirt: The Aesthetics and Rituals of British Indie Music*, Middletown, CT: Wesleyan University Press.

Frith, S. and Marshall, L. (eds) (2004) *Music and Copyright*, 2nd edition, Edinburgh: Edinburgh University Press.

Garofalo, R. (2003) 'I Want My MP3: Who Owns Internet Music?', in M. Cloonan and R. Garofalo (eds) *Policing Pop*, Philadelphia: Temple University Press, pp. 30-45.

Gay, P. du and Negus, K. (1994) 'The Changing Sites of Sound: Music Retailing and the Composition of Consumers', *Media, Culture and Society*, 16 (3): 395-413.

Gorman, P. (2001) *In Their Own Write: Adventures in the Music Press*, London: Sanctuary Publishing Limited.

Harris, J. (2003) *The Last Party: Britpop, Blair and the Demise of English Rock*, London: Harper Perennial.

Herman, E. and McChesney, R. (1997) *The Global Media: The New Missionaries of Global Capitalism*, London: Cassell.

Hesmondhalgh, D. (2002) *The Cultural Industries*, London: Sage.

Hoskyns, B. (ed) (2003) *The Sound and the Fury: A Rock's Back Pages Reader. 40 Years of Classic Rock Journalism*, London: Bloomsbury.

Hull, G. P. (2004) *The Recording Industry*, 2nd edition, New York and London: Routledge.

IFPI (2006a) 'Global Digital Music Sales Triple to US $1.1 billion in 2005 as a New Market Takes Shape', 19 January 2006, Press Release. www.ifpi.org;site-content/press/20060119.htm (accessed 19 January 2006).

IFPI (2006b) 'Recorded Music – Driver of a US $100 Billion Economic Sector', 22 June 2006, Press Release. www.ifpi.org/content/section_news/20060622.html (accessed 1 January 2009).

Jones, S. and Lenhart, A. (2004) 'Music Downloading and Listening: Finding from the Pew Internet and American Life Project', *Popular Music*, 27 (2): 221–40.

Kennedy, R. and McNutt, R. (1999) *Little Labels – Big Sound: Small Record Companies and the Rise of American Music*, Bloomington and Indianapolis, IN: Indiana University Press.

Kusek, D. and Leonard, G. (2005) *The Future of Music: Manifesto for the Digital music revolution*, Boston: Berklee Press.

McLeod, K. (2005) 'MP3s Are Killing Home Taping: The Rise of Internet Distribution and Its Challenge to the Major Label Music Monopoly', *Popular Music and Society*, 28 (4): 521–32.

Millard, A. J. (2005) *America on Record: A History of Recorded Sound*, 2nd edition, Cambridge: Cambridge University Press.

Negus, K. (1999) *Music Genres and Corporate Cultures*, London and New York: Routledge.

Popular Music (2002) 'Special Issue: Music and Television', 21 (3).

Rolling Stone (2007) 'Biz Bets on Subscriptions', 1041, 13 December: 17–18.

Ross, P. (2005) 'Cycles in Symbolic Production Research: Foundations, Applications, and Future Directions', *Popular Music and Society*, 28 (4): 473–88.

Sandall, R. (2007) 'Off the Record', *Prospect Magazine*, 7 August, (137).

Savage, J. (1991) *England's Dreaming: Sex Pistols and Punk Rock*, London: Faber & Faber.

Sawyer, M. (2008) 'Who Calls the Tune in the New Music Age?' *Guardian Weekly Global Network*, 2 February, www.scenta.co.uk/music/news/1714969/who-calls-the-tune-in–the-new-music-age.htm (accessed on the same day).

Schiller, D. (1999) *Digital Capitalism: Networking the Global Market System*, Cambridge, MA: MIT Press.

Shuker, R. (2008) *Understanding Popular Music Culture*, London: Routledge.

Telegraph Group (2008) Emma Thelwell, 'Keeping It Real and Keeping It Going', story reproduced in the *Dominion Post* (New Zealand), 23 February.

The Times (2007) 'Death Knell of the Old Music Industry', reproduced in the *Dominion Post* (New Zealand), 13 October.

15

The Internet and the Web

Lorenzo Cantoni and Stefano Tardini

Chapter overview

This essay defines and examines the internet as a medium and its relation to the world wide web. It discusses the origins of the internet, its impact on the communication world and other media and explores the new possibilities the internet provides for its users (such as user generated content, exchange and interactivity). To understand the internet as a medium of communication, it introduces a specific model (WCM) which evaluates internet communication's different dimensions. The chapter concludes by discussing the movement to web 2.0, especially the possibilities for community-building.

Introduction

According to the Webopedia, an interesting online encyclopedia dedicated to information, communication and technology (ICT), the internet

> is a massive network of networks, a networking infrastructure. It connects millions of computers together globally, forming a network in which any computer can communicate with any other computer as long as they are both connected to the internet. Information that travels over the internet does so via a variety of languages known as protocols.
>
> (www.webopedia.com/DidYouKnow/Internet/2002/Web_vs_Internet.asp)

This global network of computers is spreading more and more widely, both in our everyday and professional life, and is increasingly changing our practices (Cantoni and Tardini, 2008). The internet, for instance, is changing the way we buy and sell, allowing us to 'go' shopping while staying in front of a computer screen (e-commerce); it is changing the way we learn (e-learning), the way we interact with banks (e-banking) or with public administrations (e-government), the way we communicate with physicians and treat ourselves (e-health), the way we play (video) games, the way we meet people, and so on.

The internet is not the first 'technology of the word' (Ong 2002) to bring changes in social life: all previous communication technologies have caused more or less deep changes in the societies within which they have been introduced. The invention of *handwriting*, for instance, made it possible for the first time to communicate between persons who were separated both spatially and temporally (Danesi 2006); according to Walter Ong, writing initiated 'the separation of the word from the living present, where alone spoken words can exist' (Ong 2002: 82). The alphabetic letterpress print, invented by Johannes Gutenberg in 1456, made the word itself 'into a kind of commodity. The first assembly line, a technique of manufacture which in a series of set steps produces identical complex objects made up of replaceable parts, was (, , ,) one which produced a printed book' (Ong 2002: 118). The diffusion of print precipitated very important social and cultural changes: for instance, it had a normalising effect on national languages and fostered the rise of national literatures; it helped the birth of specialised knowledge and modern science on one side, and started the way to universal alphabetisation on the other; and so on (Cantoni and Tardini 2006: 18–23).

In respect of these technologies of the word, the internet must not be confused with the world wide web (www – or simply the web), although the two terms are often used interchangeably. The www is just a way of accessing information over the internet. The web transmits data using one of the languages 'spoken' over the internet, namely the HTTP (HyperText Transfer Protocol). However, information data can be exchanged over the internet also through other languages or tools, such as email, the File Transfer Protocol (FTP), instant messaging (IM) systems, and others.

In this chapter, the origins and the historical evolution of the internet and of the web will be presented in the first section; in the second one, the main tools of the web (websites) and of so-called web 2.0 will be introduced from a communicative perspective, i.e. they will be introduced as tools for communicating rather than as mere technological artefacts; the third section will focus on the main features of online communication, stressing the opportunities ICTs offer and the limits they impose; the final section will focus on the potential of web 2.0 tools in building new forms of online communities.

History of the internet and the web (www)

The origins of the internet are usually traced back to 1957 when the Soviet Union launched *Sputnik I* into space; as a reaction to this, in 1958 the US founded the Advanced Research Projects Agency (ARPA), a special agency under the Department of Defense, whose mission 'was to develop long-term highly innovative and hazardous research projects' (Cantoni and Tardini, 2006: 26). ARPANET, the first prototype of the internet, was developed by the ARPA department, and saw the light of day properly in 1969 when four US universities (the University of California Los Angeles, the Stanford Research Institute in Palo Alto, the University of California Santa Barbara and the University of Utah) were connected by a network of computers. The development of this first computer network was made possible by the application of *packet switching* to the concept of a *distributed network,* two fundamental concurrent inventions in the field of computer science. Packet switching is a computer process that allows division of a message into packets and sending of them to their destination following different routes; once all the packets arrive at their destination, they are recomposed into the original message. The concept of a distributed network was developed in the 1960s by Paul Baran, who was conducting a research funded by the US Air Force at the Research and Development (RAND) Corporation, research aimed at developing a telecommunication network that had to survive in case of a nuclear war. Distributed networks are networks that have no hierarchy and no predetermined routes between nodes, thus being much more secure than centralised and decentralised networks (see Figure 15.1), which are 'obviously vulnerable as destruction of a single central node destroys communication between the end stations' (Baran 1964).

The growth of ARPANET accelerated in the second half of the 1980s, thanks to the communication protocol TCP/IP (Transfer Control Protocol/Internet Protocol), which was adopted by ARPANET in 1983 and is still the core of the internet today: 'the transition to TCP/IP was perhaps the most important event that would take place in the development of the internet for years to come. After TCP/IP was installed, the network could branch everywhere' (Hafner and Lyon 1998: 249). In 1983, after the end of ARPANET's experimental phase, the network was split into two: a civilian network for the computer research community (ARPA internet) and a military one (MILNET). In the late 1980s ARPANET had already lost its role as

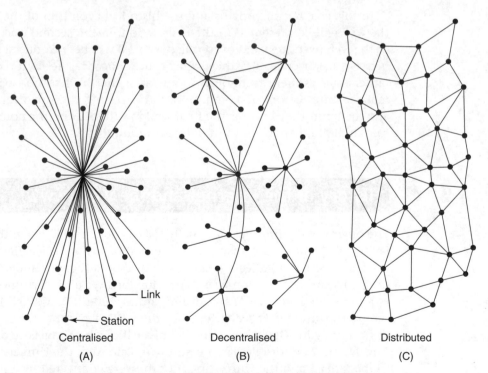

Centralised   Decentralised   Distributed
(A)   (B)   (C)

Figure 15.1 Centralised, decentralised and distributed networks

Source: From Baran, P. (1964) On Distributed Communications: I. Introduction to Distributed Communications Networks, RM-2420, Rand Corporation Memorandum p. 2. (www.rand.org/publications/RM/RM3420). Reproduced with permission of Rand Corporation via the Copyright Clearance Centre.

the spine of the internet, replaced by NSFNET, an academic network developed by the National Science Foundation. In 1990 ARPANET was officially decommissioned, and in 1991 commercial use of the internet was allowed.

However, despite the big growth of the internet in the second half of the 1980s (in 1982 ARPANET had 235 hosts, in 1990 there were 313,000), one issue remained unresolved: 'the world of computers and that of the internet remained completely separated until the end of the 1980s, because the graphic level and the multimedia richness of offline computers were still inaccessible to network applications' (Cantoni and Tardini, 2006: 29). This gap was filled in 1993, thanks to the invention of the world wide web (www) by Tim Berners-Lee, who put together hypertext and computer networks (Berners-Lee 2000). The diffusion of the web caused a radical change in the use of the internet, which shifted from the 'messenger' model to the 'hypermedia' model: the internet was no longer intended primarily as a tool for information exchanges (via textual chat systems) between human beings, but as a place for searching, retrieving and consulting documents of all kinds. Furthermore, the web determined the success of the internet as the predominant networking system: as a matter of fact, until 1995 the internet was just one networking system among many others, such as Usenet, America OnLine, Fidonet, Minitel, AT&T, and so on; with the advent of the web, the internet became by far the most important networking system.

The most recent step in the evolution of the internet and the web is so-called *web 2.0*: proposed for the first time in 2004, web 2.0 has captured a great deal of attention since then (O'Reilly 2005). The term itself – drawn from the field of software development – suggests a new version of the web, a more advanced and stable one (and due to its suggestive power the term has been frequently overused for commercial purposes, or just for fashion). In fact, web 2.0 does not provide any new protocol or completely new technologies, although a range of related technologies has been developed around it (like Ajax); it represents mainly a different use of the web itself, characterised by different expectations, goals and practices (Kolbitsch and Maurer 2006). Three core elements may be listed here:

1 A further enlargement of the number of people publishing online (UGC – User Generated Content); the web has lowered the publication threshold, making it possible for everybody with a little technical competence to publish online. Indeed, new applications and services are making this even more simple, not requiring any programming skill, nor – in some cases – the mediation of a computer (a telephone can be sufficient).

2 The web is interpreted and approached more like a town square than a library, transforming into a public place where people go to meet, to share and discuss knowledge.

3 Closely related to the previous elements, Web 2.0 is fulfilling the multimedia promises of the web; in fact, the web can be considered as a huge hypertext/medium, but – in reality – it has been for years more like a low-quality book: lots of texts and some images. The availability of large bandwidth connections makes possible a wider use of multimedia: good quality pictures, as well as audio, videos and animations are now populating web 2.0.

The tools

As we have seen, the internet is composed of different communication tools, such as e-mail, chat systems, instant messaging systems, desktop conferences, websites, peer-to-peer applications, Voice over IP (VoIP) systems, and so on. In this section we will focus only on the tools of the web, i.e. – roughly stated – on the resources that can be accessed through a browser.

The most fundamental resources of the web are *websites*: a website is a 'site (location) on the World Wide Web. Each Web site contains a home page, which is the first document users see when they enter the site. The site might also contain additional documents and files. Each site is owned and managed by an individual, company or organization' (www.webopedia.com/TERM/w/web_site.html).

From the point of view of its internal structure, a website is basically a hypertext, or – better – a *hypermedium*. As we have seen, the concept of hypertext/hypermedium was the basis of the invention of the web. Hypermedia can be defined as a set of *nodes*, i.e. of content units (texts, images, animations, videos, audio, etc.), and *links* that connect the nodes with one another (Nielsen 1995; Cantoni and Paolini 2001; Cantoni and Tardini 2006: 71–6). But a website is much more than its hypermedia structure: it is first of all a communication event, and as such it must be designed, developed, run, maintained, promoted and evaluated, in order to make it a real tool for effective communications (van der Geest 2001).

A comprehensive model, thus, is needed in order to have a complete understanding of the different dimensions of a website: we introduce here the website communication model (WCM), which resembles one of the most well-known communication models, the one developed by Russian linguist Roman Jakobson. In Jakobson's model each communicative event has six dimensions: an *addresser* sends a *message* to an *addressee* in a certain *code* by means of a *contact/channel*; the message refers to a *context* (Jakobson 1981). Similarly, the WCM identifies five main dimensions to be taken into account when considering a website (see Figure 15.2; see also Bolchini *et al.* 2004; Cantoni and Tardini 2006: 97–149).

According to the WCM, the following are the dimensions of a website:

- *Contents* and *services* (pillar I), i.e. information transmitted and activities permitted, such as following a link, downloading a document, writing a message, voting, gambling, buying, and so on. A very important issue related to this pillar is that of the *quality* of the information and the services provided, i.e. of their characteristic of meeting or exceeding customer expectations (Eppler 2003); this issue is particularly relevant in the www due to the ease of publishing online contents.

- The channel through which messages are sent are the *technical tools* that make contents and services available (pillar II) and, in particular, hardware, software, network connection and visual interfaces.

- In a web communication, the addressers are the persons who *publish* the website (pillar III), with all the activities related to the publishing of a communication activity: projecting, producing, maintaining, promoting, evaluating, improving, etc.

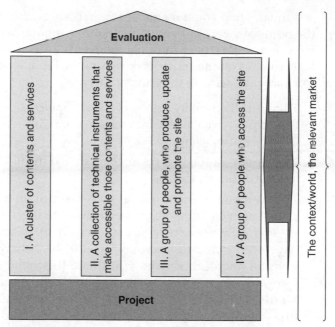

Figure 15.2 The website communication model (WCM)

Source: Adapted from Cantoni, L., Di Blas, N. and Bolchini, D. (2003) *Comunicazione, Qualità, Usabilità*. Apogeo: Milano, Italy. Reproduced with permission.

● The addressees are the persons who *visit* the website (pillar IV): the issue of the visitors of a website is pivotal in the www, as well as in any other communication, and is strictly related to two fundamental activities:

1 The analysis of the *usability* of a website, i.e. of the extent to which a website 'can be used by specified users to achieve specified goals with effectiveness, efficiency and satisfaction in a specified context of use' (ISO 1998: n. 11);

2 The analysis of the *actual usages* of the website: as a matter of fact, through the analysis of the logfiles of a website or other means, a lot of relevant communicative insights can be gathered, such as what the contents or services that have been accessed more frequently are, how long visitors stay with a given content, when and where they connect from, through which keywords users have found the website in a search engine, and so on. As can be easily understood, these insights are fundamental, for instance, to planning all the promotional activities of the website.

The fifth dimension, the context/market in which the website is immersed, affects all other pillars (in this case, the context of a website can only partially be associated with Jakobson's context). The dimension WCM does not take into account is the 'code', which in websites has a twofold nature: it refers both to the natural language or semiotic code in which the message is published and to the programming language in which the website is developed, and in this case it can be assigned to pillar II.

Fundamental components of the web are *search engines* (Battelle 2005). From the point of view of internet users, search engines are web services that help people search and retrieve information over the web by allowing them to make full-text searches on the contents of web pages. From a technical perspective, they are software that perform three main activities:

1 They surf the web by means of robots (*spiders* or *crawls*, i.e. pieces of software) that collect web pages and insert them into the search engine's database (*spidering* or *crawling*).

2 They index all the web resources gathered in the database by means of a ranking algorithm (*indexing*).

3 They respond to users' queries by presenting in a specific ranking the web resources that are (supposed to be) relevant to users' searches (*responding*). In order to offer only relevant results to users' queries, for some years search engines have been trying to take into account the behaviours of people who publish websites and of those who visit them: this trend can be seen as a 'pragmatic' turn of internet search engines, in the sense given by semiotician Charles W. Morris to 'pragmatics', i.e. the relation of signs (the web pages) to interpreters (the publishers/visitors) (Cantoni *et al.* 2006; Morris 1971).

When it comes to the list of web 2.0 features, it is difficult to come up with clear definitions. According to McKinsey (2007), the features can be organised into nine different families:

1 *blogs*: simple websites which offer a very easy publication interface, organise contents according to a temporal axis, and allow for reaction by readers;

2 *collective intelligence tools*: tools which help in collecting and organising pieces of information coming from members of a group in an attempt to represent group knowledge (Surowiecki 2004);

3 *mash ups*: aggregators of contents coming from different web sources, which combine to generate a new service (many of them are based on combining digital mapping services with other info sources);

4 *peer-to-peer networks*: services which allow access to data stored in other users' computers instead of downloading them from a single server, or allow a direct connection between two computers similar to a telephone call;

5 *podcasts*: audios or videos distributed via the internet, collected through aggregators and eventually played on portable devices;

6 *RSS (Really Simple Syndication* or *RDF Site Syndication,* where RDF stands, in its turn, for Resource Description Framework): they allow subscription to automatic distribution of news (RSS feeds);

7 *social networking*: services whose goal is to support social exchanges in given groups, allowing for data and knowledge sharing, social mapping, finding the right persons, etc.;

8 *web services*: services which support exchanges among different applications through automatic agents;

9 *wikis*: websites which support collaborative document editing.

Online communication

The communications that take place through the mediation of ICTs have rather peculiar features which depend on the tools used: communicating via chat is not the same as communicating via e-mail, publishing a website is not the same as interacting in 3D virtual environments. Generally speaking, online communication shares some features with both oral and written communications: for instance, instant messaging systems allow (quite) synchronous written communications; some authors write, with respect to this feature of online communication, of 'Netspeak' and of 'written speech' (Crystal 2001).

In this section, then, we will present the main features of web communication according to a four-layer taxonomy that can be useful when analysing each technology of the word (Cantoni and Tardini 2006: 23–5, 54–7).

The first layer considers what a communication technology is able to crystallise outside the evanescence of an oral communication. In this perspective communications via the web have very interesting features: first of all, they allow production of *multimedia* texts, i.e. communicative acts where written texts can be combined with images, animations, graphics, sounds, movies; potentially, in each electronic document texts elaborated in different semiotic codes can be integrated with one another. Furthermore, web communications are *persistent* in that they always leave a persistent trace that can be recorded somewhere in the digital world and can be recalled back when necessary (Erickson 1999). Two examples are worth mentioning here:

1 some web services (e.g. the 'Way Back Machine' – www.archive.org) regularly record a great number of web pages published around the world, thus making them available for web surfers once they are not online anymore;

2 every single interaction with a website leaves a trace in logfiles, where it is recorded and coded according to specific protocols; as already mentioned, from logfiles every interaction can then be analysed.

The second layer deals with the activities, processes, costs and resources needed for producing, modifying, replicating and keeping a communication object in a given technology. As regards the production of electronic documents, the relative ease with which digital texts, pictures, movies, etc. can be produced and published has raised the issue of digital literacy and the related one of the digital divide, i.e. the inequalities that exist in internet access from the point of view of both publishing and accessing online information (Hill 2004). Indeed, electronic tools make it very easy not only to publish online information, but also to modify and reproduce it, thus making it impossible to distinguish in the electronic world the original document from its copies; for instance, a wiki can be easily modified by anyone on the web, in a process of text production that is potentially endless. As for the reproduction activity, it must be noticed that, even if this is not a peculiarity of electronic texts, since every artefact produced by humans can always be reproduced by humans (Benjamin 1973), nonetheless digitisation has brought this process to an end, simply because in the digital world it is also very easy to reproduce only parts of a text and to paste electronic texts (or part of them) into one another.

Another important feature of electronic documents is *customisation*: websites, for instance, can be customised much more than other kinds of mass communication, i.e. they can be designed to closely meet the needs of single users or specific groups. In other words, web applications are more and more often designed as *adaptive*, i.e. in a way that they can adapt themselves to the users, presenting different contents and different links to different users (Brusilovsky *et al.* 2007). One field where the electronic world still presents many uncertainties is that of the preservation of electronic documents: as a matter of fact, due to the rapid changes in hardware and software standards and to the frailty of digital supports, we do not know how long an electronic document will be preserved, while we still have, for instance, manuscripts written many centuries ago.

The third layer concerns the possibility of moving communication artefacts in space through some physical support: because of the linguistic nature of the electronic world (Cicognani 1998), digital documents are *immaterial* and, as a consequence, very easy to transport; when they are published online, they cannot even be located spatially, thus overcoming the problem of moving them in space.

Finally, the fourth layer considers what one needs to access and interpret communication artefacts. Electronic documents are rather interesting in this respect: in fact, on the one hand they cannot be accessed directly by human senses, since they need the mediation of hardware and software in order to be seen and read; furthermore, they cannot be accessed as a whole, since only part of them appears on the monitor at one time. However, on the other hand, if electronic documents are published online they can be accessed potentially without any limit of time and space: a website is always close to its readers, provided they have internet access, unlike a book or a CD-ROM that are spatially located in a physical environment.

Community building in web 2.0

The features of online communication and, in particular, the three above mentioned characteristics of web 2.0, can offer us guidance in understanding the communities that shape it. In fact, user generated contents exemplify a further popularisation of the web, which includes publication: desktop publishing, photography, audio and video production. This popularisation of production is not to be understood as an enlargement in the number of authors in a library; rather, it has to be understood more as the expansion of numbers of people taking part in a public discussion. Their contents do not aim to be stable, they are mainly produced like actual communication exchanges. The third characteristic, a larger use of multimedia, explains why people can actually engage in extensive conversations/discussions, being able to rely also on audio and video channels which are less cumbersome and less time consuming than linguistic text production.

According to the WCM, a website itself can be considered a community of people running and accessing that website: people who share website contents (sometimes) get in touch with each other, for instance via e-mail. In fact, the internet itself has changed mass communication in that it allows for more extensive feedback/doubled ways communications. According to a semiotic interpretation of communities, there is a distinction between paradigmatic and syntagmatic communities (Tardini and Cantoni 2005). The first requires that people share a set of characteristics, for instance, the 'community of those who bet online'. Syntagmatic communities are built when people not only share given common characteristics, but also embark on actual communication exchanges; for example, people who share and comment on each other's photos or videos, or recommend each other for professional purposes, or get to know each other through any other common interests. Moreover, online communities can be distinguished depending on the way they support a community which gathers also offline, or a community whose exchanges take place exclusively online.

While the web has supported and fostered a number of old and new communities since its very beginning, web 2.0 goes even further in this direction. As noted above, users perceive the web less as a library and more as a place to meet other people. If, for instance, we think of the most famous wiki, i.e. Wikipedia (www.wikipedia.org), and map it as an online encyclopedia, we must observe that its authority is always in question, less authoritative (unless one really is an absolute relativist in respect of scientific knowledge), compared with a printed encyclopedia which has been refereed and subject to quality control. Nevertheless, we can map it as a place where people interested in a certain subject can discuss and collaboratively produce a document about the subject itself, hence giving birth to a new genre.

Web 2.0 also offers new tools to information research, pushing further the pragmatic turn of search engines. In fact, information-seeking is reinterpreted as expert-seeking, or seeking people with similar interests (and then, possibly, with specific expertise). As an example, we can mention search engines offering the possibility to publish questions and answers – where real people ask in natural language and provide fresh answers. We might also mention so-called *folksonomies* – user generated taxonomies which help to overcome the information overload problem, as well as to solve the impossibility of providing a universal semantic language (a task which can be performed, in fact, only in given applicative areas: the semantic web). Through folksonomies people can freely label web contents according to their own concerns. Those labels, provided they are numerous enough, can provide a relevant map for resources, helping people find what they actually need.

Questions

1 Digital literacy and the digital divide: what practices/activities are inconceivable without the internet today? What would be the cost of not having access to the internet in terms of your social life?

2 Information on the web: are the information/resources one can find on the web as reliable as the ones that can be found offline? How can the reliability of web sources be evaluated?

3 Online communities and social networks: what is the difference between being part of an online social network and part of an offline one? In what ways are the interactions and the relationships in each kind of social network different?

Further reading

Battelle, J. (2005) *The Search: How Google and Its Rivals Rewrote the Rules of Business and Transformed Our Culture*, New York: Portfolio. A detailed and interesting investigation into the power of online searches and search engines. It offers detailed historical information on the evolution of online search markets and interesting discussions on the issues it raises.

Berners-Lee, T. (2000) *Weaving the Web: The Original Design and Ultimate Destiny of the World Wide Web by Its Inventor*, with M. Fischetti, New York: HarperCollins. The story of the invention of the www in the words of its inventor. Tim Berners-Lee reflects also on the impact of the www and tries to predict its future directions.

Cantoni, L. and Tardini, S. (2006) *Internet* (Routledge Introductions to Media and Communications), London: Routledge. A comprehensive introduction to the internet and the www from a communication perspective; with in-depth investigations on ICT mediated communication, hypertext, websites and internet search engines.

Crystal, D. (2001) *Language and the Internet*, Cambridge: Cambridge University Press. An in-depth analysis of the communicative and linguistic aspects of the internet and of online conversations. The author's thesis is that 'netspeak' is a radically new linguistic medium that cannot be ignored.

Gillies, J. and Cailliau, R. (2000) *How the Web Was Born: The Story of the World Wide Web*, Oxford: Oxford University Press. A detailed story of the birth of the web. With a useful timeline at the end of the book.

Hafner, K. and Lyon, M. (1998) *Where Wizards Stay Up Late: The Origins of the Internet*, New York: Touchstone. A very detailed story of the birth and the early years of the internet, with many 'behind the scenes' anecdotes.

O'Reilly, T. (2005) 'What Is Web 2.0. Design Patterns and Business Models for the Next Generation of Software', 30 September 2005, available at www.oreillynet.com/pub/a/oreilly/tim/news/2005/09/30/what-is-web-20.html?page=1. The seminal paper on web 2.0, written by one of the inventors of the concept. The paper illustrates the principal features of web 2.0 by offering rich examples of web 2.0 applications and comparing them with web 1.0 ones.

Rivoltella, P. C. (ed) (2008) *Digital Literacy. Tools and Methodologies for Information Society*, New York: IGI Publishing. The book provides a rich conceptual framework for the issue of digital literacy in the so-called information society, stressing in particular the impact of digital media on educational processes.

Websites

www.archive.org - internet archive: a huge digital library of internet sites and other cultural artifacts in digital form; it also includes the WayBack Machine, an interesting web service that allows people to browse web pages that are no longer available online, archived from 1996.

www.itu.int - ITU - International Telecommunication Union: the website of the leading UN agency for information and communication technologies provides important reports and resources about the state of the information society.

http://jcmc.indiana.edu - Journal of Computer-Mediated Communication: an online quarterly publication, published since 1995, covering the issue of computer mediated communication in all its many different aspects.

www.webopedia.com – Webopedia – Online Computer Dictionary for Computer and Internet Terms and Definitions: a complete and reliable encyclopedia about ICT.

References

Baran, P. (1964) 'On Distributed Communications', Memorandum RM-3420, RAND Corporation. www.rand.org/publications/RM/RM3420/.

Battelle, J. (2005) *The Search: How Google and Its Rivals Rewrote the Rules of Business and Transformed Our Culture*, New York: Portfolio.

Benjamin, W. (1973) 'The Work of Art in the Age of Mechanical Reproduction', in W. Benjamin (ed) *Illuminations*, with an introduction by H. Arendt, London: Fontana Press, pp. 211–44.

Berners-Lee, T. (2000) *Weaving the Web. The Original Design and Ultimate Destiny of the World Wide Web by Its Inventor*, New York: HarperCollins.

Bolchini, D., Arasa, D. and Cantoni, L. (2004) 'Teaching Websites as Communication: A "Coffee Shop Approach"', in L. Cantoni and C. McLoughlin (eds) *Proceedings of ED-MEDIA 2004*, Norfolk, VA: AACE, 4119-24.

Brusilovsky, P., Kobsa, A. and Neidl, W. (eds) (2007) *The Adaptive Web: Methods and Strategies of Web Personalization*, Lecture Notes in Computer Science, Vol. 4321, New York: Springer.

Cantoni, L. and Paolini, P. (2001) 'Hypermedia Analysis: Some Insights from Semiotics and Ancient Rhetoric', *Studies in Communication Sciences*, 1 (1): 33–53.

Cantoni, L., Faré, M. and Tardini, S. (2006) 'A Communicative Approach to Web Communication: the Pragmatic Behavior of Internet Search Engines', *QWERTY. Rivista Italiana di Tecnologia Cultura e Formazione*, 1 (1): 49–62.

Cantoni, L. and Tardini, S. (2006) *Internet* (Routledge Introductions to Media and Communications), London: Routledge.

Cantoni, L. and Tardini, S. (2008) 'Communicating in the Information Society. New Tools for New Practices', in P.C. Rivoltella (ed) *Digital Literacy: Tools and Methodologies for Information Society*, New York: IGI Publishing, pp. 26–44.

Cicognani, A. (1998) 'On the Linguistic Nature of Cyberspace and Virtual Communities', *Virtual Reality*, 3: 16-24.

Crystal, D. (2001) *Language and the Internet*, Cambridge: Cambridge University Press.

Danesi, M. (2006) 'Alphabets and the Principle of Least Effort', *Studies in Communication Sciences*, 6 (1): 47–62.

Eppler, M. J. (2003) *Managing Information Quality: Increasing the Value of Information in Knowledge-intensive Products and Processes*, Berlin: Springer.

Erickson, T. (ed) (1999) 'Persistent Conversation', *Journal of Computer-Mediated Communication*, 4 (4), http://jcmc.indiana.edu/vol4/issue4/.

Hafner, K. and Lyon, M. (1998) *Where Wizards Stay Up Late. The Origins of the Internet*, New York: Touchstone.

Hill, E. (2004) 'Some Thoughts on E-Democracy as an Evolving Concept', *Journal of E-Government*, 1 (1): 23-39.

ISO (1998) *ISO 9241. Ergonomic requirements for office work with visual display terminals (VDTs)* – Part 11: 'Guidance on usability'.

Jakobson, R. (1981) 'Linguistics and poetics', in S. Rudy (ed) *Selected Writings. Vol. III: Poetry of Grammar and Grammar of Poetry*, New York: Mouton, 18-51.

Kolbitsch, J. and Maurer, H. (2006) 'The Transformation of the Web: How Emerging Communities Shape the Information We Consume', *Journal of Universal Computer Science*, 12 (2): 187-213.

McKinsey (2007) 'How Businesses Are Using Web 2.0. A McKinsey Global Survey', *The McKinsey Quarterly*.

Morris, C. W. (1971) 'Foundations of the Theory of Signs', in C. W. Morris (ed) *Writings on the General Theory of Signs*, The Hague: Mouton.

Nielsen, J. (1995) *Multimedia and Hypertext: The Internet and Beyond*, Cambridge, MA: AP Professional.

O'Reilly, T. (2005) 'What Is Web 2.0. Design Patterns and Business Models for the Next Generation of Software', 30 September 2005, available at www.oreillynet.com/pub/a/oreilly/tim/news/2005/09/30/what-is-web-20.html?page=1

Ong, W. J. (2002) *Orality and Literacy: The Technologizing of the Word*, New York: Routledge.

Surowiecki, J. (2004) *The Wisdom of Crowds: Why the Many Are Smarter Than the Few and How Collective Wisdom Shapes Business, Economies, Societies, and Nations*, New York: Doubleday.

Tardini, S. and Cantoni, L. (2005) 'A Semiotic Approach to Online Communities: Belonging, Interest and Identity in Websites' and Videogames' Communities', in P. Isaías, P. Kommers and M. McPherson (eds) *Proceedings of the IADIS International Conference e-Society 2005*, IADIS Press, pp. 371–8.

van der Geest, T.M. (2001) *Web Site Design Is Communication Design*, Philadelphia: John Benjamins.

16

News Agencies

Oliver Boyd Barrett and Terhi Rantanen

Chapter overview

News agencies are defined as organisations whose primary but not necessarily sole goal is business-to-business or wholesale provision of news information to other communications media, for them to repurpose and repackage for their retail news consumers. The chapter discusses the origins and evolution of an interdependent global news system of global or transnational, regional, domestic and local news agencies. The system has both been challenged by and accommodated to processes of contemporary globalisation, although some agencies have adapted much more successfully than others.

What are news agencies and why are they important?

News agencies were classically defined (e.g. Boyd-Barrett 1980) as *wholesale* media, gathering and packaging 'news' (much of it about currently developing events in the political, economic and sporting arenas) for the purpose of distributing it to other – *retail* – media, mainly newspapers and broadcasters, who then packaged this material for their own distinctive readers and audiences. In today's world the classic definition may be refined by requiring that for an organisation to be considered a 'news agency,' the business-to-business provision of news content and allied services for other media should be a salient feature of its operations. But in addition to their traditional 'wholesale' role, classic news agencies have also become increasingly important as 'retail' sources of information, providing tailored services not only for media, but also for non-media institutions and *individual* people as clients.

This has been evident for some time in the provision of financial news services for financial institutions, investment banks, brokers and traders, but is everyday more in evidence in the provision of general news through the internet. Even on the internet, however, clients typically access news agency news through secondary, or 'retail' agents consisting of web portals such as Yahoo!, news aggregators including Google, corporate websites, including the websites of newspaper and television stations, and blogs (Paterson 2006). Associated Press (AP) established The Wire, an online news service accessible through the sites of AP member media, in 1996, and began offering online access to its Photo Archive in 1997. In 2004, the first client for its online Financial News service was Yahoo! The 'wholesale' role of news agencies is therefore still important even though it is easier for the individual news consumer to access large quantities of news agency content without other editorial intervention.

The 'classic' news agencies, established as such well before the age of the internet, do not possess a monopoly on membership of the 'news agency' club, since this should include publishers, broadcasters and internet providers who also gather, package and repurpose news for other media. This phenomenon is an old one – since it includes syndicated news services such as the New York Times News Service, and could extend to the sale of television news channels to cable distributors. Some 'classic' news agencies buy into 'retail' media. Examples include Reuters' 20 per cent ownership (at the time of writing) of Independent Television News (ITN), the flagship of television news for commercial terrestrial television in the UK, or the ownership by Xinhua (national news agency of China) of the leading financial newspaper in Shanghai.

Origins of the international news system

News agencies were among the first highly visible manifestations of 'globalisation' in the 19th century, a process of the inter-linking of different local and national economies through the activities of transnational economic and financial trade. However, the agencies (especially those deemed to be, or self-described as, 'national') have been important symbols of national identity as well as contributing to the development of the nation-state by rationalising the national organisation of news collection and dissemination and centring these processes in major and 'capital' cities thus forming an international news exchange system (Boyd-Barrett 2000a; Rantanen 2009).

In postulating five stages of globalisation, Robertson (1992) argues that a second phase began in Europe in 1750–1870. While he places international communication only in his third, 'take-off' phase (1875–1925), news agencies had started their transnational operations earlier. If we define globalisation, as Tomlinson does, as the ever-thickening network of interconnections and interdependences that characterises modern social life (Tomlinson 1999: 2), it is significant that news agencies operated as the first electronic media transmitting news instantaneously and simultaneously to and from many different parts of the world.

Nor should we overlook the relationship between geographic centres of political, economic and military power, and the major hubs of worldwide news gathering and dissemination. Global processes are not neutral nor egalitarian in their operations and impacts: the global news system that is their informational component should be investigated not merely as an economic or business phenomenon but also as one with important hegemonic ramifications.

The Havas agency, predecessor to Agence France Presse (AFP), and founded in 1832 in Paris, is widely considered to be the world's first news agency. It started as a private firm owned by ex-banker Charles Havas, by translating items from domestic and foreign newspapers. AP was founded in New York as a press cooperative in 1846. A second major European agency, Wolff, was founded in 1849 in Berlin. Its owner, newspaper proprietor Bernhard Wolff, delivered economic news to his own newspaper *National-Zeitung* and then extended the service to other newspapers and enterprises. A contemporary of Wolff, Julius Reuters (originally Isaac Beer), founded a news agency in Paris where both Reuter and Wolff had once worked for Havas. The new Reuters agency soon had to move, first to Aachen and then to London, where it started operations in 1851. Establishment of these agencies was subsequently followed by a *national* agency in almost every European country. By the end of the century most European countries had their own news agencies and the trend has continued worldwide.

News transmission has always been transnational, crossing the boundaries of nation-states. Before the first news agencies, newspapers delivered foreign news mainly by quoting foreign newspapers or, if they could afford it, reports from their own correspondents. When the news agencies started operations, foreign news-gathering became primarily their responsibility. Even in their early years, foreign news transmission played a major role. The three pre-eminent European agencies – Havas in France, Wolff in Germany and Reuters in Britain – each transmitted foreign news from the first years of their operation, while other agencies continued to operate mainly within a national framework. Reuters actually began as an international agency. A separate agency (the Press Association) was established in 1868 to provide domestic news to national newspapers in the UK and Ireland. These major agencies specialised in political and financial news, above all else, and their clients were mainly news media, financial institutions and governments. Political and financial affairs have always had a strong international component, and transnational links of this kind had grown much stronger and more intense with industrialisation.

Simultaneously, news was commercialised and monopolised. The news agencies established exchange arrangements between themselves to further reduce costs, rationalise operations, control competition and protect markets. The first extant and verifiable agreement among the three big agencies was signed in 1859. These arrangements were revised periodically and constituted the foundation of a powerful news cartel that lasted for more than 70 years. Although the cartel itself was dismembered in the 1930s, its long period of operation established an institutional hierarchy or global news system which bequeathed very significant advantages to some of its leading members, notably, Reuters, Havas and its successor – Agence France Presse – and finally, to Associated Press, which had originally been a junior member of the cartel.

Through the cartel agreements, the global agencies allocated themselves control over given territories on an exclusive or shared basis. For example, according to the 1909 agreement, Reuters controlled outside its 'home' territory the following: Canada, India, most of the Far East, Australia, New Zealand, and its dominions in Africa, while it shared certain other territories with Havas. Each global agency was to negotiate appropriate agreements with a national agency in its domain. The national agencies obtained through these agreements exclusive rights to the news from the global agencies. News from the cartel agencies would be funnelled through to the national agency by the particular global agency with which a national agency had to deal. Inevitably, this stoked concern among some national agencies and their respective governments about the ways in which news of the world was represented by the global agency, and about how the global agency represented news of their countries to the rest of the world through the cartel. In signing these agreements, national agencies relinquished their right to transmit news abroad, either directly or through any other agency. They could send this news only through the global agency with which they had concluded the agreement. In addition, the national agencies paid commission to the global agencies, not vice versa (Rantanen 1990).

There were several attempts to break the cartel by national agencies, but it was only the partnerships established with other national agencies by the two rival US agencies – namely, the United Press (UP, founded by Edward W. Scripps in 1907, later to become United Press International or UPI) and AP, founded by Moses Yale Beach – that finally crushed the system. The German Wolff lost its position as a global agency after the German defeat in World War One, and its former territories were acquired and redistributed between Reuters and Havas. UP, which had operated outside the cartel, already served South America – previously Havas territory – and AP followed. AP managed to extract a major concession from the cartel in 1918, when it concluded a separate agreement with Havas that gave the AP a free hand in South America (Rantanen 2009).

Both US agencies were interested in the Asian market. While UP operated outside the cartel and successfully competed with it, AP became more and more anxious to operate freely without the restrictions set by the cartel (AP became a formal member of the cartel in 1927). UP was free to start operations in Asia, therefore, but AP faced the problem that the Far East belonged to Reuters, which was much stronger there than Havas had been in South America. The cartel finally collapsed in 1934 with the US agencies playing the decisive role. If World War Two had not broken out when it did, the US agencies would have become completely global by the late 1930s. The US became the only country to have two global, general news agencies in the world's news market. Indeed, for several decades there were three, including Hearst's International News Service (INS). Today, the US is home to only one of the surviving giant general news agencies, AP. UPI has greatly diminished in stature. But, additionally, the US is home to major financial news agencies Bloomberg and Dow Jones. The other two principal Western agencies that now dominate the global news market are the French AFP, founded in 1944 as direct successor of Havas, based in Paris, and Reuters, based in London and, at the time of writing, in the process of being acquired by Thomson, a Canadian media conglomerate.

The global news agencies

News agency identity has a variety of geographical markers. Most celebrated of the genre are the major global print news agencies, including AFP, AP and Reuters. While these do operate globally, gathering news independently from most countries of the world, and selling it to clients in most countries of the world, each of the three big agencies also has a long-established national identity (though

Reuters rather less than the other two), and two of the 'Big Three' have a strong European identity. The history of news agency research has been driven for the most part by Western scholarship which in turn has tended to concentrate its attention on the Western news agencies and, among these, their general news operations. While these may have been and perhaps still are the most significant organisations of their kind, on some indicators, there are evident ideological and definitional problems with the manner in which many other agencies with significant international reach have been sidelined, including 'national' general news agencies Chinese Xinhua, the German dpa, the Japanese Kyodo, the Russian TASS (now ITAR-TASS), and the Spanish EFE, among others, as well as financial or other specialist agencies, including Bloomberg (based in New York), Dow Jones (based in New York) and Interfax (based in Moscow).

Of the classic 'big three' agencies, one, Reuters, grew spectacularly wealthy from the 1980s as it redirected its core business towards computerised information and transaction services for financial markets and commodity traders, which now account for well over 90 per cent of its total revenues. The other two major agencies, AP and AFP, control substantial worldwide human resource and communications assets. They do not typically generate substantial revenues in excess of operating expenditures, nor have they been constituted for that purpose. They serve media markets, principally. Until the 1990s they derived most of their revenues from domestic markets. More recently, overseas clients account for up to half of AP's revenues (Hau 2008).

Reuters, once a private limited liability company owned by the national and provincial daily newspaper press of the UK and Ireland, is today – as Thomson Reuters – a commercial company quoted on the London and New York stock exchanges. AP is a not-for-profit cooperative news agency owned by almost all of the 1200+ daily newspapers of the US. AFP is a public entity constituted according to French law, with headquarters in Paris and controlled by a governing council on which is represented the French newspaper press, the agency's journalists and its major state clients. State clients still account for approximately half of the agency's revenue, and the bulk of this derives from French media and other clients.

Business models that long sustained the operations of news agencies have undergone continual processes of adaptation and evolution in response to changing social and political contexts, market structure, new technologies and competition. Since the 1990s, the pressures for change have emanated from several sources:

- *Merger and acquisition among both the agencies themselves (e.g. acquisition of Bridge-Telerate by Reuters and of Reuters by Thomson) and among their clients.* This has implications for the scope and intensity of competition between news agencies; and also for the diversity and influence of corporate voices on their governing bodies.

- *Weakening of the distinction between 'wholesale' news media (providing news solely for other media), and 'retail' media (providing news directly to end-users).* This extends the boundaries of what can properly be described as the market(s) for news agencies; and creates tense competitiveness between classic agencies and their media owners and clients. In some countries, the US included, declining advertising and circulation revenue has reduced the tolerance of media clients for competitive entrepreneurial services generated by agencies that the clients are supposed to own or control. Alternatively, in previously developing countries such as India and China, significant growth of outlets and of advertising revenue has provided a firmer revenue basis for national news agencies.

- *Blurring of the boundary between 'national' and 'global' news agencies.* This has implications for the sustainability of the original 'hierarchy' of news agencies worldwide and the collaborative 'systemic' properties of the global news system and also shifts the boundaries of what can properly be described as the market(s) for individual news agencies.

- *Emergence of new regional agencies.* ANSAMed, for example, is a new agency formed by a collaboration of 17 news agencies operating in Europe and in the Middle East. ANSAMed operates a newswire and website in Italian, English and Arabic (Rantanen 2006). There are indications of emergent new voices from the global 'South,' including Al Jazeera, based in Qatar, although these are primarily 'retail' services broadcasting directly to audiences.

- *Competition from emergent web-based services and blogs* sometimes impacts news agency revenue streams, but also creates new clients for classic agencies. AP depends on online services for 15 per cent of its overall revenues. Reuters sells news services to large numbers of corporate and other websites.

- *Declining dependence on traditional sources of revenue.* There has been a general decline in the proportion of revenues drawn from membership assessments, in the case of cooperatively owned agencies, or from government subsidies in the case of government-sponsored agencies and, in the case of almost all agencies, from content-based income streams in favour of revenues earned from other categories of service. By 2007, the largest cooperative agency, AP, depended on its US newspaper members for only 30 per cent of its revenues, with 37 per cent of revenue being generated by global customers for its broadcast services, 15 per cent for online services and 18 per cent from other international clients and clients for photographic services (Hau 2008).

- *Intensified competition for new sources of revenue in niche markets* such as financial information services and trading platforms, specialist content fields such as sports and weather information, infrastructural support such as copy-editing and page preparation for client media.

- *Blurring the boundaries between news and entertainment, opinion and information.* (Rantanen 2009)

Sources of revenue for traditional news agencies have generally extended beyond media subscriptions to include, at various times, government subvention, advertising placement, leasing of communications networks and, most significant of all in the case of Reuters, financial information and trading platforms for institutions such as banks, brokers and traders. Reuters announced in 2007 that the board of Canadian Publisher Thomson Corp. had agreed to buy Reuters for approximately $17.2 billion. The Thomson Corporation would control about 53 per cent of the new company. The merger would intensify the business rivalry between Reuters and another leading supplier of business information and trading platforms, Bloomberg. Combined, Thomson and Reuters would control 34 per cent of the market for financial data, and Bloomberg 33 per cent. Also in 2007, News Corporation secured the consent of the owners of Dow Jones, publishers of the *Wall Street Journal* and of Dow Jones wire services to News Corporation's bid for ownership. For the first time in news history, four of the world's wealthiest news agencies, AP, Bloomberg, Dow Jones (now owned by News Corporation) and Reuters would be controlled by businesses based in North America, specifically the US and Canada.

The world's largest agencies had otherwise achieved a measure of financial and structural stability by 2007, following years of market turbulence. Many agencies that looked fragile in 2001 were notably healthier by 2007. Worldwide, most news agencies, whether global, regional or national, showed signs of convergence, in whole or in part, towards a market-based business model (Boyd-Barrett 2002, 2007). The world's single most celebrated example of cooperative ownership, the not-for-profit AP, was dependent on membership assessments for less than a third of its income by 2006 – these same members contributed a third of AP's US daily state news (Hau 2008). What had once been one of the world's most celebrated examples of government ownership and finance of a news agency, Xin Hua, the national agency of China, depended on self-generated revenue for 30–50 per cent of expenditure from 1985.

Bloomberg, of which approximately 70 per cent is owned by the agency's founder (and for many years Mayor of New York), Michael Bloomberg, reported sales in 2006 of $4.7 billion, an increase of 14.6 per cent over 2005. Reuters staged a recovery from several years of decline or stagnation, with overall revenues of $5.1 billion, a growth of 6.5 per cent over 2005. Dow Jones and Co. reported 2006 revenue of $1.93 billion, showing a year on year growth of over 16 per cent. In 2005, AP reported net income of $18.5 million on overall revenue of $654.2 million, a 3.8 per cent increase on 2004. In 2006, AP's overall revenues increased to $654.2 million. Whereas 94 per cent of Reuters revenue has derived from non-media commercial services in recent years, the corresponding percentage for AP has been 20 per cent.

Other major international agencies, and national agencies with significant international reach, also showed signs of innovative, profit-driven development. In 2006, Agence France Presse reported net profit of $3.9 million (contrasted with a corresponding loss the previous year), a result described by its CEO as the 'best result since 1979'. Dpa, the largest news agency of Germany, reported 2006 sales of $124.4 million, and earnings after tax of $7.8 million, an increase of 30 per cent over the previous year. Earnings in 2005 had registered the first increase in turnover in five years. The British Press Association (PA) increased its underlying operating profit in 2006 by 5 per cent to $12.8 million, on turnover which increased by 15 per cent to $173.4 million.

The internet had initially seemed more a threat than an opportunity for news agencies, because it reduced the costs of market entry for news-gathering and distribution. Yet by 2007 the larger news agencies had successfully accommodated to a multi-media universe. All the major agencies now ran internet news and information services for direct client access, as well as news and information packages for client websites and mobile telephony services. Thus, the internet had greatly expanded the number of potential clients for agency services, increased agency flexibility in generating novel information packages, and reduced the costs of distribution so that a greater proportion of expenditure could be dedicated to content and service quality. Many client media during this period reduced the strength of international news gathering and came to depend more heavily on the major agencies. Among the new generation of alternative news sites and blogs, few had the resources to compete with major agencies and most depended heavily on the news services, direct or indirect, of the agencies.

The world of commercial television news agencies (therefore excluding the Eurovision exchange of news among European public service broadcasters) has been reduced to two major players, Reuters Television News and APTV (which absorbed what had been the third largest player, WTN, in 1998), and there were signs in 2000 of retrenchment by Reuters Television News while the company played out multi-media and internet strategies.

The global news agencies represent the archetype of 'syndication' and they highlight the issue as to whether the apparent diversity of 'retail' media is much less than it seems. The major agencies reflect 'Western' news values (e.g. priority to elite nations, elite sources, recency, negativity). They are primarily in business to provide news of major 'national' stories of economic, political and military affairs, sport and entertainment, as well as news of international relations and conflict. They are interested in events more than processes. Notwithstanding and perhaps in part *because* of their commercial adaptability, news agency coverage of many parts of the world and on many issues and topics is extremely thin (see Davies 2008, for a severe critique).

National news agencies

The global news agencies are sometimes regarded as the most significant players of a global news system made up of global, national and city news media. Global news agencies monitor local media, they often develop stories that have been first identified in local media, and they customise local news for distribution to and consumption in global markets. Their local clients include national news agencies with whom they often maintain close ties. National news agencies are popular: most nation-states have them and new nation-states are generally quick to establish them. They may be seen as component parts of the iconography of nationhood (Boyd-Barrett 2000a). National news agencies are often the largest domestic news-gathering organisations, connecting central and peripheral media in a network with the national agency at its centre, collecting news from the different provinces, compiling a service of national and regional news for national dissemination. Some national agencies were originally established directly by or with the aid of the global agencies, and many were junior partners in a global network of news exchange in which the global agencies were dominant.

The global agencies typically supply their international news services to national agencies. Directly, or indirectly through national agencies, national media take international news from the global agencies (which are often the sole first-hand news sources for such news), and their news priorities are influenced by the global agencies. Local media usually have access to other sources of international news, including the international press and broadcasters. There has been significant internationalisation from news suppliers of the 'south', including Inter Press Service (Rome), Al Jazeera (Qatar) and Telesur (Caracas). Such international 'retail' media are not necessarily first-hand sources, since their international coverage may have been influenced by and to a varying extent drawn from the global news agencies, even while they are also adding valuable and sometimes more in-depth coverage of leading news events and issues.

Many national agencies also engage in news exchange networks with other national agencies, to augment supplies of regionally-relevant news and compensate for perceived deficiencies in the news portfolios of global news agencies. For example, the Organization of Asia Pacific News Agencies (OANA, established in 1961), provides a forum for the engagement of 41 national news agencies (in 2007) from 33 countries of Asia and the Pacific-rim in discussion of issues of mutual interest and concern. OANA has also developed a regional news exchange for the mutual benefit of members, generating approximately 50,000 stories each year.

Early in the 21st century, many national news agencies appeared vulnerable in the face of a range of external and internal problems; the nature of the problems varied between different kinds of news agency. A year 2000 review (Boyd-Barrett 2000b; Boyd-Barrett and Rantanen 2000) of European news agencies argued that the industry as a whole could be described as in a state of crisis. While some sources of this crisis persist, it appeared, by 2007, that many if not most national news agencies were not only surviving, but some were thriving.

Most national news agencies in Europe demonstrate some features of 'cooperative' structure, in as much as they depend on the cooperation of different and possibly competing media that share a common interest in securing a cheap and reliable source of news, or, sometimes, on the cooperation of private media, public media and state agencies. Cooperative agencies often experience tensions between the interests of their owners in saving money as against the interests of their managers in improving/conserving service, between owner preference for exclusivity of membership (to shut out competitors) against management preference for universality of service to maximise revenue, between owners' minimalist goal of covering costs as against managers' entrepreneurial ambitions to explore new markets and services even where these conflict with private business interests of their owners and, finally, between the owners' vision of a closed 'business-to-business' operation, as against managers' interest in a more open 'business to customer' ethos.

More fortunate managers have persuaded owners to allow national agencies some entrepreneurial freedom in return for rate reductions on the mainstream news services. Less fortunate managers encounter reluctance among owner-clients to maintain desired levels of investment and rates of subscription. Rate restrictions imposed by owners are a common cause of dispute between owners and agency managers. These tensions may be most in evidence in the case of those cooperative agencies that depend very heavily for their income on media markets and therefore have the furthest to move in order to diversify into new services and markets. Some of the older, cooperative agencies are among those most heavily wedded to traditional media markets: this was the case, for example, of the Swedish national news agency, whose cooperative structure fell apart in 1999.

Globalisation presents a somewhat different threat to the traditional news agency. Media members of a national news agency cooperative increasingly find themselves subsumed within larger international corporations that may have little sensitivity or respect for local news markets, needs or customs, and have a strong interest in cost reduction and profit maximisation. The result may be pressure to reduce staff and lower rates, or even to develop separate agencies whose sole mission is to serve the news needs of their respective owner corporations. This may be particularly dangerous in markets that are characterised by a high degree of concentration. In these cases, a small number of corporations control both the media and the national news agency which serves them: if one of these corporations withdraws from the cooperative then it undermines the agency's claim to be 'national', and its economic viability. Many national agencies in Europe have experienced competition that emerges from within their memberships, although to date most such efforts have been repulsed or contained by incumbent national agencies. Such competition may sometimes take the form of regional challenges to centrally dictated news agendas.

National news agencies that have or have had strong ties to their respective national governments, among them the agencies of Central and Eastern Europe, face a somewhat different range of problems. Just as dependence on government for subsidy or for custom is itself a problem for agencies that are dependent on such funding, equally so, and for different reasons, are reductions in government subsidy or custom – a worldwide trend in the wake of processes of deregulation and political transition. These same processes simultaneously open the doors to competition from the global agencies which may establish national or financial news services for local markets. The post-cold war states of Central and Eastern Europe have had to develop new models for the relationship of state and news agency, and a variety of solutions have emerged, of which some offer substantial protections from undue political interest, but mostly have made their national agencies prisoners of the state.

In response to the aforementioned challenges of globalisation, news agencies are under great pressure to 'diversify'. The range of diversification strategies includes services for: internet portals, aggregators, blogs and websites; supply of news to mobile telephony service providers; sale of advertising space and the distribution of advertising to client media; specialised country, county, issue, industry, sports and classified advertising; consultant and media management (information, market assessment, feasibility, negotiating deals); public relations wires; copy-editing for client media groups; direct print-to-customer pagination; screen-ready and teletext services; specialist statistics or data (e.g. financial, sports); financial (share prices, performance graphs, unit trust company information and graphics, investment analysis graphics), weather news (national, regional and international weather graphics, symbol charts, text forecasts and reports, comparative data, detailed analysis, world temperature tables, satellite pictures), television listings, special features; and management of supply of client news to databases such as Lexis-Nexis. Some news agencies, such as the Australian Associated Press, cover the entire costs of their traditional news-gathering activities from revenues generated by such entrepreneurial initiatives. Such entrepreneurship may be more international than the original news business it was designed to serve, as is the case with the British Press Association's foray into European sports and weather services.

Issues

This chapter addresses a number of key issues. A principal issue of concern is diversity of supply. Are there enough sources of international and national news supply? Do the international and national agencies represent a sufficiently comprehensive (including geographical, ethnic, political) diversity of voices, topics, issues and interests? A second issue has to do with revenue generation. Can these agencies survive economically while maintaining a commitment to their core mission as news-gatherers and suppliers? How far do pressures to diversify their economic base in order to generate additional revenue, or in other ways to adjust to the new conditions of deregulated and globalised markets, conflict with their core mission? Thirdly, we should ask how far are traditional structures of ownership and control – including the different examples available of cooperative and state ownership – suited to the new world order in which the agencies find themselves, and to the pressures on them to diversify economically and to demonstrate credibility by maintaining independence of political and corporate interests? A fourth issue has to do with new technology and, in particular, the impact of the internet. What are the likely implications for cost reduction, news-gathering practices, service delivery, revenue structure (for example, does the internet suggest a future of greater dependence of agencies on advertising as opposed to subscription revenue or, less directly, on clients who are themselves more and more dependent on advertising revenue), and market competition?

In the previous edition of this book we considered that the biggest question of all was whether there was still a role for national news agencies and, if so, how that role should best be performed in a global economy. It seemed self-evident that there was such a role in developing countries where the few media were likely to be concentrated in urban areas, and where there was a strong need for a communications vehicle that could be harnessed to developmental campaigns, for example, of agriculture or education, and where the national agency could provide a national news service that was also a contribution to the government's own internal channels of information. There was more of a question, we suggested, about the strength of the case for news agencies in media-saturated, developed countries, where the clarity of role might be less obvious, which in turn might indicate the need for a fundamental reclarification of purpose and potential about the very nature of the news agency business at national level. In the event, market challenges to the business models of traditional retail print and broadcast media in the developed world, associated with declining circulations, audiences and advertising revenue, have actually intensified retail media dependence on news agencies for supply of news, just at the time that news agencies have become more proficient in cost control, exploitation of the opportunities of the internet, and the development of alternative sources of revenue that they can use to cross-subsidise traditional news-gathering and sales.

As we have seen, many agencies that looked fragile in 2001 were notably healthier by 2007, in many cases because they were converging towards a market-based business model. In some cases this was achieved through a radical change in ownership structure and/or business model, as in the case of the New Zealand Press Association (NZPA) which, under pressure of intensifying business rivalries among its increasingly concentrated owner-client newspaper base, transitioned from a media cooperative model to a conventional business model in 2006. In a further sign of growing confidence among both news agencies and governments alike, the national news agency of Indonesia, Antara, transitioned in 2007 from being principally a government financed agency to being an independent business entity. But rather than just abandon the news agency to the cold new world of entrepreneurship, the Indonesian government provided $45 million start-up capital, with a view to the news agency achieving sustainability within a five-year period, a possible prelude to it then going public on the stock exchange. Rationalisation of its legal status would enable partnerships with private enterprises. Equally important – because the measure acknowledged the importance both of the public role of news agencies and the duty of government to enable the fulfilment of that role – the government committed to continue underwriting the news agency's public service operations, subject to regular parliamentary scrutiny. The Indonesian example may suggest there lies a 'third way' between older ideas of either media or government-*subsidised* news agencies, on the one hand, and the neo-liberal solution of 'out-sourcing' public service functions to the discipline and mercy of the marketplace, on the other.

Questions

1 What is the distinction between 'wholesale' and 'retail' media? Why has this been important in the past? Is it still important?

2 What are the contributions of news agencies to the gathering, distribution and social construction of news?

3 In what ways might the operations of news agencies be said to facilitate or to impede plurality of news sources for print and broadcast media?

4 How do news agencies contribute to globalisation?

5 How important are traditional news agencies as national agenda setters for news?

Further reading

Boyd-Barrett, O. (1980) *The International News Agencies*, London: Constable. This study is the first by a social scientist of the growth and development of news agencies worldwide, focusing mainly on international but also on national news agencies. It includes interview, survey and observational evidence from news agency journalists across all continents.

Boyd-Barrett, O. and Rantanen, T. (1998) *The Globalization of News*, London: Sage. This edited collection includes chapters on the international print, television and financial news agencies and case studies of national and regional news agencies in different transitional contexts from dictatorship to democracy, state socialism to deregulation, apartheid to pluralism. The book makes substantial progress towards the theorisation of news agencies.

Rantanen, T. (1990) *Foreign News in Imperial Russia: The Relationship between International and Russian News Agencies, 1856–1914*, Helsinki: Federation of Finnish Scientific Societies. While this is a very specialised work, it offers what is probably the single most detailed insight into the competition between international news agencies and between international and domestic news agencies in the 19th century.

Read, D. (1998) *The Power of News*, 2nd edition, Oxford: Oxford University Press. While there are many histories of individual news agencies this is probably the most substantial news agency history ever written, and the first to draw comprehensively from the Reuters' archives, following their restoration and cataloguing in the 1990s.

References

Boyd-Barrett, O. (1980) *The International News Agencies*, London: Constable.

Boyd-Barrett, O. (2000a) 'Constructing the Global, Constructing the Local: News Agencies Re-Present the World', in A. Malek and A. P. Kavoori (eds) *The Global Dynamics of News*, Stamford: Ablex, pp. 299–321.

Boyd-Barrett, O. (2000b) 'National and International News Agencies: Issues of Crisis and Realignment', *Gazette: The International Journal for Communication Studies*, 62 (1): 5–18.

Boyd-Barrett, O. (2002) 'Towards the "New Model" News Agency' in APA – Austria Presse Agentur (ed) *The Various Faces of Reality: Values in News (Agency) Journalism*, Innsbruck: StudienVerlag, pp. 91–6.

Boyd-Barrett, O. and Rantanen, T. (2000) 'European National News Agencies: The End of an Era or a New Beginning?' *Journalism*, 1 (1): 86–105.

Davies, N. (2008) *Flat Earth News*. London: Chatto and Windus.

Hau, L. (2008) 'The News Business: Down on the Wire', *Forbes*, 14 February.

Paterson, C. (2006) 'News Agency Dominance in International News on the Internet', Papers in International and Global Communication No. 01/06, Centre for International Communications Research, Leeds University, http://ics.leeds.ac.uk/papers/cicr/exhibits/42/cicrpaterson.pdf (accessed 20 June 2008).

Rantanen, T. (1990) *Foreign News in Imperial Russia: The Relationship between International and Russian News Agencies, 1856–1914*, Helsinki: Federation of Finnish Scientific Societies.

Rantanen, T. (2006) 'News Agencies. Their Structure and Operation Revisited'. European Association of News Agencies Conference, Geneva.

Rantanen, T. (2009) *When News Became New*, Oxford: Blackwell.

Robertson, R. (1992) *Globalization, Social Theory and Global Culture*, London: Sage.

Tomlinson, J. (1999) *Globalization and Culture*, Cambridge: Polity Press.

17

News Media

Jackie Harrison

Chapter overview

In this chapter I define news and news journalism as both an ideal and as something real that occurs within the setting of the news media. The news media are themselves currently being subject to two major interrelated vectors of change which combine to challenge their role and remits as providers of news. The first vector of change is referred to as 'technological' and the second 'journalistic'.

Defining news and news journalism

At its simplest and most basic level news can be defined as an interest in and reports of contemporary events. Certainly, at its most fundamental our interest in reports of contemporary events is well attested to by anthropologists, historians, psychologists and sociologists. Human beings it seems are always interested in events beyond their immediate purview and, correspondingly have always relished reports that purport to explain such events. Indeed, some analysts such as Shoemaker and Cohen (2006) believe that biological and cultural evolution combines to form the basis for our need for news. Be that as it may, I shall side step the issue of the origin of our need for news and side with those media historians who conveniently date what we call and recognise as news, i.e. *mediated* reports of contemporary events, with the development of the printing press from the late 15th century onwards. It was from this time on that news and technology became inextricably and forever linked together in a significant way as the processes of news mediation became ever more technologically expansive and sophisticated and the requirements made of news journalism ever more demanding.

Over time the growing sophistication of news mediation had an impact on three functions undertaken by news media: news gathering; news production; and news dissemination. These three functions became the framework within which news journalism operated and ultimately this framework was what shaped the role of the news media themselves. News and news journalism became linked together in a conventional organisational model where particular news organisations sought to undertake one or more of the following:

- report contemporary events (news gathering);
- package those reports via news production into some form or another, for example a newspaper, radio programme, TV bulletin and website (news production), and
- distribute them to as many people as possible (news dissemination).

Parallel to this and at some ill-defined point in time, the requirement for these reports to be truthful accounts also emerged as a correlate of what constituted news journalism good practice. In other words, news journalism acquired a set of normative values that defined it in an ideal way and were therefore to be aspired to. Of course no one can say with any historical or philosophical certainty just when the ideal of truthfulness and truthful reporting was used to distinguish news and news journalism from other forms of mediated content, but once news and news journalism and the requirement for truthfulness and truthful reporting became linked together the news media assumed a special role in their relationship to people who wanted to know and understand what was happening in the world. This role is best understood and analysed in terms of the relationship between what news and news journalism should be (the ideal) and what, in the setting of news media organisations, they actually are (the real). It is only by assessing this relationship that we actually arrive at an accurate account of the news and new media, what they are, what they do and ultimately what their value is to us. Figure 17.1 shows this diagrammatically (cf. Harrison 2006, 2007 and 2008c).

Figure 17.1 is meant to show how news and news journalism can be disassembled and broken down into artificially separate layers that reveal that when we talk about news journalism and the news media we must constantly bear in mind the distinction and the relationship between the ideal form of news journalism and what news selection criteria are actually used on a daily basis by news organisations (the real). By examining the way the ideal form of news journalism and real news organisations' selection factors work together and the way the two conflict and contradict each other we can determine the kind of news we have. Where the relationship is one of mutuality, good (and frequently admired news journalism) is produced and is recognised; where the relationship is one of conflict and contradiction, we complain that the news and news journalism have lost sight of what they should be doing and have descended into trivia of one form or another – the 'dumbing down argument', and/or have ceased to have an orientation towards truthfulness, becoming more concerned with celebrity, popularity, persuasion or propaganda.

One thing though is important to note. I am not saying that the ideal is the same as the high minded, or that in the real settings of news media organisations the dominant tendency is to produce trivia as news. For example as the recent history of newspapers shows the old British taxonomy of dividing newspapers into:

- newspapers, which are variously referred to as positioned upmarket, also known as broadsheet or qualities (this now includes compacts and Berliner midi sizes);

DEFINITION OF NEWS

● Truthful reporting and reports of contemporary events

DEFINITION OF NEWS JOURNALISM

● Disposition towards truthfulness
● Interest in understanding contemporary events

THE NORMATIVE AND IDEAL VALUES OF NEWS JOURNALISM (THE IDEAL)

Disposition towards truthfulness

● Accuracy. The virtue of reporting how things are only when the report is the outcome of sufficient investigation to make it likely to be true
● Sincerity. The virtue of communicating only how you take things to be (Blackburn 2007)

Interest in understanding and reporting contemporary events

● Critical interpretation of events which are understood to be located in relational and ambiguous space and time

NEWS SELECTION CRITERIA USED BY NEWS MEDIA ORGANISATIONS (THE REAL)

● Derived news factors: newsrooms have their own socialised dynamics that account for news selection. What counts as news is learned by a news journalist 'doing the job' as, it is argued, new journalists acquire their understanding of newsworthiness from more senior or experienced members of the newsroom and what the particular news organisation they are working for regards itself as standing for and the audience/readership it serves. In this way news factors are vocationally and organisationally derived.

● Intrinsic news factors: events are deemed to be self evidently newsworthy because they have certain characteristics that make them recognisably news. A contemporary event is newsworthy if it has certain intrinsic news factors.*

Figure 17.1 Definitions and layers

*I have compiled a list of intrinsic news factors in Harrison (2006: 137). These entail that an event has one or more of the following: a) there are pictures or film available (television news); b) they contain short, dramatic occurrences which can be sensationalised; c) they have novelty value; d) they are open to simple reporting; e) they occur on a grand scale; f) they are negative or contain violence, crime, confrontation or catastrophe; g) they are either highly unexpected or, h) they contain things which one would expect to happen; i) the events have meaning and relevance to the audience; j) similar events are already in the news; k) they provide a balanced programme; l) they contain elite people or nations; m) they allow an event to be reported in personal or human interest terms.

● those that are positioned as middle market, also known as popular or black tops;

● those that are positioned downmarket, also known as tabloid or red tops; and

● those that position themselves as alternative to the mainstream (Atton 2002) and typically refer to themselves as radical, underground or, under special circumstances samizdat,

no longer really applies as papers now seek to combine different approaches to news within the same edition (Harrison 2008a) and use their copy to supply other platforms (a development known as 'convergence' or 'technological integration', see 'The technological vector of change for news media', below). The growth of 24-hour news and the use of user generated content have challenged long-established practices and assumptions in the traditional broadcasting sector. This has been particularly the case for public service broadcasters who have to reconcile the tension between their value of accuracy and the authority accuracy engenders (traditionally provided by flagship appointment news programmes), with the need to take a risk and be the first to break a story via their 24-hour news channels and websites. In order to provide news in a way that is seen to be more relevant to the needs of modern audiences the traditional broadcast media have had to rethink their priorities. The relationship between the ideal and the real, and the way it is worked out in practice, can therefore be seen in the rapidly changing news media and in particular in the organisational settings where professional news journalism is responding to technological change and audiences' expectations.

News media and vectors of change

The changes discussed above can be broadly broken down into two broad vectors of change: technological and journalistic. Interestingly both vectors of change can be understood via the same concepts, *convergence* and *personalisation* and both serve to provide an account of today's news media which are full of unresolved contradictions and uncertain futures. Paradoxically we are witnessing the increasing convergence of technology (and ownership, see 'Converging news media ownership', below), which has meant that companies from different economic sectors are now chasing the same news markets, via very similar products. At the same time we are seeing the increasing capacity for and concern with diversification of news provision, where news is a personalised product anyone can both receive and generate. The former should suggest a more homogeneous newscape, the latter points to something entirely different.

The technological vector of change for news media

Digital technology has undoubtedly had an impact on the news media and the extent of this and its significance is much debated. Therefore what follows in this section is a high level account of the two dominant technological scenarios for the immediate future of the news and the news media. It needs, however, to be remembered that in reality these two scenarios are much more complex than I can present them here and overlap in an ever increasing number of permutations both corporate and individual. Nonetheless these scenarios do serve to represent and highlight the stark reality facing the news media and their news services when judged from the impact of technological change.

Scenario one: news convergence

Today the news media encompass 'the globalised, the regional, the national, the local, the personal media; the broadcast and interactive media; the audio and audio visual and the printed media; the electronic and the mechanical, the digital

and the analogue media; the big screen and the small screen media; the dominant and alternative media; the fixed and the mobile, the convergent and the stand
alone media' (Silverstone 2007: 5). Traditional news media companies know this
only too well. Their newscape is no longer served by one particular platform or
specific locale but by many and, while television still remains the most dominant
form by which we in the UK obtain our news, it is still the case that other news
sources are becoming more and not less important. Traditional news organisations can no longer confine themselves to one platform; they have to become
multi-platform. In the case of private sector news media organisations this is critically important since economically the requirement for a multi-platform news
presence is seen as necessary to retain and possibly to increase advertising revenue. In the case of public sector news services a multi-platform service is seen as
a concomitant extension of their public purpose role in extending the availability
and reach of their news services (see 'News journalism and personalisation of
news', below).

Consequently, traditional media companies are increasingly converging their
news operations and services and becoming multi-platform news suppliers. In
short, providing news for, and disseminated according to, the different formats of
print, television (including broadband, web TV and internet protocol TV – IPTV)
and web newssites, using the capacities of each to cross promote their news content and news services to maximum effect. Essentially convergence works on the
basis of integrated digital technology. Horizontal convergence occurs when media
organisations offering the same or very similar products merge to establish cross
platform and cross promotional opportunities, where a media company simultaneously owns interests in print, broadcasting and the internet. Vertical convergence occurs when news organisations merge with other news organisations to
undertake activities at different levels of the news chain (merging news gathering
and news production with news dissemination).

According to an American report by the Project for Excellence in Journalism
there is growing evidence for the economic benefit to traditional news media
companies of adopting a strategy of convergence.

> There is more evidence that advertisers are reluctant to spend money without a clearer
> sense of its effect. The technology for measuring audience is about to leap forward,
> including methods for showing whether TV viewers are skipping the ads. The hope that
> internet advertising will someday match what print and television now bring in appears to
> be vanishing. Former enemies, newspapers and classified job websites are now creating
> partnerships. . . .   (State of the News Media 2007)

According to the convergence scenario it is through the myriad forms of multi-
platform technological partnerships that a secure future for the traditional private
sector news media is based, particularly the print sector. At the same time the
requirement for and necessity of these partnerships often requires another form
of convergence, the convergence of ownership and the development of larger
news media organisations. I will look at how the convergence of ownership affects
the news, below.

Scenario two: the personalisation of the news

In an article for the magazine *Wired*, called 'The Media Lab at 10', Fred Hapgood (1995) records that it was in the 1970s that Nicholas Negroponte (2000), the founder of the MIT Media Laboratory, first considered an interactive media in which:

> Your newspaper could track what you skipped and reread and where you paused, then use those cues to evolve into a composite 'Daily Me' that would carry only the news you cared about most. Advertisements would watch people watching them and continuously adapt to their responses,

and so was unleashed the holy grail of a personalised news service accompanied by customised adverts based upon knowledge of 'who you are', which in turn was derived from profiling individual's news habits. Since then and in one form or another the pursuit of web-based retail opportunities, based upon personalised knowledge of the consumer, has inspired information, communication and technology companies (ICTs) to enter the news market and to challenge the previous supremacy of traditional news media companies by offering more and more sophisticated versions of the 'Daily Me' replete with customised adverts. With the launch of Amazon in 1995 and then with the launch of Google in 1998, the ICT sector has seen the growth and financially successful deployment of software that facilitates more and more elaborate and accurate customer profiling and relevant personal recommendation services (Making It Happen 2008). Accompanying this was the expanding ability and option for ICTs to offer what was originally called web-based aggregator news services.

In essence an aggregator news service is either a piece of software or web-based application that profiles a variety of news sources and either compiles them into an easy to use compendium and/or synthesises them into news bullets. These news bullets are branded as the ICT's own news service. Conventionally the news sources are online newspapers; online television news services; blogs or vlogs; podcasts and other web-based news content sources.[1] The aggregated product is then provided to users as either a value added service attached to other services the ICT provides, or as a discreet web-based news channel.

Using the developments in customer profiling and personal recommendation software these aggregated news services could increasingly provide news content directed to the user that is regarded as individually customised or tailor made. It is the ability to customise which is seen by the ICTs as defining the news markets of the future. In short, ICT news services could take account of *who I am* and *what I want* through the knowledge they have gained about *me*. This knowledge is acquired by looking and building a profile of me via my news habits, my news story priorities and my views. From this profile ICTs can seek to provide advertisers with the opportunity to customise their adverts according to what type of person they think I am; how I could fit into a particular marketing strategy and what I am most likely to want to buy. At the moment, however, although it is possible to provide such a service, no one is absolutely certain of the demand for this type of 'Daily Me' envisaged above, although RSS (Really Simple Syndication) already makes it possible for people to keep up with their favourite websites in an automated manner with content that can be piped into special programmes or filtered displays. It does seem clear though that as consumers are increasingly being put at the heart of news media customisation and customer loyalty towards specific brands dwindles, further personalisation of news provision is inevitable.

The journalistic vector of change for news media

When the news media are looked at from the point of view of what changes are affecting the future of news journalism we see that both the ideas of *convergence* and *personalisation* are again applicable. The former describes the patterns of ownership of news, the second describes changes to news journalism.

Converging news media ownership

The first issue raised by the convergence of ownership of news organisations is that given an open and free private sector media is regarded as essential to the good order of a working democracy, to what extent does a highly converged private news commercial sector provide for the kind of news that sustains deliberative democratic activity? To which there are two very different answers. First, it is via the existence of a competitive marketplace and the degree of freedom the media have from control via legislation, regulation and governmental interference which guarantees a range of free and independent news services which accurately report contemporary events. Second, private sector news organisation companies cannot be trusted with news and meeting public purposes since, when it comes down to it, making money has for them priority over democratic obligations.[2] Where you stand on these answers is where you stand on the benefits or risks of news market domination by a handful of private sector transnational news media organisations and how you feel about the necessity to insure against news distortion by publicly funding a news organisation charged with specific public purposes of the kind that the BBC has (www.bbc.co.uk/info/purpose/).

The second issue raised by the convergence of ownership of news organisations is the charge that although they are often transnational in nature, these dominant news organisations do in fact share much the same set of political values. The similarity arises because the largest media companies in the world, with their giant news organisations, are primarily American (and secondly European). Such companies, it is said, tell the story of the world from an essentially American or Eurocentric perspective which supports and promotes (with varying degrees of difference, but not enough to dispute the idea of a consensus) news coverage where events are judged by their conformity to, or challenge of, Western democratic liberal values. In short, news coverage becomes nothing but the endorsement of these values, or an account of how they are threatened by people who do not share 'our' way of life and 'our' political philosophy. How true this is and to what extent an homogeneous news consensus exists is much debated. On the one hand it has been said that the Western news media do have certain ways of reporting, certain favoured topics are routinely covered, certain predispositions and assumptions are evident in the copy or coverage (El-Nawawy and Iskandar 2002; Philo and Berry 2004), but on the other that they are also capable of and are sufficiently independent to discover and uncover unpalatable truths, expose corruption and get to the truth of events, officials and those vested interests that would otherwise rather remain hidden (Gregory 2004).

The final issues raised by the convergence of ownership of news organisations is the assertion that such convergence (a) puts profits before news integrity and/or (b) produces a dominant ideological version of the news.

Evidence for (a) usually relies on the following range of considerations which themselves are much debated:

- that all of the largest media companies have with their news media organisations varying and very different types of news products and services;

- that some news organisations run news services at a loss because they wish to have the public esteem (some would say value added) of such a service within their portfolio;

- that shareholder power and corporate governance limit the predatory powers of media moguls (who are figures from a bygone age);

- that competition between media companies ensures news diversity;

- that most interestingly there is no global converged media since news tastes remain essentially parochial (Hafez 2007).

Evidence for (b) is that more and more news organisations are being created and entering the news market and some of these have very different news perspectives from the American and European news media giants. The most famous of these new news organisations is Al Jazeera (and its English language sister company, Al Jazeera International) and the accompanying growth of Arab news broadcasting across the globe.[3]

The growth of satellite technologies has meant that television news produced in the 'homeland' can also be made available to isolated individuals or diasporic communities around the world and so 'transcend national divides' (Pickerill and Webster 2006: 413). This developing transnational communication space gives individuals access to news channels such as Al Jazeera (in English or Arabic), CNN (English), BBC World (English), RAI-24 (Italian), Russia Today from Moscow (English), CCTV-9 from Beijing (English), NDTV 24x7 from Delhi (English), Bloomberg (English) and CNBC (English), EuroNews (multilingual), France 24 (in English, French or Arabic). The ability simultaneously to share common images from the 'homeland' with a dispersed population or diasporic groups has significance for the development of a transnational imagined community and identity formation (Ogan 2001). The popularity of satellite and cable television is growing amongst diasporic communities which often choose to watch homeland programming rather than that of the host country and is a phenomenon over which the host nation-state and its own news media often has little control (Georgiou 2003). The increasing popularity of Al Jazeera, which has around 50 million viewers around the world, is testament to the growing demand for personally relevant transnational news provision.

News journalism and the personalisation of news

The old adage that convergence (both technical and ownership) ensures that the 'Martini Principle' of 'Anytime, Anyplace, Anywhere' content access is guaranteed needs to be updated to include 'Anyone'. It is the role of this 'Anyone' which now needs to be looked at as it lays down challenges to news journalism and provides further opportunities for news media organisations.

The personalisation of news content described above was essentially a description of what can be supplied to ICT customers by virtue of technological developments. What it failed to describe is the way platforms have interactive capacities that allows 'me' (anyone) to become a news journalist and supply news organisations with news stories. The advent of so-called citizen journalism; participatory journalism; public insight journalism; public journalism; open source journalism or crowdsourcing journalism and user generated content (UK); user distributed content or video created content (USA) is upon us. Even though they differ in detail from each other, I shall for the sake of simplicity and brevity collectively refer to them under the generic title of 'citizen journalism' (for examples, see Allan 2006: 143–67).

'Citizen journalism' is regarded by many as 'a variant form of news based upon a democratically free, truth-directed discussion of contemporary events,' and 'occurs where people who either do not work for a professional media organisation' and are untrained news journalists, 'contribute to the creation of news agendas and the subsequent dissemination of news in two main ways: either by a variety of peer to peer methods, or by passing on their own news stories, sources or views of news stories to a professional news organisation' (Harrison 2008b). Today both public and private news organisations are increasingly turning toward the use of 'citizen journalism' to provide news content. This news content can take one of two forms:

- Primary news content, which may break a story, change an already running story and may well involve the stimulation of further investigative activity by the mainstream news provider.

- Secondary news content is requested by news organisations, either because they want footage and pictures taken by mobile devices before their own crews arrive, or because they want to bulk out a story which is already running, or because by actively encouraging people to contribute their own content, news media organisations now feel themselves to be duty bound to be seen routinely to welcome and even make space for user generated content on a daily basis (Harrison 2008b).

At the moment it is too soon to know what the impact of 'citizen journalism' is likely to be. But the claim that it can be undertaken by 'anyone' either independently or working on a shared basis is still very topical and the significance for news media still much debated. On the negative side one could argue that 'citizen journalism', which routinely gives audiences the right to contribute to the output of news media, could, aside from disaster and trivial news, eventually develop to do little more than produce news based upon what Stanley Cohen in 1972 famously called 'seven familiar clusters of social identity' and 'panic discourse' (Cohen, 2002). These persistent types of news story are negative and judgemental in focus and subject area concentrating on: young, working class, violent males; school violence, bullying and shootouts; wrong drugs, used by wrong people at wrong places; child abuse, satanic rituals and paedophile registers; sex, violence and blaming the media; welfare cheats and single mothers; refugees and asylum seekers, flooding our country, swamping our services – to which of course we could add our own 21st century categories. In short 'citizen journalism' could be used to confirm the 'gatekeeper' role and reinforce the agenda of traditional news media organisations.

On the positive side is the idea that citizen journalism enables minorities and members of exiled or scattered communities to produce their own news as well as find out what is going on back home. Rather than stereotyping, marginalising and scape-goating certain groups, 'citizen journalism' can, even via the traditional news media, allow new voices and opinions to be heard.

How precisely the developments outlined above will evolve is uncertain. It is, however, clear that in parallel to the traditional reliance on the production of newspapers, magazines, radio or television news programmes, news consumers are increasingly adopting new ICT and satellite technologies that facilitate the development of a more dynamic, community defined and, ultimately customised and personalised newscape, that is unrestricted by territory. Although it is perhaps too soon to talk of 'diasporic public spheres' emerging from an ICT stimulated and active civil society across diverse territories, it is clear that at the same time as traditional news media with their top-down methods of news dissemination multiply, diversify and explore new means to entice news consumers to 'pull' news from their news media, 'the means for citizen-led alternatives' (Allan 2006: 172) are also developing. Given the speed and scale of change the biggest challenge facing traditional news media is how to retain their position in the new news media ecology.

Questions

1 Compare and contrast a public sector and private sector news provider in any European country.

2 Despite increasing concentration of news media ownership, the newscape will become more and more pluralist. Discuss.

3 Consider the differences between news provided for consumers and news provided by citizens.

Notes

1 Currently a news aggregator does not or is not required to pay the news sources from which it takes its news content since it is usually derived from free and open access websites. Consequently, traditional news media companies which place their content on the web are now seeing

255

their news re-presented by news aggregators without receiving any fee and therefore without any contribution to the cost they incur in gathering and producing the news.

2   Evidence for the second view is usually provided in the form of News Corporation and its agreement to remove the BBC from its satellite service to China. Google's acceptance of internet censorship in China was heavily criticised, when it allowed its search results to be filtered via filters, sometimes referred to as 'The Great Firewall of China'.

3   Although a more free media environment may be developing in the Middle East, the Arab satellite TV charter, 'Suggested Guidelines and Principles for Organizing Satellite TV in the Arab World', signed by the Arab League's Ministers of Information on 12 February, aims to regulate the work of around 500 TV channels currently broadcasting via the Arab Sat and Nile Sat satellites. The charter could have an impact on freedom to broadcast.

Further reading

Ferrell Lowe, G. and Hujanen, T. (eds) (2003) *Broadcasting and Convergence: New Articulations of the Public Service Remit*, Göteborg: Nordicom. Collection of essays based on the Re-visionary Interpretations of the Public Enterprise (RIPE) conferences.

Georgiou, M. (2003) 'Mapping Diasporic Media Across the EU: Addressing Cultural Exclusion', *The European Media and Technology in Everyday Life Network, 2000–2003 Report submitted to the EU*, London: Media@LSE, London School of Economics and Political Science. Important document potentially informing future policy in the area.

Harrison, J. (2006) *News*, London: Routledge. Introduction to the range of topics associated with news media.

McNair, B. (2006) *Cultural Chaos: Journalism, News and Power in a Globalised World*, London: Routledge. Characteristically sharp analysis of the globalisation of journalism.

Ofcom (2007) *New News, Future News: The Challenges for Television News After Digital Switch-over*, London: Ofcom. Also available at http://www.ofcom.org.uk/research/tv/reports/newnews/newnews.pdf. Report examining the environment in which television news currently operates, and assesses how that may change in future (after digital switch-over and, in 2014, the expiry of current Channel 3 and Channel 5 licences). It identifies particular issues that will need to be addressed and suggests some specific questions that may need to be answered.

Sunstein, C. (2007) *Republic.com 2.0*, Princeton, New Jersey: Princeton University Press. Valuable discussion of news overload, though mainly with US examples.

References

Allan, S. (2006) *Online News*, Maidenhead: Open University Press.

Atton, C. (2002) *Alternative Media*, London: Sage.

Blackburn, S. (2007) www.phil.cam.ac.uk/~swb24/reviews/Williams.htm.

Cohen, S. (2002) *Folk Devils and Moral Panic: Creation of Mods and Rockers*, 30th anniversary edition, London: Routledge.

El-Nawawy, M. and Iskandar, A. (2002) *Al-Jazeera: How the Free Arab News Network Scooped the World and Changed the Middle East*, Cambridge, MA: Westview Press.

Georgiou, M. (2003) 'Mapping Diasporic Media Across the EU: Addressing Cultural Exclusion', *The European Media and Technology in Everyday Life Network, 2000–2003 Report submitted to the EU*, London: Media@LSE, London School of Economics and Political Science, www.lse.ac.uk/collections/EMTEL/reports/georgiou_2003_emtel.pdf.

Gregory, D. (2004) *The Colonial Present,* Oxford: Blackwell Publishing.

Hapgood, F. (1995) *The Media Lab at 10,* www.wired.com/wired/archive/3.11/media.html (accessed 8 February 2008).

Harrison, J. (2006) *News,* London: Routledge.

Harrison, J. (2007) 'Critical Foundations and Directions for the Teaching of News Journalism', *Journalism Practice*, 1 (2): 175–89.

Harrison (2008a) 'News' in B. Franklin (ed) *Pulling Newspapers Apart: Analysing Print Journalism,* London: Routledge.

Harrison, J. (2008b) 'Citizen Journalism' in G. Creeber (ed) *Television Genres,* 2nd edition, London: British Film Institute.

Harrison, J. (2008c) 'Exploring News Values: The Idea and The Real' in J. Chapman and M. Kinsey (eds) *Broadcast Journalism: A Critical Introduction*. London: Routledge.

Harrison, J. and Woods, L. (2007) *European Broadcasting Law and Policy*, Cambridge: Cambridge University Press.

Hafez, K. (2007) *The Myth of Media Globalization,* Cambridge: Polity Press.

Making It Happen (2008) http://epic.makingithappen.co.uk/ (accessed 18 February 2008).

Negroponte, N. (2000) *Being Digital,* London: Vintage Books.

Ofcom (2007) *New News, Future News: The Challenges for Television News After Digital Switch-over*, London: Ofcom. www.ofcom.org.uk/research/tv/reports/newnews/newnews.pdf.

Ogan, C. (2001) *Communication and Identity in the Diaspora: Turkish Migrants in Amsterdam and their Use of Media*, Lanham: Lexington.

Philo, G. and Berry, M. (2004) *Bad News from Israel*, London: Pluto Press.

Pickerill, J. and Webster, F. (2006) 'The Anti-War/Peace Movement in Britain and the Conditions of Information War', *International Relations*, 20 (4): 407–23.

Project for Excellence in Journalism (2007) *The State of the News Media 2007: An Annual Report on American Journalism*, www.stateofthenewsmedia.com/2007/narrative_digital_intro.asp?media=2.

Shoemaker, P., and Cohen, A. (eds) (2006) *News Around the World*, New York: Routledge.

Silverstone, R. (2007) *Media and Morality: On the Rise of Mediapolis*, Cambridge: Polity Press.

State of the News Media (2007) www.stateofthenewsmedia.com/2007/narrative_overview_ economics.asp?cat=4&media=1.

Williams, B. (2002) *Truth and Truthfulness*, New Jersey, Princeton: Princeton University Press.

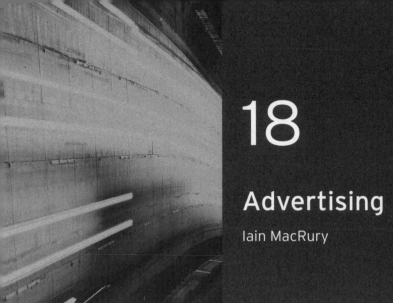

18

Advertising

Iain MacRury

Chapter overview

Advertising is a global economic and cultural industry. In 2006 global advertising expenditure increased by 5.5 per cent[1] to reach a figure above US$400,000 million.[2] Advertising has been central to the formation of the contemporary media landscape, which depends heavily upon advertising revenue. In turn advertising is dependent on the media to provide audiences – potential consumers to see, hear and appraise advertising appeals. Accelerating changes and enhancements in internet communications technology, transformations in the organisation of the industry and its institutions and shifts in audiences' relationships to advertising media, have forced advertising institutions to face up to challenging new media, cultural and marketing environments.

Advertising: growth and transformation

Advertising is the distinguishing cultural form present in all modern industrial market economies. Emerging in the US and Europe after the industrial revolution, modern advertising rapidly developed in the 20th century. As national consumer cultures grew in the US, UK, Western Europe and Japan, advertising agencies developed into highly organised corporations, often operating globally.[3] In the 21st century advertising has taken its place as one of the major visible signatures of cultural and commercial globalisation – expanding across continents from West to East and from North to South. Today, billboards and broadcasts traverse media networks from London to Beijing, from Tokyo to Sao Paulo and from New York to Cape Town, and so on round the globe. Advertisements individually and all together declaim the reach and appeal of trans-national brands in a melange of relentless glamour, part cliché and part creative ingenuity.

Whether browsing the web or flicking through a magazine, audiences' daily use of media is more than likely to involve some kind of engagement with the commercial speech of advertisers; mainly manufacturing and service industry corporations,

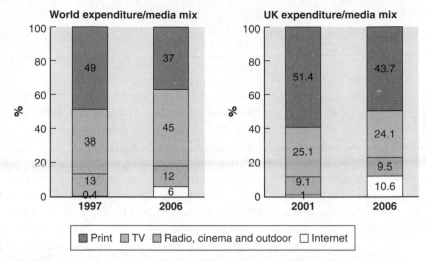

Figure 18.1 Expenditure on advertising media: percentage of total advertising expenditure for print, TV, radio, outdoor and cinema, and internet. Global comparisons 1997–2006/UK compares 2001–06

Source: Adapted from World Advertising Research Center (2007) *World Advertising Statistics Yearbook 2007.* WARC, Henley on Thames. Reproduced with permission.

but also charities, governments and political campaigners. Advertisers continue to pay millions of dollars to media owners for the opportunity to be seen or heard by potential consumers as they watch, read and listen to TV shows, radio broadcasts, and newspaper articles – and in real and virtual spaces. Figure 18.1 shows the composition of the media mix in the UK and globally – the amount of advertising expenditure allocated to the different advertising media. The rapid rise of internet advertising, as a nevertheless still small proportion of the advertising spend, is of great significance. Print and TV remain the major advertising media.

Advertisements are just one part of the much larger productive enterprise of the promotional industries. It is important to try to distinguish advertisements from the array of other promotional activities which have become central to social, economic and cultural life. Advertising represents one form (or genre) of communication which takes its place alongside a vast and intricate array of commercially produced signs and stories. These include the work of public relations, package design, corporate sponsorship, retail display and innumerable other small acts of face to face promotion. The advertisement is one communication option among many available to the corporation or other body wishing to project promotional messages into public arenas. It is an ingredient in what is known as 'the marketing mix': one which not all corporations are obliged to include.

Global advertising expenditure in 1989 was estimated at $167 billion. It grew to $276 billion[4] in 1998, the bulk (over 40 per cent) of which was spent in North America. In 2006 global expenditure was more than $400,000 million. The US remains by far the largest advertising market (at $139,000 million). However as a proportion of the total global advertising spend the US has declined slightly (relative to the enlarged global total), alone accounting for 33 per cent in 2006 (from 40 per cent in 1998).

The continuing emergence of Eastern European market economies (after the fall of the Berlin Wall in 1990), has seen some new and important emerging advertising markets, for instance China ($48,518 million, i.e. 9.9 per cent of global spend), India ($3,583 million i.e. 0.7 per cent of global spend) and Brazil ($18,302 million i.e. 3.7 per cent of global spend). These have all together contributed significantly to ongoing increases in advertising expenditure. In 2006 China, for instance, is the second largest advertising market in the world, having been 12th in 1997. The UK remains fourth in the expenditure table accounting for $25,827 million (i.e. 5.3 per cent of global spend). Recent increases in more mature advertising markets (UK, France and Germany for instance) have been relatively more modest than in, for example, the BRIC[5] economies – and with some recent declines.

At a national level advertising is a key sector of economic activity in most economies. In 2006 advertising expenditure in the five highest spending national markets was at a level of between 0.78 per cent (in Japan) and 1.23 per cent of GDP (in the US). Table 18.1 offers some insight into the levels of advertising expenditure in the five largest advertising markets in 2006.

The per capita figure (e.g. $274.5 in the UK) makes the larger national expenditure figure more readily comprehensible. Thus in the UK advertisers spend approximately £140.00[6] per person per year, in total, in purchasing media space for advertising. This is about 1.09 per cent of GDP. This figure includes only the money spent on buying media space and is exclusive of other marketing expenditures (which are far greater). For comparison, UK education spending was about 5.5 per cent GDP in 2006 – i.e. £710 per person per annum. Just over 1 per cent of GDP was spent in higher education. This figure is similar to the annual spend on media based advertising space.

The most interesting global figures come from China. The per capita expenditure remains relatively small ($36.7 per person in 2006). This reflects the size of a population which nevertheless in the main has currently far less spending power per head than in more developed economies – and with wide gaps between rich and poor. The advertising expenditure growth rate (of over 1000 per cent) is a clear index of a society in rapid transition towards a consumerist market economy – one where advertising is likely to take a prominent role in communicating between

Table 18.1 Overall increase in advertising expenditure*

National advertising market placed in rank order of total expenditure	Total spend ($)	%GDP	Per capita expenditure 1997 ($)	Per capita expenditure 2006 ($)	Percentage growth of ad spend 1997–2006
1 USA	163,036	1.23	387.4	$541.6	21.6
2 China	48,518	1.85	3.0	$36.7	1,092.3
3 Japan	34,240	0.78	265.0	$267.1	0.8
4 UK	25,827	1.09	274.5	$431.4	14.4
5 Germany	21,177	0.75	249.7	$263.2	−10.1

*Note: Adjusted and relative to $US constant 2000 prices and local currencies 1997–2006.

global and national manufacturers on the one hand, and an expanding population of newly affluent Chinese consumers on the other. Some of the growth in the UK and the US is based on the increasing success of internet advertising – a medium which has finally begun to appeal to advertisers in a variety of ways.

National and international expenditure statistics indicate some interesting patterns in advertising and the economy. Advertising and marketing, always important considerations for businesses, have become increasingly central components in the thinking and activity of corporations selling goods and providing services. The recent preoccupation with branding in developing business and other institutional models has ensured that advertising has maintained a prominent place in managerial thinking and practices – even in the face of consumers who express ongoing scepticism about advertising appeals and even while there are credible alternatives to expensive main media advertising.

For people living in contemporary societies, such expenditure levels, and the volumes of media and advertising activity they represent[7] explains one aspect of contemporary experience – the promotional ambience, the buzz that is cultivated, hyperactively, around so much that happens. The assertion that we are bound to a 'promotional culture' (Wernick 1991) seems increasingly accurate, as lives play out against a media landscape of competing images and signs, defining the look and feel of traditional media, as well as online sites and across the spaces where we live and work.

Advertising texts: authenticity and the audience

The expenditure recorded in these figures refers (Table 18.1) to a highly familiar and typically ephemeral media form: the advertisement, i.e. short, even negligible, messages inserted into the flow of broadcast programmes, websites, magazines or newspapers. Advertisements are one media-based means deployed towards marketing ends such as raising and maintaining consumer awareness or disseminating information about a particular product, service or brand. Ads invite audiences to consider imageries and propositions. They hope to garner attention, opening up a brief interlude in or interruption of audiences' experience of the main media communication (e.g. a TV show) and against the flow of other advertising communications.

There is significant and ongoing scepticism in the face of commercial appeals – however artfully made. The ad industry is familiar to us as both a source of endless unasked for ads, and as a common target for criticism of its work: criticism both casual and detailed (James 2007: 209–37; Williams 1980). Given this context, 21st century advertisers continue to have a hard job in achieving a welcome from ad weary audiences. Advertising agencies are expert in persuading advertisers that – with the right ad strategy – such resistance and restiveness can be overcome, or at least diminished.

Advertising creativity seeks to bypass audiences' critical reflexes in a variety of ways including humour, advertising self parody and by using carefully selected celebrities. For example, this 2004 French Connection ad voiceover undercuts some familiar imagery – of tanned bodies in an exotic setting – aiming to disarm defensive criticisms of stereotypes and clichés:

> Where do you think you're going? And who told you to go there? Weren't influenced by the advertising, were you? Big in your face messages like 'buy our denim'. Haven't you had enough of being told what to do, where to go, what to wear? Don't you just hate being influenced? especially by the great big offensive logos at the end?

At the same time other ads will use timeworn appeals to sex, glamour, tradition and nostalgia – and trusted formats such as 'before and after' for detergents and beauty products. It is a mistake to generalise too much about the genre, with variation in ad styles partially determined by the product sector (contrast perfume ads and, say, dog food ad formats), current ad fashions or cultural 'vibes', the sense of the audience, the advertising aims (e.g. a product launch ad is usually quite different from an ad for a long established product) and so on. Occasionally ads will seek attention by using shock tactics – risking the (not always unwelcome) controversy attaching to audience complaints and press criticism.

Nevertheless there is generic continuity of a kind evident amongst the variety exhibited in individual ads. The advert is typically held together (following the constraints of its medium) by careful design and creative layout of message elements or in the timing and spacing of the ad film/soundtrack. Ads typically use carefully crafted copy, sound, music, voiceovers and slogans – they can be highly basic or very elaborate. Ads exhibit an underlying dynamic whereby the ad text enacts or affirms an associative link between the product or brand and some hitherto unconnected resources and conjunctions of cultural meaning; a celebrity, a desirable location, a funny joke or a quirky milieu added to the meaning of the product and extends the resonance of the brand. Thus, by the generic magic of advertising, shampoos become Amazonian, shoes become Parisian and biscuits become emblems of multicultural harmony. It is in the novelty and credibility of such connections – as creatively portrayed, and, perhaps, as affirmed across other parts of a brand media strategy (e.g. via PR or sponsorship) that ads can lend meaning and value to products – even persuade us to consider buying them. But, equally, it is in the face of the predictability and familiarity of the genre – weird and wonderful as individual ads can be – that audiences can affirm boredom or cynicism, and rehearse their disdain.

Recent years have not seen radical creative departures within advertising. There have been notable campaigns that have been praised and remembered. However the sense of advertisements (in print or on screen) themselves serving as the vectors for innovative cultural change – an argument upheld particularly in the 1960s and the 1980s – has diminished. As Benedictus (2008) puts it, today: 'It is the search for credible media, rather than a credible message, which is important.'

It is in the creative selection and use of new *media* that advertising is impacting everyday lives in new and interesting ways, and in the convergence of advertising with other kinds of entertainments – so that, increasingly, through product placement and various kinds of brand-based publication and media production – the advertising function is embedded within media content – films, TV shows and so on (Donaton 2004). This is advertising in intention, but, formally, it resembles the work of PR and other kinds of marketing. A 2008 advertisement for Apple's iPhone describes a level of everyday internet functionality that goes to the heart of recent transformations. The internet alters many aspects of the organisation of consumption and provision. We can shop and search online – having goods delivered efficiently, as the market comes to the consumer rather than the consumer searching the various media and marketplaces. This is highly relevant to advertising. One of the main rationales and justifications for advertising – an expensive and intrusive intervention in media time/space – is the circulation of information within local, national and global markets. The internet enhances advertising's capacity to disseminate information, but it could as easily be said to undercut or outflank the need for traditional forms of advertising such as newspapers, commercial TV and so on. The consumer's power to sort information renders the infomatic function of traditional advertising relatively redundant. The Apple ad depicts a consumer engaging with a marketplace.

> VOICEOVER: Say you're looking to buy a new car and the salesman says, 'it's the best deal in town, guaranteed'. Of course you could spend the day shopping around, just to make sure. But with the whole internet on your phone, you don't have to.
>
> (Advertisement for Apple iPhone 2008)

And, as the accompanying visuals make clear, consumers don't have to physically shop: nor need they rely on a specific remembered fact – a USP (unique selling proposition) – drummed in by an ad. Consumers can instantly search all the relevant information, there and then and on the move – comparing price and specification via an internet phone. Mobile technologies mean that domestic and consumer spaces cut across one another (altering the quality of both). Such new media technologies provoke new and refigured anxieties about technological and commercial 'invasion' and advertising manipulation.

It should be remembered however that advertising has never proceeded by information alone. Indeed it is in the work of *culturally* framing goods and setting out persuasive arguments that ads have thrived. This function is less likely to be displaced by internet advertising in the way that the market information content is. Indeed the well placed image, properly chosen, the careful slogan and the eye catching logo all have a part to play within internet advertising. Such brand imagery operates associatively, connecting with the look of retail outlets, to product packaging, to branded imagery at marketing events, to sponsored sites, to poster imagery and other advertisements. Contemporary marketing and branding involves – and involves us, product by product – in numerous and competing orchestrated communications 'programmes' of this kind. Advertising is usually a component of such integrated marketing efforts. In each case the aim is to keep the brand prominent and in mind in appropriate ways across a range of audiences. The internet offers an important new dimension to the marketing process – and to advertising. It displaces some traditional activity, but, currently, replaces almost none.

Consumers are highly familiar with a wide array of advertising. The internet is a relatively newer advertising medium. There is a variety of formats for internet advertising.[8] Much attention has recently been given to the revenue potentials of internet based search engines which rely on advertisers buying their place on popular search engine listings (such as Google). When a consumer searches for a key term (e.g. 'electric tooth brush'), alongside the search results a series of sponsored links appear. The advertiser (e.g. a toothbrush retailer) will pay whenever a browsing consumer clicks through to the advertised site (e.g. an online chemist). In 2006 this type of advertising accounted for over 50 per cent of internet advertising expenditure/revenue.

As an adaptation of older (press) formats, 'classified' internet advertising has taken a portion of revenue away from newspapers and magazines. The enhanced searchability of internet databases – of jobs, cars, houses for sale, etc. – makes this a highly functional new advertising format. Classified is distinguished from the next category, 'display' advertising in that the reader/browser is explicitly looking for a product within the *classified* listing – a job, a car, a flight, etc. Display advertising relies on catching the eye of consumers enjoying the main media content (e.g. a news article) without the explicit intention of finding product information or imagery. Other means to achieve visibility on the internet are:

- Banners/embedded advertisements: basic banners appearing above or alongside a website. These are now less popular than in the past – having been the first type of internet ads operating when pages were more constrained by dial up connection speeds.

- Tenancies: the advertiser pays to hire space within another site (e.g. a job search database inside an online trade magazine website).

- Interruptive formats: 'pop up' ads appear in a separate window and can include rich-media content – moving images, etc. Or they can resemble static banner ads that suddenly appear. These can be quite irritating and confusing.

- We might add some kinds of email advertising – including SPAM which interrupts. However these do not make a significant contribution to ad revenue.

The internet is clearly an important new medium for advertisers – with ever growing proportions of consumer expenditure now taking place online. Advertisers' interest in online formats has contributed, in the UK, to rapid growth in this type of advertising, against a background of slower growth in other formats – suggesting a displacement effect between advertising media in favour of online. Increased connectivity, the changing age profile of internet users, the relative affluence of internet users, increased trust in e-commerce and improved payment systems are all contributory factors making Internet advertising attractive. Figure 18.2 shows the steep increases in UK internet advertising expenditure.

Social networking sites such as Facebook offer further internet advertising opportunities. Facebook, and similar social network sites turn human relations into a kind of 'media content'. Ad space is sold to run alongside Facebook pages, but the 'content' of the medium is assembled by 'audiences'/users; audiences/users who are also, in a sense, the producers and the broadcasters of the content – working within parameters defined by software and some formal and informal regulatory oversight. Ad space connected to such peer to peer media communications is attractive because it can promise a feeling of trust, personalisation and intimacy. It can capture heavy online users who (advertisers fear) are leaving press and TV behind and promises targeting linked to cultural profiles linked in turn to internet usage patterns and site selection. There is some disquiet that the commercial exploitation of e-friendship networks and more obtrusive advertising than is

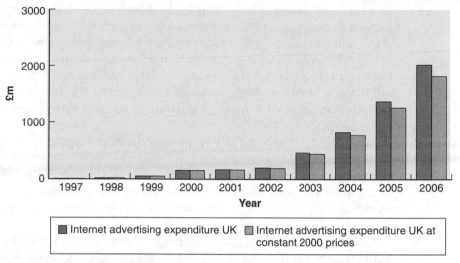

Figure 18.2 Internet advertising expenditure UK 1997–2006 (£m)

currently possible will provoke a backlash against clutter and 'media' interruption. Privacy issues with regard to tracking web use are already a concern – especially if such information is used for commercial purposes.

The expansion of the internet as a new advertising medium represents an important juncture in the development of advertising, one whose significance is usefully understood in the context of thinking about the history of advertising. Advertising has always been a genre for the mediation of the relations between consumers and producers – via paid for media. The fast growth in internet advertising marks the extension and reiteration of developments that began in the 19th century. The internet's disturbance of relations between consumers, manufacturers, retailers and the 'traditional' practices of purchasing and providing finds echoes in the history of advertising – when a similar reconfiguration of marketing processes enabled modern advertising and its institutions to emerge.

The emergence of modern advertising

Advertising and market relationships

Modern advertising has a relatively short history. The conditions and commercial tensions, which led to its emergence in the 19th century shaped the contemporary advertising industry. While 'advertising' activity of various kinds has been identified in earlier societies,[9] advertisements in the specific form we recognise, and the commercial institutions that produce them, have developed only since the early decades of the 19th century (Ohmann 1996; Presbury 1929). The key driver which provided the conditions for the emergence of modern advertising was the change in the rate and volume of manufacture and supply of goods following the industrial revolution (Ewen 2000). The key condition for advertising's development was the extension of the media infrastructure. More broadly speaking socio-cultural changes were important. Some argue that cultural changes were partly a consequence of early advertising – as consumers were 'constructed' (Ewen 2001). On the other hand there is strong evidence that the rise of 'the consumer', in the US and in Europe, was equally attached to a deep rooted long range dissolution and transformation of traditional value systems and practices, predating the industrial revolution. These changes underpinned the disposition towards consumption necessary for mass production to succeed (Marchand 1985; Campbell 1987; McCracken 1990).

Advertising, considered as a communications process, is 'a relationship' which takes place 'between a producer (or distributor) who advertises, an agency that creates the ad, and an audience to whom the ad is directed' (Schudson 1984:168–9). In the 19th and 20th centuries, as low cost and high volume industrial productivity developed, the links in this new chain of commercial relations began to grow, connect and solidify – see Table 18.2.

An 18th century household[10] was organised to produce a majority of its inhabitants' needs (clothes, food, etc.). A localised rural economy, scarcity allowing, provided the rest. By contrast a typical 21st century suburban household and its surroundings (directly) produce almost nothing, buying clothes, food technology and entertainment provided by (global) systems of manufacture, provision and marketing. This juxtaposition illustrates, at a basic level, the transformation out of which advertising institutions arose. The redistribution of production to non-local mechanised industries[11] and, in the UK, the increase of colonial imports, led to the increase in the volume (and novelty) of goods available to the market. These factors and the need to manage and ensure demand for what had been made or imported were central to the emergence of advertising. Advertising has a role when relationships to the 'system of provision' (Fine 1995:145) become less direct. The important features of these new relationships – opening space for advertising practices to develop more fully – were firstly, the *distance* separating the producer from the consumer, and secondly the subsequent mutual *anonymity* of the producer and the consumer.

As new relations between producers and consumers became more prevalent, a commercial intermediary became a necessary function. Producers sought, in the

Table 18.2 Ingredients in the emergence of the modern advertising industry

Production	Media	Consumption
Supply		*Demand*
• Sufficient levels of production achieved by industrial manufacturing. • Extended networks of distribution – including a national transport system and retail outlets – transforming local 'customers' into distant 'consumers'.	• A crucial prerequisite is the existence of national media and networks of local media channels, journals, periodicals and local newspapers.	• Sufficient levels of accessible potential consumers brought about by increasing levels of (urban) population – and improved literacy. • Culturally based legitimacy and motivation for goods consumption – a propensity to consume.

Media will grow, extending the means of mass communication as technology develops additional media

Advertising emerges alongside these developments and contributes to their acceleration. However it is difficult to pinpoint simple relationships of cause and effect between production and consumption words of 19th century economist Walter Bagehot, 'to find without effort, without delay, and without uncertainty, others who want[ed]' what they produced (Bagehot 1870 cited in Caplin 1959). Various entrepreneurial institutions and commercial roles grew out of the attempt to manage and develop the emergent networks of commerce by mediating between producers and consumers. While retail was a necessary and powerful provider of such an 'interface', producers quickly became aware of the advantages of asserting their own relationship with consumers. Numerous 'advertising agents' appeared on factory doorsteps offering to provide access to the means of communication necessary to enable manufacturers to communicate with consumers directly. Producers remained dependent upon the retail sector for distribution, but the advertising of product and price information promised a vital degree of control, in particular of retail 'mark up'.

The growing means of mass communications (which in the 19th century meant the newspapers)[12] were crucial to enable advertising, a second producer–consumer interface, to emerge. Space in the media became a commercial resource – a commodity to be traded. The first function of the embryonic 'advertising' agencies was the buying and selling of this space. Sometimes allied to the newspapers and sometimes independent, 'space brokers' or 'space farmers' (Nevett 1982) were able to offer a service to media owners and to potential advertisers; providing and selling space, and easing payment and collection of advertisers' debts (the latter function developed into account management). Agents received commission from the media owners in the process, which was a percentage of the media cost paid by the advertiser to the media owner.

The value advertising promised to businesses lay in the commercial advantage gained by increasing demand for their goods and maintaining control of prices. A necessary correlation of this was the emergence of branding. Branding, linked to the producers' practice of trade marking their goods, as it remains, was the most convenient way of distinguishing the commodities sold by one manufacturer from those of competitors. It is in this period that well-known national and international brands were born (e.g. Kodak, Guinness, Heinz and Coca-Cola).[13] It was quickly recognised that branding had the potential not only to functionally distinguish products but also to assert qualitative distinctions in the form of brand images and values. Advertising became integral to the development of branding as it assumed a form suitable not just as the vehicle for the communication of product information, but also as the carrier of cultural symbolism – transforming the commodity into a specific and meaningful 'good' and elaborating such meaning to enhance the value of the brand. The potential mistrust of faceless and placeless commodities could now be overcome by the (apparently) trustworthy symbolism of a familiar brand name. Advertising served to counteract two problems faced by large scale industrial manufacturing operations distributed across national markets:

- the logistical difficulty born of distance between consumers and producers;
- a socio-cultural difficulty born of anonymity of products for consumers; and the likelihood of diminished trust and recognition.

Advertising has often been presented as part of the solution to communications problems attendant upon restructuring of provision. For the advertising industry the use of their expertise by providers of such an ever-broadening array of products and services has contributed to the success and influence of the industry and to its social significance.

Advertising institutions

The advertising images we see around us are the product of institutions the model for which was fully formed before World War Two. In the face of new media and new marketing priorities some aspect of the way advertising is organised have changed however. In the final three decades of the 19th century advertising agencies, such as A. J. Ayer and J. Walter Thompson in the US and Mather and Crowther[14] in the UK had fully established themselves. Gradually key principles were instituted. Firstly advertising agencies became formally independent of the media owners from whom they gained commission (at 15 per cent of media cost). Secondly agencies would carry accounts from only one producer in a product sector so as to avoid conflicts of interest.

Agencies began to offer clients a range of services supplementary to basic space dealing. Making the ads was the logical step on from arranging the media space. Creative services developed quickly as the 20th century began. It was easier to sell space to a client by promising to fill it too. A copy writing department was of particular importance as early ads relied heavily on detailed written text to provide persuasive appeal (Ohmann 1996). As the century unfolded and advertising became a more visual and figurative mode of communication, artistic input (across the media) took on greater prominence under the guidance of a creative director. Research developed as another prominent element in the industry.

The lesson from history is this: advertising institutions emerged in the gap between production and consumption – to produce a media based interface to more effectively bind consumers to the productivities of industrial manufacture. This is, in essence, a dynamic evident in the contemporary era. E-commerce and key globalisation processes have shifted the means and modes of production in a number of ways. Producers of goods continue to want to engage dispersed and perhaps uninterested consumers through new interfaces – not just newspapers now, but via dynamic media including websites and text messages. This has caused a significant disturbance to the way marketers and advertisers think about media. It has also ensured some significant changes in the ways advertising work is organised, with campaigns the result of collaborative efforts coordinated by one agency – that holds the relationship with a client – but utilising specialists for research, production and creativity. Agencies have 'unbundled' with advertising institutions operating by coordinating networks locally and globally, rather than by managing departments in one building.

Advertising and the media: crisis and continuity

Marketers' shorthand has traditionally distinguished advertisements from other kinds of marketing activity in a division made between 'above the line' and 'below the line' approaches to promotion.[15] 'Above the line' referred to those communications placed in traditional media space bought, through an advertising agency, from a media owner. 'Below the line' referred to promotional activity that did not depend upon the purchase of media space and might include brochures, direct mail shots or point of sale materials.

One of the key features of the contemporary marketing environment is to blur or simply ignore the boundaries marking this distinction, which is increasingly redundant in the face of the new media environment – in particular when the internet so readily bypasses the notion of mass audience, or even audience segments, by allowing communications which are widely distributed but, also, individually sourced, targeted and accessed. Richards (2000) conveys a clear sense of the distinctive character of internet technology – and its capacity to outflank other media:

> The Internet is much more than just a medium. It is at one time a confluence of all media, a new breed of medium, a mixture of virtually all forms of marketing communication, and even a distribution channel.
>
> (Richards 2000)

Web based and digital communications technologies do a good deal to further destabilise the traditional communications models underpinning mainstream mass advertising, which is also squeezed by the success of campaigns which incorporate other marketing techniques – sponsorship, product placement, direct mail and PR for instance. Another restructuring of the marketing/media mix, sees programme sponsorship selected as an alternative to paying for a range of ill-defined national TV slots.

From its origins and by its nature advertising is intimately bound to other media. Primarily it is economic interdependence that dictates the terms of their relationship. Media and advertising companies often share personnel and technical and creative expertise in complex, formal and informal networks of association. Increasingly too, media content, ideas, images and celebrities 'inspire' advertising – and vice versa. Advertising revenue usually has great significance to a publisher or broadcaster. In commercial media, advertisers' expenditure partially or entirely underwrites the production and publication or broadcast of media 'content'. In return the media owner displays the advertisements. Advertising revenue supports media, either directly, or more usually indirectly, through a holding company or network of commissioning channels.[16] Advertising revenue provides a commercial *rationale* for the existence of the other channels of media communication, such as television, newspapers and magazines, but it does so without however being the singular *reason* for the form, existence and proliferation of other media.[17] These perform a range of social and cultural roles extending well beyond the basically commercial intentions of advertisers and media owners.

A crucial part of the organisation of an advertising campaign lies in the strategic use of what is traditionally known as the 'media mix' which offers an array of options and decisions about how and in what mode a message is communicated. The traditional strengths of the main media are outlined in Table 18.3 along with some problems advertisers (increasingly) encounter.

Table 18.3 Strengths and weaknesses of main media for advertisers

Major medium	Is an attractive advertising interface/medium because . . .	But . . .
TV: typically 30-second commercial breaks	Large national audiences offer reach and this medium offers high creative scope. Can provide regional audiences too. Digital promises smaller but better segmented audiences.	Consumers channel hop, watch videos, find ads stupid or boring, and are increasingly harder to identify and group. Digital TV has begun to fragment the audience making national reach impossible. Tivo and other digital 'anytime TV' platforms allow audiences to easily skip ads. Increases in subscription packaged based TV (e.g. Sky Movies) means that the advertising revenue based business model of the 20th century TV companies (like ITV) is under immediate threat. Internet platform TV (e.g. iplayer) technologies make some advertising formats redundant.
Radio: short 10 to 30-second slots	Ads can be related to the locality and daily routines (breakfast, drive to work, etc.), and are relatively cheap.	Audiences have now got many choices and do not tend to recall the rather low impact ads. Non-commercial radio remains popular. Many of the problems facing TV are shared by radio. In general a digital medium – especially if paid for by subscription – is not good for advertising. However radio has increased global reach via internet audiences – this extensive reach cannot be readily measured or reflected in ad pricing.
Press: newspapers, magazines	Offers frequent publications and identifiable audiences.	Readers flick past dull formats and have an immense array of choices and sections within newspapers. Classified ads in particular are better via the internet. Younger people are prone to spend less time reading papers.
Outdoor: posters, transport	They offer excellent and witty high impact ads, which improve with traffic congestion.	Viewers are typically hard to identify and target and passers-by do not pay much attention.
Cinema: 30 to 60-second slots	Captive audience, usually well segmented (by age and gender for example) sees well crafted ads in good conditions.	Audiences are relatively few in number and tend to be limited to the young.
Internet	Fast improving multi-medium, internet ads offer potential for tracking and testing ad effectiveness, which in some ad formats is very good (e.g. search and click through). Direct link to purchase sites. Improved connectivity and improving demographics/user rates.	It is not fully accessible to all segments. Innumerable web pages make targeting difficult for some ad formats. Ongoing distrust of e-commerce and web security. Low impact in all but the most rich media ads. Competition from free commercial information. Consumers irritated by pop ups and other disruptions to internet use. Low uptake of mobile internet so far.

Fragmentation and segmentation

Concerns about how advertisers use the media environment are now expressed in terms of *media* (and therefore *audience*) 'fragmentation'. Audiences are not switched off – they are switched over. Increasingly, also, they are online. A related set of problems (explored and managed by market researchers) focuses on social fragmentation. The advertiser is faced with the difficulties of catering to an ever more diverse set of lifestyle segments, social groupings and taste patterns. While these subcultures are an opportunity to forge ahead into ever new markets, they impair the effectiveness of producers' communications strategies when they hope to profit from the economies of scale afforded by selling to audiences seen as coherent cultural groupings. Once there was profit in seeking out common cultural denominators, now the denominations have become higher, and harder to scale. Advertisers addressing contemporary audiences want to use the media to hit a number of diffuse and moving targets – and even their best shots bounce off. Saturation offers one strategy. Smart targeting is an increasingly attractive alternative.

The problems of segmentation and fragmentation are multiplied by new technologies and cross platform media use. We watch TV on the internet, surf the internet via a TV remote-control, download radio shows to MP3 players and upload TV programmes to Facebook and YouTube. We telephone with Skype via our laptop computer and work on Excel spreadsheets on our mobile phones – sending and receiving emails and video-calling all the while. In such a media environment the processes of targeting, tracking – or even tracking down – an advertising audience must be unstable at best. While ad revenues remain healthy, confidence in the basic business models of mass media consumption are already under review. The ad industry is reconfiguring to better adapt to such a multi-media, multi-platform world and seeking still to engage audiences with informative and affectively rich imagery, sounds and words. The new intimacies and intrusions afforded by new data management and communications technologies will continue to afford advertisers and consumers new threats and new opportunities. Consumers, if they choose, will be able to evade messages more readily. Advertisers will feel they can get 'closer' to consumers – in real and virtual spaces.

Conclusion

In the future the advertising industry will approach the challenges of the new media and marketing environment on two fronts. The threat posed by the ever increasing fragmentation of the media audience will be confronted by ever more variegated use of the media. The trend for finding increasingly opportunistic spaces for advertising will continue. Fragmentation will be addressed by the use of ever more complex computer generated marketing data alongside novel qualitative research techniques. The attenuation of the division between main media advertising and the other aspects of the media and marketing mix will promise a tighter fit between what consumers see and hear about the marketplace and what they might want from it. This is summed up in the notion of integrated marketing communications. Whether advertising (and the market) can deliver on such a promise is, as ever, in doubt. To do this in an efficient and culturally sensitive and unobtrusive way is perhaps beyond the genre.

In so far as main media national advertising has been the 'flagship' mode of consumer communications in the past, the future will see it remain prominent but partially de-centred, making space for other modes of consumer interface under the rubric of Consumer Relationship Marketing/Management (CRM). Organisations will turn their attention more carefully to the internet, loyalty cards and other points of contact and information exchange as they attempt to satisfy more needs (real and imagined) more completely and more profitably than their competitors. Brand-style integrated marketing and management will encompass and transform advertising strategies – partially absorbing media based advertising in wide ranging arrays of branded interfaces.

There is much anxiety about the capacity of advertising to manipulate the consumer. This concern remains high on the agenda in critical commentaries on advertising's social influence (see Williams 1980; Williamson 1978 and Goldman 1992 for the detailed accounts on this position). Notably there have been renewed efforts at regulating advertising, focusing on food and youth. There has consequently been a ban on advertising many unhealthy foods around programmes associated with the young audience. The vigilance of governments and of consumer lobbyists, alongside the industry's systems for self regulation can help ensure, in different ways, that advertising adheres to codes: in detail over certain products (drink and cigarettes), in relation to certain audiences (children) and regarding certain areas of legislation (e.g. equal opportunities in recruitment advertising).

There are difficulties in enforcing some for these regulations in the face of changes to forms and formats of advertising. When products are placed deliberately in film, or when advertiser produced media content is broadcast on the web or via podcast (for instance) mechanisms for scrutiny and enforcement of regulation become complex and unclear. The reflective and morally conscientious consumer is a further and very important part of the system – inevitably haphazard as such consumer led interventions tend to be. Consumers can, and sometimes do, exercise their power of choice in the face of ethical issues linked to product promotion and advertising.

Much is pathological about the patterns and relations that constitute contemporary capitalism – and the systems of provision, distribution and communication that underpin that system. Some aspects are progressive – with evermore sensitive marketing interfaces allowing (potentially) for fuller engagements between consumers acting ethically and politically in evaluations of the costs and benefits of personal consumption in reflective ways. Advertising can have a negative role at this interface – working to evade certain truths about global economic life related, say, to the production of cheap goods. Potentially also however advertisers can use the media to state commitments to ethical issues – gaining valuable attention and 'brand credibility' in relation to ethical themes, for instance sustainability (Body Shop), fair-trade (Tate and Lyle), or gender and identity politics (Dove). Of course 'in practice' relationships between advertisements serving as signs of ethical commitment and the operational realities of branded corporations must always be scrutinised. Advertising can operate to articulate renewed commitments and promises of change. Consumers, in return can work (in limited ways) to hold brands and retailers to account – in consumption habits and brand preferences and using peer to peer internet sites to highlight concerns.

Questions

1 What threats and what opportunities confront advertisers in the new media environment?

2 Think of ways in which changes impact on the industry and on consumers.

3 Explore reasons why institutions such as universities, hospitals, government agencies and political parties increasingly use advertising in their communications strategies. Why might we be ambivalent about the use of advertising in such institutions?

Notes

1 This increase is adjusted to account for inflation and is based on a US dollar measure. 2006 was the fifth consecutive year that global advertising expenditure increased.

2 World Advertising Trends 2007 quotes $417, 677 as a figure inflation adjusted for comparability with the figure in 2000 - of $341,598.

3 Publicis, WPP, Dentsu, Havas and Omnicom are five global advertising-media holding companies that own most of the ad agencies and media companies across the world. They grew out of merged agencies in the UK, US, France and Japan.

4 Global and international statistics have been taken from *World Advertising Trends 2000* and *2007* and the *Advertising Statistics Year Book*. Figures are adjusted to allow for inflation. The figures provided are estimates based on the best evidence available. Particular caution is advised with regard to international and historical comparisons. Figures are exclusive of production costs which can run to £1 million for a 30-second spot.

5 BRIC, i.e. Brazil, India, Russia and China.

6 At current estimated exchange rates (2008).

7 The figures cited are exclusive of the far larger marketing expenditure which underwrites much of the commercial imagery and marketing activity in contemporary societies.

8 Following typologies of internet advertising formats from the Internet Advertising Bureau.

9 Samuel Johnson is famous amongst advertisers for remarking, in 1758, on what has come to be known as advertising 'clutter', that: 'Advertisements are now so numerous that they are very negligently perused and it is therefore become necessary to gain attention by magnificence of promises and by eloquence sometimes sublime and sometimes pathetick' (Johnson cited in Caplin 1959: 17).

10 This production depended, on agriculture, other modes of subsistence living and, for the wealthy, the domestic labour of household staff.

11 A key change in provision is that agriculture has developed from a local concern to become a national and global industry in the period of the 19th and 20th centuries.

12 Which had expanded circulation in the 19th century due to urbanisation, improving literacy and deregulation of the press. As other media developed, along with governmental restrictions on the commercial use of their airtime, advertising agencies dealt in their space too. Commercial television, which began in 1955, has consistently been the second largest advertising medium.

13 The 1875 Trade Marks Registration Act gave legal protection in the UK to manufacturers who wanted to use a sign to identify their products against imitation. Similar US legislation was passed through Congress in 1870 and 1905.

14 The forerunner of Ogilvy and Mather, now based in London's Canary Wharf which is, like J. W. Thompson, amongst the largest, now global advertising agencies.

15 This distinction is an artefact of accounting procedures in marketing departments of advertisers – with media expenditure records 'being placed above the line' on the accounts page and 'below the line', below it.

16 Typically revenue for magazines or newspapers will be composed of cover price revenues and revenue from the sale of advertising space. For instance the *Daily Mail* gets over half (c. 60 per cent) of its revenue from advertisers.

17 As numerous other chapters in this volume attest.

Further reading

Danesi, M. (2005) *Brands*, London: Routledge. This book provides a clear outline of the complex processes underpinning branding and an important context for understanding advertising.

Donaton, S. (2004) *Madison and Vine: Why the Entertainment and Advertising Industries Must Converge to Survive*, London: McGraw Hill. Examines the convergence of ads and entertainment.

MacRury, I. (2008) *Advertising*, London: Routledge. Introduction to all aspects of the advertising mix.

Williams, R. (1980) 'Advertising: The Magic System' in R. Williams (ed) *Problems in Materialism and Culture*, London: Verso. The classic essay on advertising, offering a powerful polemic to consider when thinking about contemporary advertising and our relationships to the genre.

Website

http://www.warc.com – The World Advertising Research Center (WARC) provides access to comprehensive industry research archives and lively case studies in virtually all areas of advertising, marketing and media activity worldwide.

References

Benedictus, L. (2008) 'The Adman as Artist', *Prospect* (April) at www.prospect-magazine.co.uk/article_details.php?id=10089 (accessed 6 March 2009).

Campbell, C. (1987) *The Romantic Ethic and the Spirit of Modern Consumerism*, Oxford: Blackwell.

Caplin, R. (1959) *Advertising: A General Introduction*, London: IPA.

Donaton, S. (2004) *Madison and Vine: Why the Entertainment and Advertising Industries Must Converge to Survive*, London: McGraw Hill.

Ewen, S. (2001) *Captains of Consciousness: Advertising and The Social Roots of Consumer Culture*, New York: Basic Books.

Fine, B. (1995) 'From Political Economy to Consumption', in D. Miller (ed) *Acknowledging Consumption*, London: Routledge, pp. 127–63.

Goldman, R. (1992) *Reading Ads Socially*, London: Routledge.

James, O. (2007) *Affluenza*, London: Vermilion.

Marchand, R. (1985) *Advertising the American Dream: Making Way for Modernity 1920–1940*, Berkeley, CA: University of California Press.

McCracken, G. (1990) *Culture and Consumption: New Approaches to the Symbolic Character of Consumer Goods and Activities*, Bloomington, IN: Indiana University Press.

Nevett, T. (1982) *Advertising in Britain: A History*, London: Heinemann.

Ohmann, R. (1996) *Selling Culture: Magazines, Markets, and Class at the Turn of the Century*, London: Verso.

Presbrey, F. (1929) *The History and Development of Advertising*, New York: Doubleday.

Richards, J (2000) 'Interactive Advertising Concentration: A First Attempt', *Journal of Interactive Advertising*, 1 (1): Fall 2000, at www.jiad.org/article3 (accessed 6 March 2009).

Schudson, M. (1984) *Advertising, The Uneasy Persuasion: Its dubious impact on American society*, New York: Basic Books.

Wernick, A. (1991) *Promotional Culture: Advertising, Ideology and Symbolic Expression*, London: Sage.

Williams, R. (1980) 'Advertising: The Magic System' in R. Williams (ed) *Problems in Materialism and Culture*, London: Verso.

Williamson, J. (1978) *Decoding Advertisements: Ideology and Meaning in Advertising*, London: Marion Boyars.

Part 3

THE MEDIA ENVIRONMENT: POLICY, ECONOMICS AND INSTITUTIONS

Introduction

Daniele Albertazzi and Paul Cobley

The economics of media, issues of policy, the state of public service broadcasting and how censorship and regulation take place (the topics covered below) all have a fundamental role in determining the kind of media we 'get', i.e. they are *inside* the media in very crucial ways. If you think about it, all these areas of investigation can in fact be discussed in terms of the very practical impact they have on our *freedom*, *access* to the media and the degree of *pluralism* our societies enjoy. That is, they determine more or less precisely the media products with which we interact: importantly, these issues are still as crucial in contemporary Europe as they have ever been.

If in our introduction (above) we have been at pains to stress how processes of digitisation have dramatically increased the availability of different media and have empowered consumers in unprecedented ways (putatively a positive development), what should also be stressed is that it is *precisely* digitisation and convergence which have very much facilitated a process of concentration of ownership in the media, too. This process has accelerated in recent years and is making concerned observers of the European media landscape increasingly uneasy about the quality of the messages we get and the *interests* these messages serve (European Federation of Journalists 2006). Huge (especially cross-media) concentration creates new imbalances in the public arena between those who can invest massively in creating and promoting the messages they put into the public domain and those who (while now enjoying unprecedented access to new technologies that provide them with new channels of communication) simply do not have the financial and organisational muscles to compete. Chapter 22 (Censorship and Freedom of Speech), addresses these issues head on, explaining why freedom of speech can never be absolute (which, in fact, would not even be desirable). Clearly the media *must* be regulated to limit the extent to which they are able to invade people's privacy, disseminate rumours about individuals and organisations that these might not be in a position to publicly disprove, misrepresent groups and cultures, etc; also, every society inevitably shares some sense of what material should be considered as 'offensive' (or even potentially damaging to certain sectors of the population) and the availability of which needs to be regulated. However, as this chapter indicates, censorship does not concern exclusively the activities of governments and regulators but also 'the workings of market forces' (p. 318) and the more subtle ways through which certain content is restricted or promoted. Inevitably, therefore, there appear to be less 'noble' reasons why all out censorship or informal pressures end up being exercised on the media by governments, regulators and, interestingly, media proprietors themselves. The case study covered in this chapter is that of Italy, which in a recent report of the US-based non-governmental organisation Freedom House (2006) was classed as 'partly free' due to the (still unresolved) conflict of interest of Silvio Berlusconi as media tycoon, leader of the largest party in the country and several times Prime Minister. Rather than dismissing Berlusconi's case as an anomaly, students should ask to what extent Italy has become archetypical of an unhealthy specific kind of relationship between politics and the media that has already spread to the rest of Europe, too.

The dire predicament Italy finds itself in now has been much facilitated precisely by the total *lack* of regulation of the television market that was typical of the country in the 1980s, when Berlusconi built his media empire. This teaches us how naïve it is to think of 'regulation' by state or EU authorities as necessarily 'bad' and as automatically curtailing media freedom, and also reminds us why media students need to understand the different kinds and variety of media policies which are put in place 'to coordinate, promote, address and sometimes control media industries' (Chapter 20, page 293). A misguided, excessive insistence on 'freedom of enterprise' or on individual liberties can in fact conceal (when the individual in question is, say, Rupert Murdoch) that media industries represent a very special case. Their fundamental role as 'educators' of the citizenry in an age in which the older institutions that promoted socialisation (e.g. churches or political parties) have lost much of their influence and appeal, means that they must be treated very differently from the producers of other commodities (say, soap or crisps). The centrality of the media derives from the fact that they are a fundamental means by which citizens gather political intelligence, monitor the activities of the elites and in general make sense of the world around them. They are also seemingly ubiquitous and prone to proliferation of their activities. As such, it is necessary for them to be regulated.

In this context, there is clearly still an important role for public service broadcasters (PSBs) to play across the continent. One good reason for thinking about this, as we do in this part of the book, is that PSBs across Europe are facing huge challenges in still focusing on their mission, providing good quality content and justifying their privileged positions in receipt of a licence fee in a multimedia environment where, technically, access to a wide variety of media is no longer a problem (Chapter 21). In this context, the question is posed, why should one organisation – no matter how virtuous it argues to be – gain public funding at the expense of all others? And why shouldn't we leave the market to decide how to deliver high quality content to those who are happy to pay for it? That PSBs manage to redefine what they stand for and how to deliver it in the digital age and in the context of media systems dominated by the new ideology of choice and competition, is arguably crucial and goes to the heart of the debate about the extent to which contemporary Europe is concerned to preserve some level of pluralism within its borders. Attacks on the core principles of PSB rely heavily on what is supposed to be a widespread distrust among the public of public subsidy of media organisations, as well as, conversely, a presumption that commercial media, within the context of different markets, will deliver choice and quality at affordable prices. The financial crisis Europe is experiencing as we move into the second decade of the 21st century and the new interventionist approach increasingly taken by European governments to 'save the economy', might perhaps go some way towards reversing this tide of distrust towards the 'public'. Public service broadcasting, with its distinctive mission of fostering diversity, pluralism and range, noncommercialist values, as well as focus on social purpose, might even benefit from the new economic climate in which the concept of the omnipotence of the market is now in disrepute. Aptly, then, Chapter 19 shows that the economic determinants of media products reveal 'a great deal about the characteristic "content" of those products' and, in the end explain 'why those products exist in the first place' (p. 291). In other words, democratic societies have proven unable to do without probing, critical and independent PSBs which are forced by their charters and mission statements to eschew the idea that media products are mere 'commodities'.

References

European Federation of Journalists (2006) 'Media Power in Europe: the Big Picture of Ownership', www.ifj.org/assets/docs/245/202/08737f5-ec283ca.pdf (accessed 7 March 2009).

Freedom House (2004–06) 'Map of Press Freedom', www.freedomhouse.org/template.cfm?page1/4251&year1/42006 (accessed 11 October 2006).

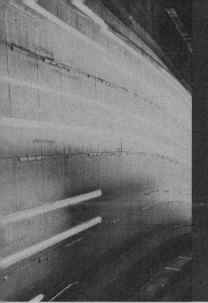

19

Economics

John Sedgwick and Guglielmo Volpe

Chapter overview

Media commodities vary greatly in terms of their form, technology, history and uses. As a consequence each commodity-type needs to be understood as a bundle of commodity characteristics that differentiate it from other commodity types. Following Fine and Leopold (1993) we term each bundle a 'system of provision' using the movie business as an example. Then, drawing on examples derived from the movie, newspaper and television broadcasting industries, we go on to show how prices are assigned, how markets clear, and the level and nature of competition between the various 'players'. We maintain that this framework of analysis is essential to a first understanding of media since it allows students to conceptualise differences between the various media and yet identify what they all have in common within and across territories as commercial entities operating in the marketplace.

Introduction

The media take many forms: material, as with newspapers and magazines, or immaterial, as with the consumed end product of the technology of radio and television broadcasts, the movies, and the internet. In each case, distinctive industrial organisations have emerged to facilitate the production, distribution and consumption of the commodity that is characteristic of a particular medium of communication – what Ben Fine and Ellen Leopold have termed 'systems of provision' (Fine and Leopold 1993). These organisations have evolved over time and, if efficient, will maximise the production output that can be derived and distributed from a given set of resource inputs (i.e. the resources needed to sustain film-making, programme-making, magazine publication, etc.), or minimise the quantity of resource inputs necessary to produce and distribute a given output.

As a consequence of the emergence of new technologies, these industrial arrangements are subject to change, even transformation. In capitalist economies new technologies are generally adopted when they bestow competitive advantage; usually, that advantage entails profit. However, the scale of investment involved in the setting up of new technologies may be prohibitive. So in those circumstances in which new technologies are perceived to be in the public interest and can be easily shared – such as in the case of broadband internet access or digital broadcasting – the state may attempt to ensure that the investment takes place and that the technologies are as widely available as possible. It does this through a variety of instruments, including regulation, control and ownership.

Drawing upon examples in the film, television and newspaper industries in the UK, and making references to other media, this chapter proposes that while each medium has its own system of provision – its own way of organising consumption and production – underpinning that level of detail are certain fundamental commodity characteristics such as price, market mechanism and market structure which the media share in common. Taking film as an example, we will begin by discussing the nature of a medium as a *commodity*.

Media commodities

Media commodities exist simply to allow a flow of information: this flow goes from suppliers to consumers. Yet, whilst all media commodities have this in common, it should be noted that they differ from one another as commodities in terms of both form and function. Thus, the creators of MySpace or YouTube have developed commodities that allow consumers to use a particular software technology to communicate with other users by means of the internet. Based on a different set of technologies, British Telecom supplies a commodity that allows consumers to communicate by telephone to other telephone users. Deploying print technologies, News International produces a number of national daily newspapers in the UK (and elsewhere) whose editors make available to newspaper readers items of news, opinion and comment, etc.; using very similar print technologies, the publishers of this book produce academic texts which they hope will be attractive to students, and, like newspaper proprietors they may also be interested in offering their portfolio of commodities in electronic form through dedicated websites and e-book formats. The BBC uses broadcast technologies to diffuse television and radio programmes that it either makes itself or acquires, at a price, from other programme makers. Warner Bros., as a film distributor, seeks to place movies made, wholly or partly, by itself, or acquired from other film-makers, on various media platforms – with cinema exhibitors (theatrical release), retail distributors (DVD) or broadcasters (television, podcasts, online iplayer viewing, downloads), who in turn make them available to audiences.

The business firms mentioned above produce distinctive commodities, each of which has a distinctive set of characteristics, defined by the technologies peculiar to it and the system of provision by which it is both supplied and consumed. To arrive at the 'ontology' of a commodity – a definition of how it exists – a number of questions need to be asked: how is the commodity reproduced? How are property rights assigned to it? How do consumers access and use it? How are prices organised?

Sedgwick and Pokorny (2005: 12–15) consider film as a commodity:

- each film released is a physical record of information (traditionally as reels of celluloid on which are imprinted the edited sequences of photographic representations of the film's content, but lately as digitally recorded signals inscribed on DVD), which

- under the appropriate conditions (traditionally in a movie theatre projector, but lately by being 'read' from a disc in a computer or a DVD player),

- makes the film available in the form in which it can be consumed in the mind of the person who has elected to see the film, i.e., as a unique combination of immaterial sensual images that can be varied in size (made bigger or smaller), which

- are non-diminishable in consumption, so that one person's consumption of those images does not reduce the stock available for other consumers.

Furthermore, film images can be reproduced infinitely but, unlike, say, the services provided by lighthouses, they are also 'excludable' – consumers can be excluded from the consumption of films in theatrical release if they are not willing to pay the price of admission to the movie theatre. A particular consumption characteristic of film is that the set of unique images that comprise each film is generally enjoyed more intensely on the first screening, with most consumers preferring not to watch most films a second time; but if they do, they very rarely watch it for a third time. This is an example of an empirically based law, which economists term the principle of diminishing marginal utility: i.e. the maximum 'utility' of the film for the audience resides in the first viewing. This principle is firmly embedded in the operations by which films are offered to the viewing public. The system of provision that has been built around film is depicted in Figure 19.1.

The contracts between the economic agents featured in Figure 19.1 – producer, distributor, exhibitor, retailer and broadcaster – apportion property rights that commonly specify temporal constraints on how the film may be shown: typically, films are exhibited theatrically before going into DVD release approximately six

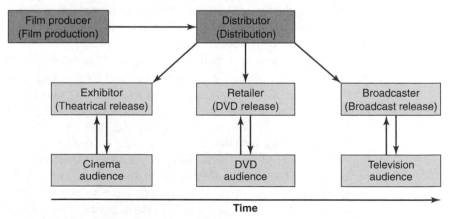

Figure 19.1 Movies as a system of provision

months later, before, in turn, going through the various stages of broadcasting release – normally in the order of cable, satellite and terrestrial. Once the film is made, the distributor is at the hub of the diffusion process through time and space (actual and virtual), serving as the agent for the film producer in securing rents from each of the various media owners and charging a fee for its services.

'Systems of provision' diagrams comparable to Figure 19.1 can be drawn for each media industry, reflecting the unique and idiosyncratic set of characteristics that comprise the commodities they produce. However, when comparing commodities within or between media, consumers need to compare not just the utility (satisfaction) they are likely to derive from consumption but also the cost to them. Likewise producers need to transform the utility they make possible into revenue from which to meet their costs of production and generate profits. Prices serve both functions.

Prices

Media commodities are part of what Karl Marx (1818–83), in the opening sentence of volume 1 (1867) of his famous work, *Das Kapital* (*Capital*, in its English translation), identified as an 'immense collection of commodities, which make up the wealth of societies in which the capitalist mode of production prevails' (Marx 1976: 125). Commodities can be distinguished from non-commodities on the basis of their being able to sustain a presence in the market: that is, suppliers are able to generate revenues by normally (but, not always, as will be shown) selling output at a price per unit in sufficient quantities to cover long term costs of production, meaning that consumers have been suitably attracted by the commodity to buy it in those quantities. Some quasi-commodities such as films supported by state financed film corporations are sustained on the market by means of subsidies – in effect the benefactor pays part of the price. If a product cannot fetch a price on the market its production is essentially a hobby. The market enables consumers to contemplate commodities 'abstractly'; thus consumers may compare the prices of commodities with the utility (pleasure) they would expect to derive through the consumption of those commodities.

Economists conceive markets to be in equilibrium when consumers buy from the market the commodities put onto it by producers. Changes in prices serve to move markets towards equilibrium, with surplus numbers of commodities on the market causing prices to fall and shortages of them causing prices to rise. Yet, this is not the end of the explanation of how prices are determined and how profit is made. Consider the case of newspapers. Newspapers, magazines and books can be found at various retail outlets and acquired for a particular price, usually determined by the retailer. Thus the five October 2007 editions of the UK Sunday newspaper the *News of the World* sold on average 3,019,183 copies in the UK at the retail price of £0.90, generating a gross revenue of £2,717,264.7 per edition, whereas the average gross revenue accruing to the *Observer* (also a UK Sunday paper) per edition during this same period was £926,090.4, the result of selling 487,416 papers at price £1.90 (ABC). Of course this tells us nothing about the profitability of either paper because data about the average costs of production are not available for public consumption. The matter is made even more complex because both newspapers are owned by multiple-newspaper owners, News International and Guardian Newspapers, respectively, which are likely to spread certain costs – e.g. printing, news-gathering – across their various titles.

In the example of the film business developed earlier, the price paid by audiences for admission to a cinema, for the ownership of a DVD, or for 'on demand' access on a pay-per-view television channel seems completely 'visible'. However, things become more complicated where the provision of a film on other modes of television transmission is concerned. With commercial subscription television from companies such as Sky, the issue is not the visibility of the price but the 'bundling' policies of the providers. Special interest groups, such as film (and sports) fans, must pay hefty supplementary subscriptions for access to the movie and sport bundles of cable and satellite television channels. In the case of 'free to air' commercial television the price is no longer 'visible' in any obvious sense. In these cases, the commercial channels seem to provide films 'for free', although it takes little imagination to realise that, in fact, the channel merely implements films to deliver particular kinds of audiences (or consumers) to advertisers. Viewing the matter in this light, it could be said that it is the advertisers who *appear to* make gifts of films during, and between which, they advertise, in the expectation that audiences consume the message implicit in the adverts – 'appear to' because of course television audiences in their capacity as consumers pay prices for commodities that cover the advertising component of marketing costs. Even in public service broadcasting, it has to be acknowledged that advertising and pricing play their part. In the case of the BBC, programmes, including films, are financed through the licence fee – the price of films is arguably 'visible' in what licence payers cough up. Additionally, though, the BBC is compelled by the terms of its charter to provide competitive programming and thus win audiences with comfortable to those of programmes (commodities) the commercial channels. Even this is not the end of the search for industry prices in the film business, because of the role of distributors. Distributors also demand a price from the exhibitors/retailers/broadcasters, normally set as some proportion of box-office revenue, whereby the more popular a film is, the higher is the proportion of the box-office specified in the contract (De Vany 2004: 31).

Each system of media provision will have its own set of relationships and its own way of pricing. Consequently, prices are a very important indicator of economic activity, signalling as they do the nature of the relationship between buyers and sellers. For students of the media it is worth gaining an acute awareness of the diverse manner in which prices are charged, including the seemingly irrational practice of charging consumers a zero price for some commodities, such as happens for certain internet services such as MySpace and YouTube. For instance, producers and actual (as opposed to virtual) retailers of music have been greatly troubled in recent times by the rapid diffusion of digital music, the new method of (virtual) retailing that accompanies it, and the explosion in illegal downloading (piracy) that has been made possible (see Chapter 14). Pirates pay a zero price for their music commodities, representing a loss of potential revenue for record producers and retailers, a practice that ultimately threatens their continued existence in the marketplace. Thus, the digitisation of music and the speed of its take-up has very greatly affected the system of recorded music provision, requiring us to understand a new set of relationships that stretch upstream to the manufacturers of MP3 players and computers and downstream to everyone in the world with a computer and an internet connection.

Knowing how prices and profits are generated and why they are as they are ultimately tells us about the nature of economic relationships and motives of the various agents in the business.

The market mechanism

Economists treat consumers as utility seekers who are rational, in that they prefer more to less utility. Yet, generally, as we have seen, it is assumed that consumers experience diminishing amounts of extra utility as they consume increasing amounts of a commodity. In the context of film going, audiences prefer Film A to Film B if the former promises higher levels of 'cinematic utility', but the repeated viewing of the same film reduces dramatically the additional pleasure derived, leading to the result that, as a general rule, adult mainstream audiences (as opposed to specialists, academics or 'film buffs') do not watch the same film over and over again. Economists also apply the concept of opportunity cost to consumption, maintaining that in choosing Film A ahead of Film B film goers understand that the cost of making this choice is the loss of utility that occurs as a consequence of not viewing Film B. However, although Film A may be viewed in preference to Film B, it might well be the case that a first viewing of Film B is then preferred to a second viewing of Film A – in this case the opportunity cost of not seeing Film B is greater than the anticipated benefit of watching Film A for a second time.

With most commodities that are scarce in supply, relative to demand for them, consumers are willing to pay more for something that yields higher levels of utility – of course, if it were something that is scarce in supply, but nobody wanted it, then nobody would be willing to pay a price for it at all! As examples of 'scarcity sensitivity', one has only to think of the prices that some football supporters are willing to pay to watch their favourite football team play in the final of a major international competition, or the prices that ballet lovers are willing to pay to watch their favourite dancer in a ballet that they adore. Film lovers would behave in exactly the same way, if they needed to, but of critical importance in understanding the nature of film as a commodity is the fact that they do not need to, and the reason for this is that the movie business is built around technological and organisational capabilities that allow it to meet the demand for a movie wherever it may emerge, with the proviso that a profit can be made by the agents involved in its supply. Hence, unlike the hypothetical football match or ballet performance, although the utility promised by particular films may be extremely high for very many consumers, the industry ensures, through distribution and exhibition practices, that films that are popular with audiences are made less scarce in supply than films that are less popular – a phenomenon known as 'adaptive contracting' (De Vany 2004: 30–2). The consequence of this is that, as a general rule, cinemas maintain a common admission price irrespective of the attractions being screened: film audiences are not required to pay a higher premium for film quality (subjectively defined), no matter how compelling the promise of cinematic utility may be.

All mass media industries work this way, rapidly responding to changes in demand through the distribution of extra production – making goods in greater demand less scarce. Clearly for this to occur two conditions must hold: (1) distribution networks have to be in place so that producers can respond rapidly to changes in consumer demand, and (2) production can be easily increased or reduced. Now consider the way in which the internet has facilitated this process and influenced the competitive environment faced by media producers.

Competition

Over the past decade the media industries have experienced considerable changes in market conditions, with the internet as a major influence, spawning a range of goods and services and modes of consumption that were inconceivable to the bulk of consumers 10 years ago. For instance, the digital technologies that have emerged around internet shopping have brought about the emergence of new retail business systems for supplying music and books in their traditional format – CDs, books as books, etc. As a consequence, the demand for books bought from bookshops has declined relative to the rise in demand for books purchased through internet suppliers such as Amazon. Furthermore, other variants of the technology have resulted in changes to the pattern of music consumption, with the growth in demand for digital music growing relative to the demand for CDs. At the time of writing this chapter, publishers are investing heavily in e-book technologies in response to the widely perceived demand for alternatives to the traditional book format. The point is that the flux in market conditions is an ever-present reality, made more dynamic through the strong association between media and digital technologies.

Economists make the distinction between competitive and non-competitive markets. Firms functioning as capitalist entities in pursuit of profits would like, ideally, to operate in markets in which they supply a commodity that has no available substitutes and for which demand is high and not sensitive to prices. Under these circumstances, the producer will be a monopolist or at least have a very high market share and enjoy a level of profitability much higher than that necessary to sustain its market presence. It will enjoy these profit levels for as long as it takes

- rival firms to put a comparable commodity onto the market, and
- for demand to remain steady.

At the time that this chapter is being written, the Apple i-phone holds such a position in the smartphone market. Now contrast this to the years of negative profits (losses) endured by Amazon as it sought to build a new retail business for selling books, based upon online retailing technology. In Amazon's case alternative bookselling services were available and the commodity was price sensitive. In order to make in-roads into this market Amazon needed to compete on price and

Table 19.1 Market shares (%) in the UK TV industry

Year	BBC1	BBC2	ITV1	Channel 4	five	Digital broadcasters
1981	39	12	49			
1986	37	11	44	8		
1991	34	10	42	10		4
1996	33.5	11.5	35.1	10.7	2.3	10.1
2001	26.9	11.1	26.7	10	5.8	19.6
2004	24.7	10	22.8	9.7	6.6	26.2
2005	23.3	9.4	21.5	9.7	6.4	29.6
2006	22.8	8.8	19.6	9.8	5.7	33.3

Source: From Broadcasters Audience Research Board Ltd (BARB) Annual % Shares of Viewing (Individuals) 1981–2008 (www.barb.co.uk/facts/annualShareOfViewing) (accessed 28 February 2008). Copyright © BARB Limited. Reproduced with permission.

service, and although it achieved a sizable market share in the UK and US, it did so by making annual losses, while at the same time encouraging other retailers into the online sector of the market.

Table 19.1 depicts the market shares of the five terrestrial channels plus the digital broadcasters (including the digital channels operated by the terrestrial channels), which together make up the UK television industry. The story is one of dramatic decline in the market share of the principal two broadcasters, BBC and ITV, over the 25-year period, hastened by the similarly dramatic growth in market share achieved by the digital channels. For ITV its declining market share brings about pressure on advertising revenues as advertisers reach fewer people and, because of this, on its stock market value as a company. However, as Table 19.2 shows, for the week ending 6 January 2008, the two terrestrial broadcasters still produce the most popular programmes.

Indeed, it is interesting to note that although between them the digital channels attracted over 40 per cent of the total audience during that week, the largest audience for any single programme broadcast by a digital channel was a mere 1,405,000, for a live football game transmitted on New Year's Day on Sky Sports 1. Between them the five terrestrial channels transmitted 136 programmes during the same week that garnered higher viewing figures. Typically, audiences for programmes on digital channels are small to tiny and lie to the right of the statistical distribution of the 150 most popular programmes depicted in Figure 19.2. The increased market share of these channels, collectively identified in Table 19.1, is accounted for by the fact that an increasing proportion of households have paid for access through satellite or cable technology. The largest of these is BSkyB, which although running some 30 channels, attracted an average daily audience of 11,279,000 during the first week of January 2008 – less than half the daily average of 25,715,000 who watched a BBC1 broadcast during the same week.

As argued elsewhere (Sedgwick 2006), different business models are in operation. The Ofcom Report of 2004 shows that Sky spends considerably more per viewer than the industry average, while the BBC spends less than the industry average, from which it is possible to deduce that the BBC is relatively efficient in

Table 19.2 Programme ratings for week ending 6 January 2008

Rank	Programme	Audience	Broadcaster
1	Coronation Street (Fri 1933)	11.44	ITV
2	Coronation Street (Wed 1931)	11.35	ITV
3	Eastenders (Thu 1930)	11.34	BBC1
4	Eastenders (Fri 1959)	10.54	BBC1
5	Coronation Street (Sun 1929)	10.06	ITV
6	Eastenders (Wed 1957)	9.61	BBC1
7	Eastenders (Tue 1931)	9.37	BBC1
8	Coronation Street (Mon 1934)	9.37	ITV
9	Coronation Street (Mon 2031)	8.9	ITV
10	Emmerdale (Wed 1859)	8.85	ITV
11	Emmerdale (Fri 1902)	8.77	ITV
12	Eastenders (Mon 1959)	8.55	BBC1
13	Heartbeat (Sun 2001)	8.51	ITV
14	Emmerdale (Thu 1902)	8.44	ITV
15	Match of the Day (Sat 1804)	7.92	BBC1
16	Casualty (Sat 2035)	7.76	BBC1
17	Emmerdale (Mon 1903)	7.37	ITV
18	Foyle's War (Sun 2104)	7.37	ITV
19	Emmerdale (Tue 1900)	7.03	ITV
20	Midsomer Murders (Tue 2104)	6.62	ITV
21	Antiques Roadshow (Sun 2002)	6.49	BBC1
22	The One and Only (Sat 1920)	6.28	BBC1
23	Match of the Day (Sun 1745)	6.21	BBC1
24	Holby City (Tue 2013)	6.15	BBC1
25	Six O'clock News (Wed 1800)	6.05	BBC1
26	Film: Bruce Almighty (2003) (Wed 2027)	5.79	BBC1
27	Match of the Day (Sat 1706)	5.78	BBC1
28	Celebrity Mastermind (Tue 1901)	5.76	BBC1
29	Film: Sense and Sensibility (1995) (Sun 2100)	5.74	BBC1
30	New You've Been Framed! (Sat 1852)	5.66	ITV

Source: From Broadcasters Audience Research Board Ltd (BARB) Weekly Top 30 Programmes (www.barb.co.uk/index1.cfm) (accessed 28 February 2008). Copyright © BARB Limited. Reproduced with permission.

using budgets to attract audiences, but Sky is relative efficient in turning audience figures into revenue.

One way to view the competitive structure of the industry is through analysis of the degree to which it is differentiated. Economists use the following concepts:

- *horizontal product differentiation* – this depicts differences in characteristics between commodities that attract distinct groups of consumers ('taste politics');
- *vertical product differentiation* – depicts a running of qualitative differences between examples of a genre or commodity-type.

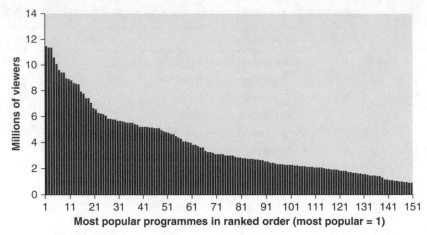

Figure 19.2 Audience sizes of the most popular 150 programmes broadcast during week ending 6 January 2008, ordered by rank

In the first case, think of the similarities between the UK soap operas *EastEnders* and *Coronation Street* and compare these to *Hollyoaks* and *Echo Beach* (which failed to be recommissioned for 2009). In all four soaps, criteria can be used to identify the salient characteristics of each, which in turn serves to distinguish them, so that they can be conceived of as 'near neighbours'. The basis of their relation as near neighbours can involve a number of things such as production values, scripts, the way they are recorded (film vs. video), etc. Organised on the basis of their characteristic profiles, horizontally differentiated commodities can be positioned along a continuum in which any new commodity can be placed between two existing commodities, with 'near neighbours' in close proximity and 'distant neighbours' far away. Clearly, within any media, commodities within a particular genre will share similar characteristics, be 'near neighbours, and be close substitutes'.

Consider, now, the case of vertical product differentiation. Figure 19.2 indicates that while some television programmes are extremely popular among audiences, most are not. If the diagram included all programmes broadcast each week, the median and mean programme would represent an audience of much less than a million viewers. Commodities that provide a superior level of utility for the bulk of consumers represent the top end of a vertically arranged continuum in which the most popular is ranked highest and the least popular lowest. As is apparent in Table 19.2 the Top 30 programmes weekly are dominated by 'near neighbour' soaps. Thus, there is vertical product differentiation which can be witnessed between programmes at the top and bottom ends of the graph of viewing figures i.e. where one programme is seen to be 'better' than another – *EastEnders* and *Coronation Street* are to be perceived qualitatively superior to *Hollyoaks* and *Echo Beach*; and there is horizontal differentiation, which is seen in differences that are to do with nuances within a genre and that are difficult to figure as one product being (at least economically) 'better' than another.

Conclusion

In the previous section the television industry was cited to illustrate market competition, but it could just as easily have been the music, newspaper, magazine, film, radio or internet-media business that generated the data found in Tables 19.1 and 19.2 and Figure 19.2. The competitive process in each case involves consumers making judgements about the quality of the bundle of characteristics that define, in their minds, each commodity that they choose, and producers wanting to both create and satisfy consumer needs. Once established, new episodes of television and radio programmes, or the next edition of a newspaper or magazine, work around the unique formula that makes the commodity attractive to audiences. In putting new commodities onto the market, producers take high risks, because audiences/consumers need to experience commodities to be in a position to make an assessment of their utility. It is for this reason that big budget Hollywood TV producers devote so much time and effort in trailing and marketing their new commodities. However, in all cases, because of the low marginal cost of replication (often zero) associated with media production, whereby highly popular commodities can easily be made less scarce than unpopular commodities, the choices made by consumers determine corporate performance, no matter whether it is measured by sales, audience numbers, revenues, advertising revenues or share price.

The task of big budget producers of film, television programmes, music albums, magazines, newspapers, books and internet communication services is to become market leaders. They do this by convincing audiences/customers that their commodities share similar characteristics and qualities with existing commodities (horizontal differentiation), for which there is a high level of demand, or are qualitatively different (vertical differentiation) and superior to existing commodities, sufficiently for audiences/consumers to become attracted by, for example, their novelty. Of course, many media commodities are not made with this purpose in mind, but rather to garner sufficient audience/consumer attention to cover costs and make a positive return on the investment made. Whatever the case, for the student of media it is imperative to know the economic determinants of media products: they reveal a great deal about the characteristic 'content' of not only the products but also why they exist in the first place.

Questions

1 Do you think that the government should intervene in the music market? Why? (Hint: in February 2008 the UK government suggested that internet service providers should be made responsible for any illegal downloading of music.)

2 In recent years, in many European and American cities, 'free newspapers' such as *Metro* have appeared on local underground and transport systems. How can a 'free newspaper' survive in the market? Do you think that the arrival of these 'free newspapers'

resembles the changes in the music industry? Should more established newspapers such as *The Times* and the *Guardian* also become free newspapers?

3 Many households install wireless routers in their homes so that the internet can be accessed anywhere in the household. However, often households make sure that the signal is password protected. What is the economic rationale for such a behaviour?

Further reading

Doyle, G. (2002) *Understanding Media Economics*, London: Sage. Explains the fundamental concepts relevant to the study of media economics; considers the key industrial questions facing the media industries today; relates economic theory to business practice; covers a wide range of media activity – advertising, television, film, print media, and new media; and looks at the impact of economics on public policy.

Hoskins, C., McFadyen, S. and Finn, A. (2004) *Media Economics: Applying Economics to New and Traditional Media*, London: Sage. Emphasises economic concepts that have distinct application within media industries, including corporate media strategies and mergers, public policy within media industries, how industry structure and changing technologies affect the conduct and performance of media industries, and why the US dominates trade in information and entertainment.

Michel, N. J. (2006) 'The Impact of Digital File Sharing on the Music Industry: An Empirical Analysis', *Topics in Economic Analysis & Policy*, 6 (1): Article 18, also available from http://norbertmichel.com/files/EmpiricalPaperAug2006.pdf (accessed 2 February 2009). Using household-level data from the Consumer Expenditure Survey, this article shows that file-sharing has decreased sales.

IFPI UK Music Market Statistics, www.ifpi.com/content/library/RIN-UK-07.pdf (accessed 2 February 2009).

References

ABC (2008) 'ABC Data', www1.abc.org.uk/cgi-bin/gen5?runprog=nav/abc&noc=y (accessed 28 February 2008).

De Vany, A. (2004) *Hollywood Economics: How Extreme Uncertainty Shapes the Film Industry*, London: Routledge.

Fine, B. and Leopold, E. (1993) *The World of Consumption*, London: Routledge.

Marx, K. (1976) *Capital*, Volume 1, Harmondsworth: Penguin.

Sedgwick, J. (2006) 'Economics of British TV', in D. Gomery and L. Hockley (eds) *Television Industries*, London: BFI.

Sedgwick, J. and Pokorny, M. (2005) 'The Characteristics of Film as a Commodity', in J. Sedgwick and M. Pokorny (eds) *An Economic History of Film*, London: Routledge.

20

Policy

Marco Gambaro

Chapter overview

This chapter looks broadly at the policies in respect of media that are implemented across Europe. It begins with a definition of policy and gives some reasons why policy is needed. It then goes on to look specifically at the economic and market reasons for regulation of the media. It then considers how policies get commissioned. Particular attention is paid to the convergence of broadcasting and telecommunications.

Introduction

Media policies encompass a large array of activities and interventions carried out by governments and institutions to coordinate, promote, address and sometimes control media industries. While there are several sectors in which governments and international agencies play an important role in coordinating and regulating economic activity, media industries represent a special case. The media industry is heavily regulated with detailed government interventions, but at the same time independence from government is crucial to the public's perception that the industry is delivering products of high quality.

The media are 'special' in many respects. Not only has the consumption of information been growing over the past decades, but media output has replaced other means by which social integration might be achieved. It has affected how people behave in different social contexts and how they interact with others, a function performed in the past by other social agencies, such as the family, the education system and/or the Church. Furthermore, the attention devoted to media represents a substantial part of people's time, after sleeping and working. In many European countries people devote from four to six hours per day to the consumption of media, with television getting the larger share.

Media industries can be described as two-sided markets where the same platform (the media outlet) sells different goods to different clients. On the one hand, radio, television, newspapers and magazines offer information to consumers; on the other, they also sell consumers' attention to advertisers. Media act as platforms enabling interaction between the two sides, consumers and advertisers, trying to get both on board through product differentiation and appropriate pricing. In theory, the two groups can interact directly. For instance companies can directly contact potential clients with sales calls or direct mail and consumers can look for product information in shops or exhibitions, but, for both sides, the transaction costs can become prohibitive. In general a market can be considered two-sided if the demands of two groups of customers are interrelated, when the consumption of one class of customers affects the utility and the usage of the other side. When considering media behaviour, market performance and obviously the making of public policies, this two-sidedness has to be taken into account. Prices in two-sided markets are determined by demand side factors and not costs. Therefore, defining oneself in the market can be a serious problem because there are multiple demands which are interrelated and several prices. For a magazine the profitability of a cover price increase depends not only on the impact of the lower circulation that might ensue, but also on the advertising revenues (the other side of the market). That means market definition must be based on the impact of price increase on both sides (consumer *and* advertising) and not just on one side of the market (Veljanovski 2006).

In Europe, different media are subject to different degrees and different kinds of regulation. While the record industry is relatively neglected by regulation, television attracts strong attention, both in terms of its market structure and the behaviour of firms. Entry into television is strictly regulated and in many countries the set of choices in programming and the advertising market is restricted. Book publishing and film production are both supported by specific programmes of financing but the former is much less strictly regulated than the latter. Newspapers are the focus of more policies and more financing than magazines, while the professional press operates at the edge of public attention.

The choices of regulators are not only driven by the perceived social and cultural impact of a certain industry. In Europe it is considered unacceptable to subject newspapers and books to censorship; however, cinema and television are treated differently, probably because the images they convey are considered more powerful and more direct. Some general trends characterised media sectors in the past decades and affected policies of regulation. Concentration grew or remained high, despite the enlargement of the market. Many media sectors still operate in conditions of oligopoly, while newspapers frequently operate even as local monopolies.

Purposes and instruments of media policy

The availability of adequate information is one of the most important conditions that allows markets and political systems to work efficiently. The power of influencing, enhancing or concealing information on certain events may have relevant consequences for consumers and citizens. There are multidimensional relationships between the quality of information supplied by mass media, the competition in information and good markets, and the making of public policies.

The information available to citizens/consumers can be distorted for different reasons. In media markets, concentration can reduce variety and pluralism, or journalists can distort or select information in order to sell more copies. Media can be captured by government through financing and regulation or by companies through public relation and promotional activities. There are three main groups of reasons for public intervention in the media sector. Two are typical economic interventions related to:

1 consumer protection, and

2 economic development of different media industries.

The third, related to:

3 freedom of expression and pluralism,

is more embedded in socio-political factors. We will start by analysing this last kind of intervention, because this kind of policy characterises the whole history of mass media.

The spread of information through mass media results in positive outcomes for citizens and the whole of society because the media contribute towards the formation of an environment which is more informed, where choices are generally taken with more awareness and where strategic information (such as political broadcasts or advertising claims) can be more easily verified. Morevoer, mass media can lower the search costs and simplify the activities of information gathering within this framework of greater awareness. The news printed each day in a newspaper or broadcast in a television newscast are only a fraction of the information theoretically available to news agencies, and the selection process is a significant component in the work of a media organisation. Yet the simple growth of the quantity of information available does not guarantee that consumers and citizens will receive the adequate information they need in order to make informed decisions and in order that information imbalance will be reduced generally.

Mass media supply citizens with cultural and political messages which, in different ways, influence people's behaviour in collective life. A first aim of media policy is therefore to ensure that there is enough of a variety of information and that, above all, the news is not distorted. Since it is difficult, if not impossible, to impose quality of information by law, seemingly the best option is to promote information pluralism through competition between different media outlets. If different sources compete with each other, the argument goes, citizens can compare the news and get richer, and therefore truer information.

Pluralism is generally associated with diversity in the media. Political pluralism relates to the representation of different political positions from left to right, or from government to opposition, so that voters can detect and understand different views on issues. If a single voice becomes too dominant, democracy might be threatened. Cultural pluralism is about the need for a variety of cultures reflecting diverse identities within society. Cultural diversity and social cohesion may be threatened unless the cultures and values of all sections of a society (religious, linguistic, cultural, lifestyle of minorities, etc.) are reflected in the media (Doyle 2002). Yet, especially in the political field, the number of media outlets is not always a sufficient condition for pluralism. If all the media outlets are controlled by the same person, as in the case of a local monopoly, the variety of opinions and points of view can be reduced – particularly when the core interests of that media owner are at stake.

Many authors distinguish between internal and external pluralism. The former indicate the diversity of opinions and voices within a single media organisation, while the second links the pluralism to separate ownership, with different and possibly conflicting interests among media organisations. Internal pluralism has been especially developed in television, in those cases when European countries' public broadcasting systems operated as a monopoly: sometimes the traditional independence of public television assured the representation of the main (but not always of all) political voices, while in other countries different public television channels endorsed different political views. Internal pluralism can be considered a second best solution and it is pursued when scale economies and high fixed costs prevent the emerging of many competing channels. Traditionally newspapers are not required to develop an internal pluralism as occurs in television.

The standard economic justification for public intervention in economic activities is market failure, a situation in which individuals' pursuit of self-interest leads to unsatisfactory results for society as a whole – not an unusual situation in media industries, one must add. Many public policies can be considered the means to correct such a failure if it occurs. In mainstream economics, market failures are caused primarily by monopolies, externalities and public goods. Information, the main output and raw material of media industry, can be considered a public good. Since consumption of information by one person does not reduce the possibility of consumption by another person, a market can emerge only with some specific device that transforms the public good into a private one. The conditional access system for pay television is an example of this: it excludes non-paying viewers and allows it to sell subscriptions at a positive price. The other way to obtain a market is to change the nature of the good offered: in this case, it is the viewers or the market for consuming advertisements that is being sold.

Externalities happen when the economic effects of an economic transaction are not completely covered by prices. Price and quantity in such cases do not respond to incentives and a company can produce too much or too little of a specific product. If the media have a positive effect on the whole society – i.e. when the available information choices are more informed and both markets and political system work better – it can be desirable for the society to subsidise production and dissemination of information.

Many media industries are concentrated because of their scale economies; bigger companies or monopolies possess the power to fix high prices. Where information is concerned – say, a football match – there needs to be a high fixed cost for the live event and this cost needs to differ from the low and variable cost of any highlights of that match that are subsequently sold. Furthermore, in broadcast television the cost of opening an extra advertising spot is zero (or to be precise is negative, i.e. reduces the time for the expensive activity of filling the slot with actual programmes); in this scenario, TV advertising should carry no charge. Yet, in such a scenario, there would be no hope of recovering the fixed costs of the information or programmes.

The second reason for media policy intervention (see point 2 above) is to promote the economic development of an emerging economic sector, especially for media that exhibit significant network externalities and are characterised by a rapid and dynamic technological change. This is particularly true for the internet, radio and television where there is a separation of hardware and software provision. At the beginning, hardware manufacturers are the most interested in the new product and service diffusion. Moreover in order to sell hardware, they often finance software production to reach the critical mass that allows the virtuous circle of autonomous development. Radio manufacturers financed early radio stations, telecommunication operators financed and incubated internet companies. When the support of the hardware sector is not sufficient to promote the new industry, the industries often ask for public interventions that promote or protect them, often with reference to the traditional argument of international competition.

In network industries technological change requires a lot of coordination because hardware and programmes need to evolve together. The deployment of digital terrestrial television is linked to the adoption of digital TV sets. If few digital programmes are available, consumers do not buy digital TV sets, and, with too little potential audience, incentives for digital television channels are reduced. When many different new technologies compete for an application, several agents can prefer a 'wait-and-see' strategy. If everyone agrees to a single standard the diffusion of new technology is faster, but the standard game is a strategic one, and the battle can delay innovation. The state can coordinate the choice and promote the national industry with a standard setting activity, with regulation or with public investments.

When, in a sector, there are many competing innovative technologies, investments by companies and by consumers can be delayed and the market does not necessarily select the best technology available, especially when several actors are involved. Public intervention may simplify coordination problems; moreover, a public commitment can shift the balance and accelerate the selection process. In Europe we had a successful case in the adoption of the GSM standard for mobile phones that allowed a more unified market on a continental basis. But public regulators can also perform worse than the market, and promote the least auspicious technology, sometimes following a lobbying effort exerted by well established industries. A European example of failure in standard setting activity, is the promotion of high-definition television (HDTV), through the development of a European standard (MAC in the 1980s) that absorbed huge public research and development funds, but never took off.

Several actors operate in the landscape of media policy, determining a complex and multi-layered approach, where national and international interventions interact with each other. At a broader level, some international organisations like the United Nations (UN) or the World Trade Organization (WTO) outlined a broad framework, sometimes adopting mandatory conventions. Other international bodies, like the International Telecommunication Organization (ITU), operate mainly in the standard setting activity that is particularly critical in media that exhibit strong network externalities, like the internet, or hardware/software interactions, such as radio and television.

The European Union, while failing to build a full and comprehensive media policy, has been gaining a growing influence over media industries with several specific directives, later adopted by member states, and through the ongoing activity of DG one of its Directorate – Generals, Competition, and the adoption of antitrust decisions. At the national level, governments are evidently major players. In each country they approve laws and build an institutional architecture of media policies. Media are subject to general regulation (common to other economic activities), to property rights definition (particularly in the area of intellectual goods) and to several specific measures, ranging from concentration limits to content regulation.

While governments take major decisions, practical implementation is often delegated to National Regulation Authorities (NRAs), formed in the past 20 years in most European countries, such as Ofcom in the UK, Agcom in Italy or Csa in France. Such authorities were created mainly to manage the liberalisation of the telecommunication industries and, at the beginning, only a few countries adopted a multimedia model, with a jurisdiction over media and telecommunication. This, in fact, later emerged as the mainstream model, with the transformation of Oftel into Ofcom in the UK. The rationale of NRA are twofold. Media and telecommunication industries require a long-term regulatory approach, and governments lack the technical competences needed to regulate the complex interactions that take place in these industries. Therefore, they often tend to look more at the short-term political influence instead of considering the long-term developments of the industry. The boundaries between government and NRA activities are often flexible and change from country to country, but NRAs are usually in charge to pursue specific goals, like pluralism and concentration control, with instruments different from standard antitrust regulation. Hence, in many countries there is an overlapping with antitrust authorities particularly in the case of mergers or when dominant position situations are noted.

Policy regulation and competition

In the past 20 years authorities surveying competition have increasingly fulfilled the role of determining the framework in which media industries operate. Convergence between media and telecommunications, technological innovation and market development, determined several mergers between companies previously operating in separate markets and a wave of horizontal and vertical integration ventures, requiring a swathe of antitrust legislation.

This happened both at national and at European level through Articles 81, 82 and 86 of the Treaty of Amsterdam. These forbid anticompetitive agreements and the abuse of dominant positions (not illegal *per se*), mainly in the private sector but, with Article 86, also in the public sector. Under competition policy, the European Commission has direct authority to make decisions which are not subject to the approval of the Council of Ministers or the European Parliament, but only by review of the European Court of Justice. Following the 1989 European Directive 'Television Without Frontiers', there was a dramatic increase in the number of cross-national media mergers and joint ventures, and in the subsequent decade the European Commission made over 50 decisions in the media sector, the majority of them positive, i.e. allowing mergers (Harcourt 2005). The decisions are made so as to promote competition and to facilitate the creation of a larger continental market in the media sector, as has happened in other industries.

For some critics this role of the Commission has been too biased toward an economic approach, with technocratic solutions and mainly economic principles underpinning regulatory activity, which has left out important aspects of media institutions rooted in social reality and the promotion of the positive role of the media in representing cultural values and in promoting democratic representation.

In general, it is possible to distinguish two different approaches to regulation and policy making, as far as media institutions are concerned (as in other economic sectors). In the first approach, government defines in advance which course of action the companies in the market can take. The rules are usually very detailed, cover technical as well as behavioural aspects, and take into account every possible exception. In the second approach, oriented to ex-post interventions, government state only some general principles and let the courts and antitrust authorities evaluate the conduct of firms on a case by case basis; in the former, *ex ante*, approach the costs of regulation are high since the government must collect a lot of information that is often private, but the costs of enforcement are low, since no information gathering activity is required at a later stage; in *ex post* regulation the contrary happens. Here the costs to produce the regulation are fairly low, but the enforcement is expensive since in each case it is necessary to collect information and to perform comprehensive economic analyses. The *ex post* approach requires little activity at the beginning and can easily deal with fast changing industries, where innovation deeply transforms products and services during the time in which the regulation is in force. As a result, it is often referred to as 'light regulation' because fewer public administrative bodies are required. However, *ex post* regulation cannot deal easily with positive actions oriented to promote, or to forbid, particular services, and to support specific industries.

Positive (or negative in case of bans) actions in public policies can be explained by reference to the theory of merit goods (Musgrave 1959) and reflect paternalistic concerns about the consumption of these goods. The basic idea is that the government provides such a good on the basis of 'merit', because it can better provide for individual welfare than allowing consumer sovereignty. Health care or cultural goods are classical examples of merit goods. There can be numerous reasons for these positive actions. Societies may want to preserve their cultural heritages (and support theatre and classical music, for instance) on the basis of the assumption that these enhance the capabilities to appreciate beauty of the general public; alternatively, societies may want to promote vaccinations because if more people are vaccinated, some diseases will be eradicated (sometimes easing pressure on government-funded health services). In this case, public bodies can evaluate better than the single individual what the benefits of pursuing certain policies might be for society as a whole.

Content restrictions, both in advertising and in editorial content, are widespread in many European nations. They are usually stricter in television than in the press because television is putatively more intrusive into the domestic sphere. They influence the conduct of companies and limit choices by the consumers. When government want to restrict the consumption of a 'demerit' good (like cigarette advertising or a violent TV programme), sometimes the same effects can be better reached with taxation rather than a ban. Moreover, if the consumption of non-merit goods is taxed, governments can gather economic resources to make information campaigns on that particular topic.

The support of minority voices is an important issue of positive media policies. In countries with various languages, the aim is to sustain the use of the minor languages, while in other situations religious or social minorities are supported. If a market is too small and there are scale economies, then there is a rationale for public intervention. At the same time the protection of minority voices has the effect of enhancing diversity in society. If there are too many minority voices that compete for public funds, the choice of which minority voice to support can become problematic, since the risk is to listen to groups that shout louder and to make choices that are not welfare enhancing.

The same argument applies to the support of media firms that experience difficulties, following technological or market changes. For instance, in some European countries the local movie industries are heavily subsidised, and newspapers often get public support and finance. When this happens, it is important to control the alignment of objectives, means and effects. When newspapers are given public money proportionate to the copies sold or with a reduction of postal rates for subscriptions, bigger newspapers end up receiving larger subsidies. Sweden adopted an interesting way to finance the newspaper industry. Local newspaper markets tended to become monopolies and usually the second best-selling paper experienced economic difficulties, while the local leader (best-selling newspaper) realised significant profits, a process well documented in other countries like the USA. Therefore, to maintain variety in local news, the Swedish government decided to finance only the second best-selling paper, using an inverse relation with the market share, and not to waste public resources to support profitable leaders.

While in European countries freedom of expression is usually not at stake, and censorship is always only a potential danger, the rules by which journalists look for stories and information must balance the right to inform of the media with the right to privacy of citizens. Following the European Convention on Human Rights (Article 10) 'Everyone has the right to freedom of expression. This right shall include freedom to hold opinions and to receive and impart information and ideas without interference by public authority and regardless of frontiers' (European Convention on Human Rights 1950). The rules for the right to impart information and the practical enforcement of the rules can enhance the capability of journalists to scrutinise the behaviour of government and elites and therefore can enlarge the countervailing role of media.

Multilayer television policy and convergence with telecommunications

The case of television can illustrate the multilayer dimension of media policy and regulation. At the international level, the legal frameworks of the World Trade Organization and the United Nations state some very general principles, while the technical aspects of broadcasting regulation and standard setting have largely been coordinated by the International Telecommunication Union that now operates as a UN agency. Moreover, various international bodies such as UNESCO are concerned with the regulation of television content, considering its social and cultural impact. The result is a profusion of international instruments, the binding legal force of which varies, from international treaties to other recommendations and customs. Even measures that cannot be argued to have any binding legal force, may be politically important and have an impact on legislative proceedings and, for that reason, cannot be ignored (Open Society Institute 2005).

At the European level, broadcasting is subject to fairly extensive regulation, based primarily on some milestone directives. Directives are not binding in themselves, but must be adopted by member states, leaving them some discretion over measures and country specific regulation. The 'Television Without Frontiers Directive' was adopted in 1989 after five years of negotiations and was aimed to create a single European audiovisual market establishing a legal framework for cross border transmission of television programmes. Other provisions included: the protection of minors, the imposition of quotas for European audiovisual production and for independent producers and a ceiling on advertising time (20 per cent hourly and 15 per cent daily). In December 2007 TWF was amended by the Audiovisual Media Services Directive that reaffirms the pillars of Europe's audiovisual model, but added clauses regarding independence of national media regulators, the distinction between linear service (traditional television) and the growing non-linear services such as video on demand, plus more flexible rules for advertising and product placement.

In 2002 the European Union adopted five directives grouped in a Regulatory Framework for Electronic Communication. The Framework Directive introduces three other directives on access, universal services, authorisation and a decision on radio spectrum. While the debate on traditional terrestrial broadcasting networks is left on one side – perhaps in order to avoid the politically delicate issue regarding public service broadcasting's competitive position – the issues related to pay TV are directly addressed through a mandatory standardisation of set-top-boxes and a regulation of a possible bottleneck (of premium content) in retail distribution.

If confirmed and consolidated, the positions adopted on frequencies management and universal service could have important implications on audiovisual matters. An auction is proposed as the system that can best guarantee the objective of spectrum efficient allocation; potentially this approach may be extended to public television services, since, regarding universal service, there is strong emphasis on public subsidies and on possible distortions of competition.

As a whole, the conceptual references and the underlying market models are borrowed from the prevailing economic analysis in telecommunications. But, despite convergence, telecommunication and broadcasting remain different. As a consequence, some of the future interventions in broadcasting policy risk being inadequate, possibly creating a legal context distant from real market dynamics.

At a national level the existence of a European common framework encourages a push towards convergence in several media policies; yet, at the same time, specific historical and national patterns of policy remain strong. In multi-language countries, the market and institutional structure of television reflect this important feature (for example, Switzerland or Belgium). In Italy the long absence of regulation in the television sector left a strict duopoly market structure, with a concentration level significantly higher than other comparable European countries. In Germany the post war occupation zones created the regionalisation of public television that endures today.

With the transition to digital terrestrial television there is a more efficient use of the radio spectrum and the technical capacity to transport television signals, in a given portion of frequencies, increases. Thus, at least potentially, the number of channels available to viewers can grow. But spectrum scarcity is not the main reason for concentration in television markets. Scale economies in content production and programming provide better explanations of this phenomenon. Therefore, the advantages supposedly brought by digitalisation to consumers might not be immediately apparent to them. Without a clear immediate benefit DTT adoption can be long, and the role of governments in promoting and coordinating this significant technological transition, that involves several different stakeholders, becomes crucial. The public commitment to switch off analogue channels at a certain time (2012 in many countries), is essential to encourage consumers to buy new devices, manufacturers to present new products and broadcasters to deploy new digital networks. But the commitment must be credible, and it could prove politically sensitive to switch off analogue channels if a significant proportion of television sets (on average, two per family) continues to be analogue and not digital.

Emerging issues

Recent technological developments and changes in media markets draw attention to some new emerging issues in media policy that are not addressed by the current legislation. A number of them relate to the internet, both as a specific medium and as a platform for other media. On the net, the boundary between editorial space and advertising space is not well defined and the possibility to spread strategic commercial information, dissimulating it as user contribution, is high and potentially dangerous. Staff of certain companies can participate in blogs or discussion groups posing as ordinary users. When such practices are exposed this destroys the credibility of such information spaces.

Internet and mobile phones offer new interactive ways to communicate for advertisers, but pose new problems, spam being one of the biggest. The political and social debate on the method for controlling online advertising and spam seems to revolve around the benefits of implementing an 'opt-in' as opposed to an 'opt-out' approach. Should the public be required to 'opt-out' whenever an unwanted message is received? Or, should the public 'opt-in' before any information can be sent? The US, Japan and Korea adopted a legislation called opt-out where the companies can send commercial and advertising messages to consumers, unless they signal they do not want to receive those messages. In Europe there has been a move from an initial opt-out approach, to a more strict opt-in orientation, where companies must receive consensus from the consumer *before* they send any promotional message, and the Electronic Communication Directive extended the opt-in approach to SMS.

The European Union considers privacy a fundamental human right and has strong regulation in place regarding the processing of personal data. Each member state appointed a Data Protection Authority with the power to enforce the privacy directive. Though European privacy law strictly regulates corporate behaviour, it largely exempts government actions. Every database in the EU must be registered with the government and consumers have the right to review data collected on them and correct errors.

Another example, is IPTV. IPTV represents a typical convergent service where the internet is the platform over which television programmes are delivered. The initial business model was similar to cable television, with a basic package, some premium channels and, on top, video on demand programmes. IPTV is usually supplied by businesses through 'bundling' internet access and telephone services, thus creating triple play package where content (programmes) can be accessed. More advanced services include user generated content and self-scheduling of television programmes. The European Commission, following the Lisbon strategy, sees IPTV as an important service for the information society and a way to promote the development of new knowledge industries. Very different services are bundled together and television programmes, with several public service obligations, are sold with and co-exist alongside telecommunication services. A relevant question is therefore which kind of regulation will apply to IPTV – telecommunications regulation or broadcasting regulation? The EU distinguishes between linear service, where the service provider selects the content and the moment of transmission, and non-linear service, controlled by the user and characterised by lighter regulation. But if different services are bundled together, it becomes difficult to distinguish between the two.

The diffusion of new digital distribution platforms, and of IPTV, depend also upon the availability of major TV programmes and audiovisual contents, so that the viewer can access the full range of TV channels and use only one remote control (rather than having to switch between different systems in the home). Established pay TV operators can buy programme rights also for other minor distribution platforms and exclude them from the market. Or, alternatively, they can refuse to carry some TV channels, which are then unable to reach a sufficiently large audience to be viable. Regulation which stipulates that IPTV packages *must* contain certain features can help to prevent some of these anti-competitive behaviours.

While in the US such regulation tends to protect the small and weak local television station from the exploitation of pay TV operators (cable and satellite), in Europe equivalent regulation may force the leading terrestrial channels to supply their content, on an equal and non-discriminatory basis, to every distribution platform. The rules are therefore oriented to protect the infant industry of advanced digital platforms from the possible preemptive competition of established pay TV operators (mainly satellite), and from discriminatory practices derived from the television channels owning the digital distribution networks.

Digitalisation has been overcoming the traditional bottleneck of the television market, mainly based on transmission capacity and control of physical assets. With the expansion of transmission capacity, the number of distribution channels has increased, and enough minority content can reach a sufficient market to exist on a global basis. But attractive content remains scarce and is expensive to produce. As Chapter 12 argues, 'content is king'. Therefore, the source of market power in the television industry is progressively shifting toward content control and exclusivity. The regulation of programme rights and exclusives is thus becoming more and more important in order to secure sufficient competition in the television industry.

Conclusion

Media are undergoing constant change in many countries and the convergence with telecommunication, made possible by digitalisation, has resulted in a number of new possibilities and significant transformations. While in the past different media were mainly separate industries with their own production facilities and distribution channels, the convergence process enables new products, new substitution patterns and a different kind of competition. The same media product can be distributed through several channels and a single platform can accommodate several different kinds of content. The informative websites of newspapers and television appear much more similar than the original media they 'serve', i.e. they all carry text news, photos and videos, sometimes from the same global sources. So, there would appear to be a demand for regulation to become more horizontal and media independent, too.

In short, the evolving media landscape poses new problems that national and European institutions will have to address in order to maintain and promote the social and economic functions of the media that are vital to foster democracy across Europe.

Questions

1 Why can media be considered two-sided markets?

2 What are the aims of competition policy and sector-specific regulation in controlling concentration in the media?

3 List the main purposes of media policies.

Further reading

Doyle, G. (2002) *Media Ownership: The Economics and Politics of Convergence and Concentration in the UK and European Media*, London: Sage Publications. An introductory discussion on the topic of rising concentration in media industries and the effects on pluralism and diversity, with an eye on the UK.

Harrison, J. and Woods, L. (2007) *European Broadcasting Law and Policy*, Cambridge: Cambridge University Press. A critical and non technical review of European policy and regulation in the television sector, ranging from advertising to ownership control.

Seabright, P. and von Hagen, J. (eds) (2007) *The Economic Regulation of the Broadcasting Market: Evolving Technologies,* Cambridge: Cambridge University Press. A diverse collection of essays that analyse economic regulation of media and discuss pluralism.

References

De Bens, E. (ed) (2007) *Media Between Culture and Commerce*, Bristol: Intellect Books.

Doyle, G. (2002) *Media Ownership: The Economics and Politics of Convergence and Concentration in the UK and European Media*, London: Sage Publications.

European Convention on Human Rights (1950) www.hri.org/docs/ECHR50.html (accessed 20 March 2009).

Harcourt, A. (2005) *The European Union and the Regulation of Media Markets*, Manchester: Manchester University Press.

Musgrave, R. (1959) *The Theory of Public Finance*, New York: McGraw-Hill.

Open Society Institute (2005) *Television in Europe*, Budapest: OSI Monitoring Program.

Television Without Frontiers Directive (1989) http://ec.europa.eu/avpolicy/reg/tvwf/index_en.htm (accessed 20 March 2009).

Veljanovski, C. (2006) *Network Effect and Multi Sided Markets*, Masters in Economics and Competition Law, London: Kings College.

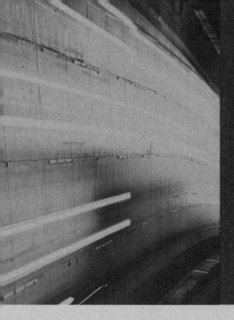

21

Public Service Broadcasting in Europe

Jérôme Bourdon

Chapter overview

Public Service Broadcasting (PSB) started as a pragmatic arrangement, supported mostly by professionals and a small managerial elite, and was soon plagued by criticism about, respectively, its lack or excess of independence, while claiming to provide cultural excellence and, more problematically, unbiased coverage of events. PSB was defined with more precision in a second moment, when it started being threatened by deregulation and commercialisation (some 20 years ago). The notion of a 'European model' of PSB is fragile, as there are many differences between Public Service Broadcasters in Europe. The BBC was for a long time the major inspiration for PSBs across the continent; in general Northern European public service broadcasters (including Germany) have been better funded and have enjoyed more independence and institutional stability than those in the South, where political influence, lack of consensus about public service, poor resources and early commercialisation weakened public service and led to a more radical deregulation than in the North. While academics and intellectuals have been mostly defending public service, its relevance is now under scrutiny due to competition from commercial broadcasters and people's easy access to a great variety of sources and media. This chapter discusses these themes and asks whether there is still a need for strong public service broadcasters (including radio) in contemporary Europe.

Introduction

'Public service broadcasting in Europe' might sound like a well trodden field. Much literature has been devoted to the topic, as Europe has been widely seen as the stronghold of public service broadcasting (PSB). However, it is a field that remains difficult to chart, as each of the three terms just mentioned ('public service', 'Europe', and even 'broadcasting') raises specific problems. As history will show, public service broadcasting has been to a certain extent 'self-evident' (de Bens and Brandt 2000: 7), i.e. in no need of grand theorising (which came only later, when PSB entered a phase of decline). In this context, theories of PSB have always inevitably been partisan – i.e. they were promoted by supporters of PSB against its looming assailants, the commercial broadcasters. Even the small numbers of scholars who claim PSB is no longer relevant are by no means supporters of commercial broadcasting as such. Overall, the analysis of PSB cannot be separated from value judgements. Most scholars have difficulty escaping nostalgia, especially British scholars who feel (and they have strong non-British allies) that the UK had created something that most closely resembles the public service 'ideal'. The best example of this approach is Michael Tracey's (1998) beautiful and highly idealistic paean to PSB.

The European dimension is also by no means clear. The creation of the European Union and the funding of much 'European research' have engendered a rather dangerous trend to 'reunify' Europe retrospectively. This European 'invention of tradition' is rather complicated to pursue. Indeed, the whole idea that public service broadcasting is a 'European' idea was part of the above mentioned efforts, to protect PSB against a deregulatory and commercial offensive, Europe being an elastic continent, with its centre located, surprisingly enough, somewhere in the North-West. Much writing about public service generalises from a very small number of cases. National cultures still differ, however, and so does PSB in different countries, while some degree of European convergence is taking place, ironically enough, through the market (the arch-enemy of PSB).

Finally, although one writes about PS *broadcasting*, most analyses (and this writer is no exception) have focused on television, neglecting the distinct contribution of public service radio. This is paradoxical, as radio has had less trouble than television in preserving its distinctiveness from its private counterparts. Radio programming in general has been under-researched, despite the fact that overall, although the future of PSB may be bleak, public service radio has a better chance of survival than PS television. Even this chapter, however (which reviews much of the available literature), will focus on television, as a rapid glance at its bibliography will show.

The history of PSB: bedrock or fragile consensus?

PSB has been defined with some precision only in retrospect. Until the years of deregulation, when numerous authors embarked on a search for the precise meaning of this elusive notion (Broadcasting Research Unit 1985; Blumler 1992), there was a common feeling across countries that television should belong to the public domain. PSB was often defined negatively, as an activity 'not of the commercial kind' as the German Constitutional Court put it in a 1961 judgment (Humphreys 1996: 163). The fact that PSB was the product of a complicated set of evolving political and social circumstances, as well as the 'internal contradictions of public service philosophy' (Ang 1991: 104) would only be perceived later.

According to the most often quoted analysis of PSB in Europe (Blumler 1992) public service broadcasting can be defined by 'geographical universality' (since its signal should reach everyone), 'ethics of comprehensiveness' (by providing information, education and culture, not just entertainment), 'generalised mandates' (by having general, but official and binding statements of missions), 'diversity, pluralism and range' (by providing a wide range of opinions and tastes, including minorities), 'non-commercialism' (by not focusing exclusively on maximising audiences, and by not targeting only audiences of interest to advertisers) and 'place in politics' (it should be the place of choice for political coverage).

The theorist, and the public service supporter, can be contented with a list of somewhat abstract criteria. Not the historian, however, especially the historian of an elusive Europe. Basically, 'comprehensive programming' and 'non-commercialism' were indeed present from the onset. As for the rest . . . The ideal model of the 1990s is in fact the result of a slow accumulation of criteria from a variety of different intellectual and social sources. Much depended on professionals defending PSB against politicians who were officially in charge of setting up PSB institutions. Official mandates, in particular, were often defined late, especially in Southern Europe. Moreover, the attention towards ethnic minorities is absent in the early history of PSB (on the contrary, PSB culture strived to be homogeneous, that is, nationally homogeneous). Finally, the final criterion, 'place in politics', can be considered as the Achilles' heel of PSB, as proximity to the state has not always been compatible with pluralism. In many cases, it has been hard to distinguish proximity to the state as a guarantor of the national interest from proximity to the governing party, and PSB was perceived as *endangering*, not protecting, political pluralism – with people arguing that this was more easily provided by the private, commercial print press (see below).

Even in the UK, which can boast the most detailed and earliest formulations of the notion, PSB was not an *a priori* doctrine, but 'a concept grafted onto an initial pragmatic set of arrangements between the Post Office and the British radio industry to establish a broadcasting service that would create a market for radio receiving equipment' (Scannell and Cardiff 1991: 5). Indeed, two key features of the British broadcasting system were established without an *a priori* ideological rationale: the licence fee and the monopoly. In 1922, when the British Broadcasting Company was founded by a group of companies selling wireless sets, the main profit of broadcasting, it was thought, would come from the sale of receivers. The Post Office started charging a licence fee, half of which went to the BBC. It was the Sykes Committee (1923) which first defined broadcasting as a 'public utility' (not a public service), as a national service to be developed 'in the public interest'.

The notion of a non-profit making organisation, enjoying a public monopoly, and broadcasting programmes with high cultural standards, was born then, and this can be considered as the first definition of public service broadcasting. This organisation also had a quite national, if not nationalistic, character: broadcasting had to be a universal service not only on the basis of egalitarian principles, but because it should cement the nation, especially around major events, and because it should bring the best of the nation to the rest of the world. There was no room for cultural, linguistic or religious minorities here – indeed the very word 'minority' meant little at a time when 'the nation' was still seen as an absolute value, the community which superseded all other forms of collective belongings, and had a right, as a European nation, to impose its ideals on vast parts of the world: British

PSB had an imperialist dimension, as in all countries that were also the centre of colonial empires. This dimension of PSB has eventually been forgotten later on, as PSB was increasingly idealised.

In many countries, the early days of broadcasting were characterised by complications, as broadcasting evolved from being private, to being partly private and finally to be controlled by the state – or at least supervised by it, as, for instance, in Germany, Italy or France. In the end, PSB was increasingly being trusted to public corporations, often after a long period of direct control by the government. In pre-war Germany (including pre-Nazi Germany) and in Italy, broadcasting was closely tied to the executive.

The BBC's Royal Charter (from its first version of 1927 to its subsequent revisions, up to the latest one in 2006) has influenced European broadcasters in its insistence on the triple mission of informing, educating and entertaining. Yet, while PSB managers in Europe have often quoted these aims over the years, not many legal texts have provided such (relatively) clear mission statements. In West Germany, some kind of 'broadcasting constitution' was enshrined in the 1949 Basic Law of the new Republic. Article 5 assigned three political (as opposed to cultural) functions to broadcasting in the new parliamentary democracy: 'to disseminate information; to assist in the process of formation of public opinion (. . .); and to exercise a (. . .) function of critique and control' over the government (Humphreys 1996: 133). The need to break away from the Nazi past is apparent here, while culture is not central to this national mandate partly because, in a federal country such as Germany, culture belongs to the jurisdiction of the *Länder* (i.e. the states). In France, a general mandate was couched in Article 4 of the 1964 Law which reformed PSB: the public broadcaster was in charge of the 'national public service of radio and television . . . with the aims of satisfying the needs of information, culture, education and entertainment of the audience' (Bourdon 1990: 40).

Assuming that the triple mission was seen as relevant everywhere, its implementation left much to be desired right from the very start. In general, the second objective (i.e. to educate) has been central in Europe. The term 'education' (which is clearer, but rather narrow and not very appealing given the popular nature of television) and 'culture' have both been used, with culture eventually becoming the preferred term; it had the advantage of being flexible, however it also carried with it the risk of vagueness, especially as the term 'popular culture' was also becoming widespread. From the beginning, what it meant to 'inform' the public was hotly debated, and only in a few cases the notion was operationalised in a manner which satisfied (almost) everyone. Critics never relented, they only changed tacks, by either criticising PSB for its alleged political bias (broadcasting was said to be partisan, i.e. pro-governmental) or rather by accusing broadcast news, especially those shown on television, of being trivial. As for the third objective of PSB, i.e. 'to entertain', this was the object of much disdain in the early days, and yet it was present everywhere. Professional entertainers and television hosts were despised, however they were seen as a necessary evil. As competition grew in the 1980s their importance, if anything, increased. A focus on entertainment carried with it the danger of Americanisation. Although PSBs tended to emphasise their national characters, discrete adaptations of American entertainment formats took place early in most countries (Bourdon 2008).

The history of PSB should not be complete without a gallery of its legendary managers. PSB was increasingly associated with certain personalities and managers who played a key part in the nostalgic discourse about PSB, although they cannot be separated from the professionals, mostly producers and/or directors, who worked under their guidance or protection and ended up celebrating them later on. Again, the BBC, with the figure of its first director-general John Reith (1889–1971), reigns supreme. The son of a Scottish church minister, Reith was an engineer with great hopes in the power of technology; he was a great supporter of Public Service Broadcasting, which he saw as a major educational tool for the masses. The 'brute force of the monopoly', as he would phrase it before the Pilkington Committee of 1962, should be used, he argued, to enlighten the audience, letting them access 'the best' of a culture. Reith actively and successfully pushed for the transformation of the British Broadcasting Company into the British Broadcasting Corporation in 1927. An independent public corporation was the best tool to fight what Reith viewed as its two major enemies, i.e. political interference and commercial pressures. Although he left the BBC in 1938, his heirs preserved and valued Reith's heritage, even in the television sector (which Reith was suspicious of).

The German Reith was Hans Bredow, the founder of German public radio during the pre-war years. Appointed Broadcasting Commissioner of the Imperial Ministry of Communication in 1926 and later dismissed by the Nazis, Bredow still played a major role in the post-war period as chairman of the administrative council of one of the public broadcasters in the Land of Hesse. Like Reith, Bredow was keen to use radio as a way to 'civilise' and unify the German nation. Unlike Reith, he viewed the state (the radio being its instrument) as a civilising agent, and wanted to keep it free from party interference: again, from the very beginning the problem was how to make sure that information services were not going to be subjected to external pressures. In Italy, Ettore Barnabei was editor of *Il Popolo,* the party newspaper of the Christian Democrats who would rule the country for almost 50 years following the end of World War Two. Acting as the public service broadcaster's director-general from 1960 to 1969, Barnabei famously stated that RAI (the Italian public broadcaster) was there to help the Italians 'get down from the trees' (Musso and Pineau 1990: 24), this being an elitist version of the 'brute force of the monopoly' argument. In France, television professionals long celebrated the memory of Jean d'Arcy, director of television programmes from 1952 to 1959, who came directly from the world of politics but fought to turn television into an innovative, artistic and educational medium.

North/South: the great divide?

Beyond the common aspiration to imitate the British public broadcaster, there was much diversity. As in other domains, one can draw attention to the existence of a North–South divide in Western Europe – a much repeated claim in comparative political studies, which has been adapted by media researchers (Heinderycks 1998).

Most recently, this claim has been appropriated by Hallin and Mancini (2004) who proposed a typology of media systems which mentions three models rather than two. They distinguish between: (a) a 'polarised pluralist model', typical of France, Italy, Spain, Greece and Portugal, which is characterised by low levels of newspaper circulation and journalistic professionalisation and high levels of both political parallelism (media structured according to the way in which it 'parallels' political divisions) and state intervention; (b) a 'democratic corporatist model' (in Scandinavia, the Benelux countries, Germany and Austria), characterised by high levels of all the above mentioned criteria: newspaper circulation, professionalisation, political parallelism, state intervention; (c) a 'liberal model', typical of the UK, Ireland and the US. The main difference between (c) and (b) is the low level of state intervention typical of the liberal model, which places the British system somehow 'outside' Europe. This type of classification poses a major problem as far as PSB is concerned. PSB supposes, by definition, a high level of state intervention, which means that it then becomes necessary to define 'types' of 'state intervention'. One should distinguish between limited political intervention typical of the 'corporatist' and 'liberal' models (which played a role mostly when PSB was established) and the highly politicised interventions typical of the 'polarised pluralist' model – which tended to weaken PSB. In Southern Europe, PSB all too often became a tool in the hands of political parties (what Hallin and Mancini call 'political parallelism'), either by simultaneous sharing (i.e. Belgium and Italy, where the phenomenon was christened 'lottizzazione' (sharing out)) or by the fact that the parties in power would take turns in influencing the service (which still applies to Spain to an extent). The threat of privatisation loomed mostly in Southern Europe, although it took place only in France in 1987 for the first public channel TF1.

In the South, PSB was more likely to yield to government pressures: obviously this applied to repressive regimes (e.g. Spain, Portugal and Greece), but also to some extent France and Italy, where governments always tried to appoint heads of news divisions they perceived as friendly and dismiss those they saw as 'too independent' (e.g. Grasso 1992: 112; Bourdon 1990: 84). In France, in December 1971, a left-wing intellectual (and television critic) left the set of a famous prime time debate programme with a parting shot which would become legendary: 'Messieurs les censeurs, bonsoir' (Bourdon: 2004: 128), and indeed there were many cases of censorship, not only in the news but also in current affairs programmes. In the South, historically left-wing opposition parties have been the most vocal critic of public service broadcasting, often with good reasons.

Although they were more stable, Northen European public broadcasters also suffered, mainly due to governmental critics irritated by what they perceived as the extreme independence of PSBs. In the UK, the main incident occurred in 1971. The recently defeated British Labour Party, and especially the former Prime Minister Harold Wilson, were infuriated by a sarcastic programme that targeted some Labour politicians, *Yesterday's Men* (Briggs 1985: 356). In Germany, the Christian Democrats 'increasingly blamed the "red" public-service broadcasting corporations, and the fact that the "red" NDR (the Northern Broadcaster) furnished the ARD with its main national news service', for its 1972, 1976 and 1980 electoral defeats (Humphreys 2004: 182). Party allegiance increasingly affected professional practices, and conservative politicians accused journalists of left-wing bias.

This politicised state intervention was problematic not only because of politicisation and instability: there was no consensus about finance, and public financing of PSB has in fact remained limited. In general, licence fees in the North have been higher than in the South, and while commercial revenues have been growing everywhere, the growth started earlier and has been higher in the South. In 2007, the licence fee cost €116 in France and €104 in Italy – politicians in both countries having been reluctant to increase it. In Northern Europe, broadly speaking, rates more than double. In Germany, it was €204 in the same year, €195 in the UK and €210 in Sweden. In some countries (the Netherlands in 2000, Portugal in 1992), the licence fee has been abolished and replaced by public funding from the state budget. In Spain, public television was financed mostly by advertising from its inception. There still are no advertisements on PSB in the UK and in Scandinavia. Everywhere else, advertising has been introduced: in Germany this happened in 1956, in Italy the year after, in France in 1968 (the delay being caused by intense lobbying by the press).

Differences in funding levels and political uncertainties account for the differences in production capacities. The two strongest producers of fiction have almost always been the UK and Germany (Buonanno 1999), while big 'Southern' countries, including France, have been weak producers. Until the years of deregulation, Southern European drama constituted mostly of one-shots or short-series. This was congenial to those considering themselves artists among the professionals, mostly directors, while producers' concerns for extended narratives have been more important in Northern Europe. Ever since, Southern European broadcasters have been struggling to produce long series. So far, Spanish private producers have been the most successful, but their series do not export well (although some series formats were replicated). Again, history weighs on the present.

More than a clear divide, we should talk of a European 'continuum', with the UK closest to the ideal model of PSB, Northern Europe following suit, then France and Italy, and finally relatively recent European democracies such as Spain, Portugal and Greece, where PSB is the weakest. In France, the February 2009 reform which has cancelled commercial advertisements on PSB will only serve to weaken the institution further.

In addition, much work remains to be done about PSB outside Europe. In global reviews of public broadcasting, there is a tendency to oppose Western Europe, allegedly the model of public service broadcasting, to a whole world of weaker, more authoritarian or dictatorial broadcasting systems, partly if not wholly submitted to the state, where public service ideals have been absent. While this might be true when thinking about the news, researchers should also fruitfully study the implementation of public service ideals that have to do with education and culture in quite varied cultural contexts, especially in the early days of radio or television, when the faith in the power of the new medium to change society was stronger. A good case study could be the televising of Shakespeare outside Europe, for example in Argentina (Varela 2005) or India. Indeed in some respects, PSB has been a widespread, if not even global, ideal.

Crises and weaknesses

The crisis of PSB has been repeatedly diagnosed since the 1970s, to a point where the notion of crisis has become almost useless, unless one cares to classify its uses. First, there is a constant 'crisis' of PSB since it reached the majority of the population, in the late 1960s in most of Europe; that is to say that PSB has suffered a chronic weakness as a result of attacks from its opponents. The status of PSB has even been used, in a very political manner, to exemplify the crisis of the welfare state. Its alleged poor management and the power of the unions have relentlessly been taken to task, to a point where one should ask, first, whether those problems are 'real', and second, to what extent they should be seen as specific to public service broadcasting. PSB has been under constant attacks for obvious, structural reasons. Commercial lobbyists have always tried to get a bigger slice of the advertising cake and have encouraged criticism; in addition, the fact that PSBs had a monopoly of TV news made them the target of criticism by political parties. This problem seemed particularly acute in the 1970s: despite national differences, it could be argued that Briggs' comment that at the time 'the BBC had more critics than ever before both on the right and on the left' (Briggs 1985: 355) describes the situation of several European countries.

As it happens, criticism became louder precisely at the time when efforts were made to solve the problems of PSB, or when sheer social pressures forced media systems to embrace liberalisation and competition. In 1974, the French monolithic ORTF was broken into different companies, of which three were for television and one for radio, and more autonomy was given to the channels of the Italian public broadcaster RAI. This paved the way to more pluralism, as well as more criticism. In the history of public television, reforms were never perceived as being successful and seemed only to provide more fuel to the fire of criticism.

The term 'crisis' – as a phenomenon which is circumscribed chronologically – is more relevant to describe the debates and deep changes which occurred in the 1990s, in the wake of deregulation and commercialisation. The wild process of deregulation Italy embarked upon since the late 1970s was copied by France and Germany, with the UK following later on (Tunstall and Machin 1999). As for the European Union, the mix of liberal creeds and Euro-illusions about the project of a 'truly' European television system have contributed to a process whereby Euro-deregulation, like national deregulations, has not at all strengthened the national television industries. On the contrary, Hollywood and private television channels have emerged as the major winners. While public service television has retained a sizable share of the audience, despite many prophesying that this would much reduce, it has had to pay a high price for this. News has been 'tabloidised', documentaries have been denied prime time slots or have been transferred to theme channels, and entertainment has grown. Many public service channels try to shun reality television (or at least to develop a public service version of the genre), however the BBC has been a major promoter of some reality formats and talk-shows, and the difference between public service and commercial television has become thin. However, it would be excessive to claim that PSB does not maintain some of its originality, especially if one considers the proportion of news and current affairs, which remains higher on PSB channels (especially on radio).

As the BBC is still seen as the most prestigious and able PSB, it is interesting to notice that even this venerable corporation has become vulnerable, despite pursuing a remarkably aggressive and innovative policy in the past 20 years, when compared to its European counterparts. Following Tunstall and Machin (1999: 175–82), it could be argued that the BBC now faces a number of dilemmas. The (relatively high) licence fee will probably not rise much in the near future, which means that new sources of revenue have to be found. However, 'big money-spinners' of the future (interactive shopping, game shows, pay movies) are either unsuitable to its brand or out of reach in a competitive environment. Among public broadcasters, the BBC has been most successful in marketing commercial products derived from its popular programmes: books, DVDs, etc. As for broadcasting itself, in order to generate new 'large blocs of popular programming', the BBC needs rich partners, which means commercial partners, at the risk of damaging its distinct identity. Indeed, the BBC signed a major agreement with American cable television giant TCI in 1998. And other European PSBs are following the same path, or trying to. All those weaknesses, and perils, became clear when the BBC went digital, trying to promote a number of channels and spreading its resources very thin. In short, even the mother of all PSBs is bound to see its share of the market, and its place in the public arena, decrease.

Does PSB still matter?

Does public service broadcasting still matter? The people who think so can be recruited mostly from academic circles. Nicholas Garnham has been a leading supporter of PSB, from a seminal article published in 1983 to a recent defence of it in 2003. For Garnham, the market is the enemy, as it reduces viewers' choice to few options and exploits technological changes for the worst by reinforcing inequalities (between enterprises and between consumers). Conversely, PSB can satisfy a wide range of tastes across various genres, 'rather than only those tastes that show the largest profit' (quoted in Collins 2004: 42). Garnham connects the PSB ideal not to the state but to the Habermasian public sphere, a third term distinct from both state and market, a space for rational universalistic politics. Richard Collins has suggested another genealogy of the PSB ideal: he notes its indirect filiation to the Enlightenment. Indeed, the philosopher Kant might have provided the best rationale for PSB when he wrote:

> Tutelage is man's inability to make use of his understanding without direction from another. Self-incurred is this tutelage when its cause lies not in lack of reason but in lack of resolution and courage to use it without direction from another. Sapere aude! Have courage to use your own reason – was the motto of the enlightenment.   (Kant 1784, quoted in Collins 2004: 44)

However, 'for any single individual to work himself out of the life under tutelage which has become almost his nature is very difficult' (Kant 1784, quoted in Collins 2004: 44). Much later, PSB would be seen by Habermas as a late heir of the

Enlightenment (to some extent), as an institution which can assist individuals to work themselves 'out of the life under tutelage'. Heir of the Frankfurt School, Habermas thus supports what was taken to task as a typically bourgeois institution, or 'state apparatus', in the 1970s. Theodor Adorno had showed him the way in 1966, when he was interviewed by Umberto Eco on Italian TV. While Adorno had once been a scathing critic of the bourgeois state, he claimed to support public television in his own country, Germany: 'In the United States, commercial television is the instrument of a monolithic, commercial taste. In Germany, said Adorno, public television had played a very positive role at some critical junctions of our political life' (Grasso 1992: 199).

While the support for public service might still be dominant among communication scholars, another trend has emerged, which considers elitist public service as increasingly irrelevant in a more open, wider market of representations and ideas. In 1987 John Fiske coined the phrase 'semiotic democracy', reiterating how television viewers 'produce' and manipulate meanings, including those of 'pure' entertainment programmes. In a Fiskean way, Elisabeth Jacka (2003) has challenged the view that PSB (represented in particular by one genre, journalism) can play a central role in democracy. New forms of democracy and citizenship, she claims, are emerging, centred on other genres and less related to a homogeneous national culture. Jacka highlights a new dimension of cultural citizenship (a fourth one besides the civil, political and social ones), which she calls, following Hartley, 'do-it-yourself' citizenship. It consists in 'the practice of putting together an identity from the available choices, patterns and opportunities on offer in the semiosphere and the mediasphere' (Hartley 1999: 178). Unfortunately, this libertarian conception of the post-modern individual cannot easily be related to media consumption practices, where aggressive commercial television and an increasingly commercial voyeuristic internet perpetuate old inequalities of access and consumption and reinforce the domination of genres which can only hesitantly be labelled as offering freedom of choice (i.e. talk-shows, reality TV, good old game-shows, soap operas, not to mention pornography).

The supporters of PSB still have an existing, and relatively strong, institution they can defend, although they all agree that the fortress is under siege and increasingly aping its enemies. The critics might exalt the multi-faceted individual constructing his or her identity from a pool of increasingly variegated sources. However, behind the exaltation of the post-modern self-created individual, some basic facts need to be remembered. Commercial television still is the main source of information and entertainment for the majority of the population – especially those who are not connected to the internet and to cable and satellite TV, who will remain a sizable minority of Europeans for many years (and the majority of the world population for even longer). In addition, cable and satellite television are busy repackaging old genres and formats. As for new media, potential interactive access to different forms of information does not necessarily translate into much more active patterns of consumption. The most popular websites often are tied to the most popular old media (press and television), or are devoted to commercial transactions online. In short, the free-willing postmodern individual seems to be, first and foremost, a not so free-willing consumer exposed to an increased variety of products and advertisements. The fact that these products include, especially in reality-shows, self-improvement (including self-marketing and self-help) tools is still a far cry from the ideal 'do-it-yourself' democracy dear to Hartley and his followers.

On the other hand, if we still think that democracy matters, and if democracy still means that citizens are to be connected to some sort of public sphere through media with a sizable audience share, it is hard, for all its weaknesses, to completely dismiss PSB. The main challenge here is to convince the powers that be that PSB needs decent financing to reach its audiences and to address the important issues of the day, which are increasingly global (from finances to ecology). PSB might not be the best tool for this, but it remains certainly better than commercial channels with their menu of national infotainment and gossip.

Questions

1 Among the three requirements of PSB, i.e. to 'inform, educate and entertain', it is the first two which have been discussed the most. Discuss the public service value of entertainment programming by using specific examples.

2 What is the relevance of public service broadcasting to democratic ideals in the context of a multi-channel/multi-platform environment? Discuss.

3 Choose a country outside Western Europe. Gather some material on its public service broadcaster (for instance its regulation and history), and see whether it has fulfilled all or part of the ideals of PSB as they were formulated in Western Europe.

Further reading

Bourdon, J. (2007) 'Unhappy Engineers of the European Soul: The EBU and the Woes of Pan-european Television', *The International Communication Gazette*, 69 (3): 263–81. Includes a history of European policies meant to encourage European unification through public television. Discusses why and how those policies failed in the context of increased commercialisation.

Collins, R. (1998) *From Satellite to Single Market: New Communication Technology and European Public Service Television*, London: Routledge. Same theme as Bourdon (2007) above, but focuses more specifically on satellite television in the 1990s.

Curran, J. and Park, M. (eds) (2000) *Dewesternizing Media Studies*, London: Routledge. A path-breaking reader which puts public service broadcasting into a global context. Good chapters on PSB in Israel and France.

Ferrell Lowe, G. and Jauert, P. (eds) (2005) *Cultural Dilemmas in Public Service Broadcasting*, Göteborg, Sweden: Nordicom. Includes rare, specific discussion of cultural policies by public service broadcasting.

Ouellette, L. and Lewis, J. (2004) 'Moving Beyond the "Vast Wasteland": Cultural Policy and Television in the United States' in R. C. Allen and A. Hill (eds), *The Television Studies Reader*, London: Routledge. A refreshing text for the European reader, explaining how PSB is seen in a country in which commercial television has always reigned supreme. While Europe has been blaming its public service broadcasters, others have been dreaming about a full-fledged public service they never got in the first place.

References

Ang, I. (1991) *Desperately Seeking the Audience*, London: Routledge.

Blumler, J. G. (ed) (1992) *Television and the Public Interest: Vulnerable Values in West European Broadcasting*, London: Sage.

Bourdon, J. (1990) *Histoire de la Télévision sous de Gaulle*, Paris: Institut national de l'audiovisuel/Anthropos.

Bourdon, J. (2004) 'Old and New Ghosts. Public Service Television and the Popular, a History', *European Journal of Cultural Studies,* 7 (3): 283–304.

Briggs, A. (1985) *The BBC, The First Fifty Years*, Oxford: Oxford University Press.

Broadcasting Research Unit (BRU) (nd c. 1985) *The Public Service Idea in British Broadcasting, Main Principles*, London: BRU.

Buonanno, M. (ed) (1999) *Shifting Landscapes. Television Fiction in Europe*, Luton: University of Luton Press.

Collins, R. (2004) '"Ises" and "Oughts": Public Service Broadcasting in Europe', in R.C. Allen and A. Hill (eds) *The Television Studies Reader*, London: Routledge.

De Bens, E. and Brandt, K. (2000) 'The Status of TV Broadcasting in Europe', in J. Wieten, G. Murdoch and P. Dahlgren (eds) *Television Across Europe. A Comparative Introduction*, London: Sage.

Grasso, A. (1992) *Storia della Televisione Italiana*, Milano: Garzanti.

Hallin D. and Mancini P. (2004) *Comparing Media Systems. Three Models of Media and Politics*, Cambridge: Cambridge University Press.

Hartley, J. (1999) *The Uses of Television*, London: Routledge.

Heinderycks, F. (1998) *L'Europe des médias*, Bruxelles: Editions de l'université de Bruxelles.

Humphreys, P. (1996) *Mass Media and Media Policy in Western Europe*, Manchester: Manchester University Press.

Jacka, E. (2003) 'Democray as Defeat: The Impotence of Arguments for Public Service Broadcasting', *Television and New Media,* 4 (2): 177–91.

Musso, P. and Pineau, G. (1990) *L'Italie et sa Télévision*, Paris: Institut national de l'audiovisuel et Champ Vallon.

Scannell, P. and Cardiff, D. (1991) *A Social History of British Broadcasting*, London: Blackwell.

Tracey, M. (1998) *The Decline and Fall of Public Service Broadcasting*, Oxford: Oxford University Press.

Tunstall, J. and Machin, D. (1999) *The Anglo-American Media Connection*, Oxford: Oxford University Press.

Varela, M. (2005) *La Television Criolla (1951-1969)*, Buenos Aires: Edhasa.

22

Censorship and Freedom of Speech

Julian Petley

Chapter overview

Most people would agree that freedom of expression is a hallmark of democratic societies, and one of the traits which distinguishes them most strongly from non-democratic ones. But, of course, even in democratic societies, freedom of expression is never absolute. As the Law Lords stated in 1936: 'free speech does not mean free speech; it means speech hedged in by all the laws against blasphemy, sedition and so forth. It means freedom governed by law' (quoted in Robertson and Nicol 2008: 2). But in modern democracies, laws are by no means the only factors which hedge in freedom of expression, and nor are the state and its agents the only censors. Thus this chapter will argue that, in order fully to understand how the freedom of the media is circumscribed today, we need to define censorship in a broad sense so as to include not only the activities of governments and the operations of the law but also the modus operandi of regulators of one kind or another, the workings of market forces, and indeed more nebulous but nonetheless extremely important factors such as the ideological tenor of the times. Derek Jones usefully defines censorship as 'a variety of processes . . . formal and informal, overt and covert, conscious and unconscious, by which restrictions are imposed on the collection, display, dissemination, and exchange of information, opinions, ideas, and imaginative expression' (2001: xi), and in this chapter I wish to explore the operations of censorship in the European media from this particular perspective.

The European Convention on Human Rights

Let us, however, begin with a brief consideration of the law. Inevitably, laws governing expression vary considerably in different European countries, and in the context of a chapter such as this it is neither possible nor desirable to attempt a *tour d'horizon* of the laws affecting freedom of expression in every European country. However, it is safe to say that there are certain areas which are everywhere likely to be hedged around by legislation and regulation – for example, child pornography, national security, defamation and confidentiality are all areas particularly liable to censorship of some kind.

There is, however, a pan-European measure which has considerable significance for how freedom of expression is exercised in Europe. This is the European Convention on Human Rights (ECHR), which came into force in 1953 and has now been ratified by all member states of the Council of Europe. The UK was the first country to ratify the Convention but did not in fact incorporate it into domestic law until 1998 with the Human Rights Act.

Article 10(1) of the European Convention on Human Rights states that: 'everyone has the right to freedom of expression. This right shall include freedom to hold opinions and to receive and impart information and ideas without interference by public authority and regardless of frontiers'. And in 1976, in a case involving *The Little Red Schoolbook* (which encouraged young people to challenge social norms, particularly at school, and which was successfully prosecuted in the UK for obscenity), the European Court of Human Rights expanded on this principle, arguing that:

> Freedom of expression constitutes one of the essential foundations of a democratic society and one of the basic conditions for its progress and for each individual's self-fulfilment. It is applicable not only to 'information' or 'ideas' that are favourably received or regarded as inoffensive or as a matter of indifference, but also to those that offend, shock or disturb. Such are the demands of pluralism, tolerance and broad-mindedness without which there is no 'democratic society'.
>
> (Quoted in Robertson and Nicol 2008: 44)

However, anyone who believed that Article 10 guaranteed absolute freedom of expression would soon find themselves sadly disappointed, as Article 10(2) is concerned precisely with the *limits* of freedom of expression, noting that:

> The exercise of these freedoms, since it carries with it duties and responsibilities, may be subject to such formalities, conditions, restrictions or penalties as are prescribed by law and are necessary in a democratic society, in the interests of national security, territorial integrity or public safety, for the prevention of disorder or crime, for the protection of health or morals, for the protection of the reputation or rights of others, for preventing the disclosure of information received in confidence, or for maintaining the authority and impartiality of the judiciary.

Entirely contrary to those who see the ECHR as part of a plot to create a European superstate, Article 10(2) of the ECHR in fact allows a great deal of leeway – too much, some might argue – for individual European states to censor the media in line with their own particular standards or perceived needs. For example, on 19 October 1988, during the Irish 'troubles', the British Home Secretary Douglas Hurd, using powers contained in the BBC Licence Agreement and the Broadcasting Act 1981 enabling the government to ban any programme or type of programme which it sees fit (or, rather, unfit), made it illegal to broadcast words spoken by representatives of 11 Irish organisations, and indeed words spoken in support of these organisations. The ban was unsuccessfully challenged in the UK courts by the National Union of Journalists, who then took their case to the European Commission on Human Rights (which at that time acted as a filter for the European Court of Human Rights). But here too they lost, the Commission rejecting the case on the grounds that the ban was prescribed by law, that it concerned 'one aspect of a very important area of domestic policy' (Council of Europe 1994: 92), and that the extent of its interference with freedom of expression was limited. Noting 'the difficulties involved in striking a fair balance between the requirements of protecting freedom of information – especially the free flow of information from the media – and the need to protect the state and the public against armed conspiracies seeking to overthrow the democratic order which guarantees this freedom and other human rights' (ibid.), but also drawing attention to 'the margin of appreciation permitted to States' (ibid.) in matters such as this and 'the importance of measures to combat terrorism' (ibid.), the Commission concluded that the ban's interference with freedom of expression was 'not disproportionate to the aim sought to be pursued' (ibid.).

The ban, which caused a significant diminution in the number of Republican voices heard on the UK airwaves, was finally lifted in September 1994 as part of the Northern Ireland peace process. However, section 81(4) of the current BBC Licence Agreement states that 'the Secretary of State may give the BBC a direction in writing that the BBC must not broadcast or otherwise distribute any matter or class of matter, specified in the direction, whether at a time so specified or any time' (BBC Licence Agreement 2006). Similarly, section 336(5) of the Communications Act 2003 gives the Secretary of State the power, at any time, to require Ofcom, which licenses all broadcasters in the UK other than the BBC, to direct them 'to refrain from including in their licensed services any matter, or description of matter specified by the Secretary of State' (Communications Act 2003: 296).

Article 10(2) also allows governments which are signatories to the ECHR generous leeway in the regulation of content which is not explicitly political. Thus, in spite of their ringing defence of freedom of expression in the *Schoolbook* case quoted above, the European Court actually found *in favour* of the British government, because

it is not possible to find in the domestic law of the various Contracting States a uniform European conception of morals. The view taken by their respective laws of the requirements of morals varies from time to time and from place to place, especially in our era which is characterised by a rapid and far-reaching evolution of opinions on the subject.

(Quoted in Robertson and Nicol 2008: 65)

Clearly, then, Article 10 of the ECHR allows individual European states a wide margin of appreciation to determine what they regard as the acceptable limits to freedom of expression within their own boundaries, and is not as stout a defence against censorship as some imagine it to be. Thus the laws of the various nation states which make up the EU vary greatly in the extent to which they circumscribe (or indeed liberate) the media in those countries. Here, however, we cannot adumbrate all the laws and other regulations across the EU which impinge upon media freedom. Furthermore, to concentrate purely on these would be to ignore the wider political and economic, structural and systemic, factors which also act as agents of media censorship in the broad sense of the term. Let us now, therefore, move on to a broad overview of the most significant of these factors.

Dreams of freedom

At the start of the 1990s, it was possible to imagine that the European media faced a future of greater freedom. The collapse of the Communist regimes in Eastern Europe spelled the end there not only of a particularly virulent form of state censorship but also made it much more difficult for Western European governments to invoke the Communist bogeyman and 'national security' as pretexts for their own acts of censorship. Meanwhile, new forms of communication such as satellite broadcasting and the internet, no respecters of national boundaries or jurisdictions, seemed to hold out the promise of censor-free communication. However, ensuing events were to confound many of these dreams of freedom. Many of the new governments of countries in which free expression had long been confined did not suddenly embrace it with gratitude. Furthermore, with the overnight arrival of a cut-throat brand of 'booty' capitalism, many of the newly democratised Eastern European states awoke to find that their media had been gobbled up by foreign companies. Meanwhile, in Western Europe, the behaviour of many of those same companies was increasingly giving rise to concerns about the growth of cross-media concentration, overweening proprietor power, rampant commercialism, and threats to public service broadcasting – in short, what has increasingly come to be known as market censorship.

And then, with 9/11 and the subsequent terrorist attacks in various European countries, many of the features of the Cold War returned to haunt the European media, with the spectre of Communism being replaced by the shadowy threat of 'Islamic fundamentalism'. Once again, civil liberties – including freedom of expression – found themselves sacrificed to 'national security' (particularly in the UK, closely identified as it is with American foreign policy). And as the Danish cartoons affair all too clearly showed, many media organisations came to practise self-censorship when dealing with Muslims and Islam – some out of a well-meaning desire not to offend religious feelings (the revival of which has been a particularly striking feature of parts of the post-millennial European landscape) but others merely out of fear of reprisal. This was not simply paranoia, however, as illustrated by the *fatwa* passed on Salman Rushdie in 1989 and the murder of the Dutch journalist and film-maker Theo van Gogh in 2004, whose killer fixed to his victim's body a letter directly linking the murder to his negative comments on Islam, and in particular to his film *Submission* which had recently aired on Dutch television.

Goodbye to freedom?

Journalists frequently bear the brunt of the various processes which constrain media freedom, and it is thus particularly significant that in 2007 the Association of European Journalists (AEJ) produced a report on the state of the media in 20 European countries worryingly entitled *Goodbye to Freedom?* Its editor, the former BBC foreign correspondent William Horsley argued that, across Europe, 'journalists and news organisations face multiple barriers to their work from restrictive laws, unjustified interventions by government authorities and a mixture of overt and unseen pressures to manipulate or distort their work' (2007: 1).

Of course, journalists within the EU are very rarely killed – the ultimate form of censorship – as happens in some of the countries of the former Soviet Union (although one should not forget the murders of Veronica Guerin in the Republic of Ireland in 1996 and of Martin O'Hagan in Northern Ireland in 2001). However, in many EU countries, according to a recent update of the AEJ survey:

> Security-related laws are being used more aggressively by European governments to block access to official information and to threaten journalists with jail or fines for defamation, revealing state secrets or refusing to disclose confidential sources . . . The AEJ finds a marked trend for national governments around Europe to use harsher methods, including heavy official 'spin' and tighter controls on journalists' access to information, to block media criticism. Journalists are coming under more pressure to censor themselves or toe a political line and not to challenge authority. (Horsley 2008: 3)

For example, in August 2007, prosecutors in Munich, Frankfurt, Hamburg and Berlin opened criminal investigations under Article 353b of the criminal code against 17 journalists for 'involvement in disclosing state secrets' (Horsley 2007: 29). The case related to the alleged leaking of classified papers from a parliamentary committee's inquiry into alleged government complicity in secret CIA 'rendition flights' using German airfields, as well as into the activities of the German intelligence service in Iraq at the time of the US-led invasion in 2003. The investigation targeted journalists from many of Germany's leading print media, including *Der Spiegel, Die Welt, Die Zeit, Süddeutsche Zeitung* and *Stern*. And although by the end of the year the prosecutors' offices had all dropped their cases, this did nonetheless represent what the AEJ considered an attempt to deter the media from investigating the covert activities of government. It also prompted the German journalists union, the Deutscher Journalisten-Verband, to note that in Germany since 1986, 180 lawsuits alleging 'involvement in disclosing state secrets' have been brought against journalists. And, of course, the fact that many of these failed does not lessen their inevitable 'chilling effect' on serious journalism.

Far less fortunate were the civil servant David Keogh and the political researcher Leo O'Connor who, in the UK in May 2007, were jailed under the Official Secrets Act 1989 for leaking a secret memo detailing discussions between Tony Blair and George Bush in August 2004 about an alleged American proposal to bomb the Arabic television channel al-Jazeera. On 22 November 2005 the *Daily Mirror* revealed some of the memo's contents, following which the Attorney General warned that any further publication by any medium would be met with prosecution under section 5 of the Act, which makes it an offence to have come into possession of government information, or a document from a crown servant, if it has been disclosed without lawful authority. The government then attempted to have the entire trial held in secret on the grounds that open disclosure of the memo in court could have a serious impact upon the international relations of the UK and could damage the promotion and protection of UK interests. Remarkably, the trial judge, Mr Justice Aikens, agreed, arguing that if the contents of the memo were thus to be read throughout the world, some individuals, parts of the media, and 'even some states' might react 'very unfavourably' to its contents

(Norton Taylor 2006). Unsurprisingly, he also produced the trump card of 'national security', arguing that it was legitimate for 'the court to bear in mind the ever-present threat to national safety which is posed by the possibility of terrorist acts by extremists in the UK' (ibid.).

In the event, only part of the trial was held in secret, but it was also the most important part, as it involved the contents of the memo. However, after passing sentence, the judge then imposed draconian gagging orders under the Contempt of Court Act 1981, permanently preventing UK journalists from publishing a comment in open court by David Keogh about the memo. He also said that allegations already in the public domain could not be repeated if there was any suggestion they related to the contents of the document, although he did allow that the allegations could be 'recycled' if they were published on a separate page of a newspaper from that containing references to the trial. Seventeen media organisations immediately appealed these orders, and in July the appeal court relaxed them to allow the media to publish a degree of speculation about the contents of the memo, and to report that Keogh was said to have described the contents as 'abhorrent', 'illegal' and as exposing Mr Bush as a 'madman'. However, the court also ruled that any suggestion that such speculation accurately represented evidence given in secret during the trial still risked being in contempt of court, and that the media could not publish a particular phrase uttered in open court by Keogh when asked about the document. Consequently, in the UK it is still difficult to write openly about this case without risking contempt.

The Keogh/O'Connor case is particularly important in that it represents the most extreme and authoritarian example of a worrying EU-wide trend – the abandonment of fundamental rights, in this case the right to freedom of expression, in the face of the terrorist threat; a threat which, ironically, has frequently been greatly exaggerated by the media themselves. But as Agnes Callamard (2007), executive director of Article 19 argued:

> Whistleblowers should be protected when they disclose evidence of wrongdoing in the public interest. The memo disclosed by David Keogh and Leo O'Connor is as clear an example of serving the public interest as it is possible to imagine. Furthermore, no legitimate national security interest is served by keeping this information secret. Indeed, information such as this should be subject to mandatory disclosure under an access to information law where, again, the overall public interest should trump secrecy exceptions.

Market censorship

And yet, scandalous though this case was, it actually attracted relatively little attention from the mainstream media. Of course, it could be argued that newspapers (such as Rupert Murdoch's) which supported the Iraq war would have found this an awkward subject about which to wax indignant, (Greenslade 2003) and that the BBC, having been thoroughly chastened by Lord Hutton's inquiry into the Andrew Gilligan/David Kelly affair, would have treated any matter concerning Iraq with extreme caution. But whilst there may indeed be some truth in such explanations, this episode also demonstrates how, in today's media environment, 'hard' news and 'difficult' subjects frequently find themselves pushed to the margins, along with other less easily 'consumable' types of content. Across Europe, due to the imposition of various forms of 'deregulation' since the 1980s, the media environment has become far more intensely competitive, and this has inevitably led to the increased commercialisation, commodification and standardisation of media content. Public service broadcasters have been particular victims of these processes, finding themselves forced increasingly to compete with purely commercial channels on the latters' terms. In consequence, citizens' rights to be informed – and indeed to be treated as citizens as opposed to merely consumers – have been seriously eroded. The same processes of 'deregulation' have also led to a situation in which more and more media of every kind are owned by fewer and fewer corporations, which puts democratically unhealthy amounts of power over public consciousness in the hands of a few media barons and their institutional shareholders. Furthermore, in pursuit of policies friendly to their business interests, media owners have shown themselves all too ready to employ their media for their own purposes, backing those governments which support their economic interests and excoriating those which do not. All of these factors give rise to forms of censorship and restriction which are best described as structural and systemic, but which are no less damaging to media freedom for being less immediately obvious than cuts, bans and other more 'old-fashioned' forms of overt proscription. As John Keane (1991: 90) puts it:

> Communications markets restrict freedom of communication by generating barriers to entry, monopoly and restrictions upon choice, and by shifting the prevailing definition of information from that of a public good to a privately appropriable commodity. In short, it must be concluded that there is a structural contradiction between freedom of communication and unlimited freedom of the market, and that the market liberal ideology of freedom of individual choice in the marketplace of opinions is in fact a justification for the privileging of corporate speech and of giving more choice to investors than to citizens. It is an apology for the power of king-sized business to organise and determine and therefore to *censor* individuals' choices concerning what they listen to or read and watch . . . Market competition produces market censorship. Private ownership of the media produces private caprice. Those who control the market sphere of producing and distributing information determine, prior to publication, what products (such as books, magazines, newspapers, television programmes, computer software) will be mass produced and, thus, which opinions officially gain entry into the 'marketplace of opinions'.

Instances of these processes at work across Europe are legion. The activities of Rupert Murdoch furnish a well-known example, but, as we shall see, there are many others. In the UK, Murdoch has propelled his papers towards lowest common denominator journalism in pursuit of commercial gain and thereby encouraged his competitors to do likewise (Williams 1998: 220–5); used his papers vociferously to support the Thatcher regime in return for his being allowed in 1981 to take over *The Times* and *The Sunday Times* without any reference to the Monopolies and Mergers Commission (Page 2003: 227–78; Belfield *et al.* 1994: 67–87), and in 1990 to take over British Satellite Broadcasting behind the back of the Independent Broadcasting Authority, and thereafter to run BSkyB as a purely commercial enterprise largely exempt from the public service obligations of his terrestrial competitors (Belfield *et al.* 1994: 192–277); and used his papers (rather less vociferously) to support 'New Labour' in return for the Communications Act 2003 considerably relaxing the restrictions on cross-media ownership, thereby enabling him to buy his way into terrestrial television as well (Page 2003: 443–4). Responsible as he now is for nearly 40 per cent of UK national newspaper circulation, and owning as he does a satellite television monopoly, he is a titanic force within the UK media, and one whom politicians both court assiduously and fear horribly. The irony is, however, that he is largely a force of their own creation.

However, Murdoch is by no means the only 'market censor' in the European newspaper market. For example, in the Czech Republic, German and Swiss companies own 80 per cent of 'Czech' newspapers and magazines, whilst German, Austrian, Swiss, French and Scandinavian companies dominate the print media of Bulgaria, Hungary, Poland and the Baltic States. Given the importance of the press to the way in which people understand how their societies work and what their politicians stand for, such massive domination by outside interests cannot but be unhealthy for the state of the polity.

Turning to the matter of concentration, in the UK a mere five groups – Trinity Mirror, Newsquest, Northcliffe Newspapers, Johnston Press and Archant – account for 76 per cent of local newspaper circulation, and regional monopolies and 'cluster publishing' have developed as the major owners have carved up the country between themselves. The resulting economies of scale have meant that these companies have been able to dispense with large numbers of journalists – with all too predictable consequences for the content of their papers. (It should also be pointed out, in this context, that the parlous state of ITV in the newly competitive broadcasting environment, allied with Ofcom's 'deregulatory' approach to broadcast regulation, has led to a very serious diminution in the amount of local news on commercial terrestrial television.)

Meanwhile in France, Socpresse, which is largely owned by the aircraft and weapons manufacturer Dassault, and Hachette Filipacchi Médias (HFM), which is part of the French industrial conglomerate Lagardère, another major manufacturer of arms and planes, whose owner Arnaud Lagardère is a close friend of President Sarkozy, have built up large holdings in regional newspapers (which, in France, are far more widely read than national ones) and in the highly popular magazine sector (where around 1300 magazines are sold for every 1000 inhabitants). At the level of the national press, both *Libération* and *Le Monde* have faced severe financial crises due to falling circulations, making them easy prey for wealthy industrial groups. *Libération* became the property of Edouard de Rothschild in 2005 – job cuts, a strike and accusations of editorial interference followed. Meanwhile at *Le Monde*, the famous system by which the paper is part-owned and controlled by its journalists is constantly under threat from would-be new owners (such as the ubiquitous Lagardère), whose price for an admittedly much-needed injection of cash would undoubtedly be a significant diminution of employee power. In April 2008, after a management shake-up, it was announced that 130 jobs would be cut, most of these in the paper's newsroom, which employs some 340 journalists. *Le Figaro* was acquired by Socpresse/Dassault in 2004, which immediately resulted in changes in the newspaper's leadership and accusations that the new owner, Serge Dassault, a mayor and senator from the ruling Union pour une Mouvement

Populaire (UMP) and the father of a member of the French National Assembly from the same party, was meddling in editorial matters. Things were not helped by Dassault stating that he could not understand why only journalists, and not shareholders, were allowed to write newspaper articles and that 'newspapers must promulgate healthy ideas . . . left-wing ideas are not healthy ideas' (Anon. 2004). Finally, in 2007, France's most influential business newspaper, *Les Echos*, was sold to the LVMH group, which includes Louis Vuitton, Kenzo, Céline and Dior and is owned by Bernard Arnauld, one of France's richest men. Immediate concern was expressed about the owner of leading stock market companies controlling the country's foremost business newspaper, whose role is to provide reliable and independent business information to the business sector and the public (Horsley 2007: 25–7).

This chapter has attempted to demonstrate just some of the multifarious ways in which media censorship operates in European societies, ranging from outright bans and cuts through to more diffuse and systemic, but no less damaging, forms of restriction. It will conclude by examining media censorship in Italy, a country in which all these different mechanisms have come to coalesce in a particularly disturbing fashion.

Sua Emittenza

In the 1980s the building magnate Silvio Berlusconi either established or took over three commercial television networks, Canale 5, Rete 4 and Italia 1, in effect a monopoly of commercial television under the control of his company Mediaset, in clear breach of the Italian constitution. That he was originally able to do this was thanks to the patronage of Bettino Craxi, then leader of the Italian Socialist Party, and since Craxi's departure Berlusconi has managed to sabotage all attempts to remedy this situation. By 1983, his channels were achieving higher ratings than those of the public broadcaster RAI. Furthermore, by the following year, RAI, which is only part-funded by a licence fee, was showing 46,080 advertisements totalling 311 hours, and the Mediaset channels 494,000 advertisements totalling 3468 hours. Some 53 per cent of all Italian advertising budgets are spent on television, and by 2003 Mediaset was responsible for over 60 per cent of the entire television advertising market. No wonder, then, that Berlusconi rapidly acquired the nickname *Sua Emittenza* – His Broadcastingship.

Inevitably RAI ended up aping Mediaset and competing with it on its own terms – undemanding entertainment in pursuit of high ratings. As Paul Ginsborg put it: 'a grotesque duopoly was created: on the one side a flagging public broadcasting system, on the other the suffocating pre-eminence of Berlusconi's three channels. The combination produced a deeply conformist, repetitive and uncritically consumer-oriented television system' (2004: 51), in which diverse and demanding content was increasingly conspicuous by its absence. In other words, what has been called the 'savage deregulation' of Italian television produced a particularly acute form of market censorship.

But worse was to come. By 1993, the two largest Italian political parties, the Christian Democrats and the Socialists, had been totally wiped out as a consequence of both the investigations into political corruption known as *Mani Pulite* (Clean Hands) and the emergence of the separatist Northern League. It was thus expected that the next elections would be won by the Democratic Party of the Left and their allies in the Progressive coalition. Well aware that the Left was hostile to his media empire, Berlusconi formed the political movement Forza Italia (whose name echoes the football chant 'Come on, Italy!') in 1993 and on 26 January 1994 announced he was contesting the forthcoming elections. Forming an alliance with the Northern League and the 'post-fascist' Italian Social Movement (later renamed as the National Alliance), he immediately launched a massive electoral campaign on the Mediaset channels – and not simply in the advertising slots. At one point, Raimondo Vianello, the presenter of *Pressing*, Italia 1's top sports show, announced on air his backing for Berlusconi; at another, a young starlet, Ambra Angiolini, proclaimed during a show featuring 13-year-old dancers that 'God is for Berlusconi, Satan is for Occhetto' (the leader of the Left) (Stille 2006: 167). Berlusconi won the elections, with Forza Italia gaining 21 per cent of the vote, the highest percentage of any single party. He was appointed Prime Minister, but his term in office failed to last the year, mainly because of the inherent contradictions in his coalition.

However, in 2001 Berlusconi again became Prime Minister, this time as leader of the centre-right coalition House of Freedoms which once again included Forza Italia, the National Alliance, the Northern League and some small centrist parties. In spite of the inevitable conflicts within the coalition, Berlusconi managed to stay in power until the 2006 elections, when he was narrowly defeated by the centre-left coalition led by Romano Prodi. This collapsed in January 2008. A few months earlier, Berlusconi had announced the formation of People of Freedom, a new party in which the National Alliance and Forza Italia agreed to merge, fighting and winning the elections held in April 2008.

As Tobias Jones puts it: 'having a politician who owns three television channels turns any election into the equivalent of a football match in which one team kicks-off with a three-goal advantage' (2003: 126). But, in his periods as Prime Minister, Berlusconi has also controlled RAI as well, thus being responsible for 90 per cent of Italian television viewership. But 'responsible' is a word few would use to describe how he has used this extraordinary fusion of media and political power. One presenter on Rete 4, Emilio Fede, who is also the channel's news director, has been nicknamed 'Fido' because of his faithfulness to his boss. For example, on the early evening news programme Fede once stated: 'to me Berlusconi is eternal' and followed this up with 'I love Silvio Berlusconi'. As Paul Statham (1996: 96) puts it:

> It is not only the personal ownership of the means of public communication by Berlusconi that has been seen as a threat to pluralism, but also the willingness of his television networks to employ communication strategies that break the traditional norms and practices of independent public broadcasting, which are designed to ensure a degree of political objectivity. The television news channels on Berlusconi's networks select versions of events that are explicitly favourable to Berlusconi personally and to Forza Italia. On the news programmes of Retequattro and Italia Uno, the presenters intervene to explain the news, explicitly defending statements made by Berlusconi and attacking those of his

adversaries. The television news often finishes with staged interviews with people on the street who offer eulogies to Berlusconi and denigrate his opponents, or the news concludes with unscientific opinion polls that give much higher ratings to Forza Italia than independent sources. The image and voice of Silvio Berlusconi are omnipresent, but in a controlled and stylised format usually recorded on video. Feature films are interrupted to bring news of his latest speech, and subliminal advertising techniques have been used to communicate political messages in non-political television programmes. Popular celebrities extol the virtues of Forza Italia on mainstream talk shows and other programmes, such as the *Wheel of Fortune* game show. Vittorio Sgarbi and Giuliano Ferrara, established political commentators with long-standing programmes on Berlusconi networks, both used their programmes to promote Berlusconi and Forza Italia. They then assumed key state positions on media and culture in his government.

Source: From Statham, P. (1996) 'Berlusconi, the Media and the New Right in Italy', *Harvard International Journal of Press/Politics*, 1 (1): 87-105. Copyright © 1996 Sage Publications. Reproduced with permission.

In 2002 Daniele Luttazzi, Michele Santoro and Enzo Biagi could no longer work for RAI after Berlusconi had very publicly accused them of being 'criminal' in their use of state channels. During the election period in the previous year, Luttazzi, the host of the satirical talk-show *Satyricon*, had interviewed Marco Travaglio, the author of a book which explored the origins of Berlusconi's wealth. Santoro had done likewise on his programme *Sciuscià*. In the same period, the veteran journalist Biagi had, on his programme *Il Fatto*, interviewed the comic actor Roberto Benigni, who had ridiculed Berlusconi in no uncertain terms. Subsequently both *Sciuscià* and *Il Fatto* were not recommissioned. By the end of April, new directors of the RAI channels had been appointed. Admittedly RAI had always been carved up by the main political parties (in a process known as *lottizzazione*, i.e. 'sharing out'), and this continued under Berlusconi. Thus RAI 3 remained in the hands of the Left, but RAI 1 was headed by Fabrizio del Noce, a Forza Italia stalwart, and RAI 2 by Antonio Marano of the Northern League. The news programmes on these channels were now headed by Clemente Mimun (Forza Italia) and Mauro Mazza (National Alliance). Thereafter, the claims of political interference and connivance continued unabated. For example, in February 2003 RAI refused to provide live coverage of a huge demonstration in Rome against the Iraq war (of which Berlusconi was a supporter), and in the following November Mediaset filed a suit for defamation against the first episode of RAI's new satirical show *RaiOt*, which caused the remaining five episodes to be pulled.

As John Carlin (2004) put it:

To say that Berlusconi, who is the richest man in Italy . . . has crossed the line between big business and politics would be a ludicrous understatement. Never in history – at least not in the history of western democracy – has anything like it ever been seen. It's as if Rupert Murdoch were president of the US, but in addition to owning Fox he also owned CBS and NBC. But Berlusconi, in the Italian context, is actually more than that. He is a mix of Murdoch and Bill Gates, laced with a generous measure of Mohamed Al Fayed. Berlusconi – or, in some cases, his wife and children – owns virtually all of Italy's commercial TV networks, the country's biggest advertising company, the biggest publishing house, the biggest film distribution business, two national newspapers, 50 magazines and internet service providers. He is a big player in the construction business and insurance, and he is president of Italy's most glamorous football club, current European champions AC Milan. On top of all that, as head of a political party that he – or rather his advertising company, Publitalia – created in two months in 1994, he has been elected prime minister of Italy twice.

This quite extraordinary situation, which raises the most serious concerns about the plurality and independence of the media in Italy, and which clearly gives rise to various forms of both direct and indirect censorship, has been the subject of critical resolutions in the European Parliament and the Council of Europe, and has been attacked by the Organisation for Security and Co operation in Europe (OSCE), Reporters Without Borders, the International Federation of Journalists and many others. One of its most trenchant critics has been *The Economist*, which never tires of pointing out that the case against Berlusconi includes not simply staggering conflicts of interest and the gross abuse of media power but money laundering, complicity in murder, connections with the Mafia, tax evasion, and bribing politicians, judges and the tax police. On 28 April 2001 it pronounced that 'Mr Berlusconi is not fit to lead the government of any country, least of all one of the world's richest democracies' (Anon. 2001) and on 2 August 2003 it condemned his behaviour as 'an outrage against the Italian people and their judicial system' and 'Europe's most extreme example of the abuse by a capitalist of the democracy within which he lives and operates' (Anon. 2003).

The arguments for Berlusconi as censor, then, are that he has greatly narrowed the range of programming available on all Italian television, debasing vast tracts of it to the level of *panem et circenses* (bread and circuses). This may be popular with some sections of the audience, but it has also served to narrow the choices of other sections and so deny them their full communicative rights. In political terms he has used his Mediaset channels consistently to extol Forza Italia and People of Freedom whilst excluding or excoriating his political opponents, and, during his periods as Prime Minister, attempted to neuter RAI both politically and commercially. More generally, his numerous critics, both in Italy and elsewhere, accuse him of narrowing, trivialising and commodifying all political discourse on Italian television. Tobias Jones has called Berlusconi the 'Italian anomaly' (2003: 106), but Paul Ginsborg, noting that 'his is the most ambitious attempt to date to combine media control and political power', shares the present writer's concern that this potent fusion may be an alarming harbinger of the European future, re-marking that 'we may choose to regard him as a prototype or as an exception, and time will tell which of these views is closer to the truth' (2004: 10).

If Berlusconi is indeed the shape of things to come elsewhere in Europe – and I write these words the day after his third election victory in April 2008 – the future for media freedom, in the fullest sense of the term, looks bleak indeed. For Berlusconi's Italy exemplifies, in a particularly stark fashion, many of the forces explored in this chapter which impinge upon media freedom in contemporary Europe: the growth of cross-media empires accountable to no-one but their share-holders, excessive power over the political process and popular consciousness in the hands of a coterie of media barons, the steady attrition of serious journal-ism by media owners and managers whose only concern is with the bottom line, the abuse of legal process to silence and discourage dissent, and, above all, the increasing convergence of state and corporate power, which means that the media act less as a watchdog over the establishment and more as an increasingly crucial part of it.

Questions

1 In what ways does the European Convention on Human Rights both protect and limit freedom of expression?

2 Does the 'deregulation' of media markets necessarily lead to greater freedom of expression for the media?

3 Does it harm freedom of expression if media ownership is concentrated in a few hands? If so, why?

Further reading

Croteau, D. and Hoynes, W. (2006) *The Business of Media: Corporate Media and the Public Interest*, 2nd edition, Thousand Oaks, CA: Pine Forge Press. A detailed and wide ranging account of the economic and structural factors which constrain media freedom.

Nicol, A., Millar, G. and Sharland, A. (2001) *Media Law and Human Rights*, London: Blackstone Press. A useful guide to the implications for freedom of expression of the European Convention on Human Rights.

Page, B. (2003) *The Murdoch Archipelago*, London: Simon and Schuster.

Petley, J. (2001) 'Silvio Berlusconi' in D. Jones (ed) (2001) *Censorship: A World Encyclopedia*, Vol. 1, London and Chicago: Fitzroy Dearborn, pp. 217–20. A detailed account of why Berlusconi should be considered a censor.

Petley, J. (2007) *Censoring the Word*, London: Seagull Books. A succinct account of the main arguments for, and threats to, freedom of expression.

Rolston, B. and Miller, D. (1996) *War and Words: The Northern Ireland Media Reader*, Belfast: Beyond the Pale Publications. Contains a series of excellent accounts of the censorship of news of the Irish conflict in the British media, and a particularly useful chronology of the victims of the Hurd ban.

Summers, C. (2007) 'When Should a Secret Not Be a Secret?', *BBC News*, 10 May (http://news.bbc.co.uk/1/hi/uk/6639947.stm).

References

Anon. (2001) 'Fit to Run Italy?', *Economist*, 28 April.

Anon. (2003) 'Dear Mr Berlusconi . . .', *Economist*, 2 August.

Anon. (2004) 'M. Dassault Veut une Presse Aux "Idées Saines"', *Le Monde*, 12 December.

BBC Licence Agreement (2006) www.bbc.co.uk/bbctrust/assets/files/pdf/regulatory_framework/charter_agreement/bbcagreement_july06.txt (accessed 3 March 2009).

Belfield R., Hird, C. and Kelly S. (1994) *Murdoch: The Great Escape*, London: Warner Books.

Callamard, A. (2007) 'Public Interest in Leaking Blair-Bush Memo', *Guardian*, 12 May.

Carlin, J. (2004) 'All Hail Berlusconi', *Observer*, 18 January.

Communications Act (2003) www.opsi.gov.uk/Acts/acts2003/ukpga_20030021_en_31 (accessed 3 March 2009).

Council of Europe (1994) *Yearbook of the European Convention on Human Rights*, The Hague/London/Boston: Kluwer Law International.

Ginsborg, P. (2004) *Silvio Berlusconi: Television, Power and Patrimony*, London: Verso.

Greenslade, R. (2003) 'Their Master's Voice', *Guardian*, 17 February.

Horsley, W. (ed) (2007) *Goodbye to Freedom? A Survey of Media Freedom Across Europe*, The Association of European Journalists, www.aej-uk.org/survey.htm (accessed 3 March 2009).

Horsley, W. (ed) (2008) *Goodbye to Media Freedom? Spotlight on Europe: An Update of the AEJ Media Freedom Survey*, The Association of European Journalists, www.aej-uk.org/survey.htm (accessed 3 March 2009).

Jones, D. (ed) (2001) *Censorship: A World Encyclopedia*, Vol. 1, London and Chicago: Fitzroy Dearborn.

Jones, T. (2003) *The Dark Heart of Italy*, London: Faber and Faber.

Keane, J. (1991) *The Media and Democracy*, Cambridge: Polity.

Norton Taylor, R. (2006) 'New Evidence Clears up Whether Bush Sought to Bomb Al-Jazeera. But We Are Not Allowed to Hear It', *Guardian*, 13 October.

Page, B. (2003) *The Murdoch Archipelago*, London: Simon and Schuster.

Robertson, G. and Nicol, A. (2008) *Media Law*, 5th edition, London: Penguin.

Statham, P. (1996) 'Berlusconi, the Media and the New Right in Italy', *Press/Politics* 1 (1): 87–105.

Stille, A. (2006) *The Sack of Rome*, New York: Penguin.

Williams, K. (1998), *Get Me a Murder a Day! A History of Mass Communication in Britain*, London: Edward Arnold.

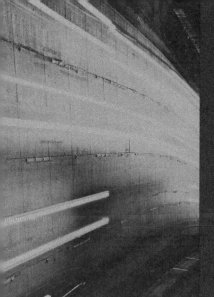

Part 4

AUDIENCES, INFLUENCES AND EFFECTS

Introduction

Daniele Albertazzi and Paul Cobley

Part 4 of this volume features four overview essays on audience studies. Audience studies has been central to the study of the media from the outset, but the field saw a resurgence of research into audiences during the past 30 years. For students of media, it is crucial that you have a sense of how communication of all kinds has an understanding of audience, general or specific; it is also crucial to gain an understanding of how businesses, including the media industries, might conceptualise their audiences. Yet these are not the only reasons for this part's existence. As you will see, there is ongoing debate about audiences – a debate which should help you establish your own understanding of media, your position on events in the world of media and even your own general political views. Do people receive media messages passively? Or do they receive them actively? If it is the former – what are the results? Does the message pass over them? Or are they brainwashed into behaving in a certain way?

What is clear is that media organisations have sought to gain as much information as possible about audiences in order to effectively target them with *messages*. Sending expensively constructed messages to uninterested audiences is, after all, a waste of money. Yet, despite this long history, the question remains: how have media organisations researched audiences and what features of audiences have they been able to find out about? One of the most common conceptions regarding audiences concerns the idea that 'the media' has an 'effect' on people. This has a residual aspect in the media's own research of audiences in the sense that media organisations try to predict what media product will encourage people to turn on, turn off, download, click through, and so forth. Yet the other idea of 'effect' on audiences – as deleterious and automatic – is often touted, often unselfconsciously, by the media themselves. Indeed, it is one instance where 'the media' is treated as an undifferentiated monolith (undifferentiated, that is, except for the distinction between the media outlet claiming the effect and the rest of the media). So, do the products of the media have the 'effect' of making children more violent, causing adolescents to be listless, inciting a man to rape a woman, developing a girl's eating disorder?

Or is the idea of media 'effects' a lazy way of latching onto flawed research in order to ignore more complex determinants of social ills?

Aside from these large questions, we certainly need to have a sense of what audiences actually do. For commercial media organisations, audiences are commodities that can be sold to advertisers; they are also targets for those organisations' own products. Nevertheless, audiences are made up of people. You are a member of a media audience no matter how analytically you approach topics in media. As such, you will have demographic characteristics – age, occupation, a postal address, etc. – but you will also have a complex array of personal characteristics. To be sure, some of these are individual and not susceptible to measurement. However, many are shared with others, despite their complexity. They might be aspects of your identity that are pretty much visible in society – for example, gender. Or they might be less visible but strongly felt – you enjoy archery. What roles do these play in your existence as part of the audience for media products? Will they enable you to negotiate media output in a way that makes you sceptical or immune to many messages? Or will they make you prone to certain kinds of suggestion? Does the repetition of certain kinds of media output make you think in a particular way because it echoes features of your understanding of life? Or do you find you can see through media output because it conflicts with your understanding of life?

It is up to you to decide where you stand on these matters. It is also up to you to decide how your standing will help you in your understanding of the media. The discussions in the essays that follow will help in these processes.

23

Administrative Research of Audiences

Michael Svennevig

Chapter overview

Audience research aims to provide the media industries with reliable and representative information about the people using the services on offer. It offers insights into how people use television, radio, newspapers and magazines, cinemas, PC- and internet-based services and content, and the growing range of mobile access applications. Audiences and users of specific media are estimated using a range of research techniques, including meters attached to TV sets, 'listening' devices which people keep with them, surveys of people's activities and opinions, and software 'counters' based in internet-linked PCs. The range and scope of audience research has changed rapidly in the past few years following the growth of digital technologies in old and new communications services, together with the application of these technologies to research methods themselves. Media users can now access different types of content across an expanding array of digital communication devices. These changes have increased demand for audience research which informs decision making among media owners, advertisers and sponsors. Also, the regulatory environment for the electronic media has become more complex and also requires research input for decision making.

Introduction

The producers of television and radio programmes, the makers of films and DVDs, national and transnational broadcasters, newspaper and magazine editors, website owners, mobile phone service operators, on-demand TV channels and services, media owners and advertisers all require information about their audiences and/or users. Advertising agencies, media consultants and market research agencies also need data on audiences in order to advise their clients, and to plan communications strategies. The 'ratings' (the percentage of the population who encounter specific content) achieved by individual programme or content producers, by broadcasters, television or radio stations, the circulations and readerships obtained by the print media, numbers of cinema attendances, and of people passing poster sites, and the volume of visitors ('hits') to websites, online advertising sites, and internet search engines are all crucial to those involved in one way or another with the various media industries.

Research-based empirical quantified data are the key basis for determining the success or failure of media services and, importantly, constitute the basic 'currencies' for negotiating advertising and sponsorship fees for commercially-funded media services. These industries are large in terms of turnover: the most recent estimates (2007 data) for advertising revenue earned by the UK media and communications sector was over £19 billion (Advertising Association 2008).

Equally, for the BBC – whose broadcasting and internet services are directly funded by the UK public through the household TV licence fee which in 2007 raised £3.2 billion (BBC 2008) – audience research offers evidence that its various outputs (radio, TV and internet) serve the UK public and offer value for money. Furthermore, the regulatory framework of electronic communications has changed in recent years. The previous UK media regulatory bodies (the Independent Television Commission, the Radio Authority, the Broadcasting Standards Commission) were replaced in 2003 by the Office of Communications (Ofcom). Ofcom sets performance targets for the organisations it regulates, and tracks their actual performance through subscribing to existing audience and market research, as well as commissioning its own studies, particularly in respect of television and radio broadcast services.

The purposes of audience research

The primary purpose of audience research in all its forms is to provide both quantitative and qualitative feedback on the size, composition, product and media usage, lifestyles and opinions of audiences to an increasing range of media and media-related services. Quantitative research is designed to *measure* media use: for example, numbers of people using a medium and their characteristics (e.g. age, gender, social grade, occupation, education, UK region), types and strength of opinions held, media-related behaviour. Qualitative research methods are primarily designed to *understand* media use: discovering people's preferences and dislikes, motivations and emotional responses to media content, and the role of the media in everyday life. The bulk of 'routine' media research is quantitative, though, and usually undertaken by the various media organisations for management, promotional or regulatory purposes and these various research strands are what this chapter focuses upon.

To simplify matters, the term 'audience' is taken here as a broad term which includes the following main categories and groups:

- newspaper readers (national and regional/local),
- magazine readers,
- radio listeners,
- television viewers,

- cinemagoers,
- digital video recorder and personal video recorder/Sky+ users,
- internet and online service users,
- mobile communications users (cell phone, PDA, Blackberry, etc.),
- people encountering posters and other public display advertisements.

These are not necessarily mutually exclusive categories: a person using a PC or a mobile phone, a PDA, a wireless-enabled laptop with broadband internet, and who also watches TV and some days reads a newspaper or magazine, or sees a poster, can be classified as all of these in one way or another. What is clear is that there are potentially many different ways that could be used to define a 'user' of a particular medium. How long does a visitor have to look at a website to be 'using' it? Is 'live' radio or TV use the same as listening to a recording or download of the same output, which can be halted or replayed at will? Is looking at a newspaper website the same as holding and reading a physical newspaper?

These questions reflect the needs of media industries for relevant information about the users (audiences) of their services in order to manage these services efficiently and at the same time to meet and anticipate user needs.

The audience research industry is driven mainly by the needs of buyers and sellers of opportunities to target audiences through advertising. All the major sources of audience research are to a greater or lesser extent the product of a necessary cooperation between media organisations/owners and the advertising industries who together finance research into the public's media habits. In the following sections, the key media research systems operating in the UK are outlined. These sections cannot give full details of each medium and associated research methods, but are intended to provide sufficient information to allow the reader to have a sound grasp of the methods and main outputs available, and their strengths and weaknesses. The References section at the end of the chapter gives contact details for the various organisations and research suppliers covered.

The beginnings of broadcasting audience research

In the UK the BBC pioneered broadcasting audience research in the late 1930s, which has been developed in one form or another in the present day multimedia environment. Back then, the BBC began 'The Daily Survey of Listening' in which specially trained interviewers across the UK each day asked a different sample of people what they had listened to on the previous day. These data were then used to estimate the audience size and composition for each radio service and for each programme. At the heart of that method, and all other subsequent audience research methods, is the statistical concept of *sampling*: using a relatively small number of individuals to represent the total population. When the BBC began TV transmissions on a national basis in the late 1940s, the survey was enhanced to include TV questions, becoming the Daily Survey of Listening and Viewing which continued until the early 1980s.

Television audience research

The commercially-funded ITV service started in London in 1955, and was rolled out across the other ITV regions over the next few years. Initially each regional ITV company made their own arrangements for audience research, since they and the advertising agencies required evidence of the channel's performance in each ITV transmission area. The research in some areas involved interviews similar to the BBC's method. In others a 'set meter' was used: an electronic device connected to a TV set which identified which channels were viewed over time using a sample panel of ITV-receiving households. A panel is the term used for a sample of people and/or households which is continuously used over time, rather than just once. In 1964 the advertising industry and the ITV companies set up a standardised audience measurement system for all of the UK ITV regions. This resulted in set meters being used across the UK and standard analysis rules being applied in all ITV regions.

The peoplemeter

The UK research company AGB developed what in the 1970s they termed a 'peoplemeter': this still used a set meter, but also collected data on who was actually viewing that set. Each person aged four or over in the household is asked to push a button on a small handset when they start watching TV and again when they stop or leave the room – each viewer being identified by their own button on the special handset. The system also downloads all the data from the sample of homes via the telephone. For the first time ever, programme-makers and schedulers could get interim ratings the morning after transmission: the so-called 'overnights'. The peoplemeter is now used in a wide range of countries across the world and is effectively the standard way of measuring TV audiences.

In 1977, the Annan Committee on the Future of Broadcasting recommended the setting up of a joint BBC/ITV audience measurement system. In 1981 a single system – based around the peoplemeter – was established which involved creating the Broadcasters' Audience Research Board (BARB) jointly owned by the BBC, the ITV companies, and the Institute of Practitioners in Advertising. A reduced version of the BBC's Daily Survey was retained, though, in order to measure BBC radio audiences. Over the following years Channel 4 joined BARB, followed by BSkyB and then by Five. BARB sets the detailed criteria for the service, and appoints the research companies which run the service and undertakes quality control. It also plans for future changes.

BARB's audience measurement service is based on a panel of over 5100 homes (around 11,500 individuals aged four or older) that are representative of the UK as a whole, and have peoplemeters installed on all their TV sets. This panel is run by AGB Nielsen Media Research for BARB and started in 2002. TV programmes recorded on a VCR, DVD recorder or PVR and then played back on the TV set are also monitored. Each year, an Establishment Survey of some 52,000 homes is undertaken to establish and track changes in TV reception and viewing characteristics –

numbers of TV sets and TV recorders, acquisition of multichannel services (cable, digital satellite or digital terrestrial TV), and details of television viewing households in the various ITV and BBC regions. The panel in each region is balanced by size of household, presence of children, age of housewife, presence of working adults, and socio-economic status and educational status of the head of household.

The central data storage unit is contacted in the early morning by telephone from the research agency's data centre (telephone ringing is suppressed) and the stored viewing information is downloaded. Audience 'overnight' figures become available the next day – after data from all the panel homes have been downloaded. Some data analyses obviously require longer to produce, such as weekly viewing patterns, 'Top 10s', monthly summaries of viewing, etc. Table 23.1 shows an example of the 10 highest audiences (in thousands of viewers aged 4+) for the

Table 23.1 Viewing figures: five UK terrestrial channels and Sky 1 (week ending 25 January 2009)

	000s
BBC1	
1 EastEnders (Mon 20:00)	9,490
2 EastEnders (Thu 19:29)	9,059
3 EastEnders (Fri 20:00)	8,737
4 Casualty (Sat 20:26)	7,176
5 The National Lottery – In It To Win It (Sat 19:36)	6,962
6 EastEnders (Tue 19:29)	6,834
7 Antiques Roadshow (Sun 18:59)	6,579
8 Six O'clock News (Tue 18:00)	6,490
9 Lark Rise to Candleford (Sun 19:59)	6,313
10 Hustle (Thu 21:00)	6,297
BBC2	
1 Masterchef (Thu 20:02)	3,946
2 Victorian Farm (Thu 21:02)	3,704
3 Masterchef (Wed 20:34)	3,518
4 Masterchef (Mon 20:31)	3,458
5 Masterchef (Tue 20:30)	3,294
6 Oz and James Drink to Britain (Tue 19:59)	3,197
7 University Challenge (Mon 20:01)	3,186
8 The Natural World (Fri 20:01)	2,491
9 Eggheads (Wed 18:05)	2,310
10 Obama: His Story (Tue 18:59)	2,296
Channel 4	
1 Big Chef Takes On Little Chef (Wed 21:00)	4,312
2 Big Chef Takes On Little Chef (Tue 21:01)	4,013
3 Celebrity Big Brother (Fri 21:59)	3,654
4 Big Chef Takes On Little Chef (Mon 21:01)	3,502

	000s
5 Celebrity Big Brother (Mon 22:03)	3,417
6 Dispatches (Thu 20:01)	3,393
7 Celebrity Big Brother (Fri 20:29)	3,292
8 Celebrity Big Brother (Wed 22:03)	3,200
9 Celebrity Big Brother (Thu 21:00)	2,837
10 Celebrity Big Brother (Tue 22:04)	2,712
Five	
1 CSI: Crime Scene Investigation (Tue 21:01)	3,980
2 CSI – New York (Sat 21:15)	3,250
3 NCIS (Fri 21:01)	2,410
4 Film: The Contractor (Wed 21:01)	2,220
5 CSI: Crime Scene Investigation (Tue 21:59)	2,058
6 Ice Road Truckers (Wed 20:01)	1,916
7 Neighbours (Thu 17:29)	1,821
8 Neighbours (Mon 17:29)	1,740
9 Neighbours (Wed 17:29)	1,697
10 Neighbours (Fri 17:29)	1,663
ITV1	
1 Coronation Street (Mon 19:33)	10,622
2 Coronation Street (Wed 19:30)	10,199
3 Coronation Street (Mon 20:30)	9,935
4 Coronation Street (Fri 19:33)	9,807
5 Coronation Street (Fri 20:30)	9,139
6 Dancing on Ice (Sun 18:29)	8,580
7 Emmerdale (Mon 19:02)	7,784
8 Emmerdale (Wed 18:59)	7,564
9 Wild at Heart (Sun 20:29)	7,475
10 Emmerdale (Thu 19:01)	7,393
Sky 1	
1 Lost (Sun 21:00)	1,195
2 The Simpsons (Sun 19:00)	910
3 The Simpsons (Sun 19:31)	754
4 The Simpsons (Wed 19:00)	717
5 24 Season 7 (Mon 21:03)	696
6 The Simpsons (Mon 19:34)	691
7 The Simpsons (Thu 19:31)	608
8 The Simpsons (Thu 19:00)	596
9 The Simpsons (Wed 19:31)	551
10 The Simpsons (Fri 19:32)	548

five UK terrestrial channels and for Sky 1. In this particular week, *Coronation Street* and *EastEnders* both obtained audiences of over 9 million viewers.

Television audience ratings

The main currency within the TV industries for the measurement of television audiences is the 'rating', or TVR, rather than millions of viewers, although both can be used. The TVR (TeleVision Rating) measures the popularity of a programme, daypart, commercial break or advertisement, by comparing its audience to the population as a whole. One TVR is numerically equivalent to 1 per cent of a target audience. For example, if *Coronation Street* achieved a women TVR of 20 in the Yorkshire ITV region, this means that an estimated 20 per cent of all women in the Yorkshire region watched an average minute of *Coronation Street*. In reality, audience size varies throughout the duration of a programme and is measured for each individual minute, and these minute-by-minute ratings are then averaged over the whole of the programme.

Ratings are calculated for advertisements by taking the TVR for the minute in which the advertisement began. Advertisers and their agencies then add these ratings over all the 'spots' (showings) for a given advertising campaign. The figures will, of course, no longer be a true percentage since they can exceed 100, but it is taken as a measure of the 'weight' of the advertising campaign. There are other useful measures such as 'reach' – the net number or percentage of people who have seen at least some of a particular element of broadcast output (e.g. a programme, or a series of programmes, a specific channel, or a TV advertising campaign). Ratings also reveal the regional and demographic characteristics of each audience.

Commercial broadcasters also need ratings for each commercial break as a guide for selling air-time to advertisers. Highly rated breaks (with large audiences) command a higher price. Other high-value advertising spots are those where there is a particularly attractive audience: wealthier people, or people with a specific demographic profile (younger, upmarket men, parents of young children, etc.). Equally, programme-makers and schedulers need feedback on the success or failure of their efforts. If, for example, TVRs for a new series start high and then decline, this may well be a sign of a production that has little appeal. Or, if TVRs for existing channels decline, this may be a sign of changes in rival channels' schedules. Figure 23.1 shows longer-term changes within the TV market arising from the expansion of channel capacity since 2002. The 'others' category includes over 250 digital channels available via Virgin, Sky and Freeview. The chart shows how the combined audiences to the dozens of additional channels now available has made the 'others' category the largest, gradually reducing the level of use of the five original terrestrial channels.

Future developments in television audience research

As it stands, the BARB peoplemeter-based system is coping reasonably well with recent changes in TV content delivery. Programming recorded off-air by a VCR or DVD recorder, or via a PVR or Sky+, and played back within seven days is added to

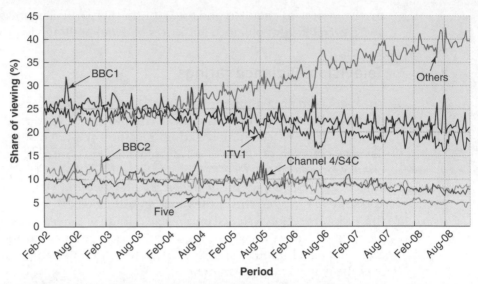

Figure 23.1 TV viewing shares (February 2002–August 2008)

Source: Adapted from Broadcasters Audience Research Board Ltd (BARB) TV Viewing Shares (February 2002–August 2008), www.barb.co.uk/report/index, Copyright © 2009 BARB Limited. Reproduced with permission.

the relevant channel's ratings. However, a clear weakness of the peoplemeter is the fact that it is based on the TV set in the home. Peoplemeters cannot measure out-of-home viewing, such as watching in other people's homes, or viewing major sporting events in pubs and clubs. Nor can they currently measure internet-based TV viewing via PCs, or via mobile phones or PDAs. For the present at least these are manageable breaches in the TV set's long-established monopoly on delivery of content. But there is a growing need to develop ways of obtaining reliable estimates of the sizes of audiences accessing media content through these new routes, especially among younger people.

The current BARB contract runs until 2010, when a revised system will be rolled out which makes provision for the possibility of using recently-developed lightweight Portable Personal Meters (PPMs) carried by people during the day, together with in-home fixed peoplemeters, and also has provision for introducing measurement systems for other delivery routes such as IPTV (internet protocol TV) content viewed via PC or other broadband-enabled internet devices.

Radio audience research

The measurement of radio audiences is more complex than measuring TV viewing. First, listeners are not always aware of which station they are listening to, given the wide choice now available in many parts of the UK via FM analogue and DAB digital radio services, as well as internet-based radio services. At present there are over 390 radio stations in the UK, most being regional or local. Second, radio listening is often casual and a secondary activity while doing other things (working, driving, etc.), or used just as background. Being in a room with a television switched on (and peoplemeter attached) is a much more straightforward concept than the idea of 'presence' when a radio can be heard. Third, listeners tend to be mobile, with 20–35 per cent of listening taking place outside the home, often on radios not owned by or tuned in by the listener. This creates problems either for asking people to recall their radio use or for diary-keeping. Fourthly, radio is a highly fragmented and rapidly expanding service.

Radio data collection

Until 1992 the BBC and independent local radio undertook separate radio audience research. In 1992 a new company, Radio Joint Audience Research Ltd (RAJAR), was established to operate a single audience measurement system for the radio industry as a whole, meaning the end of the BBC's Daily Survey. RAJAR is jointly owned by the Commercial Radio Companies Association (CRCA) and the BBC. It covers all BBC national and local stations, UK licensed stations and most other commercial radio stations. It also covers both analogue and digital (DAB) radio services, and a range of reception/delivery methods: AM/FM analogue radio and digital reception via DAB digital radio, DTV via Sky, Freesat, Freeview or cable, and via the internet.

The radio listening diary

RAJAR has always used seven-day self-completion diaries to gather listening data, covering Monday to Sunday. Each year across the UK, over 130,000 adults are contacted by interviewers, household and individual details collected, and radio listening diaries covering seven consecutive days' listening are placed and collected a week later. The interviewers also check which radio services each person uses at all, and ensure that a 'personalised' listening diary, covering the services used, is left with the interviewee. The explanatory example given to all RAJAR participants is shown in Figure 23.2.

The diary records actual radio listening. If the person listens to the radio for at least five minutes in any quarter of an hour, they draw a line through the appropriate time segment boxes for that particular radio service. They are also asked to indicate where they listened – at home, in a vehicle, or at work/elsewhere, and what medium was used (radio, DTV, internet).

The data are then analysed to give population estimates for each service within its transmission area. The standard measures for each radio service measured are:

- reach – the number of different people listening to each specified service over a period of time expressed as a percentage of the total population of the transmission area;

- total hours – the overall number of hours of listening to a service per day;

- average hours – average hours per listener to the service calculated from total hours divided by reach.

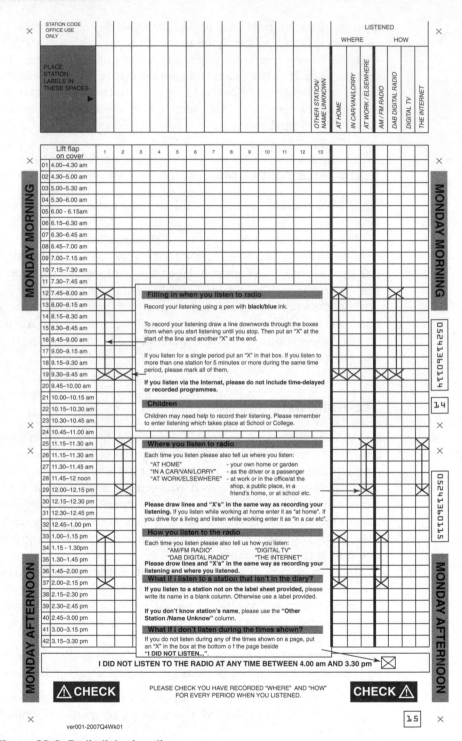

Figure 23.2 Radio listening diary page

Source: From Radio Joint Audience Research Ltd (RAJAR) www.rajar.co.uk/docs/about/RAJAR_diary_example_page.pdf. Copyright © RAJAR Ltd. Reproduced with permission.

The future of radio audience research

The present research design drawn up by RAJAR only began in 2007 and will run until 2009, but it included an 'experimental' element in addition to the established methods described above. The new element would involve a potential switch from a diary-based manual method to electronic detection of radio services heard. This would involve a two-year London test panel using a portable people meter (PPM) in collaboration with BARB. The PPM is a device carried by individuals designed to 'listen' for broadcast content which is in use in a number of countries around the world for measuring both radio and TV use. The device is recharged on a daily basis, and while recharging it downloads data. Both RAJAR and BARB, after experimenting with PPMs, currently remain committed to their established methods but are also committed to continue exploring more flexible methods such as portable metering.

Newspaper and magazine readership

The commercial importance of readership research stems from the fact that newspapers and magazines carry substantial amounts of advertising and are highly dependent upon the revenue obtained from it: the purchase or cover cost rarely covers production, promotion and distribution costs. Equally, advertisers depend upon research-derived estimates of readership to determine the allocation of their spend between the many different titles available. Readership estimates are the 'currency' in which advertising space in the print media is traded. Readership data can also be important in helping editorial decisions.

Measuring readership

'Reading' is a complex concept to define, and difficult to measure. It ranges from glancing at the headlines in a newspaper, skimming through an article or looking at pictures in a magazine, moving from factual reporting to fiction, through to a deep involvement with content.

The face-to-face interview is the preferred method of data collection for readership assessment in the UK. The National Readership Survey (NRS), using this method, has been the key source of UK readership data for over 50 years. It is based on an annual sample of 40,000 interviews conducted in-home across the year with adults (aged 15 or older). This procedure allows small readership publications to accumulate research evidence over time, and also allows seasonal variations to be detected. The survey covers over 260 daily, weekly and monthly publications, and the list is growing. The sample of addresses used is randomly selected from the Royal Mail's Postcode Address File, containing over 28 million addresses.

The NRS interviews are conducted in-home by specially-trained interviewers, using a laptop-based system. This allows the interviewer to display key questions, lists of publications and examples of front pages to the interviewee on a separate screen, while entering responses onto the laptop. The first part of the interview is a series of classification and lifestyle questions. The second part asks which publications the respondent has read. The interviewee is shown screens which contain the titles of around 280 newspapers or magazines laid out in a standard typeface. The respondent is asked to say which titles they have read or looked at for at least two minutes in the past 12 months.

The interviewer then returns to each of these titles in turn on the screen. The interviewee is then asked two key questions about their reading:

- the *recency* question (*when did you last read a copy of . . . ?*), and
- the *frequency* question (*how often do you read . . . ?*).

These two measures are used to produce the key readership statistics. Readerships are usually measured in terms of *Average Issue Readership* (AIR) – the number of different people who read a single issue of a publication, averaged across issues. If they claim to have read an issue in the last publishing interval, i.e. yesterday for a daily newspaper, within the last seven days for a weekly newspaper or magazine, within the past four weeks for a monthly magazine – they are counted as a reader of that edition of the publication.

Frequency data are used to calculate reading probabilities for each title. These are used to estimate cumulative readership across a number of issues of a given title. Readers of all titles are also asked where they obtained the most recent issue they read, and also asked about the time they usually spend reading an issue of the publication. There are also a number of questions about the use of other media: television, radio, cinema and internet.

The final section of the interview comprises further classification questions, in which the respondent is asked the age, sex, marital and occupational status of each member of the household. This part of the interview also covers lifestyle questions, such as motoring, travel, use of a range of products, personal qualifications, financial activity, and household income. The NRS has over the years been seen as the 'gold standard' for survey research in general, because of the quality and size of the samples of the UK population that it uses. It sets the standard not only for readership measurement, but also for demographic classification of the UK population, and provides the basic 'yardstick' for most of the other media audience research systems operating in the UK. Social grading as defined by the NRS has become the standard for the whole of the UK market research industry. Social grade quota setting and weighting of many surveys is often undertaken with reference to the findings of the NRS.

Film audience measurement and evaluation

The cinema industry has always been able to monitor basic information such as audience size through counting numbers of tickets sold. The main source of UK cinema admissions data is that commissioned by the Cinema Advertising Association (CAA). This provides weekly estimates of the total number of audience admissions to all circuit and independent screens that carry advertising. The trend over the past years shows a growth in cinema-going from a low point in the 1980s (Figure 23.3).

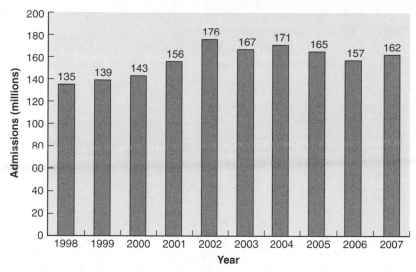

Figure 23.3 UK cinema admissions 1992–2008

Source: CAA / Gallup / Nielsen EDI. Copyright © 2008 Cinema Advertising Association (CAA). Reproduced with permission.

Starting in 1983, the CAA commissioned an annual research project – Cinema and Video Industry Audience Research (CAVIAR) – to enable cinema media owners to better understand their audiences' behaviour and attitudes towards cinema and other media. The CAA also set up the Film Monitor which runs every quarter, and provides the industry with audience profiles of new releases.

The cinema market has changed significantly since 1983 with multiscreens virtually the norm, online viewing and rental; to match that change the CAA in 2007 created Film Audience Measurement and Evaluation (FAME) to replace CAVIAR. This is an annual survey of cinema-going, conducted online with around 3000 people. FAME provides greater insight into film viewing across cinema, DVD, online and new emerging formats, and how people are deciding which films to see and where to see them.

Posters

Posters, unlike the media mentioned so far, are not embedded in personal information or entertainment. They are not consciously 'used' in the ways other media are, and contact with them is often fleeting, and essentially a matter of chance rather than intention. This means that people cannot sensibly be asked to recall what posters they have recently seen. Poster research is aimed at estimating how many people are likely to see or pass by a particular panel and with what frequency. Into this also has to go some measure of visibility. The advertising value of each site has to be assessed so that advertising campaigns using combinations of sites can be planned. The current system called POSTAR (for POSTer Audience Research) was launched in 1996, and is funded by the Outdoor Advertising Association (OAA) and the Institute of Practitioners in Advertising Outdoors (IPAO). In the UK there are almost 250,000 poster panels which have been assessed by POSTAR in terms of audiences.

It is a complex system which uses a combination of sources to generate estimates of numbers of people seeing posters in everyday life:

● traffic estimates (based on local authority and government traffic counts) at roadside poster panels;

● visibility studies and eye movement tracking at different types of location;

● regular travel surveys based on samples of around 7000 members of the public in different areas of the UK.

However, from February 2008 the POSTAR system is being redesigned. The new system will be based around automatic tracking methods involving a sample of 20,000 people keeping small GPS tracking devices with them during the day, enabling their movements to be followed. The data from these will then be 'married' with the known characteristics of poster sites encountered and estimates of seeing posters calculated.

The Target Group Index

The Target Group Index (TGI), run by the UK research company BMRB since 1969 is a markedly different form of audience-related research. Rather than focusing upon a specific medium, the TGI focuses primarily upon the individual and their interests, tastes, habits and opinions, and on a wide range of usage questions about the media, shops, services and products. In practice the TGI involves a very traditional methodology, using a sizeable self-completion questionnaire which is completed by a very large and rigorously recruited representative sample of around 24,000 individuals aged 15 or older drawn from the general UK population along lines similar to the NRS. There is also a separate Youth TGI devoted to 7–19 year-olds.

Some of the specific questions in the TGI match or are compatible with data from other research sources, allowing a technique called 'data fusion'. In this, two individuals who have taken part in different studies and have a sufficient number of similar key attributes in common can be mathematically 'fused' into a single 'person'. So, for example, a member of the BARB panel could be fused with a TGI informant with a similar demographic and media use profile to produce a fused individual with known TV and shopping, as well as holidaying habits and a range of other attributes. While not perfect, studies to date do seem to show that this technique can work well enough to be a genuine advantage.

The internet and digital media

Until a relatively few years ago, it was possible for each of the separate media to go their own, somewhat idiosyncratic and specialised ways through the audience research jungle. Each pre-digital medium was distinct in terms of what it offered to the user, how it was delivered, and where it was located. These features of the pre-digital world meant that each medium had acquired its own traditional way of being researched in terms of assessing its users and audiences. From the mid-1990s, though, it rapidly became clear that the internet had arrived as a mainstream, popular and cost-effective multifaceted communications service. Digitisation has meant that content previously carried by 'traditional' media can increasingly be carried by the internet more efficiently, in great detail and in reproducible form.

This flexibility means that assessing how people access digital media, and the use of content, services and applications is a far more complex task than measuring single medium use. The internet can deliver the printed page, adverts, live performances, stream live and archived TV and radio programmes, act as a low-cost telephone service, and create virtual social networks. This ever-changing nature means that measuring the various activities undertaken by internet users is not an easy task. The internet is not a medium in the traditional sense of being able to offer a clearly defined set of benefits in forms which are specific to that medium.

There are two main research strategies which seem best suited to internet measurement: monitoring individual users and monitoring individual websites. Both of these strategies have been adopted by the two major research organisations dominating the field: ComScore Media Metrix and Nielsen NetRatings. ComScore uses a worldwide panel of over 2 million internet users who have agreed to have tracking software on their computers. The panel is recruited from random surveys of internet users. The software reports back to ComScore on the panellists' internet use, including all sites visited and pages visited within each site and time spent there, adverts seen online, and products and services bought and the price paid. The system is passive, in that the PC user does not have to do anything at all after agreeing to take part and load the ComScore software. Personal details held on computers are excluded from ComScore's analysis. In exchange for taking part, ComScore offers free virus protection, encrypted data storage on the home PC and sweepstakes for prizes. In some ways, these data are not quite what they seem: the figure for 'Google sites' includes the millions of searches made by people using Google as a search engine, but also includes all visits to the very successful social networking site MySpace, now part of Google (see Table 23.2).

Nielsen NetRatings use a very similar approach, and operate national panels of internet users in a number of countries including the UK. NetRatings also measures web traffic and search engine use, based on measuring the numbers of visitors to websites (see Table 23.3).

There is debate about the two systems' methods and accuracy. At times they produce very similar findings, at others they differ. In part these differences are to be expected given the measurement methods. It is not clear whether people on the internet user panels are always identified by the measurement systems: if person A was logged in and tracked by a measurement system and then person B takes over without logging in separately, then the change is not recorded. However, there is little doubt that the basic measures of number of users and numbers of visits to websites are generally reliable. Less reliable are data on specific users and specific uses of sites. For example, the increasing numbers of people who are illegally uploading or downloading copyright video and music material are very unlikely to volunteer to be surveyed.

Table 23.2 Top 20 most-visited websites in the UK

Sept 08 Rank	Aug 08 Rank	Property	Total unique visitors (000) Sep 08
N/A	N/A	Total internet: total audience	35,980
1	1	Google Sites	31,769
2	2	Microsoft Sites	28,828
3	3	Yahoo! Sites	21,015
4	4	eBay	19,769
5	6	FACEBOOK.COM	18,410
6	5	BBC Sites	18,181
7	7	AOL LLC	16,793
8	9	Wikimedia Foundation Sites	13,641
9	8	Ask Network	13,565
10	10	Amazon Sites	11,417
11	12	Apple Inc.	10,168
12	11	Fox Interactive Media	9,989
13	13	Lycos Europe Sites	9,529
14	14	DMGT	8,688
15	15	CBS Corporation	8,470
16	16	Sky Sites	7,706
17	27	Glam Media	6,845
18	19	Tesco Stores	6,487
19	17	Home Retail Group	6,423
20	18	Yellow Book Network	6,367
21	20	News International	6,102
22	24	Adobe Sites	5,937
23	30	WordPress	5,422
24	23	Viacom Digital	5,213
25	26	The Royal Bank Of Scotland	5,181

Notes: Top 25 properties by number of UK unique visitors. Total UK, age 15+, home and work locations.
Ranking based on the top 100 UK properties in August 2008.
Source: Adapted from The Nielsen Company (http://uk.nielsen.com).

Also, use of internet-delivered TV content – whether from established broadcasters or from pirate or web-only sources – is currently not measured in any reliable form. In principle, a software-based peoplemeter-type solution is a possibility, but as yet is not developed.

Mobile devices

The most recent change in media content delivery is in the rapid growth in mobile access to internet services, including television and video, using an increasingly wide array of portable devices such as iPods, PDAs, and mobile phones.

Table 23.3 Top 10 company websites visited and patterns of use by UK home internet users

United Kingdom: Top 10 parent companies
Month of December 2008
Home panel

Property name	Unique audience (000)	Reach %	Time per person
Google	25,299	84.98	01:17:14
Microsoft	23,172	77.83	02:06:12
Yahoo!	15,198	51.05	01:09:03
eBay	15,134	50.83	01:32:31
BBC	14,493	48.68	00:36:39
Facebook	13,632	45.79	04:28:37
Amazon	13,221	44.41	00:24:51
AOL LLC	9,845	33.07	02:06:30
Apple Computer	9,039	30.36	01:08:32
InterActiveCorp	8,552	28.72	00:06:40

United Kingdom: average web usage
Month of December 2008
Home panel

Sessions/visits per person	34
Domains visited per person	71
PC time per person	31:56:52
Duration of a web page viewed	00:00:50
Active digital media universe	29,772,512
Current digital media universe estimate	39,541,956

Source: Nielsen Online (http://uk.nielsen.com). Copyright © Nielsen Online. Reproduced with permission.

For internet use, some of this activity can be tracked using existing methods – ComScore in the UK for example can produce estimates of TV use via mobile devices, and some portable peoplemeter systems could be adapted to new tasks. Several other research companies and organisations such as BARB are also working on a range of possible strategies and methods to assess the use of mobile communications devices and the range of content which can be delivered by them.

At present, the situation remains confused, with rival methods and systems in the field. For many purposes, tried and tested methods – interviews and/or questionnaires – can provide basic details of patterns of use of almost any technology. What they cannot deliver is the very fine details: how many seconds was this looked at? Where did the user move on to? However, given the increasing complexities of people's interactions with technologies, there will continue to be a pressure for 'passive' methods – real or virtual devices that track behaviour without disrupting that behaviour at the same time.

Conclusions

In the UK in December 2008 over 93 per cent of people used TV at least once a week, and similar proportions listened to radio. The average viewer spent between three and four hours a day viewing television, and radio users spent about three hours per day listening to the radio. Daily newspapers in 2008 were read by over 40 per cent of adults on an average day, and about 20 minutes per day were spent reading a newspaper or a magazine. It is worth noting, though, that six out of the Top 10 magazines read in 2008 were TV guides (data from BARB, RAJAR and NRS websites, accessed 10 January 2009).

Over the month of December 2008, the average home internet user in the UK spent just under 32 hours on the web, and one of the most visited websites was the BBC with 14.4 million hits from UK-based users (Nielsen UK Online website, accessed 10 January 2009). Consuming broadcasting is still a major pastime, over and above actually viewing.

The seemingly straightforward processes of measuring audiences/users to one medium or another have become far more difficult to operate, both theoretically and practically. The historic separation of different media because of their separate forms and delivery mechanisms is rapidly breaking down. This undoubtedly is a source of major benefits both for the consumers and for users of media content, while representing major challenges for the media and research industries themselves. At present, the research industries are engaged in crossing the methodological divide from separate to combined or harmonised media research methods. Without such an evolutionary process, the media industries and the companies that fund these industries through advertising or other means would themselves suffer from the inability to predict the future (and also to look back into past radical media shifts such as the introduction of TV).

Questions

1 To what extent does the media industries' research about audiences offer data that might help us understand audiences beyond measurement of who consumed what?

2 To what extent is the 'audience' to a particular medium a creation of the procedures used to measure it?

3 How can the complexity of a typical internet user's online activities be meaningfully 'captured' by research?

Further reading

Brooker, W. and Jermyn, D. (eds) (2003) *The Audience Studies Reader*, London: Routledge. Covers a wide range of theories of and approaches to different media and types of audiences.

Livingstone, S. (1998) *Making Sense of Television*, 2nd edition, London: Routledge. A detailed study of UK audiences' interactions with and uses of TV programming.

Mytton, G. (1999) *Handbook on Radio and Television Audience Research*. UNESCO/UNICEF: Geneva, available free of charge at www.cba.org.uk/audience_research/documents/ar_handbook_2007_complete.pdf, accessed 10 January 2009. A detailed but non-technical guide to the main techniques used in audience research, written by the former Head of Audience Research for the BBC World Service.

Websites

www.adassoc.org.uk
The Advertising Association UK

www.barb.co.uk
TV audience measurement

www.bbc.co.uk/bbctrust/assets/files/pdf/consult/purpose_remits/audience_research.pdf
(BBC)

www.carltonscreen.com *or* www.tnsglobal.com/news
For Fame and other cinema research

www.mrg.org.uk/evening_mth.asp
The Media Research Group, which has evening meeting presentations by members on its website

www.nrs.co.uk
For National Readership Survey

www.ofcom.org.uk/research
Regulatory research

www.postar.co.uk
Poster

www.rajar.co.uk
Radio

Media research companies

www.agbnielsen.net

www.arbitron.com

www.bmrb-tgi.co.uk

www.comscore.com/metrix or www.nielsen-netratings.com (internet)

www.gfknop.com

www.ipsos-mori.com/media

www.tnsglobal.com

References

The Advertising Association (2008), www.adassoc.org.uk/Ad_stats_yearbook_2008_8june08.pdf (accessed 10 January 2009).

BBC (2008) *Annual Report 2007*, London: BBC, www.bbc.co.uk/annualreport.

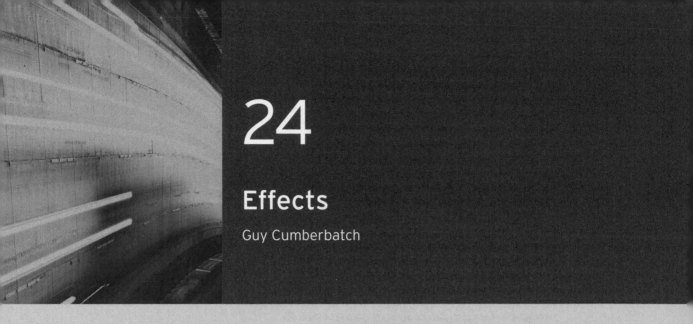

24

Effects

Guy Cumberbatch

Chapter overview

Concerns about media effects have a long history, changing little with the arrival of each new medium, and often focusing on the media's potential to aggravate crime and violence in society. In the last decade a notable US–UK divide has appeared where the majority of American reviews of the research evidence conclude that media violence is clearly harmful whereas the majority of UK reviews of the same literature disagree.

History of concerns

As Geoffrey Pearson (1983) has pointed out, there has been a long history of moral panics about the possible harmful effects of popular culture. In the 16th century 'popular songs too often presented criminals as heroes' while in 1776 Joseph Hanway suggested that 'debasing amusements' and newspapers were among the causes of 'the host of thieves which of late years has invaded us' (cited by Pearson 1983). In 1869, Greenwood complained that 'penny dreadful' comics 'may sow the seeds of immorality among as many boys as a town may produce'. By 1905, violence on the streets of Manchester was blamed on 'the horrible murders and terrible tragedies' enacted in popular theatres. Almost from their inception, the technological advances of cinema, radio and television provoked similar concerns. Since then, the unexpectedly rapid spread of video recorders in the 1980s, computer games in the 1990s and the mainstreaming of internet use in the new millennium, all seem to have inherited the legacy of fears and anxieties about earlier media without altogether eclipsing them.

Of course, the range of concerns raised about the possible effects of the mass media is extremely wide, from the almost mythical phenomenon such as alleged subliminal advertising/persuasion (Cumberbatch and Wood 1998) to more tangible issues, such as the preoccupation with overt media content (Millwood-Hargrave and Livingstone 2006). The most prevalent concern is that people – children especially – may be harmed by the mass media, and particularly that crime and violence in the media may fuel crime and violence in society. Indeed, an ICM poll taken in 2003, which asked the UK public 'Do you believe that on-screen violence (in the form of films, television and computer games) encourages violence in society or not?' found that 73 per cent of respondents (and 86 per cent of those over 45) thought that it did. Similar results have been reported for the USA (Potter 2003).

On-screen violence has also been one of the most enduring of concerns, providing the initiative for a wide variety of legislation aimed at controlling the media – including the establishment of the British Board of Film Censors (BBFC) – as early as 1912. However, it also provided the focus for some of the earliest research in mass communications and helps to illuminate some of the many methodological and conceptual problems which pervade the study of effects.

Early research

Perhaps the most notable of early studies were those by the Payne Fund which was set up in New York in 1928 to study the impact and influences of motion pictures on youth. It produced 12 independent studies with a summary volume written by Charters (1933). There was some disagreement between the researchers about the true influence of film. Most of the studies found that delinquents and truants went to the cinema more often than others – but was it possible to establish a relationship of cause and effect between the two, or was cinema just somewhere to go? Charters was unwilling to attribute delinquency to the effects of the films, concluding that, despite public anxiety about the new medium, any influences were fairly modest and fairly superficial in such visible things as fashion, rather than morals.

Somewhat similar conclusions were reached in the UK in 1951 by the Departmental Committee on Children and the Cinema (the Wheare Committee) which sponsored a very large survey of all juvenile offenders appearing before the courts over a six-month period. This produced an impressive sample of 38,000 young offenders – perhaps too many to study in any depth. Nevertheless the committee considered that, of these, perhaps in 141 cases (i.e. just under 0.4 per cent) the offending behaviour might be related to cinema attendance (Home Office 1951).

The most broadly based studies of media effects were carried out as television was being introduced extensively to the UK (Himmelweit *et al.* 1958) and to the USA (Schramm *et al.* 1961). Both these studies were able to compare areas which had begun to receive television with those which were still waiting for the new medium. They make fascinating reading, not the least in how people found the time to accommodate the new medium. Himmelweit *et al.* introduced the concept of 'functional similarity' to explain why some activities declined (like cinema attendance and comic book reading) but left others untouched (such as teenage social activities and sports). However, the bulk of the time found for television seems to have been drawn from essentially time-wasting activities (like watching raindrops run down a window pane).

In terms of harmful effects, very little support was found for the popular concerns about television, although it should be noted that many of the measures used were fairly cursory. Schramm *et al.*'s conclusion was a classic in circumspection:

> For *some* children under *some* conditions, *some* television is harmful. For *other* children under the same conditions, or for the same children under *other* conditions, it may be beneficial. For *most* children under *most* conditions *most* television is probably neither particularly harmful nor particularly beneficial. (Schramm *et al.* 1961: 1)

Despite the generally reassuring tone of much of this early research, the 1960s saw a rapid growth of psychological research into media aggression, largely stimulated by the laboratory experiments of Albert Bandura at Stanford University and Leonard Berkowitz at Wisconsin.

Imitation

In the early 1960s Bandura published a series of experiments demonstrating that when young children were exposed to a film clip of someone behaving aggressively, they were more likely to play in a similarly aggressive manner than a control group of children who had not seen the film. This research has become something of a classic and is one of the most cited in psychology textbooks. Bandura soon became quite convinced that violence on television would lead to observational learning by children – imitating what they saw – and became involved with various campaigns against violence on television.

Bandura's experiments were certainly impressive in the results obtained. Up to 88 per cent of the children imitated the aggressive acts which they had seen on television (Bandura 1994). However, some details of the experiments are worth noting. Pre-school (3–5 year-old) children were used – mostly recruited from the university crèche. The specially prepared film clip featured a model (initially an adult but, in later experiments, another child) assaulting a large inflated plastic clown called a 'Bobo' or 'Bozo' doll which, due to its weighted base, would bounce back up again when hit. The model engaged in various 'aggressive' acts, uttering comments from a prepared script such as 'Pow!' and 'Whack it, eh!' After being exposed to the model's curious antics, the children were led from the viewing room to the laboratory where they would be observed. On the way there, they passed some very attractive toys, which the researcher invited them to admire and handle asking if they would like to play with them, only to be told 'well you can't!' The children, described by Bandura as 'frustrated', then entered the laboratory, which contained a three-foot high Bozo doll and various other toys. The children were ostensibly left alone to play but were secretly observed through one-way mirrors and their behaviour logged in terms of imitative (i.e. copying something seen in the film) or non-imitative aggressive behaviour.

Limitation

Of course, one key observation might be that this kind of imitative behaviour cannot be classified as aggression after all, since there is not much else one can do to a Bozo doll except hit it. Indeed my own Bozo doll was wrecked due to the enthusiasm of an elderly professor who could not resist the temptation to kick it (giggling unashamedly as he did so) whenever he came to my office! Ironically, other research using the Bandura paradigm has found that the novelty of the toy was a big factor in producing imitation – when children had been allowed to play with the doll before the experiment, imitation of the model tended to be much less frequent.

Another limiting factor is that the films were somewhat contrived (for example each aggressive act was repeated three times). Grant Noble, who carried out a large research programme on young children using TV programmes and commercially available films, maintained that he rarely observed more than 5 per cent of cases of imitation. He also suggested that children may not behave naturally in such studies but take their cues from the experimenter. He quotes one shrewd four-year-old who, on her *first* visit to a Bandura-like laboratory, was heard to whisper to her mother:

'Look, mummy! There's the doll we have to hit!'   (Noble 1975: 134)

In more naturalistic settings, results have been equivocal. For example Gadow and Sprafkin critically reviewed 20 naturalistic field experiments where young children were exposed to various film clips or television programmes. They noted that, while the aggressive material often produced high levels of aggressive behaviour, sometimes the control film produced even more. Even fast-paced pro-social educational programmes (like *Sesame Street*) resulted in more aggressive responses than the control film. They conclude that the available literature 'provides little support for an effect which is peculiar to aggressive content' (Gadow and Sprafkin 1989: 404).

Finally, despite concerns that violent video games might encourage imitation because they involve aggressive role play, Irvin and Gross (1995) failed to find such imitation (of Nintendo's *Double Dragon*) in seven-year-olds even though their experiment had been designed to 'maximise modelling cues' (Irvin and Gross 1995: 347).

The simple notion of imitation cannot do justice to the more sophisticated theory of social learning which Bandura developed. Such learning is an important part of socialisation and obviously some children – and even adults – do *sometimes* imitate what they see on television. Indeed, in one study of young video gamers (between seven and 16 years-old), almost six out of 10 (58 per cent) interviewees said they had seen somebody copying from video games and, of these, 77 per cent spontaneously mentioned fighting. However *all* the young people that had been interviewed thought that when children copied violent games, they were enacting *pretend* violence, not serious violence (Cumberbatch *et al.* 1994). The crucial issue here must be whether crime and violence in society are aggravated by people imitating what is carried by the media.

Realisation

A good authority on this subject is James Ferman who, for more than a quarter of a century, was Director of the BBFC (now the British Board of Film Classification). Whenever some crime occurred where claims were made that it was linked to violence on the screen, he had to investigate. Did he think that there were cases – as routinely reported in the mass media – of such imitation? After all, in 1987 Michael Ryan shot dead 16 people with a Kalashnikov rifle in the sleepy English village of Hungerford, allegedly imitating Rambo in *First Blood*. It said so in the newspapers. When Ferman was questioned about this by the House of Commons Home Affairs Select Committee in 1994, he replied:

> I do not know of particular cases where somebody has imitated a video and gone out and actually committed a serious crime as a result of what they have seen.
>
> (Home Affairs Committee, Fourth Report 1994: 5)

Similar conclusions were reached in the flagship documentary *Panorama* by Kate Adie (the BBC's chief news correspondent) and her team. In 1988, they thoroughly researched six cases where a crime had been confidently 'linked' to the mass media. None of the cases, including the massacre in Hungerford, were supported by the evidence.

Red herrings

Since then there have been regular reports of media inspired crime in the UK, none of which has been substantiated. Perhaps the best known of these has been the murder of a two-year-old toddler, James Bulger, who was battered to death on a railway line in Merseyside by two 10 year-old boys. In sentencing them, the judge, Mr Justice Moorland, claimed that 'exposure to violent video films may, in part, be an explanation'. Newspapers quickly identified *Child's Play 3* as the film which the boys had re-enacted. The *Sun* newspaper (26 November 1993) even organised a public burning of the video. However the investigating police officer – Detective Superintendent Albert Kirby – had specifically looked for any media links and concluded there were none. It is true that Neil Venables, the father of one of the boys, had rented the film some three months earlier but since his son, Jon, was not living with him at the time, Kirby concluded that it was unlikely that the boy might have had the opportunity to see it. Moreover, the boy disliked horror films and was upset by violence in videos – a point confirmed by later psychiatric reports. Of course, such mundane facts could not be allowed to spoil a good story or the campaigns calling for a 'crackdown' on video violence.

Perhaps equally notorious is the murder of 14-year-old Stefan Pakeerah who was stabbed and repeatedly beaten with a claw hammer by his 17-year-old friend Warren LeBlanc. Stefan's mother maintained that there were strong similarities between this tragic event and the '18' rated video game *Manhunt* and called for it to be banned. Among the more restrained headlines, one read: 'Killing incited by video game' (the *Guardian*, 29 July 2004). However, only the local newspaper emphasised that the police had decided that there was no link between the crime and the video game and that both 'The prosecution and defence barristers insisted at Leicester Crown Court that the video game played no part in the killing' (the *Leicester Mercury*, 3 September 2004).

This tragedy is particularly interesting since the BBFC referred to it to explain why they had refused to certificate *Manhunt 2*, noting that the original *Manhunt* had 'achieved notoriety when linked to the murder of Stefan Pakeerah'. They added in parentheses that '(The Board is aware that this link has not been proven)', nonetheless suggesting there was something in it after all (evidence to Video Appeals Committee, 26 November 2007: 4).

Damning links

Probably the biggest concern about media violence has been that of possible cumulative effects on the development of young children. Although it might seem relatively simple to investigate this, it has become something of a minefield. The early Payne Fund studies had certainly identified a 'link' between cinema attendance and delinquency, while a number of other studies conducted before World War Two had found that delinquents made use of comic books more often than others – thus fuelling concerns about the negative influence of the media (Howitt and Cumberbatch 1975). However the problem is interpreting the link between the two – i.e. is the delinquency the *root* or the *fruit*? Does the medium *cause* delinquency or vice versa? Considering the cost of research, it is astonishing that so much effort has been put into trying to establish a link, rather than attempting to unravel it.

The sample sizes of the numerous surveys conducted on the topic run to hundreds of thousands of respondents and the majority have revealed some association between consumption of violent media and some degree of aggression. However, the effect size is small. Paik and Comstock (1994) reported an average correlation (r) of +0.19 in their meta-analysis of 410 results – thus less than 4 per cent (3.61 per cent) of the variance in aggression could be predicted from television viewing patterns. Additionally, many of the results are inconsistent and contradictory. For example, one of the best early studies by McLeod, Atkin and Chaffee in 1972 found the correlation between the amount of television violence watched and aggression was three times higher in girls than boys even though other contemporary studies quite consistently reported no significant results for girls (see Cumberbatch and Howitt 1989).

Missing links

As might be expected, boys tend to consume more violent media and tend to be more aggressive than girls. Thus any study combining the results of boys and girls would show an overall correlation between violent media and aggression entirely due to gender differences. Sadly this point does not seem obvious to all researchers. For example, Anderson and Dill (2000) report a significant relationship between video game play and feelings of insecurity and mention almost as an afterthought that this becomes insignificant when gender is controlled for!

There are numerous variables, such as gender, which can produce spurious links between the media and aggression. Another of these would be social class. For example, in the UK at least, C2DE children watch almost one third more television than their ABC1 counterparts (Cumberbatch 2004) and are also more likely to become delinquent (Halloran *et al.* 1970; Flood-Page *et al.* 2000). TV consumption and aggression are also age related in children, both rising until the early teens, when TV viewing starts declining. Another example of a variable which is rarely controlled for is provided by Singer *et al.* (1999) who found that preferences for violent programmes were correlated with self-reported aggressive behaviour in a sample of 2245 young people. However, witnessing violence in the *real world* was correlated *three times* more strongly with self-reported aggression. Similarly Ferguson *et al.* (2008) concluded that exposure to family violence was a crucial variable to control when looking at the potential effect of violent video games (which did not show any causal link to aggression).

Slater *et al.* (2003) showed that personality traits, such as sensation seeking and aggressivity, lead to selective exposure to media violence and hypothesised that this exposure reinforces aggressivity (the 'downward spiral model'). Although the model is speculative, more importantly they concluded that:

If the same predispositions that lead to aggressive behavior also lead to using violent media content, many of the relationships found in cross-sectional and even longitudinal studies might be called into question.

(Slater *et al.* 2003: 715)

Time bomb . . .

Although there are a certain number of longitudinal studies that have been conducted (including that of Slater *et al.* mentioned above), the first of importance was completed in 1972. Eron and Huesmann had measured aggression and television violence exposure in eight and nine year-olds and followed them up 10 years later. They claimed a 'Rip Van Winkle' or 'sleeper effect' where *early* television viewing predicted *later* aggression. While this is true of one of their measures of aggression in boys, two other measures did not support the hypothesis and none of the measures were significant in girls. Stronger claims were made for their more modest cross-national study in Australia, Finland, Holland, Israel, Poland and the USA where children were followed up over three years. Huesmann and Eron (1986) again claimed a sleeper effect and that the findings were 'robust' and 'travel well'. Gunter writes that the results support the idea of 'a sensitive period – probably up to the age of 10 – during which television can be especially influential' (Gunter 1994: 174).

. . . or damp squib?

On closer examination the results show a very mixed pattern:

- The Dutch researchers concluded that their results simply did not provide evidence of any effects of television and refused to allow them to be included in the edited book (Wiegman *et al.* 1992).

- In Australia there were no significant correlations between early television violence viewing and later aggression.

- In the USA, after controlling for initial aggression, the relationship between early violence viewing and later aggression was only significant in girls.

- In Israel, significant effects were found in the city samples but not in the Kibbutz samples.

- In Poland, while the authors recognised that the house style of the book should concur that 'a greater preference for violence viewing was predictive of greater aggression' they also admitted that 'nevertheless the effects are not large and must be treated cautiously'.

- In Finland the researchers concluded that 'our study in Finland can be taken to corroborate the previously obtained results that the amount of aggressive behavior in children is related to their viewing of violence on TV . . .' However the results were not significant for girls and it is apparent from the full report (Viemero 1986) that, while there is indeed a relationship in boys, it is actually negative (-0.324). In other words, the more boys watched violent television, the *less* aggressive they became later!

Although, in principle, longitudinal studies hold the promise of illuminating any possible cumulative effects of violent media, in reality they almost all suffer from failures to control the 'confounding' variables which we know correlate with both media use and aggression. Anderson and Bushman (2002) claim that the average correlation found in these studies between early TV violence and later aggression is $+0.17$ (i.e. explaining less than 3 per cent of the variance in aggression). However, in reality this figure is quite inflated by the confounding variables.

Despite a fanfare of publicity in the late 1990s for a UNESCO Global Study on Media Violence, the research turned out to be quite cursory and the interpretation lame. The Swedish coordinator, Jo Groebel, concluded that 'There is a link between the preference for media violence and the need to be involved in aggression oneself' (see Carlsson and von Felitz 1998: 16). But is the link causal?

Priming aggression

Perhaps the strongest claims that the media can have harmful effects have come from the laboratory experiments that followed in the footsteps of Leonard Berkowitz since the 1960s. Berkowitz suggested that observing (media) violence 'triggers' or 'primes' aggressive thinking and emotions and incited aggressive be-haviour. Although the experimental designs evolved over time to become quite complex and his theoretical position became more sophisticated, essentially the studies involved showing either violent or 'neutral' film clips to university stu-dents and measuring their aggression. Half of the participants were 'anger aroused' (by a confederate of the experimenter insulting the participants) and half were treated neutrally. They were then given the chance to deliver electric shocks to the confederate (who did not suffer since the delivery was faked). Berkowitz con-cluded that violent film clips produced aggressive behaviour (i.e. electric shocks) in those who were angry, especially when the violence in the film was justified (see Berkowitz 1993). Support for his theory is claimed from a variety of experi-ments including some where firearms were casually left around the laboratory to test the hypothesis that such aggressive stimuli might induce aggression. When weapons were present, participants produced more aggression – leading Berkowitz to conclude that, to some extent, it is 'the gun that pulls the trigger' (see Anderson *et al.* 1998).

This idea that media violence stimulates aggressive thinking has been popular – perhaps not the least because it allows experimenters to use fairly simple quanti-tative measures. One example of this is the measurement of the reaction time to 'aggressive words'. (There are, of course, practical and ethical problems with mea-suring actual aggression.) Craig Anderson has been one of the most prolific re-searchers in this field. His *General Aggression Model* embraces both priming and imitation theories but also includes the notion that through the mass media peo-ple can learn aggressive 'scripts' (which are sets of 'rules' about how to interpret, understand and deal with a variety of situations, such as conflict). There is some overlap here with the 'cultivation theory' of George Gerbner who claimed that we develop a 'mean world' view by watching violence (see Signorielli and Morgan 1990). However, the idea of 'scripts' originates from the work of Rowell Huesmann in the 1980s (see Anderson and Huesmann 2003).

Particularly over the past 10 years, Anderson has blitzed journals with research evidence about the harmful effects of media violence – especially video games (e.g. Anderson *et al.* 2007). However, he persistently reports only findings that support his case and glosses over those measures which do not (e.g. Cumberbatch 2000; Cumberbatch 2004). Ferguson (2007) agrees, pointing out that Anderson's claims about the overall effect of video games merely show the publication bias of journals which favour this kind of results. After re-examining Anderson's results, Ferguson computed a correction for this publication bias and showed that the overall effect then became effectively zero.

Training kids to kill?

Although media scholars in the UK have been more than sceptical about this tra-dition of effects research for decades (e.g. Gauntlett 2005) such critics are very much a minority in the USA. There have been some exceptionally insightful cri-tiques (e.g. Freedman 2002), however dissenting voices are quite marginalised.

The most recent report *Violent Television Programming and Its Impact on Children* by the Federal Communications Commission (2007) is quite unequivocal:

These findings make clear, and the Commission today affirms, that exposure to violent programming can be harmful to children.   (Chairman Kevin J Martin, FCC 2007: 25)

Following a four-year inquiry, the Commission recommended to Congress that legislation should be passed to curtail television violence, advising that this would not be incompatible with freedom of speech. Over the years the majority of relevant professional bodies have supported the view that the research evidence points 'overwhelmingly to a causal connection between media violence and aggressive behavior in some children'. (In 2000, a joint statement agreeing this wording was issued by the American Academy of Pediatrics, the American Academy of Child and Adolescent Psychiatry, the American Medical Association, the American Psychological Association, the American Academy of Family Physicians and the American Psychiatric Association (Anderson *et al.* 2003: 82).) For some years, media violence has been presented as a public health threat. The evidence has been alleged to be as strong as that between smoking and lung cancer (Huesmann and Taylor 2006).

... or just torturing data?

In the UK, reviews of the research evidence on media violence commissioned by regulatory bodies have reliably pointed to the weaknesses (see Brody 1976 (for the Home Office); Cumberbatch and Howitt 1989 (for the Broadcasting Standards Commission); Cumberbatch 1995 (for the Council of Europe); Harris 2001(for the Home Office); Boyle and Hibberd 2005 (for the Department of Culture, Media and Sport); Byron 2008 (for the Department for Children, School and Families)). In their deliberation on *Manhunt 2*, the Video Appeals Committee (2007) noted that members had had to read a considerable amount of research literature. However, they concluded that 'there are substantial limitations to the research. Firstly, most of the research is from North America, it is inconsistent and the most vociferous proponent of a causal link between video game playing and violence, Dr Anderson, has been roundly criticized by many and his evidence has not been accepted in courts in the United States' (Judgment, 11 December 2007).

This intriguing suggestion, i.e. that effects research may not have persuaded everyone in the USA, can be checked via the Entertainment and Software Association's website (www.thesa.com/archives) where court rulings can also be found. In each case, the judge has decided that the research evidence supporting the idea that media violence causes harm was unconvincing. Adjectives such as 'tentative', 'speculative' and so on are more in line with UK perspectives.

Violence in the media

Although some researchers seem to think that they know what kind of media violence poses the greatest risk of harm to children (e.g. National Television Violence Study 1997; Gunter *et al.* 2003) this attitude must be considered quite reckless for two reasons. First of all, the research is deeply flawed. Secondly, there is no pattern in the aggression outcomes anyway. The most ambitious attempt to identify the kinds of media content which might 'cause' later aggressive behaviour in youths (Belson 1978) have found that non-violent television, comics, comic books and newspapers also correlated with later aggression.

More than this, there is not any convincing evidence that the effects of violence in video games is any different from that of MTV (Gentile *et al.* 2004) or rap music (Anderson *et al.* 2003) or that carried by the news (Pierce 2005). Indeed, Anderson *et al.* (1998) found that aggressive stimuli as printed words were more effective at priming aggression than pictures! Davies *et al.* (2004) report that nursery rhymes have a rate of 52 violent scenes per hour – 12 higher than television and ask: 'Could nursery rhymes cause violent behaviour?' Coyne and Archer (2005) report that the rate of indirect aggression on TV (e.g. making nasty comments) is much higher than direct physical aggression and conclude that it may have more influence on viewers. All of the above suggests that there is really no hiding place unless viewers are to be fed a media diet with the stimulating properties of porridge, healthy though this might be.

Violence to the media

The most notable feature of the vast research literature on media effects is for strong conclusions about harm to be reached on rather weak data. The devil is always in the detail and only close scrutiny reveals the inconsistencies in the findings. Of course, attempting to disentangle media effects when the media are so embedded in our culture presents practical problems. Much of the 'evidence' relies merely on establishing a link whereby, for example, aggressive children may be shown to enjoy media violence. But this can tell us little about how such individuals are *changed* by the process, if at all. Indeed, in the UK at least, the pattern emerging from Hagell and Newburn's (1994) study of young offenders was that, compared with a school control group, the delinquents reported having *fewer* television sets, were *less* able to name favourite television programmes or characters they would like to be like and were *less* likely to go to the cinema. As Messner (1986) concluded, the pattern for delinquents is for them to be out on the streets offending rather than to be at home watching television – violent or otherwise.

As a final point, perhaps the largest deficiency in the various studies lies in the grossly oversimplified approach to both media content and media experiences. For example, Viemero's (1986) study, carried out in the 1980s, categorises the following UK programmes as having the same 'violence score': *The Benny Hill Show*; *Bergerac*; *Magnum*; *Dallas* and *Woody Woodpecker*. In most studies the old *Batman* series are considered 'violent' even though the heroes are portrayed as excessively moral beings (Cumberbatch 1994). Whether children perceive these moral narratives is, of course, another matter (Buckingham 1996) but it is as much a disservice to research as it is to children or to the media not to ask. As Marvin observes:

Understanding how cultures circulate meanings about the exercise of physical force requires a richer background language and thicker description and appraisals than can be found in the

simplifying presumption that such representations are inevitably coarsening, frequently dangerous and always to be avoided.
(Marvin 2000: 148)

Quite so.

Questions

1 In what different ways do we 'circulate meanings about the exercise of physical force' in our culture?

2 What would you say to a Home Secretary who felt that a 'crackdown' on media violence was necessary?

3 Taking any *one* social problem (such as crime; drink-driving; child abuse; racism; unsafe sex; unhealthy lifestyle) what various roles might the media play in aggravating or ameliorating it as a social problem?

4 If US and UK reviews disagree on what conclusions can be drawn from the research evidence on media effects, why might this be?

Further reading

Barker, M. and Petley, J. (eds) (2001) *Ill Effects: The Media/Violence Debate*, 2nd edition, London: Routledge. A lively account and critique of media violence as a moral panic.

Cumberbatch, G. (2004) *Video Violence: Villain or Victim?* London: Brittania, www.videostandards.org.uk/downloads/video_violence.zip (accessed 20 February 2009). A comprehensive, critical review of research evidence on media violence.

Gauntlett, D. (2006) *Moving Experiences: Media Effects and Beyond,* 2nd edition, London: John Libbey. A clear exposition of old and new directions in effects research.

Goldstein, J. (ed) (1998) *Why We Watch: The Attractions of Violent Entertainment*, New York: Oxford University Press. A fascinating collection of essays from a wide variety of disciplines covering a wide variety of forms of entertainment.

Millwood-Hargrave, A. and Livingstone, S. (2006) *Harm and Offence in Media Content: A Review of the Evidence*, London: Intellect. Particularly useful in covering the original programme of research by the Broadcasting Standards Commission.

Weaver, C. K. and Carter C. (eds) (2006) *Critical Readings: Violence and the Media*, Maidenhead: Open University Press. Very useful sourcebook of reprints.

References

Anderson, C., Benjamin, A. J. and Bartholow, B. D. (1998) 'Does the Gun Pull the Trigger: Automatic Priming Effect of Weapon Pictures and Weapon Names', *Psychological Science*, 9 (4): 308-14.

Anderson, C. A. and Bushman, B. J. (2002) 'Media Violence and the American Public Revisited' *American Psychologist,* 57(6-7): 448-50.

Anderson, C. and Dill, K. E. (2000) 'Video Games and Aggressive Thoughts, Feelings and Behavior in the Laboratory and in Life', *Journal of Personality and Social Psychology*, 78 (4): 773-90.

Anderson, C. A., Gentile, D. A. and Buckley, K. E. (2007) *Violent Video Game Effects on Children and Adolescents,* New York: Oxford University Press.

Anderson, C. A. and Huesmann, R. L. (2003) 'Human Aggression: A Social Cognitive View' in M. A. Hogg and J. Cooper (eds) *Handbook of Social Psychology.* London: Sage, pp. 296–323.

Anderson, C., Berkowitz, L., Donnerstein, E., Huesmann, L. R., Johnson, J. D., Linz, D. Malamuth, N. M. and Wartella, E. (2003) 'The influence of media on youth', *Psychological Science in the Public Interest,* 4 (3): 81–110.

Bandura, A. (1994) 'Social Cognitive Theory of Mass Communication' in J. Bryant and D. Zillman (eds) *Media Effects: Advances in Theory and Research*, Hillsdale, NJ: Lawrence Erlbaum, pp. 61–90.

Belson, W.A. (1978) *Television Violence and the Adolescent Boy*, Farnborough: Teakfield.

Berkowitz, L. (1993) *Aggression: Its Causes, Consequences and Control*, New York: McGraw-Hill.

Boyle, R. and Hibberd, M. (2005) *Review of Research on the Impact of Violent Computer Games on Young People*, http://www.culture.gov.uk/reference_library/publications/3539.aspx (accessed 19 February 2009).

Brody, S. (1976) *Screen Violence and Film Censorship*, London: Home Office.

Buckingham, D. (1996) *Moving Images: Understanding Children's Emotional Responses to Television*, Manchester: Manchester University Press.

Byron, T. (2008) *Safer Children in a Digital World*, www.dcsf.gov.uk/byronreview/ (accessed 19 February 2009).

Carlsson, U. and von Felitzen, C. (eds) (1998) *Children and Media Violence Yearbook*, Gothenburg, Sweden: Nordicom.

Charters, W. W. (1933) *Motion Pictures and Youth: A Summary*, New York: Macmillan.

Coyne, S. M. and Archer, J. (2005) 'The Relationship Between Indirect and Physical Aggression on Television and in Real Life', *Social Development*, 14 (2): 324–8.

Cumberbatch, G. (1994) 'Legislating mythology: video violence and children' *Journal of Mental Health* 3: 485–94. www.academicarmageddon.co.uk/library/CUMB.htm (accessed 19 February 2009).

Cumberbatch, G. (1995) *Media Violence: Research evidence and policy implications*, Strasburg: Council of Europe, www.academicarmageddon.co.uk/library/EURO.htm (accessed 19 February 2009).

Cumberbatch, G. (2000) 'Only a Game?' *New Scientist*, 10 June (2242): 44–5.

Cumberbatch, G. (2004) *Video Violence: Villain or Victim?* London: Brittania/Video Standards Council.

Cumberbatch, G and Howitt, D. (1989) *A Measure of Uncertainty: The Effects of the Mass Media*, London: John Libbey.

Cumberbatch, G. and Wood, G. (1998) *The Evidence of Things not Seen: Television Images of Short Duration*, London: ITC.

Cumberbatch, G., Maguire, A. and Woods, S. (1994) *Children and Video Games: An Exploratory Study*, London: ELSPA.

Davies, P., Lee, L., Fox, A. and Fox, E. (2004) 'Could Nursery Rhymes Cause Violent Behaviour?' *Archive of Disease in Childhood,* 89: 1103–5.

Federal Communications Commission (2007) *Violent Television Programming and Its Impact on Children*, Washington D.C. FCC 07-50.

Ferguson, C.J. (2007) 'The Good, The Bad and The Ugly: A Meta-analytic Review of Positive and Negative Effects of Violent Video Games', *Psychiatric Quarterly,* 78 (4): 309–16.

Ferguson, C. J., Rueda, S. M., Cruz, A. M., Ferguson, D. M., Fritz, S. and Smith, S. M. (2008) 'Violent Video Games and Aggression: Causal Relationship or Byproduct of Family Violence and Intrinsic Violence Motivation?' *Criminal Justice and Behavior*, 35 (3): 311–32.

Flood-Page, C., Campbell, S., Harrington, V. and Miller, J. (2000) *Youth Crime: Findings from the 1988/1989 Youth Lifestyles Survey,* Home Office Research Study 209, London: Home Office.

Freedman, J. L. (2002) *Media Violence and Its Effect on Aggression: Assessing the Scientific Evidence*, Toronto, Canada: University of Toronto Press.

Gadow, K. D. and Sprafkin, J. (1989) 'Field Experiments of Television Violence', *Pediatrics*, 83 (3): 399-405.

Gauntlett, D. (2005) *Moving Experiences: Media Effects and Beyond*, 2nd edition, London: John Libbey.

Gentile, D. A., Lynch, P. L., Linder, J. R. and Walsh, D. A. (2004) 'The Effects of Violent Video Game Habits on Adolescent Hostility, Aggressive Behaviors and School Performance', *Journal of Adolescence*, 27 (1): 5-22.

Gunter, B. (1994) 'The Question of Media Violence' in J. Bryant and D. Zillman (eds) *Media Effects: Advances in Theory and Research*, Hillsdale, NJ: Lawrence Erlbaum, pp. 163-211.

Gunter, B., Harrison, J. and Wykes, M. (2003) *Violence on Television*, London: Lawrence Erlbaum.

Hagell, A. and Newburn, T. (1994) *Young Offenders and the Media*, London: Batisford.

Halloran, J. D., Brown, R. L. and Chaney, D. C. (1970) *Television and Delinquency*, Leicester: Leicester University Press.

Harris, J. (2001) *The Effects of Computer Games on Young Children - A Review of the Research,* RDS Occasional Paper No. 72, London: Home Office.

Himmelweit, H. T., Oppenheim, A. N. and Vince, P. (1958) *Television and the Child: An Empirical Study of the Effect of Television on the Young*, London: Oxford University Press.

Home Office (1951) *Report of the Departmental Committee on Children and Cinema*, London: Home Office.

Howitt, D. and Cumberbatch, G. (1975) *Mass Media Violence and Society,* London: Elek.

Huesmann, L. R. and Eron, L. D. (eds) (1986) *Television and the Aggressive Child: A Cross-National Comparison*, Hillsdale, NJ: Lawrence Erlbaum.

Huesmann, R. L. and Taylor, L. D. (2006) 'The Role of Media Violence in Violent Behavior', *Annual Review of Public Health*, 27: 393-415.

Irvin, A. R. and Gross, A. M. (1995) 'Cognitive Tempo, Violent Video Games and Aggressive Behavior in Young Boys', *Journal of Family Violence*, 10 (3): 337-50.

Marvin, C. (2000) 'On Violence in Media', *Journal of Communication*, 50 (1): 142-9.

Messner, S. F. (1986) 'Television Violence and Violent Crime: An Aggregate Analysis', *Social Problems*, 33 (3): 218-35.

Millwood-Hargrave, A. and Livingstone, S. (2006) *Harm and Offence in Media Content: A Review of the Evidence*, London: Intellect.

National Television Violence Study, Vol. 3 (1998), Thousand Oaks, CA: Sage.

Noble, G. (1975) *Children in Front of the Small Screen*, London: Constable.

Paik, H. and Comstock, G. (1994) 'The Effects of Television Violence on Antisocial Behavior: A Meta-analysis', *Communication Research,* 21 (4): 516-46.

Pearson, G. (1983) *Hooligan: A History of Respectable Fears*, London: Macmillan.

Pierce, T. A. (2005) 'Violence in the News: Attachment Styles as Moderators of Priming Effects' *Journal of Media Psychology*, www.calstatela.edu/faculty/sfischo/Violence_in_the_News.html.

Potter, W. J. (2003) *The 11 Myths of Media Violence*, Thousand Oaks, CA: Sage.

Schramm, W., Lyle, L. and Parker, E. B. (1961) *Television in the Lives of Our Children*, Stanford, CA: Stanford University Press.

Signorielli, N. and Morgan, M. (eds) (1990) *Cultivation Analysis: New Directions in Media Effects Research*, Newbury Park, CA: Sage.

Singer, M. J., Miller, D. B., Shenyang, G., Flannery, D. J., Frierson, T. and Slovak, K. (1999) 'Contributions to Violent Behavior Among Elementary and Middle School Children', *Pediatrics,* 104 (4): 878-904.

Slater, M. D., Henry, K. L., Swaim, R. C. and Anderson, L. L. (2003) 'Violent Media Content and Aggressiveness in Adolescents: A Downward Spiral Model', *Communication Research,* 30 (6): 713-36.

Viemero, V. (1986) *Relationships between Filmed Violence and Aggression,* Åbo Akademi, Finland: Akademisk Avhandling Monograph Supplement 4.

Wiegman, O., Kuttschreuter, M. and Baarda, B. (1992) 'A Longitudinal Study of the Effects of Television Viewing on Aggressive and Pro-social Behaviours', *British Journal of Social Psychology*, 31 (2): 147-64.

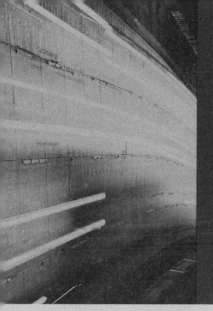

25

Impacts and Influences

Jenny Kitzinger

Chapter overview

This chapter summarises debates about media effects/influence and introduces readers to recent research around this issue. It briefly reviews historical developments and critically examines assumptions about direct media impacts while also challenging those who dismiss questions of media influence. The chapter then goes on to outline qualitative studies which address the complexity of people's engagement with media coverage of contemporary events. Such studies, I argue, constitute a valuable body of 'new effects/influence research' which demonstrates multiple ways in which mass media representation can influence how we understand, and engage with, the world around us.

The effects of communication: a brief history of theoretical approaches

A long history lies behind questions about how communication affects or influences people.[1] Even in one-to-one conversations each of us implicitly mobilises theories about how to influence our listeners. We communicate in order, for example, to seek cooperation or invite confidences, to reassure or to inform. We may wish to make others understand how we feel, invite debate or simply want to entertain our friends. We tailor our words to different audiences, depending on our relationship and what we know about them. Sometimes we consciously alter what is said, or the *way* we say it, in order to maximise its impact.

Public speaking, and the printed word, involves a different type of relationship. In this case the communicator is often addressing many different people at the same time and may be separated from them by both time and space. It is not possible to know one's audience in the same way or, necessarily, directly, to observe their response and tailor communication accordingly. Formal theories about how best to communicate to a wider audience have been consciously explored throughout history by political, religious and military leaders, as well as philosophers, playwrights and poets. The ancient Greeks, for example, developed highly sophisticated hypotheses about how to impress listeners through the spoken word. Aristotle's 'Treatise on Rhetoric' (fourth century BC) was concerned with theorising the art of speaking. It examined 'the recesses and windings' of the human heart, in order to discover 'how to "to excite, to ruffle, to amuse, to gratify or to offend it"' (Copleston 1810 cited in Eldridge *et al.* 1997).

In the 20th century, mass communication studies developed as a distinct discipline with a focus on television and newspapers and, to a lesser extent, cinema and radio. Mass communication technologies developed which reached thousands or even millions of people simultaneously, and a single programme could be viewed nationally, or even globally. Questions about effect thus became all the more pressing, as well as complex.

The origin of modern media studies is usually located in 1930s Germany associated with work by scholars such as Adorno, Marcuse and Horkheimer. It is these writers who coined the term 'mass culture' – a concept originally suggested by the Nazi Propaganda machine. Their theories were developed in response to Germany's descent into fascism. This work, collectively known as 'the Frankfurt School', theorised that social disintegration left people vulnerable to propaganda. The Frankfurt School promoted a 'hypodermic model' of media effects whereby messages were directly absorbed into the hearts and minds of the people (rather like a drug injected directly into the bloodstream).

Many other theories and approaches to the media have developed since then. The Frankfurt School's 'hypodermic model' was challenged by subsequent work highlighting the importance of personal influence. These studies showed how social mediation and opinion leaders within communities filtered and shaped how messages were received by the general population (Merton 1946; Katz and Lazersfeld 1955). Other researchers argued that people select from media messages for their own purposes and that the media is therefore more likely to be used to *reinforce*, rather than to change existing attitudes (Blumler and McQuail 1968).

From the 1970s onwards a new strand of audience research developed which revealed the diverse ways in which different people may respond to the same television programme. Such work highlights the fact that the messages 'decoded' by audiences are not necessarily those intended by the programme producers (Hall 1973). Research exploring how different groups of people engage with the media shows that we are not blank slates ready to uncritically absorb whatever we see or hear. How we respond to a particular programme or newspaper article may be influenced by class, gender, sexual and ethnic identity as well as wider cultural context. Fascinating data has been collected through comparing sub-cultural, cross-cultural and cross-national 'readings'. A traditional Western which casts cowboys as heroes and 'red Indians' as savages can still be enjoyed by some Native Americans who identify with the cowboy character and see him as representing a free and autonomous way of life akin to Native American values. An American soap opera understood by some viewers as a display of consumer-capitalism, will be seen by others as a critique of mainstream American values. (For further discussion see Eldridge *et al.* 1997: Chapter 12.)

The trajectory of media and cultural studies during the past 50 years increasingly insisted that we recognise audience diversity and see people as 'active' rather than passive consumers of media images (see Chapter 26). The hypodermic model of media effects has been thoroughly discredited. The growth of the new media, and breakdown of traditional relations between some 'audiences' and media producers has seemed to confirm the irrelevance of any focus on media power.

Straw-men, babies and bath water: discrediting the question of effects/influence

The fact that the hypodermic model has been exposed as too simplistic should not mean that we totally dismiss the question of media effects or influence. To do so risks, if I may mix my metaphors horribly, setting up a 'straw-man' and throwing out the baby with the bath water as well. So-called 'effects research' has become associated with a very narrow and methodologically weak strand of work. Indeed, it is even suggested that the very word 'effects' is problematic because it implies that the media influence operates rather like 'a bat hitting a ball' (Hodge and Tripp cited in Gauntlett 1995: 12). Gauntlett, for example, presents a thorough requiem for the traditional effects model in his book *Moving Experiences* (1995). He rightly condemns crude stimulus – response approaches and unreflective confusion of correlation with causation. He also attacks the politics of the traditional effects model: its focus on children and negative outcomes and its tendency to scapegoat television for problems such as crime whilst ignoring other possible factors such as inequalities (Gauntlett 1995: 116). His review of the field concludes that:

> The cumulative 'message' of this monograph is not so much that there should be no concern about television content . . . but that, scientifically speaking, you're on your own . . . The search for direct 'effects' of television on behaviour is over, every effort has been made, and they simply cannot be found. (Gauntlett 1995: 115, 120)

The problem with such conclusions is that the lack of evidence for direct, observable effects on behaviour, similar to that of 'a bat hitting a ball' is used to imply that there is no evidence that media representation is important at all. Such conclusions also ignore a whole body of new research into effects and influence which *does* justify 'concern about television content' and clearly demonstrate how media images impact on viewers' perceptions. There is, in fact, a great deal of in-depth qualitative work with audiences which provides compelling evidence about the media's role in helping to shape public understandings. I would include in this category work by, among others, Jhally and Lewis (1992), Gamson (1992), Corner, Richardson and Fenton (1990) and much of the audience reception work produced from the Glasgow Media Research Group. Such research constitutes a significant body of evidence that might usefully be identified as 'the new effects/ influence research'.

Evidence of effects and influence: 'the new effects/ influence research'

The following section outlines a range of projects developed during the late 1980s and into the 1990s which explore media influence and effects. At the time I identified these as 'new effects' research, to try to differentiate them from the old discredited work in the area. This is, of course, a label which rather dates the work! These projects are, however, quite different from those routinely reviewed in attacks on 'effects research' (and such attacks often continue in the 21st century as if alternative approaches have never been tried). The 'new effects/influence' work from this period do not pursue a simplistic search for crude correlation or adopt a shallow stimulus-response model. They all also, to a greater or lesser extent, are sensitive to audience diversity and the broader cultural context of reception. There may, of course, still be weaknesses in the method or conclusions of such studies. However, in combination, they make an important contribution to debates about effects/influence. I cannot do justice to each study here. However, I hope that a brief outline of their approach and sample of their findings will stimulate students to read the primary texts on which these summaries are based.

Jhally and Lewis's study of *The Cosby Show*

Jhally and Lewis studied audience reception of *The Cosby Show*, a situation-comedy which revolves around a black American middle class family (the parents are a doctor and a lawyer). They were interested in this programme's role in a society where, in reality, most black people are not professionals and most are much poorer than white people. Their study was designed to 'delve into the complex interaction between the program and the viewer. . . . [to] look into the delicate ideological suppositions that inform the sites where program and viewer meet to create meaning and pleasure' (Jhally and Lewis 1992: 9). They conducted 52 focus groups with white and black viewers in the US to explore whether 'television influences the way we think' (Jhally and Lewis 1992: xv). Through close attention to how people discussed the programme they conclude that there is clear evidence of influence. *The Cosby Show*, they argue was used by white people to make judgements about the position and behaviour of black people, 'observations that their actual experience of black people did not equip them to make' (Jhally and Lewis 1992: 32). The growing image on TV of black middle classes helps to create the illusion that racism is 'a thing of the past' and fuels resistance to affirmative action. *The Cosby Show* and programmes like it, they argue, obscures the class-race nexus, diverting attention from class-based causes of racial inequality (Jhally and Lewis 1992: 70).

Gamson's study of politics

Gamson's work is a similarly fascinating and in-depth study. Gamson bases his analysis on 37 focus groups in which people talked about four political issues: affirmative action, Arab-Israeli conflict, nuclear power and troubled industry. He examined how people talk about such issues and how this related to media treatment, particularly media 'frames' (the overall conceptual approach). His writing is self-consciously respectful of his participants and certainly avoids the 'cultural dope' approach so criticised in relation to conventional effects research. He also thoroughly explores how people draw not only on the media, but also on experiential discourse and popular wisdom and argues that 'people read messages in complicated and sometimes unpredictable ways' (Gamson, 1992: 6). However, he points out '[f]rames . . . invisible in mass media commentary rarely find their way into [people's] conversations. Systematic omissions make certain ways of framing issues extremely unlikely' (Gamson 1992: 6). In his final chapter he also suggests a particular way of thinking about 'effects' as 'effects *in use*'. Media content, he argues, serves as:

> an important tool or resource that people have available, in varying degrees, to help them make sense of issues in the news. When they use elements from media discourse to make a conversational point on an issue we are directly observing a media effect . . . The causal relationship is complicated and bidirectional as the tool metaphor implies.   (Gamson 1992: 180)

Corner, Richardson and Fenton's study of nuclear power

The third example I wish to draw attention to is work by Corner, Richardson and Fenton. They examined people's responses to different programmes about nuclear power. Again, this study has little in common with the traditional hypodermic effects model but does tell us a great deal about how media effects (influence or impact) can operate. Corner and his colleagues place themselves in a tradition of reception studies that examines 'the "creative" processes of interpretation' but are still concerned with audience 'responses' and 'understood meaning' (Corner *et al.* 1990: 47).

Corner, Richardson and Fenton examined four programmes about nuclear power and analysed discussions among nine groups of viewers. They looked in detail at how people respond to different images (such as steam rising from a pond next to a nuclear power plant), presentation of facts (such as information about leukaemia pockets) and also to programme structures. For example, one documentary programme was generally interpreted as suggesting that the Sellafield nuclear power plant was implicated in causing leukaemia. This was in spite of the programme's presentation of many explanations which problematised or even rejected this suggestion. Through close attention to their research participants' conversations, Corner and his colleagues suggest why the programme operated in this way. They argue that the documentary's imagery and structure, built around one family's search for answers about their child's leukaemia, was more powerful than the programme's abstract speculation about risk.

> At one level, it [the programme] focused on a particular instance of illness and the legal battle that was beginning around it. At another level, it engaged more broadly with questions of risk probability in the nuclear industry. But the sheer power of the depiction it offered of one family's tragedy, backed up by the programme's own 'dark' framing of the industry . . . tended to crystallise meanings at the lower level for our respondents, leaving the wider reach of speculation relatively unassimilated. (Corner *et al*. 1990: 100)

These authors comment that their research engages with questions of influence by demonstrating how 'television images can exert a "positioning" power upon viewer imagination and understanding of a kind which may prove more resistant to counter-interpretation than the devices of commentary, interview and voice-over' (Corner *et al*. 1990: 105). They go on to comment that divergence between the groups in how they related to the programme 'should not be allowed to obscure the more important *convergence* – the power of the affective dimension, even on groups who reject its legitimacy, comes through in many ways. This may be of considerable significance in the shaping of public opinion about the issue' (ibid.). Corner and his colleagues conclude:

> . . . though our findings suggest that, indeed, there is a good deal more at issue than many traditional approaches [e.g. the hypodermic effects model] have assumed, they also suggest that taking the power of television seriously is as important as recognising the considerable extent to which it falls well short of being omnipotent. (Corner *et al*. 1990: 108)

Audience reception work at the Glasgow University Media Unit

The final set of research projects which I want to highlight in this chapter are a series of studies developed by researchers at Glasgow University. These projects involved focus group discussions about contemporary issues such as industrial disputes, BSE, conflict in Northern Ireland, AIDS and breast cancer. In most of the projects research participants were invited to write their own media scripts, such as a news report or dialogue from a soap opera. These scripts were then used as a basis for discussion and reflection. (For descriptions of this technique see Kitzinger 1990 or Philo 1990.)

These projects show how the media conveyed facts which influenced public beliefs, assumptions and actions. Concrete examples are located where misinformation had been conveyed, for example leading to inaccurate public beliefs about the shooting dead of three IRA members in Gibraltar (Miller 1994). This body of work demonstrates how patterns of media coverage and routine associations can influence beliefs and assumptions, invoking, for example, fear of people with mental illnesses and impacting on people's willingness, or not, to believe that BSE was a threat to humans (Reilly 1999). Close attention to people's talk shows how images and themes from the media are used as rhetorical reference points to explain or justify a point of view (rather like the 'effects in use' discussed by Gamson). It also reveals how dramatic personal accounts may have greater impact than statistics, for example in assessing breast cancer risk (Henderson and Kitzinger 1999). More specifically some of this research examined how words, images, story lines or themes can become integrated into people's conversation and arguments and inform public understandings.

My own work while I was at Glasgow included an extensive study of audience understandings of AIDS. The 52 focus group discussions conducted for this project suggested that widespread media adoption of the phrase 'body fluids' contributed to some people's belief that saliva was a route of HIV infection ('because it is a body fluid'). This research also demonstrated the impact of vivid media images of people dying from AIDS on people's understanding of HIV (mass media images undercutting health education messages). It also revealed how health education advice such as 'If you're not 100 per cent sure of your partner, use a condom' interacted with cultural conditions to produce, in some case, an anti-safe sex message. More general cultural associations were also explored. For example, the media implicitly associated HIV transmission with 'unnatural' and 'perverse' acts – feeding into incorrect inferences by a significant proportion of the public that lesbians were a 'high-risk' group. This research project also showed how the media contributed to a racist formulation of associations between AIDS and 'Africa' (Kitzinger and Miller 1992) and highlighted the importance of 'social currency' in determining whether, and how, media accounts came to be reiterated through social networks (Kitzinger 1993).

Similar findings, around the significance of specific images, phrases, and the 'social currency' of particular stories, emerged from a subsequent study of audience understandings of child sexual abuse. Analysis of the 49 focus group discussions in this project also highlighted the significance of historical analogies which, I argue, operated as media 'templates'. Participants' discussions illustrated the way in which one scandal around allegations of abuse ('the Orkney case') was successfully associated with two previous scandals, cases already seen as proven examples of professional malpractice. The earlier scandals acted as a template for telling the story, and interpreting the meaning, of unfolding events in Orkney several years later (Kitzinger 2000).

Comparing this focus group data with interviews with incest survivors during the 1980s highlighted the significance of media representation even in the interpretation of personal experience. The media's sudden and dramatic discovery of child sexual abuse, particularly incest, during the second half of the 1980s led many women to name and speak out about their own abuse for the very first time. Prior to that, without any social recognition, their own experience seemed unspeakable, or even unbelievable. Interviewees and focus group research participants described how media recognition of sexual abuse during the 1980s and 1990s allowed them to confront their memories or abuse. It allowed some to 'put together pieces of a jigsaw' and others to identify what had been done to them as wrong or redefine it as abuse instead of a consensual affair. The media in this case played a crucial role in facilitating dramatic personal and social transformations (Kitzinger 2001: 2004).

A continuing enquiry: audience research in the 21st century

The strand of research into audiences established in the 1990s has continued to develop in the 21st century. Although many scholars choose to focus on questions around audience agency (e.g. in many studies around fandom and in many enquiries around interactivity and the new media), questions of influence remain pertinent. Key events such as '9/11' and the attack on the twin towers, the Iraq war and other on-going conflicts have all been the focus of detailed studies exploring how the media represent such issues, and how publics and policy makers respond (with subsequent impacts on issues such as whether or not people buy GM food, or support their governments' military and foreign policy (Lewis 2008)). A major study of television news coverage of Israel–Palestine, for example, highlighted the lack of context provided in news reports, and linked this to the fact that many research participants had little sense of the history of events, believing that the Palestinians were occupying the occupied territories or that it was simply a border dispute between two countries (Philo and Berry 2004). Other work examines a wide range of topics from the effects of different framings of foreign nations (Brewer *et al.* 2003), to the impact of a scandal about the safety of a vaccination (Boyce 2007), from the way in which celebrity culture influences public debate (Couldry and Markham 2007) to the influence of reading blogs (e.g. Sweetser and Kaid 2008). The rich seam of work help to connect media studies to key issues of the day, including debates about contemporary events, theories about citizenship, emerging media trends and the implications of new technologies.

Understanding different ways of assessing audiences is crucial to a sophisticated approach to researching the media's role in contemporary society. Audience research can take many forms, but we ignore questions about influence at our peril. However, sometimes an alternative focus may be more appropriate – it is a question of context, and of assessing the costs and benefits of different foci. Although my own research, for example, has often focused on effects/influence, in recent work I was particularly concerned about the myths that were being promulgated about a simplistic media 'effect' in the area under study. My colleagues and I were examining the representation of stem cell research and human cloning (Haran *et al.* 2008). We found that policy makers often blamed the media in general, and science fiction in particular, for public concerns about such emerging biotechnologies. However, our focus group data suggested that although such media could resource public imaginings, people's concerns were often informed by a much wider repertoire of understanding. Questions about implications and use/abuse of biotechnologies were linked to understanding of the social and political contexts of science and their trust in government (a trust which had been shaken by scandals around health or foreign policy). In writing up this research, we therefore focused on questioning the simplistic model of 'media effects' and sought to replace it with a more nuanced understanding of why people might wish to challenge some 'advances' being promoted by scientists and policy makers (Haran *et al.* 2008).

I went on to do in-depth tracking of all references to science fiction in 20 focus groups debating a series of emerging 21st century technologies (GM crops, stem cell and nanotechnology). This revealed that references to science fiction are often used in everyday conversation to *discredit*, rather to warrant, opinions. People might, for example, express worries about how human cloning, but then follow this up with a dismissive or apologetic comment such as 'it sounds stupid, it sounds like a film'. Science fiction, its place in hierarchies of taste, and its rhetorical use thus may sometimes undermine opportunities to seriously address concerns, rather than, as policy makers claim, serve to 'scare-monger'.

Further detailed analysis also showed that science fiction was not necessarily only associated with a message of fear, but could be seen as reassuring, or even as implying hope. *The Boys from Brazil* (1976), for example, is a film which is usually read as a dystopian text, raising the alarm about human cloning. However, the film can be interpreted as a *positive* representation. One research participant declared that, having seen the film, he reckoned that 'The actual idea in there [producing cloned human babies] was probably okay in my eyes, it was just the way he went about it was wrong'; another felt the film left her with 'A positive message, that the evil will not out, the good will out.'

The way in which science fiction might resource positive imaginings was even more striking in the discussions of nanotechnology. Most people had not heard of nanotechnology – but those who had associated it with fiction, rather than fact. They linked it to films such as *The Fantastic Voyage* (1965) (involving a mini-submarine implanted into a human being) or television programmes such as *Star Trek: The Next Generation* (where 'the Borgs use nanotechnology to strengthen their bodies'). This had left them predisposed to link 'nano' with very positive associations focusing on its potential to create wonderful consumer goods or to facilitate medical treatments. A striking exception to this positive predisposition, however, was evident in a group of Muslim research participants. These individuals were very concerned about the potential of nanotechnology to be used in covert surveillance and the erosion of civil liberties – a view they explicitly linked to their experience of increasing Islamophobia in contemporary Britain.

Conclusion

Awareness about media influence is not the same as treating the media as all powerful or assuming that audiences are a homogeneous mass of dupes. The mass media are an important site of influence. There is now an established body of research which demonstrates how the media help to define what counts as a public issue, organise our understandings of individual events, shape suspicions and beliefs, and resource memories, conversations, actions and even identities. Such media effects/influence cannot be dismissed simply because these processes are complex, multi-mediated, and sometimes successfully resisted. Nor should any attempt to theorise influence be dismissed simply because simplistic ideas about media effects are often misused.

Research on audience reception highlights how some messages are conveyed particularly effectively because of features such as: reiteration of key phrases and themes, coherence of narratives, use of metaphor or particular images. Patterns are evident across studies. Several different studies, for example, highlight the role of particular formats and structures (e.g. the impact of personalised accounts or family drama). Others emphasise the impact of story trajectory and timing (e.g. how a story is initially framed and first emerges into the mass media). Particular themes recur across studies such as the importance of 'social currency' (the value of an item of media information in conversation) and the power of tapping into pre-existing discourses or ways of thinking about the world. Detailed investigations of how people relate to media representations can thus help us to refine how we analyse media content and hypothesise about the meanings and likely impact of media coverage.

A growing critical mass of 'new effects/influence research' shows that complex processes of reception and consumption *mediate*, but do not necessarily *undermine* media power. Acknowledging that audiences can be 'active' does not mean that the media are ineffectual. Recognising the role of interpretation does not invalidate the concept of influence. A major task for the next generation of researchers is to further explore and consolidate our understandings of how media effects operate, both now and with the on-going development of new communication policies, practices and technologies.

Questions

1 What is wrong with the traditional model of media effects operating like a hypodermic syringe?

2 How can analysis of how people *relate* to television programmes or newspaper articles inform our analysis of media content? What are the limitations of content analysis on its own?

3 How do developments in communication technologies (such as the internet) inform how we might consider questions of influence?

4 Collect newspaper clippings and video tape news reports around a particular one-off event such as a crash, scandal or crisis. Several weeks later ask people to recount their memories and thoughts on the event. Compare what they say with your media archive. What were the images, explanations or phrases recalled by your interviewees? Were these directly taken from the media coverage, from a shared cultural repertoire, or from other specific sources? What facts have been forgotten or ignored? How did people come to the opinions they did?

5 Ask a group of friends to talk about an issue (perhaps one that you care about passionately, or simply one that has had a great deal of media coverage). Encourage them to assert their own beliefs and debate the rights and wrongs of the issue. Try to identify the source of the information, images and ideas that they use in the discussion. How difficult is it to determine the source of ideas? Pay close attention to the difference between people and the way in which they interact, share information, jokes and stories or challenge one another.

Note

I Synonyms for 'effect', according to my thesaurus, are words such as 'outcome', and 'consequence'. Synonyms for 'influence' include 'control', 'power', 'sway', 'rule', 'authority' (and 'effect') (Windows 97, tools). Chambers dictionary defines 'influence' as 'power of producing an effect, especially unobtrusively' and 'ascendancy, often of a secret or undue kind'. Oddly, within the media studies literature the term 'effects' is sometimes used to imply crude models of media impact, whereas 'influence' is seen as a more sophisticated term. This allows for conceptual slippage when dismissing 'effects research': I therefore deliberately chose to use both terms.

Further reading

Curran, J., Morley, D. and Walkerdine, V. (eds) (1996) *Cultural Studies and Communications,* London: Edward Arnold. Includes a lively exchange between James Curran and David Morley about developments in audience research.

Kitzinger, J. (2004) 'Audience and Readership Research' in J. Downing, D. McQuail, P. Schlesinger and E. Wartella (eds) *Handbook of Media Studies*, London: Sage, pp. 167–81. This gives an overview of some of the different research designs and methods than can be adopted to explore audiences.

Kitzinger, J. (2004) *Framing Abuse: Media Influence and Public Understandings of Sexual Violence Against Children,* London: Pluto Press. This book presents a detailed analysis of how media influence plays out in how people understand sexual violence. It explores the impact of media recognition of a social problem, the effects of the *analogies* that journalists adopt, and the impact of story visuals, the way in which a news event is *labelled*, and how it is *located* in time and place. Reflections on how the findings relate to research method and theory may help students consider how to explore media influence in relation to a range of different issues.

Philo, G. (ed) (1999) *Message Received*, Harlow: Longman. This brings together audience work from the Glasgow Media Group exploring audience understandings of issues such as immigration, AIDS, BSE and mental illness.

References

Blumler, J. and McQuail, D. (1968) *Television in Politics: Its Uses and Influences*, London: Faber.

Brewer, P. R., Graf, J. and Willnat, L. (2003) 'Media Influence on Attitudes Toward Foreign Countries', *International Communication Gazette*, 65 (6): 493–508.

Boyce, T. (2007) *Health, Risk and News: The MMR Vaccine and the Media,* London: Peter Lang.

Corner, J., Richardson, K. and Fenton, N. (1990) *Nuclear Reactions: Format and Response in Public Issue Television*, London: John Libbey.

Couldry, N. and Markham, T. (2007) 'Celebrity Culture and Public Connection: Bridge or Chasm?' *International Journal of Cultural Studies*, 10 (4): 203–421.

Eldridge, J., Kitzinger, J. and Williams, K. (1997) *The Mass Media and Power in Modern Britain*, Oxford: Oxford University Press.

Gamson, W. (1992) *Talking Politics*, Cambridge: Cambridge University Press.

Gauntlett, W. (1995) *Moving Experiences: Understanding Television's Influences and Effects,* Acamedia Research Monograph 13, London: John Libbey.

Hall, S. (1973) *Encoding and Decoding in the Television Discourse*, in S. Hall, D. Hobson, A. Lowe and P. Willis (eds) (1981) *Culture, Media, Language: working papers in cultural studies 1972-79*, London: Hutchinson.

Henderson, L. and Kitzinger, J. (1999) 'The Human Drama of Genetics: "Hard" and "Soft" Media Representations of Inherited Breast Cancer', *Sociology of Health and Illness*, 21 (5): 560-78.

Haran, J., Kitzinger, J., McNeil, M. and O'Riordan, K. (2008) *Human Cloning in the Media: From Science Fiction to Science Practice*, London: Routledge

Jhally, S. and Lewis, J. (1992) *Enlightened Racism: The Cosby Show, Audiences and the Myth of the American Dream,* Oxford: Westview Press.

Katz, E. and Lazersfeld, P. (1955) *Personal Influence: The Part Played by People in the Flow of Mass Communication,* New York: Free Press.

Kitzinger, J. (1990) 'Audience Understandings of AIDS Media Messages: A Discussion of Methods', *Sociology of Health and Illness*, 12 (3): 319-35.

Kitzinger, J. (1993) 'Understanding AIDS - Media Messages and What People Know About AIDS', in J. Eldridge (ed), *Getting the Message*, London: Routledge.

Kitzinger, J. (2000) 'Media Templates: Patterns of Association and the (Re)construction of Meaning Over Time' *Media, Culture and Society*, 22 (1): 64-84.

Kitzinger, J. (2001) 'Transformations of Public and Private Knowledge: Audience Reception, Feminism and The Experience of Childhood Sexual Abuse', *Feminist Media Studies* 1 (1): 91-104.

Kitzinger, J. (2004) *Framing Abuse: Media Influence and Public Understandings of Sexual Violence Against Children,* London: Pluto Press.

Kitzinger, J. and Miller, D. (1992) 'African AIDS: The Media and Audience Beliefs' in P. Aggleton, P. Davies and G. Hart (eds) *AIDS: Rights, Risks and Reason*, London: Falmer Press.

Lewis, J. (2008) 'The Role of the Media in Boosting Military Spending' in *Media, War and Conflict*, 1: 108-17.

Merton, R. K. (1946) (with the assistance of M. Fiske and A. Curtis) *Mass Persuasion*, New York: Harper & Brothers.

Miller, D. (1994) *Don't Mention the War*, London: Pluto.

Philo, G. (1990) *Seeing and Believing*, London: Routledge.

Philo, T. and Berry, M. (2004) *Bad News from Israel*, London: Pluto Press.

Reilly, J. (1999) 'The Media and Public Perceptions of BSE', in G. Philo (ed) *Message Received,* Harlow: Longman.

Sweetser, K. D. and Kaid, L. L. (2008) 'Stealth Soapboxes: Political Information Efficacy, Cynicism and Use of Celebrity Weblogs Among Readers', *New Media and Society*, 10 (1): 67-91.

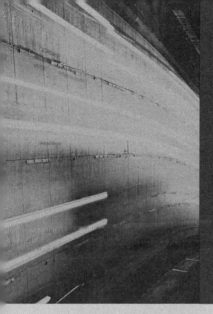

26

Active Audiences

Joke Hermes

Chapter overview

This chapter will consider academic debates in which the term 'the active audience' was introduced. Discussions about influence and effects tend to assume that the audience is 'passive', no more than the recipient of a message produced elsewhere. Media scholars sought to challenge this (implicit) view, by arguing the case of audiences as 'meaning producers'. This essay argues that debates about the 'active' audience sought to lay bare issues of power in the relationship between audiences and the media, but also in the relationship between media researchers and audiences.

Introduction

'Active', according to my *Concise Oxford English Dictionary*, means 'energetic', or 'doing things'. In relation to audiences, 'the active audience' calls forth a vision of audiences who act upon what they see. The addition of 'active' suggests that normally audiences are passive. It is fairly easy to visualise what could be meant by the 'passive' audience, whether as a concept or as a description of an everyday practice: someone sitting on a sofa with crisps or biscuits and a remote control, zapping from station to station. Here we run into a problem, though, as even the zapping would constitute an act. Perhaps the implicit 'passivity' of audiences is not so much a suggestion of total inactivity, but rather of a compliant going along with whatever is on offer.

Mainstream media and communication research has not so much visualised audiences asleep on their couches in front of the television set, remote control on the floor; rather, they seem to have been conceived as hypnotised by what is on offer, out of contact with their critical faculties. The *raison d'être* of mass communication research has been to reconstruct how media influence works in order, presumably, to be able to guard ourselves against it. Metaphors and concepts, such as 'hypodermic needle', or 'magic bullet', but also 'two-step-flow' and 'spiral of silence', all captured the scientific and social imaginations alike. Media scholars have been cast in the role of keepers of our collective sanity in times in which, supposedly, the opium of the people has all but drugged most of us. However, it is important to remember that most of the eminent scholars in the field were wary of the popularised thesis of media influence. For there was one problem with the widespread, concerned view of how the media work: there was no evidence. Klapper (1960) famously concluded after reviewing all the research available at the time that it could not be proven that publicity or media exposure led to changes in, for instance, voting behaviour. Furthermore, media audiences love opinion polls: polls suggest the possibility of predicting an outcome, while also allowing the fear that they may themselves influence the outcome of elections. However none of this has ever been proven beyond reasonable doubt, and this remains the case to date.

In media and communication handbooks there is simply no entry for the 'passive' audience. Indeed, passivity of audiences is (still) seen as business as usual. Much research on the media has implicitly understood the researcher, and others 'in the know', as enlightened, as ahead of the masses, aware of the possible dangers of the media. As a result, defining the audience as 'active' may be considered by some as a deviation from the norm. In fact, neither 'active' nor 'passive' refer to audience activity in a direct manner, nor was 'active' introduced in media studies theory as a twin to 'passive'. The notion of 'the active audience' is the product of critical interventions in the history of mass communication research that will be discussed below. 'Active' in these traditions means different things, varying from indeed using the media to accomplish specific goals (to be informed about what is happening in the world; to be able to engage in small-talk with colleagues; not to feel alone), to the basic act of making media texts meaningful: that is, to translate coded words and images into stories, ideas that either are or are not relevant to how we understand the world around us.

'The active audience' is a phrase that can be dated back to different historical periods, but only to two academic paradigms. The best known of these is the uses and gratifications approach (1950s–), a body of empirical work that was said to ask not what it is that the media do with people, but what do people do with the media. It questioned why there is such audience interest in staple media genres (an early example being Herta Herzog's research on radio soap opera in the late 1930s and 40s). Later on, in the 1970s, uses and gratifications research was interested in what, exactly, people use the media for: personal guidance, relaxation, adjustment, information (McQuail 2000: 387). It would take the interdisciplinary projects in what came to be known as cultural studies, the second paradigm, to really reconceptualise the audience in terms of subjectivity rather than individuality and in terms of meaning production rather than effects and influence (1980s–). This opened up a space to reflect critically upon the diverse and complex relations between media texts and their users. Unlike uses and gratifications research, media and cultural studies research does not foreclose the possibility of fruitfully combining research focusing on the audience with research that focuses on the text.

Uses and gratifications versus media and cultural studies

In the early 1970s McQuail, Blumler and Brown published results of research conducted into the goals served by media use, not for society as a whole, but for media users. They assumed media and content choice to be rational and aimed at fulfilling specific goals. Audience members were taken to be conscious of the choices they make. In general these choices (what McQuail calls 'personal utility') are a more significant determinant of the grouping of people into distinct audiences than aesthetic or cultural factors. Blumler and McQuail assumed that these factors could be measured (McQuail 2000: 387–8) and offered a typology of the interaction between media and audiences which included: diversion, personal relationships, personal identity and surveillance (or information seeking) goals (McQuail *et al.* 1972). Market research took up this model and continues to use versions of it. Retrospectively, McQuail is critical of his own earlier work, and suggests that social origins and ongoing experience are important in understanding those audience–media relations which fall outside the initial behaviourist and functionalist leanings of the research he carried out earlier. Social origins and ongoing experience, however, are not so easily measured (McQuail 2000: 389). Social origins – anybody's class background, for example – can be translated into quantitative indicators (e.g. as more or less formal and informal schooling), but ongoing experience may, for any one person, take a multitude of forms that need not even relate directly to one another. These range from what one learns from an individual film or article in a magazine, to witnessing everyday racist behaviour or parental neglect in the street, to boredom doing a job that had once seemed so exciting.

The 'uses and gratifications' approach was never developed theoretically to the full. Critics have argued that it is impossible to separate uses and gratifications, as it is impossible to establish whether uses precede gratifications chronologically, or whether 'gratifications' are somehow made legitimate by identifying 'uses' related to them. If the latter is the case, the uses and gratifications model would not be able to free us from the dominant paradigm: audiences would still be seduced by the media, to such an extent that needs could be said to be 'invented' for what is basically imposed on us by capitalism (through the commercial media) or a paternalist nation-state (through public service broadcasting). It is important to stress that 'gratificationist research', as it has also been called, was not initially understood to be a mainstream or conservative approach to the study of the media. On the contrary, it appeared to depart from the tradition which focused on effects (mass communication research) or texts (such as the film criticism of the British journal *Screen*), in order to gather intelligence about audiences.

Gratifications research at least focused on people, making them part of the media–meaning–society equation. It is only when gratificationist research is used as a spearhead in debates about the possible convergence of quantitative and qualitative traditions in media research (the first seen as conservative and mainstream, the second as its challenger), that media critics such as Ien Ang strenuously oppose it. For them, it is a matter of the difference of the 'ethnographic' method against individualistic quantitative research, requiring a closer look at what is meant by the term 'active audience' (Ang 1989). Ang suggests that it is basically impossible to bring the quantitative and qualitative traditions together in mass communication research. The social scientists who work with quantitative methods in uses and gratifications research and have here been labelled 'mainstream' may superficially be seen to use the same terms that the 'critical' scholars (Ang's term) use, but this does not mean that the two agree over the way in which the object of study needs to be conceptualised, or, in fact, over the goals and aims of science or social research as an enterprise (Ang 1989: 101). What is important here is that especially from the perspective of mainstream media research the term 'the active audience' was introduced in support of the idea that a process of convergence between the two traditions was desirable. After all, if everybody agrees that the (television) audience is 'active' (rather than passive) and that watching television or other forms of media use is a social (rather than an individual) practice, this is not saying all that much after all, according to Ang. And yet, from the perspective of mainstream media research it is saying a lot. In line with McQuail's (self)criticism of earlier uses and gratifications research, to give up such tenets as the basic measurability of audience behaviour is tantamount to owning up to defeat for mainstream media and communications research.

As part of the discussions between the supporters of mainstream communication research and scholars from within the area of cultural studies that took place in the 1980s (Jensen 1987), the phrase 'the active audience' was often used. In retrospect, it could be argued that this was done to assure cultural studies researchers of the good faith of the supporters of mainstream research and their willingness to incorporate a number of terms that were alien to their earlier work. 'Active', in this discussion, referred to the fact that the meaning of texts is always subject to negotiation. It suggested that researchers on both sides of the divide were aware of the role of ideological formations: the 'active' audience was conceived as battling against media institutions from a specific background, the bastion of class positions, of the values, ideas and perspectives that come with being raised in a particular milieu. Ang's critical response to the convergence tradition makes clear that, as one of the leading figures in qualitative audience studies, she was not at all taken with this forceful invitation from the other camp. Though the audience might be labelled 'active', there still was no room for a conceptualisation of context: mainstream social researchers were and are interested in gathering quantitative data and therefore needed to be strict on what they could allow to be conceived as variables in their models and what they could not. As will become clear, this is totally against the grain of qualitative audience research which was to take a turn towards ethnography in precisely that period.

Ethnographic approaches are characterised by an initial wide focus which is only gradually narrowed down. Perhaps, more importantly, Ang pleads the incommensurability of the goals audience research was to serve in both projects. Social scientists bent on reaching 'scientific' results, finding 'the truth' and predicting audience behaviour (a highly valuable type of knowledge in the media production marketplace), certainly were not much interested in audience ethnography – a political project for critical researchers who want to 'give a voice' to the respondents. This is felt to be important as it challenges official knowledge that is used to monitor and control people, by countering apparatuses of dominance and by giving credence to forms of pleasure and resistance that have no place in mainstream media research.

So, what was qualitative media and cultural studies research like? What was meant by the term 'active' in this tradition? Ang invited readers of the Dutch women's magazine *Viva* to write to her about their experience of viewing *Dallas*, a much debated prime time soap serial. Her advert read: 'I like watching the TV serial *Dallas* but often get odd reactions to it. Would anyone like to write and tell me why you like watching it too, or dislike it? I should like to assimilate these reactions in my university thesis. Please write to . . .' (Ang 1985: 10). Following the publication of this ad, Ang received 42 letters, mostly from women, on the basis of which she reconstructed what kind of pleasures watching *Dallas* offered to these Dutch viewers. Ang's goal was not simply to describe how viewers made sense of and found pleasure in watching *Dallas*; she was also determined to contribute to a debate that was taking place in the Netherlands and in other European countries about the alleged cultural imperialism of American television shows by taking a stand against those who denigrated popular culture and its users. By using qualitative methods inspired by the ethnographic tradition, Ang was able to gain access to the various pleasures members of the audience enjoyed by watching (and sometimes hating) *Dallas*; she was also able to identify the ways through which a dominant ideology conveyed by mass culture structure social debate and individual evaluations of popular culture (even if they cannot rigidly determine audience pleasure). While Ang's starting point is the 'activity' of meaning production on the part of audiences, she is well aware that audience activity is always bounded by the norms, values and rules that make it possible to talk about any subject in a given period.

The second, important reason why Ang chose to work with readers' letters is political, as this scholar helped to establish a new, more radical forum where feminist debates about popular culture, women's genres and women readers could take place. The feminist work on popular culture at that time consisted primarily of text-based analysis. As has been implied above, text-based analysis that is used also to understand audiences too often ignores audience activity and hence understands audiences, implicitly, as passive. In the early 1980s such a text-based view was offered in Tania Modleski's (1982) work on women's genres (which included soap opera). Modleski combines her decoding of the narrative structure of romances, Gothic novels and soap operas with psycho-analytical and clinical psychological views. As a result, some critics see her work as ultimately contradicting her own goals. Instead of generating respect for female audiences she ends up stigmatising them as hysterics (the romance readers) or else stereotyping them as housewives (the users of soap opera) whose distracted frame of mind, crucial to their efficient functioning as cleaners and caretakers in the household, fits appropriately with the structure of daytime television soap operas (a characteristic of which are its multiple and fragmented plotlines).

In a nutshell, then, this debate about the prime-time soap opera *Dallas* and its daytime counterparts provides an overview of the different conceptualisations of the 'audience' put forward in media and cultural studies research against paradigms developed within the social sciences, as well as approaches based on textual analysis. On the one hand, social scientists gave little credence to the contextuality of audience negotiation with media texts; on the other, research in the humanities tended to focus especially on the text and exclude the audience altogether. Media and cultural studies researchers maintained that to understand how popular genres are interpreted by audiences the social context in which they are used needs to be taken into account. Moreover, analyses based exclusively on the text generate difficult questions about the status of the researcher. Is she the enlightened expert? Can she, unlike the women she describes, withstand the enticements of the text? For instance, Modleski's analysis clearly sets her apart from the people she writes about. Compare this to Ang's invitation to *Dallas* viewers that they should write to her about their experiences ('I like watching . . . *Dallas*, but often get odd reactions to it.'). Ang's claims to 'authority' appear to be more 'dialogical' in nature, in tune with ethnographic work. Ethnographers, after all, tend to spend much time in the field in order to get to know respondents well; moreover, they talk, as well as observe. In dealing with her respondents, Ang made clear that she felt she was also a member of the audience, not simply an observer. Rather than arguing that she could provide an 'objective' account of the pleasures one gains by watching soap operas, Ang offered a reflexive reading of the series based on the accounts of viewers and on her own analysis of *Dallas* as a televisual text. What issues are raised by this charting of the active audience? Ang was concerned about American cultural imperialism, but she did not try to find as fine-tuned a method as possible to determine its effects. She reconstructed the pleasures gained by her respondents, as well as their dislikes, by identifying what she labelled as 'the ideology of mass culture', i.e. an ideological framework through which a large number of *Dallas* haters accounted for their displeasure (Ang 1985: 95) and *Dallas* lovers excused their 'weakness'. Abhorrence of American cultural products and concern for their influence is part of this ideology, which is a vehicle for what Bourdieu called the 'bourgeois aesthetic' (Ang 1985: 116). Ang was thus interested in the ideological or discursive functioning of popular television, as well as how popular television became meaningful to viewers given such an ideological context.

Insofar as the rhetoric of media effects has a place in Ang's reconstruction, it would be in the ideology of mass culture itself when it professes concern for manipulable and vulnerable audiences. To some extent, this is exactly what classical or mainstream mass communication research does. Rather than giving a voice to media consumers, it is customary to come to some sort of conclusion about them, for instance the degree to which they are influenced by a programme, or, in the context of viewing *Dallas*, they may be said to be 'victims' of American cultural imperialism (e.g. Liebes and Katz 1986). While mainstream research tells us what the media do with audiences, what it does not tell us is what audiences do with the media. Media and cultural studies research offers a more complex and theoretically interesting discussion of this topic. As well as strong support for the view that audiences are not so much duped by the media, media and cultural studies suggests audiences have to operate within the constraints set by society, including mixed systems of state and commercial efforts to control publics: whether as fodder for advertisers, or as unruly subjects that should be disciplined to be fully rounded citizens. While the pressure of these disciplinary efforts should be taken very seriously, media and cultural studies also poses the counter question: what is in it for audiences to comply with these roles? What pleasures, in short, are gained by being a member of an audience, and how are these contextually determined and enabled? No matter whether these pleasures are either bad or good for you, analysis and evaluation of media practices has to start from the assumption that audience members are neither stupid nor duped but that they, as do media scholars, have valid reasons for their choices.

Questioning media and cultural studies research on audiences

Above it has been made clear that the notion of the active audience was the intellectual property of two highly different research traditions: gratificationists from a social science background on the one hand, media and cultural studies scholars from an interdisciplinary background (inspired by both the humanities and the social sciences) on the other. Although uses and gratifications research would seem to offer an attractive prospect, it is very much part of a hard-nosed scientific community, in which the term 'active audience' in practice is reduced to a gimmick. That at least was the claim of media and cultural studies scholars in the debate about 'the active audience' of the late 1980s – the theory of media 'dupes', again – which in some fora is still rekindled (Schroeder 2000).

To concentrate solely on the difference between these two traditions which deploy the term 'active audience' would obscure the fact that in both camps there are major differences between practitioners, whether we consider mainstream social scientists or else the media and cultural studies camp. To elucidate the full importance of the adjective 'active' let us return to Ang's criticism of gratificationist research and the discussion about combining mainstream and cultural studies research (Ang 1989). In a review published in 1989, Ang discusses David Morley's work, who is seen, like Ang, as one of the founders of audience research within media and cultural studies. In 1980 David Morley had published *The Nationwide Audience*, part of a study of a popular British current affairs programme that he undertook together with Charlotte Brunsdon. The book is based on group interviews with students, workers and managers about *Nationwide*. Its most pressing question was whether audiences would subscribe to the dominant ideology, or whether they would occupy a variety of positions, as suggested by a model Stuart Hall had sketched in an occasional stencilled paper at the then Centre for Contemporary Cultural Studies at the University of Birmingham ([1974] 1980). The variety of opinions and views that Morley gathered convinced him that audiences are not necessarily positioned as subjects or ideologically 'placed' by a programme so as to reproduce the dominant ideology. The audience, in short, cannot be conceptualised as a puppet which is pulled by the strings of an individual text. Programmes become meaningful through a combination of the positions offered by the text and the social background of its viewers, which includes the codes and discourses viewers are familiar with. Therefore, television programmes can never be seen as an unproblematically shared referent for all members of the audience.

Six years later Morley published another study focusing on audiences, *Family Television* (1986). Ang reviews it by portraying it as a study which balances mainstream communication research and cultural studies, in contrast to Morley's earlier work. Indeed, in the book Morley pleads against 'unproductive form(s) of segregation' (1986: 13) between questions of interpretation and questions of use. However, to her dismay, Ang cannot locate Morley as an author within the text. As a writer, he appears as a totally disembodied subject, driven by a disinterested wish to contribute to scientific progress (Ang 1989: 107). The political thrust of his analysis does not become clear. In fact, like uses and gratifications research, Morley appears primarily interested in difference, in the range of audience experiences. The experienced reader, however, says Ang, will discern important differences between Morley's approach and uses and gratification research. Where the latter is interested in drawing up typologies, Morley, as a media and cultural studies scholar, sees some differences as far more significant than others. Family television is also very much a book about the power structure within families. Reviewing Morley's interpretation and the debate between the author and Brunsdon which is reported in the book, Ang concludes that: 'What emerges here is the beginning of an interpretive framework in which differences in television viewing practices are not just seen as expressions of different needs, uses or readings, but are connected with the way in which historical subjects are structurally positioned in relation to each other'(1989: 109). The 'concentrated viewing mode' of many of the men in Morley's study and the 'distracted mode of watching television' that characterised many of the women, are constituted in relation to one another. They are not individual choices, they are two sides of one coin. How television is used (literally) and how programmes are interpreted, the two dimensions of audience activity, need to be understood as issues having to do with power relations.

This debate between Ang and Morley, whose work is usually understood as closely related, shows how media and cultural studies scholars were less interested in the activities of audiences as such than in how to come to a self-reflexive theoretical understanding of how people cope with the media. Although I started out this chapter by simply defining 'active' as 'meaning making', and by stating that 'the active audience' was a phrase coined by different research traditions, I now have to retract this. Media and cultural studies would seem to have very little interest in audience activity as such. Within this framework, audience activity is only the beginning of an engaged trajectory of getting to know viewers, of interviewing them, of understanding their lives and backgrounds in order to develop critical theory. Whereas social scientists, in a sense, lament the unruliness of audiences and their unpredictable behaviour, the key to media and cultural studies research is political engagement and criticism. Research and writing styles are therefore key ingredients of ethnographic audience research; the key element of this research practice has been to look not only for regularities but also for exceptions. For instance, if the designated readers of women's magazines are female, how do men read them (Hermes 1995)? Such strategies will take us beyond the assumption that audiences are active meaning producers, by allowing us to theorise *how* they are meaning makers, and also what the role of the text might be in all this.

To do so has become all the more important now that, in contrast to concerns about what the media do to us, there is also a fair amount of ungrounded optimism about what we can do with the media. Studies on computer-mediated communities and fans are, from time to time, suggestive in this respect. The marketing of computer software to schools indeed relies on the notion that all things to do with computers and screens will be popular with young people and help them learn (Buckingham 2007). Neither concern, nor an overly eager and naïve acceptance of media texts and media use, are a useful start in media research or in social discussions of the role of the media. Respect for audience members is the logical outcome if we conceive audiences as active meaning makers. Recently, scholars within media and cultural studies have come up with some strong suggestions for addressing this issue.

Starting from classical sociological theory, David Gauntlett (2007) suggests that if, as researchers, we want to know how audiences build identities in relation to media texts, we must engage them in creative work. As identities are neither especially logical nor linear (in the way a well-reasoned scientific argument is), verbal exchange is not always the ideal method to study processes of identity construction. This is especially the case when interviews are limited in time, thus leaving little room to build trust and to explore the meandering multi-layeredness of how we unveil our autobiographies (Gray 2003). Gauntlett invited groups of informants to make drawings or build objects with Lego and let interviews be inspired by such activities, thus enabling a more associative and open conversation. Collective storytelling and media production (e.g. for websites), is another venue that can be explored to do justice to how audience members interpret their lifeworlds. Collaborative media ethnography, as recently developed by Marie Gillespie (2007), also supports a respectful and open approach to audiences and allows for a deep understanding of how media texts are appropriated and made sense of by audiences, while giving due attention to how the media operate.

While new computer technology is indeed shifting the balance between producers and the media, and while we are becoming more and more adept at being 'prosumers' (producers and consumers), there is little reason to believe that the distinction between 'consumers' and 'producers' of media messages will disappear altogether. For one thing, much of the user generated content offered by websites is of fairly low quality. Although youtube.com has gained enormous popularity, only a fraction of the material uploaded to the site is of really good quality. Secondly, several of the websites that rely on user generated content are run by media corporations. This suggests that although the rhetoric of a new relationship between media and audiences is gaining ground (labelled, for example, web 2.0), everyday media practice still needs to be understood in terms of unequal power relations. A respectful and reflexive approach is needed to understand 'new' media practices, just as much as it is needed to approach more traditional media use. Shallow and unreflexive use of the term 'active' would lead to ungrounded celebrations of the creativity of the audience, for instance by pointing out that small groups of gamers cross over to the ranks of game developers. Indeed, so far this has appeared to be a marginal and severely underpaid group. It is questionable who benefits the most from this type of 'audience activity', whether the industry or gamers themselves (Humphreys 2008; Nieborg and Van der Graaf 2008). Even more importantly, such cases do not defuse older arguments about the vulnerability of audience members. This shows how thinking in terms of the 'activity' of audiences, should not be limited to thinking about audience 'pleasures' but should rather address the question of the power of the media and the strategies of audiences to deal with, and at times even oppose that power.

Conclusion

That single adjective 'active' stands for more than just 'doing things', or 'energetic'. In the context of mainstream media and communication research it is better translated as 'unpredictable' or 'uncontrollable'. 'Active', when used to describe what audiences do with the media or with media texts, refers to a discussion between researchers relying on quantitative or qualitative methods that took place in 1980s, but also to more recent, and sometimes overly optimistic, talk about the ways in which the web is supposedly allowing media users to become producers. The debate of the 1980s may now seem as a thing of the past. But the 'battle' over the nature of the audience was never won by anyone and issues surrounding how 'active' audiences are remain contentious. It remains important to reflect on how we relate to those we study and on issues of positionality, whether or not we are part of the groups under investigation ourselves. Equally, it remains important to think of the goals we wish our research to serve. Should our research be a means to improve the quality of programming, or to increase advertising revenue? Should it help support the identity struggles of paternalistic public broadcasters or the attractiveness of often costly digital games? Would it at all be possible to really make a difference in the lives of all those ordinary people out there through our research efforts? These are difficult questions.For media researchers, whether established in the field or just starting out in their professional careers, such questions demand an interrogation of whom the adjective 'active' should describe. *We* need to be 'doing things', as the *Concise Oxford English Dictionary* tells us. Personally, I have opted for continuing my research in terms of cultural citizenship (Hermes 2005). If one thing has become clear in the discussion around the 'active' audience, it is that – notwithstanding the public and media-fed mourning of Princess Diana in 1997 – media use seldom moves us to act collectively. Yet our media use can make us feel part of real or virtual communities: as readers of a particular genre, as discussants on a mailing list. These can be a means to take up our responsibilities as citizens or to make good on our civic rights and duties. For me, active still means 'meaning making'. Those meanings are potentially against the grain, and possibly steps forward towards a better world, incorrigible optimist that I am . . . , they challenge the dominant pessimism concerning the media and how they influence our lives.

Questions

1 List the arguments for and against combining quantitative and qualitative audience research, by focusing on the logic of both approaches.

2 Prepare an interview about everyday television use by interviewing yourself. How would you answer questions about the programmes you really like (what makes them such fun to watch, or to talk about)? Which programmes irritate you but are you familiar with nonetheless? (Do you often watch programmes not of your own choice but because you share your living space and TV set with others?)

3 Ethnographic audience study wishes to reconstruct media use from the perspective of the audiences themselves. To that end researchers try to find and use 'members' categories' (an anthropological term); and as evidence of the authenticity of their reconstruction they introduce large segments of interview texts in their academic publications. Some have argued that within such a framework asking so-called leading questions does little harm. After all, the ethnographer only uses them to challenge interviewees, in order to get them to talk back. Simple yes or no answers are no good in qualitative research. Also, we all have finite cultural capital and use our own terms and categories to explain our point of view as media users. Argue why you do, or do not agree with this point of view.

Further reading

Classic studies

Ang, I. (1991) *Desperately Seeking the Audience*, London: Routledge. This book documents the ideological background of different forms of quantitative audience research used in the television industry.

Ang, I. (1997) *Living Room Wars*, London: Routledge. This is a collection of articles discussing the critical project of engaging with audience practices.

Morley, D. (1980) *The Nationwide Audience*, London: BFI (undertaken with Charlotte Brunsdon) and (1986) *Family Television*, London: Comedia. Both discuss the nature of audience activity and how that should be conceptualised.

Examples of empirical work

Hermes, J. (1995) *Reading Women's Magazines*, Cambridge: Polity. This book reconstructs the meaning of women's magazines from the point of view of readers.

Hermes, J. (2005) *Rereading popular culture*, Oxford: Blackwell. This book uses audience interpretations of popular culture to reconstruct the underlying social issues and ideological tensions which are addressed via popular texts such as sport, television, crime series and detective novels.

References

Ang, I. (1985) *Watching Dallas*, London: Methuen.

Ang, I. (1989) 'Wanted Audiences: On the Politics of Empirical Audience Research', in E. Seiter, H. Borchers, G. Kreutzner and E. Warth (eds) *Remote Control. Television, audiences and cultural power*, London: Routledge, pp. 79–95.

Buckingham, D. (2007) *Beyond Technology: Children's Learning in the Age of Digital Culture*, Cambridge: Polity Press.

Gauntlett, D. (2007) *Creative Explorations: New Approaches to Identities and Audiences*, London: Routledge.

Gillespie, M. (2007) 'Security, Media and Multicultural Citizenship: A Collaborative Ethnography' in *European Journal of Cultural Studies*, 10 (3): 273-93.

Gray, A. (2003) *Research Practice for Cultural Studies: Ethnographic Methods and Lived Cultures*, London: Sage.

Hall, S. (1980) 'Encoding/decoding', in S. Hall (ed) *Culture, Media, Language*, London: Hutchinson, pp. 197-208.

Hermes, J. (1995) *Reading Women's Magazines: An Analysis of Everyday Media Use*, Cambridge: Polity Press.

Hermes, J. (2005) *Rereading Popular Culture*, Oxford: Blackwell.

Humphries, S. (2008) 'Ruling the Virtual World: Governance in Massively Multiplayer Online Games', *European Journal of Cultural Studies*, 11 (2): 149-71.

Jensen, K.B. (1987) 'Qualitative Audience Research: Towards an Integrative Approach to Reception', *Critical Studies in Mass Communication*, 4 (1): 21-36.

Klapper, J. (1960) *The Effects of Mass Communication*, New York: Free Press.

Liebes, T. and Katz, E. (1986) 'Patterns of Involvement in Television Fiction: A Comparative Analysis', *European Journal of Communication*, 1 (2): 151-71.

McQuail, D. (2000) *McQuail's Mass Communication Theory*, 4th edition, London: Sage.

McQuail, D., Blumler, J. and Brown, J. (1972) 'The Television Audience, a Revised Perspective', in D. McQuail (ed) *Sociology of Mass Communication*, Harmondsworth: Penguin, pp. 135-65.

Modleski, T. (1982) *Loving with a Vengeance. Mass-produced Pleasures for Women*, New York: Methuen.

Morley, D. (1980) *The Nationwide Audience*, London: BFI.

Morley, D. (1986) *Family Television, Cultural Power and Domestic Leisure*, London: Comedia.

Nieborg, D. and van der Graaf, S. (2008) 'The Mod Industries? The Industrial Logic of Non-market Game Production', *European Journal of Cultural Studies*, 11 (2): 177-95.

Schroeder, K.C. (2000) 'Making Sense of Audience Discourses: Towards a Multidimensional Model of Mass Media Reception', *European Journal of Cultural Studies*, 3 (2): 233-58.

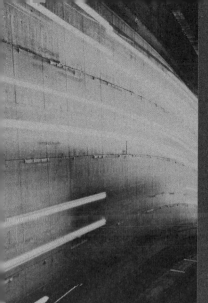

Part 5

MEDIA REPRESENTATIONS

Introduction

Daniele Albertazzi and Paul Cobley

This part of the book is devoted to essays about the representation in different media of various facets of life. That said, the media and forms that tend to dominate in this section are television, film, magazines, newspapers, news and advertising. One reason for this – and the reason that representation is so important – is that these media seem to be so omni-present. Furthermore, although the media are clearly industries and part of national and continental media systems, most *consumers* of media encounter media through representations. This is where they interact with media most directly, in spite of the fact that the economic bearing of the media industries may be having an impact on their lives in different ways. In fact, the essays in this part seek to demonstrate that representations not only contribute to how we experience facets of life, but often representations actually *create* those facets in order that they *can* be experienced.

Three concepts are important, here, and are worked through in these chapters. These are: representation, ideology and discourse. You need to gain a sense of what each of these means by the way that they are used in each of the chapters in this part, by the recommended further reading and by your own reading round the topic. (The following offer a good start to the latter task: Hall (1997) on representation; Eagleton (1991) on ideology; and Coupland and Jaworski (2001) on discourse). However, a few words on the topics are offered here to orientate your reading.

Because the *rendering* of any object in the world *cannot be* that which it renders, representations are never straightforward *presentations*. Rather, they are always *r*epresentations of the world and the relationships between people in it. What is common to understandings of the act of representation is that represent*ing* is not a simple reflection of the world but a *creation* of something that is almost new. It is impossible for us to think of ourselves, our gender, 'race', sexuality, for example – without involving the changing images, ideas and values associated with facets of our identity which surround us: representations. These representations are ubiquitous and make such a contribution to the production of our 'common sense' understandings of the world that we can hardly imagine being without them. Yet, of course, they are not without problems: much mainstream portrayal of, say, religious issues, bodies, sexualities and national identities, to mention just a few of the topics covered in this part, is said to share stereotypical notions of what is acceptable or unacceptable, of how people 'should' experience and express their sexuality, what is 'appropriate' to their age or gender, how they are affected by their national identity, how their religious beliefs are supposed to make them behave, and so on. These stereotypes can be said to serve specific interests and have very real effects – think, for example, of the extent to which certain representations of Islamic communities can contribute to heightening tensions in society following 9/11 and how such a climate of fear can be used to justify the approval of draconian anti-terror legislation. Representations can (and indeed do) serve specific interests, held by specific groups, individuals and/or organisations in specific historical and social circumstances. In other words, representations are *ideological*.

Insofar as the term 'ideology' is used in everyday speech, it usually refers to the realm of 'ideas' and 'values'. Moreover, there are clearly 'ideas' behind all representations. However, ideology also operates beyond the realm of representation. It operates in people's *concrete* experience, giving coherence, consistency and 'naturalness' to our lived existence. Yet, all the time, it serves to perpetuate and extend existing power relations which may serve the interests of some at the expense of others. Ideology precedes media representations but it also charges representations with the task of disseminating nutshell versions of the complex configurations of our identities and *re*presenting them as fixed or 'obvious': hence the appearance of the aforementioned *stereotypes* in the media – images that we know (with some thought) to be, simultaneously,

- very condensed or simplified;
- 'false';
- containers of some recognisable 'truths' (if stereotypes did not contain some truth they would garner no notice at all and be all too easy to dismiss).

Representations can contain specific ideologies (ideas about how the world is) and can be considered to be ideological in general. This latter is because, if representations contain stereotypes – and, sometimes, even if they do not – the act of representation will *exclude* many features and ways of understanding the social world.

One can therefore see in representations the workings of ideology, sets of ideas which exist prior to the representation. Yet, in the act of *re*presentation there is also a construction of that which one can have an ideology about. Put another way, the very act of communication actually *produces* the objects about which one can have an ideological understanding. So, in talking about things, writing about them, representing them in the media, we participate in the creation of a *discourse* about those things. Discourses, like the representations that uphold them, have self-constructed boundaries that allow us to communicate about some things but not about others. There are various discourses of identity: we know that there are discourses of class, nationality, gender, sexuality, age, race and ethnicity. Representations of all of these facets of identity are considered in the following essays. Nowadays, it is commonplace for us to consider each of these facets as being made up of ideas, in spite of the fact that we feel them deeply – sometimes bodily – as we inhabit different classes, genders, age groups, sexualities, races, nationalities, and in spite of the fact that, with the exception of class, they are usually taken to be 'natural' or biological. Thus, we can see identity as an object created not just by nature but also by *discourse*. For any such discourse to be maintained, there must be representations that feed it. But are there only discourses and representations which are directly about facets of identity? Obviously not; in fact, there are numerous discourses which are upheld by representations and these do a number of things, while contributing to discourses about identity as well. Some of them are considered in the following chapter. One chapter is on the body, health and illness, matters which are supposedly biological but have supreme importance for our identities. Others are on sport and sex acts, bodily activities which, when media representations of them are analysed, tell us much about the discourses which maintain them at the centre of European society. Finally, there is a chapter on the representation of religion, a discourse which, in its many competing forms, has been a focus for much contestation at the level of representation in the past decade.

References

Coupland, N. and Jaworski, A. (2001) 'Discourse' in P. Cobley (ed) *The Routledge Companion to Semiotics and Linguistics*, London: Routledge.

Eagleton, T. (1991) *Ideology: An Introduction*, London: Verso.

Hall, S. (1997) 'The Work of Representation' in S. Hall (ed) *Representation: Cultural Representations and Signifying Practices*, London and Thousand Oaks, CA: Sage.

27

Sexualities

Charlotte Ross

Chapter overview

This chapter explores the representation of sexualities in a variety of media forms, paying attention to the ways in which readers and viewers may be influenced by normative portrayals of sexuality in the mainstream media. The chapter discusses the construction of sexual stereotypes and how to go about critically interpreting media representation of sexualities. As an illustration, the chapter offers a case study of the representation and regulation of female sexuality in Italian magazines, television and the internet.

Introduction

In a consumer society we are constantly exposed to sexually-charged images through advertising. These images predominantly seek not to broaden our attitudes to sexuality, but to persuade us to part with our cash by acquiring products that may enable us to emulate dominant, idealised modalities of sexuality. While the representation of sexuality is obviously not in itself a problem, much mainstream portrayal of it, as in the example of advertising, seems bound by narrow, stereotypical notions of what is acceptable or unacceptable, or of how people 'should' experience and express their sexuality. Scholars debate the ways and the extent to which different social groups are influenced by the representations of sexuality they encounter or seek out, but there is general agreement that our sexual behaviour is indeed influenced by what we read and see in the media, which provides a pervasive form of sexual socialisation (Brown 2002). Moreover, the ways in which a particular culture represents sexualities can tell us a great deal about that culture's priorities, anxieties and concerns. It therefore becomes essential to question the messages embedded in the representations of sexuality by which we are surrounded.

Critical discussions of sexuality emphasise its socially-constructed nature: that is, sexual acts, identities and behaviours do not result purely from our biological instincts, nor do they carry a universally valid, fixed meaning. Instead, sexual identities and expressions of sexuality differ in meaning and form depending on the context in which they occur; in other words, cultural contexts influence both how our sense of ourselves as sexual beings is produced, and how, why, where, when and with whom we may choose to engage in, or refrain from, sexual activities of any kind. Gender theory is based on the premise that gender identity (masculinity and femininity) does not derive from our biology, but is formed through a series of culturally imposed, learned acts and behaviours (see Chapter 28). These behaviours are shaped by social norms of 'proper' masculinity and femininity, and impact on everything from the aesthetic cliché of pink frills for girls and plain blue for boys, to the way we walk and talk, and the career paths and social roles we feel we 'should', or are able to, follow. Similarly, sexuality is constructed through a system of power relations channelled through legal, religious and state institutions, as well as through the mass media and social norms, that direct and determine culturally 'acceptable' expressions and understandings of sexuality: whether it is appropriate to engage in sexual acts in public (and if so what kind of acts?); whether homosexuality is considered a crime or simply a differently-oriented sexual desire; what 'normal' sexuality is for a 15-year-old girl; and where the line is drawn by censors evaluating sexually-explicit material, for example.

According to theorists of gender and sexuality, the system of sexual power relations that dominates in the Western world imposes a norm of 'compulsory heterosexuality' that disallows gay, lesbian, transsexual and bisexual identities by making their expression illegal, or socially and morally unacceptable (Rich 1980; Butler 1999: 155). However, rather than obediently remaining within the confines of this system, individual subjects are able to push at and breach its boundaries, redefining and multiplying the models of sexuality that are available, visible and accepted in a particular cultural context (Butler 1999: 39). In this view, norms of sexuality are both imposed upon individuals and open to redefinition by them. We are given a set of rules to obey, but we also have the power to rewrite them, to a certain extent, and to shape our own sexualities.

This chapter explores some of the tensions around the representation of sexuality in a variety of media forms, paying attention to the ways in which readers and viewers are influenced by normative portrayals of sexuality in the mainstream media (those that reinforce sexual norms or stereotypes), but are also able to see beyond 'compulsory heterosexuality'. However, although we are theoretically in a position to *choose* how to live our sexuality and sexual orientation, rather than obediently following the norms set out for us by others, this may not be a straightforward process. The chapter begins with an account of sexual stereotypes and some of the ways in which they are constructed and function in mainstream media. This is followed by a discussion of how to go about critically interpreting media representations of sexuality. As an illustration, the chapter offers a case study of the representation and regulation of female sexuality in Italian magazines, television and the internet. Through specific examples I argue that while an increased range of sexual identities is now visible across different media formats, which offer a substantial challenge to narrow (hetero)normative, stereotypical depictions of sexuality (ones that privilege norms of heterosexuality), the frequency with which we are exposed to normative images and views of sexuality mean that one nevertheless has to work hard in order to discover alternatives to the norms.

Sexual stereotypes

Stereotypes of any kind hold themselves up as 'common', 'representative' depictions of certain groups of people, playing on reductive, generic and often prejudicial understandings of the characteristics they might embody. Stereotypes bundle individuals into groups, and through frequently disseminated generic portrayals, assert that people associated with those groups inevitably fit particular patterns of behaviour. Furthermore, the implications that stereotypes carry about certain social groups are naturalised as though they already existed before the stereotype was made popular, when in reality we often derive our understandings of social groups from stereotypical representations (Dyer 2000: 248). This leads to the problematic, circular argument, 'Of course s/he did that; it's because s/he is gay/straight/black/young etc.', trapping people into rigid roles, denying their individuality and even attributing to them characteristics that they do not possess.

In Western media production, stereotypes have long operated to reinforce perceived barriers between notions of masculine and feminine gender identity, of female and male sexuality, of heterosexuality and homosexuality, among other categories, which are often presented as clear and distinct opposites. Stereotypes promote the view that there is a 'natural' and irreducible difference between men and women, that heterosexuals and homosexuals are clearly distinct groups of people or that male sexuality contrasts strongly with female sexuality, when in reality there are often significant degrees of similarity and areas of overlap between these categories (Carter and Steiner 2004; Dyer 2000). In this way, stereotypes claim that sexual orientation is clear and fixed, which social constructionists would deny. How can we account for polysexuality if sexual orientation is fixed? What about people who change their sexual orientation (from hetero- to homosexuality or vice versa)?

Sexual stereotypes are often based on a notion of the 'otherness' or fundamental difference between men and women, hetero- and homosexuals, nurtured by an unfounded, prejudiced conviction of the superiority of certain identities over others (Enteman 2003). Patriarchal ideology, which privileges the interests of certain men over other social groups (including other men), in a male-centred, male-dominated society, produces stereotypes of sexually powerful men who control and regulate female sexuality (Johnson 2005). Male (hetero)sexuality has been traditionally portrayed as active, driven by an almost constant need that is based on a biological impulse to reproduce (Holloway 1996: 86). 'Real' masculinity has come to be seen in mainstream representations as fundamentally based on sexual prowess. It is embodied by men who 'prove' themselves through their sexual dominance, reinforced through idealised narratives of physical strength and mechanical or violent sexual power, which is evident in slang terms used to refer to the penis such as 'tool', 'piston' and 'weapon'. This has been theorised as hegemonic male sexuality (Plummer 2005: 180–7). In contrast, stereotypes of women have tended to veer between simplistic, binary opposites; the 'good', nurturing, wife and mother is set against the sexually available or 'loose' woman, who is objectified and commodified: that is, her humanity and individual character are erased and she is viewed and treated like a sexual object that can be bought and sold. Clearly the implications of these stereotypes are potentially enormously harmful. In the representation of sexual crimes against women, the biological discourses surrounding male sexuality may seem to at least partially exonerate aggressive male sexual urges as 'natural', while female victims are often portrayed as sexually enticing, active participants in the violence (Sunindyo 2004). This scenario is captured in the sadly commonplace expressions relating to male sexual violence against women: 'She was asking for it', or 'He just couldn't help himself'. Additionally, there may be a racist or homophobic dimension to depictions of sexuality in the media; for example bell hooks argues that in the US media, black women have been stereotypically portrayed as prostitutes (hooks 1996: 217). Stereotypes of gay men on TV often depict them as outrageously flamboyant, hyper-emotional beings, obsessed by sex. Due to the historical criminalisation and marginalisation of gay men (among other groups), many people only encounter gay culture through these media stereotypes, which serve to reinforce perceived divisions between gay and straight people.

Why are stereotypes so pervasive and powerful? One reason is that it sometimes feels easier to put people into established categories rather than to deal with the complexities of their identities and characteristics that do not fit into these boxes. This allows one group to almost instantaneously measure itself against another group and provides reassurance about who one is and who the other is, never mind how inaccurate these notions might be. Imposing stereotypes on people can also disempower them whilst empowering those doing the imposing. Some argue that one reason for the sexual objectification of women through contemporary media stereotypes was that it worked to prevent women from displacing men from positions of social and political power, once they had been granted the vote (Heller 2000: xii). As gender equality increases and women have more access to positions of public responsibility, sexual equality seems to be decreasing, and we are surrounded by ever more images of women depicted as little more than sexual playthings. Similarly, homophobic or racist sexual stereotypes derive at least in part from a desire to disempower and vilify the perceived 'other', and to reinforce the boundaries of sexual identities that are legitimised by social norms.

Analysing media constructions of sexuality

When approaching media representations of sexuality, key questions to be asked include: who is the image or text aimed at? In what format does it appear? What ideas does it communicate? Does it challenge or reinforce sexual stereotypes? Sexualised images tend to be aimed at specific groups, such as gay men or heterosexual men, and are packaged accordingly: we have magazines for straight men, gay men, lesbians, girls, young women, older women and so on, each promoting a particular type of sexuality. In mainstream media production, patriarchal ideologies have a significant influence on representations of sexuality, with the result that women are often portrayed as decorative, sexualised and seeking validation of themselves through male attention. Women offer themselves up on the pages of our magazines (for both men and women), in advertising and in mainstream, blockbuster films, to be admired not for what they do or think, but for how they look and how sexually attractive they are to men. Often women are depicted scantily clad, reclining in inviting poses that imply they are sexually available and willing to please. (Heterosexual) men too are increasingly bombarded with images of male sexuality. As the male body too becomes a target for fashion retailers and beauty product manufacturers, companies use depictions of hegemonic male sexuality as a hook to capture the male viewer's attention, promising the achievement of 'real' manliness through association with their products. A recent advertisement by Dolce and Gabbana dramatises some of these tensions, as we see a man watched by other men, holding down a woman as if about to have sex with her. Highly problematic in its evocation of a gang rape scene, this scenario has been glamorised by the models' designer clothing and their physiques, which conform to idealised norms of slenderness and hairless skin for women against glistening, muscled torsos for men. Thus on one reading we see a performance of hegemonic male sexuality admired by male witnesses who seemingly aspire to emulate both the 'look' and the deed, enacted on a woman whose sexually inviting pose suggests that she craves this type of dominance and attention. When this advertisement provoked complaints from consumers in Spain for its 'glorification of sexual violence', Dolce and Gabbana withdrew it from the Spanish market, but accused Spain of being 'behind the times' asking 'What does an artistic photo have to do with the real world?' (Nash 2007).

Articles in women's and girls magazines turn predominantly around the issue of physical attractiveness: what exercises can be done, what clothes can be worn, make-up applied, and sexual techniques mastered in order to emulate the ideals of female sexuality promoted on their pages? This type of advice can be analysed as a way of regulating female sexuality by indicating clearly how, and how *not* to behave and present oneself, which reinforces social norms. When you look through magazines, think about how stereotypes of sexuality feature in them. Quizzes and 'how to' articles often assume that all readers will want to achieve the same end result, for example that all women are predominantly concerned with pleasing and keeping their man, rather than experiencing pleasure themselves.

In magazines aimed at (heterosexual) men, women on display are objects to be desired; this is especially true in UK men's magazines such as *Nuts* and *Zoo*. Features which invite readers' girlfriends to send in photographs of themselves in erotic poses serve to consolidate a sense of presumed male sexual entitlement over women. Furthermore, by implication these photos extend the apparent sexual availability of the girlfriends featured to all 'ordinary' women, not only to professional models and celebrities. Media representation of male sports stars, who regularly receive a large amount of female attention, repeatedly collapses sporting and sexual prowess, and seems to exonerate male sporting heroes for exploitative treatment of women, including sexual assault. When 'successful' masculine sexuality is heralded as triumph of power over women, there is little space for the development of more sensitive models of sexuality, which the advent of the 'new man' in the 1990s seemed to suggest might be possible. However, some theorists have begun to explore more nuanced expressions of male sexuality that depart from and dismantle hegemonic discourses (Plummer 2005: 189).

To analyse visual representations of sexuality, helpful questions to ask are: who is doing the looking and who is being looked at? With what intent? What is the power balance – or imbalance? Are gay and lesbian viewers excluded from images aimed at a heterosexual public and vice versa? Critical analysis should pay attention both to the stereotypes depicted, and to the ways in which stereotypes are challenged or resisted. For example, analyses of female sexuality in women's magazines have criticised the unachievable stereotyped ideals of (white, heterosexual) femininity they promote, which require women and girls to buy into the multi-million pound beauty industry as the pathway to success (Woolf 1990). More recently, however, feminist scholars have found that even mainstream women's magazines now manifest a form of 'popular feminism', depicting alongside these familiar, reductive stereotypes alternative identities, such as different ethnicities or lesbian sexuality. Moreover, while sexuality remains the bedrock of female identity in media representation, its construction is no longer exclusively for male pleasure and consumption but for women themselves, and a layer of 'knowing' self-awareness has endowed these publications with a sense of fun and even irony (McRobbie 1996: 189). Nevertheless, you might want to ask whether a touch of irony is enough to undo the effects of the normative images of sexualised women that dominate elsewhere, or of symbols associated with this form of female sexuality such as the infamous 'Playboy bunny'. Playboy bunny merchandise has been marketed to extremely young girls who arguably are unable to assume a 'knowing' stance as regards the sexual implications of this icon. This suggests that attempts to redefine female sexuality on women's terms have yet to make lasting inroads into the popular culture industry.

As regards format, there are clearly differences between television, print media and the internet in terms of how we access representations of sexuality. These differences affect whether images are still or moving, whether we see them briefly or can examine them in detail, and our level and mode of engagement. The internet has revolutionised the way in which we can access and be exposed to information and images, as well as encouraging a more interactive participation in cultural debate by way of blogs, forums and MUDS (multi-user domains). Research has suggested that 'sexual pursuits, ranging from visiting websites with sexual themes to intense online sexual interactions, may be the most common use of the internet' (Stern and Handel 2001: 283). Obviously, these interactions can take many forms. The internet has been celebrated by some people as a 'queer' virtual space, one in which norms of homo- and heterosexuality can be challenged and disrupted, and sexual identity becomes potentially fluid. It provides a virtual space in which previously isolated lesbian, gay, bisexual, transsexual and queer (LGBTQ) individuals, for example, can come together and find support, or in which we can actively experiment with our identities, shrugging off the cultural norms of gendered identity and heteronormativity that we encounter or perform in our everyday lives, and creating avatars of our fantasy selves. Online we can be who we want to be without fear of social stigma, unconstrained by cultural dictates based on our appearance, biology, or the expectations of others. Individuals who feel they need to hide their sexuality at school, at work or with their families, and who suffer from the lack of positive LGBTQ role models in the mainstream media can access a much broader range of information about and representations of LGBTQ issues on the internet. Virtual sites of queer experimentation have been hailed as extremely productive by some because of the multitudinous way in which they enable the development and expression of non-normative sexualities (Shaw 1997). However, the internet has also facilitated the easy and instantaneous transmission of more exploitative forms of sexuality, such as child pornography, which has led to demands for stricter regulation of websites (Jenkins 2001).

National regulation bodies, such as the Advertising Standards Agency in the UK, tread the difficult path of deciding which images of sexuality might give offence, but obviously when it comes to the internet the influence of such an agency is extremely limited (Akdeniz 1999). The question of what constitutes 'pornography' is also highly complex and contested (see Chapter 36). The freedom for humans to express their sexuality as they wish is an important human right; however, sometimes freedom of expression blurs with normative ideology confusing the freedom to represent sexuality (i.e. the sheer availability of sexually-charged images) with increased sexual autonomy for individuals (i.e. the freedom to decide oneself how one wishes to live and present one's sexuality). In other words, more sexual content on television will not necessarily encourage people to see and live beyond stereotypes.

Sexuality in contemporary Italian media production

Having presented some of the issues to take into consideration when analysing the representation of sexuality in the media, I now consider some of the points made above in relation to the Italian media context. Since the 1980s, the inescapable figure of Silvio Berlusconi has exerted a significant influence on Italian life and culture, both as a political leader who has governed the country (1994, 2001–06, 2008–) and as the owner of Fininvest, the holding company of a very large media group. Fininvest controls the advertising company Publitalia, the television group Mediaset (which operates three terrestrial networks – Canale 5, Italia 1 and Retequattro) and many other media-related businesses. In his periods in office as prime minister, Berlusconi has exerted tremendous power over the Italian media, both through his private companies and through his influence over the public service broadcaster RAI (Radiotelevisione Italiana), which in contrast with the politically-neutral position of the BBC has long been a battleground for competing political influences (Padovani 2005). After his re-election in 2001, Berlusconi began to intervene ever more directly in the running of the RAI, even in 2003 publicly criticising presenters whose views he disagreed with, who were then suspended from public broadcasting (Rothenberg 2009). Berlusconi's views on women are well known due to his many comments regarding the attractiveness of female celebrities, including, in what seems to be his highest accolade to a woman, statements to certain individuals that if he were not already married, he would marry them (Amato 2007). In his worldview, women's highest aspirations seem to be attracting powerful men through their physical attractiveness. He has used his networks to promote an ideal of the heterosexual family and to flood the channels with variety TV programmes featuring bikini-clad women who serve merely as sexual titillation for viewers, which has proved easier to achieve there than it would have done in the UK, for example, given the lack of regulation of Italian television (Ginsborg 2005). Under Berlusconi's influence, troupes of dancers known as 'veline', meaning 'tissue paper' or 'carbon copy', have populated programmes such as the satirical news show *Striscia la notizia* ('The News Slithers') on Mediaset's Canale 5. The *veline* perform energetic routines to animate the pauses between different elements of the show, but have no voice or role to fulfil other than to look 'good', according to cultural stereotypes of female attractiveness; they are slim, white (although tanned), have long shiny hair and their faces are fixed in an open-mouthed smile that strives to please or in an expression that aims to titillate the (male) viewer. There is no room for individual identity here, and the young women, who gain their coveted positions by performing a hyperbolic version of heterosexual female sexuality, remain carbon copies of one another.

This is arguably the most visible form of female sexuality in mainstream Italian media today

Source: Livio Valerio / Press Association Images

During the summer months, when *Striscia la notizia* is off-air, it is replaced by the half-hour programme *Veline* in which new recruits are scouted from around the country. This programme attracts an audience of 5,520,000, or 24 per cent of the target audience, composed of viewers aged from 15–64, making it the most popular non-sporting programme on Canale 5 (Mediaset 2008). The *veline* are thus becoming celebrities in their own right, but are decidedly anti-feminist icons, whose sexually-charged television exploits – from dancing in a shower to accidentally revealing a nipple – can be viewed freely on YouTube, but whose voices remain inaudible.

The sexual objectification of women on Italian TV provoked Adrian Michaels, an American journalist living in Milan, to write an article expressing his shock at the gratuitous use of virtually naked women to sell everything and anything in Italy, and as a device to 'cheer up' male TV viewers (2007). Michaels argues that Italy's style of advertising and programming would not be tolerated in the US and the UK, and suggests that the low percentage of women in Italian politics, in executive business positions and especially in the media, makes it hard for women to break with the demeaning sexual stereotypes reinforced by the mainstream Italian media. Female readers have written in to the women's magazine *Io donna* (*Woman*, a supplement of the daily *Il Corriere della sera*) complaining that they resent turning on the television since it actually feels like they are stepping into a bordello (Maraini 2006: 194). This stereotype of women as sexually available, eager to please men, and voiceless is widely disseminated since, as recent statistics show, 91 per cent of Italians watch TV regularly (at least three times a week; CENSIS 2008: 10); moreover, if there is nothing of any interest on TV, 58 per cent will nevertheless continue to watch, passively consuming stereotypical models of sexuality (CENSIS 2005: 24).

Alongside these highly heteronormative depictions of women, transvestite individuals have gained fame on Italian TV, such as the provocative drag queen Platinette who has appeared on several talk shows, including the 'Maurizio Costanzo Show' (the longest running Italian talk show, screened on Mediaset's Canale 5). She also hosts a daily radio programme on Radio Deejay, *Casa Platinette* ('Platinette's House'). However, some argue that figures such as these encourage an unhelpfully sensationalistic view of transvestites, and by association transsexuals, gays and lesbians. Until very recently, homosexuality has been a taboo subject in Italy; more so than in the UK or its neighbour France. This changed in 2000 when Rome hosted World Pride, against the wishes of the Pope and the Vatican, provoking much media debate of LGBTQ issues as Rome was represented as an international gay tourist destination (Luongo 2002). The success of World Pride led to hard-fought campaigns to legalise civil partnerships for same-sex couples, and to fully implement anti-discrimination legislation advocated by the EU, among other issues. The Vatican and many politicians are strongly opposed to LGBTQ individuals gaining improved civil rights, such as civil unions, as they fear this will threaten traditional marriage in some way. Thus gays and lesbians are constructed as a threat to social stability. Alongside mainstream media production, Italian LGBTQ associations have been developing their own media outlets for some time: magazines and websites that feature alternative aesthetics and modes of desire, and engage with political struggles as well as cultural production. The 'Circolo

Mario Mieli' (http://www.mariomieli.org/), founded in Rome in 1983, which offers legal, psychological and social support to LGBTQ individuals and their families, as well as organising Rome Pride and many other events, has published the monthly magazine *Aut* since 1995. The Cassero Centre in Bologna, which hosts the headquarters of Italy's largest national LGBTQ association 'Arcigay', as well as a library, and spaces for social, cultural and political gatherings, has issued *Il Cassero*, a bimonthly publication since 2002 (see http://www.cassero.it/ for more details). These magazines are free and are distributed nationally to LGBTQ centres, where they are available to all groups and individuals in the local community who meet in or drop into the centre. The magazines are also available in some other organisations such as cinemas and cafés. Italian LGBTQ websites (e.g. www.gay.it) feature online critiques of the depiction of LGBTQ individuals, communities and queer sexualities in national and international newspapers, on Italian and international TV channels, as well as in cinemas. Yet just because they represent non-normative sexual identities does not mean that these magazines are free from stereotypes; indeed, gay male media cultures in particular have been accused of relying on and promoting narrow norms of gay male sexuality based on club and consumer culture, identified as 'homonormativity' (Duggan 2002).

Front cover of *Il Cassero*, May–June 2006
Source: Courtesy of Cassero, Bologna

For lesbians however, the alternatives proposed by publications such as *Il Cassero* present a much more varied, rare vision of a self-determined sexuality that stands out amidst the troupes of *veline* on mainstream TV. Here we see the cover of the May/June 2006 issue of *Il Cassero*, depicting two women who are much more fully and comfortably clothed than the *veline*, who are implicitly intimately involved but without proclaiming that fact overtly.

The women's gazes are averted from the viewer's eyes, fixed on their own goals, rendering them less available for visual consumption. Moreover, unlike the *veline*, they are not overtly seeking approval from or attempting to please anyone except themselves. Indeed, these young women represent an alternative sexual orientation to compulsory heterosexuality as reinforced by the *veline*, and therefore are not overtly sexualised. The image dismantles hierarchies promoted by normative heterosexuality, where the woman is generally seeking approval by making herself sexually available, and refuses to act as 'lesbian' titillation for heterosexual men, as promoted in UK men's magazines such as *Loaded* or *Zoo*. These types of images do much to dismantle narrow sexual stereotypes and to encourage young women, among other groups, to break away from social norms and to define themselves on their own terms. However, despite their national distribution, the circulation of magazines such as *Il Cassero* is largely limited to LGBTQ individuals rather than reaching out to the population at large. In Italy, TV remains the dominant influence since only 38 per cent of Italians use the internet regularly (at least three times a week; CENSIS 2008: 10).

Conclusions

Sexually-charged images abound ever more frequently across the range of our media, yet this has not led to a significant diversification in terms of the models of sexuality represented; indeed, in countries such as Italy, increased representation of sexuality on television can be seen to push against the work of feminists and LGBTQ campaigners who have worked to encourage a more respectful, diverse and less stereotypical representation of women and LGBTQ individuals. Sexual stereotypes remain highly influential in the process of sexual socialisation, and may prevent individuals from expressing themselves as they wish, as well as provoking feelings of frustration and perceived inadequacy that can lead to anger and violence, against the self or others. If women have traditionally been sexually objectified in the media, men are increasingly finding themselves in a similar position, as depictions of hegemonic male sexuality persist in media culture, for both gay and heterosexual men. Given the influence of media production on our sense of ourselves, representations of sexuality must be carefully and critically evaluated. However, as Butler (1999) suggests, individuals do have the capacity to resist dominant discourses, and alternative media may prove rich sites of such resistance, where non-normative sexualities are elaborated and thrive. Theoretical and critical debates on sexuality in the media are constantly evolving to keep up with ongoing developments in socio-cultural practice as well as in technological capabilities, making this an exciting, pertinent and dynamic field of inquiry.

Questions

1 Consider the extent of nudity in magazines for male and female readers. What purpose does the nudity serve? Does it have the same connotations for male and female bodies?

2 Compare a range of magazines for heterosexual and LGBTQ readerships. What kinds of stereotypes and challenges to these stereotypes can you identify?

3 Think about the portrayal of sexualities in popular TV shows like soap operas. What norms are operating and how are 'alternative' sexualities presented?

Further reading

Arthurs, J. (2004) *Television and Sexuality: Regulation and the Politics of Taste,* New York: Open University Press. A historical and theoretical consideration of the representation of sexuality on television, which includes empirical case studies on pornography and sexuality in prime time drama.

Gross, L. and Woods, J. D. (eds) (1999) *The Columbia Reader on Lesbians and Gay Men in Media, Society, and Politics*, New York: Columbia University Press. An anthology of key readings of gay and lesbian cultures and identities, which includes a specific section on media representation.

Gunter, B. (2002) *Media Sex. What Are the Issues?* London: Lawrence Erlbaum Associates. A critical discussion of representation of sex and sexualities in the media, which details anxieties surrounding sex in the contemporary media, and explores the potential socio-cultural effects of media sex.

Keller, J. R. and Stratyner, L. (eds) (2006) *The New Queer Aesthetic on Television: Essays on Recent Programming*, Jefferson, NC: McFarland. An edited collection of essays which analyse developments in the representation of queer identities in TV programmes such as *Will and Grace, Six Feet Under*, and *Queer as Folk*.

Levy, A. (2005) *Female Chauvinist Pigs: Women and the Rise of Raunch Culture,* London and New York: Free Press. Based largely on the North American context, this is a provocative critique of 'pseudo empowerment' for women in contemporary popular culture and media.

References

Akdeniz, Y. (1999) *Sex on the Net: The Dilemma of Policing Cyberspace,* London: South Street.

Amato, R. (2007) 'Berlusconi e le Donne, Battute e Gaffe Tra Veronica, Aida e le Altre', *La Repubblica,* 13 January.

Brown, J. D. (2002) 'Mass Media Influences on Sexuality', *Journal of Sex Research,* 39 (1): 42-5.

Butler, J. (1999) *Gender Trouble. Feminism and the Subversion of Identity*, London and New York: Routledge.

Carter, C. and Steiner, L. (2004) 'Mapping the Contested Terrain of Media and Gender Research' in C. Carter and L. Steiner (eds) *Critical Readings: Media and Gender*, Maidenhead: Open University Press, pp. 11-35.

CENSIS (2008) 'Communicazione e Media' in *42 Rapporto sulla Situazione Sociale del Paese,* www.censis.it/277/280/339/6663/6667/6677/content.asp (accessed 12 February 2009).

CENSIS (2005) *Quarto Rapporto sulla Comunicazione in Italia,* Milan: FrancoAngeli.

Duggan, L. (2002) 'The New Homonormativity: The Sexual Politics of Neoliberalism' in R. Castronovo and D. Nelson (eds) *Materializing Democracy: Towards a Revitalized Cultural Politics*, Duke University Press, Durham, NC, pp. 175–94.

Dyer, R. (2000) 'The Role of Stereotypes' in P. Marris and S. Thornham (eds) *Media Studies: A Reader*, New York: New York University Press, pp. 245–51.

Enteman, W. F. (2003) 'Stereotyping, Prejudice and Discrimination' in P. M. Lester and S. Dente Ross (eds) *Images that Injure. Pictorial Stereotypes in the Media*. Westport, CT: Praeger, pp. 15–21.

Ginsborg, P. (2005) *Berlusconi: Television, Power and Patrimony*, London: Verso.

Heller, S. (ed) (2000) *Sex Appeal: The Art of Allure in Graphic and Advertising Design*, New York: Allworth Press.

Holloway, W. (1996) 'Gender Difference and the Production of Subjectivity' in S. Jackson and S. Scott (eds) *Feminism and Sexuality: A Reader*, Edinburgh: Edinburgh University Press, pp. 84–100.

hooks, b. (1996) 'Continued Devaluation of Black Womanhood' in S. Jackson and S. Scott (eds) *Feminism and Sexuality: A Reader*, Edinburgh: Edinburgh University Press, pp. 216–23.

Jenkins, P. (2001) *Beyond Tolerance: Child Pornography on the Internet*, New York: New York University Press.

Johnson, A. (2005) *The Gender Knot: Unraveling our Patriarchal Legacy*, Philadelphia: Temple University Press.

Luongo, M. (2002) 'Rome's World Pride: Making the Eternal City an International Gay Tourism Destination' in *GLQ: A Journal of Lesbian and Gay Studies*, 8 (1–2): 167–81.

Maraini, D. (2006) *I Giorni di Antigone. Quaderni di Cinque Anni*, Milan: Rizzoli.

McRobbie, A. (1996) '*More!* New Sexualities in Girls' and Women's Magazines' in J. Curran, D. Morley and V. Walkerdine (eds) *Cultural Studies and Communications*, London and New York: Arnold.

Mediaset (2008) 'Audience: Canale 5, Partenza Al Top Per "Veline", Programma Non Sportivo Piú Visto Della Giornata', 11 June, www.mediaset.it/corporate/salastampa/2008/comunicatostampa_4486_it.shtml (accessed 11 June 2008).

Michaels, A. (2007) 'Naked Ambition', *Financial Times*, 13 July (Arts and Weekend).

Padovani, C. (2005) *A Fatal Attraction. Public Television and Politics in Italy*, Lanham, MD: Rowman and Littlefield.

Plummer, K. (2005) 'Male Sexualities' in M. S. Kimmel, J. Hearn and R. Connell (eds) *Handbook of Studies on Men and Masculinities*, London: Sage, pp. 178–95.

Rich, A. (1980) 'Compulsory Heterosexuality and Lesbian Existence', *Signs* 5 (4): 631–60.

Rothenberg, N. (2009) 'Political Cleansing and Censorship in Public Television: A Case Study of Michele Santoro and Enzo Biagi', in D. Albertazzi, C. Brook, C. Ross and N. Rothenberg (eds) *Resisting the Tide: Cultures of Opposition Under Berlusconi (2001–06)*, London: Continuum, pp. 217–30.

Shaw, D. F. (1997) 'Gay men and Computer Communication: A Discourse of Sex and Identity in Cyberspace' in S. Jones (ed) *Virtual Culture: Identity and Communication in Cybersociety*, London: Sage, pp. 133–4.

Stern, S. E. and Handel, A. D. (2001) 'Sexuality and Mass Media: The Historical Context of Psychology's Reaction to Sexuality on the Internet', *The Journal of Sex Research*, 38 (4): 283–91.

Sunindyo, S. (2004) 'Murder, Gender and the Media. Sexualising Politics and Violence' in C. Carter and L. Steiner (eds) *Critical Readings: Media and Gender*, Maidenhead: Open University Press, pp. 87–103.

Woolf, N. (1990) *The Beauty Myth: How Images of Beauty are Used Against Women*, London: Chatto and Windus.

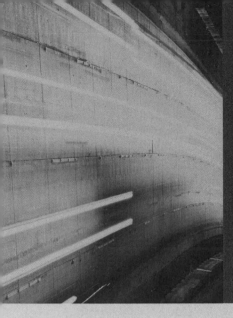

28

Gender

Rosalind Gill

Chapter overview

This essay focuses on representations of gender in the media. It outlines early feminist critique of media and illustrates how this has informed contemporary debates about gender representations. It then goes on to discuss gender representations in news (particularly sexual violence and women in politics) and in advertising, the latter of which has seen significant changes in recent years. Advertising, it is shown, has had to respond to feminist critique and has done so by using 'edgy' images, depictions of women with 'ordinary' looks and images that feature sexually assertive women. The final section looks at an important recent development in the media: the casual eroticisation of the male body.

Introduction

We live in a world that is stratified along lines of gender, race, ethnicity, class, age, disability, sexuality and location, and in which the privileges, disadvantages and exclusions associated with such categories are unevenly distributed. We also live in a world that is increasingly saturated by media, information and communication technologies. In many respects the past four decades of research on gender and the media has been an attempt to explore the relationship between these two facts. In this chapter I will introduce the study of gender representations in the media. The objective is to give a general sense of the research that is done in this field, and its main findings, as well as to focus on two areas that have received particular attention from scholars interested in gender representations: news and advertising.

Before beginning it is important to highlight three points. First, note that not all research on gender and media is concerned with representations. Many media analysts interested in gender have conducted research on audiences or on media production or organisation; the study of representations of gender in media is just one part of this wider set of interests. Secondly, it is worth pointing out that not all research on gender and the media is concerned with women. There is a growing body of research concerned with changing representations of masculinity, and some of this is discussed below. Thirdly, it may be worth making a distinction between the general body of research about gender and communication, and *feminist* media studies. The latter takes a more explicitly political viewpoint and is animated by the desire to understand how images and cultural constructions are connected to patterns of inequality, domination and oppression. To designate a piece of research feminist is to signal its concern with enduring gender inequalities and injustices, amongst a matrix of other forms of oppression, relating to race, sexuality, disability and other identities or locations. Much of the research discussed in this chapter may be understood within this broad feminist perspective.

Early feminist media critique

Early feminist media critique in the 1960s and 1970s came from a number of different sources: from academics in universities in the newly emerging fields of cultural and communication studies; from women within the media industries who were concerned about the lack of opportunities for themselves and their female peers; and from women outside both academia and the media who were pushed towards activism by their anger at what they regarded as the patronising or demeaning stereotypes through which women were represented.

Looking back from the vantage point of the early 21st century, this moment is notable for the extraordinary *confidence* of the analyses produced. Reviewing a decade of studies in the late 1970s, Gaye Tuchman (1978) unequivocally entitled her article 'the symbolic annihilation of women in the mass media' and wrote of how women were being destroyed by a combination of 'absence', 'trivialisation' and 'condemnation'. Such clear evaluations were not unique and were accompanied by similarly robust calls to action – whether these were voiced as demands for more women in the industry, campaigns for 'positive images' or 'guerilla interventions' into billboard advertisements. Writing about this period of research on gender and the media, Angela McRobbie (1999) has characterised it as one of 'angry repudiation'.

By the late 1980s 'angry repudiation' had largely given way to something more equivocal and complex. As Myra Macdonald (1995) has noted, one of the reasons for this is that media content changed dramatically over this period. The notion that the media offered a relatively stable template of femininity to which to aspire gave way to a more plural and fragmented set of signifiers of gender. There was a new playfulness in media representations, a borrowing of codes between different genres, and a growing awareness and interest in processes of image construction. Overall, media output was shaped by producers and consumers who were increasingly 'media savvy' and familiar with the terms of cultural critique, including feminism (Goldman 1992).

Contemporary shifts

The 1990s and first decade of the 21st century marked further important shifts. First, this period saw a proliferation of *different theoretical languages* for discussing media representations of gender. What Liesbet van Zoonen (1994) has characterised as the 'transmission model' of media was replaced by more constructionist, poststructuralist-influenced accounts. These tended to see meaning as more fluid, unstable and contradictory, and to emphasise the role played by media in constructing subjectivity and identity. Queer theory and postcolonial writing also exerted an influence in opening up such questions, producing 'gender trouble' (Butler 1990) and a more intersectional approach based on the understanding that social positions are multiple and relational (Phoenix and Pattynama 2006).

Secondly, as in media studies more generally, the last decade has witnessed a marked interest in questions about global media amongst gender scholars. At its most straightforward this translates into a greater international focus and more cross-national comparisons. In 1995 the first extensive cross-national study of women's portrayal in the media – covering newspapers, radio and television in 71 countries – found that only 17 per cent of the world's news subjects (i.e. newsmakers or interviewees) were women. The proportion of females was lowest in Asia (14 per cent) and highest in North America (27 per cent). This Global Media Monitoring Project gave the first truly international picture of women's underrepresentation in news. A follow-up study in 2006 found that the percentage of female news actors was still only 21 per cent. Even in those countries doing 'best', women only represented just over a quarter of news actors, and across many aspects of political and economic life women were quite literally invisible. Globally, men constituted 86 per cent of spokespeople and 83 per cent of experts, while women were more than twice as likely as men to be portrayed as victims (Global Media Monitoring Project 2006).

An interest in globalisation also produced a focus on how representations 'travel'. David Machin and Joanna Thornborrow (2003) have written a revealing study of the global brand *Cosmopolitan* magazine, examining the extent to which its depictions of femininity were globalised or tailored to specific local settings – asking, for example, how different the UK edition of *Cosmopolitan* is from the Greek or Indian or Argentinian editions? They highlight the construction of a global 'fun fearless female' across a range of different national contexts. Michelle Lazar (2004) too has produced fascinating research about globalised advertising in Asia, pointing to the construction of an almost 'identikit' image of desirable youthful femininity: the ideal model should look 'a little bit' Indian, a little bit Thai, a little bit Malaysian, and is carefully designed to exemplify a 'pan-Asian blend' of 'consumer sisterhood'.

A third shift in recent research on gender and media can be seen in the growing interest in representations of men and masculinity. This has been particularly evident in film studies, as well as in research on the proliferation of men's magazines or 'lad mags' such as *FHM, loaded, Zoo* and *Nuts* (Benwell 2003; Crewe 2003; Jackson *et al.* 2001). Some research has examined the way the media are implicated in particular dominant representations of masculinity such as the figures of 'new man', 'new lad' or 'metrosexual' (Gill 2003; Nixon 1996). A further focus (explored below) is on changing representations of the male body in media sites such as advertising or fashion magazines.

Perhaps not surprisingly another new focus of interest for gender and media researchers has been the internet. Early research looked at gendered practices in on-line sites such as chat rooms or multi-user dungeons. Approaches tended to be polarised between, on the one hand, techno-utopians who believed the web would offer unparalleled opportunities to transcend the body and to explore futures devoid of social divisions such as gender and, on the other, the cyber-pessimists who argued that the technology could never escape its origins in the military-industrial complex and who pointed to new forms of oppression that were practised in online communities, e.g. flaming or cyber-bullying. In the last few years the excesses of both positions have given way to more measured and cautious research, exploring (for example) the impact of dating sites on the way in which people conduct their intimate relationships, or the emerging forms of sociality on network sites such as Facebook or Bebo. Research on the web is still in its infancy and, like other media scholars, those interested in gender are fascinated by questions about the longer term impact of the communications revolution it has produced: the ways it might transform democracy and politics, the extent to which it offers a space for re-imagining identities, and whether it breaks down previously stable distinctions between media producers and media consumers.

The latter question has also been asked in relation to the final recent transformation in feminist media studies I will mention: notably the growing interest in new genres such as reality TV and makeover TV, and their connection to the rise and rise of celebrity culture (Biressi and Nunn 2005; Hill 2005; Hollows 2000). Feminist researchers have pointed out that the Western preoccupation with celebrity plays out almost exclusively over women's bodies, with an hysterical and punitive interest taken in celebrities judged to be too fat, too thin, to have stray armpit or bikini hair (Julia Roberts) or 'ugly hands' (Madonna) (Gill 2008). Jean Kilbourne (1995) has noted that women are now expected to meet standards of physical perfection that only a mannequin could achieve. What does the daily ubiquity of such hostile, excoriating vilification of women's 'failing' bodies mean for gender relations?

Gender representations in news

Having pointed to some general trends in research about representations of gender in media, I will now turn to the first of my two case studies, concerned with gender in news. We have already seen how news is dominated by men – as journalists, as presenters, as 'experts', as news actors more generally. However, it is not just the small numbers of women in news that is a cause for concern, but also the ways in which women are portrayed when they do become 'newsworthy'. One consistent finding from research is that most news about women focuses on their physical appearance – indeed many newspaper editors seem incapable of printing a story featuring a woman without some evaluation of her attractiveness, or at least a description of her age and hair colour. Gaye Tuchman's (1978) description of one of the 'unwritten laws' of media reporting seems as depressingly true today as it was when she wrote it 30 years ago. Almost whoever she is the media will represent a woman in one of two ways: in terms of her domestic role or her sexual attractiveness (or both). This goes for female politicians and women who become subjects of news because they are victims of crime, as much as for the entertainment celebrities who increasingly fill our daily papers.

Reporting sexual violence

A particular concern in studies of gender and news has been the examination of the role media reports might play in cases of sexual violence. An Amnesty International study about the UK, published in November 2005, found that a 'blame culture' exists around sexual violence, with a significant proportion of the British population believing that women are partly responsible if they are sexually attacked. Some 30 per cent of Amnesty's respondents thought a woman would be partly to blame for being raped if she was drunk, 26 per cent thought this was the case if she was wearing sexy or revealing clothing, and 22 per cent would be more likely to find a woman blameworthy if she had had several sexual partners in the past. A number of researchers have argued that findings such as these, together with the scandalously low conviction rates for rape (less than 6 per cent of cases that reach the courts – already a tiny minority of all cases – result in a conviction), require attention to the impact of media representations (Benedict 1992; Cuklanz 1996, 2000; Moorti 2002; Soothill and Walby 1991).

Several well-established myths seem to inform much reporting of sexual violence. These include the notion that rape is trivial ('it's just sex'), the idea that rape attackers are motivated by lust and unable to help themselves, and the myth that women 'cry rape' for revenge or in order to seek attention. This myth was mobilised powerfully in the case of a rape allegation made against footballer Jonny Evans at the Manchester United Christmas party in December 2007. British newspapers described Evans as 'a rising star' (Ducker 2007), 'a real gent' (Roberts *et al.* 2007), 'shy and well behaved' and 'one of the quietest and most intelligent players on United's books' (Roberts *et al.* 2007). Reporting highlighted his unblemished record and his nine GCSEs. In stark contrast, the women attending the party were variously described as 'scantily clad young women, some so drunk they were falling over' (Jenkins and Ducker 2007), 'unseasonably tanned bleach-blonde young women' in 'designer minidresses and Jimmy Choos' 'trying to bag a footballer for the night' (Pendlebury 2007). Meanwhile the *Sun* quotes 'a United insider' who said 'only the best looking were allowed in. They were hand-picked and very excited, almost in a state of hysteria' (Pyatt 2007). Lest these comments are not enough to discredit the allegation, the *Sun*'s front page declares as a banner: 'I'M NO RAPIST', *The Times* (on 20 December 2007) headlines with 'When claims are false lives can be destroyed', and the *Daily Mail* highlights an unnamed 'police source' saying 'many of the women were there to bag a wealthy football star, and while we have to take any allegation of rape extremely seriously we will be examining the woman's background and who she associates with closely'.

Studies from across the world have highlighted the ways in which news reporting of sexual violence sensationalises it, gives a distorted view of its incidence and

Front cover of the *Sun*, 20 December 2007

Source: Copyright © 2007 News Group Newspapers Ltd

nature, trivialises women's experiences of the attack, and reports rapes in a manner that is designed to be titillating or arousing. Female victims are frequently described in sexualised terms: 'sexy 21-year-old', 'blonde beauty', 'curvaceous model', etc. with descriptions that bear little relationship to the woman's experience of the attack e.g. 'he fondled her breasts'. Helen Benedict has noted the key role that language like this places in news reporting:

> Men are never described as hysterical, bubbly, pretty, pert, prudish, vivacious or flirtatious, yet these are all words used to describe the female victims of cases I have examined . . . male

415

crime victims are rarely described in terms of their sexual attractiveness, female crime victims almost always are . . . Even policewomen and female detectives were described as 'attractive' or 'pretty'.   (Benedict 1992: 20-1)

She asks us to imagine press reports saying 'Vivacious John Harris was attacked in his home yesterday' or 'handsome, blonde detective Paul Robinson took the witness stand today'. Of course, we cannot. Imagining reversals in this way can be a useful strategy for thinking about the representation of gender as it helps to expose our own taken for granted assumptions.

Women in politics

Another key focus of research in recent years has been the way in which those women who have made it into senior positions of public office are treated by the media, compared with their male counterparts. Female politicians receive significantly less coverage than their male colleagues, even when their relatively small numbers are taken into account. Moreover, the ways in which they are depicted fits with the patterns associated with the portrayal of women generally, in stark contrast to the representation of male parliamentarians. A comparative study of female politicians in Britain, South Africa and Australia found that women's age and marital status are routinely commented upon in news reports (unlike men's), women are frequently referred to only by their first name, photographed in domestic rather than Parliamentary settings, and have their physical appearance obsessively picked apart by journalists (Ross 2002).

In the USA, Hillary Clinton's campaign for the Democratic presidential nomination in 2008 was marked by hostile scrutiny of her appearance. Clinton's credibility was endlessly derogated with a chorus of articles about her 'boxy jackets',

Clinton's 'tears' were endlessly discussed in the media
Source: Elise Amendola / AP / Press Association Images

unflattering haircut, and failure to avail herself of a stylish enough image. The distinctly gendered nature of the coverage was also highlighted by media reactions to her apparent tearfulness early on in the campaign: speaking before the New Hampshire primary her voice seemed to crack a little and her eyes are said to have misted up momentarily as she talked about the 'frustrations' of keeping it all together. Within moments the image had been beamed around the world as journalists and commentators fought over how 'Clinton's tears' should be interpreted. In one account these were cynical, crocodile tears, turned on for the camera, designed to break her 'ice queen' image and to engineer increased public support; in the other they were *genuine* tears but this only showed that she was not tough enough (not man enough?) to be in the White House. Senator John Edwards succinctly expressed the view that was dominating much media coverage: 'I think what we need in a commander-in-chief is strength and resolve, and presidential campaigns are a tough business, but being president of the United States is also a tough business.' The implication from much reporting was clear: either she was manipulative and untrustworthy or weak and unable to cope in a crisis.

Jessica Evans (2008) has argued that this reporting is evidence of a deeply entrenched set of double standards that affect women in political life.

> 'If a woman is a strong leader she is at fault for not being a homemaker, but if she is a homemaker she is at fault for not having the qualities of the leader. The quality she needs to be a president – to hack it with the big boys – is the same quality that goes against her. If women talk loudly they are shrill; if they talk softly they are overly feminine and weak. And Clinton as a woman is described in ways that could not now be publicly used to describe Obama as a non-white; when a member of the audience at a John McCain event asked the Senator "How do we beat the bitch?" McCain's smiling reply was "Excellent question".'

Evans's argument seems to be borne out in the reporting of Segolene Royal, the Socialist party presidential candidate in France in 2007. What might be characterised as firmness or resoluteness in her male opponent and eventual winner Nicolas Sarkozy, is presented much less positively as 'steeliness' in her. Her capabilities were called into question by the media so routinely that she was moved to comment: 'It's pretty simple. If a man had been an adviser to the President of the Republic as I was to President Mitterrand for seven years, if he had been a minister three times and elected as an MP four times consecutively as I have been, if he had beaten the then prime minister in the last regional elections as I did, would he find his legitimacy contested and his capacity to govern questioned? No.' (quoted by Willsher 2006).

Newspaper and magazine articles endlessly discussed Royal's 'elegance' and 'sexiness'. *Newsweek* magazine dubbed her the 'sexy socialist' and even a think-piece in *Salon*, critical of her treatment by the media, could not resist mentioning her 'bikini-worthy' 53-year-old body. Much of the reporting veers towards constructing her as a kind of dominatrix, with emphasis on her coldness, power and ambition, and references to her apparent penchant for 'power suits' (these are just suits when men wear them, of course) and 'heels'. This construction is deployed to suggest emasculating qualities. *Der Spiegel* describes one of her male colleagues as 'Segolene's playboy' and writes that 'she doesn't even display much interest in Francois Hollande the leader of the PS and her life partner, leaving Hollande with little choice but to publicly express his hope' that things will work out 'with Madame's "plan"'. This single-mindedness admired in male politicians is suspect in Royal's case, calling into question her very femininity and apparent lack of maternal qualities (despite having had four children, three of whom were grown up at the time of the campaign): 'Who will look after your children?' she was asked. Male politicians are simply not asked such questions by journalists, yet despite decades of feminist activism they are still routinely asked of women.

Gender in advertising

One field of media where we have seen significant changes is advertising, and in the final section of this chapter I want to explore contemporary patterns of gender representation looking both at women's and men's depiction.

In the wave of feminist scholarship and activism that swept through Western countries in the 1960s and 1970s, advertising was a key target for analysis and critique. The short, condensed nature of adverts predisposed their creators to rely heavily on crude, easily recognisable stereotypes, and research highlighted the narrow range of degrading and trivialising images of women: the dumb blonde, the unintelligent housewife, the passive sex object, and so on. Throughout the 1970s and 1980s, content analytic studies documented the same consistent pattern of gender stereotyping in adverts: women were shown predominantly in the home (indeed in the kitchen or bathroom); depicted as housewives and mothers; they were frequently shown in dependent or subservient roles; their appearance was more important than anything else; and they rarely provided an argument in favour of the advertised products – voiceovers were generally done by men, indexing their greater authority. In contrast, men were portrayed in a range of settings and occupational roles; as independent and autonomous; and were presented as objective and knowledgeable about the products they used (G. Dyer 1982; Gunter 1994; Livingstone and Green 1986; Lovdal 1989).

A landmark study by the sociologist Erving Goffman (Goffman 1979) provided another way of coding gender representation in advertisements, concentrating on the way in which *non-verbal signals* communicated important differences in male and female power. Examining magazine and billboard advertising, Goffman concluded that adverts depicted ritualised versions of the parent–child relationship, in which women were largely accorded child-like status. Women were typically shown lower or smaller than men and using gestures which 'ritualised their subordination' (1979: 43), for example, lying down, using bashful knee bends, canting postures or deferential smiles. Women were also depicted in 'licensed withdrawal' (1979: 29): slightly distanced from a scene, looking into the mirror or gazing into the distance, not quite there.

Goffman's work was developed by many other writers to examine the body's presentation in advertising. Perhaps the major insight of subsequent feminist work has been the analysis of how 'cropping' is used in adverts. Many studies have highlighted the way in which women's bodies are fragmented in adverts, visually dissected so that the viewer sees only the lips, or the eyes, or the breasts, or whatever (G. Dyer 1982; Coward 1984). This frequently mirrors the text in which women's bodies are presented simply as a composite of problems, each requiring a product-solution. The effect is to deny women's humanity, to present them not as whole people but as fetishised, dismembered 'bits', as objects.

Advertising is always changing; it is in its nature to have to shift constantly to keep up with trends in music, fashion, design as well as staying abreast of changing social and cultural mores. But Robert Goldman has argued that in the late 1980s and early 1990s the nature of change intensified as advertisers were forced to respond to three previously unprecedented challenges: 'sign fatigue' on the part of many media audiences, fed up with the relentless parade of brands, logos and consumer images; increasing 'viewer scepticism' particularly from younger, media-savvy consumers who had grown up with MTV and personal computers; and feminist critiques of advertising that expressed women's anger at constantly being addressed through representations of idealised beauty.

Goldman argued that advertisers' response was to develop 'commodity feminism' – an attempt to incorporate the cultural power and energy of feminism whilst simultaneously domesticating its critique of advertising and the media. This takes many different forms. Here, I want to look briefly at three different themes or figures that can be seen in contemporary gender representations in advertising.

Edgy models and ordinary women

One response on the part of the advertising industry to feminist critiques has been to confront women's anger directly and to use more ordinary looking people or, alternatively, individuals with unusual or striking looks in adverts. The shift towards 'edginess' can be seen in various parts of popular culture including fashion, music and film, and reflects a disenchantment with the bland, packaged, squeaky clean nature of popular entertainment. It is also evidence of the increasing speed with which 'alternative' looks, values and lifestyles are commodified in late capitalist society.

It is perhaps surprising how *little* edginess in popular culture has impacted on advertising, or, to put it another way, how minutely female models must differ from the norm of 'perfection' in order to earn the tag 'edgy'. Berger (2001) cites examples of advertising agencies pointing out that the model has freckles as 'evidence' of a move away from tyrannical images of female beauty! Similarly, every time a cosmetics company chooses a woman over 40 to be the 'face' of their products – for example Madonna, Isabella Rossellini or Andie MacDowell – it makes the national and international news with reports of their 'daring' strategy.

One brand which did notably break the mould is Dove. In 2004 it launched a series of global campaigns centred on the theme that 'beauty comes in many shapes and sizes and ages', and showing 'ordinary' women. In one advert a group of women dressed only in identical white knickers and bras stand smiling under the headline 'firming the size of a size 8 model wouldn't be much of a challenge'. In another series of adverts pictures of pleasant looking and attractive women (but not models) were shown with two tick boxes giving options for viewers to respond, for example 'fit' or 'fat', 'wrinkled' or 'wonderful'. The adverts highlighted

curvy thighs, bigger bums, rounder stomachs. What better way to test our firming range?

There's not much point in testing a new firming lotion on size-eight supermodel thighs, is there? That's why Dove's Firming range was tested on ordinary women with real lives to live – and real, curvy thighs to firm. After using Dove's nourishing and effective combination of moisturisers and seaweed extracts, we asked if they'd go in front of the camera. What better way to show how they felt about the unretouched, unairbrushed results?

new Dove Firming Range
Gel Cream · Body Wash · Lotion

Attacking the beauty myth . . . to sell beauty products
Source: The Advertising Archives

women's distress at being offered only 'narrow stifling stereotypes' and suggested that Dove's claims about the product (various kinds of firming cream or gel) were more genuine or authentic than those of their competitors – through such slogans as 'our latest Dove firming results (and we haven't cheated the figures)'. The adverts were notable for generating debate and extensive media coverage about their departure from the use of very thin models, though many commentators also noted the relative slimness of the women used and their uniformly attractive appearance. The Dove advertising was also notable for the use of a 'campaign' to sell its product. But the irony of selling creams designed to slim and firm the body on the back of a critique of the beauty industry was not missed by everyone, and the campaigns produced anger and enthusiasm in almost equal measure.

From sex objects to sexual subjects

Another key transformation in the portrayal of women has been the shift from showing women as passive, mute sex objects (of an assumed male gaze), to depicting them as active (hetero)sexually desiring subjects. The shift was inaugurated by a 1994 advert for Wonderbra which pictured model Eva Herzigova in a head and cleavage shot, and hailed viewers with a quotation from Mae West: 'Or are you just pleased to see me?' The first part of a quotation – 'Is that a gun in your pocket?' with its implication that the male viewer had an erection – was left out for us as viewers to fill in. This was no passive, objectified sex object, but a woman who was knowingly playing with her sexual power. Similarly, the confident, assertive tone of a Triumph advert from the same period is quite different from earlier representations: 'New hair, new look, new bra. And if he doesn't like it, new boyfriend.' The emphasis in such adverts is on women's playfulness, freedom and, above all, choice. Women are presented not as seeking men's approval but as pleasing themselves, and, in so doing, they just happen to win men's admiration. A South African advert for She-bear lingerie, for example, featured an attractive young white woman wearing only her lingerie and a nun's habit and rosary. The slogan 'Wear it for yourself', ties the brand identity to women who dress for themselves rather than for men – even if they are not nuns. 'If he's late you can always start without him', declares another British lingerie advert in which the *mise en scène* constructs a picture of seduction, complete with carelessly abandoned underwear, but in which a sexual partner is absent.

This shift raises questions about the theoretical vocabularies gender and media scholars and activists have available for engaging with contemporary representations. The notion of 'objectification', so long the key term in the feminist critical lexicon, would seem to have little purchase to critique adverts in which women are presented not as objects but as powerful, playful, sexual subjects. Yet there are many objections that could be raised to this new form of representation. We might note its exclusions – it's overwhelmingly white, youthful, heterosexual framing. Older women, fat women and any woman living outside a heteronormative framework are conspicuously absent, and the adverts are also marked by strong patterns of racialisation. There is also much to criticise in the postfeminist mantra of choice adopted by such campaigns, the emphasis upon individual freedom and autonomy. It could be argued that this represents a shift in the way power operates – a move away from an external male judging gaze to a self policing narcissistic gaze, in which women must understand their own objectification as pleasurable and self chosen (see Gill 2008 for more discussion).

Men's bodies on display

One of the most profound shifts in visual culture in the last two decades has been the proliferation of representations of the male body. Where once women's bodies dominated advertising landscapes now men's have taken their place alongside women's on billboards, cinema screens and in magazines. However, it is not simply that there are more images of men circulating, but that a specific kind of representational practice has emerged for depicting the male body: namely an idealised and eroticised aesthetic showing a toned, young body. What is significant about this type of representation is that it codes men's bodies in ways that give permission for them to be looked at and desired (Cohan and Hark 1993; Gill *et al.* 2000; Jeffords 1994; Mulvey 1975; Nixon 1996).

The catalysts for this shift in visual culture have been considered by a number of writers (Beynon 2002; Chapman and Rutherford 1988; Edwards 1997; Mort 1996; Nixon 1996; Wernick 1991). At a general level the representations can be understood as part of the shift away from the 'male as norm' in which masculinity lost its unmarked status and became visible as gendered. Sally Robinson (2000) argues that white masculinity was rendered visible through pressure from black and women's liberation movements which were highly critical of its hegemony. Moreover, the growing confidence of the gay liberation movement in Western countries, and the increasing significance of the 'pink economy' helped to produce a greater range of representations of the male body in gay magazines and popular culture. Part of the shift can be understood in terms of these images 'going mainstream' and, as they did so, opening up space for an active gaze among heterosexual women (Moore 1988).

This transformation has prompted much discussion, with claims that 'we are all objectified now' and that idealised-sexualised representational strategies are no longer limited to women's bodies. Indeed, many concerns have been raised about the impact of this representational shift on men's wellbeing – their self-esteem, mental health, and the possibility that they will become increasingly susceptible to eating disorders and other body-image related conditions (Grogan 1999; Wykes and Gunter 2005). There is a growing sense in much writing that visual culture has become *equalised*, and that we are *all* today subject to relentless sexualisation.

However, there are good reasons for going beyond general claims about 'sexualisation' to look at the specific ways in which men's bodies materialise in visual culture. For many commentators, the representation of men as objects of the gaze, rather than as the ones doing the looking, constituted not just a change but a seismic shift. Frank Mort (1996) argued that it was nothing short of the 'visual reassembly of masculinity' and claimed that the cropping of male bodies to focus on selected, eroticised areas (e.g. the upper arms, the chest and the 'sixpack') represented a metaphorical fragmenting or fracturing of male power. Mark Simpson (1994) argued that, quite simply, male dominance and heterosexuality would not survive this transformation in visual culture.

In advertising a number of strategies were developed to deal with the anxieties and threats produced by this shift. On the one hand, many adverts used models with an almost 'phallic muscularity' – the size and hardness of the muscles 'standing in for' male power. Indeed, writing about an earlier generation of male pin-ups, Richard Dyer (1982) talked about representations of the male body having a 'hysterical' feel. Moreover, the use of photographic conventions and *mise-en-scène* from 'high art' also served as a distancing device to diffuse some of the potential threats engendered by 'sexualising' the male body. Giving the representations an 'arthouse' look through the use of black and white photography or 'sculpted' models that made reference to classical iconography, offered the safety of distance, as well as connoting affluence, sophistication and 'class'.[1]

The organisation of gazes within adverts also works to diminish the transgressive threat discussed by Simpson. Men tend not to smile or pout, nor to deploy any of the bodily gestures or postures discussed by Goffman (1979) as indices of the 'ritualised subordination' of women in advertising. In contrast, men are generally portrayed standing or involved in some physical activity, and they look back at the viewer in ways reminiscent of street gazes to assert dominance or look up or off, indicating that their interest is elsewhere (R. Dyer 1982). They are mostly pictured alone in ways that reference the significance of independence as a value marking hegemonic masculinity (Connell 1995), or they are pictured with a beautiful woman – to 'reassure' viewers of their heterosexuality.

However it is not simply the case that these representations must disavow homoerotic desire. On the contrary, gay men are a key target audience for such advertising representations, being acknowledged as fashion leaders in clothing,

Are men's bodies now equally
objectified as women's?
Source: The Advertising Archives

grooming and the purchase of fragrances. Indeed, through the figure of the 'metro-sexual' marketing professionals sought to re-articulate these interests in 'looking good' to a heterosexual agenda.

In the last few years advertising images of eroticised male bodies have undergone other shifts. In 2003 an advert for Dior broke taboos by using a naked man to promote a fragrance. Almost as significant as the showing of his penis was the presence of abundant facial and body hair on this model – marking a departure from earlier, more typical representations of the male body (that are 'manscaped' to use the current parlance). Thinner, more vulnerable-looking models have also become popular, alongside the male superwaifs in fashion and men are sometimes pictured in repose or lying down. It might be argued that representations of men's bodies are increasingly using strategies familiar from depictions of women.

Conclusion

This is an exciting moment to be interested in gender representations in the media. Media are changing rapidly in response to technological, social, political, economic, and regulatory transformations, producing a proliferation of new and contested constructions of gender. For researchers interested in gender the task is to explore how media representations may challenge or reinforce inequality, and to examine how gender is intimately connected with other identities relating to age, class, 'race', sexuality and disability. Gender and media researchers have turned their attention to a myriad of media, genres and representations and re-vealed the complex and contradictory ways in which gender and media are entangled. Beyond critiquing the media a key task remains to construct a cultural politics that can help to create more open, equal, and generous gender relations.

Questions

1 How useful is the notion of 'objectification' for thinking about the portrayal of women's bodies in the media?

2 Choose a newspaper and compare the coverage of male and female politicians. Pay attention to the photographs, descriptive language and assumptions that inform each article. What are the differences?

3 Choose an image of a male body from a fragrance campaign. Analyse the extent to which the strategies discussed above are deployed.

Note

1 A study for the British Broadcasting Standards Commission found that viewers were far more tolerant of 'tasteful' depictions of sex than they were of 'tacky' ones – a distinction that is profoundly dependent on various kinds of class markers (Millward Hargrave 1999). See also Jancovich (2001).

Further reading

Benwell, B. (ed) (2003) *Masculinity and Men's Lifestyle Magazines*, Oxford: Blackwell. A superb introduction to current writing about men's magazines.

Brunsdon, C., D'Acci, J. and Spigel, L. (eds) (2007) *Feminist Television Criticism*, 2nd edition, Oxford: Oxford University Press. An excellent collection of writing, from key media scholars.

Carter, C. and Weaver, K. (2003) *Violence and the Media*, Buckingham: Open University Press. Looks not only at the obvious examples but also at symbolic violence in adverts, etc.

McRobbie, A. (2008) *The Aftermath of Feminism: Gender, Culture and Social Change*, London: Sage. An important collection of essays from one of the pioneers of feminist cultural studies.

References

Benedict, H. (1992) *Virgin or Vamp: How the Press Covers Sex Crimes*, New York: Oxford University Press.

Benwell, B. (2003) *Masculinity and Men's Lifestyle Magazines*, Oxford: Blackwell/Sociological Review.

Berger, W. (2001) *Advertising Today*, London: Phaidon.

Beynon, J. (2002) *Masculinities and Culture*, Phildelphia, PA: Open University.

Biressi, A. and Nunn, H. (2005) *Reality TV: Realism and Revelation*, London: Wallflower Press.

Butler, J. P. (1990) *Gender Trouble: Feminism and the Subversion of Identity*, New York and London: Routledge.

Chapman, R. and Rutherford, J. (1988) *Male Order: Unwrapping Masculinity*, London: Lawrence and Wishart.

Cohan, S. and Hark, I. R. (1993) *Screening the Male: Exploring Masculinities in Hollywood Cinema*, London and New York: Routledge.

Connell, R. W. (1995) *Masculinities*, Cambridge: Polity.

Coward, R. (1984) *Female desire*, London: Paladin.

Crewe, B. (2003) *Representing Men: Cultural Production and Producers in the Men's Magazine Market*, Oxford and New York: Berg.

Cuklanz, L. M. (1996) *Rape on Trial: How the Mass Media Construct Legal Reform and Social Change*, Philadelphia, PA: University of Pennsylvania Press.

Cuklanz, L. M. (2000) *Rape on Prime Time: Television, Masculinity, and Sexual Violence*, Philadelphia PA: University of Pennsylvania Press.

Ducker, J. (2007) 'Rising Star Who Signed Up with His Dream Club as a 9 Year Old' *The Times*, 20 December: 7

Dyer, G. (1982) *Advertising as Communication*, London: Methuen Routledge.

Dyer, R. (1982) 'Don't Look Now: The Male Pin-up', *Screen* 23 (3-4): 61-73.

Edwards, T. (1997) *Men in the Mirror: Men's Fashion, Masculinity and Consumer Society*, London: Cassell.

Evans, J. (2008) 'Intimate Publics' paper presented at ESRC seminar on 'Publics', Milton Keynes, February.

Gill, R. (2003) 'Power and the Production of Subjects: A Genealogy of the New Man and the New Lad' in B. Benwell (ed), *Masculinity and Men's Lifestyle Magazines*, Oxford: Blackwell.

Gill, R. (2007) *Gender and the Media*, Cambridge: Polity Press.

Gill, R. (2008) 'Empowerment/Sexism: Figuring Female Sexual Agency in Contemporary Advertising', *Feminism and Psychology,* 18 (1): 35-60.

Gill, R., Henwood, K. and McLean, C. (2000) 'The Tyranny of the Six Pack?' in C. Squire (ed) *Culture in Psychology*, London: Routledge.

Global Media Monitoring Project (2006) London: HMSO.

Goffman, E. (1979) *Gender Advertisements*, London: Macmillan.

Goldman, R. (1992) *Reading Ads Socially*, London and New York: Routledge.

Grogan, S. (1999) *Body Image: Understanding Body Dissatisfaction in Men, Women and Children*, London: Routledge.

Gunter, B. (1994) *Television and Gender Representation*, London: John Libbey.

Hill, A. (2005) *Reality TV: Audiences and Factual Television*, London: Routledge.

Hollows, J. (2000) *Feminism, Femininity, and Popular Culture*, New York: Manchester University Press.

Jackson, P., Brooks, K. and Stevenson, N. (2001) *Making Sense of Men's Magazines*, Malden, MA: Polity Press.

Jeffords, S. (1994) *Hard Bodies: Hollywood Masculinity in the Reagan Years*, Piscataway, NJ: Rutgers University Press.

Jenkins, R. and Ducker, J. (2007) 'Boyfriend of Woman in Rape Claim "Scuffled with Footballer" ', *The Times*, 20 December: 6.

Kilbourne, J. (1995) 'Beauty and the Beast of Advertising' in G. Dines and J. Humez (eds) *Gender, Race and Class in Media*, Thousand Oaks, CA: Sage.

Lazar, M. (2004) *(Post-) Feminism in Contemporary Advertising: A Global Discourse in a Local Context*, Cardiff: Cardiff University.

Livingstone, S. and Green, G. (1986) 'Television Advertisements and the Portrayal of Gender' in *British Journal of Social Psychology,* 25: 149-54.

Lovdal, L. T. (1989) 'Sex Role Messages in Television Commercials; An update' *Sex Roles*, 21: 715-24.

Macdonald, M. (1995) *Representing Women: Myths of Femininity in the Popular Media*, London: E. Arnold.

Machin, D. and Thornborrow, J. (2003) 'Branding and Discourse: The Case of Cosmopolitan' *Discourse and Society*, 14: 453-71.

McRobbie, A. (1999) *In the Culture Society: Art, Fashion, and Popular Music*, London and New York: Routledge.

McRobbie, A. (2004) 'Notes on "What Not to Wear" and Post-feminist Symbolic Violence', in L. Adkins and B. Skeggs (eds) *Feminism after Bourdieu*, Oxford: Blackwell/The Sociological Review.

Millward Hargrave, A. (1999) *Sex and Sensibility*, London: Broadcasting Standards Commission.

Moore, S. (1988) 'Here's Looking at You Kid!' in L. Gamman and M. Marshment (eds) *The Female Gaze: Women as Viewers of Popular Culture*, London: The Women Press.

Moorti, S. (2002) *Color of Rape: Gender and Race in Television's Public Spheres*, Albany, NY: State University of New York Press.

Mort, F. (1996) *Cultures of Consumption: Commerce, Masculinities and Social Space*. London and New York: Routledge.

Mulvey, L. (1975) 'Visual Pleasure and Narrative Cinema' *Screen*, 16 (3): 6-18.

Nixon, S. (1996) *Hard Looks: Masculinities, Spectatorship and Contemporary Consumption*, London: UCL Press.

Pendlebury, R. (2007) 'United by Booze, Girls and Too Much Money' *Daily Mail*, 20 December: 8.

Phoenix, A. and Pattynama, P. (2006) 'Intersectionality' *European Journal of Women's Studies*, 13 (3): 187-92.

Pyatt, J. (2007) 'Weeping Girl's Pal Confronted a Player and Was Headbutted' the *Sun*, 20 December 2007.

Roberts, B., Disley, J. and Sloan, J. (2007) 'Man United "Rape" Claim' *Daily Mirror*, 20 December: 7.

Robinson, S. (2000) *Marked Men: White Masculinity in Crisis*, New York: Columbia University Press.

Ross, K. (2002) *Women, Politics, Media: Uneasy Relations in Comparative Perspective*, Cresskill, NJ: Hampton Press.

Simpson, M. (1994) *Male Impersonators: Men Performing Masculinity*, London: Cassell.

Soothill, K. and Walby, S. (1991) *Sex Crimes in the News*, London: Routledge.

Tuchman, G. (1978) 'The Symbolic Annihilation of Women in the Media', in G. Tuchman, A. Daniels and J. Benet (eds) *Health and Home: Images of Women in the Mass Media*, Oxford: Oxford University Press.

Van Zoonen, L. (1994) *Feminist Media Studies*, London: Sage.

Wernick, A. (1991) *Promotional Culture: Advertising, Ideology and Symbolic Expression*, London: Sage.

Willsher, K. (2006) 'Is This the Face of France's First Madame la Présidente?', the *Guardian,* 3 March.

Wykes, M. and Gunter, B. (2005) *The Media and Body Image*, London: Sage.

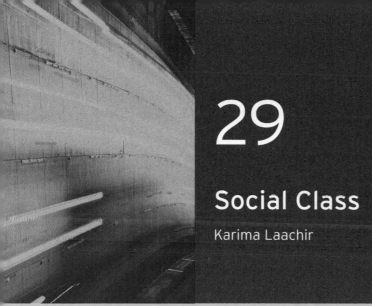

29

Social Class

Karima Laachir

Chapter overview

The media is important in producing and consolidating stereotypes about social groups, because it arguably influences our perception of the world around us. It can have the role of maintaining or challenging social divisions and prejudices. This chapter examines the representations of social class in a number of media texts, focusing particularly on magazines and films in the context of France. I analyse how written media in the form of two politically different magazines reproduces some dominant discourses on social class in their coverage of recent events in France. Visual media in the form of three recent films provides an alternative portrayal of social classes and identities in France by rejecting dominant discourses, especially those related to the working class.

Introduction

It is important to examine the ways in which social class is portrayed in the media because the latter have a crucial role in maintaining, perpetuating or challenging social divisions. In his book *Why Study the Media?*, Silverstone (1999: 1) argues that 'The media are an essential dimension of contemporary experience. We cannot evade media presence, media representation.' The media, therefore, play an important role in shaping our perceptions of the world around us (Kellner 2002: 9). They produce and reproduce ideologies, especially in their portrayal of certain social groups and identities. This chapter looks specifically at representations of social class in the media. It examines briefly how class has been conceptualised and then looks at how it is represented in a number of media texts, especially magazines and films with particular focus on France, a country that has a slightly different class history to that of Britain.

I analyse the representation of social class in two types of media texts in France: written media in the form of weekly magazines and visual ones in the form of films. The written press is traditionally perceived in France as a source of pluralistic depictions and analysis of events, unlike television representations, which are marked by a more dominant discourse on social identities (Boyer and Lochard 1998: 68). However, in recent years, and because of the fierce competition with other media, the press does not always appear to be concerned with providing nuanced and balanced analysis of events (Halimi 1997). At times, films have taken on the role of 'resisting' dominant discourses on social classes and identities (Stovall 2001). Therefore, my choice of case studies aims at demonstrating how two politically different and widely read magazines (*Le Nouvel Observateur* and *Le Point*) represent some dominant discourses on social classes in their coverage of events in France. I then analyse how three recent French films (*Resources Humaines* by Laurent Cantet (1999), *Caché* by Michael Haneke (2005) and *L'Esquive* by Abdellatif Kechiche (2004)) offer a more nuanced and alternative portrayal of social classes and identities in France by resisting dominant discourses (particularly those related to the working-class).

Class and social exclusion

Social class is an important analytical category that reveals social power relations in society. It is usually understood as the division between working-class people, those who have so-called 'blue collar' jobs, and middle- and upper-class people. It was Karl Marx who first emphasised the link between capital, cultural production and ideology (Marx and Engels 1967), arguing that the dominant ideas in society are mostly those of the dominant social class. He focused on the material nature of class inequalities and how class divisions were determined by ownership of capital in capitalist societies. Marx also stressed the importance of class consciousness among the working classes and how this could lead to their emancipation through political action. The Marxist theory of class struggle is based on the existence of different social groups with different interests and proceeds from an understanding of how the entrenched nature of class divisions produces inequalities and unevenly distributed relations of power. This classical Marxist analysis of class still continues to have some relevance for the present-day configuration of the class system; however, while it remains useful to the analysis of traditional categories of class, it is unable to account for the emergence of new social classes.

Marx's classical distinction between social classes has been blurred in many ways in the last decades because of economic and social changes. In fact, since the 1980s, a discourse has evolved about the disappearance of 'class distinctions' and hence the emergence of a supposedly classless society. Skeggs's book on *Class, Self, Culture* (2004) questions the arguments of the 'end of class' and examines the subtle links between class distinctions and cultural practices. She argues that class is 'dynamic, produced through conflict and fought out at the level of the symbolic' (2004: 5). Whereas class was previously thought to have a strict relation to economic factors such as income, it is now recognised that class involves much more than this. Class is not solely based on economic reasoning, exploitation and inequality, but also on the dynamics of representation, discourse and culture. Therefore, class continues to be an important paradigm for the understanding of various political, social and economic formations and representations.

More recently, the concept of class struggle has been replaced by the term 'social exclusion' and the notion of 'underclass' (Savage 2000). The latter refers to various groups such as poor ethnic minority groups, those on long-term state benefit, single parents, asylum seekers, etc. (Kirk 2007: 239). This language of social exclusion and inclusion presents us with a reworking of class politics but also specific problems, as it covers up social divisions among those who are 'included' in society – as if they shared the same interests and values and as if nothing could divide them. The problem in this case is to bring those who are 'excluded' to the heart of society. This discourse generally denies the existence of classes, choosing to speak about an 'underclass' instead; ultimately, this perspective denies class divisions, while simultaneously emphasising them at the same time by positing an underclass and a unity of all the other classes. It serves as a consolidating discourse for middle-class values when it might be expected to force reflection on the plight of the underclass (Kirk 2007: 239). The idea here is that class divisions still play an important role in power relations; by no means everyone outside the underclass will agree with bourgeois prescriptions, yet there is an assumption that a consensus exists on the way in which people should live. Class divisions are still deeply rooted in society even though class identities are generally weak nowadays despite people's awareness of belonging to a particular class (Savage 2000).

Moreover, social class is no longer the single most important aspect of our identity, as gender, 'race', and sexuality are all just as important as class is in defining us. Social structures, therefore, are increasingly complex and fragmented. They are characterised not just by class stratification but by other divisions arising from differences in identities. Later in this chapter, I discuss the links between 'race' and class, especially in the French context where African immigrants and their descendants have inherited working-class status in the secluded *banlieues* or outer-city suburbs of France's big cities. Phillips and Sarre argue that if social classes are mostly seen as social collectivities with shared cultures, lifestyles and 'forms of exploitations', one cannot overlook 'the role of "race" and ethnicity in class formations' (1995: 77). They stress that 'race' should not be seen simply as a minority experience, since in a racialised labour market white people (especially middle-class ones) 'commonly gain privilege from their positions in a racialised labour process, whereas black people often find disadvantage' (ibid.). 'Race' is important in the formation of class identities, since the majority of ethnic minority groups are at the bottom of the social ladder and often suffer from social discrimination, due to both their 'race' and social class. Class analysis remains important, however, because as Day (2001:18) suggests, 'Class provides an account of the origin of inequality from which other forms of oppression arise.'

Big Brother: reality TV and class

British Reality TV has often pathologised working-class 'problems' in recent years. The celebrity *Big Brother* saga – one that took place in January 2007 and dominated headlines in the UK for weeks – is an example of this form of class representation. Bollywood actress Shilpa Shetty faced bullying and abuse by three other housemates, most aggressively from Jade Goody, a former winner of Big Brother House and a tabloid darling. The comments addressed to Shetty by Goody were interpreted as racist, which led to over 30,000 complaints to the media regulator Ofcom. What interests us in this example, as I will explain below, is the way this event was used to reinforce the alleged 'moral superiority' of the 'better-educated' middle classes and brand the working classes as racist.

So what happened during the programme? Two issues emerged in relation to class portrayal in the media: the first had to do with the promotion of a certain image of India and its affluent classes through that of the glamorous actress Shetty. The second was linked to the way the working-class background of Goody was blamed as the cause of her 'racist' comments.

On entering the contest, Shilpa Shetty announced that she was representing the Indian nation. It seems that as India finds its place within the community of big global players in the world economy, it endeavours to reconcile its economic successes with the deepening inequalities that still spoil its social landscape and self-image. Therefore, the Indian government is obsessed with disseminating the myth of the nation as middle-class, professional and successful. The task of projecting that image often falls on the shoulders of the female professionals of India's flourishing glamour industry (Gopal in the *Guardian,* 25 January 2007). Hence, told by Goody to 'go back to the slums', Shetty kept repeating that she did not actually come from them. The one thing on which the pair seemed to agree: that economic disenfranchisement was a matter of personal failure and not of processes of exclusion and marginalisation.

If Shetty was selling the idea of middle- and upper-class India as a world of beauty and entrepreneurial success, Goody and her 'chav' milieu were under attack by the self-congratulatory political correctness typical of middle- and upper-class white Britons, as though racism was an exclusively working-class phenomenon. Racism is, however, entrenched in higher social echelons, too (uttered in private parties or environments). Some sections of the British national media explained Goody's behaviour as emanating from her working-class background and her lack of 'education' and culture, despite her wealth (see Wilson's article 'So Who Are the Savages Now?' in the *Daily Mail,* 20 January 2007). Therefore, it is the middle and upper classes who are seen as dictating 'good' manners, taste and values.

Other British television comedy shows, such as *The Royle Family* and *Shameless,* shown on BBC Two and Channel Four respectively, expose the lives of working-class people to middle-class audiences through various discourses that reinforce the latter's misconceptions and stereotypes. Class divisions, therefore, are still important in contemporary societies. As Kirk (2007: 226) puts it, 'The making of class, then, is a process of production and positioning, and it is within dominant strategies of projection and appropriation, through relations of representation and exchange, that class is fixed over time and space.'

Bourdieu and the production of the elite in France

It is often claimed that in Britain class divisions run deeper than in other countries such as France, where workers and employers are alleged to be 'united', and the US, a country of opportunity and social mobility (Marwick 1980). However, a closer look at both French and American societies reveals various forms of class divisions and privileges. In his analysis of how a social class maintains a dominant position, the French sociologist Pierre Bourdieu (1984) shows how a class-specific 'habitus' or way of living contributes to the production of class structures. It is the transmission of 'cultural capital' (which includes 'good' taste, manners, appreciation of 'high' culture) or cultural knowledge that has already 'accumulated' in the family that fosters the preservation of a dominant position. Bourdieu has made the issue of 'taste' a social issue by introducing the concept of 'cultural capital' (Bourdieu 1984). He claims that our tastes and appreciation of forms of 'high culture' such as classical music, art, etc. are determined by our social class and upbringing. 'Cultural capital' allows people to dominate and remain in a position of power.

Bourdieu's discussion of 'cultural capital' and 'habitus' is based on his investigation of the French elite and the way they maintain economic and cultural dominance in a country that prides itself on being meritocratic. Bourdieu claims that the educational system in France helps to reproduce class structures. The dominant classes no longer think that it is sufficient to pass on economic capital to their offspring to maintain their class dominance. Rather, it is the gaining of prestigious educational degrees which allows them to occupy top positions in all domains. Even though France's prestigious *Grandes Écoles* are public and free to all students, they are dominated by children of the middle and upper classes, since their family's privilege and social positioning facilitate easy access. Middle- and upper-class students often benefit from good schooling (since they live in wealthy and leafy neighbourhoods where good quality state schools can be found) and financial support from their parents, which allow them to have private tuition to prepare for tough entry exams to these institutions. They can also rely on family networks that facilitate the processes of application and access. Students from lower and poorer social backgrounds find it very difficult to compete in entry exams because they often do not receive good quality schooling (schools in deprived neighbourhoods are often poor, parents are unable to pay for private tuition, etc.). Therefore, students from privileged backgrounds have a higher success rate in accessing these *Grandes Écoles* and hence they consolidate their social and economic privileges by acquiring top jobs in both the public and private sector after graduation. As Hartmann (2000: 243) puts it, 'For Bourdieu, the "incorporated cultural capital" of the individual – the core of class-specific habitus, socialised within the family – remains the key to acquiring coveted academic qualifications granted by a select handful of institutions such as the famous French *Grandes Écoles*. A *grandes-écoles* diploma, then, documents the possession of "cultural capital", indispensable to securing a top-level position, in an objective and universally-recognised form.' In this way, the dominant classes maintain their grip on key positions in all areas of French political, economic and social life. 'The "new elite" thus does not trace its legitimacy back to birth or wealth, but rather to its "intelligence", in which "all claims to legitimation" cumulate' (ibid.). It is this 'new elite' which dominates the media in France with their ideas and perceptions.

In fact, the French working-class population, despite being the largest group in the country, have become invisible in the French media in recent decades because of the lack of positive reference to them (Beaud and Pialoux 1999). In 2002, the highly-respected French broadsheet newspaper *Le monde* published a series of articles on the 'forgotten French people', i.e. the working classes. The articles focused on how the Communist and Socialist parties had abandoned any positive reference to the working classes. They also pointed out that the place of the working classes had been taken over to a considerable degree by the figure of the 'immigrant'. Therefore, the term 'working class' had become largely linked, in the media and in certain political discourses, with the inability to 'integrate' into French society.

In the next section, I explore how class in France has become identified with geographic divisions that have created the peripheral outer-city suburbs or so-called *banlieues* (where most of lower working-class people reside) and how the latter are represented in the media.

Class and space in France

The *banlieues* are a set of small neighbourhoods located on the outskirts of France's big cities. They are in the 'suburbs', but unlike the suburbs in Britain, which are predominantly middle-class areas, the *banlieues* or *HLM cités* (low-income housing estates) are to an extent similar to inner-city areas (council estates) in Britain. These neighbourhoods, which sprang up in the early 1960s to provide better housing for the French working-class populations, are still designated to people on the lowest rung of the social ladder. In the 1960s, they were known as '*Les banlieues rouges*' or 'red suburbs' because they were run by local Communist party members. They had a strong working class culture, consciousness and organisation, especially in terms of political mobility, trade-union activism, etc. (Dubet 1991: 3). Even though these 'red suburbs' were poor and marginalised, they had strong working-class ties and communal links; they also generated a great deal of fear and anxiety because of the militancy of the workers. When the economic crisis hit France in the early 1970s, with its processes of de-industrialisation and the decline of the Communist party, the *banlieues* lost their strong working-class militancy and 'redness'. They, thus, became closely associated with negative images of unemployment, crime, poverty and violence (Begag and Delorme 1994; MacMaster 1997) and are now mainly inhabited by ethnic minority groups of North African and African origin.

The term *banlieue* is not only loaded with negative connotations in the French popular media, but the *banlieues* are usually referred to, in a derogatory way, as '*quartiers en difficulté*' (deprived areas) or '*zones sensibles*' (trouble spots). Since the 1990s, dominant sections of the French media have played on the image of the 'threatening immigrant' taking over the nation and hence contributed to the negative representation of the *banlieues* (Taranger 1994: 59–71). The media have often focused on distorted and selective representations of crime and violence, hence emphasising the image of the *banlieues* as the space of a threatening 'other' (Hargreaves 1996: 613). Therefore, the *banlieues* are usually equated with insecurity, crime, violence and a total rejection of 'French values' on the part of their predominantly 'ethnic minority' working-class inhabitants.

Class, ethnicity and the *banlieues*

Even though the *banlieues* are made up of groups of diverse ethnic origin, including white French people, they have been mostly defined in ethnic terms (Waquant 2007; Mucchielli 2002). Class in France is thus strongly linked to ethnicity. The *banlieues* have been ethnicised and spatially segregated as they are claimed to reject the dominant culture (i.e. 'civilisation'), because of their 'cultural difference', whereas beneath this argument lies the fact that this ethnicising of territory allows the concealing of social inequalities and exclusion. The French state has continually practised policies of spatial exclusion of poor immigrants and their descendants. They mostly live in deprived areas with poor schooling, poor access to social services and political institutions, which deprive them of social mobility. In other words, they mostly live in zones of economic, social and political exclusion (Dubet and Lapeyronnie 1992; Silverstein 2004). As Tissot (2007: 376–8) puts it, 'The language of class helped recast socio-economic problems as ethnic problems, and class antagonism as cultural tensions. But such ethnicisation did not only mean obscuring the role of class [. . .], it also – paradoxically – served to obscure the way race has been a factor in the economic woes of the *banlieues*.' Class is an important factor in the exclusion of the *banlieues* residents, but racial discrimination has also an important role in fostering this exclusion. If the 'red banlieues' with their predominantly white working-class population were seen as a threat in the past because of their revolutionary militancy and their attempt to change the capitalist system in favour of the working classes, the *banlieues* today – mostly populated by poor and marginalised ethnic minority groups – are perceived as a threat to national security and stability.

Popular uprising in the *banlieues* and the media

In their coverage of the recent riots that rocked France's big cities in November 2005, most sections of the French media focused on social and economic deprivation as their main cause. However, images of the young rioters in the media have served to reinforce the links between their working-class, or even under-class, status and their ethnicity with crime and violence. French public opinion has bought into these violent representations since their knowledge of the *banlieues* is limited to these sensational reports. In March 2006, a few months after the *banlieues* riots, France was hit again by another wave of massive disturbances. This time, it was mainly university and college students from middle-class families protesting fiercely against the adoption of the CPE (First Employment Contract) by the government of De Villepin. I will now compare the depiction of the popular *banlieues* disorder with that of the middle-class rioters in two French weekly magazines. My choice of the two weekly magazines: the left-wing *Le Nouvel Observateur* and the centrist *Le Point* derives from the fact that both magazines enjoy a wide readership among diverse classes in France. According to Kuhn (1995: 75), the two Paris-based magazines 'fill a gap left by a lack of quality Sunday newspapers which in Britain, for example, provide a source of political analysis and commentary'. Therefore, both magazines play an important role in influencing public opinion in France.

Le Nouvel Observateur devoted a whole issue (10–16 November) to the *banlieues* disturbances. The front cover showed a picture of the young rioters in the background, surrounded by fire, with at least two policemen in the foreground; the headline read 'Banlieues: the causes of the conflagration', with subheadings about the effects of segregation on a desperate generation of working-class youth.

The tone of the magazine was quite inquisitive in this instance, as journalists raised questions about the poverty and marginalisation of the working-class

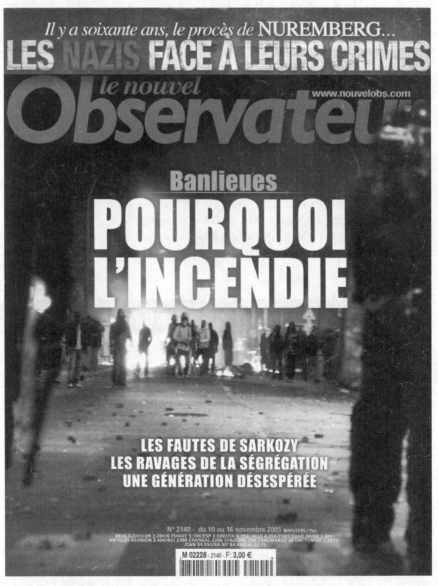

Front cover of *Le Nouvel Observateur*, 10–16 November 2005

Source: © Le Nouvel Observateur 2005

population of the *banlieues*. *Le Point,* on the other hand, had devoted two issues to the subject (10 November and 17 November 2005) and had adopted a more sensationalist style in reporting these riots. The cover of the 10 November issue showed a picture of a black, hooded youth hiding his face from the camera with the headline, 'Banlieues: what we don't dare to say'.

The headline was explained in an editorial by Claude Imbert, who stated that France had to face up to the 'truth' that the *banlieues* riots were the result of a lack of integration among the immigrants and their descendants, whose culture was incompatible with French values. It is apparent how the working-class rioters had

Front cover of *Le Point*, 10 November 2005
Source: © Le Point 2005

been ethnicised here and portrayed as foreign (even though the majority were French citizens, born and brought up in France). In the rest of the article, 'immigrants' were represented as a threat to the stability of the French nation by being portrayed as 'aliens' to the French language and culture, 'immigrants whose culture is incompatible with the French one', 'sick' due to educational failure, violence and drugs (Imbert in *Le Point*, 10 November 2005: 3). This negative image of the *banlieues* fosters much scaremongering among the French public. Moreover, the youth of the second and even third generation (the descendants of immigrants) end up being seen as 'belonging' to an 'alien' culture, even though most of

Front cover of *Le Point*, 17 November 2005
Source: © Le Point 2005

them were born and have been brought up in France and have been much influenced by French culture. Poverty and deprivation are attributed to them being 'foreigners' and not to the deprived socio-economic conditions which are typical of the areas where they live. In the same article (ibid. 3), Imbert stresses how the rioters are damaging the international reputation of France and the integrity of the nation. In the second issue (17 November 2005), the front cover was dominated by a picture of the then president, Jacques Chirac, giving a televised address to the nation; the caption read: 'Banlieues: the political price'.

Clearly, the headline of the magazine was sympathetic to Chirac's right-wing government and the political price it 'had' to pay because of these popular uprisings. Overall, *Le Point* reinforced stereotypes about the working-class youth in the *banlieues* by relating their ethnicity to their supposed 'criminality' and by denationalising them as outsiders. Unsurprisingly, *Le Point* did not devote any such front-cover headlines to the predominantly middle-class student riots in the centre of Paris and other large cities in France, despite the fact that they were as violent as those in the *banlieues*. The magazine only dedicated a few articles to the massive demonstrations of the students.

The left-wing *Le Nouvel Observateur* instead devoted its front cover (30 March–5 April 2006) to the student rioters, with a picture of De Villepin in the foreground and the students in action against the police force in the background; the cover headline spoke about a 'revolt' and accused De Villepin of provoking the disorders. Though the magazine was sympathetic in its depiction of the *banlieues* protests, it did not attribute them to the state's policies.

The analysis of the portrayal of the two events mentioned above thus demonstrates that the working-class youth were more markedly demonised than their middle-class counterparts. In the next section, I shall examine the representation of social class in some recent French films which provide a much more nuanced representation of evolving class identities in France.

Representation of class in French cinema

Cinema is a widely-accessible medium and has an important role in French culture and society. My decision to analyse the representation of class in three recent French films stems from the fact that these represent a wave of films that have focused on social class in the 1990s. O'Shaughnessy (2007: 56) argues that there is a switch to social class in some recent French films and an attempt to break the silence about the loss of working-class identities and militancy; he states that 'considering how unfashionable a term class has become, the relatively high number of films that are explicitly or implicitly organised around it bears testimony to some of French cinema's refusal of the consensual order' (ibid.). O'Shaughnessy claims that this 'resistant cinema', with its refusal to accept the way working classes are predominantly represented in negative terms, recognises a major shift in the organisation of class structures and accepts, to some extent, the 'defeat' of class struggle. However, it offers resistant alternatives and perceptions (ibid.). I discuss *Resources Humaines*, *Caché* and *L'Esquive* as being part of this

De Hollywood à Malibu
LOS ANGELES La ville mythe

le nouvel
Obs⬤teur
www.nouvelobs.com

Spécial
LA REVOLTE

VILLEPIN L'INCENDIAIRE
LES NOUVELLES FORMES DE VIOLENCE
POURQUOI LES JEUNES SE SENTENT SACRIFIÉS

N° 2160 · du 30 mars au 5 avril 2006

M 02228 - 2160 - F: 3,00 €

Front cover of *Le Nouvel Observateur*, 30 March–5 April 2006
Source: © Le Nouvel Observateur 2006

cinematic trend that resists dominant discourses about class identities and offers alternative perceptions.

One of the most important recent French films to have documented the 'defeat' of class conflict, but which still uses the old language of 'class struggle', is Cantet's *Resources Humaines* (Human Resources) (1999). The film is centred around the character of the working-class father who has spent all his life toiling in a factory to be able to give his son a better future. The story starts with the son returning to his home town to take up a managerial job placement in the factory where his father works. The son has attained social mobility and his future seems bright and promising, which suggests the idea that boundaries may after all be fluid (O'Shaughnessy 2007: 88). This character has the ability to relate to older working-class workers and the managerial elite of the factory because of his working-class background and education. However, soon he becomes aware of the implicit hierarchy and exploitation characteristic of the existing social order. Being part of an oppressed social group, the father keeps his distance from his son, recognising the existing status quo and social ranking. The son shows his anger at his father for not fighting for his rights, especially when he is made redundant because of his old age. The film reflects on this 'defeat' of the class struggle. However, a certain degree of resistance emerges at the end among the workers who call for a strike and rebellion on the part of the exploited. As O'Shaughnessy puts it, 'rather than the film simply making visible a defeat [. . .], it works to show that the apparently defeated still have resources (languages, resources, knowledge) with which to resist' (ibid. 89). The film, therefore, represents the class struggle as central and significant and problematises the French notion of social mobility and fluidity.

Haneke is an Austrian film-maker based in France; most of his films are in the French language and deal with French society. *Caché* (*Hidden*) (2005) explores, among other issues, the class divide in France, by focusing on the life of a middle-class family made up of a literary TV show host, Georges Laurent, and his book publisher wife Anne. The couple, portrayed as successful media intellectuals, live with their young son in a nice, affluent area of Paris. However, their peace of mind is shattered when they start receiving videotapes showing that they are being constantly filmed and observed in their own home. When a videotape arrives showing a child's drawings of a face with blood running from his mouth, Georges remembers a flashback from his childhood and his relationship with Majid, an orphan of Algerian origin temporarily fostered by his parents (Majid's parents were killed in Paris in an anti-colonial demonstration in October 1961). Georges recalls that because of his own jealousy and lies, Majid was not adopted by his family in the end. He now suspects Majid of taking revenge by observing his family and by sending the recordings to them. Instead of facing his own conscience and memory, Georges threatens and harasses a distressed Majid who denies any wrongdoing, until he commits suicide in a horrific scene at the end of the film.

What is important for us in the film is the way it represents the class contrast between the affluent middle-class French family and the poor and deprived world of Majid, the French citizen of Algerian origin. Once again, the working-class character is a descendant of immigrants, hence the link, mentioned earlier, between ethnicity and class. The world of the Laurent family typifies the French bourgeoisie with all its ease, comfort and 'good taste': for instance, the walls of their luxurious sitting room are filled with books and videotapes. Georges's status as a media celebrity suggests the dominance of the middle classes over the media. This is suggested in one of the scenes in the film, when we observe Georges performing acts of censorship by cutting out parts of a debate he has hosted on the release of a book on the French writer Rimbaud.

The film clearly contrasts the home in which Georges lives with that of Majid, on a council estate in the *banlieues*. When Georges visits Majid in his place, a shot clearly shows the geographical distance between the world of the affluent middle classes (the chic and quiet areas of Paris) and the world of the poor in the deprived *banlieues,* whose huge, ugly and badly-kept council estates reflect social and economic exclusion.

The film also explores issues of class, historical memory and trauma. It specifically refers to the bloody events of 17 October 1961, when thousands of Algerian workers and their families took to the streets of Paris to demonstrate against the Algerian war and were savagely repressed by the French police. The descendants of those Algerian workers are represented by the character of Majid who does not seem to have benefited from any social mobility outside the marginalised space of the *banlieues. Caché,* therefore, highlights class distinctions between the residents of the affluent middle classes and those of the *banlieues,* through the use of space, camera, costume and design. It also reflects on lack of social mobility in France and the way in which the figure of immigrant descent ends up inheriting working-class status.

Class and language in *L'Esquive*

Adblelltaif Kechiche's *L'Esquive* or *Games of Love and Chance* (2004) explores the world of working-class youth. The film focuses on the life of a handful of high school students of diverse origins on a council estate in a Parisian *banlieue.* Constructed around the teenagers' interest in theatre and their rehearsals to perform Marivaux's play *Le Jeu de l'amour et de Hasard* (Games of love and chance), Kechiche's film deconstructs mainstream depictions of the working-class youth of the *banlieues* as uncultured and violent. The interest of this youth in theatre, a cultural practice usually associated with the middle and upper classes, suggests a breakdown of class stereotypes.

Marivaux's play claims the essentialist nature of social positions. It concerns the story of Sylvia, the daughter of a rich bourgeois who is being wooed by a man of her class. She disguises herself as her own maid to test her lover, and he does the same with his man-servant. This works well as the master and mistress, dressed as servants, fall in love with each other and the servants follow suit. According to Nettelbeck (2007: 313–14), 'The resonances between the real life story and the text of the play allow Kechiche to display a touchingly funny contrast of social conventions. He makes the accurate and affectionate observation that the relationships between the young people of the *cité* are just as mannered, just as governed by rules and ritual, as life in Marivaux's period bourgeois setting. The nub of the conflict between daily life and the world of the play is in the language they use to express themselves.' The mixing of the language in the film is significant as it moves between the refined language of the 18th century play and the sophisticated slang of the *banlieues*, a movement that deconstructs the binary opposition between high and popular culture.

The teenagers in the housing estate are all French of different ethnic origins: white, from North and Sub-Saharan Africa, Spanish, etc. Their friendship transcends the rigid notion of ethnicity as the basis of alliance and extends to other clusters of identifications such as that of class and the dynamics of exclusion. Their common working-class background and their shared life on the council estate provide them with a strong bond of affiliation and their choice of linguistic codes plays a role in establishing their group identity. The use of the Parisian *banlieue* slang – which is made up of colloquial French and some Arabic expressions – aims at transforming the French language and appropriating it for the group's own use. It also has to do with the forces that determine the relationship of these teenagers with the languages in question, in terms of the way they appropriate the French language to transpose it for their own use. Language in this case becomes a denominator of class and a tool of group empowerment.

Marivaux was considered to be emblematic of the French literary canon and hence of the kind of French promoted by the French Academy. He was, however, accused by his contemporaries of using bizarre words and expressions that were not common in his time (Palissot 1968: 966). The illegitimacy of 'his' language (even though he was part of the powerful bourgeois class) is thus juxtaposed with the illegitimacy of the slang deployed by the youth in the film. *L'Esquive* challenges the stereotype of a violent and uncultured working-class youth since the latter move comfortably between the *banlieue* slang and the elitist language of the play. It shows how they interact with theatre as a form of art and their mastery of it. It deconstructs French classical artefacts and the way they are used to foster the exclusion of certain classes.

In one of the most important scenes in the film, during the rehearsal of Marivaux's play in the classroom, the debate on social positions emerges as central to the students and the teacher (who is in charge of the production of the play). The leading character in the film, Lydia, who is taking the role of the bourgeois woman disguised as her own maid, complains to the teacher that her friend Frida – who is playing the role of the maid disguised as her mistress – misinterprets her role since she should be more subservient as a maid even in her own disguise. The teacher then responds by emphasising that one cannot escape his or her social class, which for her is determined by certain manners, use of language, particular use of expressions and the way people behave. Even though the students in the classroom look uncomfortable with the teacher's logic, there is no attempt to challenge her directly. However, ironically, since the teacher stresses that it is the use of language that reveals one's class position, the working-class students seem very confident and comfortable in their mastery of Marivaux's bourgeois language and environment. One can propose that the students' easy movement between the bourgeois language of Marivaux and the slang of the working class *banlieues* deconstructs this essentialisation of class positions. Kechiche's film invites the audience to rethink social classifications and the mainstream perception of a violent *banlieue* by challenging social stereotypes about the use of language, class, taste and culture.

Conclusion

There is a strong connection between class distinctions and cultural practices. Class divisions are not only linked to economic inequalities, but also to cultural dominance, representation and governance. Skeggs (2004: 186) argues that class analysis must move beyond the economic to develop an understanding of the 'consequences of cultural struggle' and the way it determines processes of 'appropriation, exploitation and governance'. It seems that the working classes continue to be the subject of negative representations in most sections of the media, as they are associated with 'unruliness', lack of taste and culture, and lack of integration into mainstream society. In France, the descendants of immigrants are often portrayed in the media as the heirs of working-class people, although their exclusion in the marginalised space of the *banlieues* is often said to be a consequence of their 'ethnicity' rather than social and economic inequalities. However, some sections of the media challenge these negative representations and question their legitimacy while providing alternative images and identities for the working classes.

Questions

1 How are the middle and upper classes represented in the media? Does the media perpetuate or challenge stereotypes about class?

2 How is class perceived in France? What is the link between class and ethnicity in France? How are the *banlieues* represented?

3 Choose three different media texts and analyse images and stereotypes about social class. What are the codes used to convey social class? And what is the intended audience for each of these media texts?

Further reading

Gallie, D. (1983) *Social Inequality and Class Radicalism in France and Britain*, Cambridge: Cambridge University Press. While this book is now outdated, it offers an interesting comparison between the class histories of France and Britain.

Milner, A. (1999) *Class: Core Cultural Concepts*, London: Sage Publications. An excellent analysis of the major theories and concepts addressing 'social class' and their development.

Munt, S. (ed) (2000) *Cultural Studies and the Working Class. Subject to Change*, London: Cassell. This book offers a sound examination of the representation of working-class identities and life in different media and cultural practices.

Silverstone, R. (1997) *Why Study the Media*, London: Sage. This book offers convincing arguments on the importance of studying the media and the way they influence our social, cultural, economic and political life.

References

Beaud, S. and Pialoux, M. (1999) *Retour sur la Condition Ouvrière*, Paris: Fayard.

Begag, A. and Delorme, C. (1994) *Quartiers Sensible*, Paris: Seuil.

Bourdieu, P. (1984) *Distinction*, London: Routledge.

Boyer, H. and Lochard, G. (1998) *Scènes de Télévision en Banlieues 1950-1994*, Paris: L'Harmattan.

Day, G. (2001) *Class*, London: Routledge.

Dubet, F. (1991) 'Regards sur l'Actualité', *Mensuel* (172), July.

Dubet, F. and Lapeyronnie, D. (1992) *Les Quartiers d'Exil*, Paris: Seuil.

Gopal, P. (2007) 'Anti-racism Has to Go Beyond a Facile Representation Game', *Guardian*, 25 January.

Hargreaves, A. (1996) 'A Deviant Construction: The French Media and the *Banlieues*', *New Community*, 22 (4): 607-18.

Halimi, S. (1997) *Les Nouveaux Chiens de Garde*, Paris: Raisons d'Agir.

Hartmann, M. (2000) 'Class-specific Habitus and the Social Reproduction of the Business Elite in Germany and France', *Sociological Review*, 48 (2): 241-61.

Imbert, C. (2005) 'Le Bûcher d'Une Politique', *Le Point*, 10 November, n. 1730.

Kellner, D. (2002) 'Cultural Studies, Multiculturalism and Media Culture' in G. Dines and J.M. Humez (eds) *Gender, Class and Race in Media*, London: Sage Publications.

Kirk, J. (2007) 'Classifying Matters', *European Journal of Cultural Studies*, 10 (2): 225-44.

Kuhn, R. (1995) *The Media in France*, London: Routledge.

MacMaster, N. (1997) *Colonial Migrants and Racism, Algerians in France, 1900-62*, London: Macmillan Press.

Marx, K. and Engels, F. (1967) *The Communist Manifesto*, London: Penguin.

Marwick, A. (1980) *Class, Image and Reality in Britain, France and the USA since 1930*, London: Collins.

Mucchielli, L. (2002) *Violences et Insécurité: Fantasmes et Réalités Dans le Débat francais*, Paris: La Découverte.

Nettelbeck, C. (2007) 'Kechiche and the French Classics: Cinema as Subversion and Renewal of Tradition', *French Cultural Studies*, 18 (3): 307-20.

O'Shaughnessy, M. (2007) *The New Face of Political Cinema; Commitment in French Film Since 1995*, New York: Berghahn Books.

Palissot, C. (1968) 'Nécrologies de Hommes Célèbres de la France', in F. Deloffre (ed) *Marivaux, Théâtre Complet*, Vol. 2, Paris: Éditions Garnier Frères, pp. 966-9.

Phillips, D. and Sarre, P. (1995) 'Black Middle Class Formation in Contemporary Europe' in T. Butler and M. Savage (eds) *Middle Changes and Middle Classes*. London: University College of London Press.

Savage, M. (2000) *Class Analysis and Social Transformations*, Buckingham: Open University Press.

Silverstein, P. (2004) *Algeria in France: Transpolitics, Race, and Nation*, Bloomington: Indiana University Press.

Silverstone, R. (1999) *Why Study the Media?*, London: Sage.

Skeggs, B. (2004) *Class, Self, Culture*, London Routledge.

Stovall, T. (2001) 'From Red Belt to Black Belt: Race, Class, and Urban Marginality in Twentieth-Century Paris', *L'Esprit Créateur*, 41 (3): 9-23.

Taranger, M. C. (1994) 'Télévision et "Western Urbain": Enjeux et Nuances de l'Information sur les banlieues', *Les Cahiers de la Cinémathèque* (59-60), Perpignan: Institut Jean Vigo, pp. 59-71.

Tissot, S. (2007) 'The role of race and class in urban marginality', *City*, 11 (3): 364-9.

Waquant, L. (2007) *Urban Outcasts: A Comparative Sociology of Advance Marginality*, Cambridge: Polity Press.

Wilson, A. N. (2007) 'So Who Are the Savages Now?', *Daily Mail*, 20 January.

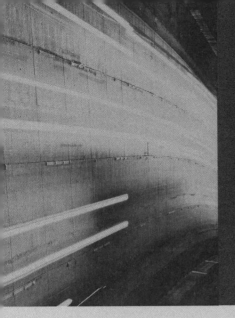

30

Race and Ethnicity

Sarita Malik

Chapter overview

This chapter outlines some of the key ways in which Black and Asian people have been represented in British television and film. By tracing back early on-screen images of 'blackness', it reflects on the complex concerns around race, ethnicity and cultural identity. The chapter takes us up to the present day by addressing issues around new media technologies and the impact that they are having on Black and Asian representation and audiences.

Introduction

The British media is a key site of contestation in matters of race and ethnicity. On the one hand, it has been seen as a problematic arena where ethnic minorities are marginalised, excluded or stereotyped, but on the other it has been recognised as a critical space in terms of how social relations are developed and ideologies around race and ethnicity are produced in broader contexts. The term 'race' in the cultural and political terrain has almost universally been aligned with Black and Asian people (those of African, Caribbean and South Asian descent) as though they are the only racial groups that 'own' an ethnicity. There have been very few occasions when 'whiteness' itself, and more specifically English people, have been depicted as a racial group with their own distinct culture, ethnicity and identity (Dyer 1997).

According to the 2001 National Census, the size of the UK ethnic minority population is 4.5 million or 7.6 per cent of the total population of the UK. Indians are the largest minority group, followed by Pakistanis, Black Caribbeans, Black Africans and those of mixed ethnic backgrounds. The 'mixed ethnic' group has the youngest age demographic, and England (compared to Wales and Scotland) has the highest number of people from ethnic minorities with 45 per cent of the UK's entire ethnic minority population living in London. The picture of UK cultural diversity is becoming increasingly complex and changeable with the arrival and settlement of a broader range of ethnic groups alongside more long-standing ones such as the Chinese, Polish and the Irish. The implication for the media, particularly for those which claim to operate within public service frameworks, is that it now has to respond to and cater for a range of diverse communities in new ways.

Alongside these demographic developments, media industries are also at a critical juncture. The emerging cultures of commercialism triggered by increasing competition, lighter touch regulation and technological developments mean that the media is engaged not just in a set of social and domestic concerns about how to manage 'difference', but also in new economic and geopolitical ones. Between 2008 and 2012 all UK television will be switched over to digital and there is considerable uncertainty about what impact an entirely digital mediascape will have on the nation's multiple publics. This is a matter not just related to questions of distribution (who gets what kind of media and how) but also to questions of public recognition (how the media responds to the claims of different ethnic groups for more and better representation). The challenge is how the relationship between ethnicity, culture and politics can be developed so as to allow for diverse cultural representation in a civil public sphere. This chapter will consider these contemporary concerns by mapping the terrain, offering a historical overview of the key moments, patterns and issues involved. We will focus on television and specifically Britain's black and Asian communities.

Different approaches to reading 'race' in the media

The analysis of race and representational practice (not unlike studies of other variables of difference, such as gender, sexuality or disability) has generally taken three forms. The first examines issues of production and consumption (the relationship between audiences and media representation or what audiences 'do' with representation); the second refers to textuality and content (an analysis which usually considers stereotyping and ideology and looks at the types of images which are used to represent ethnic minority groups); and the third focuses on power and politics (who 'controls'/is 'controlled by' media representation). Essentially, at stake in all three approaches is an analysis of representation and inclusion in relation to politics and ideology.

Most media theorists in the field of race and representation have tended to focus on issues around *textuality* and *content* by analysing how various media forms choose to select and present information on different racial groups. For example, in the late 1970s, the Centre for Contemporary Cultural Studies (CCCS) introduced the issue of 'agenda setting' particularly in relation to news and documentary reports on race. It argued that the media set the agenda/public debate on race, and denied space and access for competing ideologies and images.

Few academic or industry studies have disputed that the media, in general, have been very selective in their portrayal of Black and Asian people. Some have attributed this to the lack of ethnic minority people in key decision-making positions within media industries and argue that by employing more Black and Asian commissioning editors, writers, actors, producers, directors, etc. richer and more diverse portraits of Black people will follow. The ongoing lack of diversity in senior management was discussed at a Commission for Racial Equality (CRE) Conference on Channels of Diversity in March 1996 and also identified as a major problem by the Cultural Diversity Network (a network of UK broadcasters) in 2000. In 2007, BBC senior executives agreed to waive their annual bonuses because the Corporation was failing to meet a set of diversity targets which they had set including one to recruit 7 per cent of senior staff from Black and ethnic minority backgrounds (it had achieved 4.38 per cent). Such patterns have continued in spite of Greg Dyke's now infamous statement that 'the BBC is hideously white' following his visit around BBC departments (Dyke repeated this in a speech at the CRE's Race in the Media Awards in April 2000). In 2008, one of Britain's best-known Black television entertainers, Lenny Henry, delivered a lecture to the Royal Television Society titled 'The road to diversity is closed . . . please seek alternate route' in which he described the lack of ethnic minority decision-makers within the UK broadcast media.

Although the lack of ethnic minority inclusion in strategic and influential media roles is certainly a problem that needs to be addressed, this, in itself, is no guarantee that a particular set of images will subsequently be produced. To suggest this would be to assume that all Black and Asian people (regardless of age, gender, sexuality, class, religion, etc.) share the same political ground which implies that they are internally homogeneous. This runs the risk of denying that there are multiple voices, perspectives and politics involved in any cultural production and within ethnic groups themselves. In addition, it encourages a 'siege mentality which says that anything we do must be good' (Henriques 1988: 18).

Within this diverse range of theoretical and methodological approaches, a number of different arguments, views and positions on Black representation have emerged. Recent debates, triggered by the technological advancements in digital, satellite and the internet, have considered how the national public sphere (represented by terrestrial television and the British film sector for example) will renegotiate its relationship with Black and Asian British audiences as they increasingly engage in new types of media lifestyles in globalised, transnational contexts (Aksoy and Robins 2000). This has also involved a new focus on policy and governmentality, centring on the challenge of how national, public-facing, regulatory frameworks (for example the way in which content is regulated) can effectively be applied in the multiplatform, multichannel digital age (Born 2003).

Stereotypes: positive and negative images

Much of the debate in the area of race and representation has revolved around the issue of 'stereotyping'. Since the 1960s, this sociological term has been widely used to refer to the process by which a reductive image/impression is produced of a given social experience. During the 1970s and 1980s, many of those who were dissatisfied with representations of Black and Asian people in the cultural arena called for 'positive images' in order to balance out the 'negative images' which were all too often packaged by the media. The mid- to late-1980s, in particular, brought a series of debates in which many argued about the limitations of discussing race and representation in these terms (for example, at the Black People in British Television event which was held at Cinema City, Norwich in May 1988 and the Black Film British Cinema Conference at the Institute of Contemporary Arts in February 1988).

Given the importance of stereotyping (since it is the primary device through which representations of race circulate in media texts), it is useful to make some comments about the ways in which 'typing' functions as a representational practice. Stereotypes are shorthand; they are palatable because they help us to decode people. They appear to simplify the world and its subjects, but they are often complex in that we can associate one aspect of a stereotype with many other things; a complex web of beliefs is thus created from a seemingly glib categorisation. Thus the 'Asian immigrant', the 'Black mugger', the 'bogus asylum-seeker' or the 'British terrorist' are all labels carrying several connotations; our associations encourage us to build on basic information (issues of language, cultural values, social background, economic status, religious belief, etc. automatically follow) to create a quite detailed (though not necessarily accurate) profile of what that person constitutes. Stereotypes are social constructs designed to socially construct. They do not simply come into being from nothing and they are not 'used' in the same way by everyone. The way in which we use stereotypes in cultural production is as revealing as which stereotypes we select to represent. Stereotypes, in themselves, are not necessarily offensive or harmful, but the interests they can serve and the context in which they *can* be used have the potential to be precisely that.

Although it is useful to acknowledge the contexts, processes and interests that stereotypes might serve, leaning too heavily on the 'stereotypes/positive and negative image' rhetoric can be limiting (Malik 1996: 208–9). This is for three main reasons. First, 'typing' has to be recognised as an inevitable and necessary system of representation; secondly, there can be no absolute agreement as to what 'positive' and 'negative' mean (can the image of a gold-medal-winning Black sportsperson only be considered as 'positive'?); and, thirdly, the validity of 'positive' and 'negative' as racial categories of representation themselves need to be questioned since they do little to displace the assumptions on which the original stereotypes are based. 'Positive images' can also be stereotypes, and stereotypes can, in fact, be knowingly reproduced as forms of resistance. Examples can be found in programmes such as *Goodness Gracious Me* (BBC 1998–2000), where the British-Asian comedy team reworked well-versed stereotypes of Asians, or through a character such as Ali G who plays on the stereotype of a 'wigger' (a white, middle class person who revels in 'Black street culture') in order to satirise societal prejudice.

Early representations of 'blackness' on British television

Although there had been many Black and Asian people in Britain prior to the 1950s, the rumblings of hostility towards New Commonwealth 'visibly different' colonial migrants was to manifest itself in complex ways and the UK soon convinced itself that it had a race relations problem. Where immigrants were desperately needed to provide labour, they were also seen to be causing problems in terms of 'numbers', particularly in housing and education.

The difficulties in balancing the 'pros and cons' which Black and Asian people were perceived to have brought with them resulted in confusion. This was perfectly embodied in the British media's ambivalent approach to the treatment of these ethnic communities.

Different moral panics circulated concerning Asians and African-Caribbeans and each were seen to possess their own set of problems, often associated with the trope of a 'culture clash' or being 'between two cultures'. Asians were often seen as overly traditional, unwilling/unable to integrate, having 'language problems' or oppressed by their own communities (often in the form of arranged marriages or religious lifestyles). African-Caribbeans, by contrast, were frequently depicted as troublemakers, as muggers or rioters, or were seen to possess 'all brawn and no brains' (thus having the 'natural attributes' of athletes or entertainers) (Barry 1988). However they were located, it was always in relation to the idea of Englishness which was assumed to be central to 'normal', neutral patterns of living (Malik 2002).

A key feature of post-war television programming was the construction of the image of Black and Asian people as a social problem. The first full-length television documentary programme to examine the problems faced by Black immigrants in Britain was *Special Enquiry: Has Britain A Colour Bar?* (BBC 1955). The programme implied that the primary reason for discrimination was 'cultural difference' rather than racism. Nevertheless, it provoked emotive responses from many white viewers who felt that it was a defence of Black and Asian people in its acknowledgement that racial discrimination existed in Britain. Many documentaries at this time such as *Black Marries White* (ITV 1964), *The Negro Next Door* (ITV 1965) and *People in Trouble: Mixed Marriages* (ITV 1958) focused on 'racial problems' in British society from 'our'/the (white) audience's point of view. The classic liberal technique of *talking on behalf of* 'the victims' while simultaneously arguing that they are silenced, marginalised and denied access was a key point of contradiction in the social-democratic discourse of such representations.

These documentaries largely worked with a self-image of neutrality and balance and an apparent belief that they held the 'middle ground'. The focus on numbers and statistics typical of these programmes supported Enoch Powell's potent fears that white British people would be invaded by their racial others and Powell himself was regularly called on as an expert. (Enoch Powell, a Conservative MP, supported New Right views in the post-war period and articulated his fear of Britain being 'swamped by alien cultures' in his notorious 'Rivers of Blood' speech given in April 1968.) Pre-Powell, the media had generally restrained themselves from tackling matters of race head-on and disassociated themselves from any so-called 'extreme' views on race. The more usual approach was what Stuart Hall has called 'inferential racism' (Hall 1981: 37), which means always starting from the premise of white superiority and tolerance and the assumption that blacks and Asians are 'the problem'. The numbercentric approach to the analysis of race implied that the presence of Black and Asian people in Britain needed to be read in terms of the problematic.

You simply have to look at the programme with one set of questions in your mind: Here is a problem, defined as 'the problem of immigration'. What is it? How is it defined and constructed through the programme? What logic governs its definition? And where does that logic derive from? . . . The *logic* of the argument is 'immigrants = blacks = too many of them = send them home'. That is a racist logic. (Hall 1981: 46)

The advent of targeted ethnic minority programming in the mid-1950s operated as an extension of the BBC's core ideals of liberalism and public service broadcasting. The first programme to recognise that a space should be created for a specific racial audience was *Asian Club* (BBC 1953–61) later to be followed by *Apna Hi Ghar Samajkiye* (BBC, first transmitted in 1965) and *Nai Zindagi Naya Jeevan* (BBC 1968–82). The dominant assumption behind these programmes was that any problems which Asian people faced in Britain could be eradicated by the assimilation of 'Asianness' into 'Englishness'. However, at a time when many Asians inevitably felt alienated from the primary sources of information and entertainment in Britain, these programmes did indicate that efforts were being made to address non-English viewers.

In general, light entertainment and variety was where British television audiences were most likely to see African-Caribbean and African-American artists. There were some exceptions in dramatic productions, but not as many as you might expect given the great resource of aspiring Black actors in Britain (such as Norman Beaton, Carmen Munroe, Horace James, Lloyd Reckord and Edric Connor). Nevertheless, there were a handful of notable dramas on television (mostly written by white male playwrights) that addressed the issue of British race relations in quite unique ways. One such example was John Hopkins' British-based anti-apartheid play *Fable* (BBC1 1965) which marked a radical use of form and content compared to the dominant representations of 'race' and hallmark of documentary realism hitherto deployed in race relations discourses. Usually, however, when Black and Asian characters were included in scripts, it was in the context of dramatic conflict because of the problems their colour was assumed to cause (e.g. the white girl bringing home a Black boyfriend, or the problem of a mixed marriage). In this sense, the presence of Blacks and Asians in television drama was more a matter of their constituting racial difference (or colour), rather than dictated by the demands of their dramatic characters. One key pattern (long familiar to us from American cinema) which began to emerge in the 1970s was that of representing Black characters in 'service' roles; as nurses, chauffeurs, waiters, hospital orderlies, and so on. Within the political context of mounting pressure in Britain for more and better ethnic minority representation, this made it *look* as though black people had been included in the drama, although their roles were rarely developed into characters or written in interesting ways.

One of the most offensive recurrent images of 'blackness' could be seen in *The Black and White Minstrel Show* (BBC 1958–78), a nostalgic return to the days of the American Deep South when the good Black slaves would serenade innocent white roses. Like other emblems of 'blackness' such as the Golliwog, the 'Nigger Minstrel' debased black people and pertained to a particularly racist tradition of popular entertainment. Despite (or perhaps because of) its widespread popularity, some such as the Campaign Against Racism in the Media petitioned (as early as 1967) for its removal from our screens and the BBC finally stopped producing the programme in the late 1970s.

Another programme which generated debates about race and representation was the popular sitcom *Till Death Us Do Part* (BBC 1966–74) created by Johnny

Speight. The comedy was either understood as stridently racist, or anti-racist, or something in between – depending on your point of view. Centred on Alf Garnett, a blatantly racist bigot, Speight argued that it was precisely Garnett's bigotry that he was working against. However, members of the public routinely told Warren Mitchell (who played Alf) that they loved it when he 'had a go at the coons' (Malik 2002). Among other things, the series demonstrated the potential gap between (liberal) intention and impact (i.e. Speight could not guarantee that all members of the TV audience interpreted the programme in an anti-racist way). It also showed how representation can produce and circulate a number of different (and often competing) ideologies and meanings.

Media access and the emergence of multicultural programming

During the 1970s, ethnic minority communities alongside other different groups in society (women, gays, disabled and elderly people) were now demanding better rights and access to institutions such as the media, and pinpointing the media's limited representation of selected voices and viewpoints. Some ITV companies such as London Weekend Television (LWT) began to experiment with schedules by using low-risk off-peak slots to respond to calls to improve minority programming. *Babylon* (LWT 1979), for example, was a short series specifically targeted at young Black Londoners. This was followed by *Skin*, a 30-minute documentary series aimed at Asians and African Caribbeans. Many criticised the series, however, for explaining the Black minority to a white majority, for being *about* not *for* Black communities and for always discussing Black people in relation to white people.

During the 1970s, analysis of the media (particularly television), its functions and its effects also became central to cultural criticism and many Black and Asian people became more vocal and cohesive in their criticism of the media's racial bias. Slots such as the BBC's *Open Door* attempted to redress the balance by expressing otherwise under-represented viewpoints. For example, the Campaign against Racism in The Media used one such slot to make *It Ain't Half Racist Mum* (1 March 1979), 'a programme *about* the media and racism, *on* the media, *against* the media' (Hall 1981: 47). Such precious slots prompted many to voice their concerns about the pressure which limited space (on 'their' public service broadcaster) brought – not only the pressure to say everything in one slot, but also the pressure to please all sectors of Black and Asian communities at the same time (Gardner 1979). This impossible task has been termed 'the burden of representation' (Mercer 1994: 81).

In 1978, the soon-to-be-elected Prime Minister, Margaret Thatcher, echoed Enoch Powell's infamous 1968 'Rivers of Blood' speech when she spoke of the threat of being 'swamped by alien cultures'. In 1981 there were uprisings in St Paul's (Bristol), Toxteth (Liverpool) and Brixton (London). The politically stifling atmosphere of the 1980s acted as a catalyst, triggering off creativity and a strong desire to express and find a cohesive voice. Echoing the American Black Power movement of the 1960s, many Asian, African and Caribbean people in 1980s Britain began to use the collective term 'Black' as a political term.

In 1977 the Annan Committee promoted the concept of 'liberal pluralism', a free marketplace in which balance could be achieved through the competition of a multiplicity of diverse and independent voices. This reconceptualisation symbolised a shift in terminology and a new approach to the principle of 'public service broadcasting' on which British television had traditionally been founded. The Committee suggested that contemporary culture 'is now multi-racial and pluralist . . . [t]he structure of broadcasting must reflect this variety' (Annan 1977: 30). Discussions about the fourth channel subsequently began. British broadcasting was soon to witness one of the most radical moments in the medium's history in relation to minority group representation, with the formation of Channel 4

The 1980s was a critical period where contestation over national identity increasingly developed as a central political and social issue and as a preoccupation of emergent forms of representation. One of the most innovative interventions to emerge out of this socio-political context was Black British film in the form of Black and Asian-led grant-aided regional film collectives, many of them partially supported by Channel 4. In terms of content, documentary films such as *Handsworth Songs* (John Akomfrah, Black Audio Film Collective 1986) and *The People's Account* (Ceddo, Milton Bryan 1988) and fictional features such as *The Passion of Remembrance* (Sankofa, Isaac Julien and Maureen Blackwood 1986) and *Majdhar* (Retake, Ahmed A. Jamal 1985) tenaciously invested in the notion of contested identity. *Handsworth Songs*, in particular, with its innovative, unsettling interrogation of the 1980s Brixton 'race riots', prompted a number of debates about how to address Black and white audiences, about diaspora aesthetics and about dealing with issues of history and memory.

In the 1980s these film-makers approached the spaces they had struggled for in creative ways, and worked towards reconceptualising notions of what constitutes national identity *vis-à-vis* notions of British film and Britishness. This was a formative moment in how Black and Asian groups began to generate (self-)representational practices and a distinct theory-practice interface (around notions of Third Cinema and 'diaspora space' for example) within multicultural contexts. Towards the end of the 1980s (and for a range of complex social, political and economic reasons and as part of a more general closing up of 'minority' art spaces), many public institutions ended their commitment to these workshops, and the beginning of a single project-led commissioning structure began to arise, affecting how Black and Asian British cinema was to later develop.

The politics of multicultural programming

Multicultural programming was built into the structure of Channel 4: it was the first time ever that someone had been specifically appointed to commission programmes for a non-white British audience in the UK. By the mid-1980s, Channel 4 had built up a large number of Black and Asian programmes, which formed a significant part of its weekly schedule. These included *Black on Black* and *Eastern Eye* (1982–85), magazine programmes which were targeted towards African-Caribbeans and Asians respectively. The regularity with which the programmes were screened was unique in that there was an ongoing weekly presence of these ethnic communities on British television. Channel 4 also screened specifically 'ethnic-targeted' sitcoms such as *Tandoori Nights* and *No Problem!*, although they came under criticism for lampooning Black characters and perpetuating stereotypes about Black and Asian people (Gilroy 1983). As a response, perhaps, to a growing demise in political life of the umbrella category 'Black' to unite Asians and African-Caribbeans, the BBC's Multicultural Department (which had followed Channel 4's model) was split into the African-Caribbean Unit and the Asian Programmes Unit in 1995. Many of its subsequent series, such as *All Black* and *East*, were criticised for reiterating problem-oriented discourses and for focusing on sensationalist issues such as rent boys, prostitution, Asian pornography, girl-baby killing and Asian female self-mutilation, in an attempt to 'sell blackness' and attract a bigger audience-share in a competitive marketplace.

Besides, the very presence of specialist units and racially targeted programming sparked off debate about whether/how broadcasters can provide for Black and Asian audiences' needs. The main worry is that these units may encourage the 'ghettoisation' of ethnic minority programmes, experiences and programme-makers by containing them at the margins, and thus always ensuring they remain peripheral to mainstream television developments and portrayals. Furthermore, there is the fear that the existence of minority units lets other commissioners/ departments 'off the hook', since they rely on the specialist units to show that the company 'has a conscience' when it comes to ethnic minority audiences.

After more than 20 years, Channel 4 closed down its Multicultural Programmes Department in 2003. As the only channel to have been established with multicultural programming as part of its infrastructure and core practice, Channel 4 now repositioned multicultural representation as part of a broader 'diversity' agenda in which ethnic diversity was just one component. This supported a broader ethos of viewers as 'general viewers' rather than viewers as 'anyone-in-particular'. But in 2008, Channel 4 announced that as part of its major review of its role as a public service broadcaster, it was once again going to appoint a commissioning editor to oversee multicultural programming. Significantly, this U-turn occurred within what is now an increasingly commercially-oriented media environment; one in which the rhetorical value of officially catering for ethnic minority audiences has changed compared to the 1980s. Channel 4 is currently embarking on a public-service driven initiative, and the renewed diversity emphasis (which arguably sits at the heart of the public service ethos) is an important aspect of the channel's strategy to attract monies in a digital age in which the era of traditional public service broadcasting may be fast eroding.

New trajectories

Recent political, social and technological changes allied to the diversification of the media environment have made questions of ethnic and now religious identity highly salient (particularly since 11 September 2001). These include the shift from ethnic to religious identification, the link between identity, security and surveillance and renewed public policy concerns around social cohesion. The critical shift that has taken place in the new millennium against the idea of 'multiculturalism' and towards a positive evaluation of assimilationist style policies based around integration and citizenship, has had an important impact on the politics of cultural recognition and representation for Britain's ethnic minority groups.

Against the backdrop of such change, there have been two ways in which Black and Asian representation has become more visible in film and television since the 1990s. With regard to film, British Asian cinema (as distinct from a more general sense of 'Black British cinema') has facilitated a mainstreaming of a previously marginalised area of British cinema and provided significant examples of national cinema. British Asian narrative feature films such as *East is East* (Damien O'Donnell 1999) and *Bend it like Beckham* (Gurinder Chadha 2002) have successfully emulated the 'crossover' from art-house to mainstream cinema and have been acknowledged by critics and audiences as some of the most culturally dynamic and pleasurable examples of hybridity; fluid and transient forms of cultural mixing or syncretism (Bhabha 1994). Following a certain process of self-scrutiny about the politics of mainstreaming during the 1990s, British Asian cinema – with films such as *Slumdog Millionaire* (Danny Boyle 2008) – is now a leading example of how South Asian popular culture has been commodified. Whilst British Asian cinema appears, at least on the surface, to have untied itself from the politics of cultural marginalisation, it might be argued that it is still overwhelmed by distinct and updated expectations of 'Asianness', based around themes of traditional culture, patriarchy, family conflict and of being 'between two cultures'.

Thinking internationally, Bollywood, global cinema supreme, has become an important point of reference for Europe. The UK has the largest audience for Indian cinema outside India. These developments within South Asian cinema – UK home-grown and imported – symbolise a phenomenal success story with regards to how the South Asian diaspora has come to occupy a prominent position within British cinema both in terms of production but also amongst audiences. Although there have been a few critically-acclaimed Black British feature films such as *Bullet Boy* (Saul Dibb 2004), *Kidulthood* (Menhaj Huda 2006) and *A Way of Life* (Amma Asante 2004) these have not achieved the same level of economic success, public attention or crossover appeal as British Asian cinema. The cinematic work of British-Asian film-maker, Asif Kapadia (*The Warrior* 2001; *Far North* 2007), and Black-British director, Steve McQueen (*The Hunger* 2008) can also be noted as powerful examples of films which have made a critical impact on an international level.

Another significant area in which minority visibility has been expanded has been in relation to television and specifically related to the growth of lifestyle programming in the late 1990s. Today's glut of reality television models – from *Big Brother* (Channel 4 2000–) to 'talent' shows such as *X Factor* (ITV 2004–) to 'self-improvement' programmes like *How Clean Is Your House?* (Channel 4 2003–) to 'lifestyle-change' series such as *Wife Swap* (Channel 4 2003–) – routinely feature participants from a range of ethnic and social backgrounds. Reality television, now so ubiquitous, has become one of the racially varied forms of programming today with ethnic minority people an important part of the mix; cast in order to be representative of 'real' lived diversity.

Of course, the reality television genre, just like any other form of cultural representation can also highlight patterns of inferential and overt racism. 2007's *Celebrity Big Brother* (Channel 4) exemplifies precisely these issues around ethnic minority representation and the politics of recognition. The reality series attracted international attention when the Bollywood actress, Shilpa Shetty, was bullied and racially taunted by some of her fellow 'celebrity' housemates (on this, see also Chapter 29). The response to *Celebrity Big Brother*, as Channel 4 found out when unprecedented complaints were made to the media regulator Ofcom, serves as a sharp reminder that UK audiences have communication rights and cultural sensitivities that need to be acknowledged by broadcasters. Furthermore, with *Big Brother* as an international media brand, this response also exemplifies that there are now not just local but also global expectations about how the media respond to issues of race and racism.

Conclusion: future scenarios

The British media must be recognised as an influential site where ideologies about race are shaped. In spite of recent developments, the reality of a lived multiculturalism is not represented on British television and the media in general can by no means be seen as ethnically neutral. Recent changes in the television infrastructure have meant that, generally speaking, commercialism, ratings and revenue are being prioritised over what are assumed to be 'minority' needs. These are issues now confronting terrestrial programme-makers as competition from non-terrestrial suppliers rapidly increases with a plethora of 'specialist channels' marketed towards niche audiences of which Black and Asian people are an integral part.

The old order, with its requirements for the media to serve the public in unified and yet distinct ways, is undergoing radical transformation and ethnic minority audiences play a significant role here (Karim 2003). Audience research, viewing figures and industry reports continue to suggest that terrestrial television is a turn-off for Black and Asian audiences. British Asians are showing a particularly strong inclination to 'go elsewhere' by tuning into digital and cable television options (Ofcom 2007) and going to cinemas in droves to watch popular Asian films 'imported' from the Indian subcontinent. Attracting the Black and Asian television viewer and cinemagoer is speedily becoming not just a moral but also an economic imperative. On the one hand, there is a belief that the rise of new media technologies and processes (cable, satellite, digital compression, pay-per-view, etc.) will serve as one possible avenue through which each person can be granted their 'cultural rights' in more specific and varied ways. On the other, there is concern that an increasingly global future can, in fact, mean a 'downgrading of cultural specificity in themes and settings and a preference for formats and genres which are thought to be universal' (McQuail 1994: 112).

Competition from global media channels puts an interesting kind of pressure on the British broadcast media to secure the loyalties of Black and Asian British audiences driven by a range of imperatives in a post-multiculturalism society. In the light of these changes, the media – their programmes, role, value, past, future, economics, and relation to nationhood, citizenship and the public – are being re-evaluated and strategically modified.

Questions

1 Identify some common stereotypes about Black and Asian people in the British media and discuss how they have been constructed or deconstructed in various media texts.

2 What are the arguments for and against having specialist 'minority' programmes targeted at specific ethnic minority audiences on British television?

3 What impact do you think new media technologies are having on the relationship between Britain's ethnic minority groups and traditional media services?

Further reading

Cere, R. and Brunt, R. (eds) (2009) *Postcolonial Media Culture,* Basingstoke: Palgrave Macmillan. A diverse collection of essays about media texts and productions about, for and by ethnic minority communities in Britain.

Hall, S. (1981) 'The whites of their eyes: racist ideologies and the media' in G. Bridges and R. Brunt (eds) *Silver Linings: Some Strategies for the Eighties,* London: Lawrence & Wishart. A seminal essay outlining the key approaches to representing Black people in the British media, which identifies a dominant 'grammar of race' based on three stereotypes: the native, the slave and the entertainer.

Korte, B. and Sternberg, C. (2004) *Bidding for the Mainstream? Black and Asian Film since the 1990s,* Amsterdam, New York: Rodopi. A critical overview of the processes and politics of mainstreaming of Black and Asian British cinema and television in the 1990s and early 2000s.

Malik, S. (2002) *Representing Black Britain: Black and Asian Images on Television,* London: Sage. A discursive analysis and historical reflection on Black and Asian representation on British television, bringing the story up to date to outline the new pressures on traditional broadcasting to address the various needs of its culturally diverse audiences.

Mercer, K. (1988) *Black Film, British Cinema,* ICA Document 7, London: Institute of Contemporary Arts. An essential introduction to debates around Black British film theory and practice.

References

Aksoy, A. and Robins, K. (2000) 'Thinking Across Spaces: Transnational Television from Turkey', *European Journal of Cultural Studies,* 3 (3): 343–65.

Annan, Lord (chair) (1977) *Report on the Committee of the Future of Broadcasting,* Cmnd. 6753, London: HMSO.

Barry, A. (1988) 'Black Mythologies: Representation of Black People on British Television' in J. Twitchin (ed) *The Black and White Media Book,* Stoke-on-Trent: Trentham Books.

Bhabha, H. (1994) *The Location of Culture,* London and New York: Routledge.

Born, G. (2003) 'Strategy, Positioning and Projection in Digital Television: Channel Four and the Commercialisation of Public Service Broadcasting in the UK', *Media, Culture and Society,* 25 (6): 773–99.

Dyer, R. (1997) *White: Essays on Race and Culture,* London and New York: Routledge.

Gardner, C. (1979) 'Limited Access', *Time Out,* 23 February.

Gilroy, P. (1983) 'C4 - Bridgehead or Bantustan?' *Screen,* 24 (4-5): 130-6.

Hall, S. (1981) 'The Whites of Their Eyes: Racist Ideologies and the Media' in G. Bridges and R. Brunt (eds) *Silver Linings: Some Strategies for the Eighties,* London: Lawrence & Wishart.

Henriques, J. (1988) 'Realism and the New Language', *Black Film, British Cinema*, ICA Document 7, London: Institute of Contemporary Arts.

Karim, H. K. (ed) (2003) *The Media of Diaspora: Mapping the Globe,* London: Routledge.

McQuail, D. (1994) *Mass Communication Theory: An Introduction*, London: Sage.

Malik, S. (1996) 'Beyond "The Cinema of Duty"? The Pleasures of Hybridity: Black British Film of the 1980s and 1990s' in A. Higson (ed) *Dissolving Views: Key Writings on British Cinema*, London: Cassell.

Malik, S. (2002) *Representing Black Britain: Black and Asian Images on Television*, London: Sage.

Mercer, K. (1994) *Welcome to the Jungle: New Positions in Black Cultural Studies,* London: Routledge.

Ofcom (2007) *Communications Market Special report: ethnic minority groups and communications services,* 21 June.

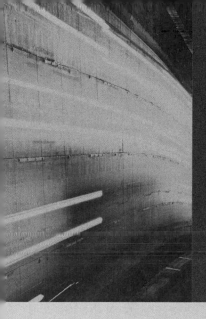

31

Media and Religion

Leen d'Haenens and Jan Bosman

Chapter overview

In general, the media tend to ignore religion unless it becomes problematic and/or religious individuals/groups behave in a disruptive fashion. Focusing on the portrayal of Islam in six Dutch newspapers as a case study, this chapter outlines some of the major ways in which the mainstream media play a visible role in constructing and reproducing multiple images of Islam. Fluctuations in the coverage are clearly event-driven, as most of the attention goes to events that have taken place in the Netherlands. Comparing the reporting of two crises, one international (9/11) and one national (the murder of Theo van Gogh), Dutch journalists appear cautious about running the risk of holding the Muslim community at large responsible for the acts of a few terrorists when dealing with the 9/11 attacks, however the opposite tendency was observed when dealing with the Van Gogh murder. Here journalists were significantly more negative about Muslims and more positive about non-Muslims in the period after the murder; the balance was restored afterwards. As to the use of framing, the framing pattern is about the same for both events. However, after the Amsterdam murder, the amount of framing drops dramatically. Assuming – as it is argued here – that bias is associated with the use of news frames, then we can conclude that Dutch journalists considered it risky to utter harsh criticism of Islam, like Theo van Gogh himself used to do.

Now that religious diversity is with us, can multicultural societies accommodate it?

The global prominence of religion in the public sphere and in the political agenda, the central position of religious diversity in debates about immigration and the stiffening of integration policies, all cast serious doubts on the thesis that religion is becoming less important in our society (Davie 2007; Stout and Buddenbaum 1996). The importance of the religious dimension in shaping ethnic cultural identities reveals a reality that has now become undeniable and that the German philosopher Jürgen Habermas (2001) has called the 'post-secular society' (Koenig 2005). The media are turning the spotlight on the crucial question of how to achieve a viable co-existence of diverse religions in a contemporary understanding of democracy, a question exemplified in debates about freedom of expression and about dress codes. But they also tend to turn their attention to religion in so far as it is problematic and in so far as religious groups or individuals behave disruptively (e.g. Bramadat 2005): take, for instance, the coverage of the numerous cases of members of the clergy accused, falsely or not, of having practised paedophilia (the so-called 'vicars and knickers' news stories). The case study we have chosen in the problem-oriented relationship between media and religion is the portrayal of Islam and Muslims in the Dutch mainstream press.

The Netherlands, often praised for its tolerance towards 'otherness', has long being characterised by the so-called 'pillarised' or segmented community model, i.e. a model of society consisting of separate social groups, each with its own institutions, based upon homogeneous religious beliefs and ideologies. As of the 1960s, with the declining role of the church, de-segmentation began with the individual assuming a much more prominent role. In view of the growing importance of about one million Muslims in the Netherlands (a country with some 16.4 million inhabitants), with Turks (328,000) and Moroccans (296,000) representing the largest ethnic minorities (CBS Statline 2007), a possible development – which goes against the general tendency towards de-segmentation that has affected Dutch society – could be the creation, at some point, of an Islamic pillar with its own daily press, political parties, clinics, etc. In reality, the formation of Muslim institutions within Dutch society has been sporadic and very much dependent on the integration strategies adopted (e.g. a multicultural, as against an assimilationist, perspective) at the national and regional levels, and the degree of empathy shown towards Muslims (Rath 2005). In all, Muslims constitute an important group in the religious spectrum of the Netherlands. How the Muslim minority is going to develop in the future – whether it is going to form a new pillar or whether it will integrate in Dutch society – is at least partly dependent on the coverage Islam will receive in the media.

The Dutch and Muslims: mutual sentiments and resentment

In two different months of 2004, June and December – i.e. before and after the ritual murder of the controversial movie-maker Theo van Gogh by fundamentalist Muslim Mohammed Bouyeri – the pollster TNS NIPO investigated how native Dutch people felt about ethnic minorities and Muslims in the Netherlands. The study revealed that between June and December 2004 native Dutch people became more anxious about the possibility of terrorist attacks by Muslim fundamentalists. In June half of respondents said they were afraid of terrorism, however in December this had gone up to two thirds. After the murder of Theo van Gogh in December 2004 one fifth of the population felt threatened by Muslims, as against one sixth in June. Rath (2005: 32) sums up the situation as follows: 'The terrorist actions in various places in the world, the war against terror, the slaying of the maverick movie-maker Theo van Gogh and so forth have nourished the distrust of Muslims and furthered governmental interference in the lives of Muslims.'

Political actors on both sides of the political divide made the perception of a 'Muslim threat' even worse. For instance, the right-wing populist politician Pim Fortuyn called Islam a backward culture, while several imams made the news with controversial pronouncements and acts. Examples are imam El Moumni, who called homosexuality a disease, and the imam of Tilburg, Ahmed Salam, who refused to shake hands with Rita Verdonk, the then Minister of Integration, because she is a woman. The criticism of Islam voiced by Ayaan Hirsi Ali, a former member of parliament for the Liberal Party (VVD), stirred up passions even more. More recently, the denunciation of Islam by the right-wing populist Party for Freedom, led by Geert Wilders, had made the party a popular political player (it gained nine seats in the 2006 elections for the Second Chamber). In short, from the 1980s onward various events and/or statements made by prominent people may have contributed to straining the relations between Muslims and non-Muslims in the Netherlands.

The media also play a role in shaping the image of ethnic minorities, and this role will be the topic of the present chapter. Just consider the publication of the 12 Mohammed cartoons in the Danish national newspaper *Jyllands Posten* in September 2005. The cartoons were reprinted by some European print media outlets in early 2006: what in the West was seen as a basic freedom (i.e. freedom of expression), was considered highly offensive in the Arab and Islamic world. (For an analysis of the Mohammed cartoons controversy in the media discourse of several countries see Kunelius *et al.* 2007.)

Media: a dark mirror of reality?

Mainstream media texts are important since they provide the main source of knowledge about a large number of issues; in informing us, the media contribute to our 'commonsense' understanding of the world. As such, media texts are believed to affect the way in which we understand ourselves and others. This chapter proceeds on the basis of the assumption that the media at least partially construct the social fabric of people's lives, especially when issues are unfamiliar and far removed from people's daily experiences; it is in these cases that the media function as substitutes for these real life experiences. Ethnic minorities argue that the Dutch media provide a one-sided and often negative portrayal of ethnic-minority groups. The image thus created is said to be an unfair reflection of the multicultural society of the Netherlands and is one of the reasons why ethnic minorities do not sufficiently recognise themselves in the media (d'Haenens *et al.* 2004: 49). As much as 63 per cent of the Muslim population in the Netherlands judges the coverage of Muslims in the Dutch mainstream media to be negative. 73 per cent of respondents believe the turning point to have been the 9/11 attacks, while 18 per cent mention the assassination of Theo van Gogh on 2 November 2004 (TNS NIPO 2005).

The criticism leveled by Dutch Muslims at the mainstream media is backed up empirically by a longitudinal content analysis (covering the period 1998–2004) (d'Haenens and Bink 2006) of the coverage of Islam and Muslim-related news in the popular daily *Algemeen Dagblad*. The analysis reveals that often news articles showed a negative slant in that they focused on terrorism, religious fundamentalism and violence. One possible explanation for this is that news is, by definition, bad news and that journalists always tend to be on the look-out for alarming and revealing news items. Good news, corrective information and data which put things in perspective are often included in later editions of a story and are given less prominence. Strikingly, however, the tone adopted in news items with an ethnic character (whether religious or not) is often more critical than in items with a non-ethnic character (Ter Wal *et al.* 2005: 947). The media often portray Muslims as fanatics, as irrational, primitive, militant and dangerous people (Shadid and Van Koningsveld 2002: 174). The most often cited shortcomings of the coverage of Islam are the following: the portrayal of Islam is too simplistic and too unsympathetic; Muslim groups are presented as the source of intractable problems and are often stigmatised; society is split into the categories of *us* and *them*; Muslims are not given an opportunity to voice their own opinions. According to Shadid and Van Koningsveld (2002: 175) the media have, since the mid-1980s, constantly and wrongfully pointed the finger at the menace allegedly posed by the Muslim world.

Research carried out in Great Britain by Elizabeth Poole (2002) shows that a mere 12 per cent of news concerning Islam deals with British Muslims, as the British press is very much focused on international news items and takes a great interest in so-called 'global Islam'. Poole also argues that British Muslims are looked at in the light of acts committed by Muslims in, for example, the Middle East (i.e. they are 'guilty by association'). Richardson (2004), too, writes about the negative portrayal of Muslims in the media in his book about the representation of Islam in British newspapers. He points out that positive actions by Muslims are not attributed to or explained by their being Muslims, while negative actions are. First, a division is produced between *us* and *them* and subsequently a negative image of Muslims is created. The outcome is that *we and they* soon translated into *we against them* or *we over them* (Richardson 2004). The articles Richardson analysed also showed, in several different ways, what kind of threat Muslims allegedly posed: whether it was a military threat posed by Muslim countries against others, the terrorist and/or extremist threat, the threat against democracy that Islam allegedly posed in the Middle East, or the threat to Muslim as well as non-Muslim women. Generally speaking, the news coverage in the seven British papers studied can be labelled as 'Islamophobic'. The picture that British newspapers sketch of Muslims is that of a homogeneous, separate, inferior and hostile group (Richardson 2004: 232).

The study by d'Haenens and Bink (2006) showed that the distinction between news coverage of domestic, as against foreign, Islam is not unimportant. News items about Islam in the Netherlands give space to several people, among whom are Dutch Muslims and Islam scholars. As a result, news about Dutch Islam can be said to be much more accurate and to reflect more shades of meaning. By contrast, news about Islam abroad is more often inaccurate, imbalanced and over-simplified, and stigmatisation and polarisation are found more often. Nonetheless, according to d'Haenens and Bink (2006), the assassination of Theo van Gogh on 2 November 2004 triggered several changes in the coverage of Islam: interest in Islam increased in the Netherlands, more non-Muslims were quoted in articles on Islam than before, these articles tended to become longer and journalists began to take a more negative approach towards Muslims, and to deal in a more positive fashion with non-Muslims. The overall result of this was increased polarisation. It is fair, then, to say – even without conducting an exhaustive overview of research in this particular field – that a good number of studies lend empirical support to the criticism levelled at news coverage about Muslims and/or ethnic minorities.

Internet discussion forums prove to be an adequate outlet to express frustration with the mainstream media. it is the place where members of ethnic minorities can talk of issues which the Dutch media do not, or hardly, touch upon. A few small-scale case studies (Brouwer 2002; Geense and Pels 2002) illustrate the diversity of the topics discussed in internet forums as well as the omnipresence of religious topics. Brouwer calls the internet a 'digital minaret'. At the end of 1998, a group of Moroccan students launched www.maroc.nl out of sheer dissatisfaction with the news coverage provided by the Dutch media (due to lack of recognition) and because it gave them the opportunity of chatting with each other in Dutch. Their intention was to set up and develop Maroc.nl as an uncensored digital platform in order to further the spread of information, communication and integration of ethnic minorities in Dutch society (see d'Haenens and Van Summeren 2006; Van Summeren 2007). Nevertheless, in this chapter we focus on coverage of Islam in the mainstream media.

Research questions

The above-mentioned study by d'Haenens and Bink into *one* popular Dutch daily served as the starting-point for a more exhaustive analysis of news about Islam and Muslims. First, we address the question of how Islam is covered in a broader range of Dutch newspapers. To that end, we will analyse articles about Islam and Muslims in the six most important national newspapers (*Het Parool, Trouw, De Telegraaf, De Volkskrant, NRC Handelsblad* and *Algemeen Dagblad*) in the year 2005. Questions related to this issue are: how often is news about Islam included? Are there any differences in the number of news items from one month to the next? Can these differences be explained on the basis of the events themselves? What are Muslims given a say on or mentioned for, and who speaks on behalf of the Islamic community? Are these persons mentioned by name, paraphrased or quoted? These questions will be answered in the cross-sectional part of our investigation. Second, we examine the degree to which the news about Islam-related issues changes in times of crisis. To this end we will analyse the coverage of Islam and Muslims in the *Algemeen Dagblad* from 2000 to 2005, a period that includes the 9/11 terrorist attacks in 2001 and the murder of Theo van Gogh on 2 November 2004. We will investigate whether the attitude towards Islam and Muslims changes due to these events and whether the ways in which Islam and Muslims are framed changes. We address these topics in the longitudinal part of our study.

News frames

Before considering the news coverage in more detail, we need to turn briefly to the concept of 'news frames'. Framing means that news is covered in a particular fashion, so that problems, causes and solutions are advanced and moral judgements are suggested (Entman 1993). Similar to what happens in the gate-keeping process, some events and aspects of a problem are presented, while others are not. Generally speaking, frames are defined as ways to ensure that a specific interpretation of a text is made more likely: 'To frame is to select some aspects of a perceived reality and make them more salient in a communication text, in such a way as to promote a particular problem definition, causal interpretation, moral evaluation, and/or treatment recommendation' (Entman 1993: 52). More recently, Entman suggested that bias is the organising concept behind framing (and agenda setting), defining bias as 'consistent patterns in the framing of mediated communication' (2007: 166). Hence, frames present topics from a particular perspective by emphasising certain aspects or, conversely, by omitting them. It is thanks to the frames that journalists, as well as the receivers of media messages, can grasp a news story, interpret it and give it a meaning. Frames are structured through the presence or absence of given key words, expressions, stereotype images, sources of information and sentences which all serve to back up a given opinion or judgement (Entman 1993). Frames help the media user to form an opinion and to arrive at conclusions about a given issue. This is different, therefore, from the concept of *agenda setting*, in which the media do not determine the user's attitude towards a given topic. By contrast, the concept of *framing* suggests that the media are actually able, by means of news frames, to determine how a topic should be interpreted. Whether they are successful in this, is yet another question, one which has so far not received an unambiguous answer.

Semetko and Valkenburg (2000) suggest that reporters usually resort to five frames. The first of these is the *conflict frame*, which emphasises conflict between individuals, groups and parties. Research shows that complicated public issues are usually reduced to a simple conflict between political parties. One outcome of this particular way of framing a conflict may be that the media thus tend to cultivate cynicism on the part of the public at large and add to people's lack of confidence in politics. The second frame is the *human interest frame*, which presents events, topics or issues from a human and emotional perspective. The news is personalised, dramatised and emotionalised in an attempt to draw the public's attention and keep it going. Next there is the *economic effects frame*, which focuses on the economic effects that an event, an issue or a topic could have on individuals, groups, institutions, countries or regions. In the fourth frame, the *morality frame*, religious principles and moral rules in their relation with events, issues and topics take a central position. News items are looked at from a religious or moral point of view. Since journalists are under the obligation to be objective, they often indirectly refer to moral rules by giving the floor to others and by letting others voice criticism. They can, for instance, quote a party involved and let him or her question the truth or value of the event or issue concerned. Finally, the *responsibility frame* emphasises the question of the responsibility or even the guilt of political authorities or individuals. Media tend to be able to convince the public of a given party's responsibility for causing or solving social problems.

Islam in the Dutch newspapers: a cross-sectional study

All articles published in the six above-mentioned newspapers in 2005 and dealing with Islam as the key theme were analysed.[1] The newspapers concerned are three national quality papers (*De Volkskrant, NRC Handelsblad, Trouw*), two national popular papers (*Algemeen Dagblad, De Telegraaf*) and the quality paper *Het Parool*, which used to be a national newspaper but which now focuses on Amsterdam and its region. In the search engine LexisNexis the terms Islam, Muslim(s) and fundamentalism were entered, specifying that articles with at least one of these terms in the headline or opening paragraph were to be listed. The term Islam in the headline yielded 208 articles, and in the opening paragraph 867 articles; Muslim(s) in the title yielded 405 items, in the opening paragraph 53; fundamentalism in the headline yielded 13 articles, in the opening paragraph 53. This procedure gave us the bulk of the news items in which Islam was the key topic. All the articles occurring twice as well as those in which Islam eventually turned out not to be the key topic were removed. In all 1130 articles were analysed.

General features

Figure 31.1 shows the greater interest in Islam and Muslims in the first three months of 2005, as opposed to 2004, which can be explained by the aftermath of the murder of Theo van Gogh on 2 November 2004. The terrorist attacks by Muslim extremists in London on 7 July 2005 resulted in a renewed focus on Islam. The third upsurge in concern with Islam came in November 2005, on the first anniversary of the murder of Van Gogh. Clearly, the coverage is to a large extent event-driven.

The highest number of the events reported in the press took place in the Netherlands (28 per cent), especially in Amsterdam (12 per cent) or Rotterdam (8 per cent), and in the Middle East (6 per cent). Most of the texts (61 per cent) are relatively long (400 words or more), which suggests that there is more room for different opinions. As a matter of fact, this is what happens in the texts under study: in 11 per cent of the short articles (with a maximum of 150 words) one or more Muslims are quoted; in medium-long texts (151–400 words) that percentage rises to 28 per cent; finally, it rises to nearly 48 per cent in long articles. A similar pattern is found with regard to non-Muslims.

Domestic issues having to do with Islam in the Netherlands are the topic of a large number of articles (38 per cent); non-region-related articles and fairly general considerations about Islam take second place (27 per cent), while coverage of Islam in other countries ranks third (25 per cent). The most frequent topics are religion

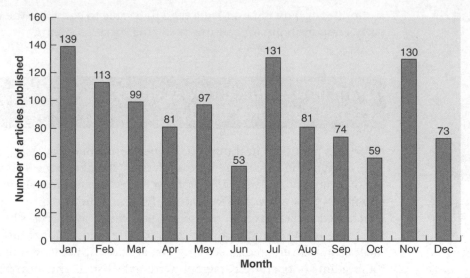

Figure 31.1 Articles on Islam and Muslims in the Dutch press in 2005 (N = 1,130)

and religious practices (27 per cent), politics (15 per cent), terrorism (13 per cent), ethnic relations (10 per cent) and criminality and violence (7 per cent). What is striking, though, is that more than one quarter (28 per cent) of the items with a religious dimension deals with fundamentalism. One article in eight (12 per cent) with a religious dimension discusses the rules laid down in the Koran. Other prominent topics are personal religious practices (8 per cent), the spread of Islam (7 per cent) and issues involving mosques (6 per cent). A large number of texts (25 per cent) treats the question of how Muslims can practice their religion in Dutch society, comparing the choices made by traditional orthodox Muslims, who strictly adhere to the rules of the Koran, with those made by modern, more liberal Muslims, who advocate a freer interpretation of Islam.

Muslim actors, relations and points of view

The 1130 articles present 2998 Muslim actors – the term 'actor' including individuals as well as organisations. The analysis focused on how many Muslim actors were mentioned, quoted or paraphrased in each article. Most Muslim actors (66 per cent) were merely mentioned; 23 per cent were quoted and 12 per cent paraphrased. The large percentage of actors who were merely mentioned can probably be explained by the fact that it is more practical and cheaper to mention actors rather than interviewing them. In 43 per cent of cases the actor involved mainly speaks for him or herself, i.e. he or she is not presented as an expert, nor as a spokesperson for a Muslim organisation, nor a person with a special role. By contrast, 14 per cent of the actors represent an Islamic organisation or institution, and 11 per cent speak for an underground movement (e.g. a terrorist organisation);

in the latter case, al-Qaeda and the Dutch Hofstad group are the most frequently mentioned groups. Entrepreneurs are underrepresented in the articles, as economic affairs and trade are the key topics in a mere 2 per cent of the texts.

Muslim actors stem from all regions of the societal spectrum, and are very diverse overall: 54 per cent of the Muslim actors who are quoted speak as citizens, 47 per cent as experts, i.e. as members of a certain organisation, a political party, the authorities or the police. Considering Muslim actors as individuals, we found that 78 per cent were men and only 22 per cent women. Men (80 per cent) were mentioned four times more often than women (20 per cent) and were quoted three times more often than women (76 per cent vs. 24 per cent)

Comparing the newspapers

We find significant differences between the six papers with regard to the number of news items included that focus on Islam and Muslims. The three quality papers together published three quarters of the overall annual number of Islam-related news items. *Trouw*, for instance, had five times more articles than the popular *De Telegraaf*. A further striking finding is that reporting on Islam had far greater highs and lows in the popular papers than the quality press. The quality papers also showed fluctuations in their interest, however these ups and downs were much less substantial than those of the popular press. Another difference is that the popular papers carried significantly more short news items with factual information, whereas the quality papers had longer items that included contextual information, and significantly more interviews, opinions and letters to the editor.

Islam in Dutch newspapers: a longitudinal study

As mentioned before, the media mainly tend to deal with religion when this is seen as a problem or when the behaviour of religious groups or individuals gives cause for alarm. This is especially true of reporting about Islam in Western countries. According to Abrahamian (2003) the news coverage about 9/11 in American newspapers was mainly framed in religious terms. At least partly inspired by Huntington's controversial article, 'The clash of civilizations?' (1993), the media have cast the 9/11 events as a battle between Islam and Western civilisation. In the following we will focus on the question of the extent to which the coverage of Islam-related news is affected by acts committed by individual Muslims. To this end, an analysis is made of Islam-related news at and around two points in time where individual Muslims received negative attention, i.e. 11 September 2001, the day when Muhammad Atta and his accomplices crashed their planes into the Twin Towers and the Pentagon, and 2 November 2004, the day when Theo van Gogh was killed by Mohammed Bouyeri.

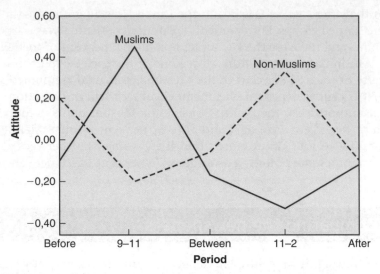

Figure 31.2 Attitude towards Muslims and non-Muslims in the reporting as a reaction to the events of 11 September 2001 and 2 November 2004

Figure 31.2 shows the attitude towards Muslims and non-Muslims in the reporting of the *Algemeen Dagblad* (AD) from 2000 to 2005. This span of five years is subdivided into five periods:

1 before 9/11 (20 months);

2 the month immediately following 9/11;

3 between a month after 9/11 and the murder of Theo van Gogh on 2 November 2004 (approximately 34 months);

4 the month immediately following the murder, and finally

5 the period beginning a month after the murder until the end of 2005 (approximately 13 months).

In the period before 9/11, reporting was slightly (but significantly) more positive about non-Muslims. Surprisingly, in the month after 9/11 the Islam-related articles became significantly more positive about Muslims and significantly more negative about non-Muslims. Apparently, journalists were cautious about running the risk of holding the Muslim community at large responsible for the acts of a few terrorists. In an attempt to balance the slant of their texts, they overshot their mark adopting some kind of self-censorship and ending up providing a positive coverage of Muslims. In the third period, the long intervening period before the murder of Theo van Gogh, the balance was restored.

We found that the reporting of the murder of Theo van Gogh followed the opposite trajectory. Right after 2 November 2004, Islam-related articles were significantly more negative about Muslims and significantly more positive about non-Muslims. In the final period the normal balance was again almost restored, however the tendency to cover non-Muslims more positively has all but disappeared.

It is worth giving some thought to the question of why the reaction to 9/11 in the Dutch newspapers was so different from that of the American press (Abrahamian 2003) and also to why the Dutch press treated 9/11 and the murder of Theo van Gogh so differently. The contrast may be due to the fact that the attack of 9/11 was close to home for the US media, and, conversely, that the murder of Theo van Gogh affected Dutch people more profoundly than the 9/11 events as it took place on Dutch soil. However, it is also possible that the two events do not stand isolated and should be interpreted in the context of a longer series of incidents involving Muslim extremists, such as the attacks in Madrid and the London bombings. From that perspective, the attacks of 9/11 and the murder of Theo van Gogh would become just two incidents in a longer series of negative events as a result of which tolerance of Islam and Muslims could be said to be gradually waning.

Figure 31.3 presents the degree of framing with which the crises of 11 September 2001 and 2 November 2004, as well as the periods before and after these two dates, were covered in the *Algemeen Dagblad*. Obviously, the amount of framing is event-driven. There is less framing in terms of economics and more framing in terms of conflict and morality, and in the case of 2 November also more framing in terms of human interest. The pattern is about the same for 9/11 and 11/2. However, after the murder of Theo van Gogh the amount of framing drops dramatically, so much so that framing is almost absent. In all, the amount of framing of Islam is clearly sensitive to the disrupting events of 11 September and 2 November. And if bias is expressed as patterns in the amount of framing, then the almost total absence of framing seems to imply that journalists have interpreted the murder of Theo van Gogh as evidence that it is risky to express unrefined opinions

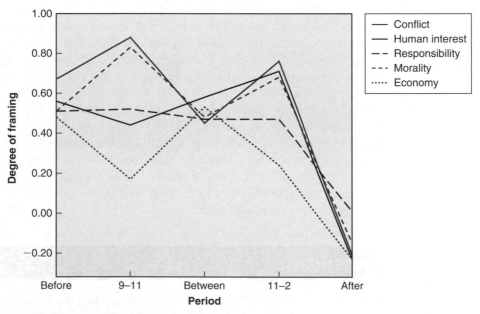

Figure 31.3 Framing of Islam as a reaction to the events of 11 September 2001 and 2 November 2004

about Islam, like Theo van Gogh used to do. This is in line with our previous finding that the relatively more positive attitude in writing about non-Muslims has almost disappeared in the last period.

Discussion

Having reflected on the representation of religion in the media, what emerges from the analysis of the press coverage and the degree of framing adopted is that the mainstream media seem to have very little counterweight to offer against black and white thinking. Fluctuations in the coverage of Islam were clearly driven by events, most of the attention going to events that took place in the Netherlands. By taking a biased look and by focusing on, for instance, interethnic conflict and religious fundamentalism, the mainstream media may even end up supporting and fostering polarising tendencies in society. The analysis also reveals that, as a response to disruptive events, the characteristics attributed to Muslim actors in news stories as part of routine reporting may shift in times of crisis. Comparing the reporting of two crises, one international (9/11) and one national (the murder of Theo van Gogh), Dutch journalists were found to be cautious about giving the impression to be holding responsible the Muslim community at large for the acts of a few terrorists when dealing with the 9/11 attacks. However, the opposite tendency emerged when dealing with the murder of Van Gogh, as journalists were significantly more negative about Muslims and more positive about non-Muslims following this event. As for the use of framing, the framing pattern was about the same for both events (i.e. more conflict and more morality framing). However, after the Amsterdam murder, the amount of framing dropped dramatically. Assuming that bias is associated with the use of news frames, this implies that Dutch journalists considered it risky to express unrefined opinions about Islam, like Theo van Gogh himself used to do.

As a complement to the changing stances and loyalties of the mainstream media, in light of the events covered, the internet is usually regarded as an interactive medium with a great potential for attracting an ethnic-minority public, which can thus broaden its horizon and obtain information framed from a different perspective (d'Haenens *et al.*, 2000). Maroc.nl is just one of the big web communities of Moroccans in the Netherlands illustrating that new media technologies can function as a bonding spot for 'soul mates' or a possibility to connect across space with other Muslims, which enables them to engage in a virtual Islamic public sphere and particularly to challenge the biased portrayal of Islam which is found in the mainstream media.

Questions

1 Select a week's routine coverage in your local or regional newspaper and compare the portrayal of Muslims and non-Muslim actors in Islam-related articles with that of a national newspaper. Do you find any differences? If so, what differences? Try to formulate

your answer by considering article length, local/regional versus national events, national versus international events. Can you identify the use of particular news frames in both newspapers? Is there any difference in the amount of framing and the kinds of frames being used?

2 Consider a crisis in which religion has played a major role (e.g. protests against the building of a mosque, Muslim women claiming the right to wear the veil at work, etc.) in your region/country and look at the coverage of it in your local or regional newspaper. Compare the portrayal of Muslims with non-Muslims. Who is being paraphrased or quoted most of the time? What is the attitude of the journalist towards Muslim and non-Muslim sources that are brought up in the article (i.e. positive, negative, mixed, unclear)?

3 Media have a choice when portraying religion. On the one hand, they can promote inter-religious exchange and mutual tolerance. On the other, they can increase conflict by providing biased coverage of religious issues. Select at least 10 different articles in which a religion is featured prominently. Do not limit yourself to Islam, but look at other religions, too (such as Catholicism, Protestantism, Buddhism, Judaism, Hinduism, etc.). Look at those who are seen as the representatives of such religions (e.g. the pope, priests, bishops, imams, muftis, etc.) and look at the ways in which these actors are described (e.g., conservative, liberal, aggressive, exotic, mystic, caring, etc.). Can you discover similarities in the ways these different religions are represented or do you see mostly differences? Can you identify recurrent patterns when a given religion is talked about?

Note

1 The groundwork for this research was carried out by Jop van Steen, who graduated in 2007 with a Master's thesis in communication science entitled 'I'm a Muslim. Don't panic!'

Further reading

Bosman, J. and d'Haenens, L. (2008) 'News Reporting on Pim Fortuyn. Framing in Two Dutch Newspapers', *Media, Culture & Society*, 30 (5): 735–48. Adopts framing analysis on the reporting of the murder of Pim Fortuyn, comparing a popular and an elite newspaper.

d'Haenens, L. (2003) 'ICT in Multicultural Society. The Netherlands: A Context for Sound Multiform Media Policy?', *Gazette. The International Journal for Communication Studies*, 65 (4–5): 401–21. Discusses the Netherlands as a multicultural society as well as its media and diversity policies.

References

Abrahamian, E. (2003) 'The US Media, Huntington and September 11', *Third World Quarterly*, 24 (3): 529–44.

Bramadat, P. (2005) 'Re-visioning Religion in the Contemporary Period. The United Church of Canada's Ethnic Ministries Unit', *Canadian Diversity/Diversité canadienne*, 4 (3): 59–62.

Brouwer, L. (2002) 'Marokkaanse jongeren en virtuele discussies', *Sociologische Gids* 49, (2): 121–33.

d'Haenens, L., Beentjes, H. and Bink, S. (2000) 'The Media Experience of Ethnic Minorities in the Netherlands. A Qualitative Study', *Communications: The European Journal of Communication Research,* 25 (3): 325-41.

d'Haenens, L. and Bink, S. (2007) 'Islam in the Dutch Press with a Special Emphasis on the "Algemeen Dagblad"', *Media, Culture & Society,* 29 (1): 135-49.

d'Haenens, L. and Van Summeren, C. (2006) 'Moroccan Youngsters as "Digital Citizens"', in F. Marcinkowski, W. Meier and J. Trappel (eds) *Medien und Demokratie. Europäische Erfahrungen/ Media and Democracy. Experiences from Europe,* pp. 161-81. Bern/Stuttgart/Vienna: Haupt Verlag.

d'Haenens, L., Van Summeren, C., Saeys, F. and Koeman, J. (2004) *Integratie of identiteit? Mediamenu's van Turkse en Marokkaanse jongeren* [Integration or Identity? Media Menus of Turkish and Moroccan Youngsters], Amsterdam: Boom.

Davie, G. (2007) *The Sociology of Religion,* London: Sage.

Entman, R. (1993) 'Framing: Toward Classification of a Fractured Paradigm', *Journal of Communication,* 43 (4): 51-8.

Entman, R. (2007) 'Framing Bias: Media in the Distribution of Power', *Journal of Communication,* 57 (1): 163-73.

Geense, P. and Pels, T. (2002) 'Allochtone jongeren op het internet', *Migrantenstudies,* 18 (1): 2-18.

Habermas, J. (2001) *Glauben und Wissen,* Frankfurt: Suhrkamp.

Huntington, S. (1993) 'The Clash of Civilizations?', *Foreign Affairs,* 72 (3): 22-49.

Koenig, M. (2005) 'Introduction', *Canadian Diversity/Diversité canadienne,* 4 (3): 3-6.

Kunelius, R., Eide, E., Hahn, O. and Schroeder, R. (eds) (2007) *Reading the Mohammed Cartoons Controversy. An International Analysis of Press Discourses on Free Speech and Political Spin,* Bochum/Freiburg: Projekt Verlag.

Poole, E. (2002) *Reporting Islam. The Media and Representations of Muslims in Britain,* London: I.B. Tauris.

Rath, J. (2005) 'Against the Current: The Establishment of Islam in the Netherlands', *Canadian Diversity/ Diversité canadienne,* 4 (3): 31-4.

Richardson, J. E. (2004) *(Mis)Representing Islam. The Racism and Rhetoric of British Broadsheet Newspapers,* Amsterdam/Philadelphia: John Benjamins Publishing Company.

Semetko, H. and Valkenburg, P. (2000) 'Framing European Politics: A Content Analysis of Press and Television News', *Journal of Communication,* 50 (5): 93-109.

Shadid, W. and Van Koningsveld, P. S. (2002) 'The Negative Image of Islam and Muslims in the West: Causes and Solutions' in W. Shadid and P. S. Van Koningsveld (eds) *Religious Freedom and Neutrality of the State: The Position of Islam in the European Union,* Louvain: Peeters.

Stout, D. A. and Buddenhaum, J. M. (eds) (1996) *Religion and Mass Media: Audiences and Adaptations,* Thousand Oaks: Sage.

Ter Wal, J., d'Haenens, L. and Koeman, J. (2005) '(Re)presentation of Ethnicity in EU and Dutch Domestic News: A Quantitative Analysis', *Media, Culture & Society,* 27 (6): 937-50.

Van Steen, J. (2007) *I'm a Muslim. Don't Panic,* Nijmegen: Radboud University Nijmegen (Unpublished Master's Degree Thesis).

Van Summeren, C. (2007) 'Religion Online: The Shaping of Multidimensional Interpretations of Muslimhood on Maroc.nl', *Communications: The European Journal of Communication Research,* 32 (2): 273-95.

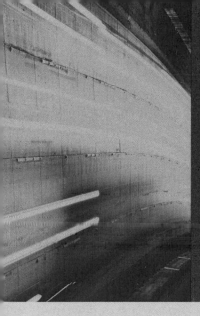

32

Youth

Bill Osgerby

Chapter overview

This chapter focuses on representations of youth in the media and the context of the growth of youth culture in the West. It uses examples from Britain, France and Germany but necessarily points to the crucible of youth culture in post-World War Two America. Beginning with an account of the recent 'hoodie' phenomenon in the UK, it proceeds to analyse the relation of media and youth with reference to the evolving concept of 'moral panic'. Youth is demonstrated to hold a particular fascination for the media as a vessel for hopes and fears, to the extent that the media are shown to create the means of thinking about youth rather than merely reflecting its existence.

'Hoodie law' in 'broken Britain': images of youth, crime and social decline

Readers of the British press in 2008 were confronted with a portrait of the nation tumbling into an abyss of juvenile crime and gang violence. That July a spate of teenage knife attacks triggered an outburst of dramatic newspaper headlines and editorials. The *Sun*, for example, conjured with images of 'Broken Britain', presenting the country as facing 'a tide of blood' and a 'new orgy of violence' (12 July 2008), while the *Daily Mail* recounted a 'terrible toll of violence and despair' as the nation was gripped by 'the scourge of knife crime' (12 July 2008). For the *Sunday Telegraph*, Britain was plagued by 'a knife crime epidemic' (13 July 2008), while a *Sunday Times* opinion poll indicated that 85 per cent of those surveyed favoured the introduction of teenage curfews as a measure to combat youth crime (13 July 2008). These media concerns about an 'appalling scale of knife crime' committed by 'a new generation of teenage thugs' (*Daily Mail*, 17 July 2008) marked the latest episode in a spree of press stories that had ostensibly spotlighted a surge in violent crime committed by antisocial delinquents.

In 2007 press outrage had followed the shooting of an 11-year-old Liverpool boy, Rhys Jones, by a young gunman. The event marked a crescendo to several years of concern among the media and politicians that Britain faced a growing problem of gun crime committed by urban youth gangs. Press stories highlighting an apparent escalation of 'gang' violence in British cities had appeared with regularity throughout 2006, 2007 and 2008 – the *Evening Standard*, for example, purporting to reveal 'the true scale of London's escalating gang culture' by naming no less than 257 youth gangs stalking the capital's streets with, the *Standard* claimed, half being 'involved in assaults or robberies, and over a quarter in murder' (*Evening Standard*, 24 August 2007).

Alarm about spiralling levels of youth crime and violence also found specific focus around the figure of the 'hoodie' (or 'hoody'). 'Hoodie' was originally a slang term for a hooded sweatshirt – attire popularised in hip-hop subculture during the 1970s, subsequently becoming a stock item of teenage streetstyle. But, from 2004, the term was increasingly used by the British press as a pejorative moniker for what was presented as a new generation of violent youths plaguing British cities. The term gained particular currency after May 2005 when youngsters wearing hooded tops or baseball caps were banned from Kent's Bluewater shopping centre as part of the store's attempt to combat crime. Subsequently, the term 'hoodie' became commonplace media shorthand for a new delinquent menace. In August 2005, for example, a *Daily Mirror* headline announced the advent of 'Hoodie Law' alongside a photograph of a youngster brandishing a replica pistol (26 August 2005), while in 2006 the *Daily Telegraph* described how a 'hoodie gang' had beaten up an Essex geography teacher (21 January 2006), and in 2007 the *Daily Mail* reported that '"hoodie" gang members' had been jailed for a 'tube robbery rampage' (20 March 2007). The *Sunday Express* even saw hooded sports tops as an active *cause* of urban crime. In March 2008, as part of its self-proclaimed campaign against 'the feral gangs of hooded youths' who were 'forcing law-abiding communities into a state of seige', the *Sunday Express* launched a crusade to 'Ban the Hood for Good' – the newspaper lobbying for 'hood free zones' in British cities, so that youngsters would be banned from raising their jacket hoods in public (30 March 2008).

However, media representations of an unprecedented 'tide' of violence committed by 'a new generation of teenage thugs' (*Daily Mail*, 17 July 2008) stood somewhat uneasily alongside empirical indices. Crime statistics, of course, are notoriously problematic. Officially recorded crime figures are often seen as an unreliable measure of 'true' crime levels because many crimes go unreported, while official crime statistics can be affected by a range of factors, including changes in the routines of law enforcement and the practices through which crimes are recorded (a thorough account of the problems presented by the use of crime statistics is provided in Coleman and Moynihan 1996). For some, the British Crime Survey (BCS) represents a more reliable index of crime levels because it asks people about their *experiences* of crime, thereby incorporating a measure of crimes that go unreported. Significantly, in 2008, a combination of *both* official police data *and* figures producd by the BCS failed to substantiate notions of spiralling levels of criminality. Instead, they revealed the longest recorded period of falling crime – with overall crime figures declining by 48 per cent since 1995 (Kershaw *et al.* 2008: 2). And, although around two thirds of the British public (65 per cent) believed crime levels were rising, the Home Office reported that levels of violent crime in Britain had actually fallen by 12 per cent compared to the previous year (Kershaw *et al.* 2008: 5).

Furthermore, statistics for knife crime did not bear out the press headlines. At 6 per cent, the Home Office reported, the proportion of violent incidents involving knives was 'not statistically significantly different' to the level of 7 per cent recorded during 2006–07, while available data indicated that the number of violent incidents involving knives had remained relatively stable 'at or below 8 per cent since 1995' (Kershaw *et al.* 2008: 75–6). Undoubtedly, youth crime and violence were important social problems, especially in the country's most deprived cities and neighbourhoods. But the nature and scale of these problems were clearly misrepresented in media portrayals of 'a knife crime epidemic' (*Daily Mirror*, 14 July 2008) in which the country was falling prey to 'gangs of hoodies' who were 'bringing terror to our streets, menacing communities, instilling fear and putting at risk the peaceful way most of us want to live our lives' (*Sunday Express*, 30 March 2008).

These concerns, moreover, were just the latest instalment of an angst-ridden succession of fears about youth, crime and social decline. According to Geoffrey Pearson, since the 19th century Britain has seen 'a long and connected history of fearful complaint and controversy' in which 'each succeeding generation has understood itself to be standing on the brink of some radical discontinuity with the past, and in which the rising generation has been repeatedly seen as the harbinger of a dreadful future' (Pearson 1984: 102). Victorians, for example, were preoccupied with an apparent explosion of street crime associated with packs of young hooligans and 'scuttlers' (as they were known) (Pearson 1984: 74–118), while 1950s Britain was haunted by the spectre of Teddy boy gangs – youngsters with a taste for rock 'n' roll and American style, who the press associated with a unprecedented wave of crime and violence (Pearson 1984: 12–24).

According to Pearson, the repeated anxieties surrounding frighteningly 'new' waves of delinquency have not addressed genuine leaps in the level of juvenile crime, but have served as a medium that condenses wider apprehensions about the nature of social change and the state of the nation. American historians Joe Austin and Michael Willard concur, explaining that 'public debates surrounding "youth" are an important forum where new understandings about the past, present, and future of public life are encoded, articulated and contested', so that 'youth' functions as 'a metaphor for perceived social change and its projected consequences' (Austin and Willard 1998: 1). Media images of youth, then, invariably articulate much wider themes and issues, representations of young people functioning as a kind of 'metaphorical vehicle' that encapsulates more general hopes and fears about trends in cultural life.

It is, perhaps, almost inevitable that conceptions of 'youth' and 'generation' feature in attempts to make sense of social change. But many authors (e.g. Smith *et al.* 1975; Clarke *et al.* 1976; Davis 1990) point to the way youth's metaphorical capacity has been powerfully extended at moments of profound transformation – for instance, the twilight years of the 19th century or the period of social and economic realignment that followed World War Two. The early 21st century might also represent such a moment, with anxieties about marauding 'hoodie' gangs serving as a focus for broader uncertainties about the nature and ramifications of change in the social, economic and political landscape.

Mod mayhem: youth, media and moral panic

Since World War Two crime, violence and sexual licence have been recurring themes in the media's treatment of youth culture, with the degeneracy of the young depicted as indicative of a wider social malaise. During the 1950s, for example, America was gripped by the perception that delinquency was spiralling out of control. In 1953 the anxieties prompted the appointment of a Senate Subcommittee to investigate the problem's cause. Headed by Esteves Kefauver, the official inquiry continued until the early 1960s, and its very existence helped confirm perceptions that juvenile delinquency – or the 'JD' phenomenon as it was often dubbed – was a major social problem. The fears were further fuelled by a torrent of media exposés in magazines, newspapers and newsreels, all purporting to depict a wave of juvenile crime frighteningly new in its severity. These accounts, however, exaggerated the problem. Notions of a quantum leap in delinquency seemed borne out by a relentless rise in crime statistics, yet James Gilbert shows this 'juvenile crime wave' was largely a statistical phenomenon produced by new strategies of law enforcement and changes in the collation of crime data (Gilbert 1986: 66–70). As Gilbert argues, rather than being a response to a genuine eruption of adolescent vice, the postwar fears surrounding delinquency served as 'a symbolic focus for wider anxieties in a period of rapid and disorienting change', with the concerns about youth crime articulating 'a vaguely formulated but gnawing sense of social disintegration' (Gilbert 1986: 77).

Similar concerns surfaced in Europe. In Britain the 1950s saw media anxieties about a 'new' form of vicious delinquency crystallise around the figure of the Teddy boy. The Ted's style of long, drape jackets and drainpipe trousers was sometimes interpreted as an adaptation of Edwardian fashion (hence the sobriquet 'Teddy' boy), but it was really a variant of the American-influenced styles that had become popular among many working-class youngsters in Britain during the 1940s – a trend inspired by the zoot-suit styles imported with the arrival of GIs during the war. First identified by the media in the working-class neighbourhoods of south London in 1954, the Teddy boy was soon being presented as a violent delinquent stalking streets and dancehalls all over the country. The negative imagery surrounding the Ted was further compounded in the sensational press coverage of cinema 'riots' that followed screenings of *The Blackboard Jungle* (1955), *Rock Around the Clock* (1956) and other films with rock 'n' roll associations. As Paul Rock and Stanley Cohen (1970: 310) have observed, these disturbances were small in scale but attracted a welter of publicity that painted the Teddy boy as an uncontrollable social menace. Once again, however, the anxieties were exaggerated and overwrought. Rather than being the result of an unparalleled tide of delinquency, recorded levels of juvenile crime were largely the outcome of changes in the scope and organisation of law enforcement and the greater formalisation of police procedures (see Davis 1990: 89–91 and Pearson 1983: 213–19).

Along with crime, the American influence evident in the styles and music adopted by the young also prompted concern. For many commentators trends towards 'Americanisation' marked an erosion of cultural standards by a tawdry and debased commercialism. As Dick Hebdige shows, the US – the home of monopoly capitalism and commercial culture – became a paradigm 'for the future threatening every advanced industrial democracy in the western world' (Hebdige 1988a: 52–3), and writers such as Richard Hoggart poured scorn on 'the juke box boys' with their 'drape suits, picture ties and American slouch' who spent their evenings in 'harshly lighted milk bars' putting 'copper after copper into the mechanical record player' – a realm of cultural experience that, Hoggart argued, represented 'a peculiarly thin and pallid form of dissipation' (1957: 248–50).

Comparable unease developed in France. Dubbed *blousons noirs*, groups of young, leather-clad motorcyclists were branded by the press as dangerously delinquent due to their provocative style and raucous 'ralleyes sauvages' that rocked the wastelands of France's new suburbs. Media and political anxiety also surrounded the large gatherings of young people that began to congregate at French coastal resorts. Perceived as antisocial gangs, they gained wide press coverage, as did the growing following for indigenous rock 'n' roll stars such as Johnny Hallyday and Eddy Mitchell. Matters peaked in 1963 when crowds of youngsters clashed with riot police after an open air rock 'n' roll concert in Paris, events that sparked a deluge of sensational newspaper headlines. (Warne 2006 provides a thorough survey of moral panics about youth culture in postwar France.)

In Germany, too, trends in youth culture provoked disquiet. As Uta Poiger (2000) shows, during the late 1940s and 1950s officials and press in both East and West Germany attacked the influence of American popular culture on young people. First targeting Westerns, gangster movies and jazz, then rock 'n'roll, the authories claimed that American imports destroyed German cultural heritage and 'barbarized' both East and West German adolescents, making them prone to fascist seduction. In West Germany the mood shifted during the 1960s, as American music and fashions were increasingly embraced as a liberating aspect of modern consumer culture, but in the East antipathy remained pronounced. Significantly, Poiger highlights the symbolic dimension to these concerns. For Poiger, debates about the influence of American culture on German adolescents were not simply about Germany becoming more American, rather they played an important role 'in the complicated processes of reconstructing Germanness in the aftermath of National Socialism and in the face of the Cold War' (Poiger 2000: 30).

In the Soviet Union postwar youth culture was also a source of alarm. In 1950s Russia, the *stilagi* were a partiular topic of controversy. Groups of relatively well-to-do urban youngsters, the *stilagi* showed little interest in official forms of Soviet culture and instead adopted Western forms of music and fashion, developing their own distinctive image – *stil'* – a (re)interpretation of American rock 'n' roll styles. Reviled as ideologically subversive and unacceptably bourgeois by the Soviet establishment, the *stilagi* faced concerted opposition from the press and state institutions. Brigades of *Kosmosol* (the official Soviet youth movement) were formed to campaign against the influence of *stil'* and, in the cities of Sverdlovsk and Ul'ianovsk, *Kosmosol* patrols were reported to have cut both the trousers and hair of local *stilagi* (Pilkington 1994: 226).

Back in Britain, by the early 1960s the Teddy boy's drape-suit and brothel creeper shoes had been largely displaced by the chic, Italian-inspired styles associated with the mod subculture. Media responses to mod style, however, often reproduced the fearful, overwrought treatment given to the earlier Teds. Like the Teds before them, the mods' appearance was often presented by the media as a symbol of national decline – an approach that peaked in press responses to the 'battles' between the mods and their leather-clad, motorcycle-riding rivals, the rockers, at British seaside resorts during 1964. In his landmark study of the events, *Folk Devils and Moral Panics* (originally published in 1972), Stanley Cohen higlighted the dimensions of sensationalism endemic to press coverage of the disturbances. According to Cohen, the total amount of violence that took place during 1964's seaside 'invasions' was actually very small, and received little coverage in the local press. But, in the absence of other newsworthy material, reporters from national newspapers seized upon the relatively innocuous events and created headlines and feature articles suggesting there had been a wholesale breakdown of public order. Cohen termed this kind of overblown media alarm a 'moral panic' in which:

> A condition, episode, person or group of persons emerges to become defined as a threat to societal values and interests; its nature presented in a stylised and stereotypical fashion by the mass media, the moral barricades are manned by editors, bishops, politicians and other right-thinking people; socially accredited experts pronounce their diagnoses and solutions; ways of coping are evolved or (more often) resorted to; the condition then disappears, submerges or deteriorates and becomes more visible. (Cohen 2002: 1)

Cohen's concept of 'moral panic' denoted processes through which the media contribute to the escalation of social problems by distorting the activities of real or imagined deviant groups – or 'folk devils'. In terms of the 1960s mods and rockers, for example, Cohen argued that these youth groups were initially ill-defined, with little enmity existing between them. The polarisation of the two camps, he contended, developed only as a consequence of the sensationalist news stories, with young people coming to identify with the 'folk devil' images of mods and rockers conjured up by the press. The melodramatic reporting, moreover, also influenced the agencies of social control. Sensitised by the early press stories, Cohen argued, the police subsequently reacted strongly to the slightest hint of trouble and, as a consequence, arrest rates soared and magistrates (also affected by the process of sensitisation) imposed harsher penalties. Media attention and exaggerated press reports, therefore, fanned the sparks of an initially trivial incident, creating a self-perpetuating 'amplification spiral' which steadily escalated the social significance of the events.

Cohen's case study focused specifically on press representations of the 1960s 'battles' between mods and rockers. His arguments, however, could easily be applied to the subsequent procession of media panics about wayward youth – from the skinheads of the late 1960s, through the punks of the 1970s, the 'New Age travellers' and 'acid house ravers' of the 1980s and 1990s, to the blade-toting 'hoodie' gangs of 2008. Repeatedly, broader social and cultural anxieties have been condensed in sprees of hysterical reporting that have cast youth as a new, uniquely degenerate generation of hoodlums.

'The teenage revolution': media representations of 'youth-as-fun'

Media representations of young people, however, have never been entirely pessimistic. A recurring duality has characterised the history of media depictions of youth, with youth culture *both* vilified as the most deplorable evidence of social decline *and* celebrated as the exciting precursor to a prosperous future. These contrasting images – which Dick Hebdige (1988b: 19) has termed 'youth-as-trouble' and 'youth-as-fun' – are obviously distorted stereotypes that bear tenuous relation to social reality. Nevertheless, their connotative power has been potent and throughout the postwar era this dual imagery of youth has been a key motif around which dominant interpretations of social change have been constructed.

At certain historical moments, media images of 'youth as fun' have eclipsed the darker, more apprehensive iconography of 'youth as trouble'. During the early 1960s, in particular, media configurations of 'the teenager' served to promote visions of liberating consumerism and social renewal on both sides of the Atlantic. The term 'teenager' was first popularised during the late 1940s and 1950s by American market researchers who used the phrase to denote what they saw as a new breed of affluent, young consumer who prioritised fun, leisure and the fulfilment of personal desires. A nascent youth market had already taken shape in the US during the early 20th century, but after World War Two it underwent exponential growth as a consequence of a general consumer boom and demographic trends that saw the American teen population rocket from 10 million to 15 million during the 1950s. Commercial interests scrambled to stake a claim in the teenage goldmine, consumer industries interacting with and reinforcing one another as they wooed a young market worth an estimated $10 billion by the end of the decade (*Life* 1959: 83).

As teenage spending emerged as a mainstay in the US economy, 'youth' also acquired powerful symbolic significance. With the growing profitability of the teen market, the media and consumer industries fêted young people as never before and by the early 1960s the 'teenager' had become enshrined as the signifier of a newly prosperous age of freedom and fun. Configured as the sharp-end of the new consumer society, 'teenagers' were presented as an exciting foretaste of affluent good times that promised soon to be within everyone's grasp. Here, Kirse May (2002) argues, images of Californian youth culture were in the forefront. During the early 1960s, the Golden State – home to surfing, hot rods and pop groups such as the Beach Boys – set the pace for America's 'New Frontier' in teenage leisure, pleasure and good living. In this context media images of monstrous delinquents slipped into the background and archetypes of 'well-behaved, well-meaning, middle-class teenagers' came to the fore as films, TV series and pop records all 'packaged California's kids as a beautiful and wholesome generation living it up on the coast' (May 2002: 119).

In Europe, too, the growth of a commercial youth market was accompanied by an iconography in which the media depicted youth as a font of energetic excitement and a vibrant contrast to the tired conventions of the past. In Britain the *Daily Mirror* was in the forefront. The theme of 'youth' (along with an explicit appeal to a young readership) became a feature of the newspaper's attempts not only to boost its market share, but also to offer a meaningful response to the pace of social change. In 1961, for instance, a television advertising campaign announced that 'the *Daily Mirror* believes in young people'. Alongside film of jitterbugging teens, the advert's voiceover pronounced, 'They look fine to us, these citizens of tomorrow. . . . The *Daily Mirror* backs the young because the young are *alive*'. As in America, then, the media deployed images of youth as a shorthand sign for flourishing modernity. And, again, themes of a dawning age of affluence and progress were condensed in the concept of the 'teenager'. The term 'teenager' did not simply denote a generational age group, but signified a new brand of liberated, classless and unashamedly hedonistic consumption. As writer Peter Laurie contended in his taxonomy of *The Teenage Revolution*, published in 1965:

> The distinctive fact about teenagers' behaviour is economic: they spend a lot of money on clothes, records, concerts, make-up, magazines: all things that give immediate pleasure and little lasting use.
>
> (Laurie 1965: 9)

Even the mod subculture could be embraced in the 1960s' celebration of youth. Indeed, at same time as they were reviled as the *bête noire* of the affluent society, the mods were also hailed as stylish consumers *par excellence*. Superficially clean-cut and well-dressed, mods were often treated as the pacesetters of 1960s élan, the press eagerly charting changes in the minutiae of their fashion and music. Even in 1964, at the height of the moral panic about the mods' seaside 'invasions' in the UK, the *Sunday Times Magazine* featured a sumptuous nine-page photospread spotlighting the mods' sartorial flair (*Sunday Times Magazine*, 2 August 1964).

The association drawn between youth and liberated modernity reached its apex in the mid-1960s. The image of 'Swinging London' – with its throbbing nightclubs and fashionable boutiques – encapsulated ideas of Britain entering an exciting age of consumer freedom. It was an image that also caught on abroad. In America, British cultural exports such as Beatlemania, mod style and Mary Quant's chic fashion designs accrued connotations of exciting 'difference', *Time* magazine's 1966 cover story on 'London: The Swinging City' capturing this sense of Britain as the font of youthful dynamism. 'Youth is the word and the deed in London', *Time* enthused, 'seized by change, liberated by affluence . . . . everything new, uninhibited and kinky is blooming at the top of London life' (*Time*, 15 April 1966).

By the end of the 1960s, however, the positive configurations of young people and social change were running out of steam. In America, the economy was faltering and liberal optimism gradually crumbled in the face of racial violence, urban disorder and the quagmire of the Vietnam War. Against this backdrop, the iconography of youthful high spirits began to give way to more negative representations of young people – with students and countercultural radicals attracting particular media venom. In Britain, too, economic downturn and a resurgence of political conflict were accompanied by more abrasive representations of youth. For example, the skinhead subculture, which first surfaced in Britain during the late 1960s, was unequivocally condemned in the media. Whereas the smoothly tailored appearance of the mods allowed them to be integrated relatively easily within discourses of prosperous modernity, the skinheads' defiantly proletarian posture (work boots, braces, prison 'crop' hairstyle) ensured the media invariably presented them as public enemy number one. As in America, media hostility also extended to elements of the counterculture. However, whereas working class subcultures such as the skinheads were stigmatised as delinquent *symptoms* of social decline, the overtly political elements within the counterculture were vilified as an even more subversive threat – and were cast as an active *cause* of social instability and cultural decline (see Clarke *et al.* 1976: 72).

The 1960s counterculture, however, was never a homogeneous movement. Rather, it was a network of loosely affiliated groups, with a disparate membership drawn from a variety of social backgrounds. Responses from the media were also diverse. While political radicalism invariably prompted criticism and reproach, the counterculture's aesthetics and lifestyles often elicited fascination, sympathy, even a degree of admiration. In Britain this attitude was evident in reactions to the Rolling Stones' drugs trial of 1967. Amid a blaze of publicity, Keith Richards and Mick Jagger were convicted and sentenced to three months' imprisonment for the possession of illegal drugs (though both walked free after an appeal). Rather than denouncing the Stones, however, significant sections of the media rallied to their defence. Famously, *The Times* published an editorial asking 'Who Breaks a Butterfly on a Wheel?' – the newspaper defending Jagger and Richards and attacking their prison sentences as unreasonably draconian (*The Times*, 1 July 1967).

The media were also fascinated by the counterculture's hedonistic lifestyles. In 1968, for instance, a feature series in *The Times* championed the 'fresh approach to living' developed by 'The Restless Generation' (*The Times*, 18 December 1968). Similar sentiments also featured in the American media. In 1969, for example, *Life* magazine was breathtaken by 'The Phenomenal Woodstock Happening', a multipage photospread describing in awe-struck tones how the Woodstock extravaganza was 'less a pop festival than a total experience, a phenomenon, a happening, high adventure, a near disaster and, in small way, a struggle for survival' (*Life*, 15 September 1969).

From 'cool Britannia' to 'violent Britain': moral panics revisited

Periodically, the 'youth-as-fun' motif has returned to centre stage. In Britain, for example, during the late 1990s an apparent resurgence in cultural creativity and entrepreneurial dynamism prompted an enthusiastic embrace of youth culture and its associated industries. In November 1996 a *Newsweek* cover story had hailed London as 'the coolest city on the planet' (*Newsweek*, 4 November 1996) and throughout 1997 'Cool Britannia' was a buzzing phrase, coined in the media to denote a rising generation of 'Britpop' bands; a new wave of young artists, writers film-makers and fashion designers; and a surge of innovative style magazines and fashionable restaurants.

Striving to present themselves as agents of forward-thinking modernity, the Labour Party also rushed to capitalise on the vitality of 'Cool Britannia'. National rejuvenation became a key theme in Tony Blair's speeches both before, and immediately after, the 1997 general election – the Labour leader promising that his government would 'make this the young country of my generation's dreams' (*Guardian*, 1 October 1995). And, once in office, Blair's attempts to forge a 'New Britain' also tapped into the cachet of contemporary youth culture. Noel Gallagher, boisterous frontman of rock band Oasis, was invited to a prestigious reception at Downing Street, while Alan McGee (founder of leading independent record label, Creation Records) was appointed as a special advisor to the government's Creative Industries Task Force (CITF) – a body where government ministers and leading media figures joined forces to map out how the economic potential of Britain's creative industries might be maximised.

But by the end of the 1990s the 'Cool Britannia' bubble had burst. Disillusioned with what they saw as Labour's failure to deliver on election promises to help young people and the poor, the grandees of Britpop deserted the Labour Party. And, as the government struggled to deal with foreign policy disasters and mounting economic problems, it shifted away from the upbeat themes of 'Cool Britannia' towards a more authoritarian stance that traded on media portrayals of a rising tide of juvenile crime. The campaign gained momentum in 2003 after two teenage bystanders were killed in a gun battle between rival gangs in Birmingham. Responding to the tragedy, both the media and the government railed against what they depicted as an upsurge of gang culture and gun crime. Lurid stories in the tabloid press painted a picture of a 'new' wave of 'gun madness' sweeping through 'Violent Britain' (*Sun*, 6 January 2003), and the following years were punctuated by recurring media alarm about levels of youth crime.

Superficially, these episodes bore many features of the classic moral panic as Cohen had originally outlined. For some theorists, however, shifts in the constitution and operation of the modern media mean that Cohen's framework requires revision. Both Angela McRobbie (1994) and Sarah Thornton (1994, 1995), for example, have argued that the classic moral panic model operated with an excessively monolithic view of society and the media. Writing about media responses to the rave and 'acid house' scenes of the late 1980s, McRobbie and Thornton argued that analysis of contemporary media culture needed to take 'account of a plurality of reactions, each with their different constituencies, effectivities and modes of discourse' (McRobbie and Thornton 1995: 564). Compared to the 1960s, for instance, the 1980s and 90s saw a greater range of agencies and experts stepping forward to challenge the media's demonisation of youth and countering the vocality of the traditional moral crusaders (McRobbie 1994: 217; McRobbie and Thornton 1995: 566). Groups such as the Freedom to Party Campaign, for instance, were effectively a mouthpiece for acid house entrepreneurs, but they still succeeded in mobilising opposition to anti-rave legislation – in 1990 a Freedom to Party rally in Trafalgar Square attracted a crowd of over 10,000 supporters. In America, too, there emerged new pressure groups working to challenge the media's 'folk devil' stereotypes. In June 2001, for example, the Hip-Hop Summit Action Network (HSAN) held the first of its annual meetings in New York. Partly financed by hip-hop business mogul Russell Simmons, the HSAN and its regional chapters drew together a wide constituency of rap artists, record industry executives, civil rights leaders and scholars who worked to promote the interests of hip-hop culture, countering claims from religious groups, the media and politicians that rap music incited violence and crime.

In these terms, then, the 'folk devils' themselves were better able to engage with, and contest, the media's distorted representations. McRobbie and Thornton argued that this had been partly facilitated by changes in the media itself. The proliferation and fragmentation of mass, niche and micro-media, they argued, had generated a 'multiplicity of voices, which compete and contest the meaning of the issues subject to "moral panic"' (McRobbie and Thornton 1995: 560). Stressing the diversity of media responses to the rave scene, McRobbie and Thornton argued that the 'classic' notion of moral panic not only failed to distinguish between different kinds of mainstream media, but also ignored the alternative accounts offered in the 'micro' and 'niche' media that had mushroomed within the youth cultures of the 1980s and 90s. In response to mass media scare-mongering about the rave scene, they argued, the subcultural press (e.g. magazines such as *i-D*, *The Face* and *New Musical Express*) 'tracked the tabloids' every move, re-printed whole front pages, analysed their copy and decried the *misrepresentation* of Acid House' (McRobbie and Thornton 1995: 568).

Overall, therefore, McRobbie and Thornton challenged the original moral panics model which, they argued, had conceptualised the media as (mis)representing an objective social reality to a gullible audience. In contemporary cultural life, they argued, social reality was increasingly constituted through *competing* media representations and decoded in a *variety* of ways by sophisticated audiences. Indeed, during the late 1980s some members of the rave scene actually greeted media condemnation with relish, since it confirmed their romantic self-image as transgressive rebels (Thornton 1994). Commercial interests, moreover, increasingly exploited (even deliberately cultivated) episodes of moral panic as a neat marketing strategy. As McRobbie and Thornton explained:

> Culture industry promotions and marketing people now understand how, for certain products like records, magazines, movies and computer games, nothing could be better for sales than a bit of controversy – the threat of censorship, the suggestion of sexual scandal or subversive activity.
>
> (McRobbie and Thornton 1995: 572)

Mixed metaphors: representations of youth in the contemporary media

Modern media respresentations of youth are often multifaceted and contradictory. There had always been a degree of slippage between the media stereotypes of 'youth-as-fun' and 'youth-as-trouble' identified by Hebdige (1988b), but these have increasingly given way to a more blurred and ambiguous set of images. Moral panics, in particular, have become more complex and conflicted. As Cohen himself has reflected, contemporary moral panics have seen the media become more self-reflective in their coverage, so that 'the same public and media discourse that provides the raw evidence of moral panic [also] uses the concept as first-order description, reflexive comment or criticism' (Cohen 2002: vii).

Rather than being rejected as outmoded and redundant, however, perhaps the moral panic framework needs review and revision. Indeed, despite the greater multiplicity of voices heard in the contemporary media, Chas Critcher has argued that some voices are more powerful than others. 'When the police, the tabloid press and the governing party conjoin in the concerted campaign', Critcher observed, 'the weak power base of the alternative media is revealed' (2000: 154). Indeed, by their very nature, 'micro' and 'niche' media are targeted at a relatively narrow market. Largely preaching to the converted, 'niche' media have only limited ability to sway wider public and political opinion. For Critcher, then, the notion of moral panic remains a sound analytical concept. Account has to be taken of the specific character of any one moral panic, of the contradictory nature of media coverage and of the complexity of social and political responses – but, Critcher maintained, in attempts to understand the media's construction of social reality and its active role in shaping events, the essential features of the moral panic model 'remain an indispensable account of the basic processes at work' (2000: 154).

Yet Critcher *did* detect a shift in the form of modern moral panics. Although the power of 'niche' media was relatively limited, Critcher suggested that during the 1980s and 90s attempts to portray youth as a threatening social menace had become harder to sustain in the face of arguments to the contrary from young people themselves, their allies and expert opinion. As a consequence, he argued, the construction of youth as folk devils had been increasingly displaced by the presentation of *children* as *the victims* of folk devils. With an eye to the mounting anxieties about paedophilia during the 1990s, Critcher speculated that the army of claim-making crusaders had 'retreat[ed] to safer ground where its moral concerns are unlikely to be challenged' (Critcher 2003: 162).

Nevertheless, as the 2008 furore about 'hoodies' and knife crime demonstrated, the 'ideological' dimension to media images of youth remains pronounced. As always, the media did not simply 'reflect' reality. Instead, they actively constructed a particular view of the social world, deploying visual codes and textual techniques to suggest specific ways of making sense of issues and problems. Media representations of youth, then, are never a straightforward 'reflection' of young people's cultures and lifestyles. Instead, they offer a particular interpretation of youth, constructing images of young people that are infused by a wealth of meanings related to a much wider set of social, economic and political discourses.

Questions

1 Using a specific newspaper story, analyse the social meanings it constructs around representations of 'youth'. What themes and connotations does the story articulate, and how are images and text deployed to communicate these?

2 How do the dimensions of gender, 'race' and sexuality influence and mediate representations of 'youth' in the media?

3 How are other generational groups represented in the media? Are there particular kinds of social meaning associated with these images?

Further reading

Critcher, C. (ed) (2006) *Critical Readings: Moral Panics and the Media*, Buckingham: Open University Press. Collection of some of the key essays on moral panics, many of them necessarily focusing on youth.

Drotner, K. and Livingstone, S. (eds) (2008) *International Handbook of Children, Media and Culture*, London: Sage. Near comprehensive collection of essays including contributions on youth films, videogames, children in pictures, policy, communication rights of young people and coverage of Africa, Asia and other areas beyond Europe.

Furlong, A. and Cartmel, F. (2007) *Young People and Social Change: Individualisation and Risk in Late Modernity*, 2nd edition, Buckingham: Open University Press. Focused on sociological issues rather than media alone, the book provides essential background to any investigation into contemporary youth.

Jamieson, P. and Romer, D. (2008) *The Changing Portrayal of Adolescents in the Media Since 1950*, New York: Oxford University Press. Very useful collection of essays, including contributions on body image and adolescence in the media, images of young people's alcohol use, tobacco and sexuality.

Osgerby, B. (2004) *Youth Media*, London: Routledge. The first sustained analysis of youth 'in the media' and 'media for youth'.

References

Austin, J. and Willard, M. (1998) 'Angels of History, Demons of Culture', in J. Austin and M. Willard (eds) *Generations of Youth: Youth Cultures and History in Twentieth-Century America*, New York: New York University Press, pp. 1–20.

Clarke, J., Hall, S., Jefferson, T. and Roberts, B. (1976) 'Subcultures, Cultures and Class: a Theoretical Overview', in S. Hall and T. Jefferson (eds) *Resistance Through Rituals: Youth Subcultures in Post-War Britain*, London: Hutchinson, pp. 9–74.

Cohen, S. (2002) *Folk Devils and Moral Panics: The Creation of the Mods and Rockers*, 3rd edition, London: Routledge.

Coleman, C. and Moynihan, J. (1996) *Understanding Crime Data: Haunted by the Dark Figure*, Buckingham: Open University Press.

Critcher, C. (2000) '"Still Raving": Social Reaction to Ecstasy', *Leisure Studies*, 19: 145–62.

Critcher, C. (2003) *Moral Panics and the Media*, Buckingham: Open University Press.

Davis, J. (1990) *Youth and the Condition of Britain: Images of Adolescent Conflict*, London: Athlone.

Gilbert, J. (1986) *A Cycle of Outrage: America's Reaction to the Juvenile Delinquent in the 1950s*, Oxford: Oxford University Press.

Hebdige, D. (1988a) 'Towards a Cartography of Taste, 1935–1962', in D. Hebdige, *Hiding in the Light: On Images and Things*, London: Routledge, pp. 45–76.

Hebdige, D. (1988b) 'Hiding in the Light: Youth Surveillance and Display', in D. Hebdige, *Hiding in the Light: On Images and Things*, London, Routledge, pp. 17–36.

Hoggart, R. (1957) *The Uses of Literacy*, London: Chatto and Windus.

Kershaw, C., Nicholas, S. and Walker, A. (2008) *Crime in England and Wales 2007/8: Findings from the British Crime Survey and Police Recorded Crime*, Home Office Statistical Bulletin, London: HMSO, July.

Laurie, P. (1965) *The Teenage Revolution*, London: Anthony Blond.

May, K. G. (2002) *Golden State, Golden Youth: The California Image in Popular Culture, 1955-1966*, Chapel Hill: University of North Carolina Press.

McRobbie, A. (1994) 'The Moral Panic in the Age of the Postmodern Mass Media', in A. McRobbie, *Postmodernism and Popular Culture*, London: Routledge, pp. 198-219.

McRobbie, A. and Thornton, S. (1995) 'Rethinking "Moral Panic" for Multi-Mediated Social Worlds', *British Journal of Sociology*, 46 (4): 559-74.

Pearson, G. (1983) *Hooligan: A History of Respectable Fears*, Macmillan: London.

Pearson, G. (1984) 'Falling Standards: A Short, Sharp History of Moral Decline' in M. Barker (ed) *The Video Nasties: Freedom and Censorship in the Media*, London: Pluto Press, pp. 88-103.

Pilkington, H. (1994) *Russia's Youth and Its Culture: A Nation's Constructors and Constructed*, London: Routledge.

Poiger, U. (2000) *Jazz, Rock, and Rebels: Cold War Politics and American Culture in a Divided Germany*, Berkeley, CA: University of California Press.

Rock, P. and Cohen, S. (1970) 'The Teddy Boy' in V. Bogdanor and R. Skidelsky (eds) *The Age of Affluence, 1951-1964*, London: Macmillan, pp. 288-318.

Smith, A. C. H., Immirizi, E. and Blackwell, T. (1975) *Paper Voices: The Popular Press and Social Change, 1935-65*, London: Chatto and Windus.

Thornton, S. (1994) 'Moral Panic, the Media and British Rave Culture' in A. Ross and T. Rose (eds) *Microphone Fiends: Youth Music and Youth Culture*, London: Routledge, pp. 176-92.

Thornton, S. (1995) *Club Cultures: Music, Media and Subcultural Capital*, London: Polity.

Warne, C. (2006) 'Music, Youth and Moral Panics in France, 1960 to the Present', *Historia Actual Online*, 11: 51-64.

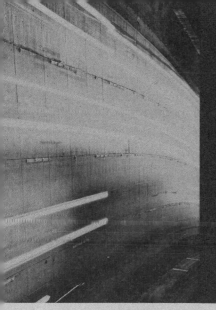

33

The Body, Health and Illness

Andy Miah and Emma Rich

Chapter overview

This chapter discusses media representations of health and illness and describes the ways in which media habitually represent the body. Issues such as disability, eating disorders, body image, genetic engineering, sexually transmitted diseases, mental disorder, cosmetic surgery, drug cultures, abortion, fertility treatment, euthanasia, gerontology, and so forth, are within the general remit of this chapter. However, it focuses on four main issues as exemplary: 'beginning of life', eating disorder, lifestyle enhancements and 'end of life' issues. These examples, it will be shown, urge consideration of the kind of ethical principles which might inform media representations.

Introduction

The disciplinary boundaries of social studies on the body, health and illness are widely dispersed and no less so when inquiring into the subject of media representations. So much research from a range of disciplines seeps into this area that it can be difficult to draw meaningful boundaries around it. Such issues as disability, eating disorders, sexually transmitted diseases, mental disorder, cosmetic surgery, drug cultures and much more, all fall within this area of concern. Moreover, debates in other areas of media inquiry are often explained through a health-related lens. For instance, discussions about computer games are repeatedly subjected to health-related discourses over whether their use leads to an increasingly sedentary, young population – a claim that is not borne out in the literature. The breadth of this subject prompts us to consider how to limit the study of media representations of health, illness and the body, when each and every action we undertake can be interpreted through this conceptual lens.

One starting point is to identify the various bodies of literature that have contributed research findings and insights to this subject area. Long-standing examples include the fields of media/communication and medical sociology, which have been brought together to examine representations of health, illness and the body (see Seale 2003). Indeed, as early as 1975, the *Journal of Communication* explored the relationship between 'Media and Medicine', marking one of the earliest encounters between the health-care professions and media theorists. In this volume, McLaughlin (1975: 184) writes about *The Doctor Shows* in which television doctors positioned themselves as *necessary* outsiders, where they purported to 'deal objectively with the facts at hand, interpret and shuffle them, and solve all kinds of problems.' In this study, one observes the attempts from the medical profession to adopt the position of expert and authority in order to extend their medical gaze. (The limitations of this are explored by Elliott and Kahn 1994.) Alternatively, studies in the sociology of health and illness have long addressed issues related to media representations (see Lupton 1999). Yet, we can also look to studies in less familiar bodies of literature, such as medical law and ethics, which have become increasingly engaged by media studies of health. Indeed, one of the key factors of research development in this area over the past five years has been the convergence of inquiries into the role of *ethics* within the cultural sphere.

An increasing number of studies have interrogated the role of ethics within cultural and media studies (Zylinska 2005), alongside ethical debates about transformations in health care and the development of scientific research more generally. For instance, consider the end of the millennium debates about the Human Genome Project – the project that promised to inform a revolution in health care, but which was also discussed as bringing the prospect of Frankenstein-like technologies. Today, an increasing number of outgrowths of the project are appearing on the market and this has exacerbated the level of public and media debate about the new moral choices they present for people. For instance, today's prospective parents must now consider whether to pay for the cost of saving stem cells from their child's umbilical cord, in case the child contracts a blood related illness. (At the time of publication, these costs are approximately €2000 from most clinics.) These tangible effects on people's lives create new populations that media scholars are gradually beginning to study and they will grow in numbers and diversity. Moreover, the vested interests to promote understanding and – often – acceptance of such innovations from various organisations of health governance, also explains why media studies in this area are flourishing.

The breadth of ethical concern in this area is also expanding and this has a bearing on how we limit media representations of health, illness and the body. For instance, debates about climate change and environmental concerns generally are often portrayed via the long-term health risks they present for people, non-human species and the ecosystem at large. Such issues are accompanied by a wide range of media artefacts, which become an integral part of this representative sphere. For example, Al Gore's docufilm *An Inconvenient Truth* (2007) occupied a mixed-zone of media space, infiltrating politics through culture. Alternatively, the fictional film *The Day After Tomorrow* (Emmerich 2004) has subsequently been studied by media researchers to understand how audiences become (mis)informed by such texts of popular culture (Lowe *et al.* 2006). A further example in the arena of health specifically is Michael Moore's docufilm on the US health care system, *Sicko* (Moore 2007). This film became a focal point for discussions within the media, which refracted on the state of health in other countries. In this case, Moore spends considerable time comparing the US health care system to that of

France and the UK in particular, concluding that each is far healthier than the USA. These artefacts feed back into political debate and become the subject of media studies as they relate to politics, which partly explains and justifies their importance as subjects of concern for media scholars.

Various specialist terms have emerged to describe this inter-disciplinary space of health and media studies. Such concepts as *biopower, biopolitics, biomedia, biosocieties* and *bioart* each appear alongside these discussions and each merits separate consideration in the attempt to convey something more precise about media representations of health, illness and the body (see Miah 2008). Such representations play a part in fashioning diverse cultural narratives that inform our understanding of what it means to be healthy or sick and the expansion of these concepts into the psycho-social domain – where sickness implies a moral transgression, rather than a biological dysfunction. As such, we identify three dimensions to this broad inquiry into these various representations. First, it is necessary to consider how medical knowledge is produced and represented by the media. Second, one should study how key actors in the mediatised process receive such information. Thus, our understanding of health and illness is inflected by processes of 'mass mediatisation' (Seale 2003) and studies exploring media reception have revealed the variance of lay public interpretation of mass media messages, and how one might integrate these into the narrative we construct about our own bodies, health and illness. Finally, one should study the influence that various agencies may have on the *production* of media. For instance, how do commercial companies in the diet and fitness industry affect what is written about health and weight within magazines? Alternatively, how do government agendas shape understandings of health inequalities? Furthermore, how will the emergence of online platforms such as Google Health transform the channels through which people access and make sense of their medical records?

Our focus connects media representations of health to the numerous institutions of medical governance that interpret our activities through a health-related lens. By these actions, they medicalise our lifestyle choices, subjecting them to the value laden terms of social responsibility and the health of the nation. This rhetoric is both the explanation for the vast media coverage that is generated by health-related issues, as well as the key factor that restricts and shapes the terms through which this conversation takes place within the public sphere. The chapter thus considers four categories of media representation, as entry points into studies of health, illness and the body:

- beginning-of-life issues,
- disordered eating,
- disability, lifestyle and enhancement technologies, and
- end-of-life issues.

Each of these themes speaks to a range of cases that can be pursued more fully with independent research. For instance, in *beginning-of-life issues*, we focus on the science of stem cell research, test tube-babies and designer genes, which promise many benefits to humanity, from repairing damaged spinal tissue to the capacity to create organ replacement farms. This subject also extends into discussions about other forms of procreative regulation, such as abortion or discussions about 'saviour siblings', where a child might be conceived in part to assist the survival of a sibling. At a time when various countries are considering the prospect of *hybrid embryos* – part human, part animal DNA – and re-visiting the legal time limit on abortions, these are crucial issues for a range of societies today.

Alternatively, *end-of-life* issues encompass the prospect of life extension, which has arisen in various formats over the last few years. This subject is made less esoteric and unlikely when one considers them in the context of more modest manifestations of such interventions that occur on a daily basis within health care. For instance, consider the concepts of life expectancy and morbidity rates and how these are affected by the social conditions within any particular region. Even within advanced countries, such as the UK, there is considerable variation across and within regions between the upper and lower limits of life expectancy. As such, it cannot be assumed that the developed world is, necessarily, a healthier world. In this capacity, the further assumption that Western health care is a model that others should attempt to follow is dubious and, with the rise in consumption of alternative medicines, there is evidence to support the claim that there is an increasing loss of confidence in such Western methods. The media play a central role in communicating these doubts and trends in understanding, as is evidenced by the recent BBC documentary series on *Alternative Medicine* (2008), presented by the science communication scholar Kathy Sykes. This final case also allows us to consider one further element – the involvement of media scholars in constituting and articulating the media-health arena. The presence of 'experts' again warrants our scrutiny.

There are also connections across the different themes. For instance, considerations of genetic selection, which fit into the *beginning-of-life* topic, also have a bearing on *lifestyle and enhancement technologies*, or indeed, *disordered eating*. Over the past 10 years, various high-profile media stories have propagated the idea that there might be such a thing as an obesity gene (see Farrar 1999; Sample 2008; Wiley 2008). A further connection arises across the first three themes and the pursuit of immortality. For one cannot pursue a range of health improvements, without also committing to some form of *life extension*. Each action that we undertake in order to promote a healthier lifestyle, affects our lifespan.

While we intend for these categories to be seen as continuous, the essay presents each of them as having been focal points of scholarly research in this area, which stand in their own right, regardless of their connections. The aim of this chapter is, thus, to survey and conceptualise the contribution of recent studies in the media representation of the body, health and illness and, in so doing, to signal emerging areas of investigation.

Beginning-of-life issues: test-tubes, designer genes and stem cells

The characterisation of certain types of issue as 'beginning-of-life' draws from terminology within medical law and ethics, though it is useful to apply in the context of media representations of certain types of health. Indeed, beginning-of-life issues have been present in media studies for at least 30 years. When Louise Brown was born on 25 July 1978, as the first child to be born of in-vitro fertilization (IVF), the media also conceived the concept of a 'test-tube' baby (see *Time* magazine cover below). In the years that followed, public discussion about assisted reproduction technologies occurred via the media, in an era when the public's participation in scientific policy was extremely limited. In an extensive study of press coverage during this period, Mulkay (1994) reveals that the discussion was always set up as a 'conflict or contest' of view points. These early technologies gave rise to new discussions about questions of (biological) identity, as kinship was affected directly by such innovations. This staging of perspectives around emerging technologies

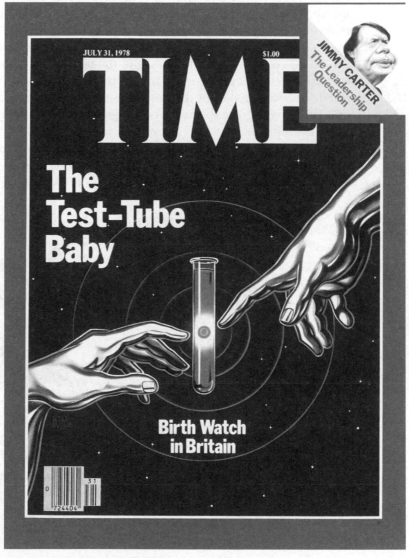

Front cover of *Time* magazine, 31 July 1978

Source: Copyright © 1978 Time, Inc.

persists in media studies where, as Mulkay notes in the case of IVF, 'Metaphors of conflict helped the press to convey a sense of drama in their reports' (1994: 37).

Studies of scientific metaphors used by the media have become a central theme in this area, with the key texts of Nelkin and Lindee (1995) and Turney (1998) articulating the parameters of this subject. For instance, the former discuss the emerging 'new genetics' that surrounded the Human Genome Project where they indicate that the cultural significance of the 'gene' far outweighs its scientific promise. They also explain how the depiction of genes as deterministic – for instance, that there are fixed entities that we may call 'selfish genes, pleasure-seeking genes, violence genes, celebrity genes, gay genes, couch-potato genes, depression genes, genes for genius, genes for saving, and even genes for sinning' (Nelkin and Lindee 1995: 2) – is cause for concern, as more and more people develop a mistaken 'genetic essentialist' view of socially determined conditions. To the extent that these pseudo-sciences give rise to commercial products that reach consumers, there emerges a loop of mis-information about what such science means and how it should be treated by either the media or the public. For example, consider the commercial release of a genetic test for performance ability in sports (see image below) (Miah and Rich 2006). In this case, the evidence to verify its meaning is limited and the range of interpretations and decisions that might follow from anyone using it multiple.

Evidence of incomplete science translating into incomplete reporting also recurs in the literature. For instance, while Mulkay reports general favour from the media on IVF, some 10 years later, the situation is remarkably different, as we enter the

Genetic test for athletic performance (2004)
Source: Genetic Technologies Limited

era of 'designer genes'. While the reality of 'designer babies' is still only partially realised, research has shown how the early days of reporting on designer genes encountered various communicative hurdles. For instance, Nerlich *et al.* (2003) describe how the idea of the 'designer baby' was first articulated in the context of the aforementioned 'saviour siblings', which is really more a case of a donor baby than a designer one, as they note. The authors also indicate that the range of metaphors used in reporting on this subject aligns it with fashion, as it details the capacity of genetics to enable us to design, engineer, and select the most desirable characteristics for our children. Indeed, the media were confronted with such a service in 1999 when Ron's Angels website came online purporting to auction ova and sperm, allowing customers to purchase the best genes for their children (see screenshot below). Within the site, it notes the ethics that underpins such practice:

> Just watch television and you will see that we are only interested in looking at beautiful people . . . our society is obsessed with youth and beauty. As our society grows older, we inevitably look to youth and beauty. The billion dollar cosmetic industry, including cosmetic surgery is proof of our obsession with beauty. If you could increase the chance of reproducing beautiful children, and thus giving them an advantage in society, would you?
>
> (Harris 1999)

Another example that fits within this 'beginning-of-life' category is that of embryonic stem cell research. Stem cells have the capacity to generate into any kind of living tissue and hold considerable promise for many reparative interventions.

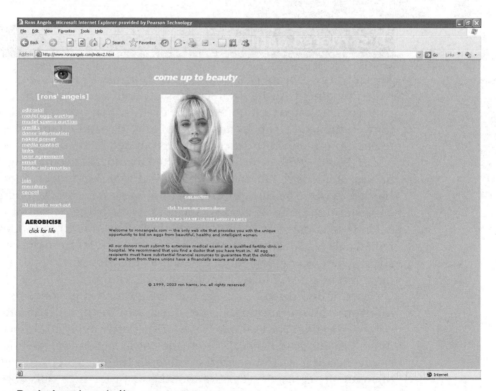

Ron's Angels website
Source: Ron Harris, Inc.

However, in this case, the debates that are present in the media involve claims about the moral status of the embryo, which has long-standing coverage through such issues as the legitimacy of reproductive/therapeutic cloning and hybrid embryos and abortion. In May 2008, the British government even re-considered its laws on abortion for the first time in 20 years. In part, this reconsideration also involved media technologies, particularly the capacity to visualise the foetus in-utero. Various news reports detail the science that claims the possibility of seeing the foetus 'smile' (Campbell 2006) and such imaging techniques have created unprecedented expectations about the moral regard one should have for the gestating foetus. However, with regard to embryonic stem cell research – perhaps the most prominent bioethical issue in recent global biopolitics over the past 10 years – the overlap between culture, politics and media has been a prominent dimension of this debate. Indeed, some of the most prominent coverage has related to celebrity involvement, particularly through Christopher Reeve of *Superman* fame and Hollywood actor Michael J. Fox. Reeve, who died in 2004, lived the final 15 years of his life paralysed from the neck down, while Fox is a Parkinson's Disease sufferer. Each campaigned for federally funded stem cell research within the US (see Goggin and Newell 2004) and each of them suffered from conditions that could benefit from the results of stem cell research. On numerous occasions, their presence in the media made manifest the importance of supporting such research by the visualisation of their suffering.

Disordered eating

Arguably, the concept of 'disorder' persists across all forms of coverage of health issues, whether it is the disordered moral boundaries that emerge through new embryonic research techniques, or the disorder that occurs from human interventions in the food chain, as might be said of 'foot-and-mouth' disease. Media representations of health are increasingly grounded in discourses of *risk* and a *politics of fear* (Furedi 2005), which are connected to wider concerns about the disordered nature of modern life and the equally disordered modern life of *nature* (see Hansen 2006). The disruption of natural processes by scientific intervention is an enduring feature of modern societies, though the degree of disruption now extends to a range of modifications that affect our consumption of nature in remarkable ways. Various cases can be considered here, from the late-1990s debates about genetically modified foods, such as the Monsanto super-Tomatoes, to the more recent crises of Mad Cow disease and Avian flu.

Cases of disordered eating are not only grounded in concerns about scientific interventions, but also speak more directly to the disordered and individualised nature of eating. For example, cases of the latter apply to the recent calls to remove pro-anorexia networks from the social networking website *Facebook*, the emergence of self-harm networks online, or the discussions surrounding the idea of an obesity epidemic. (This was not the first time such calls to censor the internet arose on this subject. In 2001 'Pro-Ana' websites faced removal from Google (see Miah and Rich 2008).) Other media representations of crises concerning confidence in medical and scientific activity are not only grounded in critique and moral panic, but are also rooted in forms of citizenship, media activism and political rights. The interest in genetically modified foods is particularly illustrative of this. Reports on this issue are mixed with parochial concerns about health, but are also infused with a moral narrative concerning emerging nations. For instance, it has been suggested that GM crops may be more drought resistant, thus offering a possible solution to the problem of famine.[1] The case of GM foods is interesting as an illustration of how media discourse can shift in its representation of particular health issues. Early moral panics linked the harmful effects of GM foods to cancer, sterility in men, and were grounded in concerns over the bound aries of science and its impact on an unknowing ill-informed public. (These issues engage us with another burgeoning aspect of media research in this area: science communication, alternatively described as the 'public understanding of science' (see Bauer *et al.* 2007).) Having supported the critique of biotechnology, media coverage quickly shifted towards a position of healthy scepticism and broader moral concerns, particularly over the destruction of experimental crops led by pressure groups, which were depicted as acts of vandalism. More recent media discourse on GM foods have been grounded in economic concerns connected to food security, particularly with reference to the European Union; 'GM crops can save us from food shortages' (*Telegraph,* 17 April 2008). Elsewhere, reports have claimed that 'farmers need to produce GM foods':

> We must relax the rules on biotechnology and ignore the 'Frankenstein Foods' headlines. The reality is that GM foods are harmless and point the way to overcoming global food shortages in the future.   (Struan Stevenson MEP, cited in Buglass 2008: 39)

The case of GM therefore reveals the fluidity of media campaigns and their multiple forms. Moreover, the portrayal of such issues in the media extends beyond concerns for health, into discussions about wider political democracy. In such cases, culture and politics are played out through debates concerning the role of citizenship and consumer rights, conveying the complexity of how health discourses are reconstituted within media activism campaigns. Indeed, the media articulates 'disordered' bodies through a series of image-based, media events and reports that engage emotions of fear around ill health and seemingly irrational living conditions. Moreover, it actively reconstitutes particular bodies that transgress boundaries of normality/health and what particular bodies come to signify. Yet, it is not a new insight to observe the media's role in stigmatising particular health conditions. Instead, we draw attention to how the mediatisation and medicalisation of health issues has focused on a renewed interest in the self-regulation of one's health.

The emergence of recent moral panics around the legitimacy of certain lifestyle choices has made it difficult to distinguish between concerns for health and the socio-political interest to preserve normality, which surrounds them. For instance, the media has treated obesity as a problem of catastrophic proportions. Reporting has taken on instructional and regulative dimensions, which implore populations to regulate and monitor their weight and health (cf. Foucault 1978 on biopower). Thus, the media consistently report that Western society is in the grip of a global 'obesity epidemic' (World Health Organization 1998), facing serious health problems and associated, imminent decline unless measures are taken to address them by central governments, health organisations, families and, most critically, individuals. This obesity discourse focuses on an assumed relationship between rising levels of obesity, health, physical inactivity and diet. Moreover, this process cultivates a 'vulnerability of people' (ibid.) and fear in order to intervene in people's private lives. In the case of obesity, young children are constructed as 'at risk' and parents are treated as deficient in their knowledge about health and their ability adequately to protect grounded in a particular moral narrative about risk as a function of both individual and collective responsibility. As Evans *et al.* (2008b) note, in this moral panic the media re-contextualises health knowledge around weight and obesity either produced 'in-house' as pseudo science, or by scientists working in primary health research. The promotion of moral imperatives to eat well and maintain a 'healthy weight' is not simply a process of disseminating information, but is influenced by media conventions, which actively shape that which they represent. In these instances, the media is mobilised as a popular and powerful mechanism through which to influence directly forms of behaviour and lifestyle change.

The proliferation of media coverage on obesity also reflects a wider process of the 'politicisation of individual lifestyles' (Furedi 2005). Ideas about obesity are not confined to traditional media, but they are increasingly embedded within popular cultural artefacts. Television and film have sought not only to *entertain* and ensure that mass communication occurs through imagery that is both populist and inherently pleasurable, but also simultaneously to *educate* and bring about certain lifestyle changes. Just as the emergence of reality television shows, such as *Supernanny,* appear to substitute traditional modes of teaching populations about how to be a good parent, new media instruct how to eat well, exercise and lose weight. (Millar (2007) notes that in the UK in 2006 the Family and Parenting Institute, set up in 1999 under the Labour Government, commissioned a poll to examine what impact the current focus in the print and broadcast media was having on parents. This was as a consequence of an explosion of reality TV programmes such as *Supernanny, The House of Tiny Tearaways, Brat Camp* and *Honey We're Killing the Kids.*) Many of these media take the format of 'reality science' (Cohen 2005) and include the vast number of 'factual' style, television programmes geared towards better informing the public about healthy living, and weight loss. Within the UK, these include *Jamie's School Dinners* (Channel 4), *You Are What You Eat* (Channel 4), *Honey, We're Killing the Kids* (BBC3), *Supersize and Superskinny* (Channel 4) and *Fighting Fat Fighting Fit* (BBC multi-programme campaign). These texts offer a clear narrative on the value of eating well, staying active and losing weight, presenting such choices as a moral imperative. Elsewhere, documentary films are also focusing on these themes, perhaps most notably the 2004 film *Supersize Me* by Morgan Spurlock, which explored the effects of fast-food culture (specifically McDonald's) on weight and health. In this case, the spectacularisation of diet is brought about by the presenter/director undergoing a 30-day all-McDonald's diet in the form of a mock-scientific experiment to witness the effects of such consumption on the body.

Many of these media events combine constructions of victimhood with responsibilisation, as a powerful but insidious exercise of biopower. The good health and lifestyle of a child is constructed as a neo-liberal rational outcome of responsible parenting and consumption, around eating, exercising and parental choice over what a child does. To illustrate, on 27 February 2007 the popular British tabloid newspaper, the *Daily Mirror*, reported the case of an 'overweight 8-year-old, weighing 218 pounds', purportedly 'four times the weight of a "healthy" child of his age'. Fearing that she may lose her child, the mother negotiated with social workers who were to 'safeguard' the boy's welfare. Such reports affect how one comes to 'read' illness, health and obesity. As Evans *et al.* (2008a: 2) note: 'Essentially these are attempts to regulate the deviant behaviours of working class men and especially women, using "panics" to either establish new or re-instate fragile social norms while leaving untouched underlying socio-economic structures, the primary determinants of "discordant", damaged and "unhealthy" lives.'

The 'responsibilisation' of family life (Fullagar 2008) within these discourses is not difficult to see, where parents are blamed as culpable for their child's poor health or lifestyle. Indeed, when one scrutinises the boundaries, then it becomes even harder to separate concerns about health, illness and the body from the broader governmental preoccupation with parenting as exemplified in the UK government's recent document 'Every Parent Matters' (DfES 2007). The discursive construction of obese children through media discourse therefore connects with a wider orientation towards welfare policies. In turn, this constructs children as in need of protection and legitimates interventions on behalf of the child's welfare, either through placing the child in care, or through the need for national action via taxation.

Disability, lifestyle and enhancement

Our third category concerns disability, lifestyle and enhancement technologies and, while each of these terms deserves a category of its own, we connect them by exploring the shift among and within them. We also suggest that they occur on a continuum that is increasingly shifting towards enhancement, which has implications for what we will come to understand as and expect from good health, as a lifestyle condition. One central link between this category and disordered eating is through their common interrogation of what it means to be normal. Thus, discourses on obesity typically presume a given notion of what normal, healthy eating involves. Similarly, the public's willingness to take into account the implications of disablement and, by extension, lifestyle enhancements, relies on expectations of what is an acceptable life that one should be entitled to live. For example, cosmetic surgery is typically conceived as less worthy of social support than the very same type of surgery that aims to treat some form of disfigurement. While there might be merit in this idea, it is important to notice that there are not shared approaches to this around the world. For instance, within the Netherlands, cosmetic dental surgery is provided via a state-funded health care system, while in the UK and many other places it is not.

Of interest here is how these various claims about lifestyle conditions are articulated through the media, but also how the alignment of lifestyle and enhancement technologies with various media industries – advertising, television, and magazines, for instance – re-constitute these norms (see King and Watson 2001). It is also important to study the moral narratives that emerge from these representations given that they often permeate the lives of people who are not at medical risk. More precisely, while obesity is medically risky and there is merit in promoting healthy lifestyles, being slightly overweight is much less so. Yet, the media imperative to reduce our size to a certain norm pervades even these non-medical cases, thus shaping our sense of responsibility to lead a particular lifestyle. Indeed, it often propels us to some other, equally unhealthy norm, as might be said of various diets or the aspiration to be the size of super-models. Again, what concerns us is how institutions – including the media – shift responsibility for health conditions in society away from themselves to individuals. In this context, the question arises as to what kinds of lifestyle are acceptable for us to lead. An integral part of this concern is how the media presents certain types of solution and response. On this basis, we begin with representations of disability before moving to lifestyle medicine and, finally, to enhancement.

Early work on media depictions of bodily difference revealed that disability is often portrayed as freakish, where disabled people fulfil roles that typically depict them as strange (Shakespeare 1994) or as a spectacle (Dijck 2002). Examples of this include documentaries that focus on the tallest, shortest or most obese people in the world (e.g. Channel 4 (2008) *The World's Tallest Woman and Me*; Channel 5 (2008) *Extraordinary People* documentary series). In addition, research has signalled the absence of disabled people within certain key media roles. As Phillips (2001: 196) notes 'We never see a woman with a visual disability holding up a bottle of Chanel perfume or a can of Pantene hair spray.' In each of these ways, disability has been marginalised within the media. However, in recent years, there are some key instances of counter examples that also deserve attention. Perhaps one of the most prominent has been the story of Oscar Pistorius, the South African sprinter and double below-the-knee amputee who, in 2007–08, campaigned to take part as an Olympian, rather than just a Paralympian at the Beijing 2008 Olympic Games. Pistorius is helpful here, as he introduces complexity to what we understand by the term disability. Thus, to the extent that disability reflects an inability of society to attend to the needs of the differently abled, Pistorius is a case where technology has circumvented this inability. Pistorius' so-called *cheetah legs* allow him to be competitive as an Olympian and bring into question the assumption that being an amputee is necessarily a disabling condition. Conceivably, his bionic prostheses allow him to achieve greater levels of capability as a runner than a biological leg. This transformation to understandings of ability/disability have also been made by Pistorius' female counterpart, Aimee Mullins. Also a double below-the-knee amputee, Mullins has made a career out of her image as a talented and desirable figure. She has been photographed by leading photographers in provocative poses and has starred in avant-garde films sporting exotic, glass prosthetic legs. Also, to counter the way in which advertising that involves people with disabilities has taken place, Mullins recent campaign for the clothing company Kenneth Cole New York conveys a retreat from disability as an imposition to a characteristic of empowerment. Both Pistorius and Mullins undertake transformative representations of disability, as their prostheses allow them to disrupt the supremacy of able-bodied performance. This is indicated by, for instance, Pistorius' role within Nike's 2007 *Just Do It* campaign in South Africa. The values articulated through Pistorius, who was one of seven athletes chosen for the campaign, read as follows:

> I was born without bones below the knee.
> I only stand 5 feet 2.
> But this is the body I have been given.
> This is my weapon.
> This is how I conquer. How I wage my war.
> This is how I have broken the world record 21 times.
> How I become the fastest man on no legs.
> This is my weapon.
> This is how I fight.

Together, Pistorius and Mullins provoke us to consider how disability might be represented in the future. Through their accomplishments we begin to see how discussions about disability are becoming intertwined with debates about the technologies of enhancement, enablement and improvement. These value-laden terms underpin the appeal of reconstructive technologies such as cosmetic surgery, botox, face reconstruction and even leg-extensions and they are justified on the dual bases of enablement and lifestyle. Parallel issues arise in the context of other technologies that have been labelled as lifestyle medicines, notably the use of such pharmaceutical products as Prozac (Blum and Stracuzzi 2004), Ritalin and Viagra (Loe 2004). In these cases, researchers have outlined how such innovations have led to patients reportedly feeling 'better than well' (Kramer 1994; Elliott 2003) and this alluring prospect has become constitutive of the appeal of lifestyle medicines.

Critically, studies of various cases such as pharmaceutical products to treat sexual dysfunction have pointed to the role of advertising in propagating certain tendencies to treat specific biological states as deficiency (see Moynihan 2003). Likewise:

> A key strategy of the alliances is to target the news media with stories designed to create fears about the condition or disease and draw attention to the latest treatment. Company sponsored advisory boards supply the 'independent experts' for these stories, consumer groups provide the 'victims,' and public relations companies provide media outlets with the positive spin about the latest 'breakthrough' medications. (Moynihan *et al.* 2002: 886)

While these studies suggest that scientific institutions and companies have been pro-active in representing dysfunction, it is also important to note that criticisms are also possible to make of the media. For instance, Seale *et al.* (2006) note how the media has been complicit in commodifying the body.

Media representations of these prospective enhancements vary considerably but many scholars have focused on cosmetic interventions, as a sub-set of the television 'makeover' genre. For instance, consider the popular US reality television programme *Extreme Makeover* (2002–06) (see Elliott and Elliott 2003; Heyes 2007; Tait 2007), which involved volunteers being transformed by major cosmetic surgery work. This format of television has been re-broadcast or replicated in various forms by a number of countries, such as *Cosmetic Surgery Live* in the UK. Research in this area has also recently drawn attention to the growing male market for cosmetic surgical interventions and has teased out the different ways in which the same products are marketed differently for men and women. As Davis notes: 'cosmetic surgery seems like such a 'natural' and unproblematic step for a woman to take, while it is a shameful and humiliating operation for a man' (2002: 61). It also indicates how, rather than an act of an oppressive, gendered society, cosmetic surgical interventions can be acts of empowerment (see Negrin 2002).

While there is no strict division between *aesthetic* and *functional* lifestyle modifications, the emergence of biological modifications that are characterised as human enhancements have become a focal point for discussions within bioethics. Concurrently, these debates have taken place within the media sphere and are, at times, integral to the prior discussions we have outlined. Nevertheless, the prospect of radical transformative enhancements occurs via discussions about emerging sciences and appears as a central tenet of various media forms. For instance, the Michel Gondry film *Eternal Sunshine of the Spotless Mind*, envisages a future where it is possible to delete memories in order to erase unpleasant recollections (Miah 2009). Alternatively, the discussion about designer genes presents the emerging possibility where selection of specific traits could be available to people in order to enhance their offspring. One of the most recent debates in this area concerns the use of cognitive enhancers, which could allow, among other things, students to cram more effectively for exams, or fighter pilots to focus on their missions in high-velocity situations. The prior example of Ritalin is one substance that has been subject to such speculations, though an increasing number of newspapers and magazines are reporting the emerging era of 'smart drugs', which speaks to the complex challenge of keeping therapeutic interventions from being applied for enhancement purposes:

> Mind-expansion may soon, therefore, become big business. Even though the drugs have been developed to treat disease, it will be hard to prevent their use by the healthy. Nor, if they are without bad side-effects, is there much reason to. And if that is so, there may be a very positive side-effect on the profits of their makers.
>
> (Anon. 2008)

End-of-life issues: dying well and living forever

Our final category consists of debates on health issues that can be broadly grouped as end-of-life. Again, this term imports language from medical law and ethics and its application to media representations offers some opportunity to infuse it with new, additional meaning. In this area, there are two types of representation that are frequently conveyed through the media, which are summarised by this section's sub-title: *dying well* and *living forever*. Together, they encompass a series of cases that span from the preservation of life by medical technology to innovations that promise to extend our lives, perhaps indefinitely.

Dying well is of considerable interest to the media, as it engages concerns about the 'innocent victim', a health-related media narrative that has recurred over the years (see Gwyn 1999). It even interfaces with some of our other categories. Recall our introductory remarks about 'saviour siblings', the practice of bearing a child who will be able to provide supplementary tissue to save the life of a sibling. Even the related science of stem cell research engages with similar questions of immortality as cell-lines could be preserved indefinitely providing a permanent resource of new tissue. Some recent cases in this category have attracted considerable media attention.

Perhaps one of the most noteworthy is the plight of baby Charlotte Wyatt, who was born with considerable health problems, to such an extent that medics considered that her life would be intolerable.[2] The ensuing debate concerned whether or not the court should require that her life-sustaining treatment be withdrawn. Regardless of the specific conditions of the case that distinguish it from others, there are crucial aspects of how the media became integral to the proceedings that are relevant to discuss. Thus, Brazier (2005) explains how such cases 'are novel in part because of the extensive publicity given to the families in the media. The earlier convention of such cases being conducted in camera and alluded to only by pseudonymous initials, were waived by the families' (ibid.: 413). The public presence of the case becomes even more complicated as the internet is harnessed as a communicative device. As the blog provider Blogger outlined to the owners of the Charlotte Wyatt blog site http://charlottewyatt.blogspot.com:

> Hello,
>
> We'd like to inform you that we've received a court order regarding your blog charlottewyatt.blogspot.com. In accordance with the court order, we've been forced to remove your blog.
>
> Thank you for your understanding.
>
> Sincerely,
> The Blogger Team   (SaveCharlotte.com, 2006 (accessed 22 May 2008))

As an increasing array of technologies becomes available, the capacity to come closer to immortality increases and, while 'Living Forever' might be a step too far today, recent reporting has intimated at the emerging culture of 'The Immortals' (Armstrong 1998) who spend significant amounts of money to achieve precisely this end. In particular, cryonics is the established practice of preserving a body at the moment of death, with a view to re-animating it some time in the future, when the technology allows this possibility. (While it is often reported that such individuals expect to be 'resurrected' in the future, the more accepted term among this community is reanimation.) For such enthusiasts, there is the option of head-only or full-body suspension, each with different price tags attached to them.

A fascination with death is present in a wide array of media episodes. Perhaps one of the most prominent is the work of Gunter von Hagens, the German physician, who created a novel method of preserving human bodies within their natural state. Von Hagens' plastinated bodies have captured the attention of worldwide audiences. This interest has extended into various media forms, from art gallery exhibitions, to documentary series' and to public demonstrations of a public autopsy (see Hirschauer 2006). While the pursuit of immortality is not really von Hagens' central message, his work has become a focal point for various considerations of how the body has been subjected to a medical gaze over the centuries and the implications of this for how we view our bodies and their relationship to medical institutions and experts.

These examples are accompanied by parallel debates about the challenges presented by an ageing population, either as a possible obstacle towards mainlining social order, but also as a source of concern about the growth of age-related illnesses. As technologies develop to reduce age-related illness, they will encounter a resulting effect of preserving people for longer and this will bring new forms of representing inter-generational differences.

Conclusion

This chapter has traced a series of key themes in the study of media representations of health, illness and the body that have emerged in recent years, including some that invite us to consider what might be studied in this field for some years to come. Together, they describe the fluid and multiple realities that are constructed through media representations of health. These subjects are infused with various moral, medicalised and aesthetic agendas, which often construct divisive/dichotomous expectations of the body, health and associated scientific endeavours. Competing advice about lifestyle, about what is 'safe', and of the perils of science against the rationality of experimentation, lead us to read specific bodily practices and science and technology in various ways. The cases offer some indication of the future landscape of what might be termed *biomedia studies*, a concept that draws on Thacker (2003: 48) when arguing that 'biology is the new medium'. Many of these cases describe issues that were previously considered distant from the everyday lives of most people, but which now have direct and clear implications for how we wrestle with some of the most fundamental choices in life. As such, biomedia studies help us understand what happens when emerging scientific discoveries or treatments clash with cultural expectations and values.

Our various examples also articulate the broad variety of disciplines that constitute studies of health and illness in the media. They explain how representations of health are part of a broader process of the construction of cultural knowledge around science and the body. We have explained that such representations do not consist wholly of discussions about risk or health care burdens. Or, rather, there are various cases that extend well beyond the purview of such concerns. Rather, each of these cases of medical intervention inhabits a distinct space of media coverage and it is important that we come to terms with the various expectations of the media in reporting these different subjects.

This chapter also urges us to consider what ethical principles should govern the reporting of health stories and the involvement of experts who provide richness of depth to these media events (Miles 2004). Over the years, various instances of dubious practices within broadcast ethics have been visible and justified on the basis that they raise awareness about important social concerns. Perhaps one of the most dramatic examples of this occurred in 2007 when a Dutch production company created *The Big Donor Show*. In this case, contestants each needed a lifesaving organ transplant and the final winner would receive this from a donor after viewers had used their mobile phones to assist on deciding who should 'win'. After some days of global news coverage prior to the broadcast, which involved exaggerated condemnations of the initiative (BBC 2007), the programme aired and, at its conclusion, revealed itself as a hoax aiming to raise awareness about the need for donor organs (Shaikh 2007). This example illustrates how, the media mechanisms that communicate health are mixed, multi-faceted and espouse various political intentions. As such, a vigilance of the media, as well an awareness of how best to harness it, is crucial to establishing how people within societies can live well, if not, even better than well.

Questions

1 What kinds of experts should the media use to communicate issues related to health?

2 Do blockbuster films help people understand some of the major health issues that societies face today?

3 Should the advertising of cosmetic health technologies such as Viagra be permitted?

Notes

1 For advanced research, consider how leading genetic scientist Craig Venter is positioning his work in 'synthetic biology' as a technology that will offer solutions to the general depletion of natural resources (fuel, water, etc.). Consider further Venter's background within the Human Genome Project and his utilisation of the media to communicate his work.

2 Other examples that are worth exploring include the US assisted-living case of Terri Schiavo, whose husband campaigned to have her treatment withdrawn, but where disputes occurred over the legitimacy of his right to act as guardian over her. Also, a further category of assisted-dying deserves separate attention, particularly through the two cases of Harold Shipman, a British physician who was convicted for unlawfully killing 215 patients (Jackson and Smith 2004) and his US counterpart Jack Kevorkian, branded by the media as 'Doctor Death' (MacIntyre 1999). Kevorkian is also notable since he broadcast his administration of a lethal solution to a terminally ill man on the US network channel CBS, as part of his long-term campaign to legalise euthanasia.

Further reading

Dijck, J. V. (2002) 'Medical Documentary: Conjoined Twins as a Mediated Spectacle', *Media, Culture, & Society*, 24: 537–56. The representation of so-called 'extraordinary' bodies through television has encountered a number of criticisms. This essay engages with the way in which this genre has been influenced by the grammar of horror films and the consequences of this for the stigmatisation of certain conditions.

Nelkin, D. and Lindee, M. S. (1995) *The DNA Mystique: The Gene as a Cultural Icon*, New York: W. H. Freeman and Co. This book is one of the earliest contributions to engaging with how the media portray an emerging science. Genetics has been of considerable attention and studies in the public understanding of science have matured through this exemplar. Genetic science suffered considerably from miscommunication due to its heightened attention at the turn of the millennium. This book situates these debates in their broader cultural context and has informed a decade of studies in science communication.

Seale, C. (2002) *Media and Health*, Sage: London. This book considers fundamental questions about why health is worthy of media inquiry, but also why the institutions of medicine should be interested in studying the media. It draws attention to how the depiction of health through the media reveals biases about social categories, such as gender. It also explains how the educative motivation of health-related media forms is rarely borne out in its reception.

Turney, J. (1998) *Frankenstein's Footsteps: Science, Genetics and Popular Culture*, New Haven and London: Yale University Press. The media often draw upon familiar narratives when conveying the implications of any new technology. This book describes how the popular imagination remains informed by the myth of Mary Shelley's *Frankenstein* and considers why this is so prominent and divisive.

References

Anon. (2008) 'Cognitive Enhancement: All on the Mind', *The Economist*, 22 May, www. economist.com/science/displaystory.cfm?story_id=11402761 (accessed 4 March 2009).

Armstrong, J. (1998) 'The Immortals: Brits Who Pay to Be Frozen When They Die', *The Mirror*, 35.

Bauer, M. W., Allum, N. and Miller, S. (2007) 'What Can We Learn from 25 Years of PUS Survey Research? Liberating and Expanding the Agenda', *Public Understanding of Science*, 16 (1): 79–95.

Blum, L. M. and Stracuzzi, N. F. (2004) 'Gender in the Prozac Nation: Popular Discourse and Productive Femininity', *Gender and Society*, 18 (3): 269–86.

Brazier, M. (2005) 'An Intractable Dispute: When Parents and Professionals Disagree', *Medical Law Review*, 13 (3): 412–18.

BBC (2007) 'Outcry Over TV Kidney Competition', news.bbc.co.uk/1/hi/entertainment/6699847.stm (accessed 4 March 2009).

Byron, T. (2008) *Safe Children in a Digital World: The Report of the Byron Review*, Department for Children, Schools and Families and the Department for Culture, Media and Sport: 224.

Buglass, D. (2008) 'Scots Farmers Need to Produce GM Foods', *Scotsman*, 11 April, 39.

Campbell, S. (2006) 'Don't Tear a Smiling Foetus from the Womb', *Telegraph*, 4 October, www. telegraph.co.uk/opinion/main.jhtml?xml=/opinion/2006/10/04/do0403.xml&sSheet=/opinion/2006/10/04/ixopinion.html (accessed 4 March 2009).

Cohen, D. (2005) 'The Rise of Reality Science', *British Medical Journal*, 330 (7501): 1216.

Davis, K. (2002) '"A Dubious Equality": Men, Women and Cosmetic Surgery', *Body and Society*, 8 (1): 49–65.

DfES (Department for Education and Skills) (2007) *Every Parent Matters*, London: DfES www. teachernet.gov.uk/everyparentmatters (accessed 4 March 2009).

Dijck, J. V. (2002) 'Medical Documentary: Conjoined Twins as a Mediated Spectacle', *Media, Culture, and Society* 24 (4): 537–56.

Elliott, C. (2003) *Better Than Well: American Medicine Meets the American Dream*, New York and London: W. W. Norton and Company.

Elliott, C. and Elliott, B. (2003) 'Logical Extreme: The Next Step for "Reality" Television', *The American Prospect Online*, www.prospect.org/cs/articles?article=logical_extreme (accessed 4 March 2009).

Elliott, C. and Kahn, J. (1994) 'Docs on the Box' *Hastings Center Report*, 24 (6): 22–3.

Evans, J., Rich, E. and Davies, B. (2008a) 'The Rise and Rise of the Child Saving Movement', International Sociology of Education Conference, London, 2–5 January.

Evans, J., Rich, E., Davies, B. and Allwood, R. (2008b) *Education, Disordered Eating and Obesity Discourse: Fat Fabrications*, London and New York: Routledge.

Farrar, S. (1999) 'Do These Genes Make Me Look Fat?' *The Times Higher Education Supplement*, 1 October, 22–3.

Fullagar, S. (2008) 'Governing Healthy Family Lifestyles through Discourses of Risk and Responsibility' in J. Wright and V. Harwood (eds) *Biopolitics and the Obesity Epidemic: Governing Bodies*, London: Routledge, pp. 108–26.

Furedi, F. (2005) *Politics of Fear: Beyond Left and Right*, London and New York: Continuum.

Goggin, G. and Newell, C. (2004) 'Fame and Disability: Christopher Reeve, Super Crips, and Infamous Celebrity', *M/C: A Journal of Media and Culture*, 7 (5), http://journal.media-culture.org.au/0411/02-goggin.php (accessed 4 March 2009).

Gwyn, R. (1999) '"Killer Bugs", "Silly Buggers" and "Politically Correct Pals": Competing Discourses in Health Scare Reporting', *Health*, 3 (3): 335–45.

Hansen, A. (2006) 'Tampering with Nature: "Nature" and the "Natural" in Media Coverage of Genetics and Biotechnology', *Media, Culture & Society*, 28 (6): 811–34.

Harris, R. (1999) 'Come Up to Beauty. Rons Angels', www.ronsangels.com (accessed 4 March 2009).

Heyes, C. J. (2007) 'Cosmetic Surgery and the Televisual Makeover', *Feminist Media Studies*, 7 (1): 17–32.

Hirschauer, S. (2006) 'Animated Corpses: Communicating with Post Mortals in an Anatomical Exhibition', *Body and Society*, 12 (4): 25–52.

Jackson, T. and Smith, R. (2004) 'Obituary: Harold Shipman', *British Medical Journal*, 328 (7433): 231.

Johnson, D. A. (2008) 'Managing Mr. Monk: Control and the Politics of Madness', *Critical Studies in Media Communication*, 25 (1): 28–47.

King, M. and Watson, K. (2001) '"Transgressing Venues": "Health" Studies, Cultural Studies and the Media', *Health Care Analysis*, 9 (4): 401–16.

Kramer, P. (1994) *Listening to Prozac*, London: Fourth Estate.

Loe, M. (2004) *The Rise of Viagra: How the Little Blue Pill Changes Sex in America*, New York: New York University Press.

Lowe, T., Brown, K., Dessai, S., Franca Doria, M. D., Haynes, K. and Vincent, K. (2006) 'Does Tomorrow Ever Come? Disaster Narrative and Public Perceptions of Climate Change', *Public Understanding of Science*, 15 (4): 435–57.

Lupton, D. (1999) 'Editorial: Health, Illness and Medicine in the Media', *Health: An Interdisciplinary Journal for the Social Study of Health, Illness and Medicine*, 3 (3): 259–62.

Macintyre, B. (1999) 'Murder Trial For "Doctor Death"', *The Times*, 23 March, 14.

McLaughlin, J. (1975) 'The Doctor Shows', *Journal of Communication*, 25: 182–4.

Miah, A. (ed) (2008) *Human Futures: Art in an Age of Uncertainty*, Liverpool: FACT and Liverpool University Press.

Miah, A. (2009) '"Blessed Are the Forgetful": The Ethics of Memory Deletion in Michel Gondry's *Eternal Sunshine of the Spotless Mind*' in S. Shapshay (ed) *Bioethics at the Movies*, Baltimore: Johns Hopkins University Press, pp. 137–55.

Miah, A. and Rich, E. (2006) 'Genetic Tests for Ability? Talent Identification and the Value of an Open Future', *Sport, Education and Society*, 11 (3): 259–73.

Miah, A. and Rich, E. (2008) *The Medicalization of Cyberspace*, New York: Routledge.

Miles, S. H. (2004) 'Medical Ethicists, Human Curiosities, and the New Media Midway', *The American Journal of Bioethics*, 4 (3): 39–43.

Moynihan, R. (2003) 'The Making of a Disease: Female Sexual Dysfunction', *British Medical Journal,* 326 (7379): 45-7.

Moynihan, R., Heath, I. and Henry, D. (2002) 'Selling Sickness: The Pharmaceutical Industry and Disease', *British Medical Journal,* 324 (7342): 886-91.

Millar, F. (2007) 'For the Sake of Children', *British Journalism Review,* 18 (1): 45-9.

Mulkay, M. (1994) 'Embryos in the News', *Public Understanding of Science,* 3 (1): 33-51.

Negrin, L. (2002) 'Cosmetic Surgery and the Eclipse of Identity', *Body and Society,* 8 (4): 21-42.

Nelkin, D. and Lindee, M. S. (1995) *The DNA Mystique: The Gene as a Cultural Icon,* New York: W. H. Freeman and Co.

Nerlich, B., Johnson, S. and Clarke, D. D. (2003) 'The First "Designer Baby": The Role of Narratives, Cliches and Metaphors in the Year 2000 Debate', *Science as Culture,* 12 (4): 471-98.

Phillips, C. (2001) 'Re-Imagining the (Dis)Abled Body', *Journal of Medical Humanities,* 22 (3): 195-208.

Sample, I. (2008) 'Gene Sequence Puts Half of UK Population at Greater Risk of Obesity, Researchers Say', *Guardian,* 5 May: 4.

Seale, C. (2003) 'Health and Media: An Overview', *Sociology of Health and Illness,* 25 (6): 513-31.

Seale, C., Cavers, D. and Dixon-Woods, M. (2006) 'Commodification of Body Parts: By Medicine or by Media?' *Body and Society,* 12 (1): 25-42.

Shaikh, T. (2007) 'Dutch Kidney Donor Show: A Hoax to Highlight Shortage of Organs', *Independent,* 2 June, http://news.independent.co.uk (accessed 4 March 2009).

Shakespeare, T. (1994) 'Cultural Representations of Disabled People: Dustbins', *Disability and Society,* 9 (3): 283-301.

Tait, S. (2007) 'Television and the Domestication of Cosmetic Surgery', *Feminist Media Studies,* 7 (2): 119-35.

Thacker, E. (2003) 'What is Biomedia?' *Configurations,* 11 (1): 47-79.

Turney, J. (1998) *Frankenstein's Footsteps: Science, Genetics and Popular Culture*, New Haven and London: Yale University Press.

Wiley, J. (2008) 'Fat? Blame Your Genes Says Doctors', *Daily Express,* 6 May, 1.

World Health Organization (1998) Obesity: Preventing and Managing the Global Epidemic: Report of a WHO Consultation on Obesity, Geneva: WHO.

Zylinska, J. (2005) *The Ethics of Cultural Studies,* London: Continuum.

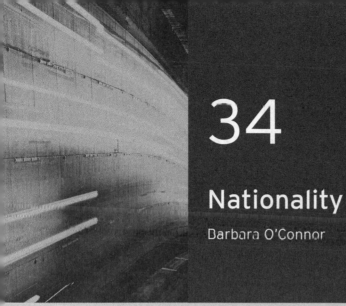

34

Nationality

Barbara O'Connor

Chapter overview

This chapter addresses the relationship between media representations and nationality, specifically the pivotal role played by media in establishing national identities. It begins by looking at the historical development of the relationship between media and nation and goes on to examine the specific ways in which images of the nation are produced in a range of print, broadcast and digital media. Examples from television news, sports, reality television and the internet are used to demonstrate how national imagery fosters a sense of collective belonging on the one hand, and of collective distancing and stereotyping on the other. Questions about the future of media representations of nationality are posed in the light of the increasing globalisation of media production and consumption. The discussion of the relationship between the national and global revolves around the process of 'glocalisation' in which global media genres are inflected in nationally specific ways, and how diasporic populations negotiate their relationship to the nation through media use. It is suggested that the national, rather than disappearing, continues to occupy a central place in the contemporary media landscape. The chapter concludes by suggesting that media representations of the nation are numerous and diverse and are continuously being reproduced, challenged and reconfigured as people use media to negotiate their collective identities.

Introduction

A billboard advertisement displays a primeval scene of intertwined and gnarled tree trunks emerging from a green sward and morphing into a team of sturdy rugby players standing in a V formation, the central figure holding a rugby ball in his right hand. The scene in earthy hues of green and brown is accompanied by the caption ' Born of Our Land' in the top left hand corner and on the bottom right 'Guinness: A Proud Sponsor of Irish Rugby'.

There are a number of key signifiers of national identity in this image. At a visual level the tree trunks connote the strength and power of the rugby team members. They also indicate their organic connection to, and rootedness in the

Guinness advertisement: Born of Our Land
Source: © Fred Gambino 2008 / Diaego plc.

land, which is also signified in the natural colour ways of the image and verbally underpinned in the caption. A sense of heroic masculinity is conveyed in the strength and sturdiness of the team as they are poised for victory, connoted in the V formation. The harp on the bottom right of the image has long been a symbol both of Irish nationalism and of Guinness. The latter, though now a global product, was established and had its headquarters for many years in St James Gate in Dublin's city centre and is now one of its main tourist attractions. The caption 'Born of Our Land' is, therefore, invited to be read as applicable to the rugby team and to Guinness, constructing them both as an essential part of Irish culture in which we should take pride. All of these signs coalesce to offer us, the viewer, a sporting (and masculine) and a consumerist sense of national identity.

The advertisement above is just one example of the myriad representations of the nation that surround us in everyday popular culture – in print and broadcast media, in performance media such as music and dance, in art forms such as painting, and on flags, banners and emblems. Other immediately recognisable examples include the team colours in the soccer World Cup, the television weather report showing the map of a particular country, the newspaper column reporting the latest 'home' news, or the green shamrock on the plane indicating its status as a national airline. These symbols can have a powerful emotional resonance that foster collective bonding expressed in tears of joy when the 'home' team wins or in irrational hatred of 'the enemy' in times of war.

The mass circulation of media representations of the nation coincide with the emergence of nation-states in Europe in the 19th century and since that time have played a key role in fostering a sense of national identity defined as the 'reproduction and reinterpretation of the pattern of values, symbols, memories, myths and traditions that compose the distinctive heritage of nations, and the identifications of individuals with that pattern and heritage' (Smith 2001:18). The historian Benedict Anderson (1991), one of the first to examine the relationship between print media and national identity, regards the nation as an 'imagined community'.

By this he means that, while most members of the nation never meet each other face-to-face, they became aware of each other's existence through print media such as national newspapers. The newspaper is printed in the national language and carries national narratives, stories deemed to be relevant to the national readership. In this way, narratives of the nation build a sense of shared economic and political interests, of collective memories and heritage, and of a common culture generally. Readers also come to see themselves as part of a national public as they are conscious of other readers countrywide reading the same news stories at the same time. While early narratives of the nation were circulated through books and newspapers, with developments in media technologies they were disseminated through broadcast media, and most recently through digital media such as the internet.

This chapter addresses three related questions: what are the narratives of the nation currently in circulation? How do they foster a sense of collective belonging? How have narratives of the nation changed over time? The first section addresses the normative role of the state in shaping national representations as well as the routine practices of media producers in generating a sense of collective national belonging, drawing on examples from television news and sport. The next section considers how media create a sense of collective distancing from certain nations and minority ethnic groups through the creation of national and ethnic stereotypes and through reflecting dominant views about which groups legitimately belong to the nation and which do not. The question of changing representations is addressed through looking at two aspects of global media, the first an example of how global media genres are inflected in nationally specific ways using the example of reality TV, and the second focused on the ways in which transnational diasporic groups engage with national discourses in their media use.

Creating a sense of national identity

Historically, the state, through government, has played a key role in shaping the nature of national narratives in broadcast media. Public service broadcast institutions might be regarded as a prime exemplar whereby broadcast legislation is interpreted and implemented in the putative interests of a national audience. Dedicated broadcasting institutions like the BBC in Britain interpreted the public service remit, through its first Director General, Lord Reith, as the duty to provide a universal service consisting of the elements of information, education and entertainment to a national audience. The BBC's tri-partite model was adopted by other nations including former British colonies such as many of the African states who were establishing their own broadcasting systems as part of nation-building projects in the 1960s.

Another way in which the state shapes representations is by determining which representations are in the public interest and which are detrimental to it through regulation and censorship. This might include individuals and groups who are regarded as posing a threat to the [nation] state such as paramilitary organisations. For example, section 31 of the Irish Broadcasting Act of 1975 prevented members of the IRA from appearing on national radio and television in the Republic of

Ireland until it was repealed in 1994. Or government concern about the health of the nation can be manifest in the banning of cigarette advertising on television. Other examples include the issuing of age-related certificates for films or confining sexually explicit or violent television to times when children are assumed to be asleep in bed. However, these direct state interventions are becoming easier to circumvent because there are so many different circuits of distribution. For instance, home viewing of film on DVD has become commonplace and the home is where computer games designed for older age groups are played by younger children.

National governments have also frequently involved themselves in promoting 'ideal' national values and practices through media use. For instance, the first rural television serial broadcast on Irish television, *The Riordans*, was originally devised as a way of encouraging farmers to adopt 'modern' farming practices. This was achieved by creating a cast of popular characters with whom audiences could identify. The serial succeeded in becoming an important national platform for negotiating 'modern' values in an era of rapid social change in rural Ireland (McLoone and McMahon 1984). India, too, has a long history of media involvement in national integration and modernising projects. A series of religious epics broadcast by the Indian state television channel between 1987 and 1990 was seen as a way of disseminating an ideal role model for women in the family and the nation (Gillespie 2005). However, Mankekar's (1999) study of women's response to these religious narratives shows that female viewers did not accept the role models on offer and the idealised femininity portrayed in the series was contested by many women who were angry about the oppression of women in Indian society. Two general points may be noted here, one is that representations of the nation can be profoundly gendered, and the second is that audiences interpret and respond to representations of the national in different ways.

With reference to broadcasting, one could say that, though the state may decide on the broad outlines of national narratives, it is the producers through their routine activities who tell the stories. Billig (1995) uses the term 'banal nationalism' to describe the unspectacular, routine ways that media invite allegiance to the nation. These are ways that we often fail to see because they appear to be so natural. It operates, according to Billig (ibid.: 93), 'with prosaic, routine words, which take nations for granted . . . [s]mall words offer constant, but barely conscious, reminders of the homeland, making 'our' national identity unforgettable'. Let us take television news as an example. Political news is always high on the agenda and we frequently see political figures making speeches and public pronouncements in which they constantly and explicitly refer to 'our country', 'the people of this country', and, 'our nation'. They also implicitly infer the nation by the use of personal pronouns such as , 'we', 'you' and 'I' in addressing the audience. Billig identifies these examples of 'deixis' as a form of rhetorical pointing that constitutes an identity between speaker and audience and links them as members of 'our' nation that is represented as the 'homeland'. Television reporters and presenters operate in a similar way when they assume that they are speaking from the position of the national homeland with references to 'the government' or 'the country'. In these cases the definite article is invariably read as the national government or country. *Nationwide* is the name of a news magazine programme currently broadcast on RTE1 where roaming reporters bring news from different locations around the country and the main presenter links news from the regions and unites them into a national discourse. The series bears the same title as a similar current affairs bulletin on UK TV in the 1970s (for discussion of national discourse in the latter see Morley and Brunsdon 1999). Media formats can also invoke the national as in the division of newspapers into sections with titles such as 'home news' and 'international news'.

Television sport is, arguably, one of the most powerful ways of mobilising a sense of national identity worldwide (see Whannel 1992; Rowe 1999; O'Brien 2004). The live broadcasting of major sports events involving national individual competitors and teams such as the Olympic Games and the Soccer World Cup helps to integrate viewers into the nation by creating a calendar of public events (Scannell and Cardiff 1991), and by enabling them to participate in a ceremonial ritual in a shared festive public space that was previously confined to the spectators at the game (Dayan and Katz 1992). McSharry's (2008) account of the 2006 Heineken European Cup Rugby Final in Cardiff between the Munster (Irish) and Biarritz (French) teams is a good example of the sharing in the ritual, the role of television in heightening the emotion, and in overcoming space and time barriers. 'Munster mania' is the term given by McSharry to describe the nationwide support for what is in reality a provincial rugby team, a term that encapsulates the intense loyalty to the team, the large numbers of supporters at home and away games, and the emotional and physical excitement that is generated. At the Cardiff game, McSharry comments on how the excitement was intensified by Sky's coverage of the game where screens at the stadium simultaneously transmitted scenes from O'Connell Street in Limerick city (the symbolic centre of Munster rugby) where thousands of supporters had gathered to watch the game. When Sky Sports executive director Martin Turner noticed how the crowds in each venue were reacting to each other he decided to linger on the shot remarking that 'it seemed like a magnificent moment. I've never seen anything like that before'. According to McSharry, 'the crystallisation of emotion was palpable in the uniting of those actually present in Cardiff, with those virtually present in Limerick' (2008: 92–3). She also makes the more general point that sport currently provides one of the few opportunities for collective physical expressions of emotion such as crying, chanting, shouting and singing in public. This is particularly true at a time when most of our daily encounters with strangers are characterised by detachment and self-enclosure. These sporting scenes of collective celebration and commiseration are thus a powerful way of realising belongingness.

The forging of collective identity is also particularly clear in situations of conflict and war. Television news generally tends to simplify these events creating an 'us and them' mentality (Liebes 1997; Philo and Berry 2004). Madianou's (2005) study of Greek television news during the 'Kosovo crisis' shows how the form and structure of the news combined to create a common 'we' aligning the Greek nation with the Serb, and uniting the Greeks against the USA and NATO. One of the media events she analysed was the television coverage of the public concert for 'peace in the Balkans' (ibid.: 97) that took place in Athens on 26 April 1999 in the context of public reaction to the NATO strikes in Kosovo. The concert was broadcast widely on public and private channels as a celebration of the Greek nation as 'united and homogenous' (ibid.: 98). This was achieved through the 'anchoring of the event in terms of Greek history and collective memory' and expressed through the journalists' verbal commentary and the use of visual cues. Journalists covering the event commented on the diversity of the crowds coming from different generations, spoke of the diversity of the participants in terms of political allegiance, and showed symbols representing different sections of Greek society such as the flags of the Byzantine Empire (associated with nationalist and religious groups) alongside that of the Communist Party. In symbolising solidarity with the Serbs, the television cameras zoomed in on the Greek and Serb flags and towards the end of the concert there was a close up shot of the two flags being tied together.

'Good' and 'bad' nations

The sense of 'us' and 'them' created in television news is applicable to media representations in general. It is commonplace to associate certain innate characteristics with members of particular nations – the French are romantic, the Italians passionate, and so on. These stereotypes can be either positive or negative depending on the context. If we look at television travel shows, for instance, countries are regularly constructed for tourist consumption in glowing terms where features such as the breathtaking landscape or the friendliness of the people are emphasised. However, this positive tourist portrayal can be challenged by other media. For example, the Northern Irish tourist board faced a strong challenge in promoting a welcoming image of Northern Ireland during 'The Troubles' because its predominant media image was as a war zone rather than a playground (Wilson 1993).

Media strategies for establishing a sense of national identity frequently involves emphasising difference from others since identity is a relational concept whereby we can only know 'who we are' by establishing who 'we are not' (Hall 1996). The Irish in the 19th century were represented in British media as ape-like, brutal and savage, childlike and lazy (Curtis 1984). These representations made sense only in the context of the historical relationship between Ireland and Britain and in particular the attempt to provide a rationale for colonial rule in Ireland. With the onset of 'The Troubles' in Northern Ireland in the early 1970s, Curtis affirms that the old stereotypes were drawn upon again to depict the Irish as savage, inhuman and psychopathic. We can witness the same media strategies currently used in US and European mainstream media to frame news about nations who are seen as a threat – among them countries in the Middle East such as Afghanistan, Iran and Iraq – emphasising the evil nature of terrorists and the freedom and democratic principles of the 'civilised' nations (Van Dijk 2006: 374).

Who belongs to the nation?

In addition to stereotyping whole nations the stereotyping of particular minority groups within nations reflects concerns about which groups legitimately belong and which do not. These concerns are currently reflected in media representations of recent migrant groups to Ireland. While it would be unfair to say that all national media representations of the new migrants are negative, there is enough evidence to suggest that the national press has been biased in terms of their relative invisibility, inaccuracy of stories referring to migrants (Ugba 2002), and the use of the term 'non-national' to describe recent migrants. A recent study of media representations of refugees and asylum seekers found that they were framed in five negative ways in news stories. The illegitimacy of asylum seeking and asylum seekers was highlighted, they were seen as a threat to national and local integrity, they were seen to be socially deviant, as criminal, and as posing an economic threat (Devereux *et al.* 2006). The press has also been accused (Fanning and Mutwarasibo 2007) of contributing to a moral panic in relation to migration around the time of the 2004 Referendum on Irish citizenship. The Referendum proposed to remove citizenship rights from children born in Ireland because it was felt in some political circles that non-Irish nationals were abusing the system. In the weeks leading up to the Referendum, the press made references to 'baby tourism'. Immigrant women in the later stages of pregnancy were reported to be flying in from abroad and presenting themselves at maternity hospitals so that their babies could be born in Ireland and thereby gain access to Irish citizenship. Fanning and Mutwarasibo claim that some newspapers, in reflecting, and failing to challenge, the dominant political agenda, contributed to the success of the Referendum.

While the media representations of the nation discussed above have a strong sense of distance and boundary maintenance, others offer a much more inclusive sense of national identity. For example, Sheehan (2007) observes that the Irish television serial drama *Fair City* has been reflecting Dublin's multi-ethnic culture by introducing characters from countries such as Russia, Iran and Nigeria and devising plotlines in which the relationships between the older and newer residents of Carrigstown, the serial's fictional location, are negotiated. There is also evidence to suggest that this re-imagining of the nation in multicultural terms is happening elsewhere. Carpentier (2003) and Matthews (2007) point to the role played by the documentary series *Video Nation Shorts* broadcast on BBC 2 television between 1994 and 2000 in reconfiguring the British nation. According to Matthews the life stories of the 'ordinary' people who participated in the series succeeded in mapping the nation 'from below' featuring as it did people from a diversity of backgrounds in terms of age, gender, region, and ethnicity talking about their personal feelings and experiences. She sees it as endorsing the BBC's website description of the series as 'holding up a mirror to Britain', as reveal[ing] our lives and ourselves' (quoted in Matthews 2007: 437). She also claims that there has been a fundamental change in the way the nation is represented and draws our attention to the fact that the participants were encouraged to tell their own stories in a narrative that focused on the private, the intimate and the subjective parts of their lives. In this way it differs from the more 'traditional' notion of the public sphere seen exclusively in terms of the public, the rational and the objective. To illustrate her point she contrasts *Video Nation* with the *Mass Observation* project that documented the lives of ordinary people in Britain in the 1930s. According to Matthews each achieved its objectives of 'mapping the nation' in very different ways – the former through observing the self and private spaces and the latter through observing others in public spaces. She argues for a 'progressive re-imagining of a diverse nation' (ibid.: 447) by insisting that the subjective and intimate aspects of life should be counted as an integral part of the national public sphere.

The national and the global: changing times?

'The country was so unified in entertainment. Everybody listened to the one radio station from Donegal down to Dingle, everybody would hear it . . . nowadays there are so many stations . . . It's so splintered' (quoted in Breen 2008: 24). These remarks of a former showband singer and musician encapsulate the fragmentation of national media audiences. We now live in a society in which there is the choice of a diverse range of media from many sources, local, national and global. As a consequence of living in a more globalised society (Rantanen 2005) are we witnessing a decrease in representations of the national and a corollary increase of the transnational and the global?

The answer to this question depends very much on where we look for evidence. Some recent writing on contemporary European film (Higson 2000; Ging 2002) suggests that it reflects a pervasive weakening of the national. However, another recent study, this time of EU news correspondents, confirms that news items are selected by national correspondents only if they are of national interest:

> There is plenty of evidence . . . to suggest that national, rather than cosmopolitan forces exert a strong influence in terms of admitting draft news stories coming from Brussels onto national media agendas (or rejecting them). The same applies to the editor's role in shaping this information flow by using news frames that resonate with local concerns. News media are still very much centred on the nation, or the region, and the news they relay from outside their territory tends to be interpreted and framed fundamentally within a national discourse.
>
> (AIM 2007: 29)

It is not just a question, though, of national and global representations being mutually opposed. The process of 'glocalisation' is a prime example of the alignment between them and reveals the ways in which global media genres continue to be inflected in nationally specific ways. One example is provided by the popular Finnish reality show *Extreme Escapades* based on a physically challenging rafting competition between two teams in the Finnish Lapland wilderness. According to Aslama and Pannti (2007) the show quite clearly promoted Finnish national identity, although they acknowledge the fact that reality TV as a genre is now a global phenomenon and that similar formats are exported and/or produced simultaneously worldwide. The 'flagging of Finnishness', according to the authors, operated in four aspects of the show: in how the issues of technology and nature were addressed; how the mythologies of Finnishness were circulated; how the competitions were constructed and acted out; and how the various modes of talk were created and realised. Finland is currently branded as a high-tech society commonly referred to as 'Nokia nation' because of mobile phone production and consumption with one of the highest penetrations of mobile phones in the world. Much was made by presenter and contestants alike of the giving up of mobile phones at the start of the competition and this was constructed as a moment of tragic drama. The use of landscape, in particular lake and forest, was another powerful symbol of Finnish national identity signifying a return to nature and cultural roots. As in many mythic tales of origin, the show presented the Lapland wilderness as 'the genius loci of the nation, the place from which all Finns have sprung' (Aslama and Pannti 2007: 58). The authors also note that the competitions organised between the teams invoked *Sisu*, a popular discourse concerning the characteristic Finnish approach to competition, war and sport. Though a difficult term to translate into English *Sisu* roughly means 'the philosophy that what must be done will be done, regardless of cost' (ibid.: 59) and is normally associated with ideas of a 'stubborn Finnishness', 'a perverse kind of pride' and even 'a special form of madness' (ibid.: 59–60). The authors note that while talk is generally a primary feature of these kinds of shows there was much less verbal interaction among the contestants in *Extreme Escapades* thereby invoking the stereotype of the 'quiet Finn'. And when contestants did talk, this was directed towards practical tasks as opposed to the therapeutic talk of other extreme reality TV shows such as *Survivor*. They also displayed a modesty in interaction when it came to making a 'sales pitch' to the voting audience and were generally unwilling to promote themselves as the most competent person. These findings lead Aslama and Pannti to the conclusion that 'what is possible or not possible on TV is connected to the mainstream values of the broader culture' (ibid.: 63) in this case Finnish national culture and that 'formats may escape national boundaries but the need for national belonging remains' (ibid.: 65). (For other examples of national discourses in reality TV see Jacobs 2007; Rejinders *et al.* 2007.)

The national and the transnational: media and diaspora

The mobility of populations from one nation-state to another can be identified as another aspect of globalisation that has led to a growth in multi-ethnic nation-states where a sense of belonging or loyalty to any one nation cannot be assured. Combined with this is the widespread access to communication technologies such as the internet. In these circumstances one might expect that media representations of nationality would be in decline as people developed more transnational communicative networks and post-national and hybrid identities (see Appadurai 1996; Poster 1999). It is instructive, therefore, to look at one kind of mobile population, diasporic groups, to see if, and in what ways, national discourses are generated through their media use. Research indicates that they imagine the nation in diverse ways; some using it to confirm traditional kinds of affiliation to the nation, some negotiating new ways of thinking about the nation, and others disavowing attachment to the nation.

Because separation from the homeland is a feature of diasporic groups, attachment to family, friends and the culture of home becomes particularly pronounced and leads to an intense search for, and negotiation of, identity (Mandaville 2001). This is borne out in a number of studies showing that one of the primary motivations for using the internet among migrant groups is to maintain relationships with family, friends and fellow nationals (e.g. Karim 2003; Mitra 2007). According to Anderson (2001) migrants who do not feel respected in their country of residence commonly develop a strong pride in their country of origin, and their media use reflects this 'long-distance nationalism' (ibid.: 42). It can take many forms one of which is simply wanting to stay in touch with fellow nationals while the more extreme versions include use of the internet for advocating extreme militant nationalist activism in the home country. While the studies referred to above indicate that media use invokes a strong sense of national identity in diasporic groups, others regard this strong emotional attachment to the homeland as a temporary state and subject to a gradual decline. Based on his study of Iranians living in Los Angeles, Naficy (1993) observed a shifting perception of the homeland which was reflected in the kind of media that Iranians produced. Mediated messages produced by recent migrants who were in between two cultures reflected a longing for home; however, this gradually gave way either to a stage where they did not see one particular place as home anymore (hybrid identity) or to one where they were more fully incorporated into the host society and developed a greater allegiance to the host nation.

Using media to connect with the homeland can also vary according to social factors such as age. A recent study (Kerr 2007) of the media use of Polish migrants living in Ireland found that older migrants were more involved in national discourses than the younger. Of the 16 respondents, only two older men reported having access to Polish language television from Poland because they wanted to keep in touch with news and sport from home. Even though some of the younger respondents had the equipment to access Polish television they did not bother watching it because they preferred to watch English language programmes and improve their English language skills.

Diasporic communities can also challenge traditional ways of understanding the nation through their media use. Chan (2005) in her investigation of online discussion boards found that students from the People's Republic of China and living in Singapore drew on multiple and contradictory discourses of the Chinese nation in negotiating their online identities. At times the discussions reflected an acceptance of the official discourses of nationalism and national identity, while at other times the official discourse of national identity were challenged or reformulated. An example of the latter is provided by these students' fantasy of China as a superpower and future empire generated partly by their perception of China as being in a weaker position than other nations and partly by their resistance to the perceived power of the USA in world affairs. This is distinct from the official Chinese government discourse about the country being a peace-loving nation, interacting with others as equals and bound by the rules of international diplomacy. Through their use of information and communications technologies including the internet young Muslims living in Europe and North America are re-imagining the *umma*, or worldwide community or 'nation' of Muslims (Mandaville 2001). These technologies give them access to interpretations of Islam that differ from traditional understandings and are relevant to their own experiences of living in the West. In this process traditional structures of religious authority based in the local mosque are refigured and, to some extent, marginalised.

Conclusions

This chapter has considered the important role of the media in producing and disseminating representations of the nation and in fostering a sense of national identity. We have seen that media narrate the nation in various ways, i.e. the sporting nation, the political nation, and so on, as well as making moral judgements about 'good' and 'bad' nations. These representations are reproduced in entertainment and informational genres, in mainstream mass media and in newer media such as internet chat rooms and websites and are inflected in different ways according to the particular historical, economic and socio-cultural contexts in which they are produced and consumed.

In trying to understand the specific ways in which media seek to establish a sense of national collective identity three specific strategies were considered. The first was the strategic role of the state in the development of public service broadcasting and the construction of a national media public through legislation and regulation. The second was through the routine practices of media producers, including their use of language which reflected the nation as their main reference point. The third, and related, practice was the live broadcasting of ceremonial and festive events and enabling audiences to participate in a shared national public space.

The media landscape that is generated by these media strategies and practices includes diverse images of the nation sometimes running in parallel directions and sometimes colliding with each other. We have seen, for instance, how top-down and bottom-up representations may exist simultaneously and how dominant discourses of the nation can be promulgated through television news, or attempts to promote 'ideal' national values through television drama. Exclusivist and essentialist versions of the nation are promulgated through negative press stereotyping of groups who are seen as outsiders. We have also seen evidence of the reconfiguration of the nation in more democratic and inclusive terms through television documentaries in which ordinary and culturally diverse people present their own lives in their own words. And we have seen how diasporic groups find a voice that may have been marginalised by mainstream media through their use of the internet.

In considering the fate of media representations of the national in the light of globalisation, it is too soon to tell if the national 'imagined community' is in decline as the evidence appears to be complex and contradictory. However, we noted that global media genres such as reality TV continue to be inflected in nationally specific ways. We also noted that one of the most transnational mobile populations, diasporic groups, continue to use the nation as a point of reference as they negotiate their identities, whether confirming traditional ideas of the nation or challenging them.

It is apparent from the discussion above that media representations of the 'imagined community' of the nation are diverse and complex. What it means to belong to a nation and the manner of expressing that belonging are continuously being reproduced, challenged, and transformed as part of an ongoing process of negotiating collective identities in a mediated world.

Exercises

1 Watch a main evening news bulletin on (a) a national channel of your choice; (b) CNN; (c) Al Jazeera English (besides CNN's and Al Jazeera's websites, you can also check availability of these channels on YouTube). Take note of the countries referred to in each bulletin and where they appear in the running order. Note the similarities and differences between the three channels.

2 Watch three episodes of a television game show such as *Who wants to be a millionaire?* produced in your own country. Take note of the ways in which the game takes aspects of your national identity (e.g. 'Irishness' or 'Britishness') for granted. You might want to focus on aspects such as the kinds of questions asked, how the competitors are introduced, etc.

3 Select either an individual sportsperson or team that recently represented your country in an international sports event. Record the coverage of that event in any national newspaper on the day before, the day of, and the day after, the event. Identify and note the variety of ways in which the coverage references the nation either explicitly or implicitly.

Further reading

Edensor, T. (2002) *National Identity, Popular Culture and Everyday Life*, Oxford: Berg. This volume addresses the relationship between national identity, popular culture and everyday life through an exploration of a range of popular cultural spheres, including spaces and places, ritual performance, material culture, and representations of national identity.

Madianou, M. (2005) *Mediating the Nation: News, Audiences and the Politics of Identity*, London: UCL Press. Based on an ethnographic study of television news in Athens, Madianou examines the discourses of the nation in national television channels, the ways people experience the nation, and the contradictory nature of national and transnational identities in modern life.

Spencer, P. and Wollman, H. (eds) (2005) *Nations and Nationalism: A Reader,* New Brunswick: Rutgers University Press. This is a critical reader on theories of nations and nationalism. It provides accounts of: the origins of nationalism, differentiates between forms of nationalism, and the relationship between national, global and cosmopolitan cultures.

Spencer, S. (2006) *Race and Ethnicity: Culture, Identity and Representation*, London: Routledge. This textbook is a good source of material on theoretical approaches to representations of race and ethnicity and presents international case studies from Australia, Malaysia, the Caribbean, Mexico and the UK. It also includes summaries, questions, illustrations, exercises and a glossary of terms.

Vitali, V. and P. Willemen (eds) (2006) *Theorising National Cinema*, London: British Film Institute. This edited volume addresses the complex relationship between national cinema and national identity in Latin America, Asia, the Middle East, India, Africa and Europe. It also considers the future of national cinema in the context of transnational culture flows.

References

AIM (Adequate Information Management in Europe) (2007) *Comparing the Logic of EU Reporting: Transnational Analysis of EU Correspondence from Brussels*, Freiburg, Germany: Project verlag: Bochum.

Anderson, B. (1991) *Imagined Communities: Reflections on the Origin and Spread of Nationalism,* revised edition, London: Verso.

Anderson, B. (2001) 'Western Nationalism and Eastern Nationalism: Is There a Difference That Matters? *New Left Review* 2 (9): 31–42.

Appadurai, A. (1996) *Modernity at Large: Cultural Dimensions of Globalization,* Minneapolis: University of Minnesota Press.

Aslama, M. and Pantii M. (2007) 'Flagging Finnishness: Reproducing National Identity in Reality Television', *Television and New Media,* 8 (1): 49–67.

Billig, M. (1995) *Banal Nationalism,* London: Sage.

Breen, M. E. (2008) 'The Showband Years', unpublished dissertation, BA Journalism, Dublin City University.

Carpentier, N. (2003) 'The BBC's *Video Nation* as a Participatory Media Practice: Signifying Everday Life, Cultural Diversity and Participation in an Online Community', *International Journal of Cultural Studies,* 6 (4): 425–47.

Chan, B. (2005) 'Imagining the Homeland: The Internet and Diasporic Discourse of Nationalism', *Journal of Communication Inquiry,* 29 (4): 336–68.

Curtis, L. (1984) *Nothing but the Same Old Story: The Roots of Anti-Irish Racism,* London: Information on Ireland.

Dayan, D. and Katz, E. (1992) *Media Events: The Live Broadcasting of History,* Cambridge, MA: Harvard University Press.

Devereux, E., Breen, M. and Haynes, A. (2006) 'Smuggling Zebras for Lunch: Media Framing of Asylum Seekers in the Irish Print Media', *Etude Irlandaises,* 30 (1): 109–31.

Fanning, B. and Mutwarasibo, F. (2007) 'Nationals/Non-nationals: Immigration, Citizenship and Politics in the Republic of Ireland', *Ethnic and Racial Studies,* 30 (3): 439–60.

Gillespie, M. (2005) 'Television Drama and Audience Ethnography' in M. Gillespie (ed) *Media Audiences,* Berkshire: Open University Press.

Ging, D. (2002) 'Screening the Green: Cinema under the Celtic Tiger' in P. Kirby, L. Gibbons and M. Cronin (eds) *Re-Inventing Ireland: Culture, Society and the Global Economy,* London: Pluto.

Hall, S. (1996) 'Introduction: Who Needs Identity' in S. Hall and P. du Gay (eds) *Questions of Cultural Identity,* London: Sage.

Higson, A. (2000) 'The Limiting Imagination of National Cinema', in M. Hjort and S. Mackenzie (eds) *Cinema and Nation,* New York: Routledge.

Jacobs, S. (2007) 'Big Brother, Africa Is Watching', *Media, Culture and Society,* 29 (6): 851–68.

Karim, K. (2003) *The Media of Diaspora,* London: Routledge.

Kerr, A. (2007) 'Transnational Flows: Media Use by Poles in Ireland' in J. Horgan, B. O'Connor and H. Sheehan (eds) *Mapping Irish Media: Critical Explorations,* Dublin: University College Dublin Press.

Liebes, T. (1997) *Reporting the Israeli-Arab Conflict: How Hegemony Works,* London: Routledge.

Mandaville, P. (2001) 'Reimaging Islam in Diaspora: The Politics of Mediated Community', *Gazette* 63 (2–3): 169–86.

Madianou, M. (2005) *Mediating the Nation: News, Audiences and the Politics of Identity,* London: UCL Press.

Mankekar, P. (1999) *Screening Culture, Viewing Politics: An Ethnography of Television, Womanhood and Nation in Postcolonial India,* Durham/London: Duke University Press.

Matthews, N. (2007) 'Confessions to a New Public: Video Nation Shorts', *Media, Culture and Society,* 29 (3): 435–48.

McLoone, M. and McMahon, J. (1984) *Television and Irish Society*, Dublin: Radio Telefís Eireann/Irish Film Institute.

McSharry, M. (2008) 'Stuck in a Ruck: The Impact of Rugby on Social Belonging' in M. P. Corcoran and P. Share (eds) *Belongings: Shaping Identity in Modern Ireland,* Dublin: Institute of Public Administration.

Mitra, A. (1997) 'Virtual Commonality: Looking for India on the Internet', in S. G. Jones (ed), *2.0: Revisiting Computer-mediated Communication and Community*, Thousand Oaks, CA: Sage, pp. 55-79.

Morley, D. and Brunsdon, C. (1999) *The Nationwide Television Studies*, London: Routledge.

Naficy, H. (1993) *The Making of Exile Cultures*, Minneapolis: University of Minnesota Press.

O'Brien, M. (2004) 'Selling Soccer' in M. Peillon and M. P. Corcoran (eds) *Place and Non-Place: The Reconfiguration of Ireland,* Dublin: Institute of Public Administration.

Philo, G. and Berry, M. (2004) *Bad News from Israel*, London: Pluto.

Poster, M. (1999) 'National Identities and Communication Technologies', *Information Society*, 15 (4): 235-40.

Rantanen, T. (2005) *The Media and Globalization*, London: Sage.

Rejinders, S., Rooijakkers, G. and van Zoonen, L. (2007) 'Community Spirit and Competition in Idols: Ritual Meanings of a TV Talent Quest', *European Journal of Communication* 22 (3): 275-92.

Rowe, D. (1999) *Sport, Culture and the Media: The Unruly Trinity*, Buckingham: Open University Press.

Scannell, P. and Cardiff, D. (1991) *A Social History of British Broadcasting,* Vol. 1. Oxford: Blackwell.

Sheehan, H. (2007) 'Television Drama as Social History: The Case of *Fair City*' in J. Horgan, B. O'Connor and H. Sheehan (eds) *Mapping Irish Media: Critical Explorations,* Dublin: University College Dublin Press.

Smith, A. D. (2001) *Nationalism: Theory, Ideology, History*, Malden, MA: Polity.

Ugba, A. (2002) 'Mapping Minorities and their Media: The National Context - Ireland', available at www.lse.ac.uk/collections/EMTEL/minorities/papers (accessed 20 February 2009).

Van Dijk, T. A. (2006) 'Discourse and Manipulation', *Discourse and Society*, 17 (3): 359-83.

Wilson, D. (1993) 'Tourism, Public Policy and the Image of Northern Ireland since the Troubles' in B. O'Connor and M. Cronin (eds) *Tourism in Ireland: A Critical Analysis*, Cork: Cork University Press.

Whannel, G. (1992) *Fields in Vision: Television Sport and Cultural Transformation*, London: Routledge.

35

Sport

Neil Blain and Raymond Boyle

Chapter overview

This chapter is on the representation of sport in the media. It notes the numerous ways in which the analysis of the representation of sport might take place as well as the array of topics on which sport and its representation impinges. It then proceeds to focus on football – especially the English Premiership – as an exemplification of the way that sport, identity, nationality, the media and finance are all imbricated.

> Murdoch tells WSJ execs: 'shorter stories, more sport'.
>
> (*Press Gazette*, 17 January 2008 reporting on the first meeting of *Wall Street Journal* bureau chiefs and their new owner Rupert Murdoch)

Introduction

The range of topics which arise from the study of media sport is wide, and research in the field has steadily diversified. We might choose (for example) to focus on matters of media genre and form. We can think about how specific sports are (say) televisually constructed through generic programming processes (sport as spectacle, sport as drama). Or, within individual sports broadcasts, we can scrutinise the formal process of selecting camera positions and subjects, or voice commentaries. Is the camera looking at the players or the spectators? Is it on or off the ball? How is coverage altered by interactive dimensions? How can football on radio be interesting? Are some sports less well adapted to mediation, and why?

At the wider level of being interesting and accessible in the media, sport can often be linked with human interest and celebrity (sometimes to the extent of getting in the way of the actual sport). More technically, sports broadcasting has led to very specific editing and assembling styles, both in the sense of cutting within or across a field of play, and also when creating montages, perhaps of weeping players after a failed penalty shoot-out, or musical sequences of Olympics highlights, or landscapes and cityscapes of the *Tour de France* or the London Marathon.

519

Research into another major topic, fandom, might range from sociological investigations of football hooliganism, or analyses of the role of official supporter clubs, to cultural analysis of the semiotics of sporting emblems and symbols.

Media sport can also be part of the study of media economics, not least because it is central to the process of acquiring audiences, which in turn attract advertising, or justify the licence fee. We might study specific sports or events, or else compare social, cultural, political or economic questions across different sports. It is possible to take a comparative approach to demographic questions of sport, for example around ethnic, gender or age issues. Demographic considerations also include those of social class. Rugby union, for example, is often regarded as a 'middle class' sport, as distinct from rugby league as a 'working class' sport. But the truth is more complex than that, since in some localities (for example, Wales) rugby union is much more likely to be associated with working class involvement than other places. There then arise interesting questions about how the media construct their own versions of difference, for example, assigning commentators with different socio-regional accents to mark out each sport as socially distinct.

Media sport is a complex phenomenon and not least in its ideological dimensions, how it constructs not just class differences or gender differences, but in its accounts of national or regional differences. In fact, across print, broadcast and online media, representations of sport are often associated with a parallel construction of demographic identities (Boyle and Haynes 2009; Brookes 2002; Rowe 2004), and 'construction' (like 'fabrication') is a useful term if it reminds us that these 'representations' are seldom neutral. In the press, representations of sport are often very highly mediated, through a variety of journalism forms, addressed to a wide variety of markets. A growth in the scope and scale of sports journalism has been one of the characteristics of European media more generally in the past decade or so, and of the UK media in particular (Boyle 2006; Steen 2008; Boyle *et al.* 2009).

In this chapter we are going to concentrate chiefly on football, because of its centrality to the functioning of media sport in much of the world, not least in Europe; and we will consider questions both of economics and of representation, because these two areas – which are in some respects linked – display media sport at its most important and forceful. And with Europe in mind, we will be especially concerned with national and cultural identities.

Most of all, however, this chapter tries to demonstrate why the combination of media and sport has become so important within contemporary societies and economies, and how it is that this fusion works with such ideological and economic force.

The media–sport nexus

Traditionally events such as the Olympic Games or the FIFA World Cup and European soccer competitions have been the vehicle for much coverage bearing on the idea of the nation. However the globalisation and internationalisation of elite sport and sports labour in the last decade have meant that issues about national identity are prevalent in discourses of sport throughout the sporting year, not simply at set-piece international events. Within football, for example, these issues are often framed in terms of the potential negative impact that imported players or athletes may have on the national game.

As in other walks of European society and economy, the twin drivers shaping contemporary sport and its deep relationship with the media are globalisation and technology. Of course, neither of these forces is played out across Europe in a universal manner. National cultures, regulatory frameworks and differing contours of political, economic and cultural life shape how these twin forces impact on life in (say) Germany, Italy or Sweden. But at the core of the debates across the continent about how everyday life is changing, and how the challenges faced by European societies are addressed, lies a dual concern about how aspects of the impact of globalisation and technological innovation are shaped or harnessed for good or ill.

To this end, a study of sport and its ubiquitous relationship with the media and communication industries offers not just an insight into the growing sports industry, but more broadly informs us about culture as a whole. As the historian Eric Hobsbawm argues:

> The dialectics of the relations between globalisation, national identity and xenophobia are dramatically illustrated in the public activity that combines all three: football. For, thanks to global television, this universally popular sport has been transformed into a worldwide capitalist industrial complex (though, by comparison with other global business activities, of relatively modest size).
>
> (Hobsbawm 2007: 90)

The narratives that sports produce, although the quotation is about football specifically – and the way these stories are delivered to and made sense of by audiences – variously reflect, reinforce and construct a range of identities of the sort we have suggested above. These operate both within particular cultural contexts and are also enacted at symbolic levels, international and global (Blain 2003).

For some critics (e.g. King 2003) the growth in prominence of events such as the UEFA Champions League has been broadly positive in its associated football fandom development, part of a wider Europeanisation of football fandom. Others (Williams 2007) are more circumspect, and emphasise the role played by capital and the media industries in shaping the broader framework and the wider parameters within which football fandom in a European context operates. But the matter is more profound than both these positions suggest. As the European dimension of the sports industry has developed over the last few decades, likewise the way that sport is run, governed, controlled and managed tells us much about how new orthodoxies have entered the mainstream of European economic thinking, with increased influence on our working and leisure lives. The English Premier League, underpinned by marketing, promotion and entertainment industry values and practices, embodies the *modernisation* of traditional industries in Britain more generally. Its influence around the globe through a range of media platforms including the internet reinforces a political discourse which views the exporting of culture and ideas as a key process conferring 'soft power' on a country which has lost much competitive advantage in more traditional areas of economic influence (e.g. manufacturing).

In other words, a study of what has been called the media–sport nexus, which is often characterised by a short-term market ethos, with vested and powerful political and media interests, increasingly global patterns of ownership, and a relocation of resources often transcending traditional national boundaries, in turn illuminates wider shifts in European industrial and corporate life. While at its heart sport remains organised play, the architecture and infrastructure that now facilitates, supports and mediates what is in essence an invention of a 19th century age of imperialism, is deeply embedded in the political, economic and cultural life of a digital 21st century Europe. Of late, separating mediated sport and 'real life' has become an increasingly difficult and complex exercise.

The next section examines why sport is important – and in what ways – in the digital media age. Then we turn our attention to some recent developments in the football–media relationship which illustrate the manner in which a study of media sport is closely associated with economic and cultural life. Throughout, we are especially concerned with the relationship between Britain and Europe.

Why sport matters in the digital age

Sport has always mattered to the media (Boyle and Haynes 2009; Brookes 2002; Rowe 2004). In the digital age of media, we have moved from an age of scarcity to potential abundance of media content delivered through a range of platforms (television, computer, mobile phone). Throughout Europe the twin drivers of digital switch-over and high-speed broadband are facilitating substantive, if uneven, change across the media landscape. We are entering an age where to talk of 'old' or 'new' or indeed 'digital' media will become redundant. There will simply be media and content delivered to screens (or increasingly pulled down by users onto those screens) wherever they may be located.

Of course there will be continuity as well as change. Print media will not simply disappear, but rather co-exist in a more complex media environment. People will still need a roadmap to find their way around the content they want, think they want (or have not yet discovered that they want). As a result, big media brands such as the BBC will remain important, and sports content and sports journalism will remain a central component of this increasingly demand-led media environment (Boyle 2006; Steen 2008).

By 2008 the television marketplace for sports had changed out of all recognition in the UK from even a decade earlier. Sky Sports, once the 'new kid on the block' who created the pay-TV sports market in the UK in the 1990s, had become part of the sports media establishment, itself under pressure from a rival in the pay sports market, Setanta, which muscled into the market in the wake of EU regulation which broke Sky's monopoly of live Premiership football. Sky and the now defunct Setanta's three-year deal (in 2007) with English football's elite division was worth £1.7 billion or £567 million a season. In 1987, by contrast, television paid £3 million a season for football rights. TV executives are now the financial underwriters of the sport as well as many other sports in the UK and elsewhere in Europe.

Tennis, golf and rugby all feed off television money and exposure as part of – in the UK alone – a staggering 36,000 hours of sports broadcast in 2007.

In 2008 the digital broadcasting market in the UK had become characterised by an increasingly fragmented audience for television with both free-to-air and pay-TV digital channels competing for viewers. Broadcasters are using a range of media platforms such as the web, and likewise on-demand technologies like the BBC iPlayer, to capture and retain audience share. A point often missed by analysts is that in Britain in 2007 audiences were watching about 10 minutes more television than in preceding years. Viewers are actually watching more television (on larger screens than ever) but less of this viewing is collective, or taking place at the same time. This rise of an 'on-demand culture' has led to live (or 'as live') 'event television' programmes such as *X Factor* (ITV) and *Strictly Come Dancing* (BBC) which cannot be time shifted, precisely because the pleasure is about the here-and-now result which the viewer can influence through voting.

Against this backdrop the premium nature of live sports events as 'event television' continues to develop. As Greg Dyke, former Director General of the BBC, argues:

> In a world were you can download anything, you can't download live sport. Anything live becomes more important. The price paid by broadcasters [for live elite sport] will continue to go up.
>
> (Oliver 2007a)

In an age when technological change, in part unleashed through a lighter regulatory framework, is restructuring how people watch and think about television, the ability of sports at major events to pull together fragmented audiences remains compelling.

In the UK it was once common (in the late 1990s) for top television shows to regularly attract over 15 million viewers. A decade later *Coronation Street* remained the most popular television programme on British screens with an average of 11 million viewers (an audience share of 45 per cent). When England played Sweden in the 2006 FIFA World Cup, ITV attracted its largest audience of the year, 18.8 million viewers. The 2007 Rugby World Cup saw almost 14 million tune into the England v South Africa final in October of that year, and as F1 motor racing enjoyed a ratings surge with Lewis Hamilton's attempt to secure the world title in his inaugural season, almost 8 million tuned into ITV coverage of the Brazilian Grand Prix that same weekend (BARB, 20 October 2007). This sporting combination of 'event' television provided a struggling ITV with the biggest-grossing advertising revenue weekend of that year. ITV sold over £16 million worth of advertising around these two events. Such is the integral nature of major international sports content (when it has a British dimension, of course) to commercial television in the UK, that when England failed to qualify for the 2008 European Championships, it was not simply football fans who lost out: ITV's advertising revenue projects for that summer were dramatically scaled back.

So sports content, in an increasingly commercial media system, remains very important for traditional broadcasters. The main public service broadcaster, the BBC, has seen its sporting portfolio diminish as the governing bodies of sport follow the money on offer from pay-TV, but is using new technology and a cross-platform presence to fight back. The 2008 Beijing Olympics, one of an increasingly small number of sporting events that cannot be exclusively captured by pay-TV, saw the BBC make 2400 hours of extra sports coverage available through the interactive 'red button' digital service. By London 2012, the Corporation aims to make BBC1 the premium Olympic channel, and show every event live via the interactive service. This kind of commitment is only sustainable through a large well-funded broadcaster such as the BBC. At a time of funding uncertainty this will continue to be sold by the Corporation as part of its distinctive public service remit. Given the massive public expenditure by government on the London Games, it can be predicted that it will support the BBC as the only broadcaster capable of promoting and making Games coverage available free-to-air and across media platforms. The BBC will make the London Games part of its political argument to keep up levels of public funding (the Games will also sustain its 'national' claims). The reality is that by 2012 the way the BBC is funded is likely to change, as the licence fee finally becomes an outdated mechanism through which to fund public service content in a multi-platform digital environment.

One key issue for both sports and broadcasters will be the extent to which sport is viewed as making a distinctive contribution to the national and cultural life of any European country, thus subject to special regulatory measures making it available for all. (This is distinct from viewing it as simply another aspect of modern life that the communications marketplace is perfectly able to support.) The marketisation of the broadcasting world will continue apace, as will the accompanying debate about when it is both necessary and useful to regulate that market for the public good (Saldaña 2008).

There is more sport on television than ever before, but much is only available live if viewers are willing to pay extra to see it, as the rights holders of sport look to the short-term money on offer, and appear oblivious to longer-term implications. For example, when Scotland played Italy in a vital qualifying match for Euro 2008, the game was exclusively live on pay-TV. Historically, such games involving the national team would have been free-to-air, forming part of a wider national cultural life and shared experience. Children in Scotland are now more likely to have seen England play live on free-to-air television than the Scottish national football team, a strange state of affairs for such a supposedly national sport.

An English league abroad

As mentioned earlier, the globalisation (or as some prefer to call it, internationalisation) of sport is one of the great forces shaping modern sports media culture. This is not a new process. However, a combination of technological innovation and a more market-oriented communications and political culture across much of Europe has strongly fuelled sports development over the last decade. As Goldblatt notes in his magisterial history of the world game, 'In the 1990s European football's long economic decline was spectacularly reversed: the ailing rustbelt of Fordist football was transformed into a booming post-industrial service sector awash with money and hubris' (Goldblatt 2007: 688). The English Premier League was created by the elite football clubs in order to generate more television revenue and allow the top-flight teams to retain this money, rather than have it redistributed throughout the game. In the television rights deal covering 2007–10 the league sold media rights packages worth in total close to £2.7 billion (selling the rights overseas generated £625 million and made it the most watched sports league in the world). While over two-thirds of the overseas deals are in Asia (Anon. 2007) it is Africa which has the Premiership's largest fan base, although the relative poverty of these fans means that it is only recently that sponsors are attempting to build markets in this part of the world.

When it started in 1992 the Premier League had 11 players who did not come from Britain and Ireland. Some 15 years later this number had grown to over 250. Players from countries such as China are brought in by clubs to expand their brand identity in these lucrative markets. In 2003 an Everton v Manchester City match saw both teams field Chinese players and was shown in China on state television to an audience of 350 million (Oliver 2007b). Even in smaller leagues a player's national identity value on the pitch is becoming increasingly fused with commercial and marketing imperatives. The presence of Celtic's Shunsuke Nakamura has resulted in the club visiting his country to promote awareness of the team, setting up a Japanese language website, and by 2007 selling over 140,000 replica shirts and 20,000 DVDs in this market (Smith 2007).

Top clubs in England now regularly have foreign managers and even more significantly, seven of the Premier League teams in 2008 including Manchester United, Chelsea, Liverpool and Aston Villa, were owned by foreign businessmen, something unthinkable back in the 1990s, but consistent with other aspects of UK plc, such as manufacturing, banking and high street retail brands.

Early in the same year, much disquiet arose in English football culture over a proposal announced by Richard Scudamore, the chief executive of the Premier League, to explore the possibility of playing an additional 'international' 39th round of Premiership matches overseas, as exhibitions of the indigenous game. Quickly dubbed 'the 39th step' the idea unleashed much comment from across the world of football:

> It is the logical step, given the League's growth and ambition – 'the only way to grow the brand', said the Birmingham City chairman, David Gold – but it is also a quantum leap. For the first time clubs will be divorced from their heritage. It begs the question, what next?
>
> (Moore, 2008)

At one level this proposal was only a minor extension of the globalisation of football. In England its 'indigenousness' was already greatly in doubt, and under constant debate, because of the major presence at the top level of overseas players, coaches and (increasingly) proprietors. The globalisation process involves intensification of the export and import of economic and cultural products (Robertson 1992) amidst accelerated space–time changes. 'Time-space compression' is one of the more succinct definitions of globalisation (Harvey 1990). The time and manner of indigenous football consumption had already adjusted to international space–time considerations, British pay TV consumers able (for example) to schedule live British and Spanish matches sequentially at weekends, and construct many similar international media packages. In any case, British sides had travelled to

Europe and beyond for decades to play club and national team football. Why not run a few Premier League matches abroad, when the English big four of Manchester United, Arsenal, Chelsea and Liverpool are judged for their success as major brands in global terms? No one could argue that the commoditisation process for football was not already far advanced.

The demographics of 21st century production and consumption create difficulties for analyses rooted in class assumptions of the previous two centuries. Benjamin's observation that the 'masses' are 'forcibly excluded from consumption' (1999: 18) is replaced in the present century by an entrepreneurial approach to consumption which squeezes profit from everywhere. C. K. Prahalad has argued that a market worth trillions of dollars is comprised by the poor of the world's developing nations (Prahalad 2004). The development of microfinance and microcredit (which fuelled the sub-prime mortgage crisis of 2007/08) illustrate a tendency in contemporary capitalism to squeeze profit from commercial operations down to (even beyond) the limits of feasibility. The English Premiership plan to play matches overseas followed the commercial logic of its time.

For overseas consumers, most consumption of English Premier League clubs is distanced, usually mediated, or through merchandise purchase. The opportunity, especially outside Europe, to consume Manchester United or Arsenal in the stadium is very rare. It is self-evident that a Manchester United v Liverpool match in almost any country in the world will be a sell-out event. In turn, the economies of both clubs, and English football in general, will benefit from further spillover activity in the purchase of merchandise and media access to Premier League games. On the surface this looks like a win–win situation for the clubs and English football.

Likewise it would seem logical to maximise team success at every phase of the operation, both on the field and in all other commercial operations. The way in which team performance, critical for profit maximisation, has been improved in the English game is through the import of overseas players and coaches. The coaches of top English sides in the first decade of the 21st century were mainly from outside England, including Scottish, French, Spanish, Portuguese, Israeli, Northern Irish and Swedish coaches. Many of the star players of the game – Thierry Henry, Didier Drogba, Cristiano Ronaldo, Fernando Torres and others – have been from overseas. One source reported that the percentage of English players in the Premier League fell from 71 per cent in season 1992–93 to 38 per cent in 2006–07 (Anon. 2008a). This has been to the large benefit of the English game as a product in terms of domestic and European success, producing a level of spectacle enhancing its international competitiveness as a product in media and other markets. For example 2008 saw, for the first time, 50 per cent of the clubs in the last eight of the UEFA Champions League drawn from the Premier League. Of those four clubs (Arsenal, Chelsea, Manchester United and Liverpool) only 25 per cent of the players active in this European competition were British. This has meant that club success has not been reflected at national level, as the pool of players from which the English national coach can draw has shrunk dramatically in the last decade.

Yet there was widespread condemnation of the plan to play Premier League fixtures abroad from across the footballing world: 'Greed will drive Premier League to more than 39th step' (Martin Samuel, *The Times*, 13 February 2008); 'All we know is money lurks behind Scudamore's plan' (Sue Mott, *Daily Telegraph*, 12 February 2008); 'What On Earth is Going On?' (Charlie Wyett, the *Sun*, 9 February 2008). The response from UEFA chief executive Michel Platini was splashed across the whole of the *Daily Telegraph*'s sports section (Bond 2008): 'You already have NO English coach, you have NO English players and maybe now you will have NO clubs playing in England. It's a joke.' While Patrick Barclay in the *Sunday Telegraph* opened his criticism of the men who control the game in England by suggesting that the Scudamore plan:

> has opened the biggest can of worms since English football (if such a term can still be used) was split up and rebranded 16 years ago [. . .] what a mess our football has got itself into [. . .] if this is globalisation, a plague on it [. . .] Scudamore is doing his best to control an organisation owned by men with no real responsibility to this country, let alone their clubs. That is the problem of letting globalisation rule football. (Barclay 2008)

There had already been, by the time that plan was floated, nearly a decade of growing concern about the saturation of the top reaches of the game by overseas professionals, and likewise, at national level, much disquiet over appointments of non-English national coaches.

Identity, media and managing 'the nation'

If it is axiomatic that football is a business, it is nonetheless also, not least in England, a repository of cultural values. It has been argued that there exists a striking directness of association characterising English soccer and English society, in essence a difficulty in dissociating football and history (Blain and O'Donnell 1998). It is possible to find much more evidence of 'indexical', or what in literary studies would be termed 'metonymic', relationships in the way in which the media account for football in England, than mere 'metaphoric' relations of comparison (Blain 2003). Put simply, English football is often read as an actual extension of English society, not least by the foreign sporting press (Crolley and Hand 2006). While people in many countries produce emotional reactions to sport, it is arguable if even the Australians are as sensitive to the implications for Australian identity of international rugby and cricket performances as England is on the question of international football. Elsewhere, football is used more flexibly as a metaphor which can be treated seriously or not, as in France or Germany (in Scotland, it is a source of both tragedy and comedy).

Now that the game has reached a more intensively globalised stage, and at a time of increased general migration to the UK, what are the new elements in the relationship between English football and English culture? Sven-Göran Eriksson's tenure as England coach, in addition to the routine vitriol from the press which the job guarantees, produced many expressions of hostility around his foreign-ness and Swedishness. When journalists reported the fans' cries of 'sack the Swede' (as happened when Northern Ireland beat England in 2005) they were in reality reporting on a discursive loop between media and fans, in which the media often took the initiative. Part of this discourse of England managers involves a process of forgetting. Even the *Telegraph*'s urbane Henry Winter allows himself to speculate that:

> Publicly supportive, the Swede's FA employers privately concede their frustration that players who shine for their clubs look so uninspired when they turn up for England duty.
>
> (Winter 2005)

In fact, this allegation had been visited on the England of coach Graham Taylor and was to become a defining characteristic of the brief reign of Steve McLaren, both native Englishmen:

> The question is not whether McLaren was a bad manager, but whether he was the worst to hold the job . . . Farewell Steve, your epitaph shall read 'worse than Graham Taylor'.
>
> (Barnes 2007)

The problem of the under-performance of England national squads (BC, that is – before Capello) in comparison to club performances had taken on chronic dimensions well before Eriksson's appearance (Carter 2007). The gambit of blaming anaemic England turnouts on Eriksson's Scandinavian temperament had never belonged to a world of logic, but rather to the internal myth-world of the populist realms of sports journalism. (Sven's characterisation as a passionless Swede was in any case incompatible with an alternative persona, 'Sven the Swordsman': 'Veteran shagger Sven Goran Eriksson is known for his love of vital statistics', begins one tabloid piece (Anon. 2008b). In the myth-world of the sports press, a hearty and wholly committed Englishman like Stuart Pearce, or a variety of other imagined beef-eating, pint-drinking Englishmen will extract genuine commitment from the players on the field, by virtue of being English (this is the Henry VIII, or Sir Ian Botham discourse of Englishness). In practice they do not, however, which is why an England coach was no longer a first choice at Premier League clubs, or the national side, by the time of Sven's arrival; earlier coach Graham Taylor's *Sun*-derived soubriquet, Turnip Head, is where the myth world leads for the unwary native manager (it surprised many that McLaren was willing to don the mantle).

Representation has its own rules in these media domains. Despite Taylor and McLaren's failures there were many media voices raised in favour of limiting the search for a coach to English contenders. We look in vain for metaphorical consistency in such accounts. The amnesiac circularity of judgements on the England situation is understood well enough by media commentators themselves:

> For England managers all beginnings are the same. The players will invariably say that team spirit is better, that they now dine together like a club side and that training is much sharper . . . There is also a sense of freshness mingling with ridiculous hope – often because your predecessor was a thorough-going disaster. (Rich 2008)

The English FA decided to appoint Italian Fabio Capello as the successor to McLaren following the failure to qualify for Euro 2008.

There were stereotype confusions in Capello's relationship with the English media from the outset. On the announcement of his appointment, the possibility that Stuart Pearce (passionate, emotional, caring, English) would be brought in to support Capello (dispassionate, pragmatic, judgemental, Italian) was introduced to soften the double blow of another European in the England job. 'Psycho turns psychologist', claims one earlier *Telegraph* article of Pearce (Barclay, 2005) noting how 'he takes a caring attitude toward his players'. 'Don't fool with Fabio Capello' says a *Sunday Times* piece (Hawkey 2007); while insiders like David Beckham and Ruud Gullit are widely quoted in the media advising not to 'mess around' with Capello, who will, according to Beckham, bring back the 'fear factor'. When Capello does get emotional, it's to 'scream at you', as several beneficiaries of his approach attest in interviews.

It quickly becomes clear that the British media will find Capello difficult to portray. One problem is the refusal of Italian coaches in general to behave in a Latin manner, instead being evidently technical, cool, detached, and well balanced, compared to the unstable temperaments found in English football among 'Anglo-Saxon' players like Wayne Rooney, or in the tortured self-doubts of English coaches (think of McLaren's strange observation on Sky News in November 2007 that 'I pick the team', something which a Spanish, French or indeed Italian coach might not have felt compelled to assert).

There was some experimentation with the account which the media wished to establish for Capello, for example covering the apparent theft of a 'top-of-the-range' hairdryer which the boss had evidently insisted on having in his Wembley dressing room: 'We thought it was a bit strange but he's the boss and we got a top-of-the-range dryer . . . Everyone is terrified about what he is going to say when he finds out it's missing' ('Fabio Capello's hairdryer is stolen from Wembley dressing room', Fricker 2008).

Nor was it clear that Capello's reaction to the loss of his hairdryer would in any case be comprehended. His initial and much-reported linguistic self-assessment, 'but in this moment my English is not so well', also happened to coincide with a new and harsher form of national attention to the question of setting standards for migrant workers. 'Britishness' has overtly become a subject of contestation in the 21st century, subject to redefinitions and loyalty tests. These have included proposals to tighten language demands on new arrivals to the country. Capello's first public ventures into the anglophone world provoked scepticism about his capacity to communicate. (These were qualified by ironic press observations to the effect that this would merely put him on a par with many of the England players; and Capello subsequently developed more poise in English as the year progressed.)

The UK of the early 21st century has been a land well suited to identity crisis. Globalisation, migration and demographic tensions have intensified the question of Englishness. Sport, so often a central medium for the expression of identity, takes on a further importance as the concept of the UK becomes more and more difficult to reconstruct and reassert.

The various ways of conceptualising how media discourses, myths and ideologies can be theoretically related to their circulation in culture and society lead to a rough consensus. Most commentators perceive a process in which the media both reflect or respond to ideologies and myths in the wider society, but also at times provide inputs and selective reinforcements, taking initiatives rather than merely reacting.

We would argue that the British media are in general conservative, and that the popular press in particular has tended to articulate socially and culturally regressive views, albeit in an uneven manner. In sport, as in news, feature and editorial coverage generally, journalists react to broader social agendas (they are, after all, usually products of their own society). However, as part of a newspaper's ideological collective, and with an eye to its market position, they may take an approach broadly typical of their newspaper as a whole, thus relating to majority belief in society in asymmetric ways.

The relentless national chauvinism of the popular press which in sports coverage includes consistent and predictable attacks, say, on the Germans and the French merely on the basis of their nationality, can sometimes appear as an idiosyncratic trait of a particular section of the media, rather than a statement of sedimented opinion in the wider society. A dozen years before Capello's arrival, for example, Euro 96 sponsors Vauxhall Motors had withdrawn advertising from the *Daily Star* and the *Daily Mirror* in protest over headlines like the *Mirror*'s 'Herr we go: Krauts gun for Tel' (24 June 1996, during Terry Venables' reign as England manager).

British radio and TV broadcasters, mindful of their need to live in a much less segmented market, tend both to avoid extremes of ideological positioning, and even sometimes to satirise or attack the popular press for its views. Newpapers will, overall, for market reasons, try to steer a course in which they believe themselves to be close to popular opinion. Also, journalists, commentators and summarisers will switch between available ways of talking about other nationalities to suit the context, expressing great technical admiration for footballers or coaches, while collapsing back into familiar stereotypes when trying to emphasise national traits or differences.

Since defining people by nationality is not in reality possible, and since the availability of stereotypes is limited, the arrival of Capello posed a number of questions. Whereas Eriksson played well to a myth of Scandinavian restraint (even depressiveness), Capello's 'hard man' persona is as close to the mythic Glaswegian character of Sir Alex Ferguson (a manager who has copyright on the use of the 'hairdryer technique') as to the 'Continental' flamboyance of Jose Mourinho.

Sampling from the first decade of the 21st century, however, it has not been difficult to find evidence of the resilience of established discursive categories both in sports coverage and in general media coverage. Even questioning national stereotypes can prolong them: 'The Germans are cold and efficient, right? Wrong. In a book that is a runaway bestseller in Germany, the Times man in Berlin debunks the myths about our Teutonic cousins.' This piece is titled: 'Sour Krauts? Not a bit of it' (Boyes, 2006). In 2005, both the *Telegraph* and the *Mirror* carried front page headlines describing the newly-elected Pope Benedict as 'God's Rottweiler', while the *Sun*'s headline was 'From Hitler Youth to Papa Ratzi'. 'Here's Hun for all the family', jests the *Sun* in the summer of 2007, fronting a piece on Nazi wartime board games (20 August 2007).

In sport, though it might be argued that the low point of xenophobic headlines from the 1990s has proved an extreme, the English tabloids are still capable of extraordinary malice. When Swiss referee Urs Meier disallowed an English goal in the quarter final of Euro 2004, the *Sun* ran a headline 'Urs hole' (25 June), and other tabloids attacked him and released personal details about him, placing him under such risk that he had to go into hiding. Sport still, as it has done for many years, licenses some of the most rabid displays of xenophobia and chauvinism, and they are at their most concentrated in the British popular press. (This has been a subject of debate on the Continent for some years now – the British popular media are viewed from Europe with a sort of horrified fascination.)

Conclusion

Any scrutiny of the internet will reveal that xenophobic and racist terminology – which the UK tabloids have (at best) made more legitimate in the eyes of some of those who use interactive sports sites – is immensely widespread. The relationship which binds English society with the English media and the sports media in particular is too complex for definition here. That the sports media still operate regressively in a number of domains (we have concentrated here on questions of nation) is unarguable.

Capello's ambivalent and, as it happens, initially mainly respectful reception by the English media (which was transformed to near-ecstasy when, in September 2009, England qualified early for the 2010 World Cup) is not by itself proof of change in discursive habits. It is England's next exposure in international competition which will properly measure any change which may have occurred since Euro 2004. What we can assert with confidence is a growing divide between discourse and action; and within discourse itself. A resilient media discourse proclaiming the virtues of Britishness and Englishness, and still often quick to offer insult to other European nationalities, has to share a real world in which the best of English football is thoroughly globalised, and at player and coach level, Europeanised in particular. And precisely because that improvement in English football depends on its globalisation, xenophobic and chauvinistic narratives have to share space with others which admiringly acknowledge the characteristics which the European world brings to British football.

The increasingly ubiquitous nature of sporting discourse in an expanded media landscape (Boyle 2006) allied with its overt commercialisation, more than ever necessitates recognising its intimate relationships with national and global economies, and with politics and culture. This is now widely acknowledged, whether through American political journalists talking about globalisation and football (Foer 2004), or cricketers writing perceptively about what sport tells us about modern life (Smith 2008).

The pace of change in the sports and media industries shows no sign of abating. Meanwhile the ability of television to remain a central mediating force in popular culture remains compelling. Broadcast sports coverage and the print and online journalism that accompanies it remain crucial in the process of legitimising the myths and narratives that surround sports culture, embedding them into deeper national and cultural narratives about ourselves and others (Boyle 2006). The study of media sport has become better at revealing how larger – sometimes quite abstract and complex – financial and economic structures increasingly shape the working, leisure and social lives of Europeans. It also casts light on their sense of identity, whether as wholehearted Europeans, or in critical dialogue, of various degrees of intelligence and seriousness, with the European idea.

Questions

1 What are the benefits and disadvantages of the 'Europeanisation' of English football in terms of:
   (a) the football business
   (b) multiculturalism
   (c) the success of the England national team?

2 Take any one sporting event and compare its coverage on radio and on television. Does your analysis challenge any preconceptions you have about each medium? Which offers the most opportunity for interaction? Consider the event itself as well as the build-up to the event and any subsequent analysis by media pundits.

3 What is the relation between sport and celebrity? Is there any coverage of sport in the media which does not presuppose a hierarchy of celebrity?

Further reading

Boyle, R. and Haynes, R. (2009) *Power Play: Sport, the Media and Popular Culture*, 2nd edition, Edinburgh: Edinburgh University Press. Latest, updated edition of key work on the relation of media and sport, covering key questions of the representation of sport as well as its political economy.

Boyle, R. (2006) *Sports Journalism: Context and Issues*, London: Sage. Analysis of sports journalism focusing on print, broadcasting, promotions, the impact of digital media and gender.

Brookes, R. (2002) *Representing Sport*, London: Arnold. Dated, but nevertheless important introduction to some of the issues covered in the current essay.

Crolley, L. and Hand, D. (2006) *Football and European Identity: Historical Narratives Through the Press*, London: Routledge. Coverage of the major European countries in relation to football, as well as nations within states (such as Corsica) and speculative chapters on the future of football and European identity in relation to Africa, America and Asia.

Smith, E. (2008) *What Sport Tells Us About Life*, London: Viking. Light but penetrating excursus which poses some of the unasked questions of sport.

References

Anon. (2007) 'English Football Scores Big in Africa', *The Economist*, 3 November.

Anon. (2008a) 'In Fact', *Prospect*, January.

Anon. (2008b) 'Sven Runs Footie Bingo Nights', *Sun*, 6 March.

BARB (Broadcasters Audience Research Board) www.barb.co.uk/ (accessed 20 October 2007).

Barclay, P. (2005) 'Psycho Turns Psychologist', *Daily Telegraph*, 4 December.

Barclay, P. (2008) 'Power Play', *Sunday Telegraph*, 10 February.

Barnes, S. (2007) 'Column', *The Times*, 23 September.

Benjamin, W. (1999) (trans. H. Eiland and K. McLaughlin) *The Arcades Project*, Cambridge, MA: The Belknap Press.

Blain, N. (2003) 'Beyond "Media Culture": Sport as Dispersed Symbolic Activity' in A. Bernstein and N. Blain (eds) *Sport, Media, Culture: Global and Local Dimensions*, London: Frank Cass, pp. 227–54.

Blain, N. and O'Donnell, H. (1998) 'Living Without the *Sun*: European Sports Journalism and its Readers During Euro '96', in M. Roche (ed) *Sport, Popular Culture and Identity*, Aachen: Meyer and Meyer, pp. 37–56.

Bond, D. (2008) 'Michael Platini Slams Premier League's Plan', *Daily Telegraph*, 9 February.

Boyle, R. (2006) *Sports Journalism: Context and Issues*, London: Sage.

Boyle, R. and Haynes, R. (2009) *Power Play: Sport, the Media and Popular Culture*, 2nd edition, Edinburgh: Edinburgh University Press.

Boyle, R., Rowe, D. and Whannel, G. (2009) 'A Crass Lack of Seriousness? Questions for Sports Journalism', in S. Allan (ed) *The Routledge Companion to News and Journalism Studies*, London: Routledge.

Boyes, R. (2006) 'Sour Krauts? Not a Bit of It', *The Times*, 21 December.

Brookes, R. (2002) *Representing Sport*, London: Arnold.

Carter, N. (2007) 'Managing the Media: The Changing Relationship between Football Managers and the Media', *Sport in History*, 27 (2): 217–40.

Crolley, L. and Hand, D. (2006) *Football and European Identity: Historical Narratives Through the Press*, London: Routledge.

Foer, F. (2004) *How Soccer Explains the World: An Unlikely Theory of Globalization*, New York: HarperCollins.

Fricker, M. (2008) 'Fabio Capello's Hairdryer Is Stolen from Wembley Dressing Room', *Daily Mirror*, 9 February.

Goldblatt, D. (2007) *The Ball is Round: A Global History of Football*, London: Penguin.

Harvey, D. (1990) *The Condition of Postmodernity*, Oxford: Blackwell.

Hawkey, I. (2007) 'Don't Fool with Fabio Capello', *Sunday Times*, 16 December.

Hobsbawm, E. (2007) *Globalisation, Democracy and Terrorism*, London: Little, Brown.

King, A. (2003) *The European Ritual: Football in the New Europe*, Aldershot: Ashgate.

Moore, G. (2008) 'Premier League Plans Games Overseas in Bid to Rule World', *Independent*, 8 February.

Mott, S. (2008) 'All We Know Is Money Lurks Behind Scudamore's Plan', *Daily Telegraph*, 12 February.

Oliver, B. (2007a) 'Sport Gears Up for Global Revolution', *The Observer*, 28 October.

Oliver, B. (2007b) '21st Century Sport: New World Order', *The Observer*, 18 November.

Prahalad, C. K. (2004) *The Fortune at the Bottom of the Pyramid: Eradicating Poverty Through Profits*, Philadelphia: Wharton School Publishing.

Press Gazette (2008) 'Murdoch Tells WSJ Execs: "Shorter stories, more sport"', 17 January.

Rich, T. (2008) 'Fans Yet to Be Convinced by Capello's England', *Daily Telegraph*, 7 February.

Robertson, R. (1992) *Globalization*, London: Sage.

Rowe, D. (2004) *Sport, Culture and the Media*, Maidenhead: Open University Press.

Saldaña, M. Muñoz (2008) 'The Future of Public Service Broadcasting in Community Law', *International Journal of Media and Cultural Politics*, 4 (2): 203–21.

Samuel, M. (2008) 'Greed Will Drive Premier League to More Than 39th Step', *The Times*, 13 February.

Smith, A. (2007) 'It's a Brand-honed Team to Play For', *Scotland on Sunday*, 1 July.

Smith, E. (2008) *What Sport Tells Us About Life*, London: Viking.

Steen, R. (2008) *Sports Journalism: A Multi-media Primer*, London: Routledge.

William, J. (2007) 'Rethinking Sports Fandom: The Case of European Soccer', *Leisure Studies*, 26 (2): 127–46.

Winter, H. (2005) 'Ireland Shatter Eriksson's Jigsaw', *Daily Telegraph*, 7 September.

Wyett, C. (2008) 'What On Earth Is Going On?', *Sun*, 9 February.

36

Sex Acts

Brian McNair

Chapter overview

This chapter gives an account of the history of the representation of sexual activity. From the ancient cultures of Greece and Rome, through the invention of pornography, to the contemporary 'pornographication' of mainstream culture, the chapter explores the links between sexual representation and media technology, and the changing attitudes to censorship and regulation which have accompanied the evolution of sexual culture. We also consider the appropriation of explicit sexual imagery by artists, film-makers and others, and the part played by these images in the politics of feminism and gay liberation.

Introduction

There has never been more sex visible in the media than we find today in the liberal democracies of the advanced capitalist world. In Europe, north and Latin America, Asia and Australasia, representation of all matters relating to sexuality, including the sex act itself – has become a common feature of a range of media, including cinema, the internet, television and print. In the space of a few decades we have moved from a position where such images were prohibited everywhere except in what John Ellis once called the 'pariah' realm of pornography (1992), and then only in the more liberal countries of Western Europe and north America, to a state of intense cultural sexualisation – what I have elsewhere called the 'pornographication' of mainstream culture (McNair 2002) – in which the explicit representation of sexual activity is no longer remarkable.

In 2007, to give an example from personal experience of just how far this process has gone, this author attended a Saturday afternoon screening of the film *Shortbus* (Cameron Mitchell 2006) at the Glasgow Film Theatre. Having read reviews of the film, I was not completely unprepared for the relatively graphic depiction of sexual activity which features heavily in *Shortbus*, but was nevertheless startled by the matter-of-fact inclusion of scenes depicting auto-fellatio, heterosexual and gay penetration, group sex, masturbation and sadomasochism, all in the context of what was essentially a light comedy. Although this film, like Michael Winterbottom's *9 Songs* (2004) and others before it, was trailed as 'the most explicit mainstream (i.e. non-pornographic) film ever made', and not without justification, it was notable that it produced neither critical controversy nor a hostile public reception on its release in the UK. Not even in the morally conservative city of Glasgow, which banned Terry Jones' *The Life of Brian* in the 1970s, and where feminists around the same time picketed Brian De Palma's *Dressed To Kill* (1980) because of its sexualised violence and perceived misogyny. (*9 Songs* was described on its release as 'the most sexually explicit film in the history of mainstream cinema' (Higgins 2004). For a discussion of the film and others of a sexually explicit nature released around that time see McNair 2004.) Like *9 Songs*, which screened in multiplexes in the UK, and before that Gaspar Noe's *Irreversible* (2002) and Lukas Moodyson's *A Hole In My Heart* (2005), and even *Baise-Moi* (Despentes and Trinh Thi 2003), the feminist rape-revenge thriller, all containing genuinely boundary-breaking material, it arrived in a climate where the explicit representation of sex had become an accepted feature of mainstream culture. The problem for *Shortbus* and other films depicting explicit sexual activity today is not that adverse publicity might lead to censorship or banning of the work, but that very few cinema goers are sufficiently interested in the subject that they can be enticed into the cinema.

This chapter explores how we got to this position, why it has happened, and how the process of cultural sexualisation has proceeded in different countries and across different media.

The history of sex acts in the media

The compulsion to represent sexual behaviour, using any available means or media, seems to be a universal feature of human societies, evidence for which is found wherever records of cultural activity survive. Prehistoric cave paintings often include images of sexual intercourse, as do paintings and artefacts found in the ancient ruins of Pompeii and Herculaem. Eroticised, explicit images of sexual intercourse occur in early Chinese, Indian and Japanese art. Human culture, in short, has always represented sex, and often in quite explicit ways.

The content of these images has varied according to the religious and moral codes of the societies which produced them. Thus, the polytheic culture of ancient Rome was comfortable with the concept of dining room paintings and tableware depicting people having sex. The ancient Greeks depicted 'boy love' as well as heterosexual activity on their pottery, reflecting that society's homophilic conventions. The rise of judeo-christianity in Europe, on the other hand, and the Augustinian strand of sexual puritanism in particular, brought in its wake a much more censorial attitude to sexuality and its representation. The early history of religious censorship of sexual representation is long and complex (see Chapter 22), and here we need note only that by the 16th century in Europe the Catholic Church's moral objection to sexual activity outside prescribed limits (i.e. marriage) extended to the depiction of sex in anything but the most asexual of terms. For the Catholic Church, at that time the dominant religious and political institution in Europe, the sex act was sacred, sanctified by God and impermissible without His blessing through the sacrament of marriage. Sex outside of marriage (adultery), homosexual sex (sodomy) and other practices were prohibited, as with rare exceptions were their depiction in culture.

The urgency with which the church policed these moral laws intensified with the invention and early spread of mass print media in the 15th and 16th centuries, when for the first time the relatively inexpensive multiple reproduction of images became possible. Where access to sexually explicit words and images had previously been restricted to the very wealthy who could afford to purchase or trade in hand-crafted books and art works, the invention of the printing press transformed the cultural environment in Europe and expanded the potential audience for media to thousands, hundreds of thousands, millions. In so doing, the emerging print media made images of all kinds, including those of a sexual nature, potentially much more dangerous, because more widely viewed. For the Pope in Rome, who around this time published the first list of banned books, it was axiomatic that words and pictures deemed subversive in various ways (morally or politically) could make those who accessed them more likely to challenge the authority of the church. For the first time, if certainly not the last, the emergence of a new communication technology was the cause of an upsurge in sexually explicit representation. Indeed, it is true to say that technological change and the spread of images of sexual activity are intimately connected. From the cave painting to the printing press to the moving image to the digital file, the capacity to make and communicate images of the sex act has often been the 'killer application' which drives a technology to the heart of a culture. More people, it is estimated, have used the internet for accessing pornography than any other category of image. When the web was still a minority interest without obvious commercial viability, online porn was one of the few things people would pay for.

The rise of pornography

And as it was with the internet, so too with the book. In the early 16th century Italian author and artist Pietro Aretino pioneered the depiction of sex in print by publishing his 'Sonnets' to accompany a series of sexually explicit engravings by an artist associate. Aretino's sonnets sold like hot cakes, provoked outrage in Rome, and were duly banned by the Pope. For cultural historian Lynn Hunt, Aretino thus became the first pornographer, in that his representations of sex 'brought together several crucial elements to form the basis of the pornographic tradition . . . particularly the explicit representation of sexual activity . . . and the challenge to moral conventions of the day' (Hunt 1993: 26).

Pornography then, as now, was characterised by the representation of the sex act for its own sake, unadorned by distractions such as plot, character development, or concern with aesthetic effect. Aretino's sonnets, like Larry Flynt's *Hustler* models, were about sex in the raw, depicted in transgressively graphic terms, and intended to sexually arouse the viewer. The sonnets celebrated sexuality in all its dirtiness and raunch – a defining feature of the pornographic text ever since.

Aretino's work, and that of the French pre-revolutionary artists and writers discussed in Lynn Hunt's book, also had a satirical element, often depicting members of the allegedly corrupt elite in explicit, exposed poses. Representation of the sex act became in this context a political instrument in the long road to the overthrow of the European aristocracies, subjecting aristocratic and clerical authority to ritual humiliation, stripping it literally naked before the ever more vocal masses. The desire to comment on the elite of his time was also a source of inspiration for the Marquis de Sade, whose disturbing (some would say disturbed) sexual imagination laid waste not only to religious notions of the sanctity of sex, but the hypocrisy and cruelty of the French ruling class. Sade's 'cataloguing of perversions', as his writings have been accurately characterised, anticipated modern pornography in their relentless focus on the sex act, and the progression towards greater and greater sexual excess in their transgressive narratives. (For a dramatised account of the life of Sade, see Philip Kaufman's *Quills* (2000), starring Geoffrey Rush as the Marquis. The film portrays Sade as a libertarian free thinker rebelling against the moral structures of the French religious establishment, and glosses over the well-documented ugliness and abusiveness of his sexual philosophy.) We will see below how the representation of sex again became politicised, two centuries later in the struggles for women's and gay liberation.

Before that, however, we note that in the four and a bit centuries since Aretino's sonnets first shocked the religious establishment in Europe, through Sade, Boccaccio, James Read, John Cleland and many others, the representation of sexual activity in literature and visual media has been the site of fierce public debate, often leading to censorship and other forms of control by the state. To the extent that such images have been judged offensive and/or obscene, they have been policed, restricted, banned, particularly in the context of the most popular media. The severity of control over the content of sexual representation has tended to be in proportion to the size and presumed educational level of the audience – thus, free-to-air, prime time TV has always been subject to greater controls than magazines, or books, or films for cinema release, or the literary works of authors such as the Marquis de Sade, whose explicit, violently transgressive sexual fantasies have long been freely available in bookshops and university libraries, branded as literary 'classics'. The explicit representation of sex acts found in such films as *9 Songs* and John Cameron Mitchell's *Shortbus* provoked little adverse public reaction because, although they *were* screened in mainstream multiplex cinemas, they were received as 'art house' movies, of little interest to the popcorn and hot dog crowd watching *Spiderman III* on the screen next door. Notwithstanding the broad cultural sexualisation which has occurred in all liberal capitalist societies since the 1960s, and which affects all media in all countries to a greater or lesser extent, images which are perceived to have been produced for cultural elites rather than the broad masses – 'art house' movies, for example, or the sexually explicit artworks of a Nobuyoshi Araki or a Jeff Koons – are able to get way with more, on the assumption that their audiences are less vulnerable to corruption by the lewd images they contain. The only exception to this general rule is sexually explicit art involving children, or art that is any way interpretable as sexualising children. Such images, whether 'innocent' or not, retain the power to provoke moral panic and censorship, as did American photographer Tierney Gearon's images of her children at play (removed by the UK police from the Saatchi Gallery in 2001), and Robert Mapplethorpe's naked portraits of children (singled out for censure by American moral conservatives in the 'culture wars' of the 1980s). The continuing 'pariah' status of sexualised images of children (or images which are perceived to be sexualised – not always the same thing) reflects current anxieties around paedophilia and child abuse which have provided moral conservatives in the media and elsewhere with the justification to attack certain artists and their work.

Such attacks are notable for their rarity, however. In the art world today, it is indeed the case that almost anything goes, be it the extreme and bloody sado-masochism of Mapplethorpe's *X Portfolio*, Jeff Koons and Cicciolina having sex in the blown up, high-definition photography of *Made In Heaven*, or Andres Serrano's equally glossy images of uroglania and other fetishistic sex acts. All of these and more can be found in any art book or museum shop.

Sex acts in the 20th century

From the time of Aretino's sonnets and engravings, the form in which sex acts are represented, and the accessibility of the resulting texts, has been determined by the state of media technology, the media marketplace, and the prevailing cultural conditions. All three factors, linked as they are, have been important in determining what can be shown, and to whom, in the field of sexuality. As a statement of the general trend, we can say that, over time, the representation of sex acts has become on the one hand more graphic and realistic, and on the other more accessible to more and more people.

Following the invention of the printing press, and with it the availability of cheap books and reproductions of visual images, followed by the invention of photography in the mid-19th century, explicit sexual representation spread throughout the early modern societies of Europe and America, leading to the emergence of the category of 'pornography'. As noted above, the representation of sex acts goes back to prehistoric human culture, and is commonplace in Roman and Greek antiquity, but in these societies it was not called 'pornography', with all the connotations associated with that term.

The word 'pornography' is usually linked back to the Greek words for 'prostitute' and 'writing', and loosely translated as 'writing about whores' (McNair 1996). The term first appears as a reference to explicit representations of sexual activity in the early 19th century, at a time when such images were first being subjected to scholarly, scientific analysis by archaeologists and others as they explored the ruins of Pompeii and Herculaem. For Walter Kendrick (1987), the gradual adoption of the term 'pornography' to describe a forbidden, morally dangerous category of image reflected the sincere desire of the educated, wealthy elites of Victorian-era Europe to protect the uneducated working classes, women and other groups they deemed vulnerable to moral corruption. In Foucault's terms, the emergence of something called pornography, to be classified and locked away in what Kendrick called the 'secret museums' of Victorian-era Europe, was part of that explosion of discourse about sex which also produced the pseudo-science of sexology, and the idea of homosexuality as an illness or condition to be treated.

Obscenity legislation was used to prohibit the circulation of naughty postcards and 'dirty books' from the mid-19th century onwards, extending into the 20th century. Pornography was hidden away, safe from the gaze of the easily-corrupted masses, pushed to the cultural underground, where it remained until the late 20th century. For the first half of the 20th century, throughout Europe and north America, moral crusaders such as Anthony Comstock ran institutions such as the Society for the Suppression of Vice to combat sexual representation, fearful that without censorship of the sexual, stable family life would collapse.

Censored or not, however, images of the sex act spread and evolved with each new wave of communications technology. The invention of the moving image in the late 19th century saw the first pornographic films, or 'stag reels', come into circulation in Europe (Tang 1999). Illegal, of course, stag reels were watched in covert, largely male environments such as smoking clubs and salons. Their content and viewing context exemplified all of the elements of straight male pornography as we know it today – a focus on sex for its own sake, as viewed from the male perspective. Thus, the objects of desire in stag reels were nearly always women, engaged in sexual acts such as masturbation, striptease or sex with other women and men. The representation of sex was undertaken almost exclusively by and for men. In conditions of patriarchy – societies in which men have superiority over women in respect of political, economic, social and cultural power – women's sexuality was invisible, denied. Women, to the extent that they were acknowledged to have any sexual desires, were expected to keep them hidden away from public view, and certainly not to indulge them through the use of pornography. For them to do so would lead, it was argued, to their moral corruption, and put the family and society at risk.

As pornography in the twentieth century adapted to the new technologies of cheap colour photography, video, cable TV and the internet, it retained this masculinist, heterosexist perspective, or gaze, typically objectifying the female body for the benefit of the male spectator. A content staple of moving image pornography became the 'money shot' – the external, thus visible ejaculation of the male on (rather than in) the body of the female (Williams 1990). Today, a major subgenre of pornography – bukkake – is devoted entirely to this particular act, sometimes involving dozens of men ejaculating on one woman.

Feminist critiques of pornography have understandably focused on the instrumentalism and inherent male-ness of this representational trope, noting that it presumes only the sexual release of the male, and indeed shows this in literal manner, placing it at the structural core of the pornographic narrative. The man in the movie or photo-spread comes, and thus achieves sexual satisfaction. The female is merely the object of his ejaculation, her skin the surface where it splatters messily, the visible evidence of his orgasm. Her own sexual pleasure is ignored, or presumed to derive from the act of satisfying her man in this passive, receptive manner. Only a man, say anti-porn feminists, could find this scenario erotic or satisfying.

As pornography evolved in the 20th century – an era of virtually unquestioned patriarchal hegemony, reflected in all aspects of culture – this male heterosexism remained dominant. Anti-porn feminists argued that sexist objectification of women was essential to the form, which was thus implicated in the broader subordination of women within patriarchy. To the older moral and religious prohibitions on explicit sexual representation was added the political objection that it was reactionary, oppressive, exploitative – the 'theory' underpinning the practice of rape, as feminist Robin Morgan famously expressed it. Throughout the 1970s and for most of the 1980s this reading of the pornographic dominated feminism, and those liberal men who wished to support feminism.

The late 20th history of pornography has challenged that reading of the form, however. Following the stag reel, pornography spread through its adoption by successive technologies – colour printing, video, cable and satellite TV. At the same time as technology made porn ever more accessible, the sexual revolution which began in the 1960s in the West made it more socially and culturally acceptable, albeit in some countries more than others. In Germany, Sweden, Denmark and the Netherlands, for example, the sexual liberalism of the 1960s and 1970s led early on to the emergence of legal, sexually explicit material in the public domain. Pornography depicting the sex act without censorship appeared in colour magazines such as those produced by Rodox and sold legally in sex shops in Amsterdam and Copenhagen. 'Educational' films about sexual behaviour, mainly made in Scandinavia, graphically depicted the sex act for the first time in 'proper' cinemas.

In America and Britain, the sexual revolution inaugurated a process which led to more and more explicit magazines coming on to the mass market, the best known and most notorious of these being Larry Flynt's *Hustler*. As Milos Forman's Oscar-winning movie *The People Versus Larry Flynt* depicts (1996), it was Flynt who took explicit sexual representation – hard core pornography, as it came to be classified (as distinct from soft core, which was much less explicit) – out of the underground and into the local convenience store and newspaper booth. Where 'soft core' porn showed the female body in relatively discrete and modest poses, hard core of the type pioneered in *Hustler* depicted models with their legs spread wide, vaginas exposed. Hard core porn, in magazines and movies, showed people having 'messy' sex as opposed to the 'varnished' movie sex.

In the early 1970s, films such as Gerard Damiano's *Deep Throat* took overtly, unapologetically pornographic content into the mainstream, in what was the first wave of 'porno-chic'. *Deep Throat* packed out box offices in New York and other American cities in the early 1970s, not only with the heterosexual men hitherto associated with the form, but 'respectable' women, retired people and others curious to see this strange tale of a woman with a clitoris in her throat.

The absurd plot of *Deep Throat*, and the anatomically impossible sex acts it depicts, reinforces the feminist critique of pornography as a fundamentally flawed form. What could be more sexist than a scenario in which a woman can achieve orgasm only by 'deep throating' the male member? And what could be more sexist than the infamous *Hustler* cover of a woman being 'fed' into a mince-making machine?

But the sexual revolution, and the cultural sexualisation which it encouraged, was not only a movement affecting straight men. Alongside sexual liberalisation in general went an emerging feminist movement, and the birth of gay liberation. If the former was founded among other things on the critique of pornography as outlined above, it also created the conditions for the 1980s split within feminism which produced the pro-porn perspectives of such as Pat Califia, Lynn Segal and then, in the popular cultural arena, Madonna and the many female artists and performers subsequently influenced by her. Feminism, for all that it was still dominated by anti-porn perspectives, had by the 1980s given rise to a cultural environment in which newly empowered, sexually confident and assertive women could produce and consume pornographic images, and be open about the pleasures to be derived from such consumption. Porn was still largely by and for straight men (as it remains today), but the notion that *only* men could or should enjoy it was eroding under the influence of expanded feminist notions of female sexuality. The idea that no true feminist could enjoy sex with a man, or enjoy looking at pictures of sex – long a core theme of anti-porn feminism, particularly in its more extreme variants – gradually gave way to the recognition that female and male sexualities were equally capable of being aroused by the transgressive, objectifying, instrumental content of porn. By the early 1990s the anti-porn hegemony of such as Andrea Dworkin and Catharine Mackinnon had given way to the pro-porn playfulness of Madonna's *Sex* book (1992), in which she is depicted having sex with men, women, and groups of both, not to mention rape fantasies and even the suggestion of bestiality.

Madonna was the pop cultural expression of the idea first floated by the pro-porn, anti-censorship feminists of the early 1980s, that women wanted access to the same kinds of sexual representation as men had grown used to since the sexual revolution. From this idea stemmed not only Madonna's sexually explicit songs, videos and photographic work, but the subsequent era of rather more sanitised female stars such as Janet Jackson, Britney Spears, Christina Aguilera and Kylie Minogue. Although these stars did not make pornography, they represented a female sexuality which delighted in provocative displays of semi-nudity and self-objectification, as did their female fans. As the 1990s progressed and became the Noughties, feminist critics such as Catharine Mackinnon, and Ariel Levy in her *Female Chauvinist Pigs* (2005) condemned what they characterised as 'raunch culture', arguing that it was a betrayal of feminism's achievements, a step backward to an earlier, pre-feminist era in which women were reduced to being the playthings of men. A more widespread anxiety focused on the apparently decreasing age of the young women and girls who were participating in this 'raunch culture', as teenagers stepped out with T-shirts proclaiming 'porn star', went shopping for the skimpiest of thongs, or taught themselves pole dancing for their boyfriends. Cultural sexualisation, it was argued, was leading to the inappropriate sexualisation of children and young adults.

If 'post-feminism', for better or worse, ended the heterosexist, masculinist monopoly of the pornographic which had been a feature of the form since the Victorian era, the gay movement, increasingly politicised and assertive after the Stonewall riots of June 1969 in New York, contributed its own desires and demands for pornographic expression. Homosexual men had always used what one commentator (Waugh 1996) calls 'fuck photos' for erotic stimulation and expression of identity, although these had of necessity been illegal, underground images. From the 1970s gay porn developed as an important sub-sector of the expanding legal market place in pornography. In gay villages such as the Castro district in San Francisco, gay porn stores flourished. In Amsterdam, sex shops routinely stocked gay as well as straight hard core porn.

Gay porn, and porn-for-women, were still porn as defined above – the representation of sex acts with the intention of provoking sexual arousal in the viewer/reader, in contexts largely devoid of plot, production values, or aesthetic worth. In the late 20th century, however, it became clear that it was not just the predatory patriarchal male of anti-porn feminist dogma who used porn, or desired to, but also gay men, gay women, straight women and couples.

From porn to art: sexual representation in non-pornographic culture

As a consequence of the 1960s 'sexual revolution' pornography expanded and diversified into the vast industry we see today, segmented into every conceivable sub-market (and some which it is hard for most to conceive as having anything to do with eroticism – amputee porn, anyone?). Where there is a sexual taste or desire, there will in the early 21st century, be a corner of the pornography market – what I have elsewhere called the 'porno-sphere' (McNair 2002) – where it can be gratified. With the rise of the internet as the latest and most efficient technology for the distribution of images, the legal–illegal distinction has become increasingly meaningless, as consumers of porn access online providers anywhere in the world. Only the production and consumption of child pornography, like the art discussed above which can be read, accurately or not, as sexualising children, is seriously policed in a consistent and rigorous manner. The pornographic representation of the sex act between consenting adults is today, in most liberal capitalist societies, routine, commonplace, unremarkable.

The technology-driven spread of pornography, and the sexual politics paralleling that trend, has remained within what is still a distinct porno-sphere, or cultural zone where such images are expected and, with variations determined by local conditions (some contemporary Islamic societies, for example, compare to the medieval societies of Europe in their strict prohibition on sexual representation of any kind), permitted. The porno-sphere of online sites, magazines, DVDs and movies has expanded and diversified in its depiction of the sex act to accommodate almost every taste and fetishistic fantasy, but it remains porn. 'We know it when we see it', to paraphrase that US Supreme court judge in an earlier era, when asked to define pornography. And we rarely see it in the mainstream cultural sphere of free-to-air TV, or journalism, advertising, cinema and so on. There has, however, been a *pornographication* of mainstream culture, by which I mean the infiltration into the mainstream of discourses *about* porn, of references *to* porn, of fashion and music trends influenced *by* porn, documentaries and parodies and pastiches *of* porn. This phase peaked in the early 1990s, when magazines such as *US* could run an entire edition devoted to 'Sex in entertainment: how far can it go?'.

In Britain in 1994, the public service Channel 4 ran a series of 42 documentaries and films about sex – the *Red Light Zone* – which frequently contained representations of the act itself. Subsequently, Channel 4 and other broadcasters produced and transmitted documentaries, docu-soaps and even musicals about porn and other sexual themes. Being 'not-porn' – these texts were clearly distinguished from the pornographic representation of sex, although they were *about* that representation – their images of the sex act were not explicit in the hard core sense, but suggestive. In *Pornography: the musical*, for example, a porn star was interviewed before and after a watersports session, in which urine-soaked sheets and hair were clear evidence of the act having occurred. Louis Theroux' *Weird Weekends* edition for BBC 2, devoted to the Los Angeles porn industry, filmed people making porn, although the sex was largely edited out of the cut transmitted on TV. In Europe similarly-themed programmes were made, such as a 1997 edition of Norwegian documentary strand *Puck* in which this author himself appeared.

Mainstream cinema also engaged in this kind of meta-discourse around pornography, in films such as Paul Thomas Anderson's *Boogie Nights* (1997) and the aforementioned *People versus Larry Flynt*. As I have suggested elsewhere (McNair 2002), these were films about the porn industry and the people who worked in it, as well as the issues which porn and cultural sexualisation in general had generated for public debate. Thus *Larry Flynt* was a film about freedom of speech; while *Boogie Nights*, like all of Paul Thomas Anderson's films up to his Oscar winning *There Will Be Blood*, was about dysfunctional child–parent relationships and the human longing for family. Such films, made in Hollywood with major stars and shown to multiplex audiences around the world, depicted variants of the sex act, often in the context of addressing issues around pornography, but without the graphic, intentionally arousing qualities of pornography itself.

More recently, however, in films made in Europe, Asia, north and Latin America, a further cultural boundary has been crossed, as films which are not 'pornographic' (at least in the eyes of their makers) become more and more explicit in their representation of the sex act. Landmark films in this category include Lars Von Triers's *The Idiots* (1997), Catherine Breillat's *Romance* (1999) and Patrice Chereau's *Intimacy* (2001). All of these works showed the sex act – fellatio, penetration, and other variations – in unflinchingly graphic terms. Rarely were they received as erotically stimulating films, instead deploying sexual representation as a vehicle for exploring relationships, societal attitudes towards disability, female sexuality, and the nature of the pornography industry. Lukas Moodyson's *A Hole In My Heart* (2004) explored the amateur end of that porn industry, depicting various extreme sex acts as they were played out in a dingy flat in Denmark. Such films became increasingly common in the Noughties, being made not just in Europe but also in Korea, Mexico and other countries. In 2006, as noted above, the US production *Shortbus* (John Cameron Mitchell) was released. Like almost all of this new wave of sexually explicit, non-pornographic movies, its sexual content was only incidentally arousing, and as 'art house' cinema, proved uncontroversial. So advanced was cultural sexualisation by this time that graphic scenes of gay and straight group sex, masturbation and sadomasochism were of little interest to the broad movie-going public, or to those who in earlier decades would have picketed cinemas and launched campaigns to prevent such scenes being shown.

Away from the art house, the trend towards more graphic sexual representation gradually fed into the big budget, mainstream movie industry. Jane Campion's *In the Cut* (2003) drew critical attention for its explicit content, but the most dramatic example of the trend as of this writing was Ang Lee's *Lust, Caution* (2007). Having worked successfully in many movie genres, and broken mainstream movie ground with his gay love story, *Brokeback Mountain*, the Oscar-winning, Taiwanese-born director adapted Ellen Cheung's short story, including in his screenplay a number of scenes which were, by the standards of Hollywood (and even more so of China, where it was co-produced) boundary-breaking. In his review of the film, Philip Kemp wrote in *Sight & Sound* magazine that 'if the much debated sex scenes are anything to go by, Lee could well become the finest porno director of all time. The scenes are not only totally credible in their context, but carry a fiercely erotic charge rarely seen in mainstream cinema' (Kemp 2008: 72).

Conclusion

Thus, we end with a director famous among other things for his adaptation of a Jane Austen novel, being described, and without obvious disapproval by an expert critic, as a potentially fine director of porn. Where Ang Lee has gone, others will follow, and the explicit representation of the sex act is likely to become, even more than it is today, a feature of the movie and pop cultural environment as routine as a kiss in a teenage rom-com.

Questions

1 What, if anything, distinguishes the representation of the sex act in films such as *Shortbus* and *The Idiots*, and that seen in pornography?

2 Is it true to say that the dissemination of explicit sexual imagery has been a driver of communication technology down the ages?

3 What, if any arguments would you present for attempts to censor and restrict sexual representation in the 21st century? Can censorship succeed as a control strategy in the era of the internet?

Further reading

Ellis, J. (1992) 'On pornography', *The Sexual Subject*, London: Routledge, pp. 146-70. Groundbreaking and still influential attempt to define pornography as the 'pariah of representational practice'.

Hunt, L. (1993) *The Invention of Pornography*, New York: Zone Books. Account of the emergence of the category of 'pornography' in early modern Europe.

Levy, A. (2005) *Female Chauvinist Pigs: Women and the Rise of Raunch Culture*, New York: Free Press. A much-discussed attack on so-called 'raunch culture'.

McNair, B. (2002) *Striptease Culture: Sex, Media and the Democratisation of Desire*, London: Routledge. Book-length study of contemporary sexual culture, including pornography, porno-chic, and other forms of explicit sexual representation.

Tang, I. (1999) *Pornography: The Secret History of Civilisation*, London: Channel 4 Books. Excellent history of sexual culture, from antiquity to the internet. Published to accompany the Channel 4 series of the same name.

References

Ellis, J. (1992) 'On Pornography', *The Sexual Subject*, London: Routledge: 146-70.

Hunt, L. (1993) *The Invention of Pornography*, New York: Zone Books.

Kemp, P. (2008) 'Lust, Caution', film review, *Sight & Sound*, February.

Kendrick, W. (1987) *The Secret Museum*, New York: Viking.

Levy, A. (2005) *Female Chauvinist Pigs: Women and the Rise of Raunch Culture*, New York: Free Press.

McNair, B. (1996) *Mediated Sex: Pornography and Postmodern Culture*, London: Arnold.

McNair, B. (2002) *Striptease Culture: Sex, Media and the Democratisation of Desire*, London: Routledge.

McNair, B. (2004) 'Not Some Kind of Kinky Porno Flick: The Return of Porno-fear?', *Bridge*, August/September, 16-19.

Madonna (1992) *Sex*, London: Secker & Warburg.

Tang, I. (1999) *Pornography: The Secret History of Civilisation*, London: Channel 4 Books.

US (the entertainment magazine) (1992) 'Sex in Entertainment: How Far Can It Go?', *US*, 175, August.

Waugh, T. (1996) *Hard to Imagine*, New York: Columbia University Press.

Williams, L. (1990) *Hard Core: Power, Pleasure and the Frenzy of the Visible*, Berkeley, CA: University of California Press.

Index

'3 for 2' policy 111
4Digital 170–1, 172
9/11 attacks 40–3, 459, 461, 465, 466–7
Abercrombie, N. 21
Abrahaimian, E. 465, 467
active audiences 381–90
  questioning media and cultural studies
    research on audiences 387–90
  uses and gratifications versus media and
    cultural studies 383–7
adaptive contracting 286–7
Adlibris 113
Adorno, T. 18–19, 315
Advanced Research Projects Agency 221
advertising 55–6, 258–72
  audience research 339
  authenticity and the audience 261–5
  display 264
  embedded 264
  expenditure 259–61, 265, 269
  fragmentation and segmentation 270–1
  and gender 418–23
  growth and transformation 258–61
  institutions 268–70
  and market relationships 265–8
  newspapers 143–4
  photography 93
  radio 168
  revenue 269
  tenancies 264
Advertising Standards Agency 403
Africa 195
Africa Cinemas 192
AGB Nielsen Media Research 338
age 360, 416, 514
Agence France Presse 235, 239
agenda setting 445, 462
aggregator news service 251
aggression, priming 361–2
Aims of Industry 122
Akdeniz, Y. 403

Aksoy, A. 446
Al Jazeera 253
Alasuutari, P. 21
Albertazzi, D. 1–11, 13–14, 75, 277–9, 333–4
Allan, S. 254, 255
Allen, K. 162, 168
Allen Lane publishers 107
Althusser, L. 20
Amato, R. 403
Amazon 287–8
  'Kindle Reader' 6, 115, 116
Americanisation 309–10, 475–6
Anderson, A. 121, 128
Anderson, B. 506–7, 514
Anderson, C.A. 113, 360, 361, 362,
    363, 364
Ang, I. 22, 29, 307, 383–5, 386, 387–8
Annan, Lord/Report 338, 451
ANSAMed 238
AOL-Time Warner 208
Appadurai, A. 513
Apple:
  i-phone 287
  iTunes 215
approaches 15–30
  ethnographic 21–2
  feminist 28–30
  Frankfurt School 18–19
  ideology 19–21
  Marxist 16–17
  political economy 17–18
  psychoanalytical 23–5
  semiotic 25–8
  uses and gratifications 22–3
APTV 240
Archer, J. 364
ARD 66, 67
Armstrong 499
Arnold, B. 156
Arnold, R. 99
ARPANET 221–3

ARTE 197
Asia 154, 195, 200, 412, 543
Aslama, M. 512–13
Association of European Journalists
    (AEJ) 110, 321–2
Astérix 79–80
Atton, C. 212, 248
audience:
    conceptualisations 385–6
    fragmentation 55
    reception work 374–6
    see also active audiences; audience research
audience research 335–52, 376–7
    film audience measurement and
        evaluation 346–7
    historical background of broadcasting 337
    hours, average 343
    hours, total 343
    internet and digital media 348–50
    measurement of readership 345–6
    mobile devices 350–1
    newspaper and magazine readership 345
    posters 347–8
    purposes 336–7
    radio 342–5
    Target Group Index 348
    television 338–42
Audio-visual Media Services Directive 301
Audit Bureau of Circulation 160
Austin, J. 473
Australia 53, 361, 416
Australian Associated Press 242–3
Austria 70, 71, 110, 114, 194, 198, 311
'Auteur Cinema' 190
authoritarian theory 62
Auton, S. 162
Autry, J. 161
Average Issue Readership 346
Azenha, G. 208, 216

BAA 132
Badger, G. 93
Baltic States 325
Bandura, A. 356, 357
Banks, J. 214
Banksy 93
banlieues 432, 433–7
banners 264
Bantam Books 107
Baran, P. 222
Barclay, P. 527, 529

Barfe, L. 207
Barnabei, E. 310
Barnard, A. 169
Barnard, S. 210
Barnes and Noble 115
Barnes, S. 528
Barnett, S. 130
Baron, M. 167
Barry, A. 448
Barthes, R. 26, 39, 82, 90, 91, 99
Batchen, G. 89, 90, 91, 102
Battelle, J. 226
Bauer (company) 155–6, 172
Bauer, M.W. 493
Bazin, A. 90, 91
BBC 48, 64–5, 165–6, 183, 340
    audience research 337, 338, 343, 352
    economics 285, 288–9
    Licence Agreement 319–20
    Multicultural Department 452
    national identity 507–8
    news media 252
    public service broadcasting (PSB) 308, 310,
        313–14
    race/ethnicity 446, 449
    radio 170, 171, 172
    Royal Charter 309
    sport 523–4
    trust issues 186
Beaud, S. 431
Becker, K.E. 100–1
Beder, S. 123
Begag, A. 432
beginning-of-life issues 487–92
Belarus 70, 71
Belfield, R. 324–5
Belgium 49, 111, 311
    cinema/film 191, 194, 198
    comics 78, 80, 81
Bellos, A. 124
Belson, W.A. 364
Benedict, H. 414, 415–16
Benedictus, L. 262
Benelux countries 80, 311
Benjamin, W. 18, 19, 90, 91, 227, 526
Bentham, J. 95
Benwell, B. 29, 412
Berger, A.A. 23, 24
Berger, W. 419
Bergfelder, T. 203
Berkowitz, L. 356, 361–2

Berlusconi, S. 71, 278, 326–30, 403–4
Bernays, E. 122
Berne Convention (1886) 107
Berner-Lee, T. 223
Berry, M. 253, 376, 509
Bertelsmann 67, 72, 107, 208
Beynon, J. 421
Bhabha, H. 453
bias 462, 468
Bias, N. 225
Big Brother 429–30, 454
BILD 66
Bilderberg group 131
Billig, M. 508
Bink, S. 460–1
Biressi, A. 413
Birmingham Centre for Contemporary
    Cultural Studies 19
Bishop, J. 208, 214, 216
Black British film 451
Black and White Minstrel Show, The 449
Blackman, L. 29
Blain, N. 519–31
blame culture 414
Bland 157
blogs 226, 238
Bloomberg 236, 239
blousons noirs 475
Blueberry: Chihuahua Pearl 79
Blum, L.M. 497
Blumler, J. 121, 307, 370, 383
body, health and illness 485–501
    beginning–of–life issues 488–92
    disability, lifestyle and enhancement 495–8
    eating disorders 492–5
    end–of–life issues 498–500
Bolchini, D. 225
Bollywood 453
Bolton, R. 90
Bond, D. 527
book publishing 106–17
    academic 108
    background 106
    business and professional 108
    consumer or trade 108
    digital developments 115–16
    economics 284–5
    educational or schools 108
    electronic 108
    historical background 106–8
    policies 294

publishers 109–10
reference 108
rights and territories 113–15
sales outlets 111–13
subsidies and prices 110–11
territories 113–15
Booth, J. 168
Bordwell, D. 40
Born, G. 446
Bosman, J. 457–68
Bourdieu, P. 93–4, 386, 430–2
Bourdon, J. 306–16
Bouyeri, M. 458–9, 465
Boyce, T. 376
Boyd–Barrett 63
Boyd–Barrett, C. 19, 21
Boyd–Barrett, O. 233–44
Boyer, H. 428
Boyes, R. 530
Boyle, R. 363, 519–31
Braithwaite, B. 155
Bramadat, P. 458
branding 109, 267
Brandt, K. 306
Brants, K. 49
Brazier, M. 499
Brazil 70, 260
Breen, M.E. 512
Brennan, M. 210
Bresow, H. 310
Brewer 376
Briggs, A. 311, 313
Bright, S. 100
British Associated Press (AP) 235, 236, 237,
    238, 239, 243
British Board of Film Censors 355
British Phonographic Industry 207
Brittain, D. 96
Broadcasters' Audience Research Board (BARB)
    338, 341, 342, 345, 351
broadcasting 63
    audience research 337, 339
    deregulation, effects of 50–2
    dual system 68
    France 67
    national identity 508
    'old' models of 48–9
    United Kingdom 64–5
    see also radio; television
Broadcasting Act (1981) 319
Broadcasting Act (1990) 166, 168, 178–9, 183, 188

Broadcasting Code 186
Broadcasting Councils 66
Broche, J. 195–6
Brody, S. 363
Bromley, M. 64
Brook, S. 172
Brookes, R. 520, 522
Brooks, K. 412
Brooks, R. 99, 132
Brouwer, L. 461
Brown, B. 22
Brown, C. 55
Brown, J. 383, 397
Brunella, E. 200
Brunsdon, C. 28, 387, 388, 509
Brunswick 132
Brusilovsky, P. 228
BSkyB 65, 145, 289, 338
Buckingham, D. 364, 389
Buddenhaum, J.M. 457
Bueno, M. 161
Bughin, J. 54
Buglass, D. 493
bukkake 539
Bulgaria 69, 71, 194, 198, 212, 325
Bulger, J. 358
Bull, M. 22
Bull, S. 88–102
bullying 184–5
'bundling' policies 285
Buonanno, M. 312
Burgin, V. 90, 91, 93
Burgon, B. 123
Burson Marsteller 132
Burston, P. 25
Bushman, B.J. 361
Business Leagues 122
Butler, J. 29, 398, 407, 412
Byron, T. 363

cable television 2, 68, 253, 315
Caché (film) 437, 439–40
Callamard, A. 323
camera obscura 89
Campany, D. 96, 98, 99
Campbell, C. 266
Campbell, S. 492
Canada 239
Canal+ 195
Cantoni, L. 220–9
Caplin, R. 267

Cardiff, D. 308, 509
Carlin, J. 328–9
Carlsen 80
Carlsson, U. 361
Carpentier, N. 511
Carruthers, S. 122
carte-de-visite portraits 92
cartel agreements 235–6
Carter, C. 28, 399
Carter, N. 528
Cartwright, L. 91
Casterman 83
CBS Corporation 72
Celebrity Big Brother 454
celebrity culture 100–2, 160–3, 492
censorship 107, 278, 438, 507–8, 535–6,
    537, 539
    see also censorship and freedom of speech
censorship and freedom of speech 318–30
    Berlusconi, S. and Italian television
        326–30
    censorship 323–6
    European Convention on Human Rights
        318–20
    freedom of speech 321–3
Central and Eastern Europe 49, 68–70, 71, 154,
    242, 260, 321
    cinema/film 195, 199, 202
    different media systems 62, 63
centralised network 222
Centre for Contemporary Cultural
    Studies 445
Chakravartty, P. 17
Chalaby, J.K. 52
Chan, B. 514
Channel 4 183, 187, 338, 340, 451, 452, 454
Channel 5 183, 338, 341
Chapman, R. 421
Charters, W.W. 355
China 115, 199, 237, 260, 261
Cicognani, A. 228
Cinema Advertising Association 346–7
cinema/film 190–203
    advertising 270
    animation 198
    art-house 190, 192, 537
    audience research 346–7
    co-financing 196–7
    co-production 196–7
    competition 199–200
    as corporate business 197–9

cinema/film *(contd.)*
 distribution 192–3, 200–2
 documentary 198
 economics 285
 Europa 192
 European and Pan-European Funds 191–2
 exhibitions 200–2
 festivals 192
 harmful effects 355, 357
 impacts and influences 370
 and music 212–13
 policies 294
 production 200
 race/ethnicity 453
 sexual activity representation 540, 542, 543, 544
 silent 212
 social class 428, 437–40
 State aid 193
 systems of provision 283
 see also France
circulation 142–3
citizen journalism 254–5
citizenship 315–16
civil society 20
Clarke, J. 473, 479
Clinton, H. 416–17
CLT/RTL 48
Cobley, P. 1–11, 13–14, 75, 277–9, 333–4
Cockerell, M. 125
Cohan, S. 421
Cohen, A. 246
Cohen, D. 494
Cohen, N. 130
Cohen, P. 21
Cohen, S. 255, 474, 476, 480, 482
coherence, problems of 128–9
Coleman, C. 472
collective bargaining 83
collective intelligence tools 226
Collins, R. 314
COMAG 157
Comcast Corporation 72
comics 77–86
 'album' culture 78–81, 85
 cultural crossovers 82–3
 e-comics 85
 economic factors 83–4
 festivals 80–1
 manga 109
 marginalisation 85–6
 respectability 81–2

 study groups 81, 82
 United Kingdom 84–5
Commercial Radio Companies Association 343
Commission for Racial Equality 446
commodities 282–4
Communications Act (2003) 168, 179, 320, 325
communications, persistent 227
Community Media Association 168
competition 287–90, 291
 cinema 197, 199–200
 news agencies 238
 policy 299–300
computer manipulation 91
ComScore Media Metrix 349, 351
Comstock, G. 359
concentration of media 64
Confessore, N. 132
conflict 247
 frame 462, 467, 468
Connell, R.W. 422
connotative meaning 26
constituents of the media 6–8
consumption 47, 445
Contempt of Court Act (1981) 323
content 147, 224
 and form 36–7
 regulation 145–6
 restrictions 299–300
 rights 50
 television 187–8
contradiction 247
control 243
 see also power
convergence 248
 active audiences 384
 horizontal 250
 impacts and influences 374
 news media 6, 249–50, 252–3
 of ownership 250
 telecommunications 300–2
 vertical 250
Cook, T. 121
cooperative structure 241
copyright 83, 84, 216
Corner, J. 35–44, 127, 371, 373–4
Cosby Show, The 372
cosmetic surgery intervention 495, 497–8
Cotton, C. 98–9
Couldry, N. 376
Council of Europe 191, 197, 329
counterculture 479

Coward, R. 419
Cox Enterprises 72
Coyne, S.M. 364
Cracknell, J. 130
Creton, L. 195
Crewe, B. 412
crime *see* effects leading to crime and violence
Crisell, A. 166, 169, 170, 171
Critcher, C. 482
Croatia 194, 198
Crofts, W. 122
Crolley, L. 527
Crook, T. 169, 173
cryonics 499
Crystal, D. 227
Cuklanz, L.M. 414
cultivation theory 362
cultural capital 431
cultural crossovers and comics 82–3
cultural diversity 196
Cultural Diversity Network 446
cultural intermediaries 207–8
cultural and media studies 382, 383–90
cultural sexualisation 540–1, 543
cultural specificity in cinema 195
culture 18–19, 47
    popular 150
Cumberbatch, G. 354–65
Curran, J. 121, 158, 160
Curtis, L. 510
customisation 228
Czech Republic 69, 192, 194, 198, 199, 200, 325

DAB 166–7, 170–1, 172, 342
Daily Survey of Listening and Viewing 337
Danesi, M. 221
Dassault, S. 325–6
data fusion 348
Data Protection Authority 303
Davie, G. 457
Davies, N. 240
Davies, P. 364
Davis, A. 121
Davis, J. 473, 475
Davis, K. 498
Day, G. 429
Dayan, D. 509
De Bens, E. 49, 50, 306
de Perthius, K. 100
De Saussure, F. 25–6, 27–8
de Smaele, K. 50

De Vany, A. 285, 287
de-segmentation 458
Deacon, D. 21, 121, 122, 127, 130, 131,
    142, 147
decentralisation 22, 66–7
Delorme, D. 432
democracy 315–16
democratic corporatist model 62, 66, 311
Denmark 2, 114, 194, 198, 214, 540
denotation 26, 90
deregulation 49, 50–2, 178, 313, 324
designer genes 488–92
Devereux, E. 511
d'Haenens, L. 457–68
diachronic approach 26–7
Digital One 166
Digital Radio Development Bureau 166
Digital Terrestrial Television (DTT) 54
digital/digitalisation 52–4, 277, 287
    audience research 348–50
    book publishing 115–16
    broadcasting 65
    cinema/film 200–1
    and its effects 4–6
    music 285–6
    news media 249
    photography 91, 94, 96
    policies 302
    radio 64, 171–3
    sport 522–4
    switchover 54
    television 55–6, 64, 183, 187–8, 289, 297,
        303–4
    audience research 340
    France 68
    see also DAB
Dijck, J.V. 496
Dill, K.E. 360
Dinan, W. 121, 122, 123, 124, 125, 130
disability 495–8
Disabled People's Direct Action Network (DAN)
    128–9
disclosure, policing of 125–6
discourses 394–5
Disley, J. 414
Disney comics 80
distributed network 221–2
distribution 187–8, 192–3, 200–2
diversification strategies 242, 243
diversity of supply 243
documentaries 42–3, 494, 496, 543

Donaton, S. 262
Doubleday 107
Douglas, A. 160
Dove 419–20
Dow Jones 236, 239
Doyle, G. 145, 295
Driver, S. 156–7
dual system of broadcasting 68
Dubet, F. 432, 433
Ducker, J. 414
Duggan, L. 406
duopoly model 48
Durham, M.G. 17
During, S. 21
Dyer, G. 418, 419
Dyer, R. 399, 422, 444
Dyson, K. 48

e-books 115
e-commerce 269
East Midlands Allied Press 155
eating disorders 488, 492–5
Eco, U. 81
economics 47, 281–91
    comics 83–4
    commodities 282–4
    competition 287–90
    effects frame 462, 467
    market mechanism 286–7
    prices 284–6
'edginess' 419–20
Editorial Intelligence 132
Edwards, E. 95
Edwards, T. 421
effects leading to crime and violence 354–65
    aggression, priming 361–2
    children 362–3
    confounding variables 361
    early research 355–6
    history of concerns 354–5
    imitation 356
    limitation 357
    links 359–60
    realisation 358
    red herrings 358–9
    'Rip Van Winkle' effect 360
    violence in the media 363–4
    violence to the media 364–5
'ego' 24
Eijinders, S. 513
El–Nawawy, M. 253

Eldridge, J. 370
Electronic Communication Regulatory
    Framework 301, 303
elitism 430–2
Elkins, J. 91
Elliott, B. 497
Elliott, C. 486, 497
Ellis, J. 161, 534
Ellison, M. 41–2
Elsaesser, T. 197
EMI 207, 208, 216
empirical approaches 21
eMusic 215
enclosure, policing of 125–6
end-of-life issues 488, 498–500
Endemol 185
Engel, M. 124
Engels, F. 20, 428
Englishness/Britishness 528–9
enhancement technologies 488, 495–8
Enteman, W.F. 399
Entman, R. 462
Eppler, M.J. 224
Erickson, T. 227
Ericson, R. 121
Eron, L.D. 360
Esquive, L' (film) 437, 440–1
Establishment Survey 338–9
Estonia 194, 298
ethics 272, 486, 491, 500
ethnic minority programming, targeted 449,
    450, 452
ethnicity see race/ethnicity
ethnographic approaches 21–2, 384–5, 386, 389
Eurimages 191–2, 193, 196, 197, 203
Euromed Audiovisuel 192
Europe 10, 277, 278–9
    advertising 258, 266
    book publishing 106, 107–8, 110, 112
    broadcasting systems/institutions 47, 48, 49,
        50, 51, 52, 54, 55
    cinema/film 190, 191–2
    digitisation 5
    magazines 153–4, 158, 160
    music 212
    National Regulation Authorities 298
    news agencies 234, 235, 237, 242
    news media 252, 253
    newspapers 140–1, 148
    policies 294, 296, 297, 300, 301, 302
    public relations 124

public service broadcasting (PSB) 88
sexual activity representation 543
sport 520, 521
youth representation 478
see also Europe and different media systems;
   European; European Union
Europe and different media systems 60–72
   Central and Eastern Europe and
      post–Communist model 68–70
   classifications 62–3
   comparisons 61
   definition of systems 61
   France 67–8
   Germany 65–7
   small states 70–1
   United Kingdom 64–5
European Commission 115, 123, 196,
   299–300, 303
European Commission on Human Rights
   319–20
European Convention on Human Rights 3, 300,
   318–20
European Court of Human Rights 319
European Parliament 123, 329
European Producers Club 196
European Union 2, 6, 108, 493, 512
   broadcasting systems/institutions 50,
      53, 56
   censorship and freedom of speech
      320, 322
   cinema/film 194, 198
   policies 297–8, 303
   public service broadcasting (PSB)
      3, 313
Evans, J. 183, 417, 494, 495
Eveno, P. 143
Ewen, S. 265–6
exception culturelle principle 67
Ezra, E. 197

Fable 449
Facebook 94, 95, 264–5
Fact (Poland) 69
Family and Parenting Institute 494
fandom development 521
Fanning, B. 511
fanzines 212
Farrar, S. 488
fashion and photography 99–100
federalism 65–7
femininity 29, 30, 398, 399, 412

feminism 25, 28–30
   commodity 419
   gender representation 411, 413, 418, 419
   materialist 30
   and photography 99
   popular 402
   sexual activity representation 539–40, 541
   and sexualities 407
Fenton, N. 371, 373–4
Ferguson, C.J. 360, 362
film *see* cinema/film
Film Audience Measurement and Evaluation
   (FAME) 347
Film Monitor 347
finance 143–4
   see also expenditure; revenue
Fine, B. 266, 281
Fininvests 403
Finland 53, 70, 111, 114, 194, 198, 361, 512–13
Flood–Page, C. 360
Foer, F. 531
folksonomies 229
Fonarow, W. 209
Fonds Sud 195, 197
Fones–Wolf, E. 122
form 35–44
   '9/11' 40–3
   and content 36–7
   formal analysis, elements of 38–40
   future of 43–4
   and interpretation 37–8
Forza Italia 327–8, 329
Foucault, M. 30, 95, 538–9
fragmentation 270–1, 512
framing 467, 468
France 2, 70, 71
   advertising 260
   Agence France Press (AFP) 63, 236, 237
   banlieues 432, 440–1, 442
   book publishing 108, 109, 110, 111,
      113–14, 115
   broadcasting systems/institutions 47, 48, 49, 53
   censorship and freedom of speech 325–6
   cinema/film 193, 194–9, 201
   co-financing and co-productions 196–7
   as a corporate business 197–9
   globalisation and competition 197
   policy and cultural specificity 195
   regulations 195–6
   comics 80, 81, 83–4
   different media systems 62

France *(contd.)*
education *(Grandes Écoles)* 431
magazines 155, 158
music 208, 212
newspapers 141–2, 143, 144, 145, 146, 147, 148, 149
public service broadcasting (PSB) 309, 310, 311, 312, 313
quotas and subsidies 67–8
youth representation 475
Frankfurt School 18–19, 370
Franklin, B. 51, 125
Freedman, J.L. 362
freedom of expression 295–6, 300
Freedom House (FH) 71
freedom of speech *see* censorship and freedom of speech
Freedom to Party campaign 480
Freesat 65
Freeview 65
Freud, S. 24, 91
Fricker, M. 529
Frith, S. 216
Frizot, M. 91
Frodon, J.M. 196
Frontline 157
Frosh 91
Fullagar, S. 495
functional similarity 355
Furedi, F. 492, 494

Gadow, K.D. 357
Gambaro, M. 293–304
Gamson, W. 371, 373, 375
Gans, H. 121
Gardner, C. 450
Garofalo, R. 215
gatekeepers 207–8
Gauntlett, D. 5, 22, 29, 43, 362, 389
Gauntlett, W. 370
gay liberation movement 421–3, 541–2
Gay, P. du 210
Geense, P. 461
gender 359–60, 410–23, 465
in advertising 418–23
contemporary shifts 412–13
feminist critique 411
identity 30, 398, 399
representations in news 413–18
sport 520
General Aggression Model 362

General Agreement on Tariffs and Trade 195
Gentile, D.A. 364
Georgiou, M. 253
Geraghty, C. 161
Germany 2, 70, 71
advertising 260
book publishing 108, 109, 110, 111, 112, 113–14, 115
broadcasting systems/institutions 47, 49, 53
censorship and freedom of speech 322
cinema/film 193, 194, 196, 197, 198, 199, 201
comics 80, 81
Deutsche Press Agentur (dpa) 63, 239
different media systems 62
federalism 65–7
impacts and influences 370
magazines 155, 158
music 208
news agencies 237
newspapers 142, 143, 144, 145, 146, 147
policies 302
public relations 122
public service broadcasting (PSB) 309, 310, 311–12, 313, 315
sexual activity representation 540
Wolffs Telegraphisches Bureau 63
youth representation 475
Gilardi, F. 51
Gilbert, J. 474
Gill, R. 28, 29, 30, 410–23
Gillespie, A. 156–7
Gillespie, M. 389, 508
Gilligan, A. 323–4
Gilroy, P. 452
Ging, D. 512
Ginsborg, P. 326, 329, 404
Gitlin, T. 128
Glasgow Media Research Group 371
Glasgow University Media Unit 374–6
Global Media Monitoring Project 412
Global Radio 172
globalisation 197, 269, 412, 512–13
news agencies 234, 236–40, 242
sport 521, 524–7
GM crops 493
GMTV 185
Goffman, E. 418, 422
Goggin, G. 492
Goldblatt, D. 524
Goldenberg, E. 125
Golding 51

Golding, P. 121, 122, 130, 131, 147
Goldman, R. 26, 272, 411, 419
Goody, J. 430
Google 95, 115–16
Gopal, P. 430
Gorbachev, M. 69
Gorman, P. 212
Gough–Yates, A. 153–63
Gould, P. 123
Government Information and Communication
    Service 125
Gramsci, A. 20–1
Grant 124, 127
'graphic novels' 85
Grasso, A. 311, 315
Gravett, P. 84
Gray, A. 29, 389
Gray, R. 132
Greece 46, 47, 70, 311, 509–10
    broadcasting systems/institutions 49, 52
    cinema/film 191, 194, 198
Green, G. 418
Green, N. 22
Greengrass, P. 43
Greenslade, R. 323
Greenwood, J. 124
Greer, I. 123
Gregory, D. 253
Gregory, M. 123
Griekspoor, W. 54
Gripsrud, J. 27, 28
Groensteen, T. 77
Grogan, S. 422
Gross, A.M. 357
Group f64 97
Gruppo Editoriale L'Espresso 144
Gunter, B. 360, 363, 418, 422
Gurevitch, M. 121
Gutenberg, J. 107
Guy, W. 125
Gwyn, R. 498

Habermas, J. 314–15, 458
Hachette 116
Hafez, K. 253
Hafner, K. 222
Hagell, A. 364
Hager, N. 123
Halimi, S. 428
Hall, S. 121, 124, 370, 387, 448–9, 450, 510
Hallin, D.C. 47, 62, 63, 64, 66, 68, 72, 311

Halloran, J.D. 360
Hamill, L. 22
Hand, D. 527
Handel, A.D. 402
Hansen, A. 492
Hapgood, F. 251
Haran, J. 376–7
Harcourt, A. 145, 298
Hargreaves, A. 432
Hargreaves, R. 100
Hark, I.R. 421
Harris, J. 363
Harris, R. 125, 491
Harrison, J. 246–55
Harrison, M. 99
Hartley, J. 315–16
Hartmann, M. 431
Harvey, D. 120, 525
Hau, L. 237, 238, 239
Havas agency 234–5, 236
Havas, C. 63, 235
Hawkey, I. 529
Haynes, R. 520, 522
Hayward, S. 197
health see body, health and illness
Hearst Corporation 155
Hebdige, D. 21, 475, 477, 481
Heffernan, R. 123
hegemony 19, 20, 30
Heinderycks, F. 310
Heller, S. 400
Henderson, L. 375
Hendy, D. 167, 173
Henriques, J. 446
Henwood, K. 421
Hepworth, D. 153, 160
Herd, H. 155
Herman, E. 208
Hermes, J. 381–90
Hesmondhalgh, D. 183, 207, 209
heterosexuality, compulsory 398
Heyes, C.J. 497
Hibberd, M. 363
Hibbert, M. 147
Higgins 535
Higson, A. 197, 512
Hill, A. 22, 25, 183, 413
Hill, E. 227
Hill, J. 191
Himmelweit, H.T. 355
Hip-Hop Summit Action Network 481

Hirschauer, S. 499
historical materialism 16–17
Hjelmslev, L. 26
HMV 210
Hobsbawm, E. 521
Hobson, D. 21, 176–88
Hoggart, R. 21, 475
Hollingsworth, M. 123
Hollows, J. 413
Hollway, W. 399
Holmes, S. 183
homeland programming 253
Honing, D. 56
'Hoodie law' in United Kingdom 471–4
hooks, b. 400
Horkheimer, M. 18–19
Horsley, R. 43
Horsley, W. 321–2, 326
Horsman, M. 168
Hoskyns, B. 212
Howitt, D. 359, 363
Huesmann, L.R. 360
Huesmann, R.L. 362, 363
Hull, G.P. 208, 211, 215
Human Genome Project 486, 490
human interest content 160
human interest frame 462, 467
Human Rights Act (1998) 319
Humphreys, P. 48, 142, 307, 309, 311
Humphries, S. 390
Hungary 70, 194, 198, 200, 214, 325
Hunt, L. 536–7
Huntington, S. 465
Hutton, Lord/Enquiry 323–4
hybridism 181
hypodermic model 370–1

'id' 24
identity 394–5
   active audiences 389
   gender 30, 398, 399, 412
   hybrid 514
   photography 88–90
   sport 527–31
   see also nationality/national identities
ideology 19–21, 29, 30, 93, 394
   patriarchal 399, 400–1
Iglesia, M. de la 78
illness see body, health and illness
Imbert, C. 435–7
imitation 356, 357

impacts and influences 369–78
   audience reception work 374–6
   audience research 376–7
   Cosby Show, The 372
   discreditation 371
   evidence and research 372
   historical background of
      communications 369–71
   nuclear power, study of 373–4
   politics, study of 373
Incal, The: Volume 1 79
Independent Television Commission 178
indexical sign 91
indexicality 95
India 199, 260, 508
Indonesia 244
influences see impacts and influences
infomediaries 132
information, communication and technology
      companies 251, 254–5
Ingham, B. 125
Institute of Practitioners in Advertising 338
institutions, models of 46–57
   analogue television 47
   broadcasting, 'old' models of 48–9
   deregulation 49, 50–2
   digitisation 52–4
   evolving model 54–6
integration model 48
intellectual respect 81
International Federation of the Phonographic
      Industries 207
   Report on Digital Music 215
International Monetary Fund 124
International Publishing Corporation 155
International Standard book number (ISBN) 108
International Telecommunications Organization
      297, 301
internet and the web 220–9
   advertising 263–4, 265, 269, 270, 271–2
   audience research 348–50
   book publishing 108, 112–13, 115, 117
   censorship and freedom of speech 321
   communication tools 224–6
   e-books 115
   e-comics 85
   e-commerce 269
   gender representation 413
   health and illness representation 487
   historical background 221–3
   magazines 162

music 210, 214–17
national identity 514
news agencies 239–40, 243
newspapers 148–51
online communication 227–8
policies 302
radio 169–70
religious issues 461
sexual activity representation 542
sexualities 403
shopping 287
see also web 2.0; websites
interpellation 20
interpretation and form 37–8
interruptive formats (pop–ups) 264
interviews 345
Iosifidis, P. 56
IPC Marketforce 157
IPTV 303
Iraq 126–7
Ireland 62, 194, 198, 235, 237, 311, 511
Irish Broadcasting Act (1975) 507–8
Irvin, A.R. 357
Iskandar, A. 253
Israel 361
Italy 2, 71, 278
    book publishing 108, 109
    broadcasting systems/institutions 47, 49,
        52, 53
    censorship and freedom of speech 326–30
    cinema/film 193, 194, 197, 198
    comics 80, 81
    different media systems 62, 72
    music 209
    newspapers 142, 143, 144, 145, 146, 147, 148
    policies 301–2
    public service broadcasting (PSB) 309, 310,
        311, 312, 313
    and sexuality 403–7
ITN 132, 234
ITV 65, 183, 186, 338, 341

Jacka, E. 315
Jackall, R. 120
Jäckel, A. 190–203
Jackson, P. 412
Jackson, T. 501
Jacobs, S. 513
Jakubowicz, K. 69
James, D.E. 17
James, O. 261

Jancovich 424
Japan 53, 116, 123, 208, 237, 258, 260, 302
Jeffords, S. 421
Jenkins, H. 22
Jenkins, P. 403
Jenkins, R. 414
Jensen, K.B. 384
Jermyn, D. 183
Jhally, S. 371, 372
Jobling, P. 99
Johnson, A. 399
Johnson, S. 155, 158
Jones, D. 318
Jones, N. 122, 123, 124
Jones, S. 215
Jones, T. 327, 329
journalism 246–7, 248, 252, 254–5
    citizen 254–5
    investigative 147
journo–lobbyists 133

Kahn, J. 486
Kaid, L.L. 376
Kant, I. 314
Kanter, J. 124
Karim, H.K. 454, 514
Katz, E. 370, 386, 509
Keane, J. 324
Kellner, D. 17, 427
Kelly, D. 323–4
Kelly, M. 63
Kemp 544
Kendrick, W. 538–9
Kennedy, R. 209
Kenyon, D. 94
Keogh, D. 322–3
Kerr, A. 514
Kershaw, C. 472–3
Kessle, P. 79
Kilbourne, J. 413
King, A. 521
King, G. 94
King, M. 496
Kirch, L. 67
Kirk, J. 429, 430
Kisch, R. 122
Kismaric, S. 100
Kitzinger, J. 369–78
Klady, L. 199
Klapper, J. 382
Klein, N. 124

Kleinsteuber, H.J. 2, 60–72
Knight, J. 203
Kodak 92, 93
Koenig, M. 458
Kolbtisch, J. 223
Korea 302
Kramer, P. 497
Krauss, R. 90
Kuhn, A. 94
Kuhn, R. 140–51, 433
Kunelius, R. 459
Kusek, D. 215

Laachir, K. 427–42
Lacan, J. 24, 93, 95
Lambert, S. 182
Lamizet, B. 67
Langer, J. 161
language and semiotics 25–8, 29–30,
    39, 91, 440–1
Lapeyronnie, D. 433
Lars 376
Lasen, A. 22
Latin America 195, 543
Latvia 194, 198
Laurie, P. 478
Lazar, M. 412
Lazersfeld, P. 370
Leigh, D. 123
Lenharat, A. 215
Lenin, V.I. 69
Leonard, G. 215
Leopold, E. 281
lesbian, gay, bisexual, transsexual and queer
    (LGBTQ) individuals 402–3, 405–7
Levitas, R. 125
Lewis, J. 50, 371, 372, 376
Lewis, P.M. 168
liberal/libertarian model/theory 62, 64, 69,
    72, 311
licensed withdrawal 418
Liebes, T. 386, 509
life extension 488
lifestyle programming 453, 488, 495–8
Lindee, M.S. 490
linear service 303
lingerie ads 420–1
Linsky, M. 130
Lippmann, W. 122
Lithuania 69, 194, 198
Livingstone, S. 354–5, 418

lobbying 123–4, 133
Lochard, G. 428
Loe, M. 497
logfile tracing 227
'Long Tail' theory 113
Longhurst, B. 21
López, B. 51
LOTIS 131
Lovdal, L.T. 418
Lowe, T. 486
Lubbers, E. 131
Lull, J. 22, 23
Luongo, M. 405
Lupton, D. 486
Lury, K. 40, 180
Luxembourg 48, 49, 70, 194, 198
Lyon, M. 222

McCharry, M. 509
McChesney, R. 17, 208
McCloud, S. 77
McCracken, G. 266
McCrum, R. 117
Macdonald, M. 411
McDonnell 171
McGrath, R. 91
Machin, D. 49, 313–14, 412
Macintyre, B. 501
Macintyre, D. 123
Mackenzie, Y. 167
McLaughlin, J. 486
McLean, C. 421
McLeod, K. 215
McLoone, M. 508
McMahon, J. 508
MacMaster, N. 432
McNair, B. 534–44
McNally, P. 172
McNutt, R. 209
McQuail, D. 47, 50, 370, 382, 383, 384, 454
McRobbie, A. 21, 28, 29, 30, 402, 411, 480–1
MacRury, I. 258–72
Madianou, M. 509
Madonna 541
magazines 2, 63, 153–63
    audience research 345
    business-to-business sector 158–9
    consumer sector 158, 159
    economics 284–5
    Europe 153–4
    France 67

industry 154–6
music 211–12
organization sector 158–9
and photography 99
production and distribution sector 156–8
and serialisations 111–13
sexual activity representation 540, 542
social class 428, 433–7
success strategies 160–3
Magnum 96
'male gaze' 25
Malik, S. 444–55
Mama Group 214
Mancini, P. 47, 62, 63, 64, 66, 68,
    72, 311
Mandaville, P. 513, 514
manga comics 109
Mankekar, P. 508
Manning, P. 121
Manovich, L. 91
Mansell, R. 18
Maraini, D. 405
Marchand, R. 266
Marcuse, H. 23
Marie, M. 197
Marien, M.W. 89, 92
market:
    failure 296
    mechanism 286–7
    mix 259
    niches 159–60
    segmentation 142
Markham, T. 376
Marqusee, M. 123
Marsen, C. 21, 25, 26, 27
Marshall, L. 216
Marvin, C. 364–5
Marwick, A. 430
Marx, K. 20, 284, 428
Marxist approaches 16–17
masculinity 29, 30, 398, 399, 412–13, 421–3
mash ups 226
Matthews, N. 511–12
Maurer, H. 223
May, K.G. 477–8
Mazey, S. 124
MEDIA 191–2, 193, 196, 203
media mix 269–70
media-centrism 121
Mediaset (Italy) 145, 326, 327–8, 329
Meehan, E.R. 30

Mercer, K. 95, 450
merchandising 198
merger and acquisition 237
merit goods theory 299
Merrin, W. 10
Merton, R.K. 370
Messaris, P. 39
Messner, S.F. 364
Metro chain 148
Metz, C. 91
Miah, A. 485–501
Michaels, A. 405
Middlemass, K. 122
Miles, S.H. 500
Millar, F. 494
Millard, A.J. 215
Miller, D. 120–34, 374, 375
Millward Hargrave, A. 424
Millwood-Hargrave, A. 354–5
MILNET 222
'mirror' stage 24–5, 93, 95
Mitchell, W.J.T. 91
Mitra, A. 514
mobile phones 302
mod subculture 474–7, 478, 479
Modleski, T. 29, 385–6
Mohammed cartoons controversy 459
Moi, T. 29
Moloney, K. 123
Monbiot, G. 132
monopoly, private sector 48
Montgomery, M. 40
Moore, G. 525
Moore, M. 42–3
Moore, S. 422
Moorti, S. 414
Moragas Spa, de M. 51
moral codes 535–6
moral panics 354, 474–7, 479–81, 482, 511, 538
    health and illness representation 493, 494
morality frame 462, 467, 468
Morgan, M. 362
Morley, D. 21, 29, 387–8, 509
Morris, C.W. 226
Mort, F. 421, 422
Mosco, V. 17
Motion Picture Association 201
Mott, S. 527
Moynihan, J. 472
Moynihan, R. 497
MTV 213–14

Mucchielli, L. 433
Muir, R. 100
Mulkay, M. 489–90
multiculturalism 450–2, 457–8
multimedia conglomerates 51
multimedia texts 227
Mulvey, L. 25, 421
Murdoch press group 143
Murdoch, R. 6, 51, 65, 67, 72, 324–5
Musgrave, R. 299
music 206–17
    festivals 214
    in film and television 212–13
    gatekeepers and cultural intermediaries
        207–8
    internet 214–17
    live 214
    MTV 213–14
    press 211–12
    radio and the charts 210–11
    record companies 208–9
    retail 209–10
Muslims *see* religion
Musso, P. 310
mutuality 247
Mutwarasibo, F. 511
Myers, K. 93

Nadin, M. 26
Naficy, H. 197, 514
Napster 5, 215
Nash 401
nation state size 2
National Magazine Company 155–6, 162
National Propaganda 122
National Readership Survey 160, 345–6
National Regulation Authorities 298
National Union of Journalists 319–20
nationality/national identities 505–15
    creating a sense of identity 507–10
    'good' and 'bad' nations 510
    national and global aspects 512–13
    national and transnational aspects 513–14
    sport 525
    stereotyping 510–12
NBC Universal Inc. 72
Negrin, L. 498
Negrine, R. 47
Negroponte, N. 251
Negus, K. 19, 207, 210
Nelkin, D. 490

neoliberalism 120
Nerlich, B. 491
Net Book Agreement 110–11
Netherlands 2
    book publishing 109, 114
    broadcasting systems/institutions 49, 53
    cinema/film 194, 198
    comics 80
    different media systems 62
    harmful effects 361
    health and illness representation 495
    magazines 158
    music 210–11
    public service broadcasting (PSB) 312
    sexual activity representation 540
Nettelbeck, C. 440
Nevett, T. 267
'new audience research' 21–2
new effects/influence research 378
New Zealand Press Association 244
Newbold, C. 21
Newburn, T. 364
Newell, C. 492
news agencies 233–44
    definition and importance 233–4
    global 236–40
    issues 243–4
    national 238, 240–3
    origins of international news system 234–6
    regional 238
News Corporation 72, 145, 239
News International 6, 144
news media 246–55
    change vectors 249
    content 254
    convergence 249–50, 252–3
    defining news and news journalism 246–9
    derived news factors 248
    dissemination 246–7
    fake 132, 133
    frames 462–3
    gathering 246–7
    gender representations 413–18
    intrinsic news factors 248
    journalism 246–7, 248, 252, 254–5
    personalisation 251–2, 254–5
    production 246–7
    selection criteria 247, 248
    strategies 121
    technological vector of change 249
    wholesale 237–8

newspapers 2, 140–51
  accounts 40–1, 43
  broadsheets 247
  economics 284–5
  France 67
  free 148
  impacts and influences 370
  in the information age 148–50
  national/regional 141–8
  paid-for 148
  policies 294, 300
  popular/black tops 248
  qualities 247
  radical/underground 248
  readership and audience research 345
  religious issues 461
  samizdat 248
  and serialisations 111–13
  tabloid/red tops 248
  United Kingdom 64
Nicol, A. 318, 319, 320
Nieborg, D. 390
Nielsen, J. 224
Nielsen NetRatings 349
Nixon, S. 412, 421
Noble, G. 357
non-competitive markets 287
non-linear service 303
Nordic countries 201
North America 52, 259, 412
  see also Canada; United States
Norton Taylor, R. 126, 323
Norway 114, 148, 212
Nouvel Observateur, Le (magazines) 433–4,
  437, 438
NRS 346
NSFNET 223
nuclear power, study of 373–4
Nunn, H. 413

objectification 421
Oborne, P. 123
O'Brien, M. 509
obscenity legislation 539
O'Connor, B. 505–15
O'Connor, L. 322–3
O'Donnell, H. 527
Ofcom 48, 54, 65
  audience research 336
  censorship and freedom of speech 320, 325
  economics 288

  magazines 162
  race/ethnicity 454
  radio 166, 168, 169–70
  social class 430
  television 179, 185
off-line media companies 64
Office of Global Communications 126
Official Secrets Act (1989) 322
Ogan, C. 253
Ohmann, R. 265, 268
oligarchy 69
Oliver, B. 523, 525
Oliver, J. 180–1
Ong, W.J. 220, 221
Open Access movement 116
opportunity cost 286
opt-in 302–3
opt-out 302
O'Reilly, T. 223
Organization of Asia Pacific News
  Agencies 241
Osgerby, B. 471–82
O'Shaughnessy, M. 437, 439
'Other' 95
Ouellette, L. 50
Ouest France 148
ownership 144–5, 243

P2P file sharing 215
packet switching 221–2
Padovani, C. 403
Page, B. 324–5
Paik, H. 359
Pakeerah, S. 358–9
Palissot, C. 441
Palmer, G. 181
Pantii, M. 512–13
Paolini, P. 224
paparazzi photography 100–1
Papathanassopoulos, S. 46–57
Papson, S. 26
paradigm 27
paradigmatic communities 229
Parker, I. 129
partisanship 146–7
Paterson, C. 234
patriarchy 30, 399, 400–1, 539–40
Pattynama, P. 412
Payne Fund 355, 359
Peacock, A. 171
Pearson (company) 107, 131

Pearson, G. 354, 473, 475
peer-to-peer networks 226
Peeters, B. 79
Peirce, C.S. 27–8
Pels, T. 461
Pendlebury, R. 414
Peoplemeters 338–9, 342, 343
performative images 99
personalisation 251–2, 254–5
personality traits 360
Petley, J. 3–4, 318–30
Phillips, C. 496
Phillips, D. 429
Philo, G. 130, 134, 253, 374, 509
Philo, T. 376
Phoenix, A. 412
phone-ins 185–6
PhotoBox 92
photography 39, 88–102
    account 41–2, 43
    anchorage 90
    and anxiety 95
    and appropriation 98
    as art 97–9
    camera phones and social networking 94–5
    clubs 94
    commercialisation 92–3
    connotation 90
    deadpan art 98–9
    and desire 95
    documentary 95–6
    as entertainment 99–102
    as evidence 95–7
    and fashion 99–100
    identity 88–90
    mass reproduction 100
    meanings 90–1
    paparazzi 100–1
    pictorialist 97, 99
    portrait 92
    snapshots 93–4
phototherapy 94
Pialoux, M. 431
Pickerill, J. 253
pictorialists 97, 99
Pilkington, H. 476
Pineau, G. 310
piracy 200–1, 216, 285–6
Pixy 79
Planet Rock 172
Platt, S. 41–2

Plummer, K. 399, 402
Plunkett, J. 172
pluralism 48, 121, 295, 296, 451
    polarised 62, 68, 311
podcasts 226
Poiger, U. 475
Point, Le 433–7
Poland 52, 69, 71, 194, 198, 200, 325, 361
policy 293–304
    emerging issues 302–4
    multilayer television policy and
        telecommunications convergence 300–2
    purposes and instruments 294–8
    regulation and competition 299–300
political conditions 47
political corruption investigation (Clean
    Hands) 327
political economy approaches 17–18, 30
political parties and newspapers 146
political society 20
politics, study of 373
politics and women 416–18
Poole, E. 460
pornography 403, 538–41
    child 542
    rise of 536–8
    sexual revolution 542
Portable Personal Meters (PPMs) 342, 345
Porter, H. 124
Portugal 46, 47, 70, 312
    broadcasting systems/institutions 49, 311
    cinema/film 191, 194, 198
post–Communist model 63, 68–70
POSTAR 347–8
Poster, M. 513
posters and audience research 347–8
Potter, W.J. 355
power 147, 445
Prahalad, C.K. 526
Premiere 67
Presbrey, F. 265
press 63, 66, 270, 436–7
    see also magazines; newspapers
pressure groups 124–5
Price, K. ('Jordan') 109
prices 110–11, 284–6
Prijatel, P. 155, 158
print on demand (POD) 115
privacy 303
Pro7Sat.1 72
product differentiation 289–90, 291

production 156–8, 200, 445
Project Gutenberg 115
'promotional culture', rise of 122–4
promotional resources 124–5
promotional strategies 127–8, 130–1
propaganda 126–7
psychoanalytical approaches 23–5
public relations 120–34
   changing trends 131–3
   coherence and division 128–9
   enclosure and disclosure 125–6
   Iraq: propaganda 126–7
   media factors 129–30
   news and media strategies 121
   'promotional culture' 122–4
   promotional resources 124–5
   promotional strategies 127–8, 130–1
public service broadcasting (PSB) 2, 3, 64–5,
   67–8, 72, 278–9
   censorship and freedom of speech 324
   economics 285
   Germany 66
   race/ethnicity 451, 452
   small states 70
   see also public service broadcasting (PSB)
    in Europe
public service broadcasting (PSB) in Europe
   306–16
   crises and weaknesses 313–14
   historical background 307–10
   importance 314–16
   North-South divide 310–12
publishing see book publishing
Putin, V. 69
Pyatt, J. 414

qualitative traditions 383–5, 390
quantitative traditions 383–4, 390
quasi-commodities 284
'Queensgate Affair' 186
queer approaches/theory 25, 412
Quinn, A. 155
quotas 67–8

race/ethnicity 30, 433, 444–55
   'blackness', early representations of in
    television 447–50
   different approaches to reading 'race' 445–6
   future scenarios 454–5
   multicultural programming 450–2
   new trajectories 452–4

social class 429, 442
stereotypes: positive and negative images
   446–7
racism 184–5, 430, 433, 450, 527–31
   inferential 118
radio 165–73
   advertising 270
   audience research 342–5
   and the charts 210–11
   commercial sector 166–7, 168
   digitisation 171–3
   expansion 165–70
   impacts and influences 370
   independent sector 166
   programming, mixed 173
   public service and commercial competition
    duopoly 170–1
   see also DAB
Radio Joint Audience Research (RAJAR)
   343, 345
Radner, H. 99
Radway, J. 29
RAI (Italy) 326, 327–8, 329, 403
Ramamurthy, A. 92, 93
Rampton, S. 123
Random House 107, 116
Rantanen, T. 63, 233–44, 512
Rath, J. 458
ratings 339–41
RCS MediaGroup (Italy) 144, 148
RDF Site Syndication 226
'reach' 339, 343
readership 142–3
realisation 358
reality television 429–30, 453–4, 494
recency question 346
reconstructive technologies 497
record companies 208–9
red herrings 358–9
refugees and asylum seekers 511
regulation 51–2, 294, 299–300, 507–8
   advertising 272
   cinema 195–6
   France 68
   light 299
Reilly, J. 375
Reith, Sir J. 64, 310
religion in Dutch newspapers 457–68
   comparison of newspapers 465
   general features 463–4
   Islam: cross–sectional study 463

religion in Dutch newspapers *(contd.)*
  Islam: longitudinal study 465–8
  and multiculturalism 457–8
  Muslim actors, relations and points
  of view 464–5
  Muslims 459–61
  Muslims, negative portrayal of 458–9, 460, 466
  news frames 462–3
  research questions 461
religious codes 535–6
Remembrance of Things Past 79
Reporters without Frontiers (RwF) 71
representation 394–5, 450
resale price maintenance (RPM) 110–11
resource-poor groups 127–8, 129
resource-rich groups 128–9
Resources Humaines (film) 437–9
Respini, E. 100
responsibility frame 462–3
restricted service licences 168–9, 170
retail:
  music 209–10
  news media 237–8
Reuter, P.J. 63, 235
Reuters 131–2, 234, 235, 236, 237,
    238–9, 240
revenue:
  advertising 269
  news agencies 238, 243
Rich, A. 398
Rich, E. 485–501
Rich, T. 528
Richards, J. 269
Richardson, C. 25
Richardson, J. 124, 460
Richardson, K. 371, 373–4
Richardson, P. 107–8
rights and book publishing 113–15
'Rip Van Winkle' effect 360
Ritchin, F. 91
Roberts, B. 414
Robertson, G. 318, 319, 320
Robertson, R. 234, 525
Robins, K. 446
Robinson, J. 153, 162
Robinson, S. 421
Rock, P. 474
Rojek, C. 102
Romania 69, 71, 191, 194, 198, 200
Rosenblum, B. 89
Rosler, M. 96

Ross, C. 397–407
Ross, K. 416
Ross, P. 209
Rothenberg, N. 403
Rowden, T. 197
Rowe, D. 509, 520, 522
Royal, S. 417–18
royalty splits 84
RSS Site Syndication 226
RTL (Luxembourg) 67, 71, 72
Russia 70, 159, 221, 237, 475–6
Rutherford, J. 421

Sabin, R. 77–86
Saldaña, M. Muñoz 524
sales outlets and book publishing 111–13
Sample, I. 488
sampling 337
Samuel, M. 526
Sanchez-Tabernero, A. 46
Sandall, R. 214
Sarkozy, N. 67–8
Sarre, P. 429
Sassoon, D. 140
Sassoon, J. 91
satellite television 2, 183, 253, 315, 321
Savage, J. 212
Savage, M. 429
Sayner, J. 15–30
Scandinavia 49, 62, 80, 191, 311–12
Scannell, P. 308, 509
scarcity sensitivity 286
Schibsted 148
Schiller, D. 208
Schlesinger, P. 121, 123
Schramm, W. 355–6
Schroder, K. 21
Schroeder, K.C. 387
Schudson, M. 266
Scott, C. 40
Seale, C. 486, 487, 497
search engines 226
searches (responding) 226
Seaton, J. 121, 158
Sedgwick, J. 281–91
Segell, G. 52
segmentation 142, 270–1
Semetko, H. 462
semiology and photography 90
semiotics *see* language and semiotics
Setanta 522

sex acts 534–44
  historical background 535–6
  pornography, rise of 536–8
  sexual representation in
    non-pornographic culture 542–4
  in the twentieth century 538–42
sex objects 420–1
sexual objectification of women 404–5
sexual orientation 399, 402–3, 405–7,
    421–3, 541–2
sexual power relations 398
sexual revolution 540, 542
sexual subjects 420–1
sexual violence, reporting of 414–16
sexualities 397–407
  analysis of media constructions of 400–3
  in contemporary Italian media production
    403–7
  stereotypes 399–400
Seymour, E. 130
Seymour–Ure, C. 46
Shadid, W. 460
Shaikh, T. 501
Shakespeare, T. 496
Shaw, D.F. 403
Sheehan, H. 511
Shetty, S. 429–30
Shingler, M. 169
Shoemaker, P. 246
Shucker, R. 206–17
Shuker, R. 5
Siebert, F.S. 69, 72
Sigal, L. 121
sign fatigue 419
signals, non–verbal 418
signification 28
signified 25–6
signifier 25–6, 27–8
Signorielli, N. 362
signs in language 25–8
Silverstein, K. 123
Silverstein, P. 433
Silverstone, R. 133, 250, 427
Simpson, M. 422
Singer, M.J. 360
Siune, K. 47
Skeggs, B. 428, 441–2
skinhead subculture 479
Sky 288, 339, 341, 522
Slater, D. 92, 93
Slater, M.D. 360

Sloan, J. 414
Slovakia 194, 198, 199, 200
Slovenia 194, 198
Smith, A. 525
Smith, A.C.H. 473
Smith, A.D. 506
Smith, E. 531
Smith, R. 501
Snow, J. 130
soap operas 179–80
social class 30, 360, 383, 427–42
  banlieues 432, 433–7
  Big Brother: reality television 429–30
  elitism 430–2
  and ethnicity 433
  and language in *L'Esquive* 440–1
  representation in cinema 437–40
  and social exclusion 428–9
  sport 520
  working class 431–2
social exclusion 428–9
social learning 357
social networking 94–5, 226
  see also Facebook
social responsibility model/theory 62, 69
Solomon, N. 131
Solomon–Godeau, A. 96, 98
Sony Corporation 72, 208
Sony Libris 115
Sony portable Reader 6, 116
Soothill, K. 414
Sorlin, P. 197
South Africa 416
South America 195, 200, 236
Soviet Communism model/theory 62, 66, 69
'space brokers/farmers' 267
Spain 46, 47, 80, 114, 161, 237
  broadcasting systems/institutions 49, 52, 53
  cinema/film 193, 194, 197, 198, 199
  public service broadcasting (PSB) 311, 312
specialist units 452
Spelman, E.V. 30
Spence, J. 94
spin doctors 122–3, 132
sport 519–31
  globalisation 524–7
  identity and managing 'the nation' 527–31
  importance in digital age 522–4
  media–sport nexus 520–2
Sprafkin, J. 357
Springer (Germany) 66, 69, 144

Squiers, C. 100
SRG SSR idée suisse (Switzerland) 70–1
Stanbury, P. 84
Starkey, G. 165–73
state involvement 46–7
  cinema 193
  comics 83–4
  see also public service broadcasting
Statham, P. 327–8
Stauber, J. 123
Steemers, J. 56
Steen, R. 520, 522
Steiner, A. 112–13
Steiner, L. 28, 399
stem cells 488–92
stereotyping 399–400, 446–7, 510–12, 530
Stern, S.E. 402
Stevenson, N. 412
stilagi 475–6
Stille, A. 327
Stone, J. 130
Stout, D.A. 457
Stracuzzi, N.F. 497
structuralist approaches 121
Sturken, M. 91
subjectivity 412
subscription services 216
subsidies 67–8, 71, 110–11
Sunindyo, S. 400
'superego' 24
Surowiecki, J. 226
Sutton, D. 94
Svennevig, M. 335–52
Sweden 49, 53, 71, 209, 312, 540
  book publishing 112–13, 114
  cinema/film 194, 198
Sweetser, K.D. 376
Switzerland 214
Sykes Committee 308
symbolic exchange 43
symbols 27–8, 506
synchronic approach 26–7
syntagm 27
syntagmatic communities 229
systematic formulation 39
systems see Europe and different media systems
'systems of provision' 281, 283–4
Szarkowski, J. 89, 97

Tagg, J. 90, 95
Tait, S. 497

Tang, I. 539
Taranger, M.C. 432
Tardini, S. 220–9
Target Group Index 348
Tarquini, B. 6, 106–17
Taylor, L.D. 364
TCP/IP 222
Tech Central Station 133
technological change 297, 521
  see also in particular digital/digitalisation;
    internet
technological integration 248, 249
Teddyboys 474–5, 476
telecommunications convergence 300–2
television 54–5, 176–88
  advertising 270
  analogue 47, 342
  audience research 338–42
  audience sizes 290
  'blackness', early representations of 447–50
  and book clubs 112
  Broadcasting Act (1990) 178–9
  cable 2, 68, 253, 315
  Channel 4 and Celebrity Big Brother 184–5
  commercial 315
  definition 176–7
  development 177–8
  drama 179–80
  event 523
  factual style 494
  financial issues 186–7
  harmful effects 355–6, 357, 360
  high-definition 297
  impacts and influences 370
  industry composition 183
  lifestyle 180–1
  loosening and losing control 187
  market shares in United Kingdom 288
  multilayer policies 300–2
  multiplication of regional and local
    private channels 51
  and music 212–13
  national identity 508–9
  news programmes, proliferation of 50–1
  'ordinary', growth of and decline of
    serious programming 182–3
  pay–per–view (PPV) 55–6
  pay–TV 64, 68
  phone–ins and trust issues 185–7
  policies 294, 303
  programme content 179

programme quality and range 50
programme ratings 50, 289
programming exports 50
programming, mixed 173
reality 181
satellite 2, 183, 253, 315, 321
serials/series 180
sexual activity representation 540
subscription 285
talent – writers and performers 181–2
terrestrial 2, 289, 339
viewing figures 340–1, 342
viewing share and revenue 51
viewing time 52
see also digital/digitalisation
Television without Frontiers Directive (1989)
    299, 301
Ter Wal, J. 460
Terzis, G. 63
Test-tube babies 488–92
Tétu, J.–F. 67
textuality and content 445
Thacker, E. 500
Think Indie 210
think tanks 133
Thomass, B. 66
Thompson 79
Thompson, K. 40
Thomson Corporation 107, 236, 238–9
Thornborrow, J. 412
Thornton, S. 480–1
Tiffen, R. 131
Till Death Us Do Part 449–50
Tilson, D. 121
Time Warner 72
Tintin 79–80, 83, 85–6
Tissot, S. 433
Tit–bits 155
Tomlinson, J. 234
Towers of Bois Maury, The: Babette 79
Town That Didn't Exist, The 78–9
Tracey, M. 307
traditional effects model 371
transaction costs 294
transformation 69
translations 113–14
transvestites 405
Treaty of Amsterdam 299
trivialities 10
trust issues 185–6
truth commission 132

truthfulness 247, 248
Tuchman, G. 411, 413–14
Tulloch, J. 21, 22, 122
Tumber, H. 127
Tunstall, J. 49, 313–14
Turner, G. 21, 22, 28
Turney, J. 490
TV 1 68

Ugba, A. 511
Ukraine 70
underclass 429
unionisation 83
United Business Media 131
United Kingdom 2, 3, 70, 71
    advertising 258, 259, 260, 261, 264, 266
    audience research 342, 346, 347
    book publishing 107, 108, 109, 110–11, 112,
        113–14, 115
    broadcasting systems/institutions 47, 48, 49,
        52, 53, 54
    censorship and freedom of speech 319, 320,
        321, 324, 325
    cinema/film 193, 194, 198, 199
    comics 78, 79, 80, 83, 84–5
    Cultural Test 196
    different media systems 62, 72
    digitisation 5
    economics 282, 288
    gender representation 416
    harmful effects 355, 362, 364
    health and illness representation 492
    'Hoodie law': images of youth, crime and
        social decline 471–4
    magazines 154, 156, 158, 160, 161, 162
    news agencies 235, 237
    newspapers 141, 143, 144, 145, 146, 147, 149
    public relations 120, 122, 123, 124,
        125–6, 127
    public service broadcasting (PSB) 64–5, 308,
        309–10, 311, 312, 313
    radio 165, 167
    sexual activity representation 540
    sport 520
    television 176–7, 178
    youth representation 474–5, 476, 478–81
United Nations 297, 300
    Educational, Scientific and Cultural
        Organization (UNESCO) 108, 113–14, 195,
        301, 361
United Press International 236

United States 2, 3
  advertising 258, 259, 260, 261, 266
  book publishing 107, 109, 114, 115
  broadcasting systems/institutions 50, 53
  cinema/film 193, 194, 195, 199, 202
  comics 78, 79, 80, 83, 85
  different media systems 72
  harmful effects 355, 361, 362, 363
  health and illness representation 486–7, 492
  magazines 153, 156, 161
  news agencies 237, 239
  news media 252, 253
  policies 302, 303
  public relations 120, 122, 123, 124, 127, 133
  public service broadcasting (PSB) 311, 314, 315
  sexual activity representation 540
  sexualities 400
  social class 430–1
  universities 10
  youth representation 474, 477–9, 480–1
user generated content (UGC) 5–6
uses and gratifications approaches 22–3, 29,
    382, 383–8

Vaijanovski, C. 294
Valkenburg, P. 462
Van Couvering, E. 18
van der Geest, T.M. 224
van der Graaf, S. 390
Van Dijk, T.A. 510
van Gogh, T. 458–9, 461, 463, 465–8
Van Konginsveld, P.S. 460
Van Steen, J. 469
Van Summeren, C. 461
Van Zoonen, L. 412
Vanderschelden, I. 199
veline 404–5
Viacom 72, 213
Vidal, J. 123, 124
Video Appeals Committee 363
video games 357
Video Nation 511
Viemero, V. 361, 364
viewer scepticism 419
violence *see* effects leading to crime and violence
Virgin Radio 172
Vivendi 72, 208
VoD 201
Volpe, G. 281–91
von Felitzen, C. 361
Vulliamy, E. 123

Walby, S. 414
Walsh-Childers, K. 130
Walt Disney Company 72
Waquant, L. 433
Ward, D. 144, 148
Warne, C. 475
watchdogs 147–8
  see also in particular Ofcom
Watson, J. 23, 25
Watson, K. 496
Waugh, T. 541
Wayne, M. 197
WCM 228–9
WDR 66
web 2.0 5, 221, 223, 226, 228–9
websites 224–7
  actual usages 225
  communication model 224–5
  crawling 226
  hypertext/hypermedium 224
  indexing 226
  links 224
  news and services 238
  nodes 224
  photography 94
  publishing 224
  robots (spiders/crawls) 226
  services 224, 226
  spidering 226
  technical tools 224
  usability 225
  visiting 225
Webster, F. 253
Weedon, C. 28
Weidenfield and Nicolson publishers 109
Wernick, A. 120, 261, 421
Wesselius, E. 132
Whannel, G. 160, 509
Wheare Committee 355
Wheeler, M. 56
whistleblowers 322–3
Whitehead, B. 132
Wiegman, O. 361
Wieringa, C. 169
Wikipedia 5, 229
wikis 226
Wiley, J. 488
Willard, M. 473
William, J. 521
Williams 539
Williams, K. 128, 146, 324

Williams, R. 19, 20, 261, 272
Williams, V. 96, 99
Williamson, J. 20, 93, 272
Willis, P. 21
Willsher, K. 417
Wilson, A.N. 430
Wilson, D. 510
Winship, J. 20
Winter, H. 528
Wire, The 234
Wolff, B. 63, 235, 236
Wombell, P. 91
Wood, G. 354
Woodward, J. 199
Woolf, N. 402
work-for-hire, fee-per-page system 84
World Intellectual Property
    Organization (WIPO) 107
World Television 132
World Trade Organization 124, 297, 300
Wyatt, W. 186

Wyett, C. 527
Wykes, M. 422

xenophobia 527–31
Xiao Pang 102
Xinhua 234, 239

youth representation 471–82
    commercialisation 477–8
    'Hoodie law' in United Kingdom 471–4
    moral panic in United Kingdom 474–7,
        479–81
    youth-as-fun 477–9, 481–2
    youth-as-trouble 481–2
Youth Target Group Index 348

Zakia, R. 26
ZDF 66, 67
Zhao, Y. 17
Zoonen, L. van 28
Zylinska, J. 486

MEDIA & CULTURAL STUDIES
TEXTS FROM PEARSON EDUCATION

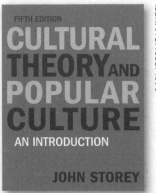
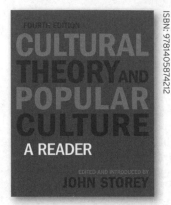
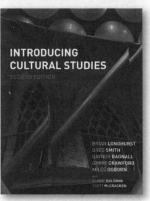

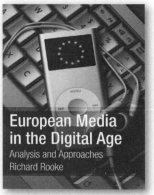